P9-CBX-091

TUTORIAL:
SOFTWARE ENGINEERING
PROJECT MANAGEMENT

RICHARD H. THAYER

**WITH ORIGINAL
PAPERS BY**

Barry W. Boehm
Fletcher J. Buckley
Richard E. Fairley
Dennis W. Fife
Norman R. Howes
Frank S. Ingrassia
Gene F. Walters
Edward Yourdon

FOREWORD BY
Winston W. Royce

IEEE Computer Society Press ◆ The Institute of Electrical and Electronics Engineers, Inc.

IEEE Computer Society Press
10662 Los Vaqueros Circle
P.O. Box 3014
Los Alamitos, CA 90720-1264

IEEE Computer Society Press Order Number 751
Library of Congress Number 87-71731
IEEE Catalog Number EH0263-4
ISBN 0-8186-0751-3 (paper)
ISBN 0-8186-4751-5 (microfiche)

Additional copies may be ordered from:

IEEE Computer Society Press	IEEE Service Center	IEEE Computer Society	IEEE Computer Society
Customer Service Center	445 Hoes Lane	13, Avenue de l'Aquilon	Ooshima Building
10662 Los Vaqueros Circle	P.O. Box 1331	B-1200 Brussels	2-19-1 Minami-Aoyama
P.O. Box 3014	Piscataway, NJ 08855-1331	BELGIUM	Minato-ku, Tokyo 107
Los Alamitos, CA 90720-1264	Tel: +1-908-981-1393	Tel: +32-2-770-2198	JAPAN
Tel: +1-714-821-8380	Fax: +1-908-981-9667	Fax: +32-2-770-8505	Tel: +81-3-3408-3118
Fax: +1-714-821-4641			Fax: +81-3-3408-3553
Email: cs.books@computer.org			

Cover concept and design by Mildred C. Thayer
Printed in the United States of America

98 97 96 95 94   9 8 7 6 5

 The Institute of Electrical and Electronics Engineers, Inc.

Foreword

Project management is a discipline that surely existed from the beginning of our civilization. Slowly through the millennia, and more rapidly within the last century, an immense body of management knowledge has arisen. Management is a discipline that must redefine itself to deal with the continuing changes arising within human institutions. For project management, technology is probably the principal driving force for such redefinition. To service the newest technological breakthrough, project management must adapt.

For example, at the midpoint of this century, the need for a new form of project management tailored to digital computer programming slowly became evident. The need to program digital computers had made its first appearance, and such programming had seemed a simple, almost self-managing, activity. A common task of the day had been programming analog computers, digital programming, by comparison, had seemed simpler and less frequently needed. However, as the incredible diversity and raw power of a properly programmed digital computer proved itself, this wrong initial impression was quickly corrected.

The term "software engineering" arose in the late 1960s and early 1970s. "Software engineering" is new enough that it is still struggling for a clear, single meaning, much as the definition of "software" struggled during its first ten years to the present meaning.

Software engineering, a discipline invented by human beings (exhibiting both their creative spark and frailties) has driven project management up new, uncharted pathways and forced its redefinition—and it continues to do so today. For all who contribute to the charting of these new pathways, it is an exhilarating experience.

This tutorial on software engineering project management collects the major published material, either by republication here or by inclusion in the complete set of references. The reader will note that many sides of the major issues are presented, for consensus has not yet been achieved. While existing, complete, and definitive solutions for the best method to achieve software engineering project management are still evolving, this tutorial is an important milestone along this uncharted pathway.

Winston W. Royce, Director
Lockheed Software Technology Center

Preface

The purpose of this tutorial is to assemble under one cover a sufficient body of knowledge about managing a successful software engineering project. A successful software development project delivers a software system on time, within cost, and meets the user's specified requirements.

This tutorial is intended for:

- *New managers.* The tutorial delivers the necessary information to manage a software development project.
- *Experienced managers.* The tutorial discusses the latest state-of-the-art in software engineering management techniques.
- *Software engineers, programmers, analysts, and other computer personnel.* The tutorial contains a general description of and problems in software engineering project management plus a number of methodologies and techniques for managing a software development project. It will also serve as a guide or goal for their future in project management.
- *College-level students.* The tutorial offers sufficient background and instructional material to serve as a main or supplementary text for a course in software engineering project management.

This tutorial presents a ''top-down view'' of software engineering project management. This top-down structure was used as a framework for selecting appropriate reprints and in assembling original material that will explain as specifically as possible how project managers manage.

One of the major premises of this tutorial is that managing a software development project is no different than managing anything else. The functions are the same: planning, organizing, staffing, directing, and controlling—only the activities to implement these functions differ. Therefore, where a software project paper was not available to address a topic, a paper on general management or management of a hardware project was substituted.

This tutorial contains unique papers and reports on software engineering project management, a Glossary of over 600 software engineering project management and software engineering terms, and a Bibliography with over 50 entries.

The chapters of this tutorial are arranged into two general groups. The first group contains Chapters 1, 2, and 3 and provides the background for software engineering project management. Chapter 1 is a general introduction to the tutorial and contains two overview papers as well as a thorough explanation of the ''top-down view.'' Chapter 2 provides a general description of software engineering and software engineering problems for the reader who may not be familiar with how large, custom-made, computer systems are built. Chapter 3 contains a general overview of project management and how it fits into the concept of software engineering. The chapter includes a description of two software development life-cycle models. It also provides the reader with an understanding of some of the difficulties involved in successfully managing a project.

The second group of papers, Chapters 4 through 8, focuses on the five functions of general management: planning, organizing, staffing, directing, and controlling. Each chapter describes one function and the project management activities that support that function. For example, under *planning* we describe requirements and goals, policies, decision making, estimating project costs and schedules, and documenting a project plan. Under *organizing* we describe the various organizational structures, different responsibilities and authority relationships, and project teams that are used to organize a software engineering project. The next chapter on *staffing* suggests how to fill the organizational structure with people who are qualified to perform their duties. Training of employees is also discussed. The next chapter on *directing* concerns itself with motivation, delegating, conflict resolution, and the leadership of software people. The final chapter on *controlling* takes into consideration standards, UDFs, reviews, walkthroughs and inspections, configuration management, audits, and other means necessary to ensure that a project is on schedule, within cost, and meets the customer's requirements.

Every attempt was made to obtain tutorial papers that would provide a basic understanding of the various facets of software engineering project management. Papers selected generally were broad in coverage. When possible, secondary sources were selected—sources which summarized earlier papers or studies.

This tutorial has a reasonably unique feature over similar tutorials. In using the top-down approach, I identified those subfunctions and areas of software engineering project management that should, by necessity, be covered by one or more papers. However in some cases, there were (and still are) management areas and activities that were not covered adequately by existing papers. To make up this difference, I contacted experienced, seasoned authors and friends in the area of software engineering and asked them to write or revise papers for this tutorial. These new or almost new papers are:

- Dr. Barry W. Boehm, "A Spiral Model of Software Development and Enhancement"
- Mr. Fletcher J. Buckley, "Establishing Software Engineering Standards in an Industrial Organization"
- Dr. Richard E. Fairley, "A Guide for Preparing Software Project Management Plans"
- Dr. Dennis W. Fife, "How to Know a Well-Organized Software Project When You Find One"
- Dr. Norman R. Howes, "On Using the Users' Manual as the Requirements Specification"
- Mr. Frank S. Ingrassia, "The Unit Development Folder (UDF): A Ten-Year Perspective"
- Mr. Gene F. Walters, "Investigative Audit for Controlling Software Development"
- Mr. Edward Yourdon, "A Game Plan for Technology Transfer"

In addition, Dr. C.V. Ramamoorthy and Mr. Atul Prakash have submitted a rewrite of their paper, "Software Engineering: Problems and Perspectives" which was originally published in the October 1984 issue of *Computer*, and I provided an overview paper, "Software Engineering Project Management: A Top-Down View."

I made every attempt to use current papers for every important topic; that is, those published later than 1980. However, in many instants this was not possible and papers in this tutorial span from 1967 through 1987. As noted above, I used the best papers on the subject regardless of year.

A number of large abstracting systems were used in the search for material, notably Dialog. However, the major method of finding articles for this tutorial was the reading of software engineering and computer science journals and magazines.

No successful endeavor has ever been done by one person alone. This is one of the measures of management, and this tutorial is no exception. I would like to thank the people and organizations that supported me in this effort, including Helen Abbot from Lockheed Palo Alto Technical Information Center; Barry S. Johnson and Sally K. Yoshihara, two students who located many suitable papers; the word processor, Barbara Dietrich; my wife, Mildred, who provided technical assistance and kept track of the immense amount of paper this task generated; and Margaret Brown, Computer Society of the IEEE Press, who motivated me to get with it and finish this tutorial.

Table of Contents

Chapter 1: Introduction to Tutorial

1. Introduction to Chapter

Project management is defined as a system of procedures, practices, technologies, and know-how that provides the planning, organizing, staffing, directing, and controlling necessary to successfully manage an engineering project. *Know-how* in this case means the skill, background, and wisdom necessary to apply knowledge effectively in practice. If the product of the project is software, then the act of managing a software project is called software development project management or, more recently *software engineering project management*. The manager of a software engineering project is called a *software engineering project manager*.

Software engineering projects are frequently part of a larger, more comprehensive system that includes equipment (hardware), facilities, personnel, and procedures, as well as software. Examples are aircraft systems, accounting systems, radar systems, inventory control systems, railroad switching systems, and so forth. These system engineering projects are typically managed by one or more system project managers (sometimes called *program managers*) who manage an organization comprised of technically qualified engineers (all types), experts in the field of the application, scientific specialists, programmers, support personnel, and others. If the software to be delivered is a "stand-alone" software system (a system that does not interface with any other system) which is being developed for or on an existing or commercial "off-the-shelf" computer, the software engineering project manager can be the system project manager.

Management can be defined as all the activities and tasks undertaken by one or more persons for the purpose of planning and controlling the activities of others in order to achieve an objective or complete an activity that could not be achieved by the others acting independently.

From the management sciences comes the *universality of management* [1], [2] which means that:

- Management performs the same functions regardless of its position in the organization or the enterprise managed.
- Management functions and fundamental activities are characteristic duties of managers; management practices, methods, detailed activities, and tasks are particular to the enterprise or job managed.

Therefore, the functions and general activities of management can be universally applied to managing any organization or activity. Recognition of this concept is crucial to the improvement of software engineering project management, for it allows us to apply the wealth of research in management sciences to improving the management of software engineering projects [3].

The application of this concept allows us to, for example, use the classic management model (see Figure 1.1) as portrayed by such well-known authors in the field of management as Koontz and O'Donnell, MacKenzie (see paper in this chapter) and others [4] to organize the chapters in this tutorial. It also allows us to select high-quality management papers from the general management world or from the management of other, non-software, enterprises for application to software engineering project management.

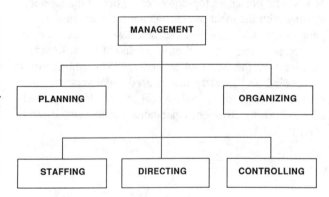

Figure 1.1: Classic Management Model

2. Overview of Chapter

The three papers contained in this chapter introduce the tutorial. The first paper by Brooks sets the stage by defining the major issues of and providing historic significance to software engineering project management. The second paper by MacKenzie is a condensed and comprehensive overview of management. The third paper by Thayer extrapolates from the general concepts of management and other papers and references and applies the concept of the universality of management to developing an overview of software engineering project management.

3. Description of Papers

No collection of papers on software engineering project management would be complete without including the classic of all classic software engineering papers, ''The Mythical Man-Month,'' by Dr. Fred Brooks. Brooks could be considered the father of modern software engineering project management; his book *The Mythical Man-Month: Essays on Software Engineering* [5] is still a best seller today. This paper, or better, the original book should be required reading for all project managers.

This paper (and his book) is the source of such now-famous quotes and sayings as:

- Adding manpower to a late software project makes it later.
- How does a project get to be a year late? . . . One day at a time.
- All programmers are optimists.
- The man-month as a unit for measuring the size of a job is a dangerous and deceptive myth.

The next paper by R.A. MacKenzie is also a classic, but in the management sciences. It is the most comprehensive and condensed description of management in existence. MacKenzie presents a top-down description of management starting with the management elements—ideas, things, and people—and ending with a detailed description of general management activities—all on one fold-out page. (Readers interested in the MacKenzie figure, ''The Management Process in 3-D,'' can buy an oversized, color version, suitable for framing, for a nominal charge from Harvard Business Publishing Division, Operations Department, Boston, MA, 02163.)

In the last paper in this chapter, Thayer expands on MacKenzie's and other papers and applies the concept of the universality of management to developing an overview of software engineering project management. His paper takes a top-down approach to establishing a set of project management and software engineering project management *responsibilities, activities,* and *tasks* that should be undertaken by any manager who is assigned the responsibility of managing a software engineering project. It covers the management functions of planning, organizing, staffing, directing, and controlling and discusses in detail the activities and tasks necessary to successfully manage a software development project.

References

1. H. Koontz, C. O'Donnell and H. Weihrich, *Management*, 8th ed., McGraw-Hill Book Co., NY, 1984.

2. H. Fayol, *General and Industrial Administration*, Sir Isaac Pitman & Sons, Ltd., London, 1949.

3. R.H. Thayer and A.B. Pyster, ''Guest Editorial: Software Engineering Project Management,'' *IEEE Transactions on Software Engineering*, Vol. SE-10, No. 1, January 1984.

4. See Table 5-1: Major Management Functions as Seen by Various Authors, from *Management: A Systems Approach*, by David I. Cleland and William R. King, McGraw-Hill Book Company, NY, 1972.

5. F.P. Brooks, Jr., *The Mythical Man-Month: Essays on Software Engineering*, Addison-Wesley Publishing Co., Reading, MA, 1975.

THE MYTHICAL MAN-MONTH

HOW DOES A PROJECT GET TO BE A YEAR LATE? . . . . . . ONE DAY AT A TIME.

By Frederick P. Brooks, Jr.

Dr. Brooks was part of the management team charged with developing the hardware for the IBM 360 system. In 1964 he became the manager of the Operating System/360 project; this trial by fire convinced him that managing a large software project is more like managing any other large undertaking than programmers believe and less like it than professional managers expect.

About his OS/360 project, he says: "Managing OS/360 development was a very educational experience, albeit a very frustrating one. The team, including F. M. Trapnell who succeeded me as manager, has much to be proud of. The system contains many excellences in design and execution, and it has been successful in achieving widespread use. Certain ideas, most noticeably device-independent input/output and external library management, were technical innovations now widely copied. It is now quite reliable, reasonably efficient, and very versatile.

The effort cannot be called wholly successful, however. Any OS/360 user is quickly aware of how much better it should be. The flaws in design and execution pervade especially the control program, as distinguished from language compilers. Most of the flaws date from the 1964-1965 design period and hence must be laid to my charge. Furthermore, the product was late, it took more memory than planned, the costs were several times the estimate, and it did not perform very well until several releases after the first."

Analyzing the OS/360 experiences for management and technical lessons, Dr. Brooks put his thoughts into book form. Addison-Wesley Publishing Company (Reading, Mass.) will offer "The Mythical Man-Month: Essays on Software Engineering", from which this article is taken, sometime next month.

NO SCENE FROM PREHISTORY is quite so vivid as that of the mortal struggles of great beasts in the tar pits. In the mind's eye one sees dinosaurs, mammoths, and saber-toothed tigers struggling against the grip of the tar. The fiercer the struggle, the more entangling the tar, and no beast is so strong or so skillful but that he ultimately sinks.

Large-system programming has over the past decade been such a tar pit, and many great and powerful beasts have thrashed violently in it. Most have emerged with running systems—few have met goals, schedules, and budgets. Large and small, massive or wiry, team after team has become entangled in the tar. No one thing seems to cause the difficulty—any particular paw can be pulled away. But the accumulation of simultaneous and interacting factors brings slower and slower motion. Everyone seems to have been surprised by the stickiness of the problem, and it is hard to discern the nature of it. But we must try to understand it if we are to solve it.

More software projects have gone awry for lack of calendar time than for all other causes combined. Why is this case of disaster so common?

First, our techniques of estimating are poorly developed. More seriously, they reflect an unvoiced assumption which is quite untrue, i.e., that all will go well.

Second, our estimating techniques fallaciously confuse effort with progress, hiding the assumption that men and months are interchangeable.

Third, because we are uncertain of our estimates, software managers often lack the courteous stubbornness required to make people wait for a good product.

Fourth, schedule progress is poorly monitored. Techniques proven and routine in other engineering disciplines are considered radical innovations in software engineering.

Fifth, when schedule slippage is recognized, the natural (and traditional) response is to add manpower. Like dousing a fire with gasoline, this makes matters worse, much worse. More fire requires more gasoline and thus begins a regenerative cycle which ends in disaster.

Schedule monitoring will be covered later. Let us now consider other aspects of the problem in more detail.

Optimism

All programmers are optimists. Perhaps this modern sorcery especially attracts those who believe in happy endings and fairy godmothers. Perhaps the hundreds of nitty frustrations drive away all but those who habitually focus on the end goal. Perhaps it is merely that computers are young, programmers are younger, and the young are always optimists. But however the selection process works, the result is indisputable: "This time it will surely run," or "I just found the last bug."

So the first false assumption that underlies the scheduling of systems programming is that *all will go well*, i.e., that *each task will take only as long as it "ought" to take*.

The pervasiveness of optimism among programmers deserves more than a flip analysis. Dorothy Sayers, in her excellent book, *The Mind of the*

Maker, divides creative activity into three stages: the idea, the implementation, and the interaction. A book, then, or a computer, or a program comes into existence first as an ideal construct, built outside time and space but complete in the mind of the author. It is realized in time and space by pen, ink, and paper, or by wire, silicon, and ferrite. The creation is complete when someone reads the book, uses the computer or runs the program, thereby interacting with the mind of the maker.

This description, which Miss Sayers uses to illuminate not only human creative activity but also the Christian doctrine of the Trinity, will help us in our present task. For the human makers of things, the incompletenesses and inconsistencies of our ideas become clear only during implementation. Thus it is that writing, experimentation, "working out" are essential disciplines for the theoretician.

In many creative activities the medium of execution is intractable. Lumber splits; paints smear; electrical circuits ring. These physical limitations of the medium constrain the ideas that may be expressed, and they also create unexpected difficulties in the implementation.

Implementation, then, takes time and sweat both because of the physical media and because of the inadequacies of the underlying ideas. We tend to blame the physical media for most of our implementation difficulties; for the media are not "ours" in the way the ideas are, and our pride colors our judgment.

Computer programming, however, creates with an exceedingly tractable medium. The programmer builds from pure thought-stuff: concepts and very flexible representations thereof. Because the medium is tractable, we expect few difficulties in implementation; hence our pervasive optimism. Because our ideas are faulty, we have bugs; hence our optimism is unjustified.

In a single task, the assumption that all will go well has a probabilistic effect on the schedule. It might indeed go as planned, for there is a probability distribution for the delay that will be encountered, and "no delay" has a finite probability. A large programming effort, however, consists of many tasks, some chained end-to-end. The probability that each will go well becomes vanishingly small.

The mythical man-month

The second fallacious thought mode is expressed in the very unit of effort used in estimating and scheduling: the man-month. Cost does indeed vary as the product of the number of men and the number of months. Progress does not. *Hence the man-month as a unit for measuring the size of a job is a dangerous and deceptive myth.* It implies that men and months are interchangeable.

Men and months are interchangeable commodities only when a task can be partitioned among many workers *with no communication among them* (Fig. 1). This is true of reaping wheat or picking cotton; it is not even approximately true of systems programming.

When a task cannot be partitioned

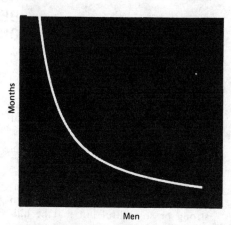

Fig. 1. The term "man-month" implies that if one man takes 10 months to do a job, 10 men can do it in one month. This may be true of picking cotton.

because of sequential constraints, the application of more effort has no effect on the schedule. The bearing of a child takes nine months, no matter how many women are assigned. Many software tasks have this characteristic because of the sequential nature of debugging.

In tasks that can be partitioned but which require communication among the subtasks, the effort of communication must be added to the amount of work to be done. Therefore the best that can be done is somewhat poorer than an even trade of men for months (Fig. 2).

The added burden of communication is made up of two parts, training and intercommunication. Each worker must be trained in the technology, the goals of the effort, the overall strategy, and the plan of work. This training cannot be partitioned, so this part of the added effort varies linearly with the number of workers.

V. S. Vyssotsky of Bell Telephone Laboratories estimates that a large project can sustain a manpower buildup of 30% per year. More than that strains and even inhibits the evolution of the essential informal structure and its communication pathways. F. J. Corbató of MIT points out that a long project must anticipate a turnover of 20% per year, and new people must be both technically trained and integrated into the formal structure.

Intercommunication is worse. If each part of the task must be separately coordinated with each other part, the effort increases as $n(n-1)/2$. Three workers require three times as much pairwise intercommunication as two; four require six times as much as two. If, moreover, there need to be conferences among three, four, etc., workers to resolve things jointly, matters get worse yet. The added effort of communicating may fully counteract the division of the original task and bring us back to the situation of Fig. 3.

Since software construction is inherently a systems effort—an exercise in complex interrelationships—communication effort is great, and it quickly

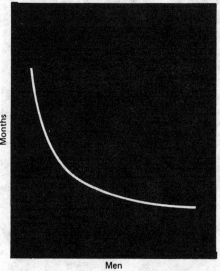

Fig. 2. Even on tasks that can be nicely partitioned among people, the additional communication required adds to the total work, increasing the schedule.

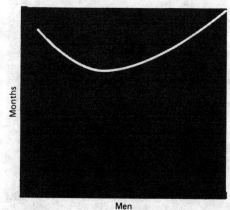

Fig. 3. Since software construction is complex, the communications overhead is great. Adding more men can lengthen, rather than shorten, the schedule.

dominates the decrease in individual task time brought about by partitioning. Adding more men then lengthens, not shortens, the schedule.

Systems test

No parts of the schedule are so thoroughly affected by sequential constraints as component debugging and system test. Furthermore, the time required depends on the number and subtlety of the errors encountered. Theoretically this number should be zero. Because of optimism, we usually expect the number of bugs to be smaller than it turns out to be. Therefore testing is usually the most mis-scheduled part of programming.

For some years I have been successfully using the following rule of thumb for scheduling a software task:

⅓ planning
⅙ coding
¼ component test and early system test
¼ system test, all components in hand.

This differs from conventional scheduling in several important ways:
1. The fraction devoted to planning is larger than normal. Even so, it is barely enough to produce a de-

of the schedule.

In examining conventionally scheduled projects, I have found that few allowed one-half of the projected schedule for testing, but that most did indeed spend half of the actual schedule for that purpose. Many of these were on schedule until and except in system testing.

Failure to allow enough time for system test, in particular, is peculiarly disastrous. Since the delay comes at the end of the schedule, no one is aware of schedule trouble until almost the delivery date. Bad news, late and without warning, is unsettling to customers and to managers.

Furthermore, delay at this point has unusually severe financial, as well as psychological, repercussions. The project is fully staffed, and cost-per-day is maximum. More seriously, the software is to support other business effort (shipping of computers, operation of new facilities, etc.) and the secondary costs of delaying these are very high, for it is almost time for software shipment. Indeed, these secondary costs may far outweigh all others. It is therefore very important to allow enough system test time in the original schedule.

two choices—wait or eat it raw. Software customers have had the same choices.

The cook has another choice; he can turn up the heat. The result is often an omelette nothing can save—burned in one part, raw in another.

Now I do not think software managers have less inherent courage and firmness than chefs, nor than other engineering managers. But false scheduling to match the patron's desired date is much more common in our discipline than elsewhere in engineering. It is very difficult to make a vigorous, plausible, and job-risking defense of an estimate that is derived by no quantitative method, supported by little data, and certified chiefly by the hunches of the managers.

Clearly two solutions are needed. We need to develop and publicize productivity figures, bug-incidence figures, estimating rules, and so on. The whole profession can only profit from sharing such data.

Until estimating is on a sounder basis, individual managers will need to stiffen their backbones, and defend their estimates with the assurance that their poor hunches are better than wish-derived estimates.

Regenerative disaster

What does one do when an essential software project is behind schedule? Add manpower, naturally. As Figs. 1 through 3 suggest, this may or may not help.

Let us consider an example. Suppose a task is estimated at 12 man-months and assigned to three men for four months, and that there are measurable mileposts A, B, C, D, which are scheduled to fall at the end of each month.

Now suppose the first milepost is not reached until two months have elapsed. What are the alternatives facing the manager?
1. Assume that the task must be done on time. Assume that only the first part of the task was misestimated. Then 9 man-months of effort remain, and two months, so 4½ men will be needed. Add 2 men to the 3 assigned.
2. Assume that the task must be done on time. Assume that the whole estimate was uniformly low. Then 18 man-months of effort remain, and two months, so 9 men will be needed. Add 6 men to the 3 assigned.
3. Reschedule. In this case, I like the advice given by an experienced hardware engineer, "Take no small slips." That is, allow enough time in the new schedule to ensure that the work can be carefully and

Fig. 4. Adding manpower to a project which is late may not help. In this case, suppose three men on a 12 man-month project were a month late. If it takes one of the three an extra month to train two new men, the project will be just as late as if no one was added.

tailed and solid specification, and not enough to include research or exploration of totally new techniques.
2. The *half* of the schedule devoted to debugging of completed code is much larger than normal.
3. The part that is easy to estimate, i.e., coding, is given only one-sixth.

Gutless estimating

Observe that for the programmer, as for the chef, the urgency of the patron may govern the scheduled completion of the task, but it cannot govern the actual completion. An omelette, promised in ten minutes, may appear to be progressing nicely. But when it has not set in ten minutes, the customer has thoroughly done, and that rescheduling will not have to be done again.

4. Trim the task. In practice this tends to happen anyway, once the team observes schedule slippage. Where the secondary costs of delay are very high, this is the only feasible action. The manager's only alternatives are to trim it formally and carefully, to reschedule, or to watch the task get silently trimmed by hasty design and incomplete testing.

In the first two cases, insisting that the unaltered task be completed in four months is disastrous. Consider the regenerative effects, for example, for the first alternative (Fig. 4 preceding page). The two new men, however competent and however quickly recruited, will require training in the task by one of the experienced men. If this takes a month, *3 man-months will have been devoted to work not in the original estimate.* Furthermore, the task, originally partitioned three ways, must be repartitioned into five parts, hence some work already done will be lost and system testing must be lengthened. So at the end of the third month, substantially more than 7 man-months of effort remain, and 5 trained people and one month are available. As Fig. 4 suggests, the product is just as late as if no one had been added.

To hope to get done in four months, considering only training time and not repartitioning and extra systems test, would require adding 4 men, not 2, at the end of the second month. To cover repartitioning and system test effects, one would have to add still other men. Now, however, one has at least a 7-man team, not a 3-man one; thus such aspects as team organization and task division are different in kind, not merely in degree.

Notice that by the end of the third month things look very black. The March 1 milestone has not been reached in spite of all the managerial effort. The temptation is very strong to repeat the cycle, adding yet more manpower. Therein lies madness.

The foregoing assumed that only the first milestone was misestimated. If on March 1 one makes the conservative assumption that the whole schedule was optimistic one wants to add 6 men just to the original task. Calculation of the training, repartitioning, system testing effects is left as an exercise for the reader. Without a doubt, the regenerative disaster will yield a poorer product later, than would rescheduling with the original three men, unaugmented.

Oversimplifying outrageously, we state Brooks' Law:

Adding manpower to a late software project makes it later.

This then is the demythologizing of the man-month. The number of months of a project depends upon its sequential constraints. The maximum number of men depends upon the number of independent subtasks. From these two quantities one can derive schedules using fewer men and more months. (The only risk is product obsolescence.) One cannot, however, get workable schedules using more men and fewer months. More software projects have gone awry for lack of calendar time than for all other causes combined.

Calling the shot

How long will a system programming job take? How much effort will be required? How does one estimate?

I have earlier suggested ratios that seem to apply to planning time, coding, component test, and system test. First, one must say that one does *not* estimate the entire task by estimating the coding portion only and then applying the ratios. The coding is only one-sixth or so of the problem, and errors in its estimate or in the ratios could lead to ridiculous results.

Second, one must say that data for building isolated small programs are not applicable to programming systems products. For a program averaging about 3,200 words, for example, Sackman, Erikson, and Grant report an average code-plus-debug time of about 178 hours for a single programmer, a figure which would extrapolate to give an annual productivity of 35,800 statements per year. A program half that size took less than one-fourth as long, and extrapolated productivity is almost 80,000 statements per year.[1]. Planning, documentation, testing, system integration, and training times must be added. The linear extrapolation of such spring figures is meaningless. Extrapolation of times for the hundred-yard dash shows that a man can run a mile in under three minutes.

Before dismissing them, however, let us note that these numbers, although not for strictly comparable problems, suggest that effort goes as a power of size *even* when no communication is involved except that of a man with his memories.

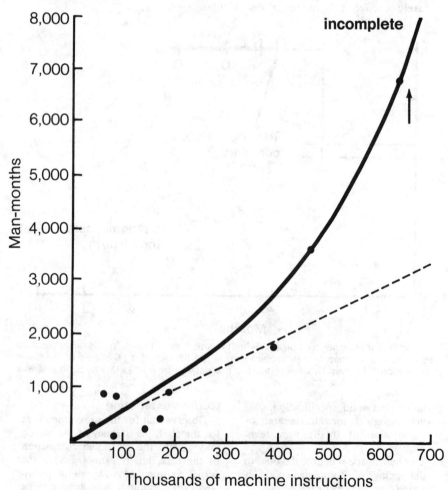

Fig. 5. As a project's complexity increases, the number of man-months required to complete it goes up exponentially.

Fig. 5 tells the sad story. It illustrates results reported from a study done by Nanus and Farr[2] at System Development Corp. This shows an exponent of 1.5; that is,

$$\text{effort} = (\text{constant}) \times (\text{number of instructions})^{1.5}$$

Another SDC study reported by Weinwurm[3] also shows an exponent near 1.5.

A few studies on programmer productivity have been made, and several estimating techniques have been proposed. Morin has prepared a survey of the published data.[4] Here I shall give only a few items that seem especially illuminating.

Portman's data

Charles Portman, manager of ICL's Software Div., Computer Equipment Organization (Northwest) at Manchester, offers another useful personal insight.

He found his programming teams missing schedules by about one-half—each job was taking approximately twice as long as estimated. The estimates were very careful, done by experienced teams estimating man-hours for several hundred subtasks on a PERT chart. When the slippage pattern appeared, he asked them to keep careful daily logs of time usage. These showed that the estimating error could be entirely accounted for by the fact that his teams were only realizing 50% of the working week as actual programming and debugging time. Machine downtime, higher-priority short unrelated jobs, meetings, paperwork, company business, sickness, personal time, etc. accounted for the rest. In short, the estimates made an unrealistic assumption about the number of technical work hours per man-year. My own experience quite confirms his conclusion.

An unpublished 1964 study by E. F. Bardain shows programmers realizing only 27% productive time.[5]

	Prog. units	Number of programmers	Years	Man-years	Program words	Words/ man-yr.
Operational	50	83	4	101	52,000	515
Maintenance	36	60	4	81	51,000	630
Compiler	13	9	2¼	17	38,000	2230
Translator (Data assembler)	15	13	2½	11	25,000	2270

Table 1. Data from Bell Labs indicates productivity differences between complex problems (the first two are basically control programs with many modules) and less complex ones. No one is certain how much of the difference is due to complexity, how much to the number of people involved.

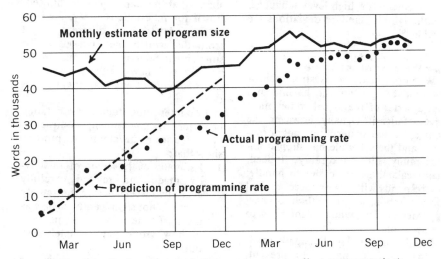

Fig. 6. Bell Labs' experience in predicting programming effort on one project.

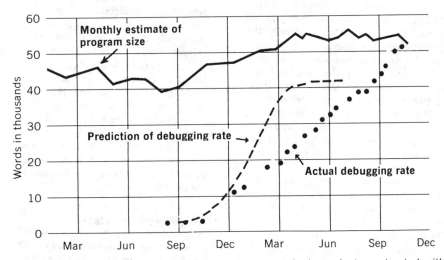

Fig. 7. Bell's predictions for debugging rates on a single project, contrasted with actual figures.

Aron's data

Joel Aron, manager of Systems Technology at IBM in Gaithersburg, Maryland, has studied programmer productivity when working on nine large systems (briefly, *large* means more than 25 programmers and 30,000 deliverable instructions). He divides such systems according to interactions among programmers (and system parts) and finds productivities as follows:

Very few interactions	10,000 instructions per man-year
Some interactions	5,000
Many interactions	1,500

The man-years do not include support and system test activities, only design and programming. When these figures are diluted by a factor of two to cover system test, they closely match Harr's data.

Harr's data

John Harr, manager of programming for the Bell Telephone Laboratories' Electronic Switching System, reported his and others' experience in a paper at the 1969 Spring Joint Computer Conference.[6] These data are shown in Table 1 and Figs. 6 and 7.

Of these, Fig. 6 is the most detailed and the most useful. The first two jobs are basically control programs; the second two are basically language translators. Productivity is stated in terms of debugged words per man-year. This includes programming, component test, and system test. It is not clear how much of the planning effort, or effort in machine support, writing, and the like, is included.

The productivities likewise fall into two classifications: those for control programs are about 600 words per man-year; those for translators are about 2,200 words per man-year. Note that all four programs are of similar size—the variation is in size of the work groups, length of time, and number of modules. Which is cause and which is effect? Did the control programs require more people because they were more complicated? Or did they require more modules and more man-months because they were assigned more people? Did they take longer because of the greater complexity, or because more people were assigned? One can't be sure. The control programs were surely more complex. These uncertainties aside, the numbers describe the real productivities achieved on a large system, using present-day programming techniques. As such they are a real contribution.

Figs. 6 and 7 show some interesting data on programming and debugging rates as compared to predicted rates.

OS/360 data

IBM OS/360 experience, while not available in the detail of Harr's data, confirms it. Productivities in range of 600-800 debugged instructions per man-year were experienced by control program groups. Productivities in the 2,000-3,000 debugged instructions per man-year were achieved by language translator groups. These include planning done by the group, coding component test, system test, and some support activities. They are comparable to Harr's data, so far as I can tell.

Aron's data, Harr's data, and the OS/360 data all confirm striking differences in productivity related to the complexity and difficulty of the task itself. My guideline in the morass of estimating complexity is that compilers are three times as bad as normal batch application programs, and operating systems are three times as bad as compilers.

Corbató's data

Both Harr's data and OS/360 data are for assembly language programming. Little data seem to have been published on system programming productivity using higher-level languages. Corbató of MIT's Project MAC reports, however, a mean productivity of 1,200 lines of debugged PL/I statements per man-year on the MULTICS system (between 1 and 2 million words)[7]

This number is very exciting. Like the other projects, MULTICS includes control programs and language transla-

tors. Like the others, it is producing a system programming product, tested and documented. The data seem to be comparable in terms of kind of effort included. And the productivity number is a good average between the control program and translator productivities of other projects.

But Corbató's number is *lines* per man-year, not *words!* Each statement in his system corresponds to about three-to-five words of handwritten code! This suggests two important conclusions:

- Productivity seems constant in terms of elementary statements, a conclusion that is reasonable in terms of the thought a statement requires and the errors it may include.
- Programming productivity may be increased as much as five times when a suitable high-level language is used. To back up these conclusions, W. M. Taliaffero also reports a constant productivity of 2,400 statements/year in Assembler, FORTRAN, and COBOL.[8] E. A. Nelson has shown a 3-to-1 productivity improvement for high-level language, although his standard deviations are wide.[9]

Hatching a catastrophe

When one hears of disastrous schedule slippage in a project, he imagines that a series of major calamities must have befallen it. Usually, however, the disaster is due to termites, not tornadoes; and the schedule has slipped imperceptibly but inexorably. Indeed, major calamities are easier to handle; one responds with major force, radical reorganization, the invention of new approaches. The whole team rises to the occasion.

But the day-by-day slippage is harder to recognize, harder to prevent, harder to make up. Yesterday a key man was sick, and a meeting couldn't be held. Today the machines are all down, because lightning struck the building's power transformer. Tomorrow the disc routines won't start testing, because the first disc is a week late from the factory. Snow, jury duty, family problems, emergency meetings with customers, executive audits—the list goes on and on. Each one only postpones some activity by a half-day or a day. And the schedule slips, one day at a time.

How does one control a big project on a tight schedule? The first step is to *have* a schedule. Each of a list of events, called milestones, has a date. Picking the dates is an estimating problem, discussed already and crucially dependent on experience.

For picking the milestones there is

only one relevant rule. Milestones must be concrete, specific, measurable events, defined with knife-edge sharpness. Coding, for a counterexample, is "90% finished" for half of the total coding time. Debugging is "99% complete" most of the time. "Planning complete" is an event one can proclaim almost at will.[10]

Concrete milestones, on the other hand, are 100% events. "Specifications signed by architects and implementers," "source coding 100% complete, keypunched, entered into disc library," "debugged version passes all test cases." These concrete milestones demark the vague phases of planning, coding, debugging.

It is more important that milestones be sharp-edged and unambiguous than that they be easily verifiable by the boss. Rarely will a man lie about mile-

> None love
> the bearer of bad news.
> *Sophocles*

stone progress, *if* the milestone is so sharp that he can't deceive himself. But if the milestone is fuzzy, the boss often understands a different report from that which the man gives. To supplement Sophocles, no one enjoys bearing bad news, either, so it gets softened without any real intent to deceive.

Two interesting studies of estimating behavior by government contractors on large-scale development projects show that:

1. Estimates of the length of an activity made and revised carefully every two weeks before the activity starts do not significantly change as the start time draws near, no matter how wrong they ultimately turn out to be.
2. *During* the activity, *over*estimates of duration come steadily down as the activity proceeds.
3. *Underestimates* do not change significantly during the activity until about three weeks before the scheduled completion.[11]

Sharp milestones are in fact a service to the team, and one they can properly expect from a manager. The fuzzy milestone is the harder burden to live with. It is in fact a millstone that grinds down morale, for it deceives one about lost time until it is irremediable. And chronic schedule slippage is a morale-killer.

"The other piece is late"

A schedule slips a day; so what? Who gets excited about a one-day slip? We can make it up later. And the other piece ours fits into is late anyway.

A baseball manager recognizes a nonphysical talent, *hustle,* as an essential gift of great players and great teams. It is the characteristic of running faster than necessary, moving sooner than necessary, trying harder than necessary. It is essential for great programming teams, too. Hustle provides the cushion, the reserve capacity, that enables a team to cope with routine mishaps, to anticipate and forfend minor calamities. The calculated response, the measured effort, are the wet blankets that dampen hustle. As we have seen, one *must* get excited about a one-day slip. Such are the elements of catastrophe.

But not all one-day slips are equally disastrous. So some calculation of response is necessary, though hustle be dampened. How does one tell which slips matter? There is no substitute for a PERT chart or a critical-path schedule. Such a network shows who waits for what. It shows who is on the critical path, where any slip moves the end date. It also shows how much an activity can slip before it moves into the critical path.

The PERT technique, strictly speaking, is an elaboration of critical-path scheduling in which one estimates three times for every event, times corresponding to different probabilities of meeting the estimated dates. I do not find this refinement to be worth the extra effort, but for brevity I will call any critical path network a PERT chart.

The preparation of a PERT chart is the most valuable part of its use. Laying out the network, identifying the dependencies, and estimating the legs all force a great deal of very specific planning very early in a project. The first chart is always terrible, and one invents and invents in making the second one.

As the project proceeds, the PERT chart provides the answer to the demoralizing excuse, "The other piece is late anyhow." It shows how hustle is needed to keep one's own part off the critical path, and it suggests ways to make up the lost time in the other part.

Under the rug

When a first-line manager sees his small team slipping behind, he is rarely inclined to run to the boss with this woe. The team might be able to make it up, or he should be able to invent or reorganize to solve the problem. Then why worry the boss with it? So far, so good. Solving such problems is exactly what the first-line manager is there for. And the boss does have enough real worries demanding his action that he doesn't seek others. So all the dirt gets swept under the rug.

But every boss needs two kinds of information, exceptions for action and a status picture for education.[12] For that purpose he needs to know the status of all his teams. Getting a true picture of that status is hard.

The first-line manager's interests and those of the boss have an inherent conflict here. The first-line manager fears that if he reports his problem, the boss will act on it. Then his action will preempt the manager's function, diminish his authority, foul up his other plans. So as long as the manager thinks he can solve it alone, he doesn't tell the boss.

Two rug-lifting techniques are open to the boss. Both must be used. The first is to reduce the role conflict and inspire sharing of status. The other is to yank the rug back.

Reducing the role conflict

The boss must first distinguish between action information and status information. He must discipline himself *not* to act on problems his managers can solve, and *never* to act on problems when he is explicitly reviewing status. I once knew a boss who invariably picked up the phone to give orders before the end of the first para-

A=APPROVAL
C=COMPLETED

*= REVISED PLANNED DATE
NE=NOT ESTABLISHED

PROJECT	LOCATION	COMMITMNT ANNOUNCE RELEASE	OBJECTIVE AVAILABLE APPROVED	SPECS AVAILABLE APPROVED	SRL AVAILABLE APPROVED	ALPHA TEST ENTRY EXIT	COMP TEST START COMPLETE	SYS TEST START COMPLETE	BULLETIN AVAILABLE APPROVED	BETA TEST ENTRY EXIT
OPERATING SYSTEM										
12K DESIGN LEVEL (E)										
ASSEMBLY	SAN JOSE	04/--/4 C 12/31/5	10/28/4 C	10/13/4 C 01/11/5	11/13/4 C 11/16/4 A	01/15/5 C 02/15/5				09/01/5 11/30/5
FORTRAN	POK	04/--/4 C 12/31/5	10/28/4 C	10/21/4 C 01/22/5	12/17/4 C 12/19/4 A	01/15/5 C 02/22/5				09/01/5 11/30/5
COBOL	ENDICOTT	04/--/4 C 12/31/5	10/25/4 C	10/15/4 C 01/20/5 A	11/17/4 C 12/08/4 A	01/15/5 C 02/22/5				09/01/5 11/30/5
RPG	SAN JOSE	04/--/4 C 12/31/5	10/28/4 C	09/30/4 C 01/05/5 A	12/02/4 C 01/18/5 A	01/15/5 C 02/22/5				09/01/5 11/30/5
UTILITIES	TIME/LIFE	04/--/4 C 12/31/5	06/24/4 C		11/20/4 C 11/30/4 A					09/01/5 11/30/5
SORT 1	POK	04/--/4 C 12/31/5	10/28/4 C	10/19/4 C 01/11/5	11/12/4 C 11/30/4 A	01/15/5 C 03/22/5				09/01/5 11/30/5
SORT 2	POK	04/--/4 C 06/30/6	10/28/4 C	10/19/4 C 01/11/5	11/12/4 C 11/30/4 A	01/15/5 C 03/22/5				03/01/6 05/30/6
44K DESIGN LEVEL (F)										
ASSEMBLY	SAN JOSE	04/--/4 C 12/31/5	10/28/4 C	10/13/4 C 01/11/5	11.13.4 C 11/18/4 A	02/15/5 C 03/22/5				09/01/5 11/30/5
COBOL	TIME/LIFE	04/--/4 C 06/30/6	10/28/4 C	10/15/4 C 01/20/5 A	11/17/4 C 12/06/4 A	02/15/5 C 03/22/5				03/01/6 05/30/6
NPL	HURSLEY	04/--/4 C 03/31/6	10/28/4 C							
2250	KINGSTON	03/30/4 C 03/31/6	11/05/4 C	10/06/4 C 01/04/5	01/12/5 C 01/29/5	01/04/5 C 01/29/5				01/03/6 NE
2280	KINGSTON	06/30/4 C 09/30/6	11/05/4 C			04/01/5 04/30/5				01/28/6 NE
200K DESIGN LEVEL (H)										
ASSEMBLY	TIME/LIFE		10/28/4 C							
FORTRAN	POK	04/--/4 C 06/30/6	10/28/4 C	10/16/4 C 01/11/5	11/11/4 C 12/10/4 A	02/15/5 C 03/22/5				03/01/6 05/30/6
NPL	HURSLEY	04/--/4 C	10/28/4 C			07/--/5				01/--/7
NPL H	POK	04/--/4 C	03/30/4 C			02/01/5 04/01/5				10/15/5 12/15/5

Fig. 8. A report showing milestones and status in a key document in project control. This one shows some problems in OS development: specifications approval is late on some items (those without "A"); documentation (SRL) approval is overdue on another; and one (2250 support) is late coming out of alpha test.

graph in a status report. That response is guaranteed to squelch full disclosure.

Conversely, when the manager knows his boss will accept status reports without panic or preemption, he comes to give honest appraisals.

This whole process is helped if the boss labels meetings, reviews, conferences, as *status-review* meetings versus *problem-action* meetings, and controls himself accordingly. Obviously one may call a problem-action meeting as a consequence of a status meeting, if he believes a problem is out of hand. But at least everybody knows what the score is, and the boss thinks twice before grabbing the ball.

Yanking the rug off

Nevertheless, it is necessary to have review techniques by which the true status is made known, whether cooperatively or not. The PERT chart with its frequent sharp milestones is the basis for such review. On a large project one may want to review some part of it each week, making the rounds once a month or so.

A report showing milestones and actual completions is the key document. Fig. 8 (preceding page), shows an excerpt from such a report. This report shows some troubles. Specifications approval is overdue on several components. Manual (SRL) approval is overdue on another, and one is late getting out of the first state (ALPHA) of the independently conducted product test. So such a report serves as an agenda for the meeting of 1 February. Everyone knows the questions, and the component manager should be prepared to explain why it's late, when it will be finished, what steps he's taking, and what help, if any, he needs from the boss or collateral groups.

V. Vyssotsky of Bell Telephone Laboratories adds the following observation:

I have found it handy to carry both "scheduled" and "estimated" dates in the milestone report. The scheduled dates are the property of the project manager and represent a consistent work plan for the project as a whole, and one which is a priori a reasonable plan. The estimated dates are the property of the lowest level manager who has cognizance over the piece of work in question, and represents his best judgment as to when it will actually happen, given the resources he has available and when he received (or has commitments for delivery of) his prerequisite inputs. The project manager has to keep his fingers off the estimated dates, and put the emphasis on getting accurate, unbiased estimates rather

than palatable optimistic estimates or self-protective conservative ones. Once this is clearly established in everyone's mind, the project manager can see quite a ways into the future where he is going to be in trouble if he doesn't do something.

The preparation of the PERT chart is a function of the boss and the managers reporting to him. Its updating, revision, and reporting requires the attention of a small (one-to-three-man) staff group which serves as an extension of the boss. Such a "Plans and Controls" team is invaluable for a large project. It has no authority except to ask all the line managers when they will have set or changed milestones, and whether milestones have been met. Since the Plans and Controls group handles all the paperwork, the burden on the line managers is reduced to the essentials—making the decisions.

We had a skilled, enthusiastic, and diplomatic Plans and Controls group on the os/360 project, run by A. M. Pietrasanta, who devoted considerable inventive talent to devising effective but unobtrusive control methods. As a result, I found his group to be widely respected and more than tolerated. For a group whose role is inherently that of an irritant, this is quite an accomplishment.

The investment of a modest amount of skilled effort in a Plans and Controls function is very rewarding. It makes far more difference in project accomplishment than if these people worked directly on building the product programs. For the Plans and Controls group is the watchdog who renders the imperceptible delays visible and who points up the critical elements. It is the early warning system against losing a year, one day at a time.

Epilogue

The tar pit of software engineering will continue to be sticky for a long time to come. One can expect the human race to continue attempting systems just within or just beyond our reach; and software systems are perhaps the most intricate and complex of man's handiworks. The management of this complex craft will demand our best use of new languages and systems, our best adaptation of proven engineering management methods, liberal doses of common sense, and a God-given humility to recognize our fallibility and limitations.

References

1. Sackman, H., W. J. Erikson, and E. E. Grant, "Exploratory Experimentation Studies Comparing Online and Offline Programming Performance," *Communications of the ACM*, 11 (1968), 3-11.

2. Nanus, B., and L. Farr, "Some Cost Contributors to Large-Scale Programs," *AFIPS Proceedings, SJCC*, 25 (1964), 239-248.

3. Weinwurm, G. F., *Research in the Management of Computer Programming*. Report SP-2059, 1965, System Development Corp., Santa Monica.

4. Morin, L. H., *Estimation of Resources for Computer Programming Projects*, M. S. thesis, Univ. of North Carolina, Chapel Hill, 1974.

5. Quoted by D. B. Mayer and A. W. Stalnaker, "Selection and Evaluation of Computer Personnel," *Proceedings 23 ACM Conference*, 1968, 661.

6. Paper given at a panel session and not included in the *AFIPS Proceedings*.

7. Corbató, F. J., *Sensitive Issues in the Design of Multi-Use Systems*. Lecture at the opening of the Honeywell EDP Technology Center, 1968.

8. Taliaffero, W. M., "Modularity the Key to System Growth Potential," *Software*, 1 (1971), 245-257.

9. Nelson, E. A., *Management Handbook for the Estimation of Computer Programming Costs*. Report TM-3225, System Development Corp., Santa Monica, pp. 66-67.

10. Reynolds, C. H., "What's Wrong with Computer Programming Management?" in *On the Management of Computer Programming*. Ed. G. F. Weinwurm. Philadelphia: Auerbach, 1971, pp. 35-42.

11. King, W. R., and T. A. Wilson, "Subjective Time Estimates in Critical Path Planning—a Preliminary Analysis," *Management Sciences*, 13 (1967), 307-320, and sequel, W. R. King, D. M. Witterrongel, and K. D. Hezel, "On the Analysis of Critical Path Time Estimating Behavior," *Management Sciences*, 14 (1967), 79-84.

12. Brooks, F. P., and K. E. Iverson, *Automatic Data Processing, System/360 Edition*. New York: Wiley, 1969, pp. 428-430. □

Dr. Brooks is presently a professor at the Univ. of North Carolina at Chapel Hill, and chairman of the computer science department there. He is best known as "the father of the IBM System/360," having served as project manager for the hardware development and as manager of the Operating System/360 project during its design phase. Earlier he was an architect of the IBM Stretch and Harvest computers.

At Chapel Hill he has participated in establishing and guiding the Triangle Universities Computation Center and the North Carolina Educational Computing Service. He is the author of two editions of "Automatic Data Processing" and "The Mythical Man-Month: Essays on Software Engineering" (Addison-Wesley), from which this excerpt is taken.

R. Alec Mackenzie

The management process in 3-D

*A diagram showing the activities, functions,
and basic elements of the executive's job*

Foreword

To many businessmen who are trying to keep up with management concepts, the literature must sometimes seem more confusing than enlightening. In addition to reflecting differences of opinion and semantics, it generally comes to the reader in fragments. The aim of this diagram is not to give the executive new information, but to help him put the pieces together.

Mr. Mackenzie is Vice President of The Presidents Association, Inc., an organization affiliated with the American Management Association. He has had extensive experience in planning, organizing, and teaching seminars for businessmen here and abroad. He is coauthor with Ted W. Engstrom of *Managing Your Time* (Zondervan Publishing House, 1967).

The chart of "The Management Process," facing this page, begins with the three basic elements with which a manager deals: ideas, things, and people. Management of these three elements is directly related to conceptual thinking (of which planning is an essential part), administration, and leadership. Not surprisingly, two scholars have identified the first three types of managers required in organizations as the planner, the administrator, and the leader.[1]

Note the distinction between leader and manager. The terms should not be used interchangeably. While a good manager will often be a good leader, and vice versa, this is not necessarily the case. For example:

□ In World War II, General George Patton was known for his ability to lead and inspire men on the battlefield, but not for his conceptual abilities. In contrast, General Omar Bradley was known for his conceptual abilities, espe-

cially planning and managing a campaign, rather than for his leadership.

Similarly in industry, education, and government it is possible to have an outstanding manager who is not capable of leading people but who, if he recognizes this deficiency, will staff his organization to compensate for it. Alternatively, an entrepreneur may possess charismatic qualities as a leader, yet may lack the administrative capabilities required for overall effective management; and he too must staff to make up for the deficiency.

We are not dealing here with leadership in general. We are dealing with leadership as a *function of management*. Nor are we dealing with administration in general but, again, as a function of management.

The following definitions are suggested for clarity and simplicity:

○ *Management*—achieving objectives through others.

1. See H. Igor Ansoff and R.G. Brandenburg, "The General Manager of the Future," *California Management Review*, Spring 1969, p. 61.

Exhibit I. The management process

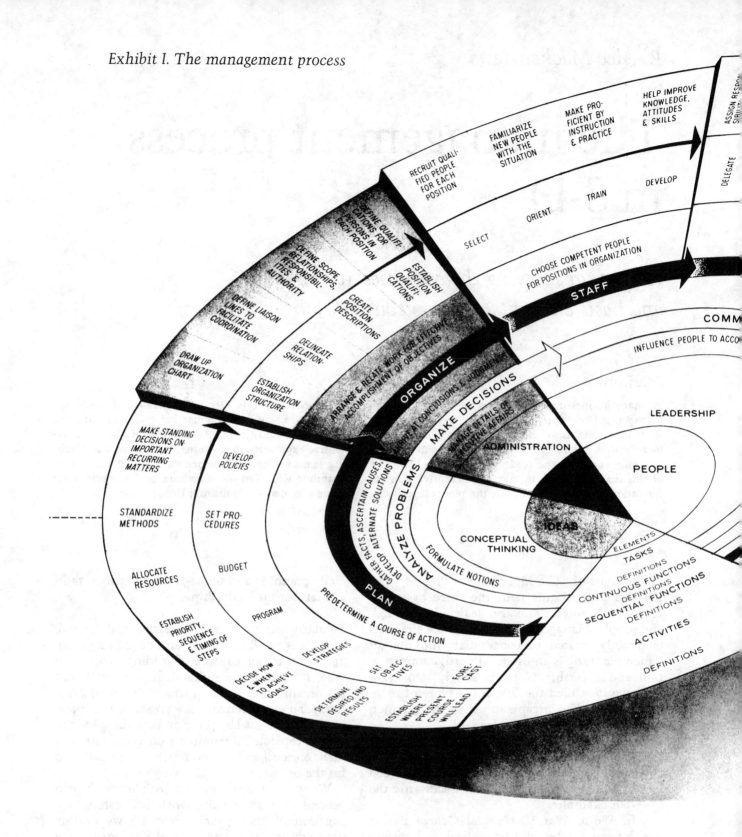

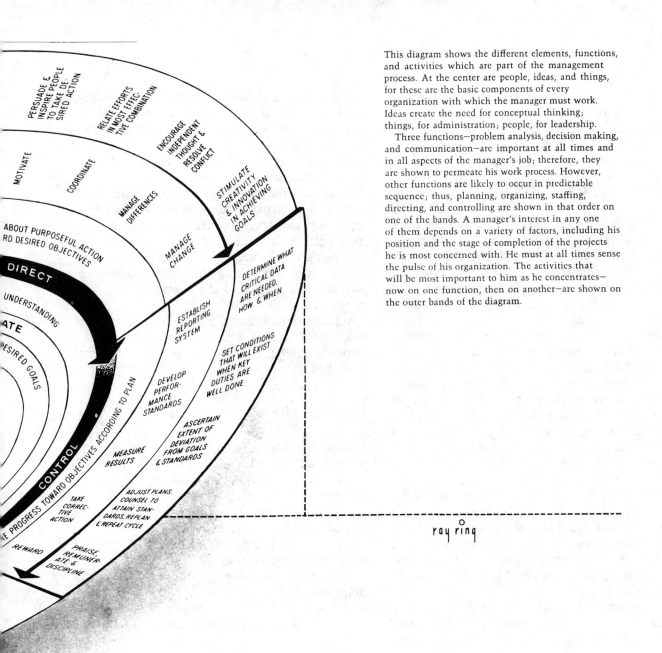

PERSUADE &
INSPIRE PEOPLE
TO TAKE DE-
SIRED ACTION

RELATE EFFORTS
IN MOST EFFEC-
TIVE COMBINATION

ENCOURAGE
INDEPENDENT
THOUGHT &
RESOLVE
CONFLICT

MOTIVATE

COORDINATE

MANAGE
DIFFERENCES

STIMULATE
CREATIVITY
& INNOVATION
IN ACHIEVING
GOALS

MANAGE
CHANGE

ABOUT PURPOSEFUL ACTION
RD DESIRED OBJECTIVES

DIRECT

DETERMINE WHAT
CRITICAL DATA
ARE NEEDED,
HOW & WHEN

UNDERSTANDING

ESTABLISH
REPORTING
SYSTEM

ATE

SET CONDITIONS
THAT WILL EXIST
WHEN KEY
DUTIES ARE
WELL DONE

DESIRED GOALS

DEVELOP
PERFOR-
MANCE
STANDARDS

ASCERTAIN
EXTENT OF
DEVIATION
FROM GOALS
& STANDARDS

CONTROL

E PROGRESS TOWARD OBJECTIVES ACCORDING TO PLAN

MEASURE
RESULTS

TAKE
CORREC-
TIVE
ACTION

ADJUST PLANS,
COUNSEL TO
ATTAIN STAN-
DARDS, REPLAN
& REPEAT CYCLE

REWARD

PRAISE,
REMUNER-
ATE &
DISCIPLINE

ray ring

This diagram shows the different elements, functions, and activities which are part of the management process. At the center are people, ideas, and things, for these are the basic components of every organization with which the manager must work. Ideas create the need for conceptual thinking; things, for administration; people, for leadership.

Three functions—problem analysis, decision making, and communication—are important at all times and in all aspects of the manager's job; therefore, they are shown to permeate his work process. However, other functions are likely to occur in predictable sequence; thus, planning, organizing, staffing, directing, and controlling are shown in that order on one of the bands. A manager's interest in any one of them depends on a variety of factors, including his position and the stage of completion of the projects he is most concerned with. He must at all times sense the pulse of his organization. The activities that will be most important to him as he concentrates—now on one function, then on another—are shown on the outer bands of the diagram.

R. Alec Mackenzie,
"The Management Process in 3-D,"
Harvard Business Review,
November-December 1969
Copyright

○ *Administration*—managing the details of executive affairs.

○ *Leadership*—influencing people to accomplish desired objectives.

Functions described

The functions noted in the diagram have been selected after careful study of the works of many leading writers and teachers.[2] While the authorities use different terms and widely varying classifications of functions, I find that there is far more agreement among them than the variations suggest.

Arrows are placed on the diagram to indicate that five of the functions generally tend to be "sequential." More specifically, in an undertaking one ought first to ask what the purpose or objective is which gives rise to the function of *planning*; then comes the function of *organizing*—determining the way in which the work is to be broken down into manageable units; after that is *staffing*, selecting qualified people to do the work; next is *directing*, bringing about purposeful action toward desired objectives; finally, the function of *control* is the measurement of results against the plan, the rewarding of the people according to their performance, and the replanning of the work to make corrections —thus starting the cycle over again as the *process repeats itself*.

Three functions—analyzing problems, making decisions, and communicating—are called "general" or "continuous" functions because they occur throughout the management process rather than in any particular sequence. For example, many decisions will be made throughout the planning process as well as during the organiz-

2. The following studies were particularly helpful: Harold Koontz, *Toward a Unified Theory of Management* (New York, McGraw-Hill Book Company, 1964); Philip W. Shay, "The Theory and Practice of Management," Association of Consulting Management Engineers, 1967; Louis A. Allen, *The Management Profession* (New York, McGraw-Hill Book Company, 1964), a particularly useful analysis of managerial functions and activities; Ralph C. Davis, *Fundamentals of Top Management* (New York, Harper & Brothers, 1951); Harold F. Smiddy, "GE's Philosophy & Approach for Manager Development," General Management Series # 174, American Management Association, 1955; George R. Terry, *Principles of Management* (Homewood, Illinois, Richard D. Irwin, Inc., 1956); William H. Newman, *Administrative Action* (Englewood Cliffs, N.J., Prentice-Hall, Inc., 1950); Lawrence A. Appley, *Values in Management* (New York, American Management Association, 1969); Ordway Tead, *Administration: Its Purpose and Performance* (New York, Harper & Brothers, 1959); Peter F. Drucker, *The Practice of Management* (New York, Harper & Row, 1954).

ing, directing, and controlling processes. Equally, there must be communication for many of the functions and activities to be effective. And the active manager will be employing problem analysis throughout all of the sequential functions of management.

In actual practice, of course, the various functions and activities tend to merge. While selecting a top manager, for example, an executive may well be planning new activities which this manager's capabilities will make possible, and may even be visualizing the organizational impact of these plans and the controls which will be necessary.

Simplified definitions are added for each of the functions and activities to ensure understanding of what is meant by the basic elements described.

Prospective gains

Hopefully, this diagram of the management process will produce a variety of benefits for practitioners and students. Among these benefits are:

○ A unified concept of managerial functions and activities.

○ A way to fit together all generally accepted activities of management.

○ A move toward standardization of terminology.

○ The identifying and relating of such activities as problem analysis, management of change, and management of differences.

○ Help to beginning students of management in seeing the "boundaries of the ballpark" and sensing the sequential relationships of certain functions and the interrelationships of others.

○ Clearer distinctions between the leadership, administrative, and strategic planning functions of management.

In addition, the diagram should appeal to those who, like myself, would like to see more emphasis on the "behaviorist" functions of management, for it elevates staffing and communicating to the level of a function. Moreover, it establishes functions and activities as the two most important terms for describing the job of the manager.

Software Engineering Project Management
A Top-Down View

Richard H. Thayer
California State University, Sacramento
Sacramento, CA 95819

Abstract—This paper attempts to identify and describe a comprehensive set of project management and software engineering project management activities and tasks that should be undertaken by any manager who is assigned the responsibility of managing a software engineering project. The paper covers the management functions of planning, organizing, staffing, directing, and controlling and discusses in detail the activities and specific tasks of software engineering project management that are necessary to successfully manage a software engineering project.

The conept of the universality of management allows us to use the management functions and fundamental activities from main-stream management as the functions and top-level activities of software engineering project management. Through th application of top-down analysis each of the five principal functons of management were partitioned into a set of detailed management activities from which the detailed activities and tasks of software engineering project management, in turn, were derived. These detailed management activities are the characteristic duties of managers. The detailed activities and tasks as defined and described in this paper are the characteristic duties and responsibilities of engineering and software engineering project management.

1. Introduction

This paper is about management, software engineering project management, and the concept of the universality of management.

Management can be defined as all the activities and tasks undertaken by one or more persons for the purpose of planning and controlling the activities of others in order to achieve an objective or complete an activity that could not be achieved by the others acting alone.

Project management, in turn, is defined as a system of procedures, practices, technologies, and know-how that provides the planning, organizing, staffing, directing, and controlling necessary to successfully manage an engineering project. *Know-how*, in this case, means the skill, background, and wisdom to apply knowledge effectively in practice. If the product of the project is software, then the act of managing a software project is called software development project management or, more recently, *software engineering project management* (SEPM). The *manager* of a software engineering project is called a *software engineering project manager* or, in this paper, just *project manager* (PM).

Software engineering projects are frequently part of a larger, more comprehensive system that includes equipment (hardware), facilities, personnel, and procedures, as well as software. Examples are aircraft systems, accounting systems, radar systems, inventory control systems, railroad switching systems, and so forth. These *system engineering projects* are typically managed by one or more system project managers (sometimes called *program managers*) who manage an organization comprised of technically qualified engineers (all types), experts in the field of the application, scientific specialists, programmers, support personnel, and others. If the software to be delivered is a "stand-alone" software system (a system that does not interface with any other system) which is being developed for or on an existing or commercial "off-the-shelf" computer, the software engineering project manager can be the system project manager.

The concept of the *universality of management* comes from the principles of management sciences [Koontz, O'Donnell, and Weihrich, 1984], [Fayol, 1949], and it means that:

- Management performs the same functions regardless of its position in the organization or the enterprise managed.

- Management functions and fundamental activities are characteristic duties of managers; management practices, methods, detailed activities, and tasks are particular to the enterprise or job managed.

Therefore, the functions and fundamental activities of management can be universally applied to managing any organization or activity [Thayer and Pyster, 1984]. The application of this concept allows us to apply many major research efforts and successes in the field of management to SEPM. Some past examples are:

- *PERT* and *CPM*—scheduling methods developed in the 1950s;

- *Work breakdown structure (WBS)*—a hierarchical method of representing the relationships between parts of a product (assemblies, subassemblies, components, parts, and so on) or activity (project, subprojects, tasks, subtasks, work packages, and so on). First applied to software development in the 1960s;

- *Matrix organizations*—a project organization method developed in the early 1960s to merge the best of a functional organization with the best of a project organization;

- *Management by objectives (MBO)*—an early motivation methodology of the 1950s;

- *Maslow's hierarchy of needs [1954]*—another motivational model; and

- *Configuration management*—the discipline of identifying the configuration of a system at discrete points in time for purposes of systematically controlling changes to this configuration and maintaining the integrity and traceability of this configuration throughout the system life cycle [Bersoff, 1984].

The importance of this topic is best illustrated by a paragraph contained in the Department of Defense (DoD) report on the DoD software engineering technology initiative called STARS (Software Technology for Adaptable, Reliable Systems), a multimillion-dollar software engineering research project. The DoD report says that:

> The manager plays a major role in software and systems development and support. The difference between success or failure—between a project being on schedule and on budget or late and over budget—is often a function of the manager's effectiveness [DoD Software Initiative, 1983].

In other words, SEPM is the key to a successful software engineering project in today's environment.

This paper attempts to identify and describe a comprehensive set of project management and software engineering project management functions, activities, and tasks that should be undertaken by any manager who is assigned the responsibility of managing a software engineering project. It covers the management functions of planning, organizing, staffing, directing, and controlling and the detailed activities and specific tasks of project management that are necessary to successfully manage a software engineering project.

Section 2 analyzes and partitions the functions of management into a detailed list of management activities. Sections 3 through 7 then partition these management activities into the detailed activities and tasks of SEPM.

2. Functions and Activities of Management

This report takes a top-down approach to establishing a set of SEPM responsibilities, activities, and tasks that should be undertaken by any manager who is assigned the responsibility of managing a software engineering project. The top-down approach involves partitioning and allocating top-level functions to lower-level activities and tasks.

The concept of the universality of management allows us to use the management functions and fundamental activities from main-stream management as the functions and top-level activities of SEPM. Figure 2.1 depicts the classic manage-

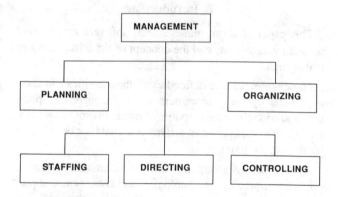

Figure 2.1: Classic Management Model

Table 2.1: Major Functions of Management

Activity	Definition or Explanation
Planning	— Predetermining a course of action for accomplishing organizational objectives.
Organizing	— Arranging and relating work for accomplishment of objectives and the granting of responsibility and authority to obtain those objectives.
Staffing	— Selecting and training people for positions in the organization.
Directing	— Creating an atmosphere that will assist and motivate people to achieve desired end results.
Controlling	— Measuring and correcting performance of activities toward objectives according to plan.

Table 2.2: Major Activities of Management

Management Functions	Fundamental Management Activities
Planning	— Set objectives or goals — Develop strategies — Develop policies — Determine courses of action — Make decisions — Set procedures and rules — Develop programs — Forecast future situations — Prepare budgets — Document project plans
Organizing	— Identify and group required tasks — Select and establish organizational structures — Create organizational positions — Define responsibilities and authority — Establish position qualifications — Document organizational structures
Staffing	— Fill organizational positions — Assimilate newly assigned personnel — Educate or train personnel — Provide for general development — Evaluate and appraise personnel — Compensate — Terminate assignments — Document staffing decisions
Directing	— Provide leadership — Supervise personnel — Delegate authority — Motivate personnel — Coordinate activities — Facilitate communications — Resolve conflicts — Manage changes — Document directing decisions
Controlling	— Develop standards of performance — Establish monitoring and reporting systems — Measure results — Initiate corrective actions — Reward and discipline — Document controlling methods

ment model as portrayed by such well-known authors in the field of management as Koontz and O'Donnell [1972], and others [Rue and Byars, 1983], [Cleland and King, 1972], [MacKenzie, 1969].

In this model, management is partitioned into five separate functions or components: *planning, organizing, staffing, directing,* and *controlling* (see Table 2.1 for definitions or explanations of these functions). All the activities of management, such as budgeting, scheduling, determining authority relationships, training, communicating, monitoring, and so forth fall under one of these five headings.

This is not to say that the five functions are totally independent of each other. Some examples of the interrelationships of management functions are:

(1) Planning for organizing the activity;

(2) Organizing for planning the undertaking;

(3) Controlling the planning function;

(4) Organizing for staffing the organization; and

(5) Staffing for the planning organization.

However, despite these interrelationships, each activity of a manager can be readily placed within one and only one of the five management functions. For instance, number (1) above is a planning function, (2) and (4) are organizing functions, (3) is a controlling function, and (5) is a staffing function.

Each of the five principal functions of management from Figure 2.1 can be further partitioned into a set of more detailed fundamental management activities (see Table 2.2) which in turn can be further divided into more detailed tasks (see Figure 2.2 to illustrate this flowdown). These activities are the characteristic duties of managers and can be applied to the management of any organization or activity. (The definitions or explanations of these activities can be found in Tables 2.3 through 2.7.)

The detailed activities and tasks that are particular to a software engineering project are defined and discussed in Sections 3 through 7. Each of these sections defines and discusses one of the five functions of management along with some of the major issues of that function. The management activities from Table 2.2 are partitioned into one or more levels of detail, called tasks (see Tables 3.1, 4.1, 5.1, 6.1, and 7.1), which are then discussed and/or illustrated in the appropriate section.

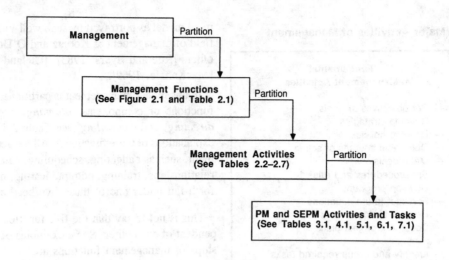

Figure 2.2: Hierarchy of management functions, activities, and tasks

Table 2.3: Planning Activities—Predetermining a Course of Action for Accomplishing Organizational Objectives

Activity	Definition or Explanation
Set objectives or goals	— Determine objectives, activities, or desired outcome or results.
Develop strategies	— Decide major organizational goals and general program of action for reaching those goals.
Develop policies	— Make standing decisions on important recurring matters to provide a guide for decision making.
Determine courses of action	— Search for and examine different courses of action.
Make decisions	— Evaluate and select a course of action from among alternatives.
Set procedures and rules	— Establish methods, guides, and limits for accomplishing an activity.
Develop programs	— Establish policies, procedures, rules, tasks, schedules, and resources necessary to reach a goal or complete a course of action.
Forecast future situations	— Anticipate future events or make assumptions about the future; predict future results or expectations from courses of action.
Prepare budgets	— Assign or allocate costs or numbers to plan/program.
Document project plans	— Record decisions, courses of action, programs/plans, expected future situations, budget, and so on.

Table 2.4: Organizing Activities—Arranging and Relating Work for Accomplishment of Objectives and the Granting of Responsibility and Authority to Obtain Those Objectives

Activity	Definition or Explanation
Identify and group required tasks	— Define, size, and group tasks to be done.
Select and establish organizational structures	— Define or select structures necessary to accomplish required duties and tasks and to control, coordinate, and communicate among these duties and tasks.
Create organizational positions	— Establish title, duties, scope, and relationships for each position.
Define responsibilities and authority	— Define responsibilities for each position and the authority to be granted for the accomplishment of those responsibilities.
Establish position qualifications	— Define qualifications for persons to fill each position.
Document organizational structures	— Record organizational structure, assignment of responsibility and authority, position descriptions, and so on.

Table 2.5: Staffing Activities—Selecting and Training People for Positions in the Organization

Activity	Definition or Explanation
Fill organizational positions	— Select, recruit, or promote qualified people for each position.
Assimilate newly assigned personnel	— Orient and familiarize new people with the organization, facilities, and tasks to be done.
Educate or train personnel	— Make up deficiencies in position qualifications through training and education.
Provide for general development	— Improve knowledge, attitudes, and skills.
Evaluate and appraise personnel	— Evaluate and record the quality and quantity of assigned work.
Compensate	— Give wages, bonuses, benefits, or other financial remuneration.
Terminate assignments	— Transfer or separate redundant personnel.
Document staffing decisions	— Record staffing decisions, training requirements and plans, appraisal records, and so on.

Table 2.6: Directing Activities—Creating an Atmosphere That Will Assist and Motivate People to Achieve Desired End Results

Activity	Definition or Explanation
Provide leadership	— Induce subordinates to accomplish their assignments with enthusiasm and confidence.
Supervise personnel	— Give assigned personnel day-to-day instructions, guidance, and discipline to fulfill their assigned duties.
Delegate authority	— Give authority and discretion to act and expend resources to subordinates.
Motivate personnel	— Persuade and induce personnel to take desired action.
Coordinate activities	— Integrate activities in the most effective and efficient combinations.
Facilitate communications	— Insure free flow of correct information.
Resolve conflicts	— Encourage differences of opinion and resolve resulting conflicts.
Manage changes	— Stimulate creativity and innovation in achieving goals.
Document directing decisions	— Document decisions involving delegation of authority, communication and coordinations procedures and policies, and so on.

Table 2.7: Controlling Activities—Measuring and Correcting Performance of Activities Toward Objectives According to Plan

Activity	Definition or Explanation
Develop standards of performance	— Set conditions or measurements that will exist when tasks are correctly done.
Establish monitoring and reporting systems	— Determine necessary data, who will receive it, and when they will receive it.
Measure results	— Determine accomplishments of, or extent of deviation from, goals and standards.
Initiate corrective actions	— Reinforce standards, adjust goals, or replan.
Reward and discipline	— Praise, remunerate, and discipline applicable personnel.
Document controlling methods	— Document the standards, methods of reporting and control, bonus plans et al., decision points, and so on.

3. Planning a Software Engineering Project

3.1 Introduction and Definitions

Planning a software engineering project consists of all of the management activities that lead to the selection, among alternatives, of future courses of action for the project and the program for carrying the actions out.

Planning involves selecting the *objectives* and *goals* of the project and the *strategies, policies, programs,* and *procedures* for achieving them. "Planning is deciding in advance what to do, how to do it, when to do it, and who is to do it" [Koontz and O'Donnell, 1972].

It is essential to recognize that every successful software engineering project starts with a good plan. Future uncertainties and changes both within the software engineering environment and from external sources make planning a necessity. Planning focuses attention on the objectives. The very act of clarifying and documenting the objectives of the project will highlight project objectives and goals.

The project plan must be efficient, i.e., the contributions of the plan must be greater than the cost of the plan and other undesirable side effects. The planning function is not a rigid, one-time-only effort. Planning should be dynamic, flexible, and subject to change when the environment or project changes.

3.2 Major Issues in Planning

The major issues (or problems) in planning for a software engineering project are:

- Software requirements (project objectives) are difficult to write correctly.
- Planning a program of action is frequently incomplete and/or neglected.
- Software costs and schedules are hard (if not impossible) to prepare accurately.
- Criteria are not available for selecting the best or most appropriate analysis, design, testing, or management methodology (procedures) for the project.

Software requirements are difficult to write correctly, completely, and unambiguously [Yeh, et al., 1984]. As a result, the project may have unclear or incomplete objectives. This vagueness can result in poor cost and schedule estimates. Costs and schedules are essential elements in a management program of action.

However, more importantly, planning is frequently incomplete or not done at all [Thayer, Pyster, and Wood, 1981]. And if done, planning becomes neglected and not maintained (updated) when conditions change.

The planning function is usually not a deliverable—only code is deliverable. Therefore, to some managers planning looks like an unnecessary overhead cost that is best discarded and the money saved for programming and testing. Even in DoD-type projects, where a planning document is usually required in the first 30 days of the project, the document is only superficially reviewed and in many cases allowed to gather dust on a shelf after it is produced.

Software budgets and schedules are hard to prepare accurately [DePree, 1984], [Ferrentino, 1981]. Numerous software cost and schedule models are on the market today [Mohanty, 1981], [Boehm, 1987], [Bailey, Frazier, and Bailey, 1986], each requiring the user to estimate the size of the project using lines of code or some other measurement from the yet–to–be–delivered system. This estimate is extremely difficult to make in the beginning states of the project and often results in an inaccurate budget and schedule for the project.

Despite the number of different software engineering development methods (often called modern programming practices) and automated tools available in the market today, almost no data are available to indicate which are the best or most cost-effective technologies. Software engineering PMs are faced with the most difficult task of selecting which methods and/or tools to use, if any. At least as difficult a task is to convince their corporate leaders that their choice is a cost-effective approach. This is, in part, one of the reasons most software development projects make little use of software tools [Zelkowitz, et al., 1984]. (See the work done by RADC and NASA/SEL and discussed in this chapter for two methods that provide help in this area.)

Table 3.1: Planning a Software Engineering Project

Project Management Activities and Tasks

Set objectives and goals	— Analyze and document technical requirements of the project: function, performance, external interfaces, design constraints, and quality attributes.
	— Analyze and document managerial requirements and constraints, e.g., available schedule and budget, required methodologies, standards, and so on.
	— Establish project goals, technical objectives, and success criteria for project.
Develop strategies	— Adopt company or top-level strategies for reaching the project goals or objectives.
	— Develop or supplement company strategies for reaching the project goals or objectives.
Develop policies	— Develop or adopt company policies that apply to software development, e.g., life-cycle phases and documents, development standards and methodologies, quality assurance and configuration management approaches, and so on.
	— Develop or adopt company policies that apply to non-technical project management activities, e.g., personnel policies (evaluations, vacation time), organizing, facilities, parking spaces, and so on.
Determine courses of action	— Analyze and develop, for each objective, possible courses of action.
	— Analyze and develop a program for each possible course of action.
	— Establish advantages, disadvantages, risks, and benefits for each course of action or program.
Make decisions	— Select appropriate courses of action based on project objectives and strategies, e.g., lowest risk, lowest cost, shortest schedule, greatest benefits, and so on.
	— Select appropriate management methods and tools to meet the project requirements and objects, e.g., what kind of authority relationships, reviews, product standards, tools (PERT, CPM, WBS, and so on) will be required.
	— Select appropriate development methods and tools to meet the project requirements and objects, e.g., life-cycle development technologies, tools, and documents.
Set procedures and rules	— Set procedures and establish methods for planning and controlling of the project, e.g., project management system.
	— Set procedures and establish methods for developing the system, e.g., standard software development methodology.
	— Set or adopt procedures for organizing and staffing the project.
	— Establish software quality assurance (SQA) plans and procedures.
	— Establish document preparation and publishing methods.
Develop programs	— Partition technical and managerial requirements into measurable tasks.
	— Determine milestones, priorities, and schedules necessary to accomplish project objectives.
	— Estimate necessary manpower and resources to accomplish project objectives.
	— Prepare contingency plans and risk-avoidance plans and procedures.
Forecast future situations	— Estimate future environment of the project, e.g., determine availability of required resources.
	— Estimate use of budgeted resources and funds.
	— Determine possible technical and managerial risks.
Prepare budgets	— Determine project costs from the project requirements, established policies, procedures and programs, and estimated staff and resource requirements.
	— Allocate budgeted resources to project tasks or cost centers.
Document project plans	— Document project management plans.
	— Prepare other planning documents such as test, software quality assurance, configuration management, staffing, and facilities.

Table 3.2: Types of Plans

Type of Plan	Definition or Explanation
Objectives	— The goals toward which activities are directed.
Strategies	— General program of action; the placing of emphasis and resources to obtain (usually long-range) objectives.
Policies	— General statements or understandings which guide decision making and activities. Policies limit the freedoms in making decisions but allow for some discretion.
Procedures	— Customary methods of handling future activities; guides to action rather than decision making. Procedures detail the exact manner in which an activity must be accomplished and allow very little if any discretion.
Rules	— Requirements for specific and definite actions to be taken or not taken with respect to a situation. No discretion is allowed.
Program	— An interrelated set of goals, policies, procedures, rules, tasks, assignments, resources to be employed, and other elements necessary to carry out a given course of action.
Budget	— A statement of activities and expected results, expressed in quantitative terms.

3.3 Planning Activities and Tasks

Table 3.1 provides an outline of the SEPM activities and tasks that must be accomplished by the PMs in planning their projects. The project manager is responsible for developing numerous types of plans. Table 3.2 contains a list of general management plans that is applicable to any software engineering project.

The balance of this section discusses and provides greater detail on the activities and tasks outlined in Table 3.1.

3.3.1 Set Objectives and Goals

The first planning step for a software engineering PM is to determine what the project must accomplish, when it must be accomplished, and what resources are necessary. Typically in a software engineering project, this involves analyzing and documenting the system and software requirements. In addition, the PM must determine the management requirements and constraints. Typical among these are resource and scheduling limitations [Yeh, et al., 1984].

Managers also must set objectives and success criteria for their projects. It can be argued that the success criteria should always be the successful delivery of a software system on time and within costs to meet project requirements. This is not always the case. For instance, success could be considered to be not only delivering the system but also winning a follow-on development contract. Other possible objectives of the PM might be to increase the size of the contract through contractor-initiated modifications or to increase the profit margin through winning an incentive award.

3.3.2 Develop Strategies

Another major endeavor of the PM is to develop and document a set of management strategies (sometime called strategic policies) for a project. Strategies are defined as long-range goals and the methods to obtain those goals. These long-range goals and methods usually are developed at a corporate level; however, the PM also can have strategic plans within his own project. This is particularly true if it is a large project. An example of a strategic plan might be to obtain a larger portion of the project (one that is being shared with another contractor or agency) and a plan for doing it.

3.3.3 Develop Policies

Policies are concerned with predetermined management decisions. The PM will establish policies within his project to aid and guide other PMs, supervisors and individual team members in making routine decisions. These policies are great timesavers. They reduce the need for the PM to interact with every decision. They also give a sense of security to the team members.

In many cases the PM does not develop new policies for the project, but selects from the policies established by his corporation. An example from a set of corporate software development policies [TRW, 1978] is:

Software Requirements Specifications Policy

Software projects shall prepare a software requirement specification to control functional, performance, and interface requirements for software end products. This policy requires projects to:

- Produce software requirements specifications prior to software requirements review in format specified by contract or corporate standards.

- Obtain written customer approval of this specification as basis for computer program and database end product acceptance.

- Obtain written corporate and customer approval for all subsequent changes to specifications.

3.3.4 Determine Courses of Action

In most projects there is more than one way to successfully deliver the project—but not with equal cost, equal schedule, or with equal risk. It is the PM's responsibility to determine a reasonable number of different approaches or programs for effectively implementing the software requirements.

For example, one approach may be very costly in terms of manpower and machines yet effectively reduces the schedule dramatically. Another approach may reduce both schedule and cost but takes a severe risk of being unable to deliver the system at all. A third approach is to stretch the schedule out, thereby reducing the cost of the project. The manager must analyze each course of action to determine its advantages, disadvantages, risks, and benefits. (See paper by Boehm [1987] for a description of a software development life-cycle model which incorporates risk-analysis and decision making.)

3.3.5 Make Decisions

The PM makes the major decisions for the project. He, along with his customer, determines the appropriate future course the project will take. He determines which of the many courses of action is most appropriate for meeting project goals and objectives.

The PM is responsible for making tradeoff decisions involving cost, schedule, design strategies, and risks (see the paper by Bunyard and Coward [1982]).

The PM is also responsible for selecting (or his company selects for him through the use of standards) the methods by which his project will be managed and developed. For example, what development strategies will be used, will the requirements be analyzed using "structured analysis" methods or "Warnier-Orr" charts? Will testing be done top-down, bottom-up, or both? Which tools, techniques, and procedures will be used in planning a software development project? Examples of project management tools are PERT, CPM, workload chart, work breakdown chart (WBS) [Tausworthe, 1980], Gantt chart, and so on [Cori, 1985].

Selecting the most appropriate and cost-effective software development tools and methods is a very difficult task. Assistance in this area is described in the research effort that follows.

R&D in Software Development Methodologies

Both the NASA Software Engineering Laboratory (SEL) at Goddard Space Flight Center and the Rome Air Development Center (RADC) have done research and development in determining methods that the PM can use to select the appropriate set of software development tools, methods, or methodologies.

Recently the SEL staff has been conducting research to determine the effectiveness of different software engineering technologies. Although NASA/SEL has been unable to find any measurable improvement in software productivity from the use of software development tools, they have found increases in software reliability through the use of modern programming practices and a regular program of quality assurance. NASA also discovered that the major factors in both software productivity and reliability continue to be personal capability and performance of the individual software developers (see discussion in Section 5) [Card, 1987].

RADC has developed a guidebook (a set of procedures) for selecting the appropriate software development methodology for a project. This guidebook is for technical managers and provides for the selection of requirements and design specifications methodologies appropriate to various software development environments and types of software. The guidelines cover the requirements analysis, architectural design, and detailed design phases of the software development life cycle [RADC Guidebook, 1985].

3.3.6 Set Procedures and Rules

In contrast to policies, *procedures* establish customary methods of handling future activities and provide guides to action rather than to decision making. Procedures detail the exact manner in which to accomplish an activity and allow very little if any discretion. A *rule*, although similar, establishes specific and definite actions to be taken or not taken with respect to a situation and allows no discretion.

The PM establishes the procedures and rules for the project. An example of a procedure might be a method of analyzing a software requirement or a set of steps to power up a computer. A rule might be the requirement to have two people on duty in the machine room at all times, or not to allow employees to smoke in the cafeteria.

Process standards (in contrast to *product standards*) are used as procedures. Standards may be adopted from the larger corporate standards or written for a particular project. Examples of standards are reporting methods, software development methodologies, and documentation preparation requirements.

As a short example, the following is a procedure for establishing a plan:

Procedures for Developing a Plan

(1) Establish the objectives of the operation for which the plan is being developed.

(2) Make assumptions about the expected future environment in which the plan will operate.

(3) Determine numerous alternative courses that will complete the objectives of the task successfully (however, not always with the same cost and risk).

(4) Evaluate the alternatives. Determine which one meets the acceptance criteria (lowest cost, lowest risk, and/or shortest schedule).

(5) Select a course of action.

(6) Formulate a detailed plan for objectives accomplishment.

3.3.7 Develop Programs

When a software engineering PM "plans" a project, he is developing a *program* of action for his project. The development program (not to be confused with a computer program) establishes all of the actions necessary to successfully deliver a project.

Typically, the manager is required to determine:

(1) The *tasks* to be performed by the software development staff in order to deliver the final software product. This usually requires the partitioning of the project product or project activities into short, measurable tasks. A useful tool for representing the partitioned process/product is the WBS [Tausworthe, 1980]. (Each task is typically assigned to a small group of developers called a programming team.)

(2) The *cost* and resources necessary to accomplish the project [Boehm, 1984].

(3) The project *schedule* by determining priorities of actions, establishing milestones, deciding when and how the milestones are to be met, and creating the detailed schedule necessary to reach the milestones and to accomplish the objectives of the project. (For a further discussion on planning see [Miller, 1978].)

3.3.8 Forecast Future Situations

The PM is responsible for predicting and making assumptions about the future as it will impact the software engineering project.

Forecasting can be addressed two ways. The first way is the forecasting of future events such as availability of manpower, predicted inflation rate, or availability of new computer hardware and the impact these future events will have on the software engineering project.

The second is the estimation of how the software engineering project will meet these future expectations and assumptions. Examples are future expenditure of available resources and project funds against the project. The PM is also responsible for estimating future risks and developing contingency plans for countering those risks.

That is, one forecast predicts the future and the other estimates how the project will react to this expected future.

3.3.9 Prepare Budget

Placing numbers on the program is called *budgeting*. The PM is responsible for determining the cost of the project and allocating the budget to project tasks or cost centers. The budget is the common denominator for all of the things contained in the management plan. Requirements for manpower, computer requirements, travel, office space, equipment, and so forth can only be compared and cost tradeoffs made when these requirements are measured in terms of a budget.

The PM is responsible for allocating the approved budget to various elements of the project. In some projects, each entity in the project has its own share of the budget and the authority to spend it to accomplish its goals.

3.3.10 Document Project Plans

The PM is responsible for documenting the project plan [Fairley, 1987] as well as for preparing other documents, such as the quality assurance plan, configuration management plan, staffing plan, and other plans such as test documents. The project plan is the PM's primary means of communicating with the other outside agencies that interface with the project and of informing them what the manager expects to do and what the manager expects from them. In addition, other plans (see again Table 3.2) should be documented and updated as necessary.

4. Organizing a Software Engineering Project

4.1 Introduction and Definitions

Organizing a software engineering project is all of the management activities that result in the design of a formal structure of software engineering tasks and authority relationships between these tasks.

Organizing involves determining and itemizing the project activities required to achieve the objects of the software development project and the arrangement of these activities into logical clusters. It also involves assignment of such group of activities to an organizational entity (frequently called a project team) within the project and the delegation of responsibility and authority to the team to carry out these activities.

The purpose of an organizational structure is to "focus the efforts of many on a selected goal" [Donnelly, Gibson, and Ivancevich, 1975]. The PM selects the optimum project structure for the existing project environment.

4.2 Major Issues in Organizing

The major issues (or problems) in organizing a software engineering project are:

- It is difficult to determine the best organizational structure for the project; e.g., project, matrix, or function.
- Responsibilities for project activities and tasks are sometimes not defined or are unclear.
- The software functional organizations and the individual staff members do not believe the matrix organizational structure is beneficial to them.

There is a complete spectrum of project organizational types ranging from the purely functional type to the all-in-one project type [Youker, 1977]. It is difficult to determine the best organizational structure for the project and for the organization building the project [Thayer, Pyster, and Wood, 1981]. The project organization is viewed as being the optimum organizational structure for developing a large software system. It creates centralized control over the project and makes one manager responsible for the final delivery of the software product. Top management and customers feel "comfortable" with this arrangement. Conversely the functional organization is viewed as being the optimum structure for nourishing highly skilled, difficult-to-hire, expensive, software engineers. Individual software developers are comfortable with this arrangement.

The matrix organization is currently accepted as being an optimum compromise between the project and functional organizations. But because of the conflicts that arise in the matrix organization (two-boss problem) and between the functional line managers, who supply the software engineers to the matrix organization, and the PM of the matrix project, the matrix organization is viewed by many managers as being disruptive to the over-all organization.

In addition, the individual software engineers believe that the matrix organization is not beneficial to their individual careers. People who are "matrixed" appear to be pushed from project to project. They have to report to both the functional manager and the PM, and they feel that nobody is looking after their career. This is particularly true with software people, who never seem to be able to advance to be PM, but only project assignees.

Functional managers, particularly where the matrix organization is new, resent losing the responsibility for software delivery. They resent running a "body shop" for the benefit of the project organizations. This is especially true in a "weak" matrix where the matrix manager shares responsibility with the functional manager. In turn the PMs resent having the functional responsibility for technology decisions such as standards and technology insertion.

This conflict is further amplified when assignment of responsibilities are not clearly made between organizations (and people). This is particularly true in a matrix organization situation. One of the major problems in any company is that if responsibilities are not clearly identified, then conflicts can arise when two organizations are trying to do the same job, or worse, a situation develops where nobody does either job.

Papers by Fife, [1987], Youker, [1977], and Mantei [1981] provide criteria for selecting the appropriate organizational structure for the software product and process. Both Stuckenbruck and Youker indicate the need for top management to give a clear project charter (document) for the matrix organization in defining responsibilities and authority for the PM as well as in defining the role of the functional departments.

4.3 Organizing Activities and Tasks

Table 4.1 provides an outline of the SEPM activities that must be accomplished by the PM in organizing a project. The balance of this section discusses and provides greater detail on the activities and tasks outlined in Table 4.1.

Table 4.1: Organizing a Software Engineering Project

Project Management Activities and Tasks

Identify and group required tasks	— Define and partition software requirements and activities into tasks. — Size and group software tasks into organizational entities.

Select and establish organizational structures	— Select organizational types:
	  • Select a line or staff organizational structure.
	  • Select a project, matrix, or functional project structure.
	  • Select team types.
	— Anticipate organizational changes as required by project life-cycle development phases, project progress, and changes in requirement.
	— Make organizational changes when required.
	— Identify and establish project customers/users relationships.
	— Recognize and use the informal organizational structure.

Create organizational positions	— Create project position titles and descriptions for each organizational position created. — Define scope, duties, and relationships for each organizational position.
Define responsibilities and authority	— Define responsibilities for each organizational position. — Define authority to be granted for the accomplishment of position responsibilities. — Establish authority and relationships between positions and tasks.
Establish positions qualifications	— Establish position qualifications for each project position. — Establish education and training requirements for each project position. — Establish experience requirements for each project position.
Document organizational structures	— Document organizational plans and assumptions. — Document organizational structure, positional responsibilities and authority, authority between tasks to be done, and relationships between organizational positions.

4.3.1 Identify and Group Required Tasks

The manager is responsible for reviewing the project requirements, defining the various tasks to be accomplished, sizing those tasks, and optimally grouping those tasks. He assigns titles and organizational entities to the assembly of tasks; for example, programmer-analysis task, operations branch, and others. This information then enables the PM to pick the best organizational structure for optimum control of these groups. For an example of this see Table 4.2.

The PM must also identify the supporting tasks needed from both inside and outside the project. Examples of internal tasks are secretarial support, word processing support, financial monitoring, project administration, and project control. Outside the project, there are tasks associated with travel requirements, motor pools, security guards, computer operation support, and so on.

4.3.2 Select and Establish Organizational Structures

Software or software systems are normally custom-built by a temporary organization called a software development project. The software development project can be organized according to several different and overlapping organizational types. For example:

- *Conventional organization structure*—can be line or staff organization type.
- *Project organization structure*—can be functional, project, or matrix organization type.
- *Team structure*—can be egoless, chief programmer, or project (hierarchical) teams.

Many PMs don't have the luxury of selecting the best project organizational type, since this is determined by policy at the company or corporate level. However, regardless of who does it, the organizational type and structure, which will match the needs and goals of the project application and environment, must be identified [Fife, 1987].

The following paragraphs describe these organizational types.

Table 4.2: Example of a Set of Software Engineering Project Tasks That Have Been Grouped and Assigned an Organizational Entity

The following is a list of software engineering project tasks logically grouped (left-hand column) and assigned to a group entity (right-hand column).

Project Tasks	Group Identifier
• Partition and allocate software requirements to SCIs	Software System Engineering
• Prepare software development plans and documents	
• Define and implement standards and practices	
• Collect and evaluate technical performance measurements	
• Audit SCI-level products for quality	
• Prepare software test documents	Software Test Engineering
• Conduct software tests	
• Support system tests	
• Maintain software development library	System Software Support
• Install vendor supplied software	
• Provide technical support on system software	
• Analyze SCI #1 requirements	Software Engineering Applications Group 1
• Design and develop SCI #1	
• Program software	
• Prepare SCI #1 documents	
• Support testing	
• Analyze SCI #2 requirements	Software Engineering Applications Group 2
• Same tasks as Group 1	

4.3.2.1 Conventional Organizational Structures: A *line* organization has the responsibility and authority to perform the work that represents the primary mission of the larger organizational unit. In contrast, a *staff* organization is a group of functional experts that has responsibility and authority to perform special activities that help the line organization do its work. All organizations in a company are either line or staff.

4.3.2.2 Project Organizational Structure: A project organizational structure is a special organization that has been established for the purpose of developing and building something that is too big to be done by only one or, at the most, a few people. In a software engineering project, the "something" is a software system. The project organizational structure can be superimposed on top of a line or staff organization. For example, a functional software engineering organization can be either a line or staff organization (see Figure 4.1 to illustrate the use of five line organizations used as software engineering functional organizations). Figure 4.1 is the organizational structure for the example in Table 4.2.

Functional Project Organization: One type of project organization is a *functional* organization; a project structure built around a software engineering function or group of similar functions. The functional organizations are normally continuous. A project is accomplished either within the functional unit or, if multifunctioned, between two or more functional units. The project is accomplished by passing the project from function to function as the project passes through the life-cycle phases. Figure 4.2 illustrates the tasks and lines of authority of a functional organization used to develop a project.

In the illustration, the software requirements analysis and specifications are prepared by the *software systems engineering group* under the supervision of the group supervisor. When finished (or believed to be finished) the system engineering group transfers the requirement specifications to the *software engineering applications group* that is most familiar with the application. The software engineering applications group, using the requirement specifications, designs the software system under the supervision of the software engineering applications group supervisor, and so on. In our illustration the applications group also programs the software system and then passes the finished code to the *software test engineering group* for testing. Tools and system support are provided by the *system software support group*. There is no one supervisor over the whole project.

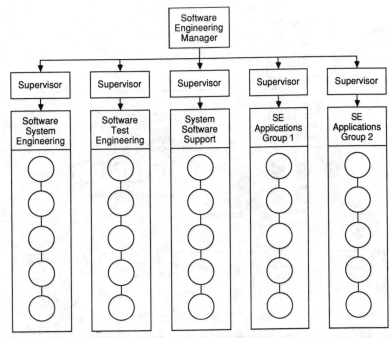

Figure 4.1: Line organizations used as software engineering functional organizations

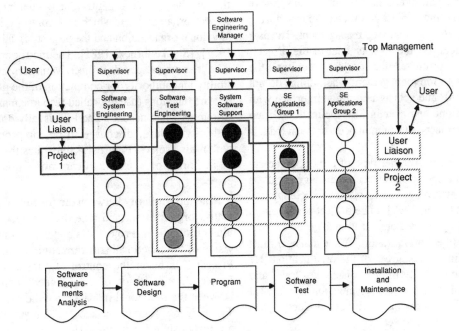

Figure 4.2: Tasks and lines of authority of software engineering functional organizations used to develop a project

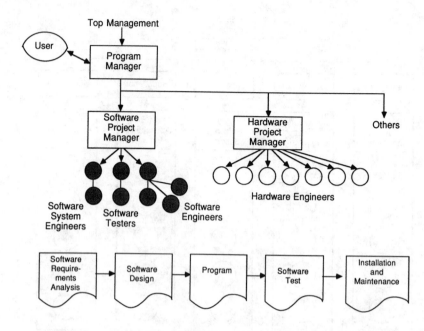

Figure 4.3: Tasks and lines of authority of project organization used to develop a project

To further discuss the example illustrated in Figure 4.2, Project 1 is under the control and supervision of the software engineering manager and Project 2 is under the monitoring of a "user liaison" who reports to top management. The user liaison does not supervise the staff or control the project. The user liaison coordinates the project, monitors the progress (reporting to top management when things do not go according to plan), and acts as a common interface with the user. Note that one engineer in SE Application Group 1 is shared by two projects—a common occurrence in today's environment.

Project Organization: Another type of project organization is built around a specific project; the manager is given the responsibility, authority, and resources for completion of the project [Middleton, 1967]. (The project organization is sometimes called a *projected* organization to get away from the term "project project organization.") The manager must meet his goal within the resources of the organization. He usually has the responsibility to hire, discharge, train, and promote people within his project organization. Figure 4.3 illustrates the tasks and lines of authority of a project organization used to develop a project.

Note that the software project manager of a project organization has total control over both the project and the assigned software personnel.

Matrix Project Organization: The third project organization is the *matrix* organization (sometimes called matrix project organization), which is a compromise between the functional organization and the project organization [Youker, 1977], [Stuckenbruck, 1981]. The matrix organization also is built around a specific project. Managers are given responsibility and authority for completion of the project. The line or staff functions (usually called resource managers) provide resources when needed. The PM usually does *not* have the authority to hire, discharge, train, or promote personnel within his project. Figure 4.4 illustrates the tasks and lines of authority of a matrix organization used to develop a project.

Note the similarity between the functional project and the matrix organization (and note the differences also). In the illustration given, Project 1 is under the control and supervision of the functional software engineering manager, and Project 2 is under the control of "top management." In Project 2, supervision of the assigned engineers is shared between the functional manager and the program manager. Typically the program manager and software project manager are responsible for the day-to-day supervision of the software engineering group and the functional manager is responsible for the career, training, and well-being of the same people.

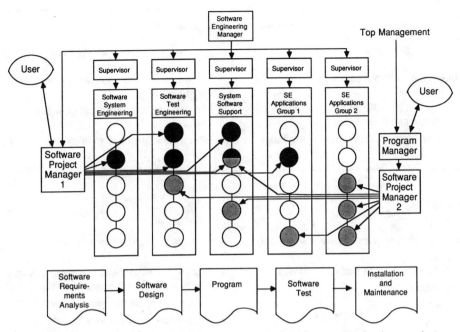

Figure 4.4: Tasks and lines of authority of matrix organization used to develop a project

Note again, as illustrated in Figure 4.4, that one (or more) engineer in the system support group is shared by two projects—a common occurrence in a matrix organization.

4.3.2.3 Project Teams: In addition to the large organizational structure discussed above, a typical software development project is organized around a number of five- to seven-member software engineering teams. Examples of these team structures are *egoless programming teams, chief programmer teams,* and *project (hierarchical) teams* [Mantei, 1981].

Egoless Programming Team: The egoless team structure was developed by Dr. Gerald Weinberg [Weinberg, 1971]. An egoless team typically consists of ten or twelve members. Discussions and decisions are made by consensus. Group leadership responsibility rotates; there is no permanent central authority.

Chief Programmer Team: The chief programmer team was first used by IBM in the now-famous New York Times Morgue Project. The team consists of from three to four permanently assigned team members—chief programmer,

backup programmer, and program librarian—plus other auxiliary programmers and/or analysts who are added as needed. The chief programmer manages all the technical aspects and makes all the managerial decisions. The librarian maintains all up-to-date documents, code, and data and performs all administrative work [Cooke, 1976].

Project (Hierarchical) Team: The project team is a structured organization in which the project leader manages senior programmers and senior programmers manage junior programmers. The project team is sometimes called a hierarchical team because of its top-down flow of authority. It can be organized by component or phase. Many project teams practice egoless reviews (walkthroughs) and use a programmer support library. Senior programmers insure quality of the product.

Strengths and Weaknesses of the Project Organizational Types: It is important in selecting a functional project, or matrix organizational structure, that the PM match the needs of the project against the various strengths and weaknesses

Table 4.3: Strengths and Weaknesses of Software Engineering Project Types

---

Functional Project Organization

Strengths	Weaknesses
• Organization already in existence (quick start-up and phase-down).	• No one person has complete responsibility or authority for the project.
• Recruiting, training, and retention of people is easier. (functional projects are people-oriented).	• Interface problems are difficult to solve.
• Standards, techniques, and methods are already established.	• Projects are difficult to monitor and control.

Project Organization

Strengths	Weaknesses
• There is a central position of responsibility and authority for the project.	• Organization must be formed.
• One person has authority over all system interfaces.	• Recruiting, training, and retention of people is more difficult (projects are product-oriented).
• Decisions can be made quickly.	• Economy of scale cannot be achieved.
• Staff motivation is typically high.	• Projects tend to perpetuate themselves.
	• Standards, techniques, and procedures must be developed (no commonality between projects).

Matrix Project Organization

Strengths	Weaknesses
• Improved central position of responsibility and authority (over functional project).	• Responsibility and authority is shared between two or more managers (unlike project organization).
• Interfaces between functions can be controlled more easily (than in functional project).	• Control or responsibility for resources (people) is shared between two or more managers (unlike project or functional organization).
• Recruiting, training, and retention are easier (than in project organization).	• Too easy to move people from one organization to another (unlike project or functional organization).
• Easier to start and end the project (than in project organization).	• Greater organizational documentation is required (than in project or functional organization).
• Standards, techniques, and procedures already established (unlike project organization).	• Greater competition for resources (than in project or functional organization).
• Better and more flexible use of people (unlike project or functional organization).	

---

of the project type. Table 4.3 displays the advantages and disadvantages of the six organizational types.

The software engineering project is either a *line* or *staff* organization. The PM must decide whether the project will operate as a functional, project, or matrix organization and whether the project will use egoless, chief programmer, or project team types. (The chief programmer and egoless teams are almost totally extinct. However the librarian concept from the chief programmer team and the egoless technical reviews (walkthroughs) are frequently used in many software engineering project teams.)

Table 4.3: Strengths and Weaknesses of Software Engineering Project Types (Cont'd)

Egoless Project Team	
Strengths	**Weaknesses**
• Democracy works best for complex and difficult problems. • Overall productivity and quality improvement. • Job satisfaction is high which reduces attrition.	• Productivity is low because communication is complex. • Works poorly in "rush" developments. • Teams select less conservative (more risky) alternatives while nobody takes the blame.
Chief Programmer Team	
Strengths	**Weaknesses**
• Jobs get completed quickly. • Works best with rigid deadlines.	• Requires very senior, experienced chief programmers. • Lowers morale in project. • Is not applicable to ill-defined problems that require brainstorming.
Hierarchical Project Team	
Strengths	**Weaknesses**
• Works best for large projects. • One person is responsible for the team's efforts.	• Works poorly with small projects, simple tasks or research projects. • Requires large supervision to staff ratio.

The majority of software engineering projects in the aerospace industry use the matrix organization with project teams. A few companies use the chief programmer team in name only. (The team supervisor is frequently not really qualified to be a chief programmer.)

4.3.3 Create Organizational Positions

Once the tasks are identified, sized, and grouped and the connections between these tasks have been identified, the manager must create titles and position descriptions for them. It is with these titles and positions that the personnel organization will recruit and/or transfer future members for this project.

Some short examples of typical software engineering titles and position descriptions are illustrated below [Source EDP, 1987]:

- *Project managers*—responsible for system development and implementation within major functional areas. Direct the efforts of software engineers, analysts, programmers, and other project personnel.
- *Software engineers*—design and develop software to drive computer systems. Develop firmware, drivers, specialized software such as graphics, communications controllers, operating systems and user friendly interfaces. Work closely with hardware engineers and applications and systems programmers, requiring understanding of all aspects of the product.

- *Scientific/Engineering programmers, programmer-analysts*—perform detailed program design, coding, testing, debugging, documentation and implementation of scientific/engineering computer applications and other applications that are mathematical in nature. May assist in overall system specification and design.

4.3.4 Define Responsibilities and Authority

Authority can be defined as "the degree of discretion in organizational positions conferring on persons occupying these positions the right to use their judgment in decision making" [Koontz and O'Donnell, 1976]. It is often stated that responsibility cannot be delegated or shared. Koontz and O'Donnell [1976] support this view by defining responsibility as "the obligation owed by subordinates to their supervisors for exercising authority delegated to them in a way to accomplish results expected." This paper takes the position that responsibility for organizational activities or tasks is assigned to the organizational position (along with the matching authority) at the time the position is created or modified. The PM is assigned and in turn assigns the responsibility and the corresponding authority to the various organizational positions and groups of tasks within the project.

The PM also establishes the lines of authority among tasks. By lines of authority, we mean which tasks will take precedence over other tasks in accomplishing an objective. For instance, analysis has authority over design, design has authority over code, and so on.

4.3.5 Establish Position Qualifications

Position qualifications must be identified for each position in the organization. What type of individual do you want for your project? How much experience is necessary in the area of the application: none, one year, three years? How much education is required: B.S. in computer science, M.S. in artificial intelligence? How much training is required, either before or after the project is initiated? Does the incumbent need to know FORTRAN, LISP, or some other language? The establishment of proper and accurate position qualifications will make it possible for the manager to correctly staff the project.

Some short examples of typical position qualifications for software engineering titles and positions are illustrated below [Source EDP, 1987]:

- *Project managers*—background in successful systems implementation, advanced industrial knowledge, awareness of current computer technology, intimate understanding of user operations and problems, and proven management ability. Minimum requirements are four years of significant system development and project management experience.
- *Software engineers*—four years experience in aerospace applications designing real-time control systems for embedded computers. Experience with Ada preferred. B.S. in Computer Science, Engineering, or related discipline.
- *Scientific/Engineering programmers, programmer-analysts*—three years experience in programming aerospace applications, control systems, and/or graphics. One year minimum with FORTRAN, Assembler, or C programming languages. Large-scale or mini/micro hardware exposure and system software programming experience desired. Minimum requirements include undergraduate engineering or math degree.

4.3.6 Document Organizational Structures

The matrix organizational structure, with its lines of authority, task, and responsibility, should be documented in an organizational plan. Justifications for decisions must be well documented and made available for future staffing of the system. Other documents include position descriptions, position qualifications, and documents assigning responsibilities and the appropriate authority.

5. Staffing a Software Engineering Project

5.1 Introduction and Definitions

Staffing a software engineering project consists of all of the management activities that involve filling and keeping filled the positions that were established by the project organizational structure. This includes selecting candidates for the positions and training or otherwise developing both candidates and incumbents to accomplish their tasks effectively. Staffing also involves terminating assigned project personnel when necessary.

Staffing is not organizing. Staffing involves people. Staffing is filling the roles created by the project organizational structure through proper and effective selection, appraisal, and development of personnel. The objective of staffing is to ensure that project roles are filled by personnel who are able and willing to occupy them.

5.2 Major Issues in Staffing

The major issues (or problems) in staffing for a software engineering project are:

- Productivity of programmers, analysts, and software engineers is unpredictable and varies greatly from individual to individual.

- Universities are not producing a sufficient number of computer science graduates who understand the software engineering process.
- Project managers are frequently selected for management positions without the benefit of management training.

One of the major issues in staffing is that productivity of programmers and software engineers is unpredictable and varies greatly from individual to individual [Thayer, Pyster, and Wood, 1981]. In the early study by Sackman and others, the difference in productivity between one programmer and another was as high as 26 to 1 [Sackman, H., et al., 1968]. In his book *Software Engineering Economics,* Boehm [1981] reports differences in productivity in personnel/team capability as high as 4 to 1. This inability to accurately match the productivity of a staff to the expected productivity of the organizational structure contributes greatly to our inability to accurately determine the cost of a software system.

Universities are not producing a sufficient number of software engineers [Thayer, Pyster, and Wood, 1981]. Most of the 2500 computer science programs in the United States are turning out theoretical computer scientists at best, or merely highly qualified programmers (coders) at worst. Most industry personnel and people involved in the hiring of the new college graduates indicate that they wished the graduates of computer science programs had more education and experience in developing large software systems—that is, software engineering skills [McGill, 1984].

Project managers frequently are assigned to their jobs without the benefit of management training. It is common practice today to elevate to the position of manager those programmers and software engineers who have demonstrated their capabilities as programmers and software engineers. The major issue today is how to go about providing an acceptable degree of training to these already proven software engineers so that they will be capable of managing a software engineering project.

5.3 Staffing Activities and Tasks

Table 5.1 provides an outline of all the SEPM activities and tasks that must be accomplished by the PMs to staff their projects. The balance of this section discusses and provides greater detail on the activities and tasks outlined in Table 5.1.

5.3.1 Fill Organizational Positions

The manager is responsible for setting position standards for positions that were established during the organization of his project. He must ensure that through these standards he is able to obtain capable and productive managers, software engineers, analysts, and programmers, as well as the various support people necessary to fully staff a project. The PM is directly responsible for selecting and recruiting qualified people for his project, and he should be certain of the qualifications and experience of the people selected to fill his positions.

In staffing any software project, the following factors should be considered in filling the organizational structure. Deficiencies in any of these factors can be offset by strengths in other factors. For example, deficiencies in education can be offset by better experience, a particular type of training, or enthusiasm for the job. Serious deficiencies should be cause for rejection.

- *Education*—Does the candidate have the minimum level of education for the job? Does the candidate have the proper education for his future growth in the company?
- *Experience*—Does the candidate have an acceptable level of experience? Is it the right type and variety of experience?
- *Training*—Is the candidate trained in the language and methodology to be used, on the equipment to be used, and the application of the software system?
- *Motivation*—Is the candidate motivated to do the job, work for the project, work for the company, or take the assignment?
- *Commitment*—Will the candidate demonstrate loyalty to the project, the company, and to the decisions made [Powell and Posner, 1984]?
- *Self determination*—Is the candidate a self-starter, willing to carry a project through to the end without excessive direction?
- *Group affinity*—Does the candidate fit in with the current staff? Are there any potential conflicts that need to be solved?
- *Intelligence*—Does the candidate have the capability to learn, to take difficult assignments, and adapt to changing environments?

Sources of Qualified Individuals: Qualified individuals to fill organizational positions may be obtained from a number of sources. One source is transferring individuals from within the project itself. It is the PM's prerogative to move people from one task to another within a project. Other software engineers are received as transfers from other projects within the same company organization. This can be done anytime but often happens when another software engineering project is either phasing down or canceled.

Other sources of experienced, qualified personnel are new hires from other companies through such methods as job fairs, referrals, headhunters, want ads, and unsolicited resumes. New hires in the form of new college graduates

Table 5.1: Staffing a Software Engineering Project

Project Management Activities and Tasks

Fill organizational positions	— Set hiring standards for capable and productive project managers, software engineers, analysts, programmers, and support personnel. — Transfer qualified people for each position from within the company. — Recruit qualified people for each position from other firms, government institutions, or college graduation classes.
Assimilate newly assigned personnel	— Orient newly assigned project members with project objectives, policies, and plans. — Familiarize and orientate newly assigned project members with facilities and company policies and procedures.
Educate or train personnel	— Educate and train managers in management and administration. — Educate and train software engineers and technical staff in the application of the project, development methods and policies, and advanced state-of-the-art techniques. — Educate and train support staff in required methods, skills, and equipment.
Provide for general development	— Develop professional knowledge, attitudes, and skills. — Broaden skill base of the company.
Evaluate and appraise personnel	— Evaluate and appraise personnel. — Establish employee objectives for the next appraisal period.
Compensate	— Determine salary scale, promotion policy, and benefits. — Compensate project personnel in accordance with their training and abilities.
Terminate assignments	— Transfer, reassign, or terminate assigned personnel at the completion of the job or when the performance of the personnel is unacceptable.
Document staffing decisions	— Document staffing plan, advancement policy, and salary scale. — Document individual training plan reflecting course work needed and progress made.

can be obtained either through interviews on campus or through referrals from last year's graduates who are now company employees.

If the PM is unable to obtain qualified individuals to fill his positions, he can hire unqualified but motivated individuals with potential and train them for those vacancies [McGill, 1984].

Selecting a Productive Software Staff: It is not enough to just select a staff, a project manager must select the best and most productive staff possible.

There are currently two metrics that are indicative of high productivity:

(1) *Amount of experience:* An experienced staff is more productive than an inexperienced staff [Boehm, 1981]. Some of the best experience comes from having worked on large software systems similar to the project being staffed.

(2) *Diversity of experience:* A diversity of experience is a reasonable predictor of productivity [Kruesi, 1982]. It is better that the individual under consideration have done well with several jobs over a period of time rather than just one.

Other qualities needed in a high productivity individual are communications skills (both oral and written) a college degree (usually in a technical field), being a self-starter, and experience in the application of the project.

If experienced personnel are not available, select an individual with a college degree. Experience and observation have shown that, in general, individuals with a college education are more versatile and can adapt more quickly to a new job than noncollege-trained individuals. Another indicator of a high-productivity staff is people who have worked their way through college by holding down part-time jobs or positions.

5.3.2 Assimilate Newly Assigned Personnel

The manager is responsible not only for hiring the people but also for familiarizing personnel with any project procedures, facilities, and plans necessary to assure their effective integration into his project. In short, he is responsible for introducing the new employee to the company and the company to the employee. Many large companies have a formal orientation program lasting several days. The orientations are frequently at the very beginning of the employment. An orientation at this time does the most good for the employee and comes at a time when the employee has the most free time.

Orientation programs include the features and history of the company; the products or services that are the main sources of revenue for the company; general policies and procedures; organization; company benefits; and the availability of in-company service organizations.

5.3.3 Educate or Train Personnel

It is not always possible to recruit or transfer employees with exactly those skills that are necessary for a particular project. Therefore, the manager is responsible for educating and training the personnel assigned to ensure that they meet the project requirements.

Education differs from training. Education involves teaching the basics, theory, and underlying concepts of a discipline with a view toward a long term payoff. Training on the other hand means teaching a skill, a knowledge of how to use, operate, or make something. It is typically needed in the near future and has a short-term payoff.

Managers should be educated in the management sciences and business techniques. They should be trained in management techniques and the duties of administration. Engineers, on the other hand, are educated in science, physics, and mathematics, but must be trained in the application of the project, the state-of-the-art techniques, and software engineering procedures used in the project. Support personnel need to understand precisely what they are supposed to do. Everyone must be familiar with the procedures, tools, techniques, and equipment they operate and use.

Some of the primary training methods to be used today are on-the-job training, formal company courses [McGill, 1984], courses through local universities and schools [Mills, 1980], self-study, and in-house formal or informal lectures. Each individual within an organization must have a training plan that shows goals and the steps that each person will take in achieving those goals. Top management must actively support a training program.

A new technique in company training that has surfaced recently is the retraining into software engineering (sometimes called "retreading") of long-time, valuable employees with technical but somewhat obsolete skills. Two examples of this technique are courses at Israel Aircraft [Ben-David, et al., 1984] and Lockheed Missiles & Space Company [McGill, 1984].

5.3.4 Provide for General Development

In addition to training, the manager must ensure that his staff can grow with the project and company. He must ensure that their professional knowledge will increase and that they have a positive attitude not only toward the project but toward the company they work for as well.

One of the purposes of providing general development for the employee is to improve company or organization effectiveness. For example, an education program at the local university in any worthwhile skill, funded by the company, will improve employee morale, aid in retaining the employees, and, in general, broaden the skill base available to the company. Even indirect skills such as typing and communication should be enhanced.

5.3.5 Evaluate and Appraise Personnel

Along with the more positive aspect of hiring people, the manager is also responsible for evaluating and appraising personnel. The PM must provide periodic appraisal or evaluation of his software engineering staff. An appraisal will provide feedback to the staff member as to the positive and negative aspects of his performance. This feedback allows the staff member to accent his better qualities and to minimize his negative qualities. A good appraisal should be done at regular intervals and should concentrate on the individual's performance and not his personality, unless his personality interferes with his performance [Moneysmith, 1984].

One evaluation technique that is applicable to project management is "management by objectives" [Maslow, 1954]. At the beginning of the appraisal period, the individual and his PM establish and agree on a set of verifiable objectives that the individual believes he will meet over the next reporting period. These measurable objectives are a verifiable goal that will form the basis of next year's appraisal. This approach is superior to evaluation by personal traits and work characteristics, such as promptness, neatness, punctuality, golf scores, and so on.

5.3.6 Compensate

The manager—sometimes directly, sometimes indirectly—is responsible for determining the salary scale and benefits of his personnel. Benefits take on many forms. Most benefits are monetary or can be equated to money such as stock options, a company car, first class tickets fo all company trips, a year-end bonus. A few are nonmonetary but appeal to the self esteem of the individual; examples are combat medals in the military, a reserved parking place at the company plant, or an impressive title on the door.

Some short examples of typical salaries for software engineering titles and position descriptions are illustrated below (all salaries are annual) [Source EDP, 1987]:

- Project managers
  Small project: $33,000 to $52,000, median $37,800;
  Medium project: $40,000 to $53,000, median $46,700;
  Large project: $45,000 to $65,000, median $55,000.
- Software engineers
  1-2 years experience: $22,000 to $30,100, median $27,000;
  2-5 years experience: $27,500 to $37,000, median $32,000;

5-7 years experience: $31,500 to $44,000, median $38,000;

Over 7 years experience: $35,000 to $51,900, median $43,000.

- Scientific/Engineering programmers, programmer-analysts

  1-2 years experience: $19,000 to $28,500, median $25,000;

  2-5 years experience: $25,500 to $35,000, median $30,000;

  Over 5 years experience: $31,000 to $46,000, median 38,000.

5.3.7 Terminate Assignments

The manager is not only responsible for hiring people, but is also responsible for terminating assignments. The term "terminate" encompasses such things as the reassignment of personnel at the end of a successful project—a farewell party is given, and people smilingly go off to new jobs. Other forms of termination are not so pleasant, such as a project being canceled early and people looking for new work. There is also termination by firing, when an employee is determined to be unsatisfactory. The PM then lets the employee seek another job within his own company or employment with another corporation.

5.3.8 Document Staffing Decisions

The PMs should document their staffing plan and their evaluation and advancement policies for all to read. Each individual within an organization should have a personal training plan reflecting course work needed and progress made. Other documents that might be produced are orientation plans and schedules, salary schedules, and promotion policies. The project manager and the individual employee should have a copy of the employee's own annual performance objectives signed by the employee and the supervisor.

6. Directing a Software Engineering Project

6.1 Introduction and Definitions

Directing a software engineering project consists of all of the management activities that deal with the interpersonal aspects by which project personnel come to understand and contribute to the achievement of project goals. Once subordinates are trained and oriented, the PM has a continuing responsibility for clarifying their assignments, guiding them toward improved performance, and motivating them to work with enthusiasm and confidence toward project goals.

Directing, like staffing, involves people. Directing is sometimes considered to be synonymous with leading (compare reference [Koontz and O'Donnell, 1972] with reference [Koontz, O'Donnell, and Weihrich, 1984]). Directing a project involves providing leadership to the project, day-to-day supervision of the project personnel, delegating authority to the lowest possible organizational entity, coordinating activities of the project members, facilitating communications between project members and those outside the project, resolving conflicts, managing change, and documenting any important decisions.

6.2 Major Issues in Directing

The major issues (or problems) in directing a software engineering project are:

- Current methods of specifying requirements, designing systems, or planning projects sometimes present a communication barrier between key organizations.
- The software development staff is not motivated to use or interested in the modern techniques of software engineering (technology transfer gap).
- Benefits, rewards, or payments that can motivate the software development staff to be more productive have not been identified.

One of the major goals of software engineering is to improve communication among the many organizations that are involved in developing a software system. Most software engineering documents are written in the English language, which is notoriously imprecise and ambiguous. Research in software engineering is trying to determine ways to develop and use tools and techniques that will make software engineering requirements specifications, design documents, and other software engineering documents communicate what they mean. Steps have been taken to improve this situation (see papers by Yeh, et al. [1984] and Ramamoorthy, et al. [1984] in this tutorial).

Technology transfer is defined as the time interval between the development of a new product, tool, or technique and its use by the consumers of that product, tool, or technique. In their paper, Redwine and Riddle [1985] estimated that this time can be on the order of 15-20 years. The cause of this transfer gap can be looked at from two viewpoints:

- Project manager's viewpoint:
  - The PMs are reluctant to introduce unfamiliar tools and methods that they have not used before that may increase the risks to their project.
  - The use of unfamiliar methods may make it far more difficult for the PM to estimate project size, cost, and schedule.
  - There is a high probability that the first time the project team uses a new tool or technique there will be an increased cost and longer schedule for the project.

Software developer's viewpoint:
  - The software developer doesn't see need for change; the old ways worked to their satisfaction and are still the best.
  - The software developers don't want to learn new techniques.
  - Many software developers believe that the new methodologies stifle creativity; that standards really can't be applied.
  - Outsiders (of the project) really don't understand the problems of the project.

Table 6.1: Directing a Software Engineering Project

Project Management Activities and Tasks

Provide leadership	— Interpret plans and requirements for the project staff. — Align the personnel goals of the project staff with the goals of the project.
Supervise personnel	— Give assigned personnel day-to-day instructions, guidance, and discipline necessary to fulfill their assigned duties. — Make short-term decisions on actions affecting the project.
Delegate authority	— Define the authority of the project staff to match this responsibilities. — Assign tasks to subgroups, teams, and individuals. — Delegate authority through lowest level of project.
Motivate personnel	— Motivate and inspire personnel to take desired action. — Initiate motivation techniques, e.g., MBO, Maslow, others. — Acknowledge special attention required for highly qualified and trained engineers and technical staff.
Coordinate activities	— Reconcile differences in approach, and bring together those differences for the benefit of the project. — Inform interested parties of actions that have affected or will affect them. — Obtain agreement on actions.
Facilitate communications	— Expedite and assist in the progress of communication, both internal and external to the project. — Disseminate project management plans and other pertinent documents.
Resolve conflicts	— Resolve disagreements between project personnel and between the project and outside agencies. — Reduce the opportunity for future conflict by removing potential sources of disagreement whenever possible.
Manage changes	— Encourage independent thought and innovation in achieving project goals. — Control change but do not eliminate it.
Document directing decisions	— Document task and authority assignments. — Document decisions on channels of communication. — Document decisions concerning change and conflict resolution.

(A plan for improving technology transfer is discussed in paragraph 6.3.8, Manage Change.)

Most software engineering personnel are well paid, work in pleasant surroundings, and are reasonably satisfied with their position in life. Therefore, in accordance with Maslow's hierarchy of unfulfilled needs, the average software engineer is high on the ladder of satisfied needs. Most software engineers are at the "esteem and recognition" level and are occasionally reaching to the "self-actualization" level. Thus, one of the issues that management is facing today is the question of what it takes to motivate software engineers into producing more and better software (called *software psychology* in some circles), since money alone doesn't seem to do it.

6.3 Directing Activities and Tasks

Table 6.1 provides an outline of all the SEPM activities and tasks that must be accomplished by the PMs in applying direction to their project. The balance of this section discusses and provides greater detail on the activities and tasks outlined in Table 6.1.

6.3.1 Provide Leadership

The PM provides leadership to his project management team. His job is to interpret the plans and requirements to ensure that everybody on his project team is working toward a common goal. Leadership is a combination of the power of the leader and his ability to guide individuals. The PM's power can be derived from his leadership position as PM (or team leader, chief programmer, and so forth); this is called *positional power*. Or the PM's power can also be derived from the manager's own "charm," skill as a manager to motivate, or charisma; this is called *personal power*.

A good leader is able to align the personal goals of his subordinates with organizational goals of his project. Problems do arise when the PM who has positional power conflicts with a subordinate within the project who has personal power. For a discussion on different uses of power by managers see [Boyatzis, 1971].

6.3.2 Supervise Personnel

The PM is responsible for overseeing the project member's work and providing day-to-day supervision and direction to the personnel assigned to him or authorized for his control. It is his responsibility to provide guidance and, when necessary, discipline to these people so that they fulfill their assigned duties.

His supervisory responsibilities involve such mundane tasks as "clocking in" the employees at the beginning of the day's work, approving vacation time, reprimanding an individual for a missed appointment, or approving a deviation from company policy. At other times, the PM can provide a crucial decision on a software design approach; make a well presented argument to top management which results in more and better tools and equipment; or is a necessary listener to a project member's personal problems.

6.3.3 Delegate Authority

The software engineering PM is also responsible for delegating authority to the project staff. He assigns tasks to subgroups, teams, and individuals, and he delegates authority to these teams so that they can accomplish these tasks correctly and properly. Typically, a good PM will always delegate authority down through the lowest level of the project [Raudsepp, 1981].

The proper delegation of the right kind of authority can free managers from time-consuming routine supervision and decisions, thus enabling them to concentrate on the important needs of their project. The individual project members should understand what authority is delegated fo what responsibility. They should also clearly understand the scope, the limitations of the authority, and the reasons for the delegation.

6.3.4 Motivate Personnel

Ordinary leadership alone is not enough. The PM is responsible for motivating and inspiring personnel to do their best. Several motivational techniques from main-stream management are applicable to software engineering projects, such as: management by objective, Maslow's hierarchy of needs [Maslow, 1954], Herzberg's hygiene factors [Herzberg, Mausner, and Snyderman, 1959], and sometimes just the charisma of the manager. The PM should always acknowledge the special attention required by the highly qualified, technically trained engineers and scientists who staff his project. Dollars will attract good software engineers to a company; dollars will not keep them. For a further discussion on motivating software development personel see [Fitz-enz, 1978]. For another paper with a unique method of motivating computer people, see [Powell and Posner, 1984].

The motivation models and techniques from Table 6.2 have been developed over the past 50 years and should be reviewed by PMs as preparation for managing a software engineering project. The following paragraphs describe several of these motivation techniques in greater detail:

Hierarchy of Needs (Maslow): Unsatisfied needs are not motivators. For example, an individual who feels safe cannot be motivated by being made to feel safer. Maslow's hierarchy of human needs in order of importance are listed below [Maslow, 1954]:

- *Biological survival needs*—basic needs to sustain human life—food, water, shelter, etc.
- *Security and safety needs*—freedom from physical danger.
- *Social needs*—need to belong; to be accepted by others.
- *Esteem and recognition needs*—to be held in esteem by themselves and by others.
- *Self-actualization needs*—to maximize one's potential and to accomplish something.

Job Factors for Computer Personnel: The following are lists of the factors, in order of declining importance, that motivate job-seekers toward taking a job (left-hand column), and that make a job dissatisfying to the job-holder (right-hand column):

Job Desirability	Job Dissatisfaction
Salary	Company mismanagement
Chance to advance	Poor work environment
Work environment	Little feeling of accomplishment
Location	Poor recognition
Benefits	Inadequate salary
Facilities/equipment	Poor chance to advance
Job satisfaction	Poor facilities/equipment
Company management	Poor benefits
Job responsibility	Poor career path definition

Case Study:
People Don't Leave For
The Same Reason They Came

A manager called in a highly valued employee, a top-flight software engineer, and explained that he was hiring a new

Figure 6.2: Motivation Models and Techniques

Motivation Model	Definition or Explanation
Frederick Taylor	— Workers will respond to an *incentive wage*.
Elton Mayo	— *Interpersonal (group) values* were superior to *individual values*. Personnel will respond to group pressure.
Kurt Lewin	— *Group forces* can overcome the interest of an *individual*.
Douglas McGregor	— Managers must understand the nature of man in order to be able to motivate him.
A.H. Maslow	— Human needs can be classified. Satisfied needs are not motivators.
Frederick Herzberg	— A decrease in *environment factors* is dissatisfying; an increase in environment factors is *not* satisfying. A decrease in *job content factors* is *not* dissatisfying; an increase in job content factors is satisfying.
Chris Argyris	— The greater the disparity between *company needs* and *individual needs* the greater the dissatisfaction of the employee.
Rensis Likert	— *Participative management* is essential to personal motivation.
Arch Patton	— Executives are *motivated* by the challenge in work, status, the urge to achieve leadership, the lash of competition, fear, and money.
Theory Z	— A combination American and Japanese management styles. People need goals and objectives, otherwise they can easily impede their own progress and the progress of their company [Ouchi, 1981].
Quality circles	— Employees meet periodically in small groups to develop suggestions for quality and productivity improvements.

man to work with him on his project. The new hire was a good engineer but younger, with less experience, than the older employee. The manager explained that the new hire would be getting more money that the older employee. The manager said he had no real choice. He needed the new hire, the project was behind schedule, and this was the only way he could get the new man to come with the company and the project. The manager carefully explained this to the older employee and hoped he would understand. The older employee grumbled a little but seemed to accept it and went back to work. The manager was on safe ground. He knew that while it took a good salary to entice a new employee, software people usually did not quit for money reasons but because of poor management. By telling the first employee about his problem, he was able to convince the employee that the management decisions made were the best for the company.

McGregor's Theories X and Y: McGregor presented two assumptions about the nature of man called Theory X and Theory Y [McGregor, 1960]. It should be noted that contrary to popular belief, McGregor did not favor one view over the other. He did not say that Theory Y was a better view than Theory X, only that there were two theories. The PM should use the best approach for his project.

Theory X Assumptions

- Average human beings have an inherent dislike of work and will avoid it if they can.

- Because of this human characteristic of dislike of work, most people must be coerced, controlled, directed, and threatened with punishment to get them to put forth adequate effort toward the achievement of organizational objectives.

- Average human beings prefer to be directed, wish to avoid responsibility, have relatively little ambition, and want security above all.

Theory Y Assumptions

- The expenditure of physical effort and mental effort in work is as natural as play or rest.

- External control and the threat of punishment are not the only means for bringing about effort toward organizational objectives. People will exercise self-direction and self-control in the service of objectives to which they are committed.

- Commitment to objectives is a function of the rewards associated with their achievement.

- Average human beings learn under proper conditions not only to accept but also to seek responsibility.

Theory Z: Theory Z is a combination of American and Japanese management styles [Ouchi, 1981]. The basic principles of Theory Z are [Arthur, 1983]:

- People need goals and objectives, otherwise they can easily impede their own progress and the progress of their company. Goals help to keep one on a forward track while a minimum amount of time is lost to non-productivity.

- Worker motivation is essential for good performance and must be both positively and negatively reinforced by management. Optimal motivation is derived from both peer and managerial recognition and to a lesser extent from promotion and reward.

- Merely having goals and motivation will not prevent people from making mistakes. Managers must correct their movement along paths that are in the best interests of the company.

- The best interests of any given company are achieved when each individual's work is standardized to ensure that similar goals are attained by similar means. In turn, any suggested improvement in one particular area of work automatically is incorporated into other similar areas.

- Goals must change as working conditions and corporate needs change. In anticipation of such change Theory Z provides the mechanism for gradual change.

6.3.5 Coordinate Activities

The PM is responsible for coordinating the activities of the project to ensure that people understand and communicate with each other. The manager wants to ensure that other personnel in contact with his project are aware of the organizational structure, the task that his organization is performing, and what he expects from other organizations.

By coordination we mean to arrange for the project entities to work together toward a common goal with a minimum of friction. Documents, policies, procedures, and so forth are viewed differently by various people. The task of the PM is to reconcile differences in approach, effort, or schedule and to bring together these differences for the benefit of the project.

Coordination is sometimes used as a substitute for communication since it means the necessity of informing interacting organizations of actions that have been or will be taken that affect the interfacing organization. Coordination is also used as a term for obtaining agreement on actions (normally in advance of the action) with an interfacing organization that will be affected by that action.

6.3.6 Facilitate Communication

Along with coordination, the PM is responsible for facilitating communication both within his project and between his project and other organizations. Communication means the exchange of information between entities that are both working toward a common goal. Facilitate, in turn, means to expedite, ease, and to assist in the progress of communication.

For example, the PM should disseminate the staffing plans and promotion policies throughout his organization as soon as practical. Nothing can destroy the morale of an organization faster than false and misleading rumors. A good PM will see to it that his project staff is kept well-informed so that rumors are quickly dispelled.

Quality Circles: While application of quality circles is primarily considered to be a motivation technique, it is also an excellent means for improving communications between the project members and the PM. One company used quality circles to enlist the software engineering team members to select the best software engineering methodologies for the company.

Although this practice of using quality circles originated in American management philosophy, it is well implemented only in Japan. Quality circles have employees meet periodically in small groups to develop suggestions for quality and productivity improvements. Quality circles can provide fertile arenas for creating a favorable environment for management. To implement a quality circle [Arthur, 1983]:

- Train managers and other project leaders on the effectiveness of the quality circle. Training must include such organizational techniques as agendas, worksheets, checklists, and, most importantly, group participation.

- Meet as a part of the company's working agenda, on company time and in company facilities. This reinforces the company's commitment to each circle as well as its need to be successful. Quality circle membership should be voluntary if it is to be viewed as an opportunity rather than a requirement.

- Organize the meeting so as not to waste the members' time. Suggestions should be acted upon and those ideas which appear most beneficial for the company's betterment should be pursued.

For a further discussion on quality circles as applied to software development organizations see [Couger, 1983].

6.3.7 Resolve Conflicts

It is the PM's responsibility to resolve conflicts among his staff members and between his staff and outside agencies in both technical and managerial matters. The PM is not necessarily expected to be an expert in all aspects of his project.

However, he should have the good judgment to recognize the best possible approach in solving a particular technical or managerial problem.

The PM should reduce the opportunity for future conflict by removing potential sources of disagreement whenever possible, e.g., team members with somewhat equal positions should have equal benefits, access to the manager, parking places, and so forth.

Another type of conflict that the PM should watch for is the conflict between the employee and himself. When this conflict reaches epic proportions it is called "burnout" [Cherlin, 1981].

6.3.8 Manage Change

The PM is responsible for encouraging independent thought and innovation in achieving project goals. A good manager will always be able to accommodate change, when change is both cost-effective and beneficial to the project. [Kirchof and Adams, 1986].

It is important that the PM attempt to control change and not eliminate it. It is clear that requirements will change, design will change, and the technology for which the software system is built will change. There will be social changes. What is acceptable to build or the procedures to build at one time will not necessarily be acceptable at another time. People change, new crops of engineers are smarter, they have been taught new ways to develop software systems. The bottom line then is not to eliminate change but to control it.

Yourdon [1987] presents a simple step-by-step plan for the transfer of a new software technology (a change) within a software development organization:

- Explain the risks and benefits of the new technology.
- Provide training for the project team.
- Prototype the technique before it is used.
- Provide technical support throughout the project.
- Listen to the users' concerns and problems.
- Avoid concentrating on the technology at the expense of the project.

As another example of controlling (taking the advantage of) change, staff turnover is usually considered a problem in most software development organization. The paper by Bartol and Martin [1983] discusses how to make the most of staff turnover and view it as a good thing, not a bad thing.

6.3.9 Document Directing Decisions

Document all tasks, assignments of authority (whom to and what for), and the outcome of conflict resolution. In addition, document all decisions concerning lines of communications, coordination, and conflict resolution.

7. Controlling a Software Engineering Project

7.1 Introduction and Definitions

Controlling a software engineering project is all the management activities that ensure that actual operations go according to plan. It measures performance against goals and plans, shows when deviation exists, and, by putting in motion actions to correct deviations, helps ensure accomplishment of plans.

The basic control process involves the establishment of plans and standards, the measurement of performance against these plans and standards, and the correction of deviation.

Control is a feedback system that provides information on how well the project is going. Is the project on schedule? Is it within cost? Are there any potential problems that will cause slippages in meeting the requirement within the budget and schedule?

The control process also requires an organizational structure. For example, who is responsible for measuring the project progress? Who will take action on reported problems?

Controlling methods and tools must be objective. The methods and tools must point out deviations from plans and standards without regard to people or positions involved. Control methods must be tailored to individual environments and managers. These methods must be flexible and be able to deal with the changing environment of the organization. Control also must be economical. It must produce a benefit, and the cost of control should not outweigh its benefits.

Control must lead to corrective action—either to bring the process back to its standard, change the standard, or, less desirably, terminate the process.

7.2 Major Issues in Controlling

The major issues (or problems) in controlling a software engineering project are:

- Many methods of controlling a software project rely on budget expenditures for measurement of "progress."
- Standards for software development activities are either not written or, if written, not enforced.
- The body of knowledge called software metrics which can be used to measure the quality of a software project is not fully developed.

The major issues in controlling involve problems associated with relying on budget expenditures for the management of progress [Thayer, Pyster, and Wood, 1981]. For example, when a PM is asked for the completion status of his software development project, he will look at the monies (or calendar time) expended. If he has spent three-quarters of his funds (or time) he will respond with sincerity that he is three-quarters of the way through the project. The obvious problem is that the relationship between monies (calendar time) spent and work accomplished is only a rough measure at best and completely incorrect at worst. One possible solution is the earned-value method of monitoring software

Table 7.1: Controlling a Software Engineering Project

Project Management Activities and Tasks

Develop standards of performance	— Develop and specify quantity and quality standards of performance.
	— Standardize and document software development life-cycle engineering procedures, deliverables, milestones, baselines, and documents.
	— Specify software quality assurance (SQA) methods.
	— Develop measurements of software engineering productivity and quality.
Establish monitoring and reporting systems	— Establish reporting and monitoring system.
	— Determine type, frequency, originator, and recipient of project reports.
	— Establish a software configuration management system.
	— Establish status reporting tools that will provide visibility of progress, not just resources used.
	— Select software tools, techniques, and indexes to monitor production, e.g., PERT, CPM, workload charts, Gantt charts, and so on.
	— Collect project data to develop more accurate forecasting and measurement methods.
Measure results	— Measure and audit actual expenditures, progress, and status of project.
	— Measure and evaluate quality and quantity of software products.
	— Determine deviation from project plan, standards, or requirements.
Initiate corrective actions	— Initiate corrective action if plans, standards, or requirements are not being met.
	— Determine best approach to initiate corrective action.
Reward and discipline	— Reward and praise successes for those who contributed to the goals of the project.
	— Take disciplinary action against those who could but did not contribute to the project.
Document controlling methods	— Document controlling procedures, measurement methods, and standards.
	— Publish periodic reports on the deviation between planned and actual results.
	— Document the action taken to correct the deviation from plan.

projects. A description of this method is in the paper by Howes [1984].

Many standards by which we measure progress are either not written or, if written, not enforced [Thayer, Pyster, and Wood, 1982]. People chafe under standards, particularly people with computer skills. Standards are frequently touted as being detrimental to a software development project because they "stifle creativity." Therefore, it is unusual for entire projects, including the manager, to ignore the company standards in favor of a local, ad hoc, and frequently inadequate, software development system.

The body of knowledge that we know as software metrics has not yet been fully developed. Software quality metrics measure the quality of the delivered software, e.g., reliability, maintainability, usability, economy, and so forth. However, our software engineering research has not yet progressed to this point. Reliability and maintainability can-

not be made an element of software design nor can they be measured accurately at the time of delivery. This has resulted in emphasis being placed on the process of software engineering in the belief that the quality of a software product comes from the quality of the process used to create it.

7.3 Controlling Activities and Tasks

Table 7.1 provides an outline of the SEPM activities that must be accomplished by the PMs in controlling their projects. The balance of this section discusses and provides greater detail on the activities and tasks outlined in Table 7.1.

7.3.1 Develop Standards of Performance

The PM is responsible for developing and specifying standards of performance for his project. These are specific software engineering standards for the software engineering project process and product. The PM either develops his own standards and procedures within his project, adopts and uses standards developed by his parent corporation, or perhaps uses those developed outside his company (see for example the IEEE Software Engineering Standards [IEEE Software Engineering Standards, 1987]).

7.3.1.1 Standards:
A standard is an approved, documented, and available set of criteria used to determine the adequacy of an action or object. A *software engineering standard* is a set of (1) procedures that define the processes for and (2) descriptions that define the quantity and quality of a product from a software engineering project.

Both process and product standards are extremely important to the task of developing high-quality software. (See [Buckley, 1987] for a discussion on how to implement a software engineering standard in a company.) Software engineering is primarily concerned with the *process* of developing software rather than the product itself. This is because software quality metrics (measuring such quality attributes as software reliability, maintainability, portability, and other ''-ilities'') is not a well developed science, and tools and techniques that do an effective job of measuring the quality of a software product are not generally available. Therefore, most software engineering standards are concerned with the process of developing software, not the product.

In addition to providing a gauge with which to measure the software engineering process, software engineering standards offer a substantial savings in software development costs. For example:

- The need for retraining engineers, designers, and programmers between projects will be reduced.
- Communications between team members can be improved.
- The transferring of staff between projects will be eased.
- Experiences and project history can be more readily shared if the software developed is based on a common method.
- The best experience of successful projects can be uniformly applied.
- Software implementation and software maintenance can be simplified.
- The standard can be controlled, resulting in controlled development.
- Standards quality assurance procedures can be applied.

7.3.1.2 Software Quality Assurance:
Software quality assurance (SQA) is ''a planned and systematic pattern of all actions necessary to provide adequate confidence that the item or product conforms to established technical requirements'' [IEEE Glossary, 1983]. SQA includes development methods (requirements and design), standards, configuration management methods, review procedures, documentation standards, verification and validation, and testing specifications and procedures. SQA is one of the major control techniques available to the PM.

7.3.2 Establish Monitoring and Reporting Systems

The PM is responsible for establishing the methods of monitoring the software engineering project and reporting the project status. Monitoring and reporting systems must be selected or developed in order to be able to determine project status at any time. The PM needs feedback on the progress of his project to ensure that everything is going according to plan. He should establish the type, frequency, originator, and recipient of project reports. He should establish status reporting tools to provide visibility of progress, not just resources used or time passed.

The PM should also select software methods, procedures, tools, and techniques to measure production. Table 7.2 lists typical SEPM monitoring and reporting systems. Some tools that aid in the controlling of a software engineering project are PERT and CPM, workload charts, Gantt charts, and so forth [Cori, 1985]. The paper by Howes [1984] presents the earned-value method of managing a software engineering project.

The purpose of the report is to provide status information to keep management informed. Table 7.3 lists examples of the types of reports that can be generated by a controlling system. It provides an opportunity to observe out-of-bounds conditions. It also provides a record from which the PM can predict the future. The manager is responsible for collecting project data to develop more accurate forecasting techniques for the future.

One of the most effective monitoring and reporting methods is the baseline management system.

7.3.2.1 Baseline Management System:
The baseline management paradigm is a management strategy that is used to control the software development. The baseline management system integrates a series of life-cycle phases, reviews, and baseline documents into a software development management system. (See Figure 7.1 for an illustration of a software development life-cycle model that is used with the baseline management paradigm.) Specifically, baseline management is:

- Based on the waterfall model [Royce, 1970].
- Partitions the project into manageable phases: requirements, design, implementation, and test.

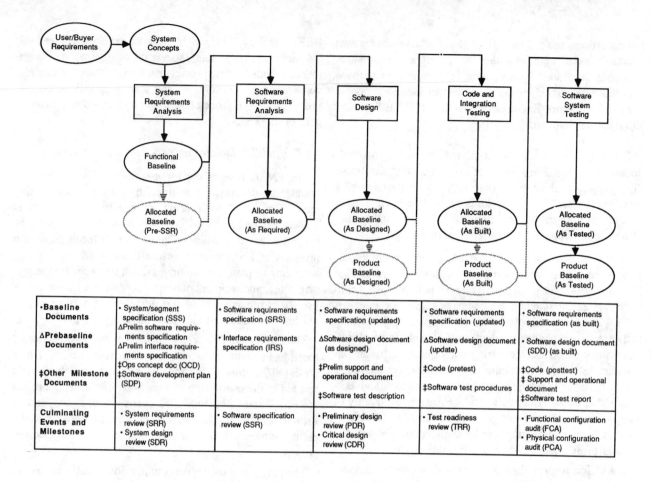

•Baseline Documents ΔPrebaseline Documents ‡Other Milestone Documents	• System/segment specification (SSS) ΔPrelim software requirements specification ΔPrelim interface requirements specification ‡Ops concept doc (OCD) ‡Software development plan (SDP)	• Software requirements specification (SRS) • Interface requirements specification (IRS)	• Software requirements specification (updated) ΔSoftware design document (as designed) ‡Prelim support and operational document ‡Software test description	• Software requirements specification (updated) ΔSoftware design document (update) ‡Code (pretest) ‡Software test procedures	• Software requirements specification (as built) • Software design document (SDD) (as built) ‡Code (posttest) ‡ Support and operational document ‡Software test report
Culminating Events and Milestones	• System requirements review (SRR) • System design review (SDR)	• Software specification review (SSR)	• Preliminary design review (PDR) • Critical design review (CDR)	• Test readiness review (TRR)	• Functional configuration audit (FCA) • Physical configuration audit (PCA)

Figure 7.1: Software development life cycle model

- Establishes milestones, documents, and reviews at the end of each phase.
- Establishes a baseline at periodic intervals.
- Uses configuration management to control the baselines.

Milestones and Milestone Charts: Milestones and milestone charts play a major part in the controlling process. A milestone is a discrete event that must be tangible and its completion must be precisely known. Quality must be evaluated and completion must be important. The buzzword is that milestones have a "knife edge" completion date or time. The completion must also be demonstrable; there must be no doubt that the milestone has been completed.

The purpose of milestones is to allow the PM to partition his project into measurable units each one terminating in a milestone, each one of which can be completed and demonstrate completeness. Examples of milestones are the completion of a software requirement specification, the completion of a software design review, the completion of code, and of course the major milestone, the completion of the project.

Formal (Milestone) Reviews: Reviews are the analysis of project processes and products by customers, users, and management in order to assess progress. A formal review (sometime called a milestone review) is a review of the management and technical progress of the software development project. Reviews are held at the end of each of the life-cycle phases (a milestone) of the software development project. For example, a preliminary design review (PDR) is held at the completion of the preliminary design phase.

Milestone reviews are usually chaired by the customer. The developer presents the current status and his progress, the work done to date, the monies expended, the current schedule, and any management and technical problems that may have surfaced since the last review. The review is a suc-

Table 7.2: Methods of Monitoring a Software Engineering Project

Method	Definition or Explanation
Monitoring the Process	
Baseline management paradigm	— A management strategy that is used to control the software development life cycle.
Budget reviews	— A comparison of estimated budget with actual expenditures by customers, developers, and managers in order to determine compliance with or deviations from plan.
Independent auditing	— An independent audit of the software engineering project for the purpose of determining compliance with plans, specifications, and standards.
Formal (milestone) reviews	— The analysis of concepts and specifications (at the completion of a milestone) by customers, users, and management in order to assess progress.
Process standards	— A standard that defines the procedures or operations used in making or achieving a product.
Software quality assurance (SQA)	— A planned and systematic pattern of all actions necessary to provide adequate confidence that the process conforms to established standards.
Unit development folder (UDF)	— A specific form of development notebook which provides an orderly approach to the development of a programming unit and provides management visibility and control over the development process.
Monitoring the Product	
Configuration management (CM)	— A method for controlling and reporting on software status.
Product standards	— A standard that defines what constitutes completeness and acceptability of items which are produced as a result of a process.
Software quality assurance (SQA)	— A planned and systematic pattern of all actions necessary to provide adequate confidence that the product conforms to established technical requirements.
Testing (unit, integration)	— The controlled exercise of the program code in order to expose errors.
Verification and validation	— The assurance that each phase of life cycle correctly interprets the specification from the previous phase and that each delivered software product functions as prescribed by its requirements.
Walkthroughs and inspection	— A critique of a software product by the producer's peers for the sole purpose of finding errors.

cess when the customer or top management gives permission to the software developer to proceed to the next phase.

Baseline Concept: A baseline is an agreed on technical configuration at some point in the software development life cycle. Baselines are typically agreed on between developers and customers and are controlled and maintained by a software configuration management system. Baselines commonly used by DoD are: functional, allocated, and product baselines.

7.3.2.2 Software Configuration Management: Software configuration management (SCM) is a method for controll-

Table 7.3: Types of Reports

Types of Report	Definition or Explanation
Budget reports	— Compare budget with expenditures and provide for making new budget estimates.
Schedule reports	— Provide status of schedule and milestones completed.
Man-hour by activity reports	— Provide a report on the number of staff hours that have been worked on a given activity.
Man-day by task reports	— Provide the number of days assigned to a given task. A task may or may not be larger than an activity.
Milestone due or overdue reports	— Provide a status of the milestones that have been accomplished or have been missed and the reason for missing the milestone.
Project progress reports	— A free-flowing narrative report indicating the status of progress or a list of activities accomplished
Activity reports	— Provide, typically over a period of time, what activities have been accomplished.
Trend charts	— Show trends in such areas as budget, number of errors found in the system, manhours of sick leave, and so on. Trend reports are used to predict the future.
Significant change reports	— A general change report indicating exceptions to the plan and significant changes both good and bad. However, it normally shows a loss of progress.

ing and reporting on software status. SCM is the discipline of identifying the configuration of a system at discrete points in time for purposes of systematically controlling changes to this configuration and maintaining the integrity and traceability of this configuration throughout the system life cycle [Bersoff, 1984].

7.3.3 Measure Results

The PM is responsible for measuring the results of the project both during and at the end of the project. For instance, he should measure actual phase deliverables against planned phase deliverables. He is responsible for determining if the project deviated from the project plan, standards, or other requirements. The results measured can be management (process) results or technical (product) results. An example of a process result would be the status of the project schedule. An example of a product result would be whether or not the design specifications correctly interpreted the requirement specifications. Some of the tools and methods for measuring results are described in the following paragraphs.

7.3.3.1 Unit Development Folders: The unit development folder (UDF) is a specific form of development notebook which has proven to be useful and effective in collecting and organizing software products as they are produced. The purpose of the UDF is to provide an orderly approach to the development of a unit of program and to provide management visibility and control over the development process [Ingrassia, 1987].

7.3.3.2 Walkthroughs and Inspection Systems: Walkthroughs and inspections are informal reviews of a software product (design specifications, code, test procedures, etc.) conducted by the peers of the group being interviewed [Weinberg and Freedman, 1984]. Walkthroughs are a critique of a software product by the producer's peers for the sole purpose of finding errors. The inspection system is another peer review developed by Michael Fagan [1986] of IBM in 1976. The inspection system was originally much more formal than the walkthrough. Recent changes to the walkthrough procedures have made them more formal. Athough the preferred term for a peer review is still walkthrough, the term inspection is becoming more popular.

7.3.3.3 *(Independent) Auditing:* The software engineering project audit is an independent review of the software engineering project to determine compliance with software requirements, specifications, baselines, standards, policies and software quality assurance plans.

An independent audit is an audit done by an outside organization not associated with the project. Occasionally it is considered appropriate to bring in an independent team for the purpose of auditing the project [Walters, 1987]. On the positive side, an independent team can provide a totally unbiased opinion. This would have the effect of reducing organizational animosity, since this team would not represent one side or the other. In the case of the need for expert knowledge, the independent team can supplement existing talent.

The negative side of the independent audit is that the audit team needs to be brought up to speed on the project. They must overcome the learning curve. The audit team requires ongoing involvement to be effective.

7.3.3.4 Verification and Validation: Two methods for determining if the product is correct are verification and validation. Verification is assuring that each phase of the life cycle correctly interprets the specification from the previous phase. Validation is assuring that each delivered software product functions as prescribed by its requirements.

7.3.3.5 Testing (Unit, Integration): Testing is the controlled exercise of the program code in order to expose errors. Unit testing (sometimes called "debugging") is the testing of one unit of code (usually a module) by the programmer who programmed the unit. Integration testing is the testing of each unit or subelement in combination with the system under test to show the existence of errors between the units or subelements and the system.

7.3.3.6 Software Configuration Audit: Software configuration audits provide the mechanism for determining the degree to which the current state of the software system mirrors the software system contained in the baseline and requirements document [Bersoff, 1984].

7.3.4 Initiate Corrective Actions

If standards and requirements are not being met, the PM must initiate corrective action. For instance, the PM can change the plan or standard, insist through overtime or other procedures that his team get back on plan, or, as a last resort, actually change the requirements, i.e., deliver less.

The PM will change the plans or standards if it is readily apparent that the original plans or standards cannot be met. This might involve requiring a larger budget, more manpower, or more checkout (computer) time on the development computer. It also might require reducing the standards (and indirectly the quality) by reducing the number of walkthroughs from reviewing all the software modules to only reviewing the critical software modules.

It is sometimes possible to get back on some part of the plan by increasing another part. For example, it is sometime possible (but not probable) to get back on schedule without reducing the product by increasing overtime. This increases the resources plan. It is also sometime possible (but not probable) to hold to the original cost by stretching out the schedule.

An example of changing the requirements involves delivering software without a full complement of documents or software that does not meet completely all the functional requirements that were laid out in the original software requirements specifications.

7.3.5 Reward and Discipline

The PM should reward people for meeting their standards or plans and discipline those who without reason cannot. This should not be confused with the compensation (usually salary) given to workers for performing their assigned duties; that is a function of staffing. This is an incentive reward (bonus, day off, "atta-boy" award) for meeting a plan or standard.

The following case example is presented to illustrate this point.

Case Study: The Project Bonus Plan

A small venture capital company was trying hard to compete with larger companies in the development of new software for medical applications. In order to improve the timeliness of the software developments the company implemented a bonus plan for all software development projects. Each project was given a required delivery date and budget and an anticipated money bonus. All members of the project shared in the bonus if the project goals were met.

7.3.6 Document Controlling Methods

The PM should document the software development and measurement methods for his project. The PM should publish periodic reports on the deviations between planned and actual results. The PM also should document the actions taken to correct the deviations.

8. Summary

In this paper and in many other documents, the terms "project management" and "software engineering project management" (SEPM) are used somewhat interchangeably. Now we can see why. The management of a software engineering project and other projects requires many of the same tools, techniques, approaches, and methods of mainstream management. As we said in the beginning, the functions and general activities are the same; only the detailed activities and tasks are different.

Following or implementing all of the project management functions, tasks, and ideas contained in the paper does not guarantee a successful project. A very good project manager can always overcome or work around deficiencies in organization, staffing, budgets, standards, or other shortcomings. A poor manager stumbles over every problem, real or imaginary, and no number of rules, policies, standards, or techniques will help. This paper is for the average project manager, who with a little luck and a little knowledge of what he is supposed to do and how he should do it, will deliver his software engineering project on time, within cost, and to the customer's satisfaction.

9. Acknowledgements

It is important to recognize that this report was based on the works of other general management experts. The author is indebted to such management experts and authors as D.I. Cleland, W.R. King, H. Koontz, R.A. MacKenzie, C. O'Donnell, H. Weihrich, and others (see References) for the basic research on identifying the major functions and activities of mainstream management on which this report is built. The works of these authors provided the structure for this report.

I would like to acknowledge the support I received from the two Lockheed technical editors, Mark Longley and Max Hosmanek, and my word processor, Barbara Dietrich, and my proofreader, Mildred Thayer.

References

[Arthur, 1983] L.J. Arthur, *Programmer Productivity: Myths, Methods, and Murphology,* John Wiley & Sons, NY, 1983.

[Bailey, Frazier, and Bailey, 1986] E.K. Bailey, T.P. Frazier, and J.W. Bailey, *A Descriptive Evaluation of Automated Software Cost-Estimation Models,* Institute for Defense Analysis, IDA Paper P-1979, October 1986.

[Bartol and Martin, 1983] K.M. Bartol and D.C. Martin, "Managing the Consequences of DP Turnover: A Human Resources Planning Perspective," *Proc. of the 20th ACM Computer Personnel Research Conf.,* ACM, Inc., NY, 1983, pages 79-86. Reprinted in *Tutorial: Software Engineering Management,* edited by R.H. Thayer, Computer Society of the IEEE, Washington, D.C., 1987.

[Ben-David, et al., 1984] A. Ben-David, M. Ben-Porath, J. Loeb, and M. Rich, "An Industrial Software Engineering Retraining Course: Development Considerations and Lessons Learned," *IEEE Transactions on Software Engineering,* Vol. SE-10, No. 1, November 1984, pages 748-755.

[Bersoff, 1984] E.H. Bersoff, "Elements of Software Configuration Management," *IEEE Transactions on Software Engineering,* Vol. SE-10, No. 1, January 1984, pp. 79-87. Reprinted in *Tutorial: Software Engineering Project Management,* edited by R.H. Thayer, Computer Society of the IEEE, Washington, D.C., 1987.

[Boehm, 1981] B.W. Boehm, *Software Engineering Economics,* Prentice-Hall, Englewood Cliffs, NJ, 1981.

[Boehm, 1984] B.W. Boehm, "Software Engineering Economics," *IEEE Transactions on Software Engineering,* Vol. SE-10, No. 1, January 1984, pp. 4-21. Reprinted in *Tutorial: Software Engineering Project Management,* edited by R.H. Thayer, Computer Society of the IEEE, Washington, D.C., 1987.

[Boehm, 1987] B.W. Boehm, "A Spiral Model of Software Development and Enhancement," *Tutorial: Software Engineering Project Management,* edited by R.H. Thayer, Computer Society of the IEEE, Washington, D.C., 1987.

[Boehm, 1987] B.W. Boehm, "Improving Software Productivity," *Computer,* September 1987, pages 43-57. Reprinted in *Tutorial: Software Engineering Project Management,* edited by R.H. Thayer, Computer Society of the IEEE, Washington, D.C., 1987.

[Boyatzis, 1971] R.E. Boyatzis, "Leadership: The Effective Use of Power," *Management of Personnel Quarterly,* Bureau of Industrial Relations, 1971, pages 1-8. Reprinted in *Tutorial: Software Engineering Project Management,* edited by R.H. Thayer, Computer Society of the IEEE, Washington, D.C., 1987.

[Buckley, 1987] F.J. Buckley, "Establishing Software Engineering Standards in an Industrial Organization," *Tutorial: Software Engineering Project Management,* edited by R.H. Thayer, Computer Society of the IEEE, Washington, D.C., 1987.

[Bunyard and Coward, 1982] J.M. Bunyard and J.M. Coward, "Today's Risks in Software Development—Can They Be Significantly Reduced?," *Concepts: Journal of Defense Systems Acquisition Management,* Vol. 5, No. 4, August 1982, pages 73-94.

[Cherlin, 1981] M. Cherlin, "Burnout: Victims and Avoidances," *Datamation,* July 1981, pages 92-99.

[Cleland and King, 1972] See Table 5-1: Major Management Functions as Seen by Various Authors, from *Management: A Systems Approach,* by David I. Cleland and William R. King, McGraw-Hill Book Co., NY, 1972.

[Cooke, 1976] L.H. Cooke, Jr., "The Chief Programmer Team Administrator," *Datamation,* June 1976, pages 85-86.

[Cori, 1985] K.A. Cori, "Fundamentals of Master Scheduling for the Project Manager," *Project Management Journal,* June 1985, pages 78-89. Reprinted in *Tutorial: Software Engineering Project Management,* edited by R.H. Thayer, Computer Society of the IEEE, Washington, D.C., 1987.

[Couger, 1983] J.D. Couger, "Circular Solutions," *Datamation,* January 1983, pages 135-142.

[DePree, 1984] R.W. DePree, "The Long and Short of Schedules," *Datamation,* June 15, 1984, pages 131-134.

[DoD Software Initiative, 1983] *Strategy for a DoD Software Initiative,* Department of Defense Report, October 1, 1982. (An edited public version was published in *Computer,* November 1983.)

[Donnelly, Gibson, and Ivancevich, 1975] J.H. Donnelly, Jr., J.L. Gibson, and J.M. Ivancevich, *Fundamentals of Management: Functions, Behavior, Models,* rev. ed., Business Publications, Inc., Dallas, TX, 1975.

[Fagan, 1986] M.E. Fagan, "Advances in Software Inspections," *IEEE Transactions on Software Engineering,* Vol. SE-12, No. 7, July 1986, pages 744-751. Reprinted in *Tutorial: Software Engineering Project Management,* edited by R.H. Thayer, Computer Society of the IEEE, Washington, D.C., 1987.

[Fairley, 1987] R.E. Fairley, "A Guide for Preparing Software Project Management Plans," *Tutorial: Software Engineering Project Management,* edited by R.H. Thayer, Computer Society of the IEEE, Washington, D.C., 1987.

[Fayol, 1949] H. Fayol, *General and Industrial Administration,* Sir Isaac Pitman & Sons, Ltd., London, 1949.

[Ferrentino, 1981] A.B. Ferrentino, "Making Software Development Estimates 'Good,' " *Datamation,* September 1981, pages 179-182. Reprinted in *Tutorial: Software Engineering Project Management,* edited by R.H. Thayer, Computer Society of the IEEE, Washington, D.C., 1987.

[Fife, 1987] D.W. Fife, "How to Know a Well-Organized Software Project When You Find One," *Tutorial: Software Engineering Project Management,* edited by R.H. Thayer, Computer Society of the IEEE, Washington, D.C., 1987.

[Fitz-enz, 1978] J. Fitz-enz, "Who Is the DP Professional?," *Datamation,* September 1978, pages 125-128. Reprinted in *Tutorial: Software Engineering Project Management,* edited by R.H. Thayer, Computer Society of the IEEE, Washington, D.C., 1987.

[Herzberg, Mausner, and Snyderman, 1959] F. Herzberg, B. Mausner, and B.B. Snyderman, *The Motivation to Work,* John Wiley & Sons, New York, 1959.

[Howes, 1984] N.R. Howes, "Managing Software Development Projects for Maximum Productivity," *IEEE Transactions on Software Engineering,* Vol. SE-10, No. 1, January 1984, pages 27-35. Reprinted in *Tutorial: Software Engineering Project Management,* edited by R.H. Thayer, Computer Society of the IEEE, Washington, D.C., 1987.

[IEEE Glossary, 1983] ANSI/IEEE Std. 729-1983, *IEEE Standard Glossary of Software Engineering Terminology,* IEEE, Inc., NY, 1983.

[IEEE Software Engineering Standards, 1987] Hardbound Edition of Software Engineering Standards, IEEE, NY, 1987.

[Ingrassia, 1987] F.S. Ingrassia, "The Unit Development Folder (UDF): A Ten-Year Perspective," *Tutorial: Software Engineering Project Management,* edited by R.H. Thayer, Computer Society of the IEEE, Washington, D.C., 1987.

[Kirchof and Adams, 1986] N.S. Kirchof and J.R. Adams, "Conflict Management for Project Managers: An Overview," extracted from *Conflict Management for Project Managers,* Project Management Institute, February 1986, pages 1-13. Reprinted in *Tutorial: Software Engineering Project Management,* edited by R.H. Thayer, Computer Society of the IEEE, Washington, D.C., 1987.

[Koontz and O'Donnell, 1972] H. Koontz and C. O'Donnell, *Principles of Management: An Analysis of Managerial Functions,* 5th ed., McGraw-Hill Book Company, NY, 1972.

[Koontz, O'Donnell, and Weihrich, 1984] H. Koontz, C. O'Donnell, and H. Weihrich, *Management,* 8th ed., McGraw-Hill Book Co., NY, 1984.

[Kruesi, 1982] Betsy Kruesi, seminar on "Software Psychology," California State University, Sacramento, Fall 1982.

[MacKenzie, 1969] R.A. MacKenzie, "The Management Process in 3-D," *Harvard Business Review,* Vol. 47, No. 6, November-December 1969, pages 80-87. Reprinted in *Tutorial: Software Engineering Project Management,* edited by R.H. Thayer, Computer Society of the IEEE, Washington, D.C., 1987.

[Mantei, 1981] M. Mantei, "The Effect of Programming Team Structures on Programming Tasks," *Communications of the ACM,* Vol. 24, No. 3, March 1981, pages 106-113. Reprinted in *Tutorial: Software Engineering Project Management,* edited by R.H. Thayer, Computer Society of the IEEE, Washington, D.C., 1987.

[Maslow, 1954] A.H. Maslow, *Motivation and Personality,* Harper & Row, NY, 1954.

[McGill, 1984] J.P. McGill, "The Software Engineering Shortage: A Third Choice," *IEEE Transactions on Software Engineering,* Vol. SE-10. No. 1, January 1984, pages 42-48. Reprinted in *Tutorial: Software Engineering Project Management,* edited by R.H. Thayer, Computer Society of the IEEE, Washington, D.C., 1987.

[McGregor, 1960] D. McGregor, *The Human Side of Enterprise,* McGraw-Hill Book Co., NY, 1960.

[Middleton, 1967] C.J. Middleton, "How to Set Up a Project Organization," *Harvard Business Review,* November-December 1967, pages 73-82. Reprinted in *Tutorial: Software Engineering Project Management,* edited by R.H. Thayer, Computer Society of the IEEE, Washington, D.C., 1987.

[Miller, 1978] W.B. Miller, "Fundamentals of Project Management," *Journal of Systems Management,* Vol. 29, No. 11, Issue 211, November 1978, pages 22-29. Reprinted in *Tutorial: Software Engineering Project Management,* edited by R.H. Thayer, Computer Society of the IEEE, Washington, D.C., 1987.

[Mills, 1980] H.D. Mills, "Software Engineering Education," *Proceedings of the IEEE,* Vol. 68, No. 9, September 1980, pages 1158-1162.

[Mohanty, 1981] S.N. Mohanty, "Software Cost Estimation: Present and Future," *Software—Practice and Experience,* Vol. 11, 1981, pages 103-121.

[Moneysmith, 1984] M. Moneysmith, "I'm OK—and You're Not," *Savvy,* April 1984, pages 37-38. Reprinted in *Tutorial: Software Engineering Project Management,* edited by R.H. Thayer, Computer Society of the IEEE, Washington, D.C., 1987.

[Novaes-Card, 1987] David N. Novaes-Card, "A Software Technology Evaluation Program," Information and Software Technology, August 1987, pages 291-300. Reprinted in *Tutorial: Software Engineering Project Management,* edited by R.H. Thayer, Computer Society of the IEEE, Washington, D.C., 1987.

[Ouchi, 1981] W. Ouchi, *Theory Z: How American Business Can Meet the Japanese Challenge,* Addison-Wesley, Reading, MA, 1981.

[Powell and Posner, 1984] G.N. Powell and B.Z. Posner, "Excitement and Commitment: Keys to Project Success," *Project Management Journal,* December 1984, pages 39-46. Reprinted in *Tutorial: Software Engineering Project Management,* edited by R.H. Thayer, Computer Society of the IEEE, Washington, D.C., 1987.

[RADC Guidebook, 1985] D.R. Addleman, M.J. Davis, and P.E. Presson, *Specification Technology Guidebook,* RADC-TR-85-135, prepared by Boeing Aerospace Company for Rome Air Development Center, Griffiss AFB, NY, August 1985.

[Ramamoorthy, et al., 1984] C.V. Ramamoorthy, Atul Prakash, Wei-Tek Tsai, and Yutaka Usuda, "Software Engineering: Problems and Perspectives," *Computer,* October 1984, pages 191-209. A corrected copy appears in the *Tutorial: Software Engineering Project Management,* edited by R.H. Thayer, Computer Society of the IEEE, Washington, D.C., 1987.

[Raudsepp, 1981] E. Raudsepp, "Delegate Your Way to Success," *Computer Decisions,* March 1981, pages 157-164. Reprinted in *Tutorial: Software Engineering Project Management,* edited by R.H. Thayer, Computer Society of the IEEE, Washington, D.C., 1987.

[Redwine and Riddle, 1985] S.T. Redwine, Jr. and W.E. Riddle, "Software Technology Maturation," *Proceedings, Eighth International Conference on Software Engineering,* Computer Society of the IEEE, Washington, D.C., 1985, pages 189-200.

[Royce, 1970] W.W. Royce, "Managing the Development of Large Software Systems," *Proceedings, IEEE WESCON,* August 1970, pages 1-9. Reprinted in *Tutorial: Software Engineering Project Management,* edited by R.H. Thayer, Computer Society of the IEEE, Washington, D.C., 1987.

[Rue and Byars, 1983] L.W. Rue and L.L. Byars, *Management: Theory and Application,* Richard D. Irwin, Inc., Homewood, IL, 1983.

[Sackman, H. et al., 1968] H. Sackman, W.J. Erikson, and E.E. Grant, "Exploratory Experimental Studies Comparing Online/Offline Programming Performance," *Communication of the ACM,* Vol. 11, No. 1, January 1968, pages. 3-11. Reprinted in *Tutorial: Software Engineering Project Management,* edited by R.H. Thayer, Computer Society of the IEEE, Washington, D.C., 1987.

[Source EDP, 1987] *1987 Computer Salary Survey and Career Planning Guide,* Source EDP, San Francisco, CA.

[Stuckenbruck, 1981] L.C. Stuckenbruck, "The Matrix Organization," *A Decade of Project Management,* Project Management Institute, 1981, pages 157-169. Reprinted in *Tutorial: Software Engineering Project Management,* edited by R.H. Thayer, Computer Society of the IEEE, Washington, D.C., 1987.

[Tausworthe, 1980] R.C. Tausworthe, "The Work Breakdown Structure in Software Project Management," *The Journal of Systems and Software,* Vol. 1, 1980, pages 181-186. Reprinted in *Tutorial: Software Engineering Project Management,* edited by R.H. Thayer, Computer Society of the IEEE, Washington, D.C., 1987.

[Thayer and Pyster, 1984] R.H. Thayer and A.B. Pyster, "Guest Editorial: Software Engineering Project Management," *IEEE Transactions on Software Engineering,* Vol. SE-10, No. 1, January 1984.

[Thayer, Pyster, and Wood, 1981] R.H. Thayer, A.B. Pyster, and R.C. Wood, "Major Issues in Software Engineering Project Management," *IEEE Transactions on Software Engineering,* Vol. SE-7, No. 4, July 1981, pages 333-342.

[Thayer, Pyster, and Wood, 1982] R.H. Thayer, A. Pyster, and R.C. Wood, "Validating Solutions to Major Problems in Software Engineering Project Management," *Computer,* August 1982.

[TRW, 1978] "Applying Corporate Software Development Policy," E.A. Goldberg, TRW, Defense and Space Systems Group, December 6, 1978. Reprinted in *Tutorial: Software Engineering Project Management,* edited by R.H. Thayer, Computer Society of the IEEE, Washington, D.C., 1987.

[Walters, 1987] G.F. Walters, "Investigative Audit for Controlling Software Development," *Tutorial: Software Engineering Project Management,* edited by R.H. Thayer, Computer Society of the IEEE, Washington, D.C., 1987.

[Weinberg and Freedman, 1984] G.M. Weinberg and D.P. Freedman, "Reviews, Walkthroughs, and Inspections," *IEEE Transactions on Software Engineering,* Vol. SE-10, No. 1, January 1984, pages 68-72. Reprinted in *Tutorial: Software Engineering Project Management,* edited by R.H. Thayer, Computer Society of the IEEE, Washington, D.C., 1987.

[Weinberg, 1971] G. Weinberg, *The Psychology of Computer Programming,* Van Nostrand Reinhold, NY, 1971.

[Yeh, et al, 1984] R.T. Yeh, P. Zave, A.P. Conn, and G.E. Cole, Jr., "Software Requirements: New Directions and Perspectives," *Handbook of Software Engineering,* Edited by C.R. Vick and C.V. Ramamoorthy, Van Nostrand Reinhold Company, NY, 1984. Reprinted in *Tutorial: Software Engineering Project Management,* edited by R.H. Thayer, Computer Society of the IEEE, Washington D.C., 1987.

[Yourdon, 1987] E. Yourdon, "A Game Plan for Technology Transfer," *Tutorial: Software Engineering Project Management,* edited by R.H. Thayer, Computer Society of the IEEE, Washington, D.C., 1987.

[Youker, 1977] R. Youker, "Organizational Alternatives for Project Management," *Project Management Quarterly,* Vol. VIII, No. 1, March 1977, pages 18-24. Reprinted in *Tutorial: Software Engineering Project Management,* edited by R.H. Thayer, Computer Society of the IEEE, Washington, D.C., 1987.

[Zelkowitz, et al., 1984] M.V. Zelkowitz, R.T. Yeh, R.G. Hamilet, J.D. Gannon, and V.R. Basili, "Software Engineering Practices in the US and Japan," *Computer,* June 1984.

Chapter 2: Software Engineering

1. Introduction to Chapter

Software engineering can be defined as:

- The practical application of computer science, management, and other sciences to the analysis, design, construction, and maintenance of software and the documentation necessary to use, operate, and maintain the delivered software system.
- An engineering science that applies the concept of analysis, design, coding, testing, documentation, and management to the successful completion of large, custom-built computer programs.
- The systematic application of procedures, methods, tools, and techniques to achieve a stated requirement or objective for a software system.

Figure 2.1 presents a first- and second-level partitioning of software engineering into its four major activities: *software development, project management, software metrics,* and *software maintenance.* This figure establishes that software engineering project management is a major element of software engineering.

2. Overview of Chapter

The three papers in this chapter introduce software engineering to the reader in order to establish what software engineering is and the relationship between software engineering and project management. The selected papers are tutorial in nature and represent the best available descriptions of software engineering and software engineering issues.

3. Description of Papers

The first paper is an overview of software engineering entitled "Software Engineering: Problems and Perspectives," (C.V. Ramamoorthy, Atul Prakash, Wei-Tek Tsai, and Yutaka Usuda). It discusses the conventional software development life-cycle model and several alternative models such as rapid prototyping and the use of very-high-level languages. The paper deals with each phase of the life cycle from software requirements through software maintenance. In addition, the paper contains a description and discussion of *software quality assurance, software reliability, software*

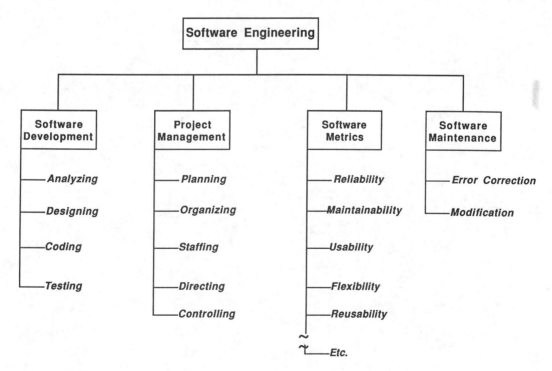

Figure 2.1: Structure of Software Engineering

reusability, and *rapid prototyping. Phase-dependent* and *non-phase-dependent* tools and techniques are discussed as well as some anticipated future trends. (This paper is a corrected copy of a paper that appeared in the October 1984 issue of *Computer*.)

The second paper by Bunyard and Coward presents another overview of developing large software systems and examines risks often encountered in software development. The objective of the paper is to focus on lessons learned and problems encountered during the past several years and to recommend alternative methods of developing software that could significantly reduce these problems. The paper concentrates on the risks and issues involved in developing very large software systems for the Department of Defense (DoD). It provides a short history of the problems faced by the DoD acquisition manager and presents a good picture of the procurement process and the problems created by the software development process. (Even small software developments have these similar problems and risks, but because of their small size the problems are not as noticeable or severe and usually can be solved by *ad hoc* procedures. However as software developments grow larger these ad hoc procedures do *not* "scale up" and the software engineering and management methods discussed in these papers and in this tutorial must be applied.)

The last paper by Barry Boehm gives the current state of the art in software engineering and project management. The paper provides a comprehensive overview of current issues in software engineering and project management and a thorough analysis on ways to "Improve Software Production." The paper discusses software cost methods and the controversy around whether or not *lines of code* is an appropriate measure of software production. Boehm's "software productivity improvement opportunity tree" is a simple and eloquent portrayal of the various ways software productivity can be improved. Boehm also provides a bibliography of "further reading" for those readers interested in more information on the subject.

Software Engineering: Problems and Perspectives

**C. V. Ramamoorthy, Atul Prakash,
Wei-Tek Tsai, and Yutaka Usuda**
University of California

As software applications become more complex, software engineering will evolve. Specification languages, rapid prototyping, complexity metrics, and maintenance techniques will be its most significant products.

Computer users first became aware of a software crisis 15 years ago. Software projects were being delivered far behind schedule, quality was poor, and maintenance was expensive. And as more complex software applications were found, programmers fell further behind the demand and their results were of poorer quality. The high demand and comparatively low productivity drove software costs up. In the US in 1980, software cost approximately $40 billion, or two percent of the gross national product.[1] Dolotta estimates that by the year 1985, the cost of software will be approximately 8.5 percent of the GNP,[2] while Steel points to 13 percent by 1990.[3] And in recognition of the importance of software engineering, the Department of Defense began a software initiative and has plans for establishing a software engineering institute.

Software engineering is a relatively new discipline. It seeks to devise techniques for software development.

Since the first software crisis, much progress has been made in this field. In this article, we discuss some important aspects of software engineering, noting past accomplishments and speculating on trends and future needs in this important area.

The software life cycle

Software systems go through two principal phases during their life cycle—the development phase and the operations and maintenance phase. Development begins when the need for the product is identified; it ends when the implemented product is tested and delivered for operation. Operation and maintenance include all activities during the operation of the software, such as fixing bugs discovered during operation, making performance enhancements, adapting the system to its environment, adding minor features, etc. During this phase, the system may also evolve as major

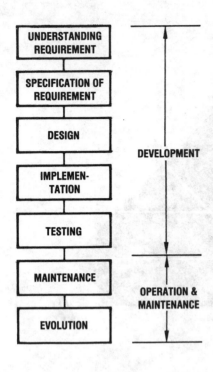

Figure 1. Software life-cycle model.

functions are added. To illustrate the software life cycle, the "waterfall model" or "conventional life cycle model" has proven convenient.[1] It is a good starting point in understanding the terminology used in software engineering.

Conventional life cycle model. The software life cycle is divided into the stages shown in Figure 1. It models the software development process from the top down. The first stage in the process is understanding the problem in question and its requirements. Requirements may have been given by the end user, or, if the software system is "embedded" within a larger system, they may derive from the system requirements. Requirements, therefore, include the context in which the problem arose, functionality expected from the system, and system constraints. At this point, the managers and software specialists decide whether it seems feasible to build the system.

During the specification stage, software specialists try to understand the requirements and define the specifications to meet those requirements. These specifications describe the external behavior of the system—*what* the system is supposed to do but not necessarily *how*. They must be carefully checked for suitability, omissions, inconsistencies, and ambiguities. Then system design begins.

Design describes *how* the system is to be implemented so that it meets the specifications. Since the whole system may be very complex, the main design objective is decomposition. The system is divided into modules and their interactions. The modules may then be further decomposed into submodules and procedures until each module can be implemented easily.

During the implementation or coding stage, each module is coded in a "suitable" language. A high-level, "structured" language might be used to improve the readability and manageability of the software.

The purpose of the testing stage is to find and correct any bugs in the program before the release. Each module might be tested separately, then in an integrated system to make sure modules are interacting properly. Currently, most of the testing and debugging is done after the system has been implemented. A large percentage of errors discovered during testing originates at requirement and design phases (Figure 2). Requirement and design errors are much more expensive to correct—typically, about 100 times more expensive than implementation errors.[1] Clearly, more effort needs to be spent in requirement definition and design, which must be considered as separate stages in software development. People must become more aware of the importance of earlier phases in the software life cycle.

Programmers need not pass through all stages of this or any other model. For example, if a small program is to be written and its purpose is well understood, it might be easier to start immediately with low-level design and coding.

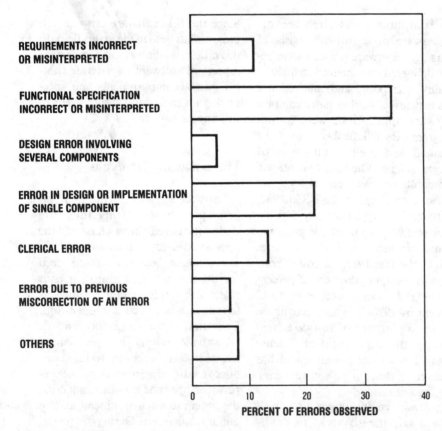

Figure 2. Sources of errors.

COMPUTER

Once in operation, the system must be maintained, which includes fixing bugs discovered during operation, adapting the system to a particular environment, and tuning it to improve performance. And if some "major" changes or improvements are made to increase functionality or performance, the system may undergo an evolution. The boundary between maintenance and evolution is fuzzy because what constitutes a major change is a subjective opinion.

Maintenance absorbs a large fraction of the cost incurred during the software life cycle (Figure 3). A major portion of maintenance activity comes from misunderstanding the user's requirements or from faulty debugging during operation, which thereby introduces errors that did not exist before. Some of these maintenance problems could be reduced if more attention were paid to development. If programmers understood users' requirements better, if they documented specifications, design, and code properly, and if they tested the system better before release, maintenance would not be so difficult and costly. To reduce maintenance costs, we advocate dividing the software life cycle into two fundamental phases—development and operations/maintenance. Software engineers must think of these phases as distinct so that both receive sufficient attention during the software life cycle.

Drawbacks of the conventional model. The conventional model requires that a large amount of time be spent developing specifications. It delays the writing code, and programmers may be impatient until they learn to accept it. In addition, the conventional life cycle model permits little feedback from the end user until the coding stage, very late in the life cycle. Then, if the system does not meet user's expectations, reexamination of the specifications, the design, and the code becomes very expensive. Therefore, some industries, like aerospace, have found it useful to receive feedback during milestone reviews.

The conventional model fails to recognize the possibility that it may often be easier to change an existing system than to redevelop the specifications and design a new system. Reusability, an important technique for developing large software, needs to be incorporated at all phases of a formal life-cycle model.

Alternative models. Alternatives have been suggested for overcoming drawbacks of the conventional model.

Rapid prototyping. In software engineering, as in other engineering disciplines, prototyping means building or designing with a new technology or for a new application while the feasibility of the design remains in question. Therefore, prototyping is basically a feasibility study that serves to demonstrate system aspects critical to the user.

It is important to note the difference between the prototype and the final system. The prototype does not usually meet all the requirements of the user. It implements only the most important aspects of the system, but it provides feedback from the user to the designer before the final system is designed; see Figure 4. By contrast, the conventional life-cycle model provides system feedback only after the system has been implemented. It is to be expected, therefore, that systems designed through prototyping have better user interfaces and respect implementation limits better than those developed through the conventional approach.

Very high level language approach. This approach emphasizes the use of languages that are very expressive and simple to use for writing program functions. Subsequently, this very high level language program can be automatically transformed to code just as a compiler transforms a source program to its object form. Its purpose is to accept certain parameters and generate an application program.

This method can usually be adapted for applications such as accounting, payroll, and banking, where software functionality is well understood. Parameters could describe the display format desired, the method of calculating interest (for banking), and any other environment-dependent factors.

By using very high level languages, programmers can generate software with few errors. They enjoy the advantages of simplicity and ease of expression, but they will find high-level languages difficult to use if they don't understand the application well. Then they must use some other approach.

Reusability approach. Hardware designers generally look first at the chips available in the market, then build the system from them. This bottom-up approach of designing systems from the basic modules and connecting them to form bigger modules eliminates the need to design modules from scratch. Reusability in software engineering involves a similar bottom-up approach, since programmers attempt to reuse as much existing software as possible.

Reusability reduces software development costs, speeds up the development process, and reduces testing needs. Of course, a new application for which little reusable software exists permits little reusability. Then development must follow a conventional approach. Nevertheless, it is to be expected that rising costs of software development will make software reusability increasingly important for many applications.

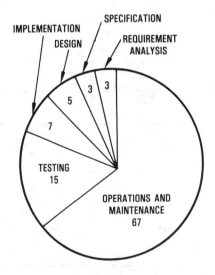

Figure 3. Distribution by cost percentage in software life cycle. Adapted with permission of Prentice-Hall, Englewood Cliffs, N.J. Source: M. Zelkowitz et al., *Principles of Software Engineering and Design*, © 1979, p. 9.

Requirements and specification

Requirements refer to the needs of the users. They include *why* the system is being designed, *what* the system is intended to accomplish, and *what* design constraints are to be observed. From an understanding of the requirements, a system analyst would have to develop some system specifications that satisfy them.

Importance of specification. Most errors found during testing and operation are traceable to poor understanding or misinterpretation of the requirements. They are the most expensive to correct once the system has been implemented. Defining and validating specifications should eliminate many errors before software reaches the implementation stage.

Natural languages are often used to describe system requirements. Although they aid users in understanding the system, they have inherent ambiguities that can lead to misinter-

pretations. Also, since it is difficult to analyze natural-language sentences, it is difficult to check the requirements for completeness and consistency. Consequently, a formal specification language is preferable since it can be tested for ambiguity, internal consistency, and completeness.

In the past few years, many formal requirement specification systems, such as Software Requirements Engineering Methodology, PSL/PSA (Problem Statement Language/Analyzer), and SADT (Structured Analysis and Design Technique), have been developed.

Functional and nonfunctional requirements. Functional requirements describe input-output behavior of the software, while nonfunctional requirements describe system simplicity, extendability maintainability, performance, reliability, user interface, etc. In successful systems, nonfunctional requirements are often as important as functional ones, and software systems incorporating many novel features

have failed to become popular just because such nonfunctional properties as the user interface were ignored.

We can test for functional requirements only by using a formal language. Most nonfunctional requirements, by their very nature, are difficult to test, so they are evaluated subjectively.

Necessary properties for a specification language. The process of generating specifications from the requirements is shown in Figure 5. A software scientist tries to understand the requirements and develop system specifications that satisfy those requirements. Some validation is then required to check whether the specifications reflect the actual requirements and whether they are complete, consistent, and unambiguous. Therefore, the specification language should have the following properties:

(1) Simplify the process of developing system specifications from informal user-requirements. The specification language should assume

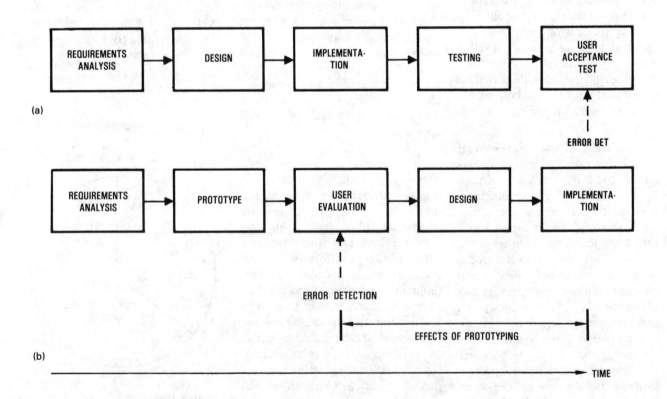

Figure 4. Comparison of life cycle models: conventional (a), and prototyping (b).

an appropriate model for software structure that simplifies the development of specifications from informal requirements.

(2) Permit the specifications to be analyzed for internal consistency, precision, completeness, etc.

(3) Facilitate validation that specifications really meet the user's requirements.

Formal specifications permit automatic analysis for internal consistency and completeness (property 2). But even with a formal specification language, it would be impossible to automate properties 1 and 3 because requirements are usually informal and not subject to automated analysis at the current state of the art.

Choice of model for specification language. It is not possible to generate specifications from informal requirements under program control, so the specification language must facilitate this tedious task. Every specification language attempts to choose a model that reflects the program behavior. Most current languages assume either a control-flow model or a data-flow model. More research (and data) is needed to determine which of these models most easily transforms the abstract ideas to a formal representation. Most probably, the appropriateness of the model is application-dependent. For example, a logic-intensive language might be appropriate for an application with highly coordinated parallel operations, such as robotics, but may not be so suitable for control-dominated applications.

Need for multiple representations. Since the main purpose of a specification language is to aid understanding of the requirements, it is useful if specifications can be read and manipulated by a variety of representations. For example, both textual and graphical representations may be provided in a specification language. It is important for graphic interfaces to be incorporated in specification languages, since they simplify considerably the task of developing specifications.

They can also, aid in explaining the specifications to the end-user, and software designers can check that the specifications reflect requirements and specifications. Some requirement specification systems such as SREM and SADT support graphics and textual representation facilities.

More than one specification language may be needed to represent the requirements adequately. For example, a language based on a data-flow model might not properly reflect the control requirements of the system, and a formal language may not be able to express nonfunctional requirements properly. Then a mixture of formal and natural specification languages is often used, with functional specifications expressed in the former and nonfunctional specifications in the latter.

Other specification language features. A specification language should support other features besides those mentioned above if it is to make a significant impact on software development methodology.

Traceability. The specification language should permit programmers to trace natural-language requirements given by the user *to* the particular set of specifications that satisfy those requirements, as well as permit them to trace natural-language requirements *from* the specifications. Traceability is important between all phases of the life cycle. For example, it should be possible to trace back from a section of the code to a portion of the design and from there back to the specifications. Traceability gives some degree

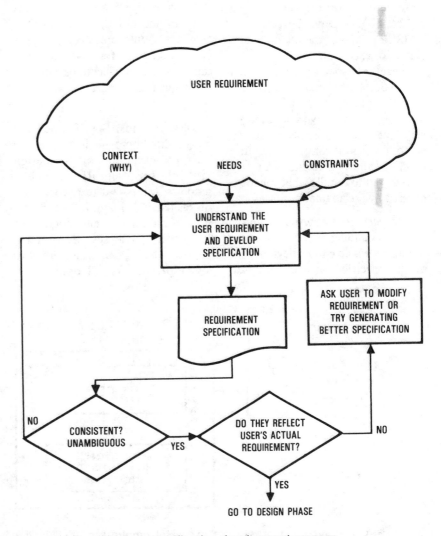

Figure 5. Requirement specification development process.

of assurance that specifications were written with user's requirements in mind, that the design indeed takes care of all the specifications, and that the code was written according to the specified design.

Executability. To specify what the system is supposed to do, a clear, simple procedure might be used to transform inputs to outputs.[4] This procedure forms the basis of executable specifications.[5] If the specifications are executable, programmers can execute them for the user, who verifies that they satisfy his needs. This idea of executable specifications has already been successfully applied to other areas of computer science, e.g., language description by means of grammars in compilers, query languages and schema languages for databases, and logic programming in artificial intelligence. In software engineering, SREM, Higher Order Software, and PAISLEY support the notion of simulation or execution.

Executable specifications present several problems: it may be difficult to estimate system performance; execution may be very slow; and it may be very time-consuming to come up with executable specifications. Therefore, other specification methods may still be required to handle what cannot be covered by executable specifications.

Summary generation. To improve the understanding of specifications, it should be possible to retrieve a subset of the specifications and generate summaries or correlate related information without going through a large formal specification document manually. Many of the existing specification languages, such as PSL/PSA, use a database to store specifications and have facilities for summary report generation, query handling, etc. Knowledge-based systems developed by artificial intelligence may soon permit storage of specifications in a "knowledge base." Then an expert system acting as a "requirement assistant" for its user could provide quick access to the relevant information (Figure 6).

Decomposability. Since the system may be very complex, system specifications must be decomposed into module specifications so that design can be carried out easily.

Concurrency. For efficient design and implementation, the specification language should preserve concurrency. It should not force activities that can be done in parallel to be expressed in a sequential manner.

Future trends. Specification languages should provide increasing support for execution or simulation, multiple representations such as graphics, tables and text, correlation of related information, and generation of summaries and documents. We expect some specification languages to be logic-intensive, like Prolog, especially for AI applications.

Highly descriptive, very high level, application-oriented languages are also likely to be useful. It is obvious from the recent development of many different kinds of specification languages that still more research and experience is required to determine appropriate models and the basic primitives that a specification language must support.

Software design

The design phase specifies how the system is to be implemented. It includes decomposition of the requirement specification into certain basic elements and partitioning the set of decomposed elements into modules (see Figure 7). Hereafter, the requirements and the specifications are used interchangeably.

First, we need to decompose the requirement specification by using divide-and-conquer and hierarchical structuring techniques. Decomposition is based on some criteria—such as functionality, data flow, or data structures—used in the program. This step ends when the decomposed elements reach the level of procedure elements.

Next, the procedure elements are partitioned into modules based on well-defined criteria. Since we need to consider the nonfunctional requirements (such as maintainability, portability, reliability, performance, and memory), the criteria for partitioning include maximizing reusability, maintainability, portability, and throughput, and minimizing complexity. Some of these criteria may conflict (e.g., performance and maintainability). Then trade-offs must be analyzed.

Finally, we must design the data structures and the algorithms within each module so that the system can be implemented easily. These data structures and algorithms should be transcribed into textual and graphical forms so that they can be easily understood. If there are several algorithms with the same functionality, we choose the one that is best based on nonfunctional requirements, executes most rapidly, and uses the least memory.

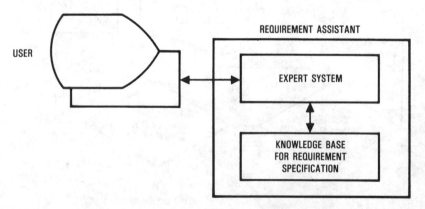

Figure 6. Use of "requirement assistant" to develop requirement specification.

Current design methodologies. *Functional decomposition* involves step-by-step division of functions into subfunctions. It requires that problem modeling and program construction be addressed simultaneously. It is most useful in applications with well understood, stable requirements, where it usually yields a good hierarchical design. However, since it does not give comprehensive criteria to decompose the given function, there could be innumerable decompositions to the same problem. For example, we can decompose functions with respect to time, shared data, data flow, and control flow.

The data-flow design decomposes the program into input modules, transformation modules, and output modules. It is best suited for design problems where a well-defined data flow can be derived from the problem specifications. Coupling and cohesiveness are the design evaluation criteria.[6,7] Coupling is the measure of the strength of association established by a connection from one module to another. Cohesiveness is the measure of strength among procedure elements in the same module. Good design is considered to have a low degree of coupling and a high degree of cohesiveness. Data-flow design decomposes the given function according to data flow, and the resulting modules usually will have very high cohesiveness. Moreover, if the concurrent asynchronous processes are to pass messages, the design is useful in distributed and parallel systems as well. However it may be difficult to identify transformations on data. Furthermore, partitioning a program into input and output branches can be artificial in many designs.

The *data-structure design* method, or Jackson methodology,[8] is primarily useful for business and other systems with well-understood data structures. It produces a program structure by designing input/output data structures. It relies on a decomposition based on the hierarchical nature of these data structures. They are partitioned into program components corresponding to the data-structure components. Since data structures for a problem specification are usually well defined and the problem mirrors the data structures, most of the people using this method will come up with remarkably similar program structures. Still, this method is too difficult to apply for highly concurrent programs with a lot of interprocess communication.

Future trends. Methodologies look simple and easy on paper, but they are sometimes difficult to apply in real design activities. Most are oriented to business applications, where features include simple and well-known transformations and emphasize input-output data structures. However, these methodologies do not address control-dominant or real-time applications. None consider performance, fault-tolerance, and security, which are becoming more important. Applications are also becoming more complex, critical, microprocessor-based, distributed, and message-oriented. Current methodologies fail to resolve all design problems so new methodologies are needed.

It would be very desirable, for instance, to have tools with which to generate an implementation automatically from a formal requirement. This would require development of design-specification languages and support

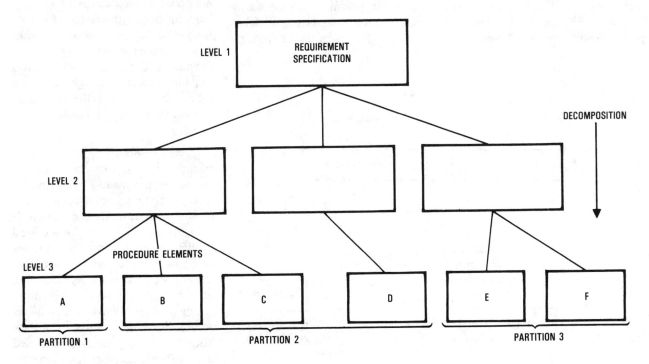

Figure 7. Decomposition and partitioning.

October 1984

environments as well as program generators. We are already beginning to see tools such as SSL, PDS, HOS, and designer/verifier assistant, which automate some parts of the design process.

Software Testing

Software testing is the process of systematic execution of a program under controlled circumstances to verify its quality. The basic steps involved are requirement analysis, program analysis, test-data selection, formulation of testing strategy, actual execution of the program, and checking that results are as expected. Testing also shows the presence of errors, but *not* their absence. Errors that are present may have been made during the requirement-understanding phase, specification phase, design phase, implementation phase, or post-test error correction.

One way of ensuring that a program is error-free is by formally proving that the program is correct. The proof is applied mainly to critical parts of the software such as the security kernel of an operating system where a single bug could compromise a whole system. It elicited a lot of interest in the 70's, when researchers observed that it was extremely difficult to check large programs. The manually generated proofs tend to be much larger and more complex than the program itself, so one wonders whether the proof was error-free. When a programs fails, it is difficult to determine whether the failure is due to an error in the program or because of its complexity. Finally, program proving may tell you whether the program contains an error but rarely tells you its cause.

Successful program proving usually requires some input-output assertions describing the desired function of the program. Generating these assertions is extremely difficult, especially for programs with high concurrency and user-interaction. Moreover, it is difficult to verify that the assertions adequately describe the functionality of the system.

Even if a program is proven correct, testing should be continued to ensure that the software meets the user's requirements and the proof process itself is correct. Exhaustive testing is not possible because there are potentially an infinite number of inputs to be tested—including both valid and invalid inputs. Test cases have to be designed to accommodate the user's need for assurance and the producer's need to economize on time and costs.

Test case design. The two basic approaches in designing test cases are the black-box and white-box approaches. Black-box test cases derive from the external specifications and requirements of the system. Methods for black-box testing include random testing, testing at boundary values, and error guessing where a list of error situations is created. It verifies the end results at the system level but does not check on how the system is implemented. Nor does it assure that all the statements in the program are executed. Nonetheless, it is good for acceptance testing because test cases are derived from the environment in which the system operates.

In the white-box approach, the test cases at the module level are derived from the internal structure of the program. It may execute all the statements or branches in the program to check on how the system is implemented. Some methods of white-box testing are statement coverage, branch coverage, and path coverage, all of which improve test coverage.

Test coverage. Since testing for all the valid as well as invalid inputs is not feasible, test cases must be selected so that a large portion of the program is verified. Test cases might be selected so that all statements are executed at least once. However, this method does not necessarily test all the branches, so bugs might go undetected. Even efforts to test all the branches are inadequate because they do not test many of the paths in the program. Path testing provides a more thorough check, but the number of paths in the loops make exhaustive testing impossible.

Quality assurance by testing. Since extensive testing does not guarantee error-free programs, when should software testing stop? Normally, the answer depends on the application. If the software is intended for a critical application, such as a nuclear reactor or a space shuttle, more testing is required. More accurate determination of software quality requires more testing, and quality assurance requires accurate estimates of software quality. Therefore, testing must be continued until software accuracy has been confirmed.

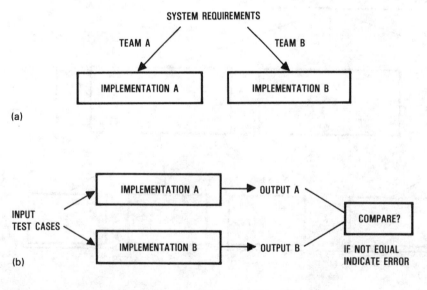

(a)

(b)

Figure 8. Dual development (a) and dual testing (b).

Testing at specification and design level. Currently, most testing follows coding. Because most errors occur during specification and design, it seems logical to test after these phases so that errors can be corrected easily. Formalization of requirement and design specifications and use of executable specifications might help in this process.

Automatic tools for testing. Although many techniques have been developed, testing is still largely labor intensive, hence expensive. The programmer still has to enter the test data, verify the results, and locate the bugs manually even though there may be guidelines and tools for each step. However, the situation is beginning to change. Many tools developed during the past few years automate test-data generation, locate potential errors, verify results, etc. These tools include static analysis, dynamic analysis, symbolic execution, and intermodule interface analysis.

Static analysis reports structural flaws such as unreachable code and potential errors like unused variables. Dynamic analysis provides facilities for executing the program, studying its behavior, and verifying any assertions during execution.

Symbolic execution can be used to generate test data and check a particular path by transmitting symbolic instead of real data objects. This symbolic execution creates system conditions that can then be analyzed in terms of the desired inputs. Intermodule interface analysis checks, as the name indicates, interfaces between modules. Other automatic tools that help in testing include the Unix "lint" program for discovering potential bugs in C programs, the Program Evaluation and Tester for assertion checking, the Fortran Automatic Code Evaluation System developed at Berkeley for NASA, and DAVE, developed at the University of Colorado to analyze Fortran programs using symbolic execution.

Untestable requirements. Real-time, critical systems, defense systems, etc., cannot be tested because actual inputs are not available. For example, if a defense system is supposed to work during a nuclear attack, few programmers would choose to test it under actual conditions. Other attributes that escape testing are constraints and nonfunctional requirements such as flexibility, evolvability, and aspects of concurrent and distributed systems.

The process called dual development and testing, however, permits programmers to overcome nontestability. It requires two implementations, each using independent designs for the same requirements (Figure 8a). Then these independent implementations are tested for the same inputs. Inconsistent results indicate an error in one or both implementations (see Figure 8b).

Dual development and testing was used in the EPRI project, which developed pilot software for nuclear power plant safety.[9] Here, timing dependencies prevented determining the correct outputs for a set of inputs. The approach eliminated the need for determining the correct outputs a priori, because it would be very unlikely that two independent implementations would have identical errors. Of course, dual development was expensive, but testing was considerably simplified and cheaper.

In some critical applications, nonfunctional requirements such as reliability and response time may be crucial. Testing can provide estimates of nonfunctional attributes such as reliability, response time, and performance. For instance, there are many models to estimate reliability of the software (degree of correctness) from the history of error detection, etc.

Software maintenance

Software maintenance usually constitutes more than 60 percent of the life-cycle cost (Figure 2). Maintenance is high because programmers often overlook it during software development. Only after the software is delivered does the maintenance cost become apparent. Since it is expensive, it is clear that better maintenance tools and guidelines are needed.

Swanson divided maintenance into three categories: perfective, adaptive, and corrective maintenance.[10] Perfective maintenance improves the software's function by responding to customer- and programmer-defined changes. It involves eliminating errors in the program. Adaptive maintenance adjusts software to environmental changes, such as a change of operating systems or system databases. Corrective maintenance refers to changes necessitated by actual errors (induced or residual bugs) in a system. Figure 9 shows the percentage distribution of maintenance in each category.

The primary sources of maintenance problems are (1) insufficient or incomplete documents, (2) inconsistency between the documents and code, (3) design difficult to understand, modify, and test, and (4) insufficient record of past maintenance. The problems come from technical or managerial mishandling, which includes inadequate management control over the software maintenance. For example, lack of documentation is often the result of administrative rather than technical incompetence.

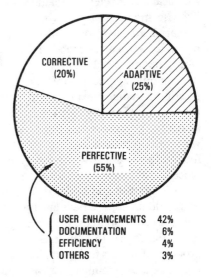

USER ENHANCEMENTS	42%
DOCUMENTATION	6%
EFFICIENCY	4%
OTHERS	3%

Figure 9. Allocation of system and programming resources to three maintenance categories.

The objectives of maintenance are to carry out the three maintenance activities, namely perfective, adaptive, and corrective maintenance, to maximize the life span of the software with minimum effort. The objectives sometimes conflict, so a trade-off has to be made.

Preventive maintenance. To reduce maintenance costs

(1) The system must be developed with maintenance in mind;
(2) The system must be maintained with future maintenance in mind; and
(3) The system must be continually upgraded to cope with future technology.

Many maintenance problems would be solved if software were developed according to precise methodologies. Formal requirement and design specifications, detailed and clear documentation, and extensive testing and validation produce economies in the maintenance phase. These preventive maintenance activities coincide with the development activities, and better development translates as reduced maintenance effort after the delivery.

Managerial approach. After the software becomes operational, there is after-the-fact maintenance, which stems from either management or technical incompetence. Solutions are likewise managerial or technical. If management were to mandate disciplined software maintenace, problems would be much reduced, particularly if such management tools as configuration management systems are used. A configuration management system is a database that stores software resources and project management information in a coherent way. Since it is a database, the information is easily queried and updated. Engineers could use it to retrieve and update the software resources, and management could use it to keep track of the progress of projects. Reports indicate that it reduces maintenance cost and effort by 50 percent.[11]

It is also important that managers determine whether to continue putting money and effort into maintenance or instead to replace the existing system. Based on the evolution of OS/360, Belady and Lehman developed guidelines to track the progress of maintenance and recommend system replacement.[12] The guidelines are based on software complexity: If it is rather complex, it may be wiser not to modify the existing code. It will be difficult to modify, and errors will creep into the program. Belady and Lehman proposed these "laws of program evolution dynamics" to characterize system maintenance:

(1) Law of continuing change. A system that is used undergoes continuing change until it is judged more cost-effective to freeze and recreate it.
(2) Law of increasing entropy. The entropy of a system (its unstructuredness) increases with time, unless specific work is executed to maintain or reduce it.
(3) Law of statistically smooth growth. Growth trend measures of global system attributes may appear to be stochastic locally in time and space, but, statistically, they are cyclically self-regulating, with well-defined, long-range trends.

These laws do not necessarily hold in all cases. In fact, the objective of maintenance is to violate these laws. Future change should be planned well ahead of time. The system should receive minimum change requests, and entropy should be well controlled.

Technical approach. On the technical side, we can treat the maintenance process as the development process with all the necessary development tools or as a unique process with special tools. As a development process, there is little difference between software development and maintenance. Maintenance is redevelopment or evolution of existing code. Proper documentation and design are then the keys for successful maintenance.

In the second method, we need four special techniques and tools to handle maintenance:

(1) techniques for helping software engineers understand the code,
(2) techniques to assist software engineers in modifying the existing software,
(3) test and revalidation techniques to ensure that the modification will not introduce new errors, and
(4) version control tools.

In the first category are program slicing and automatic tools to determine the control flow and data flow in the programs. Program slicing retrieves and displays the relevant portions of the program requested by the user. Other tools like flow-chart and cross-reference generators can also be helpful. All these tools can be considered useful for reverse engineering, since they produce information from the source code rather than from the normal software development process where the specifications are usually developed before the source code. The configuration management system should store this information because it is useful for future maintenance.

Currently, no systematic methodology is available to help software engineers modify existing code. There are tools like syntax-directed editors, which are useful in minimizing the minor errors. A rule-of-thumb is to keep the interface intact as much as possible, thus restricting the areas that require attention. In the third category, ripple-effect analysis aids in the modification of software. After the changes in a module, the ripple-effect analysis can trace and list all modules affected by the current changes.[29,30,32] In the last category, version-control systems are useful in keeping the history of maintenance, so that each version can be retrieved and stored independently.[31]

Software quality assurance

Software quality assurance aims to guarantee that the software products perform at an acceptable level before being released. Because of our society's increased dependency on computers, software engineers have become responsible for the quality of software, which we define as the totality of features and characteristics of a product or service that bears on its ability to satisfy given needs. These features include reliability, reusability, and efficiency. Quality control involves various metrics useful for quality assurance as well as for project control.

Metrics. Metrics are the measures of properties of systems. Software metrics are used to measure the quality of software systems and to control the productivity of software projects. First, we have to decide which properties to measure for a given piece of software. For example, we might want to determine complexity to estimate the effort required in testing and maintenance. Or for various metrics, we might also like to know their potential use, in what stage of software development they are going to be used, how they are going to be used, and in which kinds of projects and software environments they can be used. We then determine how to get the desired metrics from a formal model of the software. McCabe used the control flow graph of the progam as his model for evaluating the complexity, namely its cyclomatic number.[13] Once the model is decided, metrics could then be devised.

Metrics usually reflect human judgments on the properties. McCabe's cyclomatic number indicates the number of independent, or static, loops in the program. As more loops in the program make a program more difficult to test and trace, we expect a higher cyclomatic number.

Once the metrics have been designed, they must be validated against real software projects to determine their effectiveness. Unfortunately, experimental validation is usually difficult. Many factors are involved, including software development environments, the quality and number of personnel, the availability and quality of various tools, programming language of the software, and software methodologies used. Most current work on the validation of metrics for Halstead's software science and McCabe's metrics is complete, but some other metrics require further validation.[14,15]

Classes of metrics. We classify metrics into four categories: development productivity, project management, quality, and software development. Productivity metrics control cost and manpower needed to develop software. Project management metrics track the progress of a project. Quality metrics verify correctness, complexity, coupling of modules, degree of dependency of modules and variables, reusability, modifiability, testability, understandability, reliability, performance, and maintainability. These qualities can be further decomposed; for example, software complexity can be broken down into control flow and data structure complexity. Control flow complexity can be decomposed into static contol flow and dynamic control flow complexity. McCabe's cyclomatic number, which indicates the number of independent loops in the control flow graph, is a static control-flow complexity. The number of interrupts allowed during the program execution is considered as dynamic control-flow complexity.

Table 1 organizes the metrics according to the life-cycle stage at which they are used—requirement analysis, design, coding, testing, or maintenance. These metrics are used to determine the quality of the resources produced at each stage. Requirement specifications, design specifications, source code, testing programs and test data, and histories are produced at requirement analysis, design, coding, testing, and maintenance stages, respectively. Requirement complexity metrics should indicate various characteristics of the target system, but since the requirement is registered in various specification languages, there are different kinds of models at requirement level. For example, DeMarco recommends the use of a data-flow, retained data-model, and state-transition graphs to specify the requirements.[16]

Since design metrics reflect complexities, they depend on the models or languages in which the designs are expressed. For example, we use different metrics for the designs in PSL/PSA or RSL/REVS, since they are based on different models. Finally, we need metrics to indicate the difficulty of maintaining a software system. They are useful not only in determining the quality of the resources produced during the software development process, but also in development.

Project management metrics, quality metrics, and productivity metrics have ensured the quality of Bell Lab-

Table 1. Usefulness of metrics.

STAGES	RESOURCES	USEFULNESS OF METRICS AT THE CURRENT STAGE
Requirement analysis	Requirement specification	Cost estimation Design Testing Maintenance
Design	Design specification	Coding guidance Comparison of different designs
Implementation	Source/Codes Comments Documentations	Testing Maintenance
Testing	Test data Test routines	Testing Maintenance
Maintenance	All above resources and history	Maintenance

oratories' Generic Three No. 5ESS. The 5ESS project software has almost 630,000 lines of C-language code. Four hundred software engineers worked a year and a half on the project.

Metrics-guided design. Besides indicating the characteristics of the software resources, metrics can be used to guide the design process itself. For example, if the requirement complexity metrics indicate that the target control system is very involved, the target system could be described in a language such as RSL/REVS, which ex-

plicitly expresses and analyzes the contol flow. If the data structures and their manipulations are complex, then PSL/PSA may be more suitable, since its underlining model is the data flow graph. If there are alternative designs for the same requirement, the design metrics could give the data on which a selection is based. If sufficient knowledge is gathered, it is possible to have design automation for a limited range of complex requirement specifications. Design metrics may even suggest testing strategies to software engineers. We are currently building an environment system, guided by the com-

plexity metrics, which is suitable for software development and evolution.

Prediction and cost estimation models. Most current methods are based on equations derived from empirical data. Currently, estimations of time and costs are not very accurate at the earlier stages of software development, but it is expected that cost estimation models based on requirement and design metrics will be more reliable. Once accurate estimates of software characteristics are made, it will be possible to allocate more re-

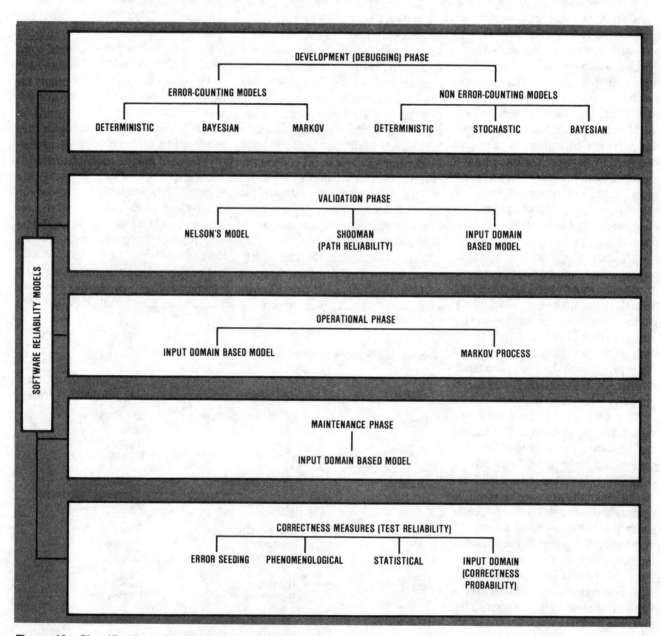

Figure 10. Classification of software reliability models.

sources (such as personnel and time) to more demanding tasks.

Software reliability. Reliable software will be produced by preventive approaches and fault-tolerant design. Preventive approaches will increase reliability before software becomes operational. Fault-tolerant design permits reliability despite errors that survive the test stage.

Since we cannot guarantee software to be error-free even after testing, it is very important to assess its reliability. Major goals of reliability assessment are estimation of the number of errors in the software and location of these errors. For location of the errors, we have already discussed methods such as path testing and symbolic testing. Two other schemes for error estimation merit attention: the error seeding and mutation model, and the reliability model.

Error seeding and mutation. Error seeding is a quantitative method for estimating reliability based on Mills' assumption[17] that the reliability of a program is related to the number of errors removed from it. Programmers other than the testers insert a known number and type of artificial errors in the program. Once testing has been completed, the number of remaining real errors can be estimated with the formula

$$\frac{\text{remaining number of real errors}}{\text{remaining no. of seeded errors}}$$

$$= \frac{\text{no. of real errors found}}{\text{no. of seeded errors found}}$$

Now the estimated number of remaining errors serves as an index to program reliability.

Mutation is similar. The program is changed by some simple mutations, usually syntactic, which change the meaning of the program. Testers search out errors and, by the formula above, estimate how effective the testing is in removing errors.

Both error seeding and mutation add artificial errors to the real ones. Because of the extra detection and correction effort, these schemes are not always practical. Other theoretical models can be used to estimate the reliability.

Reliability models. Software reliability is defined as the probability that deviation from the required output by more than a specified tolerance in a specified environment does not occur during a specified exposure period. It is expressed as

$R(i) = $ Prob (no failure over i runs) or
$R(t) = $ Prob (no failure over interval$[o, t]$)

The mean time between failure measures reliability. Reliability models predict software reliability from the history of detected errors. Many software reliability models have been proposed, specifically those for development (debugging), validation, operational, and maintenance phases.

In the development phase, errors are detected and corrected. It is often assumed that the correction of errors does not introduce any new errors, so program reliability increases with testing and analysis. Models for this phase are called reliability-growth models. They can be further divided into error-counting models and non-error-counting ones. Error-counting models estimate both the number of errors remaining in the program and its reliability, while non-error counting models estimate only the reliability of the software from the application point of view.

In the validation phase, models are applicable to highly reliable software systems like the safety control system of a nuclear power plant. However, errors are found but not corrected.

In the maintenance phase, errors are corrected, minor enhancements are made, and new features are added. The reliability of the system will be perturbed. It may be possible to estimate the change in reliability in test cases that ensure that the original features have not been altered. The new reliability can be estimated from validation phase models, of which the input domain based model alone is applicable in this phase. The classifica-tion of the reliability models is summarized in Figure 10.

Reliability growth model. Reliability growth models are based on the following assumptions:

(1) Input is selected randomly from the input domain;
(2) Consecutive inputs have the same disjoint-failure probabilities;
(3) All errors have the same disjoint-failure rates; and
(4) No new errors are introduced during error correction.

Reliability $R(t)$ is then expressed as an exponential function of time and the number of errors.

This model is simple and clear, but its applicability is limited, since many of the assumptions are not valid: Successive inputs are usually correlated in process control systems; failure rates are not independent, since earlier errors usually have higher failure rates and are easier to detect; error detection depends on the testing strategy; and faulty correction introduces new errors. Among many reliability growth models proposed, only Musa's has been found to be accurate for estimating the reliability of software in various applications.[18] In this model, the time, t, is based on the actual time required to execute the program. Other promising models have not yet been completely validated; among them are Goel and Okumoto's model[19] and the input domain model.[20]

Testing strategies. Even though reliability models are quite useful for estimating errors remaining in a program and software MTBF, they cannot guide the engineers to testing strategies. Since each strategy detects only errors belonging to a certain range, some bugs could still go undetected if testing strategies were limited.

Error size. The size of a software bug is defined as the degree of contamination in the input domain, and the difficulty of finding a bug is inversely proportional to its error size. If there is a lot of input data that will produce incorrect output, it is very easy to find the bug. If the error is small, it is harder to find it, and more input tests are needed.

Requirement errors or design bugs are usually very large. It is much more efficient to detect the requirement and design errors first, since the reliability is very low at that time. After correcting them, one should proceed to the coding errors.

Coding bugs may be very small and can be found only after extensive testing. For example, they may be in paths seldom used during program execution. They may, however, be the only remaining bugs in a very reliable program.

Magnifying the error size reduces the effort required to detect them. Since requirement and design errors are already large, it is more important to enlarge coding bugs. Certain applicative programming languages, such as SETL, and functional programming languages developed for other objectives can usually increase error size.[21]

Human intervention. Since quality assurance is very important, many companies—particularly the Japanese—are encouraging quality-control circles.[27,28] They provide the framework for structured walk-through and inspections aimed at finding errors in requirement specification, design, and implementation. They involve a team designer and a moderator who chairs the software error-detection effort. Team meetings are a part of activities in the requirement specification, design, and coding phases.

In the walk-through, one of the team members traces each line of the requirement specification, design, or code, and checks the results. During inspection, the designer or programmer reads the target documents while the participants try to detect errors using an error check list developed from past error history. These meetings are held after each life-style phase and are repeated until the document satisfied well-defined exit criteria. These criteria assure the quality of intermediate products of each phase to be above a certain level. These methods are effective in disclosing many simple errors, while testing tends to reveal the more complicated ones (Table 2). In addition, they may have an educational effect since designers and programmers can expect constructive criticism on their design and implementation.

Software reusability

Since software is so expensive, it would be very economical if some significant portion of the target system could be built from the existing software. At the end of each of the five development stages, many software resources are produced. It is expected that all software resources, not only the code, but also the other software resources, will be reusable. In fact, since source code is usually dependent on the programming language, programming style, other supporting library routines, and the system it is running on, it is easier to reuse requirement and design specifications

than to reuse code. And since the cost of coding is only 10 percent of the total development cost, reusing the existing code would not provide significant economies compared to reusing the requirement and design specifications, which constitute about 50 percent of the development costs.

Standardization and software library. Standardization of software resources is necessary to permit engineers to design the target system for reusability. It is also more important, however, to standardize the interface than the programming style or codes. Once the interface is fixed, we can ignore all the details inside each module, according to Parnas' principle of information hiding.[22]

In addition to standardization of software, methods for locating usable software resources need to be developed. It is necessary not only to have a source code library, but also requirement specification and testing libraries. These libraries should be stored in a database, such as a relational database, for easy access and update. The stored material should be of high quality, as determined by software metrics. Other desirable qualities are correctness, easy understandability, testability, simplicity, and applicability. And since reusing existing software resources is more an art than an engineering discipline, methodologies for guiding the reuse of existing resources are also needed.

Reusable program generators. If the application domain is small, it is possible to develop program generators that are highly parameterized to include several possible variations in the application. The program generator could incorporate knowledge necessary to generate application programs. The knowledge would be reused every time a new program was generated. A typical program generator is the YACC,[23] a compiler compiler that generates parsing tables and routines in the C language. We also foresee other program generators for such areas as accounting, payroll, and statistics, where the application domain is limited.

Table 2. Comparison of testing and inspection.

TECHNIQUE	INSPECTIONS	UNIT TEST
Strengths	• Simple programming blunders, logic errors • Developer blind spots • Interface errors • Missing portions • Specification errors	• Simple programming blunders, logic errors • Numerical approximations • Program dynamics errors
Weaknesses	• Numerical approximations • Program dynamics errors	• Developer blind spots • Interface errors • Missing portions • Specification errors

Rapid prototyping

Prototyping provides feasibility studies that test the principles of the new software and obtain good user feedback to solve the problems of systems that are not working according to the end-user needs. Figure 4 illustrates advantages of prototyping over conventional program development models.

Previously, prototyping was seldom used for software development, since the cost of prototype systems was considered to be very expensive. Recently, however, there have been heated debates on the effectiveness of this method. Supporters claim that rapid prototypes provide more realistic information on the system than conventional requirement specification techniques, since users' experiences on the prototype system make it easier to detect the inconsistency, ambiguity, and incompleteness of the requirement.

There are several prototyping approaches. In general, subfunctions and/or user interfaces are prototyped in an existing language. To minimize the size and cost of the systems, not all the aspects of the systems are prototyped.

Recently, various tools have become available for rapid prototyping. McCracken has reported on application generators using a database management system and report-generator capability used for the rapid prototyping/evolutionary design in application generators.[24]

Rapid prototyping can be enhanced as systematically as executable specifications. Rapid prototyping involves selection of functions to be prototyped based on software development projects, while executable specification creates a system model from a formal specification language and simulates it. In future, executable specifications and rapid prototyping tools, together with reusable program libraries, can be expected to provide an automatic software development/evolution support environment.

Table 3. New directions on software engineering.

SUBJECT	BASIC ACTIVITIES	IMPORTANCE	NEW DIRECTIONS
Requirement specification	Converting informal requirements to specifications, analyzing specifications, validating specifications against user needs	Eliminate ambiguities, requirement errors at an early stage in the life cycle	Executable specifications Multiple representation Report generation
Design	Decompose requirement specifications into modules and specify algorithms	Show how the system works Impacts on testing, maintenance, reusability, etc.	Knowledge-based automatic design
Testing	Locating existing bugs in a program	Quality assurance	Automatic test input generators, automatic verifiers Testing at requirement and design level
Maintenance	Modify program and data	Correct errors Enhance system	Configuration management system System upgrading
Quality assurance and reliability	Error data gathering Estimate reliability feedback to project	Highly reliable system	Selection of alternative test strategies
Metrics	Measure the quality to control software project	Quality control Project management	Metrics for all software resources Metrics-guided design methodology
Reusability	Reuse existing software resources	Cost reduction Quality improvement	Software library Design methodology Program generator
Rapid prototyping	Prototype a system instead of specify	Capture user's requirement from working system	Enhance the method More systematic executable specification
Cost estimation	Estimate cost before starting a project	Project management	Cost estimation based on requirement complexity

Without a reasonably accurate cost-estimation capability, we do not have a firm basis for deciding whether a project is likely to exceed its budget and/or meet its schedule. Currently, cost estimation techniques exist and are being applied to real projects, such as the Putnam SLIM Model, the Walston and Felix Model, and Boehm's Constructive Cost Model. The SLIM model[25] uses a "technology constant" obtained from past project experience to estimate the number of delivered source instructions. Boehm[1] and Walston and Felix[26] provide empirical cost estimation functions such as effort estimation and schedule estimation. The parameters of these functions include the type of software (e.g., OS, large scale), environment factors (e.g., available machine, computation time, tools), quality of personnel in the project (e.g., years of experience), and project attributes (e.g., the number of programmers, methodologies, etc.).

Although software cost-estimation techniques help managers make decisions about projects, they do have some limitations:

(1) Inability to make accurate predictions for software development using new techniques.
(2) Inaccuracy of the estimates made during the early phases of the projects (e.g., requirements and design phase; see Figure 11).

These estimation techniques calculate project schedules and efforts based on values derived from past experiences. If a project aims to develop a system with familiar tools and methodologies, the derived estimates usually prove to be quite accurate (Figure 12). However, if the project aims to develop a system based on new technology (e.g., new automation tools such as program generators), these estimates are less accurate. Therefore, we need to develop a framework for new technology as well as new application areas.

Inaccuracy at early phases comes from faulty estimates of the nature of the products. Future research directions must include a measurement of the difficulty of application areas, an evaluation of new technology—especially automation—on software development cost, methods of improving the accuracy of product size estimation, and better metrics for cost estimation.

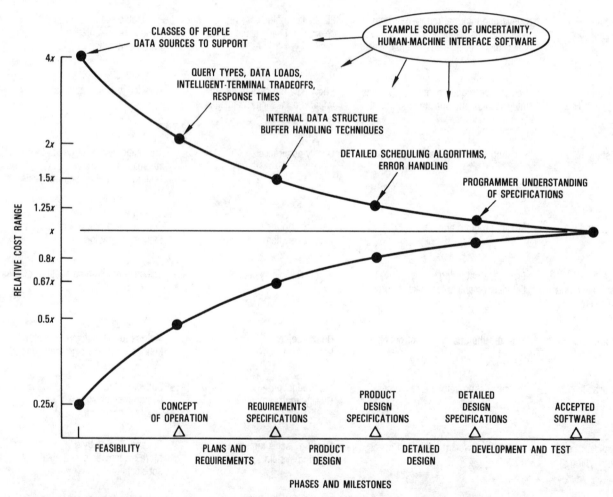

Figure 11. Inaccuracy of cost-estimate models in the early phases. Used with permission of Prentice-Hall, Englewood Cliffs, N.J. Source, B. Boehm, *Software Engineering Economics* © 1981, p. 502.

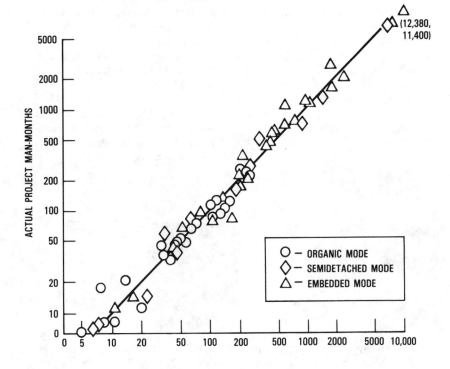

Figure 12. Effect of cost-estimation model. Used with permission of Prentice-Hall, Englewood Cliffs, N.J. Source: B. Boehm, *Software Engineering Economics* © 1981, p. 311.

There is little doubt that software engineering will continue to become more and more important in the future as applications become more complex (Table 3). The importance of research in the areas of specification languages, rapid prototyping, complexity metrics and testing has been widely acknowledged. We expect that the approaches we have summarized will solve most of the software problems, but it is clear that fault tolerance in software and distributed software design and test will likewise play a great role in future software engineering. □

Acknowledgments

We gratefully acknowledge Stephen Yau and T. Kikuno for reviewing and suggesting many improvements in an earlier draft of this article. We also thank our colleagues, K. Bannai and J. Srivastava, for numerous helpful discussions and comments as well as help in preparation of this article. This work was partially supported by the Ballistic Missile Advanced Technology Center under grant DASG-60-81C-0025.

References

1. B. W. Boehm, *Software Engineering Economics,* Prentice-Hall, Inc., Englewood Cliffs, N.J., 1981.

2. T. A. Dolotta et al., *Data Processing in 1980-85,* John Wiley & Sons, New York, 1976.

3. T. B. Steel, Jr., "A Note on Future Trends," *Information Processing in the United States: A Quantitative Summary,* edited by P. S. Nyborg, AFIPS, Montvale, NJ, 1977.

4. C. V. Ramamoorthy and H. H. So, "Software Requirements and Specifications: Status and Perspectives," ERL tech. report UCB/ERL M78/44, University of California, Berkeley, June 1978.

5. R. T. Yeh et al., "Software Requirements: New Directions and Perspectives," in *Handbook of Software Engineering,* edited by C. R. Vick and C. V. Ramamoorthy, Van Nostrand Reinhold, New York, 1984.

6. W. P. Stevens, G. J. Myers, and L. L. Constantine, "Structured Design," *IBM Systems Journal,* Vol. 13, No. 2, 1974, pp. 115-139.

7. G. J. Myers, *Composite/Structured Design,* Van Nostrand Reinhold, New York, 1978.

8. M. A. Jackson, *Principles of Program Design,* Academic Press, N.Y., 1975.

9. C. V. Ramamoorthy et al., "Application of a Methodology for the Development and Validation of Reliable Process Control Software," *IEEE Trans. Software Engineering,* Vol. SE-7, No. 6, Nov. 1981, pp. 537-555.

10. E. B. Swanson, "The Dimension of Maintenance," *Proc. Second Int'l Conf. Software Engineering,* IEEE-Computer Society, Los Alamitos, Calif., 1976.

11. K. Bannai et al., "A Total Approach to a Solution for the Maintenance Problems through Configuration Management-Maintenance Support Facility MSF," *Proc. Compsac,* 1983, IEEE-Computer Society, Los Alamitos, Calif., 1983.

12. L. Belady and M. M. Lehman, "A Model of Large Program Development," *IBM System Journal,* Vol. 15, No. 3, 1976, pp. 225-252.

13. T. J. McCabe, "A Complexity Measure," *IEEE Trans. Software Engineering,* Vol. 2, No. 6, Dec. 1976, pp. 308-320.

October 1984

14. M. H. Halstead, *Elements of Software Science*, Elsevier, New York, 1977.

15. B. Curtis, "Software Metrics: Guest Editor's Introduction," *IEEE Trans. Software Engineering*, Vol. SE-9, No. 6, Nov. 1983, pp. 637-638.

16. T. Demarco, *Controlling Software Projects*, Yourdon, New York, 1982.

17. H. D. Mills, "On Statistical Validation of Computer Programs," IBM Rep. FSC72-6015, Federal Systems Division, IBM, Gaithersburg, Md., 1972.

18. J. Musa, "Software Reliability," *Handbook of Software Engineering*, edited by C. Vick and C. V. Ramamoorthy, Van Nostrand Reinhold, New York, 1984, pp. 392-412.

19. A. L. Goel and K. Okumoto, "A Time-Dependent Error Detection Rate Model for Software Reliability and Other Performance Measures," *IEEE Trans. Reliability*, Vol. R-28, No. 3, Mar. 1979, pp. 206-211.

20. C. V. Ramamoorthy et al., "Application of a Methodology for the Development and Validation of Reliable Process-Control Software," *IEEE Trans. Software Engineering*, Vol. SE-7, No. 6, Nov. 1981, pp. 537-555.

21. C. V. Ramamoorthy and F. Bastani, "Practical Consideration for the Development of Process Control Software," Interkama 1980, Dusseldorf, West Germany, Oct. 1980.

22. D. L. Parnas, "On the Criteria to Be Used in Decomposing Systems into Modules," *Comm. ACM*, Vol. 15, No. 12, Dec. 1972, pp. 1053-1058.

23. S. C. Johnson, "YACC: Yet Another Compiler-Compiler," *Unix*, Bell Laboratories, Murray Hill, N. J., 1978.

24. D. D. McCracken, "Software in the 80s: Peril and Promises," *Computer World*, Sept. 17, 1980, pp. 5-10.

25. L. H. Putnam, "A General Empirical Solution to the Macro Software Sizing and Estimating Problem," *IEEE Trans. Software Engineering*, Vol. SE-4, No. 4, July 1978.

26. C. E. Walston and P. E. Felix, "A Method of Programming Measurement and Estimation," *IBM Systems Journal*, Vol. 16, No. 1, 1977, pp. 54-73.

27. D. Tajima and T. Matsubara, "Inside the Japanese Software Industry," *Computer*, Vol. 17, No. 3, March 1984, pp. 34-43.

28. Y. Mizuno, "Software Quality Improvement," *Computer*, Vol. 16, No. 3, March 1983, pp. 66-72.

29. S.S. Yau, J.S. Collofello, and T. McGregor, "Ripple Effect Analysis of Software Maintenance," *Proc. Compsac*, 1978, pp. 60-65.

30. S.S. Yau and J.S. Collofello, "Some Stability Measures for Software Maintenance," *IEEE Trans. for Software Engineering*, Vol. SE-6, No. 6, Nov. 1981, pp. 556-574.

31. S.S. Yau and J.P. Tsai, "GQL: A Graphic Query Language for Software Maintenance Environment," *Proc. Compsac*, 1983, pp. 218-228.

32. S.S. Yau, C.K. Chang, and R.A. Nicholl, "An Approach to Incremental Program Modification," *Proc. Compsac*, 1983, pp. 588-595.

C. V. Ramamoorthy received undergraduate degrees in physics and technology from the University of Madras, India; an MS degree and professional degree of mechanical engineer from the University of California, Berkeley; and MA and PhD degrees in applied mathematics and computer theory from Harvard University. He was with Honeywell's Electronic Data Processing Division from 1956 to 1971, then was professor in the Department of Electrical Engineering and Computer Sciences at the University of Texas, Austin. He is currently professor in the Department of Electrical Engineering and Computer Sciences, University of California, Berkeley. He also serves as editor-in-chief of *IEEE Transactions on Software Engineering*.

Atul Prakash received the undergraduate degree in electrical engineering from the Indian Institute of Technology, New Delhi. He is presently working on the PhD degree in computer science at UC Berkeley. His research interests include software engineering, computer architecture, distributed systems, and artificial intelligence. Prakash is a student member of the ACM and IEEE-Computer Society.

Wei-Tek Tsai received a BS degree in computer science from MIT in 1979 and an MS degree in computer science from UC Berkeley in 1982, where he is currently a doctoral student. He is interested in computer communication and software engineering and is a student member of the ACM and IEEE Computer and Communication Societies. ACM and IEEE Computer and Communication Societies.

Yutaka Usuda received his BS in mathematics from the Tokyo Institute of Technology, then joined Hitachi Software Engineering, Inc. Currently, he is a graduate student in computer science at UC Berkeley. His research interests include software development and evolution environments.

Address questions concerning this article to C. V. Ramamoorthy, Computer Science Division, University of California, Berkeley, CA 94720.

Today's Risks in Software Development — Can They Be Significantly Reduced?

Major General Jerry Max Bunyard, USA
James Mike Coward

During the past 15 years, there has been a significant growth in the development of complex, real-time embedded computer systems, both large and small. With this growth, the government has incurred many development problems that have resulted in poor quality of the software products. Methodologies and tools have been generated with the goal of identifying problems, resolving them early, and producing reliable, maintainable products, but software overruns still occur, schedules still slip, and software products still fall short of their goals.

According to Dr. Barry Boehm, speaking at the Software Summit Series in Los Angeles in May 1980, the cost trends for both software development and software maintenance are rising substantially and are not projected to improve (Figure 1).

Emphasis continues to be given to cost for development, with little attention being given to the overall life-cycle cost. This leads to a further rise in maintenance costs due to latent errors in the software and inflexible software design, as well as insufficient documentation and support software for maintenance. Support packages, e.g., simulations and test tools, are often treated as throwaways rather than major deliverable items that facilitate both development and maintenance. More emphasis must be placed on the required discipline and rigor early in development to ensure quality, including maintainability of the software throughout the system life cycle.

An Examination of the Problem

This article takes a look at today's risks in software development, with the objectives of focusing on lessons learned and recommending alternatives that can significantly reduce these risks. What are the primary problem areas today that lead to schedule slippages, cost overruns, or a software product that falls short of its desired goals? Some of these problem areas are original requirements that are incomplete and/or validated; software design that is not traceable to the requirements and diverges during development; software code that is not maintainable due to poor enforcement of standards; documentation of the system that

Major General Jerry Max Bunyard, USA, is Project Manager, Patriot Missile System, at Redstone Arsenal, Ala. He was previously Deputy Director of Tactical Air and Land Warfare Systems, Office of the Director, Defense Test and Evaluation, within the Office of the Under Secretary of Defense (Research and Engineering). General Bunyard holds a B.S. degree from Oklahoma State University and an M.S. degree from George Washington University.

James Mike Coward is Manager, Data Systems Department, at Teledyne Brown Engineering, Huntsville, Ala., where previously he was Project Manager for the Patriot Software V&V Project. Mr. Coward holds a B.S. degree from Lamar University and an M.S. degree from Texas A&M University.

Reprinted from *Concepts: The Journal of Defense Systems Acquisition Management*, Volume 5, Number 4, Autumn 1982, pages 73-94. U.S. Government work not protected by U.S. copyright.

FIGURE 1
Hardware-Software Cost Trends

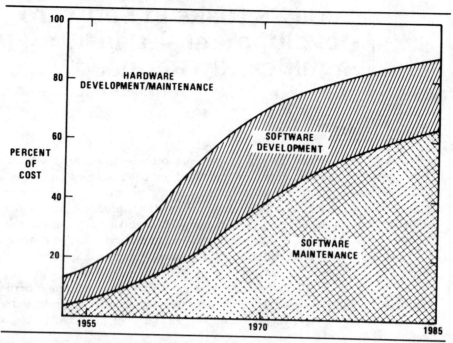

does not reflect as-built code; software that is insufficiently tested; and timing and storage budgets that are exceeded.

In software development, specific software errors are frequently classified into one of three categories: requirements errors, design errors, or coding errors. This classification is a natural result of the three major development phases that lead to fabrication of the software components. Figure 2, presented at the AIIE 1977 Software Conference, illustrates that as larger software products are considered, the number of design defects begins to exceed the number of coding defects, until design defects predominate the total errors. This implies that larger numbers of more complex defects are being introduced early in the development cycle of larger software products.

The software development cycle is often presented as a sequential set of well-defined phases, each with specific products and reviews, which provide the necessary structure to facilitate management and control by the materiel developer and project manager. Software development activities on many projects, however, continue to be burdened with management and technical problems and issues that work against a quality product end-item.

In contrast, it is important to emphasize that techniques and methodologies have been defined and are being applied to some projects. They are contributing significantly to the delivery and support of quality products. As an example, in the early 1970s, a structured, disciplined approach strengthened by employment of an independent evaluation contractor contributed significantly to reducing software risks on the Ballistic Missile Defense Systems Technology Project. As illustrated in Figure 3, presented at the 1976 AIAA Software Management Conference, the total number of errors was reduced and the error detection rate for this project was substantially shifted, resulting in early problem identification and resolution.

When large numbers of problems surface late in the development program during system integration and test, the development effort is impacted by major requirement and design issues. In Figure 4, presented by Dr. Jacques Gansler, then Deputy Assistant Secretary of Defense for Materiel Acquisition, at the 1977 AIAA Software Conference, the increased cost of correcting a requirement or design error as one progresses further into the development is illustrated. These data, used with the detection rate curves presented in Figure 3, illustrate very

FIGURE 2
Overview of Potential Life-Cycle Defects in Programming

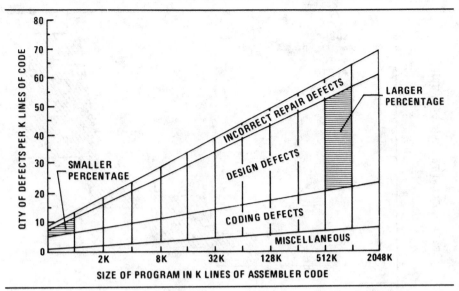

forcefully the risks associated with software costs: i.e., large numbers of errors found late in the development cycle. When errors are found late, requirements have to be revalidated, designs redesigned, software and systems retested, and documentation rewritten.

The previous paragraphs describe a major contributor to unexpected software costs. Planners don't project the costs to re-do what was not done right the first time. Since the code appears to be something that can be modified with relative ease, problem identification and resolution are often postponed until after the coding phase is completed. There is a need to recognize that there is more to fixing and maintaining software systems than making a few coding changes. Significant software risks are incurred when requirements and design flaws are not given sufficient attention early in the development cycle.

FIGURE 3
Catching Software Errors Early: Project Results

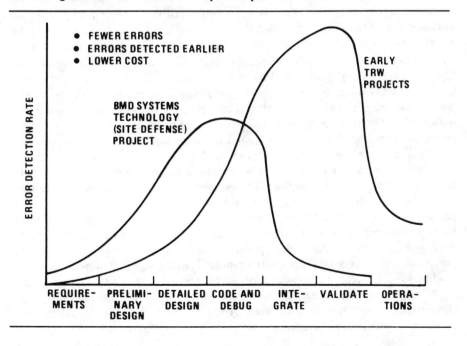

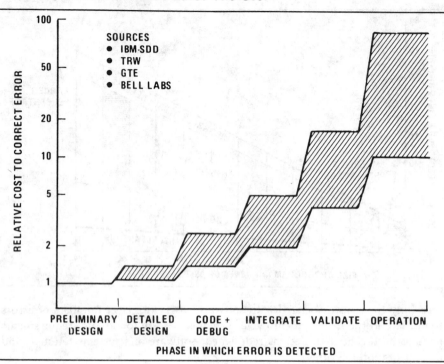

FIGURE 4
Catching Software Errors Late: The Cost

SOURCES
- IBM-SDD
- TRW
- GTE
- BELL LABS

RELATIVE COST TO CORRECT ERROR

PRELIMINARY DESIGN | DETAILED DESIGN | CODE + DEBUG | INTEGRATE | VALIDATE | OPERATION

PHASE IN WHICH ERROR IS DETECTED

Software Quality—It Begins with Procurement

THE PROCUREMENT ENVIRONMENT AND ITS IMPLICATIONS

First, let us look further at the environment in which the software development contractor works. The pressures of competition for development contracts and program funding constraints work against quality development practices as early as the proposal.

Every contractor in the world would like to propose the most thorough design job and best documentation conceivable. In fact, in costing exercises before proposal submission, such an approach might even be typical for a first cut. Competition for development contracts is intense, however, and this places extreme pressure on writers of cost proposals. This competitive pressure may also be aggravated by extremely difficult funding constraints imposed by inadequate appropriations from Congress. The result is usually that the dollars bid for software development will be cut before proposal submission and during negotiations, especially at the time of best and final offer. In making these price cuts, the contractor typically assumes that the military standards applied to the development are "loose enough" that the quality and depth of documentation and data presented at design reviews can be cut back, the requirements work can actually be carried over into the design phase, and so on through the cycle. The assumption is also made that the test program will go well and can be sized to fit whatever dollars and schedule are left when development reaches that point. This assumption basically means that the test program will be based on dollars available, not technical thoroughness, and that the tests will be completed independent of product quality. This typically will leave software problems to be fixed during operations and maintenance, after product acceptance. The contractor is also counting on his people to put in whatever hours are necessary to get the job done and is counting on contract modifications associated with new or modified requirements to help compensate for the initially insufficient funding.

When the contract is signed, the contractor is faced with still another problem: staffing. There may be only a few people left from the proposal effort who are familiar with the project. Also, a sufficient number of required personnel may

FIGURE 5
Errors in Large Software Systems

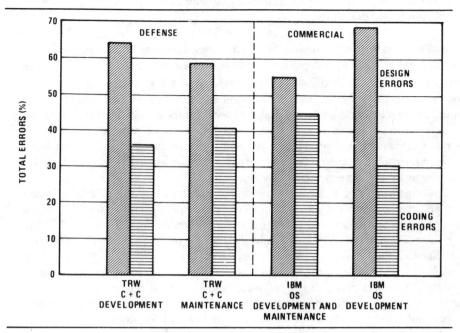

not be immediately available to assign to the project to meet staffing requirements. Thus the contractor starts understaffed, facing both hiring and training problems. This most likely was not planned for in the proposal, so work schedules will start to slip from the first day of the project.

Then begins the series of requirements and design reviews. The contractor will generally present the best picture possible of the work that has been accomplished by the time of any particular review. Because of the problems cited previously, though, this typically will be far less than initially intended. The documentation will tend to be too general, and usually there will be little analysis or data available at the time of a review to support the requirements or design being presented.

At this point, the materiel development agency has a problem. The agency will generally not be satisfied with either the content of the documentation or the review, but when they turn to standards such as MIL-STD-490 or MIL-STD-1521A, they will not find the precise, clear guidance or methods to force the contractor to make improvements. When the agency directors consider attempting to do the necessary technical analysis to validate the contractor's work in house, they find themselves lacking in technical staff and schedule time. The only remaining option is to try to "work with" the contractor, using informal mechanisms to solve individual problems, which usually takes time, and this means that data rarely become available much earlier than the contractor would have generated them anyway.

This situation is aggravated as time goes on. Because the contractor typically cannot finish his requirements definition and analysis work until well into the design phase, the requirements tend to be unstable, especially early in the design. This phenomenon may be amplified by changes directed by the materiel developer and even sometimes by Congress through funds-cutting legislation. The result is design, redesign, and more redesign, all of which must be documented, all of which cost in terms of dollars and schedule, and all of which ripple through the development cycle.

The areas of highest payoff for reducing risks associated with developing software are activities that occur earliest in the development cycle: project planning and requirements definition.

At the 1977 AIAA Software Conference, Dr. Gansler presented two illustrations of interest to this discussion. Figure 5 shows, based on four major software development programs, that *more* errors in software result from design than from actual coding. This should be expected, based on the discussion in the last section, and indicates a higher level of technical uncertainty and management stress during the requirements and early design phases. Figure 4 plots the relative cost of correcting a software error as a function of where in the program the error is found. The message is clear. To be most cost-effective, any approach to improving management techniques for software development must be directed at the early stages of the development activity.

The early stages of a development project consist primarily of project planning and requirements definition. Numerous directives developed by DOD have been prepared to help guide these efforts. As an example: DOD Directive 5000.3, as released December 26, 1979, establishes policy for the conduct of test and evaluation in the acquisition of defense systems. Under Section D. (Policies and Responsibilities, Subsection 6.) "Test and Evaluation of Computer Software," specific attention is given to the software components of a defense system and there is a call for participation by the operational test and evaluation (OT&E) agencies in "the early stages of software planning and development. . . ." The directive also calls for "Quantitative and demonstrable performance objectives and evaluation criteria . . . during each . . . phase." Performance objectives and evaluation criteria for each phase of software development are critical in reducing risks. Successful development of software cannot be based on a single, definitive test at the end of the development cycle. Experience has shown clearly that waiting until the final stages of system development to be able to measure acceptability of the software product is disastrous.

On large software development efforts, the development process may extend over 5 to 10 years. This means a high level of personnel turnover and changes in direction from higher authorities may occur before project completion. There is often no concrete, well-definable product until the final stages of development. Documentation and reviews are the primary channel of communications to assess software quality at each phase and must be taken seriously; they must not be allowed to be ignored or minimized.

In order to evaluate the software product at early stages of development, in terms of its functional and performance characteristics, more emphasis needs to be given to simulation. Only when we witness the "execution" of the large, complex software processes that are being built today do we truly understand their behavior and what they will and will not do. When this first execution is the code product, integrated into complicated, extensive hardware subsystems, we incur maximum risk.

Functional as well as analytic simulations at the system and component level can be used to ensure high quality of both requirements and design. Extensive research has been done and is under way to extend the basic concepts of such simulations, with the overall goal of writing specifications in a language that can be directly translated and executed in a computer. Other areas of research, e.g., the use of metrics to quantitatively measure quality of the software product at each phase, also appear to have future potential in the general context of evaluation criteria.

The DOD Directive 5000.29 makes a thrust in the right direction by calling for requirements validation, risk analysis, and the definition of specific criteria in measuring the attainment of program milestones. In the Army, for example, DARCOM-R-70-16, dated July 16, 1979, "implements DOD Directive 5000.29 by establishing policy and assigning responsibilities for the planning, development, acquisition, testing, training, and support of major and non-major Army battlefield automated systems employing computer resources."

Even with these advances, however, a wide range of interpretations is often applied. The current directives, standards, and guidelines are written for a wide spectrum of applications and are not intended to provide the detailed directives for a specific application. The RFP should be given special attention to ensure that the "essential ingredients" are defined to ensure visibility and control by the materiel developer for the specific development effort, as well as to ensure the quality characteristics required in the software product, e.g., maintainability. Requirements for the competitive contractors to provide software development plans, configuration management plans, design review plans, and quality assurance plans as part of their proposals can help significantly by defining early the detailed "ingredients" of the proposed approach. Typically, these documents are not called for until some months after contract award; i.e., after the software budget has been set in concrete, thus focusing the methodology to be adapted accordingly.

Today, some projects are producing better plans. The major problem is that they often do not appear until well after a project is in trouble. The requirement to submit the plans with the original proposal forces more detailed planning and provides the materiel developer with better visibility into the contractor's responsiveness to the agency's documentation and review requirements. This in turn results in a contract that "from the beginning" calls for documentation, reviews, and audits, not only by name and type, but by the requirements defining specifically what their content will be and the criteria of acceptance to be applied at each phase of development. More realistic bid pricing should also result.

With regard to software requirements definition, a recognition of the role of requirements is beginning to emerge within the entire software development community. Requirements provide the direction that guides every aspect of the design activity and are the standards against which the developed software ultimately must be validated. A candidate area for reducing risks in today's development is the environment in which requirements are developed and the tools with which they are documented. A careful review of MIL-STD-483 and MIL-STD-490, and a review of the way they are being applied on actual development programs today, suggest that attention can profitably be given to providing alternative guidelines in the area of the content of requirements documentation. These guidelines will help managers, at the outset of a project, clearly delineate the "level of detail and method of presentation" required for the requirements documentation for their particular projects.

Significant activity is currently under way in government, industry, and the universities to define languages for expressing requirements and to develop automated tools to provide management with control and analysis to the completeness, consistency, traceability, and cost of requirements expressed in those languages. The objectives of this research are to provide a means of forcing more discipline on requirements definition, provide a more precise definition of requirements, and to provide management with tools to measure the quality and status of requirements. The necessity for this discipline stems from the environment at proposal time, when decisions are made to cut cost by skimping on requirements documentation and assuming an optimistic test program. Imposing constraints to develop and maintain documentation and techniques for requirements analysis to validate requirements will raise the bid cost of development, because contractors in a competitive environment often do not bid the complete cost to thoroughly document and validate requirements.

The observation can be made that software requirements are derived from system requirements. It follows, therefore, that requirements validation entails a demonstration of some kind that the software requirements are complete, consistent, and traceable with respect to the system requirements and that the performance called for in the software requirements ensures satisfaction of performance criteria in the system specification. Major tools for performing such demonstrations are detailed simulations and models. In a similar sense, the software design can be demonstrated to satisfy requirements using similar tools. These tools need to be planned for from the beginning. In their proposals, competitive contractors should be required to present specific technical and cost data in support of simulation and test facilities to support each phase of development. In addition, those development support and test tools that are deemed useful to maintenance should be required to be formal deliverables to the government.

Another key area of risk is poor reviews at each phase of development. Agendas should be specified by the materiel developer for each review (including requirements, design, and test reviews), specifying in detail the data to be presented at each review. These data include both requirements or design data and the results of a specified set of test activities. These data should include simulation and/or analysis data for requirements and design reviews, showing explicit predicted performance against the appropriate requirements. At the preliminary and formal qualification test reviews, test data and test data analyses should be presented, demonstrating the performance of the system against all the requirements in the baselined requirements documentation. The agenda should be tailored to the particular procurement and be incorporated in the RFP and contract packages. Some contractual significance should be added to these reviews by also including specific criteria for scoring the contractor's performance at each review relating to the timeliness of completing all review agenda items (including the closing of all trouble reports, action items, and document updates resulting from the review), the quality of documentation as measured against applicable standards, and the thoroughness of data presented. Reviews should be held open until all required data are provided and all problems are closed. Incentive or award fees could be based, at least in part, on review scores.

The need to formulate an RFP that facilitates visibility and control during development activities has been discussed. An eventual contract "with teeth" that forces an orderly, structured approach requiring specified types and levels of documentation and reviews in terms of criteria for their evaluation can lead to more realistic planning on the part of the government and the development contractor.

Reducing Risks During the Software Development Cycle

A large number of critical activities, milestones, and software products are required in the development of high-quality military software systems. Visibility into and control of the development activities are essential to both the software developer and the government.

By employing an ordered decomposition of the development cycle, the identification and evaluation of major milestones and deliverables required during each phase can be considered more easily. Each milestone or deliverable can be evaluated within the scope of that particular phase of the development cycle for correctness, consistency, and adequacy. Current DOD directives, guidelines, and standards are oriented toward this approach.

In reality, however, what is often found in many of today's development efforts? A majority of the software problems are being found late in development, during software testing, and not in the particular phase in which they were created. Figure 6 depicts a typical development and test effort. In general, the majority of errors are introduced during development (up through coding), and the majority of errors are discovered and corrected after the product components have been fabricated.

Two classes of problems are encountered during testing that need to be given special attention. First, in many applications, a large number of requirements and design errors are not being discovered until late into the testing activities. These errors, present prior to coding, could have been identified and corrected much earlier with significantly less impact on the development activity. Second, coding errors are found late in the system test phase that should have been discovered in a lower-level software test. Both types of problems are symptomatic of rushing to get the product integrated into a total system. This approach, not planned but often followed, is characteristic of a high-risk development effort.

FIGURE 6
Software Development Cycle

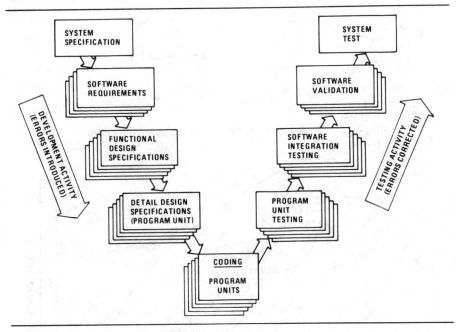

As emphasized previously in this article, it *is* possible to plan and develop software products in which software flaws are identified and corrected early, most often in the phase in which they first occur. For this to be accomplished, however, more analysis and evaluation must take place throughout the overall effort. First, the development contractor must be required to demonstrate at each phase of development the quality characteristics of the product defined for evaluation at that time. Specifics of these characteristics are explored in the subsections to follow. Second, the materiel developer needs the required resources to assess independently the quality of the software product during each phase of development.

The need for independence with regard to assessment must be emphasized. The materiel developer needs support independent of that provided by the prime contractor. In a general sense, the prime contractor has a conflict between his role as prime and any role in which he acts as advisor and assistant to the project manager. The conflict occurs because the interests of the government may differ from those of the prime contractor. The result is that, although the prime contractor is competent to advise the project manager, he is not always motivated to provide the advice most beneficial to the government. Thus the project manager needs a source of independent advice for identification of risk areas, alternative system designs, quality of documentation, actual status of development progress, and the significance of test results. Alternatives for providing this independent support range from project office staffs or in-house government laboratories to outside contractor support.

One activity of providing an independent assessment of the software development progress is commonly known today by the term "verification and validation." As illustrated in Figure 7, verification may be defined as the evaluation process designed to ensure consistency and completeness of the product at any given phase within the development cycle. Consistency is concerned with measuring the degree to which a given phase (e.g., design) is in agreement with the previous phase (e.g., requirements) in the development cycle. Completeness is a measure of the readiness to initiate the next phase in the development cycle. Validation, the next phase in the development cycle, is oriented toward the final product and is directed at test and evaluation to measure how well the product

FIGURE 7
Software Verification and Validation

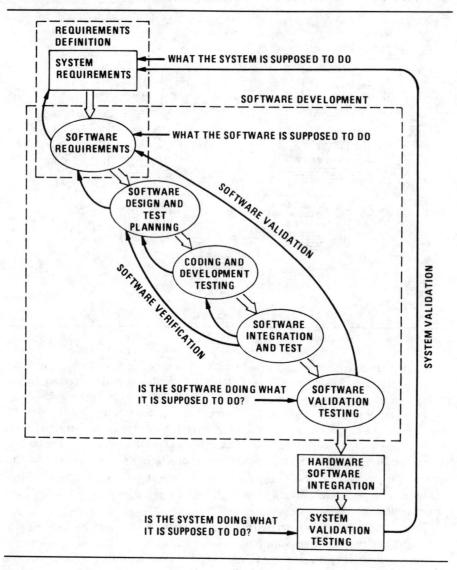

performs against established requirements. Two types of validation are illustrated: software validation and system validation.

SUPPORT SOFTWARE DEVELOPMENT

In the past, little attention has been given to support software development. From the outset (i.e., procurement phase), the significance of support software as it pertains to both development and maintenance should be evaluated. For support packages that will play a major role in either development or maintenance, the same rigor and discipline should be applied as specified for the application software. Typical support packages that are often critical to development and maintenance include compilers, requirements, simulations, software testbeds (simulating threats, environments, etc.) that support software testing, data reduction packages, and special hardware integration software. As deemed necessary, these packages should be developed as "formal deliverables" and validated to ensure the success of the role they will play. The discussion that follows, therefore, is not intended to be oriented exclusively toward the application software, but is relevant to all formal software deliverable items.

The objectives of software requirements are to provide a basis for the design activities, and to direct the planning for software validation to ensure that the software product operates according to requirements. The requirements must state what the software is to do in terms of inputs, processing, outputs, accuracy, and load. If the requirements do not accomplish these specific objectives, the following problems often occur:

—The software designer is apt to make design decisions that are not in accord with what the requirements writer intended.

—The initial development of test plans is hampered because of a lack of clear understanding of what the software product is to accomplish.

—There is no standard for judging the correctness of test results.

Examples of types of significant problems that often result during requirements definitions are as follows:

—Requirements may be ambiguous.

—Requirements may not be testable.

—The implementation of the requirements may not be feasible.

—Requirements allocations may not be adequately specified.

—Requirements may not be consistent.

When requirements have these characteristics, flaws result in both design and test planning. A detailed independent evaluation of the software requirements (often an iterative process as the requirements evolve) can play a major role in ensuring that they possess characteristics that contribute to a quality product. A representative set of criteria which may be applied during requirements analysis is presented in Table I.

As mentioned earlier, the DOD Directive 5000.29 stresses "requirements validation and risk analysis." Requirements validation may require a wide range of activities, including the conduct of extensive traceability analysis and the development or use of detailed models and analytical simulations to evaluate both functional and performance aspects of requirements.

DOD directives and military standards call for specific formal reviews to assess the quality of the software requirement specification. Formal reviews, however, are often conducted as passive tutorials for high-level management instead of an active evaluation of the specification details. Sufficient time must be scheduled for a detailed evaluation to take place before the formal review. The

---

TABLE I
Representative Criteria to Support Requirements Evaluation

Realistic - Requirements must be achievable within the capabilities of the data processing hardware.

Unambiguous - Requirements must be stated such that they are definitive and not open to subjective interpretation.

Consistent - Requirements must be consistent with one another, with interfacing subsystems, and with those at the next higher and lower levels.

Necessary - Unnecessary or overly restrictive requirements will increase the cost and complexity of the software and will also impact the design, code, and testing schedules.

Complete - The requirements must completely specify the software product to be provided in terms of accuracy, timing, throughput, interface control, and input/output.

---

significance of reviews has already been discussed, and it has been recommended that the agendas be incorporated in the RFP and contract packages. These agendas can provide guidance as to the type of documentation and data needed to demonstrate requirements validation. A formal review should be thought of in terms of days, not hours. In addition, active involvement in the formal reviews should be provided by many agencies and groups (including the user, the materiel developer, and the contractor—the systems engineers, software analysts, and test personnel).

By correcting requirement ambiguities, resolving requirement inconsistencies, rewriting non-testable statements so that they possess quantitative characteristics to measure acceptance, modeling requirements, and assessing state-of-the-art technology to ensure feasibility of their implementation, the design and test process will proceed on a more even path. Attaining this goal is an iterative process that requires maintaining the specifications as living documents.

During the software design phase, the most significant contributor to poor quality in the software is often related to the previous phase, i.e., poor requirements. Other problems may still arise, however, because of poor design practices and poor solutions to the design problems. These include poor structure caused by lack of modularity in the design, lack of traceability from design to requirement, erroneous implementation because of inconsistencies resulting from lack of design standards, and mismatched interfaces. Again, the solutions to these types of problems can be provided early in the development cycle through the use of independent evaluation by the government. A detailed evaluation of the design can help to ensure that: Documentation standards are defined and followed to reduce misinterpretation; data flow and control through all parts of the system are adequately defined; emphasis is placed on the hardware involved, data transformation, timing, and the work stations through which control passes; and the design is an accurate representation of the operations and operating rules specified by the requirements.

Design procedures and standards vary from one project to the next. Because of the complexity of the design process, standards and procedures are inherent contributors to the quality of the design specifications and should be required by the materiel developer. Examples of typical standards and procedures that should be considered for incorporation during the design phase include:
—Standards for design documentation format and content;
—Configuration control procedures for requirements and design specifications;
—Procedures to validate design concepts;
—Procedures to support traceability between requirements and design (both directions);
—Procedures for maintaining visibility into, and for the control of, schedules and problem reports.

The objective of an independent evaluation of the software preliminary design is to determine the overall feasibility of the design approach, the capability of the design documentation to support the detailed design, and the capability to test plans to accomplish testing objectives. The preliminary design should be independently traced to the requirements, thus verifying that the requirements have been allocated to the design, and identifying requirements that have been misinterpreted or not addressed. Preliminary test plans prepared in parallel with the preliminary design should be assessed as to their adequacy to accomplish the test objectives.

As the critical design review (CDR) approaches, an independent evaluation can again support status assessment with detailed design verification, test plan and test procedure evaluation, and other support documentation analysis. Functional simulations can be developed and used to verify the functional characteristics of the design. Critical algorithms can be tested using simulation to assess their validity and performance characteristics.

Figures 2 and 3 showed that for large software projects, over half of the defects incurred during development are introduced before the coding activity. When the development activity is decomposed into the three phases of design/cost/test, a general percentage rule of thumb of 40/20/40 seems to apply when defining the portion of the overall development activity that each phase may be projected to consume. This means that by the time the development effort is 40 percent complete, as many as 60 percent of the defects associated with a large development effort are already introduced into the product. A major risk factor is incurred when these defects are translated into code, and their resolution is left until the test or operational phases.

We often hear that hardware development methodology is far ahead of software development methodology, but why? Hardware developers will not expose themselves to the risks associated with fabricating a product without extensive evaluation directed at removing the design and requirements defects. It is common to proceed in software development without this evaluation.

When software developers started out by developing "small software packages" years ago, they soon learned how easy it was to let the computer help find the defects. Software was easy to change and the design could be documented after the fact if that was required. The usual approach was to "get to the code as fast as possible." This just doesn't work for large, complex software systems. Software is not so easy to change when a large number of personnel are involved. This is demonstrated by the extensive testing required after making a software change to validate that the modification fixed the problem and didn't introduce other problems. It is also demonstrated by the fractured designs and poor-quality documentation (e.g., documentation that does not match the code) often seen at the end of the development phase.

The significance of this problem is supported by the current DOD directives and guidelines calling for extensive reviews and evaluations at each phase of development. The problem is that software developers "try to do too little" and "just get by" without concentrating on the benefits of an in-depth review at each phase. Major milestones are called for during development to examine requirements and design. Risks can be significantly reduced if these milestones are taken seriously and requirements and design issues are identified and resolved prior to the coding phase.

REDUCING RISKS ASSOCIATED WITH CODE AND TEST

The coding phase of software development involves a translation of the detailed design description into a machine-readable form that, when executed, will automatically perform the functions designed. A major activity currently under way in DOD is the development of a standard higher-order language for coding future applications. The DOD Directive 5000.31 specifies currently approved languages for programming. Such a standardization is intended to facilitate both development and maintenance. However, we continue to witness flaws in software code. Examples of errors that arise during coding that contribute to risks in the development of software include: undocumented differences between design and code, lack of source-code commentary, lack of organization in code structure (usually reflected in the design), and poor configuration management of the code. The last problem results in mismatched code versions during integration and lack of visible control over changes to the code.

Independent evaluation of the code and coding standards and procedures can help to reduce the frequency of these flaws. A major code analysis activity is called for in MIL-STD-1521 as part of the physical configuration audit (PCA). In addition to this formal code audit, selective audits during the testing phase can contribute to maintaining consistency and good quality between the design as documented and as implemented in the code.

The last category selected for discussion is software testing. Actually, this activity may consume 40 to 60 percent of the development effort. Software testing, in this context, is that activity ranging from module (unit-level) testing to total system integration and acceptance. The thrust of this article has been toward doing more early in development to reduce errors so that the testing will go more smoothly, and fewer code corrections will be necessary.

Two specific classes of software tests need to be given special attention—primarily from the standpoint of emphasizing their differences and individual significance. These have been graphically named "glass box" and "black box" testing. Glass box testing suggests looking inside and is what we normally know as development testing. The major characteristic of this testing is that the design is the criterion for evaluating the test results. Special attention is given to data base structures, ranges of values of parameters, and exercising or invoking each instruction and branch statement in the code. Black box testing suggests taking a look at the outside and is what we often identify as validation testing. The major characteristic here is that the requirements are the criteria for evaluating the test results. Both software and system validations are conducted against the software and system-level specifications.

Many questions arise concerning both classes of tests: How much is required? When is it over? Where are we now in the test cycle? These questions reflect the fact that it is often not known how to measure test progress. Techniques have evolved during the past decade to help in this area—some proved and some still conceptual. One proven concept is the use of functional capabilities list to measure progress in development testing and requirements lists to measure progress in validation testing. Such lists, when developed and applied at a detailed level, can be used to decompose a complex, voluminous collection of requirements and design documents into checklists to be used by analysts and managers to guide and evaluate the test process. Not only do nominal processing paths need to be emphasized, but so do the unexpected or low probability paths associated with contingency processing.

Examples of problem areas that often arise during software testing are as follows:

—Tests are not fully traceable to the software requirements or software design, depending on the class of test under consideration.
—Unnecessary redundancy exists between test cases.
—Critical components are not adequately stressed.
—The required test data are not recorded.
—Collected data from a test are incorrectly interpreted or are not evaluated.
—Test acceptance criteria are too general and subjective.
—Sufficient test support software is not planned for and validated.

These problems contribute significantly to a high-risk program. Most of these problem areas are related to poor test planning.

Four types of documents are usually required for the test cycle: test plans, test procedures, test execution reports, and test results analysis reports. These documents encompass the planning, execution, and analysis of the test process. Each document plays an important role, and independent evaluation during its development can provide benefits similar to those discussed for other development documentation.

A key document in the test process is the test plan. An independent evaluation of a test plan can help to strengthen a weak plan by identifying the weaknesses and recommending enhancements prior to development of the detailed procedures and resources consumption activities (facilities, computers, people, time) required during test execution. A test program will be no better than the plan. Emphasis should also be given to the independent review of test results at each level of software development testing.

Discussed thus far are the types of problems often encountered during testing and how the test-related issues can be resolved early in the test cycle. If effort is expended early in the development cycle to identify and resolve requirements, design, and code problems, the usually complex and difficult job of system/software integration and acceptance testing will be simplified because fewer problems will be found in the product under test. As a result, the maintenance activity will go a lot more smoothly. Up-to-date documentation for both requirements and design will exist, and support software will be available (validated and documented) to facilitate maintenance.

Improved techniques for developing systems have been formulated during the past 15 years, but there continue to be temptations to try shortcuts in attempts to reduce current-year costs. In this sense, software development technology seems to be standing still.

Summary and Recommendations

The preceding sections have examined major risks often encountered in software development, with the objectives of focusing on lessons learned during the past 15 years and recommending alternatives that can result in significantly reducing these risks.

Primary problem areas that lead to schedule slippages, cost overruns, or software products that fall short of their desired goals have been discussed. The software development cycle, often presented as a simple sequence of well-defined phases, continues to be burdened with management and technical problems and issues that work against a high-quality product. Identifying and resolving software problems early, often in the phase in which they first occur, has been shown to contribute significantly to reducing risks in software development.

Major contributors to software schedule and cost overruns have been examined. These contributors are large numbers of requirements and design problems being found after the coding phase and large numbers of coding errors being found during system test activities. The effect of large numbers of fixes after the software package has been coded and integrated into a software system has been examined. Such fixes are very costly and have a deteriorating effect on the quality of the software product. The shift from coding defects to more serious design and requirements issues as a function of the physical size of the software package has been discussed.

The DOD has made advances in outlining what kinds of milestones, documentation, and methodology are best suited for military applications. A wide range of interpretations are often applied to these guidelines, however. The current guidelines are written for a wide spectrum of applications and are not intended to define the detailed directives for a specific application. The RFP (procurement phase) should be given special attention to ensure visibility and control by the materiel developer during software development.

To reduce risks in software development, the potential for the types of problems discussed in this article must be recognized and the necessary steps taken to either prevent their occurrence or correct them as early as possible. In simple terms, a plan must be developed and the necessary action taken to implement the plan. To be effective, the plan needs to be developed as early as possible.

Emphasis has been directed more toward the overall development concept rather than techniques that can be applied when focusing on a particular phase of the development cycle. In summary, the following recommendations are emphasized:

—Formulate an RFP that will facilitate visibility and control during development activities. A contract that forces an orderly, structured approach requiring specific types and levels of documentation and reviews in terms of criteria for their evaluation can lead to more realistic planning on the part of the government and the development contractor, and thus to less risk in the development effort.

—Plan from the beginning for independent evaluation throughout the development activity. This effort will lead to significant flaws being identified and resolved early in the development cycle, flaws that otherwise would lead to major schedule and cost impacts on the development effort.

Implementation of these recommendations will lead to an increased cost projection at the outset. For independent evaluation, a general rule of thumb for cost ranges from 10 to 20 percent of that budgeted by the software developer.

However, improved capability to develop software products of known high quality on schedule and within planned budgets resulting from the implementation of these recommendations is the primary goal. It is projected that a disciplined application of these management concepts will result in a reduction in actual system life-cycle costs through reduced development overruns and O&M expenditures.

Today's risks in software development can be significantly reduced through planning and through the application of resources to resolve errors early. ‖

Chapter 3: Software Engineering Project Management

1. Introduction to Chapter

Project management is defined as a system of procedures, practices, technologies, and know-how that provides the planning, organizing, staffing, directing, and controlling necessary to successfully manage an engineering project. Each of the five principle functions of management (portrayed again in Figure 3.1) can be further partitioned into a set of more detailed management activities (see Table 3.1). These activities, like the five management functions themselves, can be universally applied to the management of any organization or activity.

Definitions or explanations of these activities can be found in the introductions of Chapters 4 through 8. The following table served as an outline for this tutorial.

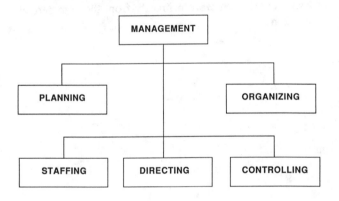

Figure 3.1: Classic Management Model

2. Overview of Chapter

The four papers in this chapter address software engineering project management and give the reader an overview of project management's role in a software development project.

The paper by Rook provides a bridge between software engineering and software engineering project management. The papers by Royce and Boehm both look at *software life cycle development models* as major management strategies for developing software. Royce discusses the older, more conventional life-cycle model called the *waterfall chart* and Boehm a new *risk-driven* method call the *spiral model*.

The paper, "Criteria for Controlling Projects According to Plan," by H.J. Thamhain and D.L. Wilemon, provides insight into the major issues of managing a project (predominantly for commercial environments) and proposes a criteria for effective project management and control.

3. Description of Papers

Despite its apparently limiting title, the paper "Controlling Software Projects" by Paul Rook, is an excellent overview of software engineering development and software engineering project management. As he states in his paper, "technical development is what is controlled and project management is the controller." The paper presents a thorough list of genuine differences between *hardware* and *software*. Then the paper goes on to say that despite these differences software development should be managed the same as hardware development.

The paper by Win Royce is another classic in this tutorial and despite its age is still the most accurate description of the software development life-cycle model which is known as the "waterfall chart." Royce shows how a software development project can be partitioned into a series of phases each one terminating with a document or specification. This bench mark paper made early note of such modern day software engineering concepts as:

- Design must precede coding.
- Represent a software design with a *specification not* with code.
- *Iterate* the design between steps as a greater understanding of the software to be delivered is realized. (Royce is often *not* credited with this concept.)
- Timing, storage, and other operational constraints must be designed into the software; they can *not* be tested in.
- Management of software development is *not* possible without a very high degree of documentation for each phase of the software development life cycle.
- *Prototype* the software system (Royce calls it "do it twice") prior to final commitment to functional and performance requirements.
- Involve the customer early in the project through life-cycle reviews.
- The use of life-cycle software engineering procedures are cost effective.

Table 3.1: Major Activities of Management

Management Functions	Fundamental Management Activities
Planning	— Set objectives or goals — Develop strategies — Develop policies — Determine courses of action — Make decisions — Set procedures and rules — Develop programs — Forecast future situations — Prepare budgets — Document project plans
Organizing	— Identify and group required tasks — Select and establish organizational structures — Create organizational positions — Define responsibilities and authority — Establish position qualifications — Document organizational structures
Staffing	— Fill organizational positions — Assimilate newly assigned personnel — Educate or train personnel — Provide for general development — Evaluate and appraise personnel — Compensate — Terminate assignments — Document staffing decisions
Directing	— Provide leadership — Supervise personnel — Delegate authority — Motivate personnel — Coordinate activities — Facilitate communications — Resolve conflicts — Manage changes — Document directing decisions
Controlling	— Develop standards of performance — Establish monitoring and reporting systems — Measure results — Initiate corrective actions — Reward and discipline — Document controlling methods

A special note: the phase Royce identified as "analysis" is generally not used anymore. The activities of analysis are handled either in the preliminary design phase or the detailed design phase.

The third paper, "A Spiral Model of Software Development and Enhancement," by Barry Boehm, describes a revolutionary new look at the software development life cycle. An earlier version of this paper was presented by Boehm at a workshop on software requirements in early 1985. The spiral model is a more general software development model than those typically in use today and treats as special cases the waterfall chart and other popular software development paradigms. The primary thrust of the spiral model is to integrate risk analysis and prototyping.

The last paper, "Criteria for Controlling Projects According to Plan," by H.J. Thamhain and D.L. Wilemon, reports on a study to investigate the practices of project managers and documents their project experiences. This study provides insight into the major issues of managing a project as reported by project managers. The paper addresses the causes of schedule slips and budget overruns and also provides a criteria for effective project management and control. The projects reported on were primarily from the commercial applications.

Reprinted from *Computer*, September 1987, pages 43-57. Copyright © 1987 by The Institute of Electrical and Electronics Engineers, Inc.

Improving Software Productivity

Barry W. Boehm, TRW

Computer hardware productivity continues to increase by leaps and bounds, while software productivity seems to be barely holding its own. Central processing units, random access memories, and mass memories improve their price-performance ratios by orders of magnitude per decade, while software projects continue to grind out production-engineered code at the same old rate of one to two delivered lines of code per man-hour.

Yet, if software is judged by the same standards as hardware, its productivity looks pretty good. One can produce a million copies of Lotus 1-2-3 at least as cheaply as a million copies of the Intel 286. Database management systems that cost $5 million 20 years ago can now be purchased for $99.95.

The commodity for which productivity has been slow to increase is custom software. Clearly, if you want to improve your organization's software price-performance, one major principle is "Don't build custom software where mass-produced software will satisfy your needs." However, even with custom software, a great deal is known about how to improve its productivity, and even increasing productivity by a factor of 2 will make a significant difference for most organizations.

This article discusses avenues of improving productivity for both custom

By 1995, a 20 percent improvement in software productivity will be worth $90 billion worldwide. Clearly, the measures outlined in this article are worth the effort.

and mass-produced software. Its main sections cover the following topics:

- The importance of improving software productivity: some national, international, and organizational trends indicating the significance of improving software productivity.
- Measuring software productivity: some of the pitfalls and paradoxes in defining and measuring software productivity and how best to deal with them.
- Analyzing software productivity: identifying factors that have a strong

productivity influence and those that have relatively little influence, using such concepts as software productivity ranges, the software value chain, and the software productivity opportunity tree.
- Improving software productivity: using the opportunity tree as a framework for describing specific productivity improvement steps and their potential payoffs.
- Software productivity trends and conclusions.

The importance of improving software productivity

The major motivation for improving software productivity is that software costs are large and growing larger. Thus, any percentage savings will be large and growing larger as well. Figure 1 shows recent and projected software cost trends in the United States and worldwide. In 1985, software costs totaled roughly $11 billion in the US Department of Defense, $70 billion in the US overall, and $140 billion worldwide. If present software cost growth rates of approximately 12 percent per year continue, the 1995 figures will be $36 billion for the DoD, $225 billion for the US, and $450 billion worldwide. Thus,

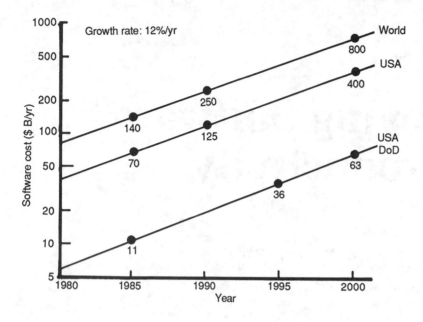

Figure 1. Software cost trends.

even a 20 percent improvement in software productivity would be worth $45 billion in 1995 for the US and $90 billion worldwide. Gains of such magnitude are clearly worth a serious effort to achieve.

Software costs are increasing not because people are becoming less productive but because of the continuing increase in demand for software. Figure 2, based on Boehm[1] and a recent TRW-NASA Space Station software study, shows the growth in software demand across five generations of the US manned space flight program, from about 1,500,000 object instructions to support Project Mercury in 1962-63 to about 80,000,000 object instructions to support the Space Station in the early 1990's.

The reasons for this increased demand are basically the same ones encountered by other sectors of the economy as they attempt to increase productivity via automation. The major component of growth in the Space Shuttle software has been the checkout and launch support area, in which NASA automated many functions

to reduce the number of people needed to support each launch—as many as 20,000 in previous manned spaceflight operations. The result has been a significant reduction in required launch support personnel but a significant increase in the required amount of software.

Many organizations have software demand growth curves similar to Figure 2. A large number of organizations simply cannot handle their increased demand within their available personnel and budget constraints, and they are faced with long backlogs of unimplemented information processing systems and software improvements. For example, the US Air Force Standard Information Systems Center has identified a four-year backlog of unstarted projects representing user-validated software needs. This type of backlog serves as a major inhibitor of a software user organization's overall productivity, competitiveness, and morale. Thus, besides cost savings, another major motivation for improving software productivity is to break up these software logjams.

Measuring software productivity

The best definition of the productivity of a process is

$$\text{Productivity} = \frac{\text{Outputs produced by the process}}{\text{Inputs consumed by the process}}$$

Thus, we can improve the productivity of the software process by increasing its outputs, decreasing its inputs, or both. However, this means that we need to provide meaningful definitions of the inputs and outputs of the software process.

Defining inputs. For the software process, providing a meaningful definition of *inputs* is a nontrivial but generally workable problem. Inputs to the software process generally comprise labor, computers, supplies, and other support facilities and equipment. However, one has to be careful which of various classes of items are to be counted as inputs. For example:

- Phases (just software development, or should we include system engineering, software requirements analysis, installation, or postdevelopment support?)
- Activities (to include documentation, project management, facilities management, conversion, training, database administration?)
- Personnel (to include secretaries, computer operators, business managers, contract administrators, line management?)
- Resources (to include facilities, equipment, communications, current versus future dollar payments?)

An organization can usually reach an agreement on which of the above are meaningful as inputs in their organizational context. Frequently, one can use present-value dollars as a uniform scale for various classes of resources.

Defining outputs. The big problem in defining software productivity is defining *outputs.* Here we find a paradox. Most sources say that defining delivered source instructions (DSI) or lines of code as the output of the software process is totally inadequate, and they argue that there are a number of deficiencies in using DSI. However, most organizations doing practical productivity measurement still use DSI as their primary metric.

DSI does have the following deficiencies as a software productivity metric:

(1) It is too low-level for some purposes, particularly for software cost estimation, where it is often difficult to estimate DSI in advance.

(2) It is too high-level for some purposes because complex instructions or complex combinations of instructions receive the same weight as a sequence of simple assignment statements.

(3) It is not a uniform metric; lines of machine-oriented language (MOL), higher-order language (HOL), and very high level language (VHLL) are given the same weight. For example, completing an application in one man-month and 100 lines of VHLL (100 DSI/MM) should not be considered less productive than doing the same application in two man-months and 500 lines of HOL (250 DSI/MM).

(4) It is hard to define well, particularly in determining whether to count comments, nonexecutable lines of code, reused code, or a "line" as a card image, carriage return, or semicolon. For example, putting a compact Ada program through a pretty printer will frequently triple its number of card images.

(5) It is not necessarily well correlated with value added, in that motivating people to improve productivity in terms of DSI may tempt them to develop a lot of useless lines of code.

(6) It does not reflect any consideration of software quality; "improving productivity" may tempt people to produce faster but sloppier code.

A number of alternatives to DSI have been advanced:

- "Software science" or program information-content metrics
- Program control-flow complexity metrics
- Design complexity metrics
- Program-external metrics, such as number of inputs, outputs, inquiries, files interfaces, or function points, a linear combination of those five quantities [2]
- Work transaction metrics

Comparing the effectiveness of these productivity metrics to a DSI metric, the following conclusions can be advanced: Each has advantages over DSI in some situations; each has more difficulties than DSI in some situations; each has equivalent difficulties to DSI in relating software achievement units to measures of the software's value added to the user organization.

As an example, let us consider function

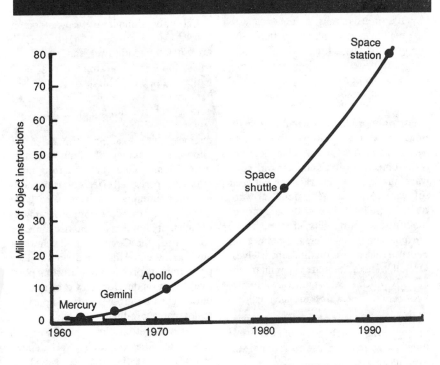

Figure 2. Growth in software demand: US manned spaceflight program.

points, which are defined as

$$FPs = 4 \times \#Inputs + 5 \times \#Outputs + 4 \times \#Inquiries + 10 \times \#Masterfiles + 7 \times \#Interfaces,$$

where *#Inputs* means "number of inputs to the program," and so on for the other terms.

Function points offer some strong advantages in addressing problems 1 (too low-level) and 3 (nonuniformity) above. One generally has a better early idea of the number of program inputs, outputs, etc., and the delivered software functionality has the same numeric measure whether the application is implemented in an MOL, HOL, or VHLL. However, function points do not provide any advantage in addressing problems 5 and 6 (value added and quality considerations), and they have more difficulties than DSI with respect to problems 2 and 4 (too high-level and imprecise definition). The software functionality required to transform an input into an output may be very trivial or very extensive. And we still lack a set of well-

rationalized, unexceptionable standard definitions for number of inputs, number of outputs, and other terms that are invariant across designers of the same application. For example, some experiments have shown an order-of-magnitude variation in estimating the number of inputs to an application.

However, function points have been successfully applied in some limited, generally uniform domains such as small-to-medium-sized business applications programs. A number of activities are also under way to provide more standard counting rules and to extend the metric to better cover other software application domains.

Thus, no alternative metrics have demonstrated a clear superiority to DSI. And DSI has several advantages that induce organizations to continue to use DSI as their primary software productivity output metric:

- The DSI metric is relatively easy to define and discuss unambiguously.
- It is easy to measure.

- It is conceptually familiar to software developers.
- It is linked to most familiar cost estimation models and rules of thumb for productivity estimation.
- It provides continuity from many organizations' existing database of project productivity information.

Software productivity-quality interactions. As discussed above, we want to define *productivity* in a way that does not compromise a project's concern with software quality. The interactions between software cost and the various software qualities (reliability, ease of use, ease of modification, portability, efficiency, etc.) are quite complex—as are the interactions between the various qualities themselves. Overall, though, there are two primary situations which create significant interactions between software costs and qualities:

(1) A project can reduce software development costs at the expense of quality but only in ways that increase operational and life-cycle costs.

(2) A project can simultaneously reduce software costs and improve software quality by intelligent and cost-effective use of modern software techniques.

One example of situation 1 was provided by a software project experiment in which several teams were asked to develop a program to perform the same function, but each team was asked to optimize a different objective. Almost uniformly, each team finished first on the objective they were asked to optimize, and fell behind on the other objectives. In particular, the team asked to minimize effort finished with the smallest effort to complete the program, but also finished last in program clarity, second to last in program size and required storage, and third to last in output clarity.

Another example is provided by the Cocomo database of 63 development projects and 24 evolution or maintenance projects.[1] This analysis showed that if the effects of other factors such as personnel, use of tools, and modern programming practices were held constant, then the cost to develop reliability-critical software was almost twice the cost of developing minimally reliable software. However, the trend was reversed in the maintenance projects; low-reliability software required considerably more budget to maintain than high-reliability software. Thus, there is a "value of quality," which makes it generally undesirable in the long run to reduce development cost at the expense of quality.

Certainly, though, if we want better software quality at a reasonable cost, we are not going to hold constant our use of tools, modern programming practices, and better people. This leads to situation 2, in which many organizations have been able to achieve simultaneous improvements in both software quality and productivity. For example, the extensive Guide, Inc., survey of about 800 user installations found that the four most strongly experienced effects of using modern programming practices were code quality, early error detection, programmer productivity, and maintenance time or cost. Also, the Cocomo life-cycle data analysis indicated that the use of modern programming practices had a strong positive impact on development productivity but an even stronger positive impact on maintenance productivity.

However, getting the right mix of the various qualities (reliability, efficiency, ease of use, ease of change, etc.) can be a very complex job. Several studies have explored these qualities and their interactions. Also, several new approaches have had some success in providing methods for reconciling and managing multiple quality objectives, such as Gilb's design by objectives and the Goals approach (Boehm,[1] Chapter 3). For pointers to additional information on these and other topics covered in this article, see the "Further Reading" box on pp. 54-55.

Metrics: The current bottom line. The current bottom line for most organizations is that delivered source instructions per project man-month (DSI/MM) is a more practical productivity metric than the currently available alternatives. To use DSI/MM effectively, though, it is important to establish a number of measurement standards and interpretation guidelines, including

- objective, well-understood counting rules defining which project-related man-months are included in MM;
- objective, well-understood counting rules for source instructions;
- a definition of *delivered* in terms of compliance with a set of software quality standards;
- definition and tracking of the language level and extent of reuse of source instructions, along with interpretation guidelines encouraging the use of VHLLs, HOLs, and reused software.

Examples of such definitions are given by Boehm[1] and by Jones.[2]

In addition, because new metrics such as function points have been successful in some areas, many organizations are also experimenting with their use, refinement, and extension to other areas.

Analyzing software productivity

We can consider two primary ways of analyzing software productivity:

(1) The "black-box" or influence-function approach, which performs comparative analyses on the overall results of a number of entire software projects, and which tries to characterize the overall effect on software productivity of such factors as team objectives, methodological approach, hardware constraints, turnaround time, or personnel experience and capability.

(2) The "glass-box" or cost-distribution approach, which analyzes one or more software projects to compare their internal distribution between such costs as labor and capital, code and documentation, development and maintenance, and other cost distributions by phase or activity.

Here, we will concentrate on two representative approaches: the black-box productivity range and the glass-box value-chain.

Software productivity ranges. Most software cost estimation models incorporate a number of software cost driver factors: attributes of a software project or product that affect the project's productivity in (appropriately defined) DSI/MM. A significant feature of some of these models is the productivity range for a software cost driver: the relative multiplicative amount by which that cost driver can influence the software project cost estimated by the model. An example of a set of recently updated productivity ranges for the Cocomo models is shown in Figure 3.

These productivity ranges show the relative leverage of each factor on one's ability to reduce the amount of effort required to develop a software product. For example, assuming all the other factors are held constant, developing a software product in an unfamiliar programming language will

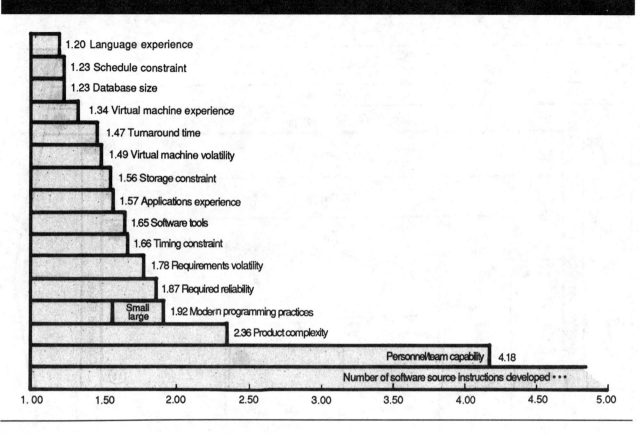

Figure 3. Cocomo software life-cycle productivity ranges, 1985.

typically require about 20 percent more man-months than using a very familiar language. Similarly, developing a product with a mediocre (15th-percentile) team of people will typically require over four times as many man-months as with a 90th-percentile team of people. The open-ended bar at the bottom of Figure 3 indicates that the number of man-months required to develop a software product increases without bound as one increases the number of instructions developed.

Some initial top-level implications of the productivity ranges are summarized as follows; more detailed implications will be discussed in "Improving software productivity" later in this article.

• *Number of source instructions.* The most significant influence on software costs is the number of source instructions one chooses to program. This leads to cost reduction strategies involving the use of fourth-generation languages or reusable components to reduce the number of source instructions developed, the use of prototyping and other requirements anal-

ysis techniques to ensure that unnecessary functions are not developed, and the use of already-developed software products.

• *Management of people.* The next most significant influence by far is that of the selection, motivation, and management of the people involved in the software process. In particular, employing the best people possible is usually a bargain, because the productivity range for people usually is much wider than the range of people's salaries.

• *Fixed features of the product.* Some of the factors, such as product complexity, required reliability, and database size, are largely fixed features of the software product and not management controllables. Even here, though, appreciable savings can be achieved by reducing unnecessary complexity and by focusing on appropriate life-cycle cost-reliability trade-offs as discussed in the preceding section.

• *Other, management-controllable factors.* The other cost driver factors are generally management controllables:

requirements volatility, hardware speed and storage constraints, use of software tools and modern programming practices, and so on can be directly factored into a productivity improvement effort.

Some primary productivity improvement strategies involving these cost driver variables are described later. See Boehm,[1] Chapter 33, for a discussion of each cost driver and Boehm et al.[3] for an example of their successful application to an integrated software productivity improvement program.

The software product value chain. The value chain, developed by Porter and his associates at the Harvard Business School,[4] is a useful method of understanding and controlling the costs involved in a wide variety of organizational enterprises. It identifies a canonical set of cost sources or value activities, representing the basic activities an organization can choose from to create added value for its products. Figure 4 shows a value chain for software development representative of

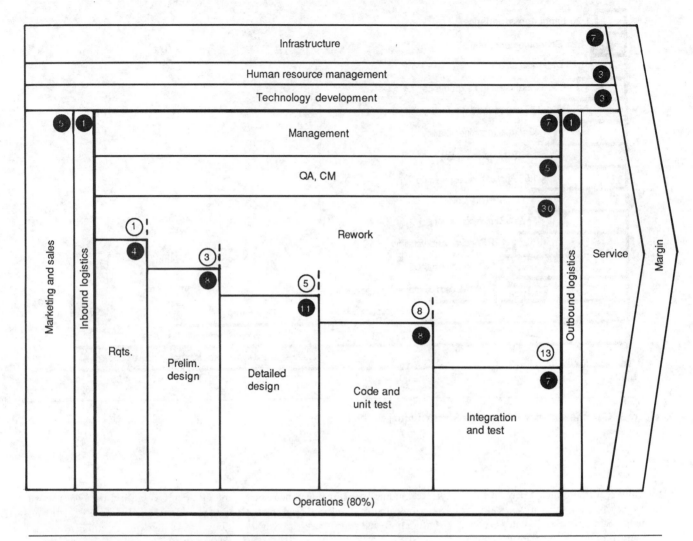

Figure 4. Typical software development value chain.

experience at TRW. Definitions and explanations of the component value activities are given by Porter.[4]

For software the largest single value chain element is Operations, which covers activities associated with transforming inputs into the final product form and typically involves roughly four-fifths of the total development outlay. In such a case, the value chain analysis involves breaking up a large component into constituent activities. Figure 4 shows such a breakup of Operations into management (7 percent), quality assurance and configuration management (5 percent), and the distribution of technical effort among the

various development phases. This phase breakdown also covers the cost sources due to rework. Thus, for example, of the 20 percent overall cost of the technical effort during the integration and test phase, 13 percent is devoted to activities required to rework deficiencies in or reorientations of the requirements, design, code, or documentation; the other 7 percent represents the amount of effort required to run tests, perform integration functions, and complete documentation even if no problems were detected in the process.

For simplicity, the service and margin components of the value chain have not

been assigned numerical values. "Margin" basically represents profits; "service" represents postdevelopment software support activities, often called "maintenance" but more properly called "evolution." Evolution costs are typically 70 percent of software life-cycle costs, but since some initial analyses have indicated that the detailed value chain distribution for evolution costs is not markedly different from the distribution of development costs in Figure 4, we will use Figure 4 to represent the distribution of software life-cycle costs.

The primary implication of the software development value chain is that the Operations component is the key to significant improvements. Not only is it the major source of software costs, but also most of the remaining components such as human resources will scale down in a manner roughly proportional to the scaling down of Operations cost.

Another major characteristic of the value chain is that virtually all of the components are still highly labor-intensive. Thus, there are significant opportunities for providing automated aids to make these activities more efficient and capital-intensive. Further, it implies that human resource and management activities aimed at *getting the best from people* have much higher leverage than their 3 percent and 7 percent investment levels indicate.

The breakdown of the Operations component indicates that the leading strategies for cost savings in software development involve

- *making individual steps more efficient* via such capabilities as automated aids to software design analysis or testing;
- *eliminating steps* via such capabilities as automatic programming or automatic quality assurance;
- *eliminating rework* via early error detection or via such capabilities as rapid prototyping to avoid later requirements rework.

In addition, further major cost savings can be achieved by reducing the total number of elementary operations steps by developing products requiring the creation of fewer lines of code. This has the effect of reducing the overall size of the value chain itself. This source of savings breaks down into two main options:

- *building simpler products* by applying more insight to front-end activities such as prototyping or risk management;
- *reusing software components* via such capabilities as fourth-generation languages or component libraries.

The software productivity improvement opportunity tree. This breakdown of the major sources of software cost savings leads to the software productivity improvement opportunity tree shown in Figure 5. This hierarchical breakdown helps us to understand how to fit the various attractive productivity options into an overall integrated software productivity improvement strategy. The next section will discuss each of these major options in turn.

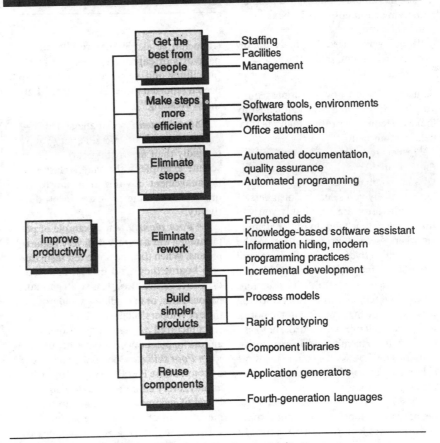

Figure 5. Software productivity improvement opportunity tree.

Improving software productivity

Following the organization of the software productivity opportunity tree, we will cover the following primary options for improving software productivity: (1) getting the best from people, (2) making steps more efficient, (3) eliminating steps, (4) eliminating rework, (5) building simpler products, and (6) reusing components.

Getting the best from people. As indicated in the opportunity tree, there are three primary options available for getting the best from people: staffing, facilities, and management.

Staffing. The productivity ranges in Figure 3 show a factor of 4.18 in productivity difference due to personnel/team capability and a combined factor of 2.52 for relative experience with the applica-

tions area, computer system or virtual machine, and programming language. Similar ranges have been determined by other studies such as the IBM productivity analysis (see Walston and Felix[5]).

Thus, if you want to increase your project's or organization's software productivity, one of the biggest leverage actions you have at your disposal is to get the best people working for your project or organization and the mediocre people working for someone else. It is worth making a significant effort to get this to happen. But it is remarkable how frequently managers are passive about key staffing decisions and how frequently they go in the opposite direction, saying things like

"I can't afford those high-salary people."

"I can't take a risk on somebody so expensive."

"I can't hire your superstar until your project gets its funds, even though that's only a month away."

"Joe has all these unassigned people charging to standby, and I have to help him out."

"I can't wait. I need somebody to show some progress on this task by next week."

Sometimes the latter two situations require you to respond, but you can generally make it a temporary rather than a permanent commitment.

The other, equally important, side of the staffing coin involves committing yourself to phase out misfits. No matter how carefully you select the members of your software team, inevitably you will find some people who do not contribute anywhere near their fair share to the team's objectives, even after several attempts to find or prepare a suitable role for them on the team. In such a situation, you will be tempted to postpone dealing with the problem, to profess not to notice it, to smooth it over with words, or to ask the other team members to do extra tasks. This may be the easy way out in the short run, but invariably it produces unhealthy results in the long run.

Phasing people out isn't easy. But if you devote enough time, thought, and sympathy to the problem, you can often create a situation in which the phaseout becomes a positive rather than a negative experience, and the person concerned finds a new line of work which suits him or her much better than a group-oriented software project. If this doesn't work, and you are left with a definite misfit, don't back away from the problem. Get rid of the misfit as quickly as possible.

Facilities. Given that software development and evolution are extremely labor-intensive activities, a great deal of productivity leverage can be gained by making software production a more capital-intensive activity. Typically, capital investment per software worker has been little different from the $2000-$3000 per person typical of office workers in general. However, a number of organizations such as Xerox, TRW, IBM, and Bell Laboratories have indicated that significantly higher investments (in the $10,000-$30,000 per person range) have been more than recaptured in improved software productivity.

Providing software personnel with private offices is another cost-effective measure, leading to productivity gains of roughly 11 percent at IBM-Santa Teresa (see Jones[2]) and 8 percent at TRW

(Boehm et al.[3]). Similar results on the payoffs of capital investments in better facilities and support capabilities have been reported in other studies (see "Further Reading").

Management. Poor management can decrease software productivity more rapidly than any other factor. Here are some examples of the major classes of management activities that most frequently contribute to losses in productivity:

• *Poor planning.* An example of poor planning was a project with very vague test plans. When the 20-person test team came on board, they found no test data, test drivers, test facilities, test strategies and procedures, or test readiness standards for the developers' code. As a result, the project incurred a 30 percent overrun in cost and a 40 percent overrun in schedule.

• *Poor skill mix.* Poor skill mix is often a result of the Peter Principle: "In a hierarchy, every employee tends to rise to his level of incompetence." The most common realization of the Peter Principle in software engineering is the practice of "advancing" good programmers by promoting them into management. Sometimes this works well, but overall it produces more mismatches, frustration, and damaged careers in software engineering than in other fields. This point has been realized by a number of organizations, which have instituted dual or multiple career paths culminating in "superprogrammer" or "superanalyst" as well as "supermanager."

• *Premature staffing.* An example of premature staffing is the following quotation from a small-project manager: "At an early stage in the design, I was made the project manager and given three trainees to help out on the project. My biggest mistake was to burn up half of my time and the other senior designer's time trying to keep the trainees busy. As a result, we left big holes in the design which killed us in the end." A related source of decreased productivity is the attempt to speed up a project by adding more people, in contradiction to Brooks's law: "Adding more people to a late software project will make it later."

• *Premature coding.* An example of premature coding is the WISCA syndrome, where WISCA stands for "Why

isn't Sam coding anything?" A counterpart is the statement, "We'd better hurry up and start coding, because we're going to have a lot of debugging to do." The most important management property of an efficient multiperson software development is the achievement of a set of thorough, validated, and stable module interface specifications, which allow the developers to operate in parallel without being swamped by interpersonal communications overhead. As early as 1961, software managers were realizing that "every sheet of accurate interface definition is, quite literally, worth its weight in gold."

• *Poor reward structure.* An example of poor reward structure is the organization which gives its top performers six percent raises and its mediocre performers five percent raises. Eventually, the good people get frustrated and leave. A great deal can be done by creative application of other rewards, such as special bonuses, grade-level promotions, travel and special courses, and recognition programs for top performers.

Making steps more efficient. The value chain in Figure 4 provides a basic set of insights on the relative productivity leverage involved in eliminating or improving the efficiency of the various steps in the software process. For example, since the process of performing code and unit test functions consumes only eight percent of the software life-cycle dollar, the productivity impact of tools to eliminate code and unit test or to make it more efficient will not exceed eight percent (unless the tools also eliminate other classes of effort, such as rework in later phases).

The primary leverage factor in making the existing software process steps more efficient is the use of software tools to automate the current repetitive and labor-intensive portions of each step.

Experience to date suggests that software tools are much more effective if they are part of an integrated project support environment (IPSE). The primary features that distinguish an IPSE from an ad hoc collection of tools are

• a set of common assumptions about the software process model being supported by the tools (or, more strongly, a particular software development method being supported by the tools);

• an integrated project master database or persistent object base serving as a unified repository of the technical and management entities created during the software process, along with their various versions, attributes, and relationships;

- support of the entire range of users and activities involved in the software project, not just of programmers developing code;
- a unified user interface providing easy and natural ways for various classes of project personnel (expert programmers, novice librarians, secretaries, managers, planning and control personnel, etc.) to draw on the tools in the IPSE;
- a critical-mass ensemble of tools, covering significant portions of software project activities;
- a computer communication architecture facilitating user access to data and resources in the IPSE.

Eliminating steps. A good many automated aids go beyond simply making steps more efficient, to the point of fully eliminating previous manual steps. If we compare software development today with its counterpart in the 1950's, we see that assemblers and compilers are excellent examples of ways to vastly improve productivity by eliminating steps. More recent examples are process construction systems, software standards checkers and other quality assurance functions, and requirements and design consistency checkers.

More ambitious efforts to eliminate steps involve the automation of the entire programming process by providing capabilities which operate directly on a set of software specifications to automatically generate computer programs. There are two major branches to this approach: domain-specific and domain-independent automatic programming.

The domain-specific approach gains advantages by capitalizing on domain knowledge in transforming specifications into programs and in constraining the universe of programming discourse to a relatively smaller domain. In the limit, one reaches the boundary with fourth-generation languages such as Visicalc, which are excellent automatic programming systems within a very narrow domain and relatively ineffective outside that domain.

The domain-independent approach offers a much broader payoff in the long run but has more difficulty in achieving efficient implementations of larger-scale programs.

Eliminating rework. The strongest opportunity identified by the value chain analysis in Figure 4 is the 30 percent productivity leverage available through eliminating rework. Actually, the leverage factor is probably more like 50 percent over the life cycle, since most of the sources of rework savings (e.g., modern programming practices and rapid prototyping) will reduce the incidence of current postdevelopment software modifications (e.g., to fix residual errors or to finally get the requirements right) as well as making the modifications more efficient.

The major rework opportunity areas identified in the opportunity tree in Figure 5 are front-end aids; knowledge-based software assistants; information hiding and modern programming practices, incremental development, improved process models, and rapid prototyping. (In addition, reusing components can significantly reduce rework.)

Front-end aids. Software computer-aided design and requirements analysis tools can eliminate a great deal of rework through better visualization of software requirements and design specification, more formal and unambiguous specifications, automated consistency and completeness checking, and automated traceability of requirements to design. Probably the most extensive of these systems is the Distributed Computing Design System, which includes a system specification language, a software requirements specification language, a distributed-system design language, and a module description language. A number of commercial front-end aids are also available, such as ISDOS/PSL-PSA, SADT, CASE, Excelerator, IDE, Cadre, and Ada Graph. Some complementary front-end aids include rapid simulation aids such as RSA and executable specification aids such as Paisley.

Knowledge-based software assistants. In many application areas, the artificial intelligence community is finding that total automation of knowledge-intensive functions falls in the "currently too hard" category but that combinations of conventional and AI techniques may be used to provide useful automated assistance to human experts in performing complex tasks. This is the primary motivation for the knowledge-based software assistant (KBSA) concept, as described by Green et al.[6]

The primary benefit of a KBSA will be the elimination of much of the rework currently experienced on software projects due to the belated appreciation that a previous programming or project decision was inappropriate. A number of prototype KBSAs are currently under development in such areas as acquisition management, configuration management, problem report tracking, algorithm selection, data structuring, choice of reusable components, and project planning and control.

Information hiding and other modern programming practices. In general, modern programming practices (MPPs) such as early verification and validation, modular design, top-down development, structured programming, walk-throughs or inspections, and software quality standards achieve their productivity leverage through avoidance of rework. As indicated in Figure 3, MPPs provide a productivity range of 1.51 during development and up to 1.92 for the life cycle of a large software product.

A particularly powerful technique for eliminating rework is the information-hiding approach developed by Parnas and applied in the US Navy A-7 project (Parnas, Clements, and Weiss.[7] This approach minimizes rework by hiding implementation decisions within modules; thus minimizing the ripple effects usually encountered when software implementation decisions need to be changed. The information-hiding approach can be particularly effective in eliminating rework during software evolution, by identifying the portions of the software most likely to undergo change (characteristics of workstations, input data formats, etc.) and hiding these sources of evolutionary change within modules.

As an example, the current requirements may specify that a particular user workstation or terminal is to be used. By also identifying in the requirements the terminal characteristics most likely to change (line width, character set, access protocols, etc.), the designers can hide these details of the terminal inside a terminal-handler module, thus isolating the remainder of the software from the usual ripple effects accompanying a change in the terminal characteristics.

This approach revolutionizes the concept of a requirements specification. Rather than being just a snapshot of a sys-

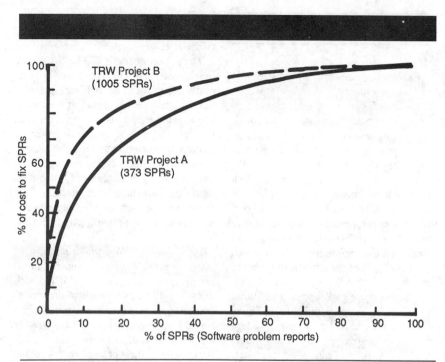

Figure 6. Rework costs are concentrated in a few high-risk items.

tem's software requirements at a single point in time, the requirements specification must also identify the most likely requirements evolution paths the system will experience. This also means that a design validation activity should address not just traceability to the current requirements snapshot but also how well the design accommodates the expected directions of change.

Modern programming practices and Ada. A major initiative to embody modern programming practices and information hiding concepts into standard programming practice has been the US Department of Defense's development of the programming language Ada. Ada has constructs such as packages that support modularity, information hiding, and reuse; strong typing that avoids rework due to common programming errors; structured programming constructs; and a number of other advanced features addressing such issues as concurrency, exception handling, and generic programs. Getting all of these features to work together has strained the state of the art in compiler development, but currently a number of effective Ada compilers are available.

Assessing the likely productivity impact of Ada is difficult because the Ada concept is also intended to include an overall programming and project environment and because most Ada capabilities are not yet fully mature. However, several studies have estimated the comparative life-cycle productivity of an Ada project and a conventional HOL project as a function of time, using as parameters the cost driver variables and productivity ranges of models such as Cocomo. The typical result of these studies has indicated an initial added cost of 12-30 percent for initial uses of Ada, a breakeven point in the 1988-89 time frame, and a long-range savings of 40-50 percent for a fully mature Ada support environment and development staff.

Improved process models. The leading current model of the software process, the waterfall model,[1] tends to focus a software project toward the production of a series of documents (system specification, software requirements specification, top-level design document, detailed design document). When used in concert with thorough front-end validation activities, the waterfall approach is very effective in reducing rework. But, frequently, the document-driven interpretation of the

waterfall model pushes a project toward more rapid production of documents rather than toward thinking through critical issues. For example, a recently proposed government software progress reporting scheme focuses on the number of unresolved elements in the software requirements and design specifications. If a project manager wants to show rapid progress, he is actually tempted to work on resolving the easy elements rather than the hard ones or to complete the document quickly by putting in arbitrary rather than well-reasoned specifications.

An important point in this regard is that rework instances tend to follow a Pareto distribution: 80 percent of the rework costs typically result from 20 percent of the problems. Figure 6 shows some typical distributions from recent TRW software projects; similar trends have been indicated in other studies. The major implication of this distribution is that software verification and validation activities should focus on identifying and eliminating the specific high-risk problems to be encountered by a software project, rather than spreading the early problem elimination effort uniformly across trivial and severe problems. Even more strongly, this implies that a risk-driven approach to the software life cycle such as the spiral model (see Boehm[8]) is preferable to a more document-driven model such as the traditional waterfall model. The spiral model organizes the software development process into a sequence of increasingly detailed definition cycles. The amount of emphasis in each cycle on documentation, simulation, prototyping, or other definition activities is determined by the relative risk of not resolving key definition issues. Thus, the spiral model focuses effort on identification and early resolution on the 20 percent of the problems that will otherwise account for 80 percent of the rework costs.

Rapid prototyping. One of the major sources of rework found in the data represented by Figure 4 were portions of a software specification based on poorly understood mission or user interface requirements. A primary example is the user who says, "I can't tell you exactly what I want, but I'll know it when I see it." A number of rapid prototyping aids have become available to improve this situation. A good many are based on the interpretive-execution capabilities of advanced artificial intelligence environments such as Interlisp. Others are based on two-phase interactive-graphics composition and execution capabilities using conventional HOLs. Other rapid prototyping systems provide risk reduction capabilities for rapid assessment of real-time performance issues or distributed data processing issues.

Building simpler products. As indicated in Figure 3, the largest productivity range available to the software developer comes from the number of instructions one chooses to develop. There are two primary options here: one is building simpler products; the other is reusing software components.

Besides their contribution to eliminating rework, the last two approaches involving rapid prototyping and improved software process models can also be very effective in improving bottom-line productivity by building simpler products to eliminate software gold plating: extra software that not only consumes extra effort but also reduces the conceptual integrity of the product.

For example, a recent seven-project experiment comparing a specification-oriented approach and a prototyping-oriented approach to the development of small-user-intensive application software products (see Boehm, Gray, and Seewaldt[9]) is illustrated in Figure 7. The experiment found primarily that

- on the average ($\bar{P}$ vs $\bar{S}$ in Figure 7), both approaches resulted in roughly equivalent productivity in delivered source instructions per man-hour (DSI/MH);
- the prototyping projects developed products with roughly equivalent performance but requiring roughly 40 percent fewer DSI and 40 percent fewer man-hours;
- the specifying projects had less difficulty in debugging and integration due to their development of good interface specifications.

The final point indicates that prototypes are not a panacea for all problems and that specifications are still very important. However, one of the telling insights in this experiment was the comment of one of the participants using the specification approach: "Words are cheap." During the specification phase, it is all too easy to add gold-plating functions to the product specification, without a good understanding of their effect on the product's conceptual integrity or the project's required effort. As Heckel[10] writes:

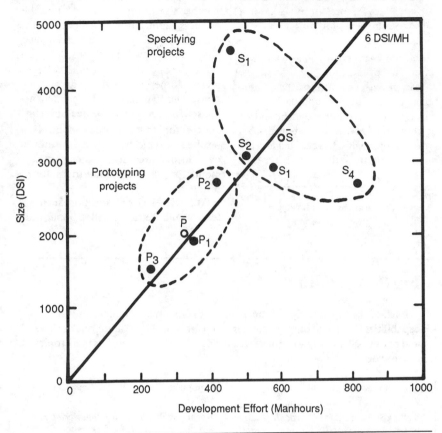

Figure 7. Prototyping versus specifying experiment: size and effort comparisons.

Most programmers . . . defend their use of a software feature by saying, "You don't have to use it if you don't want to, so what harm can it do?" It can do a great deal of harm. The user might spend time trying to understand the feature, only to decide it isn't needed, or he may accidentally use the feature and not know what has happened or how to get out of the mistake. If a feature is inconsistent with the rest of the user interface, the user might draw false conclusions about the other commands. The feature must be documented, which makes the user's manual thicker. The cumulative effect of such features is to overwhelm the user and obscure communication with your program. . . .

A further discussion of typical sources of software gold plating and an approach for evaluating potential gold-plating features is provided by Boehm,[1] Chapter 11.

Some of the newer software process models stimulate the development of simpler products. One of the difficulties of the traditional waterfall model is that its specification-driven approach can frequently lead one along the "Words are cheap" road toward gold-plated products, as discussed above. A frequent experience in the specification of large systems is that users with little feel for a computer system will overspecify on functionality and performance just to make sure the system will include what they need.

The evolutionary development model (see McCracken and Jackson[11]) emphasizes the use of prototyping capabilities to converge on the necessary or high-leverage software product features essential to the user's mission. The related transformational model (see Balzer, Cheatham, and Green[12]) shortcuts the problem by providing (where available) a direct transformation from specification to executing code, thus supporting both a specification-based and an evolutionary-development approach. The spiral model discussed above addresses the gold-plating problem by focusing on a continuing determination of users' mission objectives and a continuing cost-benefit analysis of candidate software product features in terms of their contribution to mission objectives.

Reusing components. Another key to improving productivity by writing less code is the reuse of existing software components. The simplest approach in this direction involves the development and use of libraries of software components.* A great deal of progress has been made in this direction, particularly in such areas as

---

*There is a good deal of productivity leverage in reusing software specifications, designs, and plans, as well as code.

---

mathematical and statistical routines and operating-system-related utilities. Further progress is possible via similar capabilities in user application areas. For example, Raytheon's library system of reusable business application components has achieved typical figures of 60 percent reusable code for new applications, and typical cost savings of 10 percent in the design phase, 50 percent in the code and test phase, and 60 percent in the maintenance phase. Toshiba's system of reusable components for industrial process control has resulted in typical productivity rates of over 2000 source instructions per manmonth for high-quality industrial software products.

At this level of sophistication, such systems would better be called application

generators, rather than component libraries, because they have addressed several system-oriented component compatibility issues such as component interface conventions, data structuring, and program control and error handling conventions. Similar characteristics have made Unix a strong foundation for developing application generators.

One can proceed even further in this direction to create a very high level language or fourth-generation language (4GL) by adding a language for specifying desired applications and a set of capabilities for interpreting user specifications, configuring the appropriate set of components, and executing the resulting program. Currently, the most fertile areas for 4GLs are spreadsheet calculators (Visicalc,

---

Further reading

Each of the topics in this article involves a fascinating complex of ideas and capabilities that could only be summarized. Listed below are additional articles and books that amplify some of its specific points or cover one of its main topics in more detail.

Software cost drivers and trends

Boehm, B.W., "Understanding and Controlling Software Costs," *Proc. IFIP Congress 1986,* North Holland, 1986, pp.703-714. An updated version to appear in *IEEE Trans. Software Engineering,* 1987.

Boehm, B.W., *Software Engineering Economics,* Prentice-Hall, Englewood Cliffs, N.J., 1981.

Brooks, F.P., "No Silver Bullet—Essence and Accidents of Software Engineering," *Proc. IFIP Congress 1986,* North Holland, 1986, pp. 1069-1076. Also in *Computer,* Apr. 1987, pp. 10-19.

DeMarco, T., *Controlling Software Projects,* Yourdon, New York, 1982.

Jones, T.C., "Demographic and Technical Trends in the Computing Industry," Software Productivity Research, Inc., July 1983.

Jones, T.C., *Programming Productivity,* McGraw-Hill, New York, 1986.

Walston, C.E., and C.P. Felix, "A Method of Programming Measurement and Estimation," *IBM Systems J.,* Vol. 16, No. 1, 1977, pp. 54-73.

Wegner, P., "Capital-Intensive Software Technology," *IEEE Software,* Vol. 1, No. 3, July 1984, pp. 7-45.

Software productivity and quality metrics

Basili, V., *Tutorial on Models and Metrics for Software Management and Engineering,*

Computer Society Press, Los Alamitos, Calif., 1980.

Boehm, B.W., *Software Engineering Economics,* Prentice-Hall, Englewood Cliffs, N.J., 1981.

Boehm, B.W., et al., *Characteristics of Software Quality,* North Holland, 1978.

Bowen, T.P., G.B. Wigle, and J.T. Tsai, "Specification of Software Quality Attributes," RADC-TR-85-37 (3 vol.), Feb. 1985.

Conte, S.D., H. Dunsmore, and V. Shen, *Software Engineering Metrics and Models,* Benjamin/Cummings, 1986.

DeMarco, T., *Controlling Software Projects,* Yourdon, New York, 1982.

Frewin, E., et al., "Quality Measurement and Modeling—State of the Art Report," ESPRIT Report REQUEST/STC-gdf/001/51/QL-RP/00.7, July, 1985.

Gilb, T., *Principles of Software Engineering Management*, Addison-Wesley, 1987.

Grady, R., and D. Caswell, *Software Metrics: Establishing a Company-Wide Program,* Prentice-Hall, 1987.

"GUIDE Survey of New Programming Technologies," *GUIDE 1979 Proceedings,* Guide, Inc., 1979, pp. 306-308.

Halstead, M.H., *Elements of Software Science,* Elsevier, New York, 1977.

Jones, T.C., *Programming Productivity,* McGraw-Hill, New York, 1986.

McCabe, T.J., "A Complexity Measure," *IEEE Trans. Software Engineering,* Dec. 1976, pp. 308-320.

Thadhani, A.J., "Factors Affecting Programmer Productivity During Application Development," *IBM Systems J.,* Vol. 23, Nov. 1984, pp. 19-35.

Weinberg, G.M., and E.L. Schulman, "Goals and Performance in Computer Programming," *Human Factors,* Vol. 16, No. 1, 1974, pp. 70-77.

Getting the best from people

Brooks, F.P., *The Mythical Man-Month,* Addison-Wesley, Reading, Mass., 1975.

Couger, J.D., and R.A. Zawacki, *Motivating and Managing Computer Personnel,* John Wiley, New York, 1980.

Curtis, B., *Human Factors in Software Development*, IEEE Cat. No. EHO 185-9, 1981.

DeMarco, T., *Controlling Software Projects,* Yourdon, New York, 1982.

DeMarco, T, and T. Lister, "Programmer Performance and the Effects of the Workplace," *Proc. Eighth Int'l Conf. Software Engineering,* Aug. 1985, pp. 268-272.

Hosier, W.A., "Pitfalls and Safeguards in Real-Time Digital Systems with Emphasis on Programming," *IRE Trans. Engineering Management,* June 1961, pp. 99-115.

Manley, J.H., "Software Engineering Provisioning Process," *Proc. Eighth Int'l Conf. Software Engineering,* Aug. 1985, pp. 273-284.

Metzger, P.J., *Managing a Programming Project,* 2nd ed., Prentice-Hall, Englewood Cliffs, N.J., 1981.

Weinberg, G.M., *The Psychology of Computer Programming,* Van Nostrand Reinhold, New York, 1971.

Multiplan, 1-2-3, etc.) and small-business systems typically featuring a DBMS, report generator, database query language, and graphics package (Nomad, Ramis, Focus, ADF, DBase II, etc.).

Some 4GL advocates promise factors of 10 to 100 improvement in productivity from the use of 4GLs. Are such factors achievable?

The best experimental evidence on the productivity leverage of 4GLs is provided by a six-project experiment comparing the use of a third-generation programming language (Cobol) and a fourth-generation language (Focus) on a mix of small-business-application projects involving both experts and beginners developing both simple and complex applications (see Harel and McLean[13]). Its primary findings, illustrated in Figure 8, are summarized as follows:

- On an overall average (the $\overline{C}$ and the $\overline{F}$ in Figure 8), the fourth-generation approach produced equivalent products to the third-generation approach, with about 60 percent fewer DSI and 60 percent fewer man-hours (again with roughly equivalent productivity in DSI/MH).
- From project to project, there was a significant variation in the ratio of third-generation to fourth-generation DSI (0.9:1 to 27:1), man-hours (1.5:1 to 8:1), and DSI/MH (0.5:1 to 5:1).

Although the average Cobol effort was 2.5 times higher than the average Focus effort for the same application, the effect is far from uniform across a spectrum of applications. Thus, it is difficult to predict the 4GL productivity gain for any particular application.

Guimaraes[14] provides further evidence from a survey of 43 organizations that 4GLs reduce personnel costs, reduce user frustration, and more quickly satisfy user information needs within their domain of applicability. On the other hand, the survey found 4GLs extremely inefficient of computer resources and difficult to interface with conventional applications programs. Some major disasters have occurred in attempting to apply purely 4GL solutions to large, high-performance applications such as the New Jersey motor vehicle registration system.[15]

Overall, though, 4GLs offer an

Weinberg, G.M., and E.L. Schulman, "Goals and Performance in Computer Programming," *Human Factors*, Vol. 16, No. 1, 1974, pp. 70-77.

Yourdon, E., *Managing the Structured Techniques*, 3rd ed., Yourdon Press, 1987.

Making steps more efficient

Alford, M.W., "SREM at the Age of Eight: The Distributed Computing Design System," *Computer*, Vol. 18, No. 4, Apr. 1985.

Boehm, B.W., et al., "A Software Development Environment for Improving Productivity," *Computer*, Vol. 17, No. 6, June 1984, pp. 30-44.

Green, C.C., et al., "Report on a Knowledge-Based Software Assistant," USAF/RADC Report RADC-TR-195, Aug. 1983.

Henderson, P., ed., *Proc. Second Conf. Practical Software Development Environments, ACM SIGPLAN Notices*, Dec. 1986.

Houghton, R.C., "Software Development Tools," National Bureau of Standards, NBS Special Report 500-88, 1982.

Sommerville, I., ed., *Software Engineering Environments*, Peter Peregrinus, Ltd., 1987.

Wegner, P., "Capital-Intensive Software Technology," *IEEE Software*, Vol. 1, No. 3, July 1984, pp. 7-45.

Eliminating steps

Barstow, D.R., "Artificial Intelligence and Software Engineering," *Proc. ICSE 9*, IEEE, March 1987.

"Special Issue on Automatic Programming," *IEEE Trans. Software Engineering*, Nov. 1985.

Eliminating rework

Alford, M.W., "SREM at the Age of Eight: The Distributed Computing Design System," *Computer*, Vol. 18, No. 4, Apr. 1985.

Boar, B.H., *Application Prototyping*, John Wiley, New York, 1984.

Boehm, B.W., "A Spiral Model of Software Development and Enhancement," *Proc. IEEE Second Software Process Workshop, ACM Software Engineering Notes*, Aug. 1986.

Boehm, B.W., "Verifying and Validating Software Requirements and Design Specifications," *IEEE Software*, Vol. 1, No. 1, Jan. 1984, pp. 75-88.

Booch, G., *Software Engineering with Ada*, Benjamin/Cummings, 1983.

Mills, H.D., "Structured Programming: Retrospect and Prospect," *IEEE Software*, Nov. 1986, pp. 58-66.

Parnas, D.L., "Designing Software for Ease of Extension and Contraction," *IEEE Trans. Software Engineering*, Mar. 1979, pp. 128-137.

Swinson, G.E., "Workstation-Based Rapid Simulation Aids for Distributed Processing Networks," *Proc. IEEE Simulation Conference*, 1984.

Yourdon, E., *Managing the Structured Techniques*, 3rd ed., Yourdon Press, 1987.

Zave, P., "The Operational Versus the Conventional Approach to Software Development," *Comm. ACM*, Feb. 1984, pp. 104-118.

Zelkowitz, M., and S. Squires, eds., *Proc. ACM Rapid Prototyping Symp.*, ACM, Oct. 1982.

Building simpler products

Agresti, W., *New Paradigms for Software Development*, IEEE Cat. No. EH 0245-1, 1986.

Dowson, M., and J.C. Wileden, eds., *Proc. Second Software Process Workshop, ACM Software Engineering Notes*, Aug. 1986.

Heckel, P., *The Elements of Friendly Software Design*, Warner Books, 1984.

Lehman, M.M., V. Stenning, and C. Potts, eds., *Proc. Software Process Workshop*, IEEE, Feb. 1984.

McCracken, D.D., and M.A. Jackson, "Life Cycle Concept Considered Harmful," *Software Engineering Notes, ACM*, Apr. 1982, pp. 29-32.

Reusing components

B.W. Boehm, *Software Engineering Economics* (Chapter 33), Prentice-Hall, Englewood Cliffs, N.J., 1981.

Jones, T.C., *Programming Productivity*, McGraw-Hill, New York, 1986.

Freeman, P., *Software Reusability*, IEEE Cat. No. EH0256-8, 1987.

Horowitz, E., A. Kemper, and B. Narasimhan, "A Survey of Application Generators," *IEEE Software*, Jan. 1985, pp. 40-54.

Lanergan, R.G., and C.A. Grasso, "Software Engineering with Reusable Design and Code," *IEEE Trans. Software Engineering*, Sept. 1984, pp. 498-501.

Matsumoto, Y., "Management of Industrial Software Production," *Computer*, Vol. 17, No. 2, Feb. 1984, pp. 59-70.

"Special Issue on Reusability in Programming," *IEEE Trans. Software Engineering*, Sept. 1984.

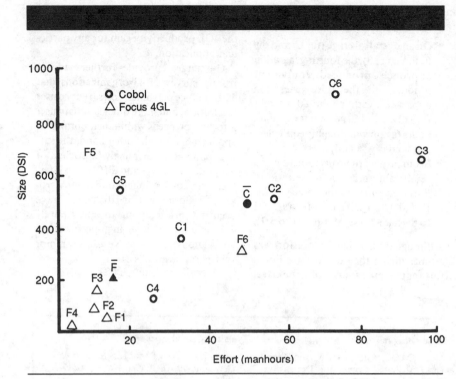

Figure 8. Fourth-generation-language experiment: size and effort comparisons.

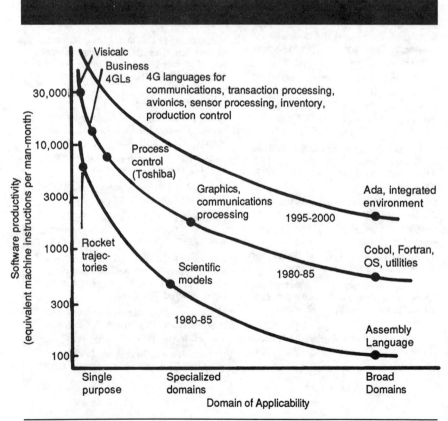

Figure 9. Software technology and productivity trends.

extremely attractive option for significantly improving software productivity, and attempts are underway to create 4GL capabilities for other application areas. Short of a 4GL capability, the other more limited approaches to reusability such as component libraries and application generators can generate near-term cost savings and serve as a foundation for more ambitious 4GL capabilities in the long run.

Software productivity trends

It is difficult to summarize such a welter of issues as those involved in improving software productivity. Figure 9 provides at least a partial summary of some of the key leverage areas. It shows our typical overall progress in improving software productivity between the 1960-65 era and the 1980-85 era, in terms of equivalent machine instructions per man-month, and it projects our potential progress by the 1995-2000 era.

The horizontal dimension in Figure 9 is a qualitative scale indicating the breadth of the domain of applicability of a given software productivity capability. It reflects the fact that our most impressive software productivity achievements to date have been made by exploiting our knowledge of particular application domains.

Thus, for example, even in the early 1960's, when most large, general-purpose systems were being developed in assembly language at a typical rate of 100 delivered machine instructions per man-month (DMI/MM), there were application generators providing productivity rates of 3000 DMI/MM and higher. Several examples were available in the area of rocket trajectory computation, where systems such as Rocket (see Boehm[16]) provided a library of reusable components (for aerodynamics, propulsion, guidance and control, earth models, etc.) and specialized extensions of Fortran for users to specify how to link components together to simulate their desired multistage rocket vehicle and flight program.

By the early 1980's, we had progressed in the power and range of domain-specific application generators, so that even higher productivity figures were being achieved in such a variety of domains as spreadsheet calculations (30,000 DMI/MM and up), industrial process control, and business fourth-generation languages. At the same time, we had extended our general-purpose capabilities from assembly lan-

COMPUTER

guage and primitive batch operating systems to HOLs with collections of tools providing on the order of 600 DMI/MM for large, broad-domain applications. According to Brooks,[17] those capabilities address the elimination of the "accidental" difficulties in developing software. The domain-specific capabilities shown on the left side of Figure 9 are aimed at reducing the "essential" portion of software acquisition costs.

Thus, for the 1995-2000 time frame, we can see that two major classes of opportunities for improving software productivity exist: providing better support systems for broad-domain applications, involving fully integrated methods, environments, and modern programming languages such as Ada; and extending the number and size of the domains for which we can use domain-specific fourth-generation languages and application generators. Examples of promising future application domains include communications processing, transaction processing, sensor data processing, broader process control areas such as avionics and job shop production control, and broader DBMS-oriented areas such as inventory control and production management.

We have seen that the magnitude and continuing growth of software costs create a strong need to improve software productivity. This implies a need to carefully define software productivity, and since our current productivity metrics are not fully satisfactory, to work on better ones. It also implies a need to develop capabilities that improve not only software productivity but also software quality.

The analyses of software productivity ranges and the software value chain led to the definition of a software productivity opportunity tree which identifies the major opportunity areas for improving productivity:

- Getting the best from people via better management, staffing, incentives, and work environments.
- Developing and using integrated project support environments, which automate portions of the development and evolution process and make them more efficient.
- Eliminating rework via better front-end aids, risk management, prototyping, incremental development, and modern programming practices, particularly information hiding.

- Writing less code by reusing software components, developing and using application generators and fourth-generation languages, and avoiding software gold plating.

As a final conclusion, one point deserves particular emphasis. In pursuing improvements in software productivity, we need to be careful not to confuse means with ends. Improved software productivity is not an end in itself; it is a means of helping people better expand their capabilities to deal with information and to make decisions. Often, helping people to do this will involve us in activities (for example, spending two weeks helping someone find an effective nonsoftware solution to a problem) that don't add points to our software productivity scoreboard. At such times we need to recall that the software productivity scoreboard is just one of the many ways we have to gauge our progress toward better use of computers to serve people. □

Acknowledgments

I would like to thank Frank Belz, Phil Papaccio, Lolo Penedo, and George Spadaro of TRW, and Bill Riddle of the Software Productivity Consortium, for substantial assistance in refining earlier versions of this article, and Bruce Shriver and the *Computer* reviewers for a particularly thorough and helpful job.

References

1. B.W. Boehm, *Software Engineering Economics,* Prentice-Hall, Englewood Cliffs, N.J., 1981.
2. T.C. Jones, *Programming Productivity,* McGraw-Hill, New York, 1986.
3. B.W. Boehm et al., "A Software Development Environment for Improving Productivity," *Computer,* Vol. 17, No. 6, June 1984, pp. 30-44.
4. M.E. Porter, *Competitive Advantage,* Free Press, New York, 1985.
5. C.E. Walston and C.P. Felix, "A Method of Programming Measurement and Estimation," *IBM Systems J.,* Vol. 16, No. 1, 1977, pp. 54-73.
6. C.C. Green et al., "Report on a Knowledge-Based Software Assistant," USAF/RADC Report RADC-TR-195, Aug. 1983.
7. D.L. Parnas, P.C. Clements, and D.M. Weiss, "The Modular Structure of Complex Systems," *IEEE Trans. Software Engineering,* Mar. 1985, pp. 259-266.
8. B.W. Boehm, "A Spiral Model of Software Development and Enhancement," *Proc. IEEE Second Software Process Workshop, ACM Software Engineering Notes,* Aug. 1986.
9. B.W. Boehm, T.E. Gray, and T. Seewaldt, "Prototyping vs. Specifying: A Multi-Project Experiment," *IEEE Trans. Software Engineering,* May 1984, pp. 133-145.
10. P. Heckel, *The Elements of Friendly Software Design,* Warner Books, 1984.
11. D.D. McCracken and M.A. Jackson, "Life Cycle Concept Considered Harmful," *Software Engineering Notes, ACM,* Apr. 1982, pp. 29-32.
12. R. Balzer, T.E. Cheatham, and C. Green, "Software Technology in the 1990's: Using the New Paradigm," *Computer,* Vol. 16, No. 11, Nov. 1983, pp. 39-45.
13. E. Harel and E.R. McLean, "The Effects of Using a Nonprocedural Language on Programmer Productivity," UCLA Graduate School of Management, Information Systems Working Paper #3-83, Nov. 1982.
14. T. Guimaraes, "A Study of Application Program Development Techniques," *Comm. ACM,* May 1985, pp. 494-499.
15. C. Babcock, "New Jersey Motorists in Software Jam," *Computerworld,* Sept. 30, 1985, pp. 1, 6.
16. B.W. Boehm, *ROCKET: Rand's Omnibus Calculator of the Kinematics of Earth Trajectories,* Prentice-Hall, Englewood Cliffs, N.J., 1964.
17. F.P. Brooks, "No Silver Bullet—Essence and Accidents of Software Engineering," *Proc. IFIP Congress 1986,* North Holland, 1986, pp. 1069-1076. Also in *Computer,* April 1987, pp 10-19.

A more extensive version of this article, including additional text, figures, and references, is available from the author. To obtain a copy, circle number 182 on the Reader Service Card at the back of the magazine.

Barry W. Boehm is the chief scientist in the Office of Technology at the TRW Defense Systems Group. He is responsible for the group's Ada Office, Technology Education Program, and Quantum Leap Software Development Program. Since joining TRW in 1973, Boehm has held several senior engineering and management positions. He is also an adjunct professor at UCLA and a member of the Computer Society's Board of Governors. Boehm received his BA in mathematics from Harvard in 1957 and his MA and PhD from UCLA in 1961 and 1964.

Boehm's address is TRW Defense Systems Group, One Space Park, R2/2086, Redondo Beach, CA 90278.

Controlling software projects

by Paul Rook

Previously published in *Software Engineering Journal*, January 1986, by the Institution of Electrical Engineers.

In recent years the software industry has seen the increasing imposition of structure and discipline on technical development activities in an attempt to improve the efficiency of software development and the reliability of the software produced. The clear emphasis in the modern approach to software engineering is to focus attention on the overall development process and the co-ordination of all aspects of software development. This paper examines the principles of managing and successfully controlling software development from a software engineering basis.

1 Introduction

The management of a large software development is a complex and intrinsically difficult task: a large software system is itself very complex and its production may involve hundreds of man-years of skilled effort with correspondingly large budgets.

Nearly every software development project is faced with numerous difficulties. When a project is successful it is not because there were no problems but because the problems were overcome. Many of the problems are technical but often the critical ones are managerial. Software development depends on documentation and communication — it is only structured if a structure is imposed and controlled. Everything that is done right in software development is done early — there is very little opportunity for catching up when things are discovered to be going wrong later in the development.

There is much discussion about comparisons between managing software development and managing hardware development. There are genuine differences between hardware and software, as follows:

- Software has no physical appearance.
- Few software quality metrics exist.
- Software has much higher complexity than hardware.
- It is deceptively easy to introduce changes into software.
- Effects of software change propagate explosively.
- Software includes data as well as logic.
- Software development makes very little use of pre-existing components.

However, in many important ways software development is like hardware development and ought to be managed and controlled using very similar techniques to those used in hardware engineering development. The genuine dissimilarities listed above are the very factors which make an engineering approach much more critical for software development.

Contributing to the difficulties of software management is the much publicised view of the programmer as the unbridled genius, whose creative process will be stifled by any of the recommended project management controls, design standards and programming standards.

Forced to contend with this view is the software manager, often a recently promoted analyst or programmer who has worked on projects managed as a collection of creative artists doing their independent thing. Management's job in these projects was to try, somehow, to steer this collection of individualists in a common direction so that their products would accomplish the project goals, be able to interface with each other, be finished within the project cost and schedule constraints, and, with a little luck, come reasonably close to accomplishing what the customer had in mind for the software. Such a software manager has been well grounded in how a project should not be managed, but has had little exposure or training in the use of effective software management techniques.

2 Structuring software development

To tackle these problems, the software industry has seen the increasing imposition of discipline on technical development activities in an attempt to improve the reliability of software development. Thus we have seen, in turn, the techniques of structured programming, structured design and structured analysis.

Structured programming provides rules for choosing the building blocks for programs. Structured design helps the designer to distinguish between good and bad designs. Structured analysis assists in the production of a specification that is correct and consistent and can be determined to be complete. The introduction in turn of each of these three techniques has thrown up problems which have been introduced through lack of discipline in the earlier stages of the development process.

In addition to this stage by stage attack on the problems of development, it is clear that all activities will have problems unless the goals of each activity are clearly stated and set within the context of the structure for the whole project.

The clear emphasis in the modern approach to software engineering is to focus attention on the overall development process. This is the aim of structured software development, which breaks down the project into a series of distinct phases, each with well defined goals, the achievement of which can be verified, ensuring a sound foundation for the succeeding phase. It also breaks down the work to be performed into a series of discrete manageable packages, and creates the basis for the appropriate organisational structure. This allows overall planning of 'how' the software is going to be developed as well as considering 'what' is going to be developed as the product.

3 Computer-based tools

An equally important development has been the introduction of computer-based tools to assist with specific tasks. The earliest tools were concerned with the production of code. These have been followed by tools which assist, for example, specification, design, estimating, planning, documentation and configuration management. In fact tools are now available to support most of the software development activities.

The right tools assist in increasing productivity and visibility of work achieved, provide a source of data for future proposal preparation, estimation and project planning, and maintain continuity between projects. They also provide automated testing and reduce iteration of work and thus aid improved quality. Tools are especially useful in detecting errors early, when they are less expensive to correct, thus leading to a more successful software project and product.

Although tools alone will not ensure success, the selection and installation of the right set of tools is seen to be necessary for an effective software development project.

4 The management of complexity

Thus the key to the management of the complex task of large software development is twofold:

- reducing complexity by imposing a structure on to the process
- using computer-based tools to make the remaining complexity more tractable.

5 Software development methodology

In planning how to develop the software, it is the responsibility of project management to ensure that a coherent system of methods and tools is chosen, integrated and supported.

However, differences in organisation structures, applications and existing approaches make it impractical to prescribe a single scheme that can be universally followed. Methods, tools, management practices or any other element of the total development environment cannot be chosen without considering each element in its relationship to the other parts of the development system.

Software engineering has introduced the term 'software development meth-

odology' to describe a systematic set of procedures followed from the original conception of a system through the specification, design, implementation, operation and evolution of the software in that system. A methodology not only includes technical methods to assist in the critical tasks of problem solving, documentation, analysis, design, coding, testing and configuration management, but also includes management procedures to control the development process and the deployment of the technical methods.

The management and technical aspects of the methodology support and gain strength from each other: the technical methods provide the basis needed for effective managerial control, while the management procedures provide the organisation and resources which enable the technical development to proceed effectively. Tools support the methodology and provide the information needed by project management.

6 Project control

The software development process is inherently subject to risks which are manifested as financial failures (time scale overrun, budget overrun) and technical failures (failure to meet requirements, over/under-engineered). The sources of risk can be placed in three main categories:

- perturbations (requirement changes, detection of problems, errors and failures)
- personnel (wrong people available, too many/too few people available)
- project environment (undefined methodology, unknown quality, errors

detected late, inadequate control, technical skill, support and visibility).

If the project is to be successful, then potential risks must be identified, and eliminated or controlled. A control system for a project is based on the usual principle of establishing suitable feedback loop(s) to ensure that the controlled system is oriented to its objective. The objective of a software development project is to produce the correct product on time and to budget.

Fig. 1 illustrates, in a simplified form, a project control system for software development. Technical development is what is controlled and project management is the controller. Estimating is a prerequisite for control, and a number of feedback loops are set up which operate via status and progress reports to compare actual progress with the plans based on the estimates.

The feedback loops operate directly from the technical development and also from the quality and configuration management systems. Fig. 1 illustrates a continuous process, as indicated by the inner product loop of feedback of intermediate development products to the activities of technical development. The quality and configuration management systems operate continuously in the development process, not only on the products finally delivered to the customer.

While the inner loop represents the work on the product, the outer feedback loops represent the basis for control. Control consists of obtaining information to make decisions and ensuring timely detection and correction of errors, thus controlling time scale and budget and minimising technical risks.

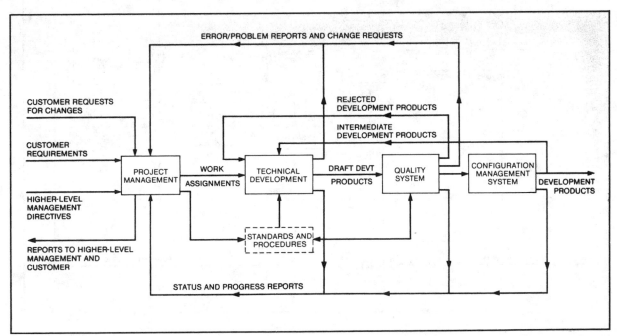

Fig. 1 Basic operation of a project control system

The upper control loops represent inevitable paths for changes, which the project manager must control through appropriate procedures, such as a change control board. The lower control loops represent the monitoring system established by the project manager to obtain information on which to make decisions and to be able to check that the consequences of those decisions are carried through and have the intended effects.

For the project to be successfully controlled the lower control loops must dominate the upper control loops. This is achieved by establishing sufficient strength in the lower loops and also by constraining the upper loops.

The operation of project control illustrated in Fig. 1 depends on an organisation with clearly defined responsibilities and disciplines related to the four functions shown — project management, technical development, quality system and configuration management system.

7 Project management

The establishment of the project environment, obtaining the personnel and dealing with perturbations (see the sources of risk listed in the previous Section) are the responsibility of the project manager. The responsibility also includes the software development methodology used on the project. In some cases a standard methodology will be available, together with the appropriate support

facilities. In other cases the project manager will have to select and establish a methodology specifically for the project. In either event, project management has the final responsibility of ensuring (or confirming) the suitability of the methodology for the project and defining precisely the details of its application.

Software development techniques such as formal specification, structured design, stepwise refinement, structured programming and correctness proofs are examples of progress in software engineering in recent years. These techniques, together with documentation standards, test methods, and configuration management and quality assurance procedures, address elements of the software development process.

The methods selected must be matched to the characteristics of the development, the imposed schedules and other operational considerations. Once selected, the methods must be implemented and controlled.

However, careful selection of software development techniques does not in itself guarantee success. Success or failure is primarily determined by the approach to project management. No matter how sophisticated the design and programming techniques, a systematic approach to project management is essential.

Project management deals with planning, defining and assigning the work to the technical development teams, monitoring status and progress, making decisions, re-planning and reporting on

the project to higher-level management and the customer.

Fig. 2 shows project management, expanded from the single box of Fig. 1, as a set of interacting processes. While the diagram is rather simplistic it does illustrate the fact that control of the project depends on the quality of information that these processes generate and the use made of it.

7.1 Decision making

The most important aspect of project management consists of making decisions (or ensuring that decisions are made), which includes making sure that timely technical decisions are made on the product as well as making the more obvious project decisions. Responsibility for decisions rests with the project manager. While he can, and must, appropriately delegate authority and decision making, he cannot avoid ultimate responsibility for customer relationship, specification, correctness of design and implementation, quality, use of allocated resources and staff, meeting time scale and budget, standards and procedures, anticipation and resolution of problems and ultimate delivery and acceptance of the product.

7.2 Planning

The planning process includes the activities of planning, scheduling, budgeting and defining milestones. This is based

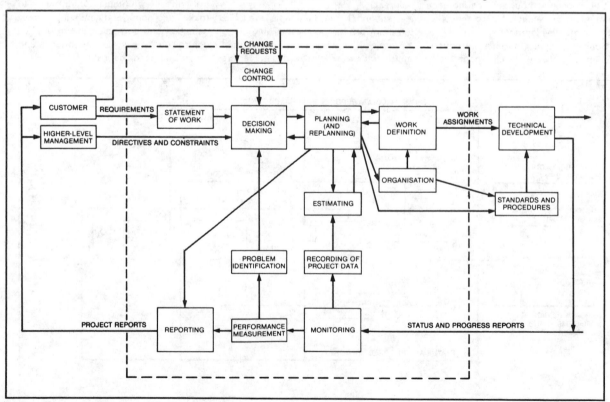

Fig. 2 The processes of project management

on the work breakdown structure (WBS) produced by the work definition process. It depends on estimating, with reference to the recorded project database derived from previous projects (and earlier stages of the current project), and, of course, is based on the input of the customer or system requirements and management constraints.

The project manager produces a project plan (to be publicly viewed and reviewed), which shows estimates, deliverable inter-relationships and timing dependencies, and the allocation of resources to produce deliverables. It is accompanied by definition of the project organisation and the standards and procedures to be used in technical development.

It is important for the project plan to be dynamic. Through the normal processes of iterative analysis, design and implementation changes, resource problems, customer or environment changes and estimation errors, the project plan will require updating and revision. Storable copies of each version of the project plan should be kept in the project history file together with the reasons for revision.

7.3 Work definition

The work definition process relies on a method of doing the work in order to be able to define the detailed work packages (the lowest level of the WBS) which are the basis for the planning process. For software development this is based on the tasks defined by the matrix of activities and phases of the life cycle model shown in Fig. 5.

These work packages define a series of products for project work and management. The WBS not only requires management and customer concurrence on the specification of the product but also requires agreement on the methodology to be used for the project.

7.4 Monitoring

The monitoring process involves measuring actual performance and handling minor schedule and resource requirements revisions that can be accommodated by the team. This process is also related to quality assurance through technical reviews and walkthroughs, and is used to maintain the project data file, which provides updated information for estimating.

Based on written reports and meetings, the monitoring process involves evaluation of expected progress in deliverables against actual progress and provides the basis for project reporting.

7.5 Reporting

The reporting process stores, analyses and filters information of project progress

fed to it by the monitoring process. It compares actual with expected performance, and yields relevant information for the project teams, management and customer.

The project manager reviews the status, progress and problems identified as a foundation for decisions, which closes the loop of internal project control.

There is also an outer loop which depends on reports to the customer and higher-level management.

The information for management should be a filtered subset of the information needed by the project manager when tracking progress within the project. The information needed by management is to answer the questions: 'Is the project on schedule?', and if not, 'Can the team handle the schedule stoppage within its own area of responsibility, or does management need to do something to help the project return to an in-control state?'

The information on measured achievement must be presented effectively to management and the customer so that project progress can be approved at critical points and the correct decisions made.

8 The life cycle model

In order to structure the software development project it is necessary to define the development process — in other words, to adopt some model of the process as an expansion of the technical development function shown in Fig. 1. A model which defines phases in the development of a software product is referred to in software engineering as a 'life cycle model'.

There are numerous life cycle models in use and described in the literature, the specific phases and names varying in detail from one model to another.

Any modern model should be easy to relate to the following phases:

- project initiation
- requirement specification
- structural design
- detailed design
- code and unit test
- integration and test
- acceptance test
- maintenance
- project termination
- product phase-out.

8.1 Baselines

Each development phase is defined in terms of its outputs, or product. The products of each phase represent the points along the development path where there is a clear change in emphasis, where one definition of the emerging product is established and is used as the basis for the

next derived definition. As such, they are the natural milestones of the development progression and offer objective visibility into that progression.

To transform this visibility into effective management control, a software development methodology based on the life cycle model uses the concept of baselines. A 'baseline' established at any stage in the development process is a set of information constituting the definition of the product at that stage.

The completion of each phase is determined by the satisfactory review of the defined products of that phase by development personnel, other project and company experts and, in many cases, customer and user personnel. These products then form the baseline for the work in the next phase. The products of the next phase are then measured and verified against previous baselines before themselves forming a new baseline. In this way confidence in project progress is progressively built on successive baselines.

The process is illustrated in the form of a V-diagram in Fig. 3. In this diagram the rectangular boxes represent the phases and the oval boxes represent the baselines. The form of the diagram shows the symmetry between the successive decomposition of the design and the building of the product by successive stages of integration and test. Each design phase is verified against the previous baseline. Each integration phase is verified against the corresponding design or specification baseline on the other side of the diagram.

8.2 Practical application of the life cycle model

The above description of the life cycle model and its representation in Fig. 3 could be interpreted as suggesting that no phase can be considered complete, and the following phases started, until all the prescribed documents have been completed to specified standards. Although the intended rigour of such an approach is commendable, it is quite unrealistic to interpret the life cycle model in such a simplistic way, particularly on large-scale software developments. For example, in a real software project:

- Exploratory work on a subsequent phase is usually required before the current phase can be completed (for example, design investigation is almost invariably required before it can be stated that a user requirement can be met).
- Problems encountered in a later phase may involve re-working the products of earlier phases — failure to recognise this leads to earlier documentation becoming inaccurate and misleading.
- The user's perceived requirement

may not remain constant during a protracted software development process, and it may be necessary to consider changed requirements and consequent design changes during later phases.

● The project plan may call for incremental development, with different increments of the product in different phases of development.

The concept of distinct phases of software development, representing the achievement of certain defined states in the development of the product, can be regarded as a device, imposed by project management to cope with complexity and improve visibility.

In practice, on a large-scale project, the precise breakpoints between the project phases are not easy to define clearly and depend to some extent on project management decision. Because completely rigid phase control is impractical, status and risk analysis at milestones is particularly important. This can only be obtained from a system of technical reviews.

However, once this reality is recognised, it does not lead to the conclusion that the life cycle model is impractical. Having escaped the simplistic interpretation, the life cycle model does represent a realistic recognition of what is actually involved in the technical work of software development.

Phases do indeed have to be imposed by project management; they will not happen of their own accord. The definitions and concepts in the life cycle model represent the best current understanding of software development methodology — gained from experience in applying software engineering to development projects.

These definitions are the worked-out basis for real control of software development, but that control has to be explicitly planned, based on an implemented methodology actually used by the development staff, and actually applied. It does not happen naturally, as is apparent from the response from some projects that the life cycle model does not correspond to reality. Project management has to *make* its version of the life cycle model realistic.

8.3 Software development life cycle phases

Listed below are the baseline outputs of each phase of the software development life cycle:

● *Project initiation phase:* A validated system architecture, founded on a design study with basic hardware-software allocations, and an approved concept of operation including basic human-machine allocations. A top-level project

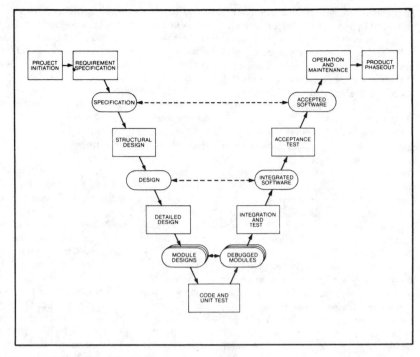

Fig. 3   The stages in software development confidence

plan, with milestones, resources, responsibilities, schedules and major activities. Defined standards and procedures.

● *Requirement specification phase:* A complete, validated specification of the required functions, interfaces and performance for the software product. A detailed project plan.

● *Structural design phase:* A complete, verified specification of the overall hardware-software architecture, control structure and data structure for the software product, along with such other necessary components as draft user's manuals and test plans.

● *Detailed design phase:* A complete, verified specification of the control structure, data structure, interface relations, sizing, key algorithms and assumptions for each program component.

● *Code and unit test phase:* A complete, verified set of program components.

● *Integration and test phase:* A properly functioning software product.

● *Software acceptance test phase:* An accepted software product handed over to the customer.

● *Maintenance phase:* A fully functioning update of the software product. This goal is repeated for each update, which follows the complete development sequence each time.

● *Project termination phase:* A completed project history document comparing estimates and plans with actual development schedule and costs as a contribution to the accumulated database of experience.

● *Product phase-out:* A clean transition of the functions performed by the product to its successors (if any).

9 Software development work

In the same way that the progress of a software development project may be partitioned into a number of discrete phases, so may the technical work involved be divided into a number of clearly identified 'activities'.

A close parallel has been deliberately adopted between the names assigned to the project phases and the technical activities, respectively. This means that, in most cases, the name of a development phase, structural design, for example, indicates the principal activity taking place within that phase. This is not to say that structural design is the only activity taking place during the structural design phase.

Conversely, not only must significant initial structural design work be performed prior to the structural design phase, but also there must be a continuing activity to deal with updates to the design during subsequent phases.

Similarly, although coding a module does not properly commence before the completion of the detailed design of that module, some programming activities must be performed during the earlier phases, such as planning coding methods and facilities, the acquisition and installation of tools and, in some cases, exploratory investigations into algorithms and operations.

Errors detected in the integration phase will require code and unit test activity even though the phase of that name has been completed.

In general, all activities continue across all phases of the project, although the emphasis shifts from activity to activity as the project proceeds from phase to phase. It follows that, in a large software development, each activity should be staffed by a distinct group of people, whose numbers might expand and contract as the emphasis of the project changes but whose existence is identifiable from project start to project end. This is illustrated in the example shown in Fig. 4.

9.1 Technical control

Since the technical activities are performed by members of a number of teams, it is vital to ensure the overall technical correctness of the product, which can be distinguished from such concerns as schedule, budget, organisation, staffing etc. which are solely the responsibility of project management. This concern with technical matters is referred to as 'technical control'.

Technical control is regarded as part of technical development (see Fig. 1) and is defined as the continuous process of making certain that what is being produced is technically correct, coherent and consistent.

It includes planning ahead for all the necessary modelling and testing. Its role is strategic in that it makes certain that the overall technical integrity of the product is not lost in the tactics of the individual technical activities. It requires an overall technical authority but does not necessarily imply managerial authority over the development staff. When sub-contractors are involved in the project, the activity of technical control becomes even more important in co-ordinating the technical aspects of all the work between the sub-contractors and the integrity of the sub-contract products.

Primary examples of technical control are the maintenance of the integrity of the design in the presence of changes following the completion of the structural design phase, and test planning. Test planning is a strategic activity from the very start of the project which defines and co-ordinates all the test methods, tools and techniques to be used throughout the life cycle. It also identifies critical components that need the most testing, what test data is required, and when it is to be prepared.

While it can be seen to be difficult to separate the two activities of project management and technical control and it is reasonable on very small projects for the project manager to undertake both activities, on large projects such a combination of roles is very rarely workable. Firstly, it is rare to find people who combine both the strong management talent and strong technical talent necessary for large projects. Secondly, and more importantly, on a project of even a reasonable size, each activity is necessarily a full-time job, or more.

It is hard for the project manager to delegate the project management tasks to allow time for technical work. It is impossible for the technical controller to delegate technical control duties without compromising the conceptual integrity of the product. It is sometimes possible to run a project with the technical control exercised by the senior manager in charge of the project and almost all project management tasks delegated to a second-in-command. It is much more usual for the project manager to be in command, with the technical controller having the technical authority. In this case it is important that the technical controller does have enough authority for decisions without being in management line above all the project teams.

9.2 Quality system

In the context of product development the word 'quality' is defined as the degree of conformance of the product to its stated requirements, i.e. 'fitness for purpose'. This definition is applied to the intermediate products of the development as well as to the final product. The development process is fundamental to the ability of the project to produce products of acceptable quality. Quality is built into the product by the activities of the software development staff as a continuous process of building the product to the specified quality.

Quality is everybody's responsibility — it cannot be added by any testing or control on the products of phases. Such testing and quality control activities do, however, provide early warning of problems; changes can be made at much lower cost than in the later stages of development, provided, as always, that proper change control procedures are followed.

The quality system comprises two distinct activities: verification, validation and test (VV&T), and quality assurance (QA).

9.3 Verification, validation and test

The terms are defined as follows:

● *Verification:* To establish the correspondence between a software product (documentation or code) and its specification — 'Are we building the product right?'
● *Validation:* To establish the fitness of a software product for its operational mission — 'Are we building the right product?'
● *Testing:* The actual running of code to produce test results.

VV&T is checking the correctness of the products of each phase (baselines) and is performed by the software development staff. The activity should, as far as possible, be carried out by staff within the project organisation, but not by the originators of the work. For this reason it is the only development activity which may be the responsibility of a series of different teams as the project proceeds through the life cycle phases.

9.4 Quality assurance

Quality asssurance (QA) is checking the correctness of the procedures being followed, i.e. whether the development staff are following the intended procedures (in all their work, not just the VV&T activities). This is carried out by QA staff either from a separate QA department or from staff assigned to QA work within the project. The checking of procedures is backed by audits (spot checks) of the quality (and conformance to standards) of the products to find out if the procedures are effective. Generally the QA staff provide an independent voice on all quality issues, especially on the setting up of standards and procedures at the beginning of the project (i.e. 'how' the project will develop the 'what' defined in the requirement specification). The responsibilities of the QA staff are:

● advising on standards and procedures
● monitoring the procedures actually employed on the project
● auditing and certifying the quality of products achieved.

9.5 Configuration management system

The successful realisation of a software product requires the strictest control over the defining, describing and supporting documentation and the software code constituting the product. It is inevitable that the definition will be subject to continuous pressure for change over the life cycle of the product, to correct errors, introduce improvements and respond to the evolving requirements of the marketplace. Configuration management provides the disciplines required to prevent the chaos of uncontrolled change.

A comprehensive approach to configuration management requires:

● clear identification of software items and documents, and their successive versions and editions
● definition of the configuration of software products, and their related configuration items
● physical control over the master files

of software code and documentation
- control of the introduction of changes to these files by a change control board and a set of change procedures
- maintenance of a system of configuration records, reflecting the definition of products in the field.

The output of each development phase should be verified and validated against the relevant preceding baselines. Configuration management disciplines ensure that all necessary corrections are introduced before this output, in turn, is baselined and that only up-to-date definitions of baselines are used by subsequent phases. The configuration management system should be able to react to the time scales needed by different phases of the project.

Once a baseline has been formally established its contents may only be changed by the operation of the formal change control process. This has the following advantages:

- No changes are made thereafter without the agreement of all interested parties.
- The higher procedural threshold for change tends to stabilise the product.
- There is always available a definitive version of the product, or of any of the controlled intermediate products (baselines).

9.6 Documentation

The output of each phase of the whole software development project consists entirely of documentation or of documentation and code. Furthermore, during the design phases, documents are the sole means by which the successive stages of the design process are recorded, and against which each phase is validated. So much of the output of a software project is in the form of documentation that it is impossible to separate the scheduling of the documentation constituting the baselines from that of the project as a whole. Therefore careful attention to the planning, structure, content, preparation, presentation and control of documentation is vital.

Documentation produced by the software development process may:

- define the software product in terms of requirement and design specifications
- describe the product to the customer or to current or future members of the development team
- support the product in the field in the form of the user's manual, operator's manual and maintenance manual.

9.7 Software development model

Having discussed all the activities of a software development project, the full list of ten activities covering all the management and technical work can be defined as follows:

- *Project management:* Project level management functions. Includes project level planning and control, contract and sub-contract management, customer interface, cost/schedule performance management, management reviews and audits, and includes acquisition of management tools.
- *Technical control:* Responsibility for the technical correctness and quality of the complete product. Responsibility for maintaining the integrity of the whole design during the detailed design, programming and testing phases. Specification, review and update of integration test and acceptance test plans and procedures. Acquisition of requirements and design verification and validation tools. Acquisition and support of test drivers, test tools and test data.
- *Requirement specification:* Determination, specification, review and update of software functional, performance, interface and verification requirements, including acquisition of requirements analysis and specification tools. Development of requirement specification level defining and describing documentation. A continuing responsibility for communication between customer requirements and the technical development.
- *Structural design:* Determination, specification, review and update of hardware-software architecture, software design and database design, including acquisition of design tools. Development of structural design level defining documentation.
- *Detailed design:* Detailed design of individual computer program components. Development of detail design level defining documentation. When a signifi-

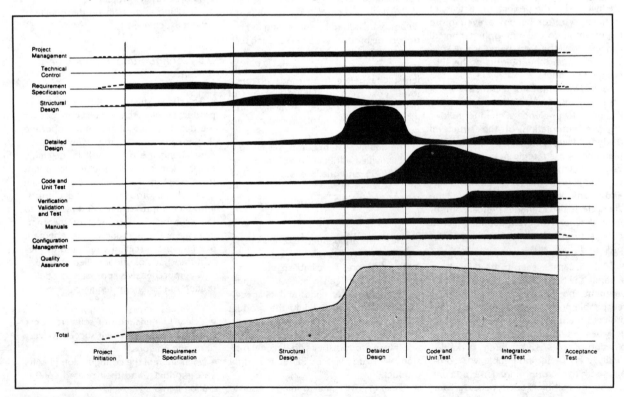

Fig. 4 Software development teams

Fig. 5 Project tasks by activity and phase

Activity	Project initiation	Reqmnt specification	Structural design	Detailed design	Code and unit test	Integration and test	Acceptance test	Maintenance
Project management	project estimating, planning, scheduling, procedures, organisation etc.	project management, project planning, contracts, liaison etc.	project management, status monitoring, contracts, liaison etc.	project management, status monitoring, contracts, liaison etc.	project management, status monitoring, contracts, liaison etc.	project management, status monitoring, contracts, liaison etc.	project management, status monitoring, contracts, liaison etc.	support management, status monitoring, contracts, liaison etc.
Technical control	technical strategy, technical plans, technical standards	system models and risk analysis, acceptance test plan, acquire V and V tools for reqmnts and design, top-level test plan	design quality, models and risk analysis, draft test plans, acquire test tools	design integrity, detailed test plans, acquire test tools	design integrity, detailed test plans, install test tools	design integrity, support test tools, monitor testing	design integrity, support test tools, monitor acceptance	design integrity, risk analysis, test plans
Requirement specification	analyse requirements, determine user needs	analyse existing system, determine user needs, integrate document and iterate requirements	update requirements	update requirements	update requirements	update requirements	update requirements	determine user needs and problems, update requirements
Structural design	design planning	develop basic architecture, models, prototypes	develop structural design, models, prototypes	update design	update design	update design	update design	update design
Detailed design	identify programming methods and resources	prototypes of algorithms, team planning	models, algorithms investigation, team planning	detailed design, component documentation	update detailed design	update detailed design	update detailed design	detailed design of changes and enhancements
Code and unit test	identify programming methods and resources	identify programming tools, team planning	acquire programming tools and utilities, team planning	integration planning	code and unit test	integrate software, update code	update code	code and unit test of changes and enhancements
Verification validation and test	V and V requirements	V and V specification	V and V structural design	V and V detailed design, V and V design changes	V and V top portions of code, V and V design changes	perform product test, V and V design changes	perform acceptance test, V and V design changes	V and V changes and enhancements
Manuals	define user's manual	outline portions of user's manual	draft user's, operator's manuals, outline maintenance manual	draft maintenance manual	full draft users and operator's manuals	final users, operators and maintenance manuals	acceptance of manuals	update manual
Configuration management	CM plans and procedures	CM plans, procedures, identify CM tools	CM of requirements, design, acquire CM tools	CM of requirements, design, detailed design, install CM tools, set up library	CM of requirements, design, code, operate library	CM of requirements, design, code, operate library	CM of requirements, design, code, operate library	CM of all documentation, operate library
Quality assurance	QA plans, project procedures and standards	standards, procedures, QA plans, identify QA tools	QA of requirements, design, project standards, acquire QA tools	QA of requirements, design, detailed design	QA of requirements, design, code	QA of requirements, design, code, testing	QA of requirements, design, code, acceptance	QA of maintenance updates

cant number of staff are involved, this activity includes team level management functions.

● *Code and unit test:* Code, unit test and integration of individual computer program components, including tool acquisition. When a significant number of staff are involved, this activity includes team level management functions.

● *Verification, validation and testing:* Performance of independent requirements validation, design verification and validation, integration test and acceptance test, including test reports.

● *Manuals production:* Development and update of product support documentation — user's manual, operator's manual and maintenance manual.

● *Configuration management:* Product identification, operation of change control, status accounting, and operation of program support library.

● *Quality assurance:* Consultancy on the choice of project standards and procedures, monitoring of project procedures in operation, and quality audits of products.

10 The complete software development model

Fig. 5 shows a matrix of the ten activities for eight software development phases. Tasks corresponding to the specific work of an activity in a phase are shown. The tasks can be sub-divided, where relevant, to sub-systems and modules of the product.

These tasks then provide the basis for the work breakdown structure for estimating, planning and assignment of work to the development team. Thus the principles of software development methodology are unified into a single model for software development project control. In fact the matrix of tasks can be considered as a slice through a cube, as shown in Fig. 6.

Having derived the matrix of tasks and already noted that the documentation system (specification and design documents) corresponds to the work of software development, we can now briefly consider the remaining slices in the cube.

10.1 Techniques and tools

Earlier in this paper it was emphasised that one of the important elements of a modern approach to software engineering is the selection of appropriate techniques and the use of computer-based tools. The careful selection and implementation of such tools is crucial to the objective of improving control and raising productivity and product quality. Mechanisation of software development processes, where practicable, in addition to increasing efficiency, encourages consistent process quality.

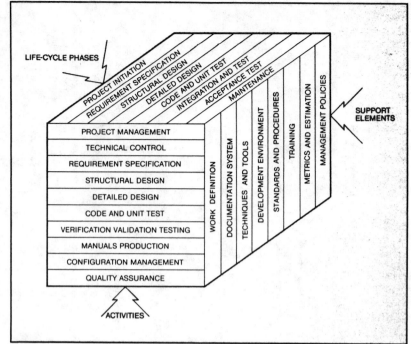

Fig. 6   The software development model

Any suggested technique or set of techniques and the supporting tools can be matched against the model to test how complete an integrated project support environment (IPSE) is provided to support all the tasks in the matrix.

This type of model provides an additional benefit: as techniques and tools are changed or improved from project to project their impact on the development process and product quality can be identified and evaluated.

10.2 Development environment

Development environment is intended to cover all aspects of the computer environment underlying the tools: namely the matters of operating system, database and file facilities, workstations, networking and mainframe computers.

10.3 Standards and procedures

A software development team can only operate effectively when each member knows the answers to the basic questions regarding the job:

● What is expected of me?
● Why is it expected?
● How do I do what is expected?
● What must I produce?
● How will my product be evaluated?
● What tools are available to me?
● What training is available to me?

A set of development procedures and standards improves communications and reduces the probability of misinterpretations among developers. Verification and validation are much easier to implement and more effective when the product is created in accordance with standards.

The model represented by the cube gives us the basis for a set of standards and procedures that are complete and non-redundant if they cover every cubicle in the cube. This is just the same method as for identifying a complete set of tools. If any standard or procedure is missing then there is a hole in the cube. Standards and procedures should be brief and to the point — they need not be bulky and complicated. In fact the cube defines a structure which can simplify the presentation of the standards and procedures documents. If everything in the cube is covered then the software development team know how they are going to develop the product.

10.4 Training

Training is vital to the success of the programming environment. Having a defined technique is useless unless every member of the team knows how to use the technique. Training should be provided not only on the techniques and tools but on all the support elements.

10.5 Metrics and estimation

We need objective metrics on both the process and the generated products (including all intermediate products for all phases). Measurements provide the immediate benefit of refining the development plan and the long-term benefit of characterising the effectiveness of the current development methodology. Whatever the measurement, it must be defined before development begins.

Collection of data, according to the activities and phases of the model, provides the basis for estimating future projects. In turn, running the project according to the model provides the means of collecting such data and the motivation to use it to succeed in controlling successful projects. All such data collection, metrics, analysis, estimation, planning and project control are much more effective when suitable computer-based tools are used.

10.6 Management policies

Management policies define the life cycle phases and the job functions. They are descriptions of what should be performed by each job function in every life cycle phase. These descriptions may be called a methodology, a corporate policy, an instruction or a procedure. Whatever they are called they must be in place at the beginning of a software development project if the project is to be managed with a high chance of successful completion on time, within budget and with a product which operates correctly to the satisfaction of the customer organisation.

11 Conclusion

The major reason for the slow evolution of software project management over the past two decades is the persistent view that programming is an art, rather than a science. This view lingers and has contributed to delays in the development of a well defined, well structured software management methodology. The problem persists despite the great advances in computer hardware technology, the introduction of software engineering, and the definition of new development approaches, such as design decomposition, structured design, structured programming, hierarchical input-output definition and team management concepts.

These factors foster the perspective in business and project management that software management must continuously evolve and change to keep up with advances in software development technology. Yet these conclusions are seldom applied to management of the rapidly advancing electronics field. Since hardware development projects, in the midst of phenomenal technology advances, can be managed in a disciplined, systematic manner based on past decades of project management experience, why should it be assumed that software projects cannot?

Software engineering recognises both technological and managerial aspects. Improvements in the technology of software development have reached the point where the major issues have been identified and considerable progress has been made in addressing these issues. Practical working tools to support improved software production are commonly available and a firm methodology for technical software development is well defined.

Published papers over the last ten years show that software development is manageable and software productivity can be significantly improved for the benefit of the business. The common denominators in the successes reported are firstly that they are usually the better developers of software making even greater improvements, and secondly that they are backed by management commitment.

Given that making software engineering methodology really work is always difficult, it follows that success depends on more than just the wish to improve control and productivity of software development: management support and the willingness to invest is necessary in order to obtain the due return on the investment.

The technical methods, tools and disciplines are the basis for the production of reliable software, on time and within budget, but it is also necessary to have an overall management framework which allows senior management to understand, and project managers to control, large software developments. The increasing complexity of the large software systems being developed and advances in software technology and tools mean that there will be a continuing evolution in technical software development, but the primary basis for the control of software development will continue to be the principles outlined in this paper.

P. E. Rook is Software Development Manager with GEC Software Ltd., 132–135 Long Acre, London WC2E 9AH, England.

MANAGING THE DEVELOPMENT OF LARGE SOFTWARE SYSTEMS

Dr. Winston W. Royce

INTRODUCTION

I am going to describe my personal views about managing large software developments. I have had various assignments during the past nine years, mostly concerned with the development of software packages for spacecraft mission planning, commanding and post-flight analysis. In these assignments I have experienced different degrees of success with respect to arriving at an operational state, on-time, and within costs. I have become prejudiced by my experiences and I am going to relate some of these prejudices in this presentation.

COMPUTER PROGRAM DEVELOPMENT FUNCTIONS

There are two essential steps common to all computer program developments, regardless of size or complexity. There is first an analysis step, followed second by a coding step as depicted in Figure 1. This sort of very simple implementation concept is in fact all that is required if the effort is sufficiently small and if the final product is to be operated by those who built it — as is typically done with computer programs for internal use. It is also the kind of development effort for which most customers are happy to pay, since both steps involve genuinely creative work which directly contributes to the usefulness of the final product. An implementation plan to manufacture larger software systems, and keyed only to these steps, however, is doomed to failure. Many additional development steps are required, none contribute as directly to the final product as analysis and coding, and all drive up the development costs. Customer personnel typically would rather not pay for them, and development personnel would rather not implement them. The prime function of management is to sell these concepts to both groups and then enforce compliance on the part of development personnel.

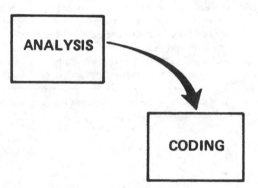

Figure 1. Implementation steps to deliver a small computer program for internal operations.

A more grandiose approach to software development is illustrated in Figure 2. The analysis and coding steps are still in the picture, but they are preceded by two levels of requirements analysis, are separated by a program design step, and followed by a testing step. These additions are treated separately from analysis and coding because they are distinctly different in the way they are executed. They must be planned and staffed differently for best utilization of program resources.

Figure 3 portrays the iterative relationship between successive development phases for this scheme. The ordering of steps is based on the following concept: that as each step progresses and the design is further detailed, there is an iteration with the preceding and succeeding steps but rarely with the more remote steps in the sequence. The virtue of all of this is that as the design proceeds the change process is scoped down to manageable limits. At any point in the design process after the requirements analysis is completed there exists a firm and closeup, moving baseline to which to return in the event of unforeseen design difficulties. What we have is an effective fallback position that tends to maximize the extent of early work that is salvageable and preserved.

Reprinted from *Proceedings of IEEE WESCON*, 1970, pages 1-9. Copyrigh
© 1970 by The Institute of Electrical and Electronics Engineers, Inc.

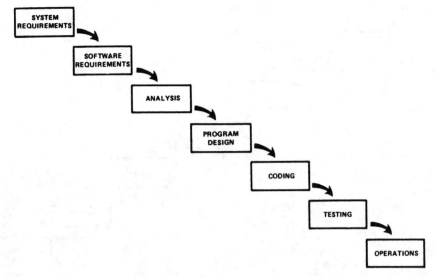

Figure 2. Implementation steps to develop a large computer program for delivery to a customer.

I believe in this concept, but the implementation described above is risky and invites failure. The problem is illustrated in Figure 4. The testing phase which occurs at the end of the development cycle is the first event for which timing, storage, input/output transfers, etc., are experienced as distinguished from analyzed. These phenomena are not precisely analyzable. They are not the solutions to the standard partial differential equations of mathematical physics for instance. Yet if these phenomena fail to satisfy the various external constraints, then invariably a major redesign is required. A simple octal patch or redo of some isolated code will not fix these kinds of difficulties. The required design changes are likely to be so disruptive that the software requirements upon which the design is based and which provides the rationale for everything are violated. Either the requirements must be modified, or a substantial change in the design is required. In effect the development process has returned to the origin and one can expect up to a 100-percent overrun in schedule and/or costs.

One might note that there has been a skipping-over of the analysis and code phases. One cannot, of course, produce software without these steps, but generally these phases are managed with relative ease and have little impact on requirements, design, and testing. In my experience there are whole departments consumed with the analysis of orbit mechanics, spacecraft attitude determination, mathematical optimization of payload activity and so forth, but when these departments have completed their difficult and complex work, the resultant program steps involve a few lines of serial arithmetic code. If in the execution of their difficult and complex work the analysts have made a mistake, the correction is invariably implemented by a minor change in the code with no disruptive feedback into the other development bases.

However, I believe the illustrated approach to be fundamentally sound. The remainder of this discussion presents five additional features that must be added to this basic approach to eliminate most of the development risks.

STEP 1: PROGRAM DESIGN COMES FIRST

The first step towards a fix is illustrated in Figure 5. A preliminary program design phase has been inserted between the software requirements generation phase and the analysis phase. This procedure can be criticized on the basis that the program designer is forced to design in the relative vacuum of initial software requirements without any existing analysis. As a result, his preliminary design may be substantially in error as compared to his design if he were to wait until the analysis was complete. This criticism is correct but it misses the point. By this technique the program designer assures that the software will not fail because of storage, timing, and data flux reasons. As the analysis proceeds in the succeeding phase the program designer must impose on the analyst the storage, timing, and operational constraints in such a way that he senses the consequences. When he justifiably requires more of this kind of resource in order to implement his equations

119

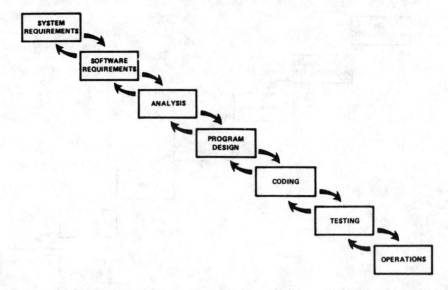

Figure 3. Hopefully, the iterative interaction between the various phases is confined to successive steps.

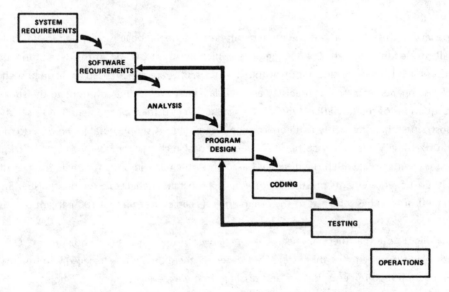

Figure 4. Unfortunately, for the process illustrated, the design iterations are never confined to the successive steps.

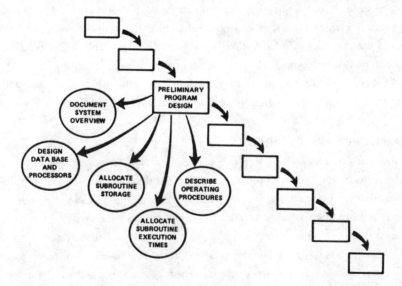

Figure 5. Step 1: Insure that a preliminary program design is complete before analysis begins.

it must be simultaneously snatched from his analyst compatriots. In this way all the analysts and all the program designers will contribute to a meaningful design process which will culminate in the proper allocation of execution time and storage resources. If the total resources to be applied are insufficient or if the embryo operational design is wrong it will be recognized at this earlier stage and the iteration with requirements and preliminary design can be redone before final design, coding and test commences.

How is this procedure implemented? The following steps are required.

1) **Begin the design process with program designers,** not analysts or programmers.

2) **Design, define and allocate the data processing modes** even at the risk of being wrong. Allocate processing, functions, design the data base, define data base processing, allocate execution time, define interfaces and processing modes with the operating system, describe input and output processing, and define preliminary operating procedures.

3) **Write an overview document** that is understandable, informative and current. Each and every worker must have an elemental understanding of the system. At least one person must have a deep understanding of the system which comes partially from having had to write an overview document.

STEP 2: DOCUMENT THE DESIGN

At this point it is appropriate to raise the issue of — "how much documentation?" My own view is "quite a lot;" certainly more than most programmers, analysts, or program designers are willing to do if left to their own devices. The first rule of managing software development is ruthless enforcement of documentation requirements.

Occasionally I am called upon to review the progress of other software design efforts. My first step is to investigate the state of the documentation. If the documentation is in serious default my first recommendation is simple. Replace project management. Stop all activities not related to documentation. Bring the documentation up to acceptable standards. Management of software is simply impossible without a very high degree of documentation. As an example, let me offer the following estimates for comparison. In order to procure a 5 million dollar hardware device, I would expect that a 30 page specification would provide adequate detail to control the procurement. In order to procure 5 million dollars of software I would estimate a 1500 page specification is about right in order to achieve comparable control.

Why so much documentation?

1) Each designer must communicate with interfacing designers, with his management and possibly with the customer. A verbal record is too intangible to provide an adequate basis for an interface or management decision. An acceptable written description forces the designer to take an unequivocal position and provide tangible evidence of completion. It prevents the designer from hiding behind the — "I am 90-percent finished" — syndrome month after month.

2) During the early phase of software development the documentation _is_ the specification and _is_ the design. Until coding begins these three nouns (documentation, specification, design) denote a single thing. If the documentation is bad the design is bad. If the documentation does not yet exist there is as yet no design, only people thinking and talking about the design which is of some value, but not much.

3) The real monetary value of good documentation begins downstream in the development process during the testing phase and continues through operations and redesign. The value of documentation can be described in terms of three concrete, tangible situations that every program manager faces.

a) **During the testing phase,** with good documentation the manager can concentrate personnel on the mistakes in the program. Without good documentation every mistake, large or small, is analyzed by one man who probably made the mistake in the first place because he is the only man who understands the program area.

b) **During the operational phase,** with good documentation the manager can use operation-oriented personnel to operate the program and to do a better job, cheaper. Without good documentation the software must be operated by those who built it. Generally these people are relatively disinterested in operations and do not do as effective a job as operations-oriented personnel. It should be pointed out in this connection that in an operational situation, if there is some hangup the software is always blamed first. In order either to absolve the software or to fix the blame, the software documentation must speak clearly.

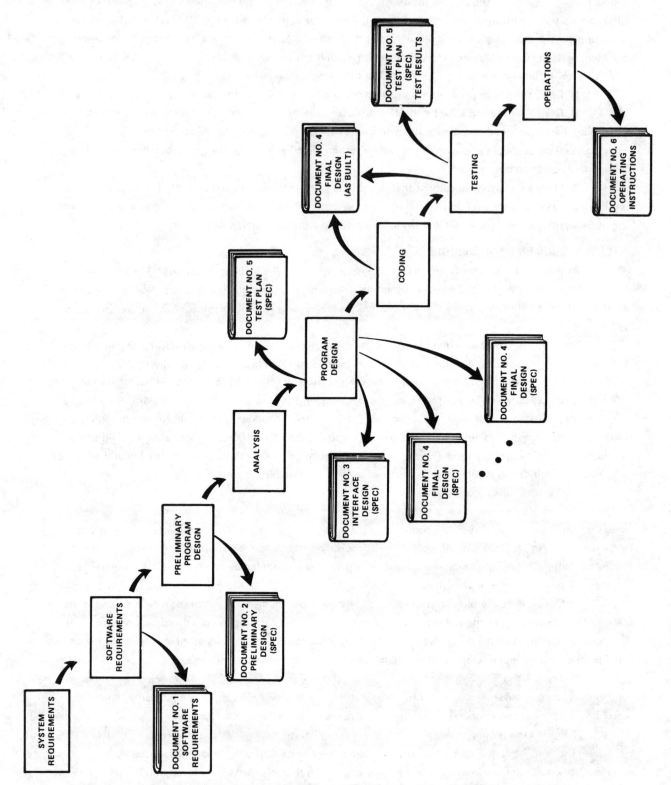

Figure 6. Step 2: Insure that documentation is current and complete — at least six uniquely different documents are required.

c) **Following initial operations,** when system improvements are in order, good documentation permits effective redesign, updating, and retrofitting in the field. If documentation does not exist, generally the entire existing framework of operating software must be junked, even for relatively modest changes.

Figure 6 shows a documentation plan which is keyed to the steps previously shown. Note that six documents are produced, and at the time of delivery of the final product, Documents No. 1, No. 3, No. 4, No. 5, and No. 6 are updated and current.

STEP 3: DO IT TWICE

After documentation, the second most important criterion for success revolves around whether the product is totally original. If the computer program in question is being developed for the first time, arrange matters so that the version finally delivered to the customer for operational deployment is actually the second version insofar as critical design/operations areas are concerned. Figure 7 illustrates how this might be carried out by means of a simulation. Note that it is simply the entire process done in miniature, to a time scale that is relatively small with respect to the overall effort. The nature of this effort can vary widely depending primarily on the overall time scale and the nature of the critical problem areas to be modeled. If the effort runs 30 months then this early development of a pilot model might be scheduled for 10 months. For this schedule, fairly formal controls, documentation procedures, etc., can be utilized. If, however, the overall effort were reduced to 12 months, then the pilot effort could be compressed to three months perhaps, in order to gain sufficient leverage on the mainline development. In this case a very special kind of broad competence is required on the part of the personnel involved. They must have an intuitive feel for analysis, coding, and program design. They must quickly sense the trouble spots in the design, model them, model their alternatives, forget the straightforward aspects of the design which aren't worth studying at this early point, and finally arrive at an error-free program. In either case the point of all this, as with a simulation, is that questions of timing, storage, etc. which are otherwise matters of judgment, can now be studied with precision. Without this simulation the project manager is at the mercy of human judgment. With the simulation he can at least perform experimental tests of some key hypotheses and scope down what remains for human judgment, which in the area of computer program design (as in the estimation of takeoff gross weight, costs to complete, or the daily double) is invariably and seriously optimistic.

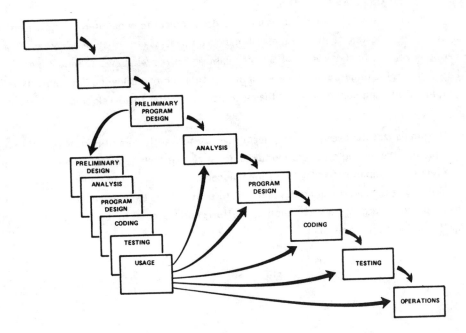

Figure 7. Step 3: Attempt to do the job twice — the first result provides an early simulation of the final product.

STEP 4: PLAN, CONTROL AND MONITOR TESTING

Without question the biggest user of project resources, whether it be manpower, computer time, or management judgment, is the test phase. It is the phase of greatest risk in terms of dollars and schedule. It occurs at the latest point in the schedule when backup alternatives are least available, if at all.

The previous three recommendations to design the program before beginning analysis and coding, to document it completely, and to build a pilot model are all aimed at uncovering and solving problems before entering the test phase. However, even after doing these things there is still a test phase and there are still important things to be done. Figure 8 lists some additional aspects to testing. In planning for testing, I would suggest the following for consideration.

1) Many parts of the test process are best handled by test specialists who did not necessarily contribute to the original design. If it is argued that only the designer can perform a thorough test because only he understands the area he built, this is a sure sign of a failure to document properly. With good documentation it is feasible to use specialists in software product assurance who will, in my judgment, do a better job of testing than the designer.

2) Most errors are of an obvious nature that can be easily spotted by visual inspection. Every bit of an analysis and every bit of code should be subjected to a simple visual scan by a second party who did not do the original analysis or code but who would spot things like dropped minus signs, missing factors of two, jumps to wrong addresses, etc., which are in the nature of proofreading the analysis and code. Do not use the computer to detect this kind of thing — it is too expensive.

3) Test every logic path in the computer program at least once with some kind of numerical check. If I were a customer, I would not accept delivery until this procedure was completed and certified. This step will uncover the majority of coding errors.

While this test procedure sounds simple, for a large, complex computer program it is relatively difficult to plow through every logic path with controlled values of input. In fact there are those who will argue that it is very nearly impossible. In spite of this I would persist in my recommendation that every logic path be subjected to at least one authentic check.

4) After the simple errors (which are in the majority, and which obscure the big mistakes) are removed, then it is time to turn over the software to the test area for checkout purposes. At the proper time during the course of development and in the hands of the proper person the computer itself is the best device for checkout. Key management decisions are: when is the time and who is the person to do final checkout?

STEP 5: INVOLVE THE CUSTOMER

For some reason what a software design is going to do is subject to wide interpretation even after previous agreement. It is important to involve the customer in a formal way so that he has committed himself at earlier points before final delivery. To give the contractor free rein between requirement definition and operation is inviting trouble. Figure 9 indicates three points following requirements definition where the insight, judgment, and commitment of the customer can bolster the development effort.

SUMMARY

Figure 10 summarizes the five steps that I feel necessary to transform a risky development process into one that will provide the desired product. I would emphasize that each item costs some additional sum of money. If the relatively simpler process without the five complexities described here would work successfully, then of course the additional money is not well spent. In my experience, however, the simpler method has never worked on large software development efforts and the costs to recover far exceeded those required to finance the five-step process listed.

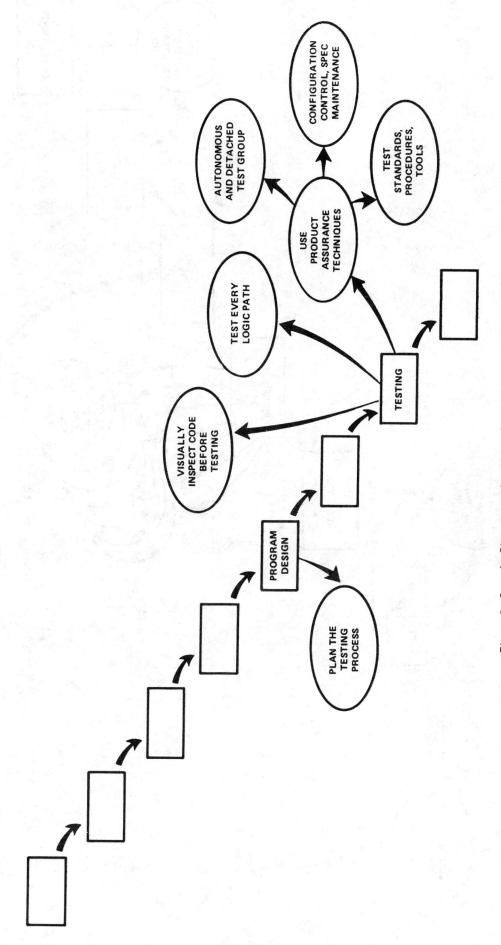

Figure 8. Step 4: Plan, control, and monitor computer program testing.

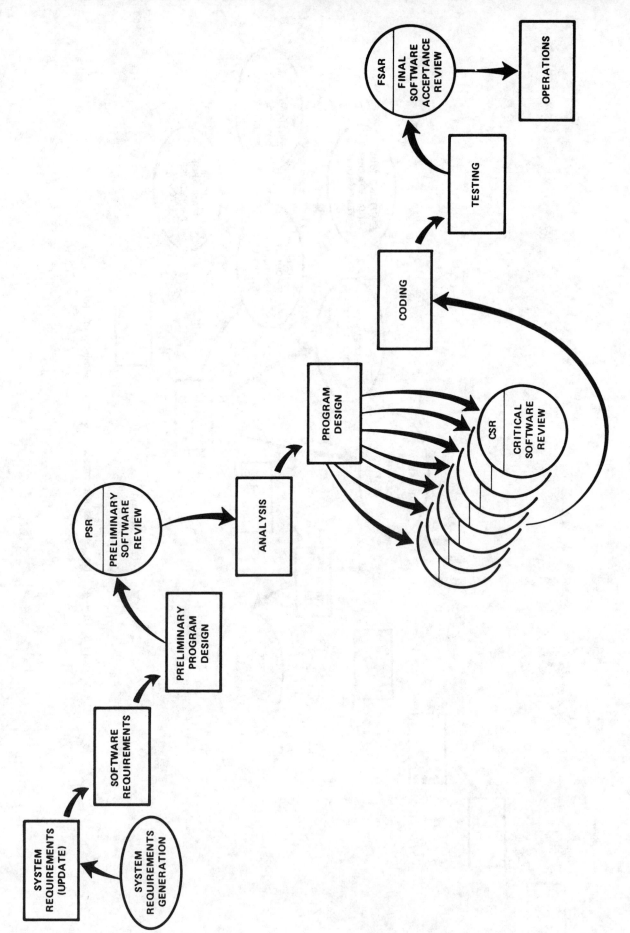

Figure 9. Step 5: Involve the customer — the involvement should be formal, in-depth, and continuing.

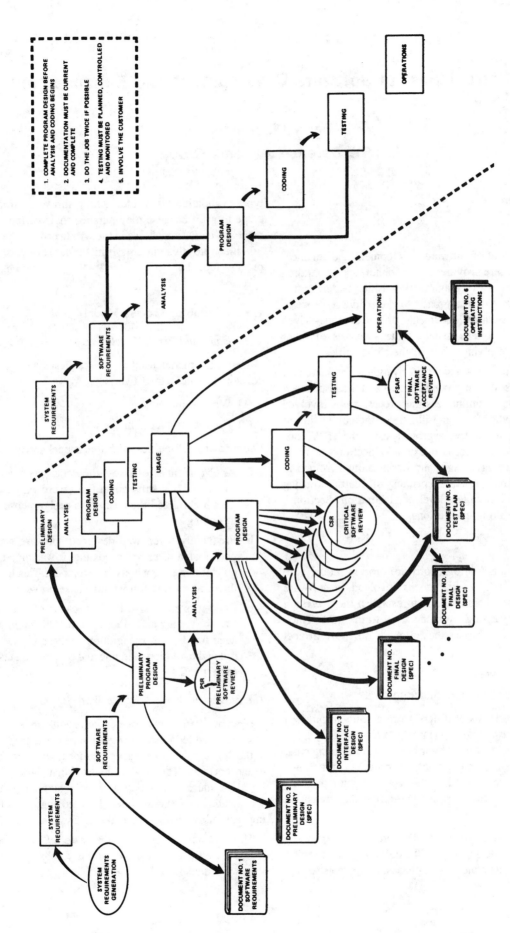

Figure 10. Summary

A Spiral Model of Software Development and Enhancement

Barry W. Boehm
TRW Defense Systems Group

1. Introduction

1.1 Overview

The spiral model of software development and enhancement presented here provides a new framework for guiding the software process. Its major distinguishing feature is that it creates a *risk-driven* approach to the software process, rather than a primarily document- driven or code-driven process. It incorporates many of the strengths of other models, while resolving many of their difficulties.

This section presents a short motivational and historical background of software process models and the issues they address. Section 2 summarizes the process steps involved in the spiral model. Section 3 illustrates the application of the spiral model to a software project, using the TRW Software Productivity Project as an example. Section 4 summarizes the primary advantages and implications involved in using the spiral model, and the primary difficulties in using it at its current incomplete level of elaboration. Section 5 presents the resulting conclusions.

1.2 Background

The primary function of a software process model is to determine the *order of the stages* involved in software development and evolution, and to establish the *transition criteria* for progressing from one stage to the next. Thus, a process model addresses the following software project questions:

(1) What shall we do next?

(2) How long shall we continue to do it?

Thus, a process model differs from a software *method* (often called a *methodology*) in that the latter's primary focus is on *how to navigate through each phase* (determining data, control, or "uses" hierarchies; partitioning functions, allocating requirements) and how to represent phase products (structure charts; stimulus-response threads; state transition diagrams).

Why are software process models important? Primarily because they provide guidance on the order in which a project should carry out its major tasks: phases, increments, proto-types, validation tasks, etc.. Many software projects have come to grief because they pursued their various development and evolution phases in the wrong order. The next section illustrates this via a short historical review of software process models.

1.3 Evolution of Process Models

The "Code and Fix" Model

The basic model used in the earliest days of software development contained two steps:

(1) Write some code;

(2) Fix the problems in the code.

The primary difficulties with this model were:

a. After a number of fixes, the code became so poorly structured that subsequent fixes were very expensive. This highlighted the need for a design phase previous to coding.

b. Frequently, even well-designed software was such a poor match to users' needs that it was either rejected outright or expensively redeveloped. This highlighted the need for a requirements phase previous to design.

c. Code was expensive to fix because of poor preparation for testing and modification. This highlighted the need for explicit recognition of these phases, and for test and evolution planning and preparation tasks in the early phases.

The Stagewise Model and the Waterfall Model

Even by 1956, experience on large software systems such as SAGE had led to the recognition of these problems, and to the development of a stagewise model [Benington, 1956][1] to address them. This model stipulated that software be developed in successive stages (operational plan, operational specifications, coding specifications, coding, parameter testing, assembly testing, shakedown, system evaluation).

The original treatment of the *waterfall model* given in [Royce, 1970][2] provided two primary enhancements to the stagewise model:

EH0263-4/87/0000/0128$01.00 © 1987 IEEE

- Recognition of the feedback loops between stages, and a guideline to confine the feedback loops to successive stages, in order to minimize the expensive rework involved in feedback across many stages.

- An initial incorporation of prototyping in the software life-cycle, via a "build it twice" step running in parallel with requirements analysis and design.

The waterfall approach was largely consistent with the *top-down structured programming model* formulated in [Dijkstra, 1970][3] and [Mills, 1971].[4] However, some attempts to apply these versions of the waterfall model ran into the following kinds of difficulties:

- The "build it twice" step was unnecessary in applications where design issues were well-understood (e.g., developing a straightforward payroll system), and subject to such unproductive phenomena as the "second system syndrome" [Brooks, 1975][5], in which the second system is overloaded with baroque embellishments.

- The pure top-down approach needed to be tempered with a "look ahead" step to cover such issues as high-risk, low-level elements and reusable or common software modules.

These considerations resulted in the *risk-management variant* of the waterfall model discussed in [Boehm, 1975][6] and elaborated in [Boehm, 1976].[7] In this variant, each step was expanded to include a validation and verification activity to cover high-risk elements, reuse considerations, and prototyping. Further refinements of the waterfall model covered such practices as incremental development [Distaso, 1980][8], developing program families and organizing software to accommodate change via information hiding [Parnas, 1979][9] and distinguishing pre-specification and post-specification activities via the "two-leg" model [Lehman, 1984].[10]

The successive stages used in the waterfall model helped eliminate many of the difficulties previously encountered on software projects. The waterfall model has become the basis of most software acquisition standards in government and industry. But even with the extensive revisions and refinements of the waterfall model, its basic scheme has encountered significant difficulties, and these have led to the formulation of alternative process models.

The Evolutionary Development Model

A primary source of difficulty with the waterfall model has been its emphasis on fully-elaborated documents as completion criteria for early requirements and design phases. For some classes of software, such as compilers or secure operating systems, this is the most effective way to proceed. But it does not work well for many classes of software, particularly interactive end-user applications. Document-driven

standards have pushed many projects to write elaborate specifications of poorly-understood user interfaces and decision-support functions, followed by the design and development of large quantities of unusable code. Further, in areas supported by fourth-generation languages (spread sheet or small business applications), it is clearly unnecessary to write elaborate specifications for one's application before implementing it.

These concerns have led to the formulation of the *evolutionary development* model [McCracken-Jackson, 1982],[11] whose stages consist of expanding increments of an operational software product, with the directions of evolution being determined by operational experience.

The evolutionary development model is ideally matched to a fourth generation language application, and well matched to situations in which users say, "I can't tell you what I want, but I'll know it when I see it." It gives users a rapid initial operational capability, and provides a realistic operational basis for determining subsequent product improvements.

But evolutionary development has its difficulties also. It is generally difficult to distinguish from the old "code and fix" model, whose spaghetti code and lack of planning were the initial motivation for the waterfall model. It is also based on the often-unrealistic assumption that the user's operational system will be flexible enough to accommodate unplanned evolution paths. This assumption is unjustified in three primary situations:

- Situations in which several independently-evolved applications must subsequently be closely integrated;

- "Information-sclerosis" situations in which temporary work-arounds for software deficiencies increasingly solidify into unchangeable constraints on evolution. A typical example is the following comment: "It's nice that you could change those equipment codes to make them more intelligible for us, but the Codes Committee just met and established the current codes as company standards."

- Bridging situations, in which the new software is incrementally replacing a large existing system. If the existing system is poorly modularized, it is difficult to provide a good sequence of "bridges" between the old software and the expanding increments of new software.

The Transform Model

The "spaghetti code" difficulties of the evolutionary development and code-and-fix models can also become a difficulty in various classes of waterfall-model applications, in which code is optimized for performance and becomes increasingly difficult to modify. The transform model [Balzer-Cheatham-Green, 1983][12] has been proposed as a solution to this difficulty.

The transform model assumes the existence of a capability to automatically transform a formal specification of a software product into a program satisfying the specification. The steps then prescribed by the transform model are:

- A formal specification of the best initial understanding of the desired product;
- Automatic transformation of the specification into code;
- An iterative loop if necessary to improve the performance of the resulting code by giving optimization guidance to the transformation system;
- Exercise of the resulting product; and
- An outer iterative loop to adjust the specification based on the resulting operational experience, and to rederive, re-optimize, and exercise the adjusted software product.

The transform model thus avoids the difficulty of having to modify code which has become poorly structured through repeated re-optimizations, since the modifications are made to the specification. It also avoids the extra time and expense involved in the intermediate design, code, and test activities.

But the transform model has various difficulties as well. Automatic transformation capabilities are only available for small products in a few limited areas: spread sheets, small fourth generation language applications, and limited computer-science domains. The transform model also shares some of the difficulties of the evolutionary development model, such as the assumption that users' operational systems will always be flexible enough to support unplanned evolution paths. And it would face a formidable knowledge-base-maintenance problem in dealing with the rapidly increasing and evolving supply of reusable software components and commercial software products.

2. The Spiral Model

The spiral model of the software process has been evolving at TRW for several years, based on experience with various refinements of the waterfall model as applied to large government software projects. The spiral model includes most previous models as special cases, and further provides guidance as to which combination of previous models best fits a given software situation. Its most complete application to date has been to the development of the TRW Software Productivity System; this application will be described in Section 3.

The spiral model is illustrated in Figure 1. The radial dimension in Figure 1 represents the cumulative cost incurred in accomplishing the steps to date; the angular dimension represents the progress made in completing each cycle of the spiral. (The model holds that each cycle involves a progression through the same sequence of steps, for each

portion of the product and for each of its levels of elaboration, from an overall concept of operation document down to the coding of each individual program). Note that some artistic license has been taken with the increasing cumulative cost dimension in order to enhance legibility of the steps in Figure 1.

2.1 A Typical Cycle of the Spiral

Each cycle of the spiral begins with the identification of:

- The objectives of the portion of the product being elaborated (performance, functionality, ability to accommodate change, etc).
- The alternative means of implementing this portion of the product (design A, design B, reuse, buy, etc).
- The constraints imposed on the application of the alternatives (cost, schedule, interface, etc.).

The next step is to evaluate the alternatives with respect to the objectives and constraints. Frequently, this process will identify areas of uncertainty which are significant sources of project risk. If so, the next step should involve the formulation of a cost-effective strategy for resolving the sources of risk. This may involve prototyping, simulation, administering user questionnaires, analytic modeling, or combinations of these and other risk-resolution techniques.

Once the risks are evaluated, the next step is determined by the relative risks remaining. If performance or user-interface risks strongly dominate program development or internal interface-control risks, the next step may be an evolutionary development step: a minimal effort to specify the overall nature of the product, a plan for the next level of prototyping, and the development of a more detailed prototype to continue to resolve the major risk issues. If this prototype is operationally useful, and robust enough to serve as a low-risk base for future product evolution, then the subsequent risk-driven steps would be the evolving series of evolutionary prototypes going toward the right in Figure 1.

On the other hand, if previous prototyping efforts have already resolved all of the performance or user-interface risks, and program development or interface-control risks dominate, the next step follows the basic waterfall approach (concept of operation, software requirements, preliminary design, etc. in Figure 1), modified as appropriate to incorporate incremental development. Each level of software specification in Figure 1 is then followed by a validation step and the preparation of plans for the succeeding cycle.

The spiral model also accommodates any appropriate mixture of a specification-oriented, prototype-oriented, simulation-oriented, automatic transformation-oriented, or other approach to software development, where the appropriate mixed strategy is chosen by considering the relative mag-

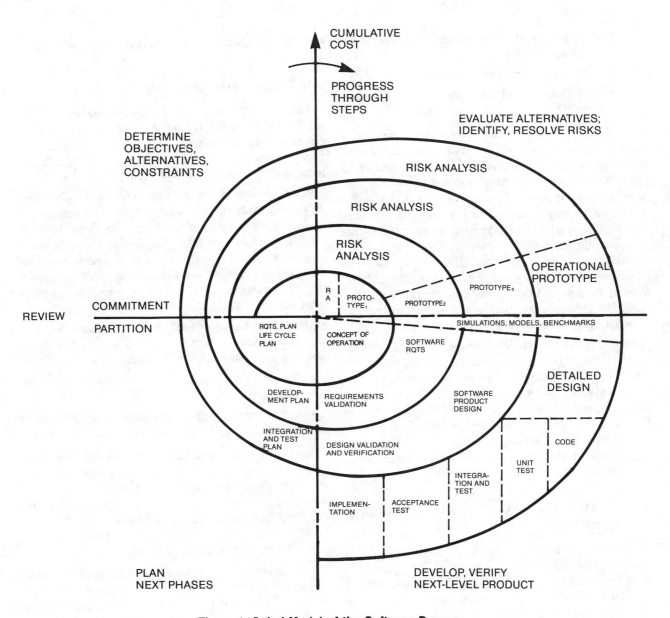

Figure 1: Spiral Model of the Software Process

nitude of the program risks, and the relative effectiveness of the various techniques in resolving the risks. (In a similar way, risk-management considerations determine the amount of time and effort which should be devoted to such other project activities as planning, configuration management, quality assurance, formal verification, or testing).

An important feature of the spiral model is that each cycle is completed by a review involving the primary people or organizations concerned with the product. This review covers all of the products developed during the previous cycle, including the plans for the next cycle and the resources required to carry them out. The major objective of the review is to ensure that all concerned parties are mutually committed to the approach to be taken for the next phase.

The plans for succeeding phases may also include a partition of the product into increments for successive development, or components to be developed by individual organizations or persons. Thus, the review and commitment step may range from an individual walkthrough of the design of a single programmer's component, to a major requirements review involving developer, customer, user, and maintenance organizations.

2.2 Initiating and Terminating the Spiral"

Four fundamental questions arise in considering this presentation of the spiral model:

(1) How does the spiral ever get started?

131

(2) How do you get off the spiral when it is appropriate to terminate a project early?

(3) Why does the spiral end so abruptly?

(4) What happens to software enhancement (or "maintenance")?

The answer to these questions involves an observation that the spiral model applies equally well to development or enhancement efforts, each of which are initiated by a hypothesis that a particular operational mission (or set of missions) could be improved by a software effort. The spiral process then involves a test of this hypothesis: at any time, if the hypothesis fails the test, the spiral is terminated. Otherwise, it terminates in the installation of the new or modified software, and the hypothesis is tested by observing the effect on the operational mission. Initiation, termination, and iteration of the tasks and products of previous cycles are thus implicitly defined in the spiral model, but not included in Figure 1 in order to simplify its presentation.

Similar spiral-type models have been defined in other fields. [Kolb, 1973][13] defines a four-stage development cycle whose stages are called divergence, assimilation, convergence, and execution. An example of its application to commercial product research and development is given in [Carlsson-Keane-Martin, 1976].[14] The book *Getting to Yes* [Fisher-Ury, 1981][15] defines a four-stage cycle for developing negotiation options; its stages are called problem, analysis, approaches, and action ideas.

3. Using The Spiral Model: The TRW Software Productivity System

The various rounds and activities involved in the spiral model are best understood via an example. This section will show how the spiral model was used in the definition and development of the TRW Software Productivity System (SPS), an integrated software engineering environment described in [Boehm et al., 1984].[16] The initial mission opportunity coincided with a corporate initiative to improve productivity in all appropriate corporate operations, and an initial hypothesis that software engineering was a potentially attractive area to investigate. This initially led to a small, extra "Round 0" circuit of the spiral to determine whether it was feasible to significantly increase software productivity at a reasonable corporate cost. (Very large or complex software projects will frequently precede the "concept of operation" round of the spiral with one or more smaller rounds to establish feasibility and to reduce the range of alternative solutions quickly and inexpensively).

Tables 1, 2, and 3 summarize the application of the spiral model to the first three rounds of defining the SPS. The major features of each round are discussed below, followed by some examples from later rounds such as preliminary and detailed design.

3.1. Round 0: Feasibility Study

This study involved five part-time participants over roughly a 2-3 month time span in 1980. As indicated in Table 1, the objectives and constraints for this round are expressed at a very high level, and in more qualitative terms: "significantly increase," "at reasonable cost," etc.

Round 0 considered a wide number of alternative approaches to significantly improve software productivity at a reasonable cost. Some of these primarily in the "technology" area could lead to the development of a software product, but these were also a number of alternatives in the management, personnel, and facilities areas which could have led to a conclusion not to embark on a software development activity.

The primary risk areas needing resolution were the possibility of situations in which the company would invest a good deal into improving software productivity and find that:

- The resulting productivity gains would not be significant; or that
- Any potentially high-leverage improvements would be incompatible with some aspects of the "TRW culture"

The risk-resolution activities undertaken in Round 0 were primarily surveys and analyses, including structured interviews of software developers and managers; an initial analysis of productivity leverage factors identified by the COCOMO software cost model (see [Boehm, 1981][16], Chapter 33); and an analysis of previous projects at TRW exhibiting high levels of productivity.

The risk analysis results indicated that it was highly likely that significant productivity gains could be achieved at a reasonable cost by pursuing an integrated set of initiatives in the four major areas. However, some candidate solutions, such as a software support environment based on a single, corporate, maxicomputer-based time-sharing system, were found to be in conflict with TRW constraints requiring support of different levels of security-classified projects. Thus, even at a very high level of generality of objectives and constraints, Round 0 was able to answer basic feasibility questions and eliminate significant classes of candidate solutions.

The plan for Round 1 involved a level of commitment on the order of 12 man-months as compared to the 2 man-months invested in Round 0 (During these rounds, all participants were part-time). Round 1 here corresponded fairly well with the initial round of the spiral model shown in Figure 1, in that its intent was to produce a concept of operation and a basic life-cycle plan for implementing whatever preferred alternative emerged.

Table 1: Spiral Model Usage: TRW Software Productivity System, Round 0

Objectives	• Significantly Increase Software Productivity
Constraints	• At Reasonable Cost • Within Context of TRW Culture — Government Contracts, High Tech., People Oriented, Security
Alternatives	• Management : Project Organization, Policies, Planning and Control • Personnel : Staffing, Incentives, Training • Technology : Tools, Workstations, Methods, Reuse • Facilities : Offices, Communications
Risks	• May be no High-Leverage Improvements • Improvements May Violate Constraints
Risk Resolution	• Internal Surveys • Analyze Cost Model • Analyze Exceptional Projects • Literature Search

Risk Resolution Results	• Some Alternatives Infeasible
	  — Single Time Sharing System : Security
	• Mix of Alternatives Can Produce Significant Gains
	  — Factor of 2 in 5 years
	• Need Further Study to Determine Best Mix

Plan for Next Phase	• 6-Person Task Force for 6 Months • More Extensive Surveys & Analysis — Internal, External, Economic • Develop Concept of Operation, Economic Rationale
Commitment	• Fund Next Phase

133

Table 2: Spiral Model Usage: TRW Software Productivity System, Round 1

Objectives	• Double Software Productivity in 5 Years
Constraints	• $10,000 per Person Investment • Within Context of TRW Culture — Government Contracts, High Tech., People Oriented, Security • Preference for TRW Products
Alternatives	• Office : Private/Modular/... • Communication : LAN/Star/Concentrators/... • Terminals : Private/Shared; Smart/Dumb • Tools : SREM/PSL-PSA/...;PDL/SADT/... • CPU : IBM/DEC/CDC/...
Risks	• May Miss High-Leverage Options • TRW LAN Price/Performance • Workstation Cost
Risk Resolution	• Extensive External Surveys, Visits • TRW LAN Benchmarking • Workstation Price/Performance
Risk Resolution Results	• Ops. Concept : Private Offices, TRW LAN, Personal Terminals, VAX • Begin with Primarily Dumb Terminals; Experiment with Smart Workstations • Defer OS, Tools Selection
Plan for Next Phase	• Partition Effort into SDE, Facilities, Management • Develop First-Cut Prototype SDE — Design-to-Cost : 15 Person Team for 1 Year • Plan for External Usage
Commitment	• Develop Prototype SDE • Commit an Upcoming Project to Use SDE • Commit the SDE to Support the Project • Form Representative Steering Group

3.2. Round 1: Concept of Operations

Table 2 provides a summary of Round 1 of the spiral along the same lines given in Table 1 for Round 0. Rather than simply elaborate on the entries in Table 2, the discussion below focuses on comparing and contrasting the features of Rounds 0 and 1:

- As mentioned above, the level of investment was greater (12 man-months vs. 2).

- The objectives and constraints were more specific ("double software productivity in 5 years at a cost of $10K/person" vs. "significantly increase productivity at a reasonable cost").

- Additional constraints surfaced, such as the preference for TRW products (particularly, a TRW-developed local area network (LAN) system).

- The alternatives were more detailed ("SREM, PSL/PSA or SADT, as requirements tools etc." vs. "tools"; "private or shared terminals, smart or dumb terminals" vs. "workstations").

- The risk areas identified were more specific ("TRW LAN price-performance within a $10K/person investment constraint" vs. "improvements may violate reasonable-cost constraint").

- The risk-resolution activities were more extensive (including the benchmarking and analysis of a prototype TRW LAN being developed for another project).

- The result was a fairly specific Operational Concept Document, involving private offices tailored to software work patterns, and personal terminals connected to VAX superminis via the TRW LAN. Some choices were specifically deferred to the next round, such as the choice of operating system and specific tools.

- The life-cycle plan and the plan for the next phase involved a a partitioning into separate activities to address management improvements, facilities development, and development of the first increment of a software development environment. (SDE).

- The commitment step involved more than just an agreement with the plan. It added a commitment for an upcoming 100-person software project to be the initial testbed user of the system, and for the environment development to focus on the needs of the testbed project. It also added the formation of a representative steering group to ensure that the separate activities were well-coordinated, and that the environment would not be overly optimized around the testbed project.

Although the plan recommended the development of a prototype environment, it also recommended that the project also employ requirements specifications and design specifications in a risk-driven way. Thus, the development of the environment followed the succeeding rounds of the spiral model.

3.3. Round 2: Top-Level Requirements Specification

Table 3 shows the corresponding steps involved during Round 2 in defining the SPS during early 1981. Since a number of these Round 2 decisions and their rationale are covered in [Boehm et al., 1984],[16] we will not elaborate on them there. Instead, we will summarize two of the highlights dealing with risk management and the use of the spiral model.

- The initial risk-identification activities during Round 2 showed that several system requirements hinged on the decision between a host-target system or a fully portable tool set, and the decision between VMS and Unix as the host operating system. These requirements included the functions required to provide a user-friendly front-end, the operating system to be used by the workstations, and the functions required to support a host-target operation. In order to keep these requirements in synchronization with the other requirements, a special mini-spiral was initiated to address and resolve these issues. The resulting review resulted in a commitment to a host-target operation using Unix on the host system, at a point early enough to work the OS-dependent requirements in a timely fashion.

- Addressing the risks of mismatches to the user-project's needs and priorities resulted in substantial participation of the user-project personnel in the requirements definition activity. This led to several significant redirections of the requirements, particularly toward supporting the early phases of the software life-cycle into which the user project was embarking, such as an adaptation of the Software Requirements Engineering Methodology (SREM) Tools for requirements specification and analysis.

It is also interesting to note that the form of Tables 1, 2, and 3 was originally developed for presentation purposes, but subsequently became a standard "Spiral Model Template" used on later projects. These templates are useful not only for organizing project activities, but also as a residual design-rationale record. Design rationale information is of paramount importance in assessing the potential reusability of software components on future projects.

3.4. Succeeding Rounds of the Spiral"

Within the confines of this paper, it is not possible to discuss each round of the spiral in detail. But it will be useful to illustrate some examples of how the spiral model is used to handle situations arising in the preliminary design and

Table 3: Spiral Model Usage: TRW Software Productivity System, Round 2

Objectives	• User-Friendly System • Integrated Software, Office-Automated Tools • Support All Project Personnel • Support All Life-Cycle Phases
Constraints	• Customer-Deliverable SDE → Portability • Stable, Reliable Services
Alternatives	• OS : VMS/AT&T Unix/Berkeley Unix/ISC • Host-Target/Fully Portable Toolset • Workstations : Zenith/LSI-11/. . .
Risks	• Mismatch to User-Project Needs, Priorities • User-Unfriendly System — 12-Language Syndrome, Experts-Only • Unix Performance, Support • Workstation/Mainframe compatibility
Risk Resolution	• User-Project Surveys, Requirements Participation • Survey of Unix-Using Organizations • Workstation Study
Risk Resolution Results	• Top-Level Requirements Specification • Host-Target with Unix Host • Unix-Based Workstations • Build User-Friendly Front End for Unix • Initial Focus on Tools to Support Early Phases
Plan for Next Phase	• Overall Development Plan — for Tools : SREM, RTT, PDL, OA Tools — for Front End, Support Tools — for LAN, Equipment, Facilities
Commitment	• Proceed with Plans

detailed design of components of the SPS: the preliminary design specification for the Requirements Traceability Tool (RTT), and a detailed design go-back on the Unit Development Folder (UDF) tool.

The RTT Preliminary Design Specification

The Requirements Traceability Tool (RTT) establishes the traceability between itemized software requirements specifications, design elements, code elements, and test cases. It also supports various associated query, analysis, and report generation capabilities. The preliminary design specification for the RTT (and most of the other SPS tools) looked different from the usual preliminary design specification, which tends to show a uniform level of elaboration of all components of the design. Instead, the level of detail of the RTT specification was risk-driven:

- In areas involving a high risk if the design was wrong, the design was carried down to the detailed design level, usually with the aid of rapid prototyping. These areas included working out the implications of various "undo" options, and the effects of various control keys used to escape from various levels of the program.

- In areas involving a moderate risk if the design was wrong, the design was carried down to a preliminary-design level. These areas included the basic command options for the tool, and the schemata for the requirements traceability data base. Here again, the ease of rapid prototyping with Unix shell scripts supported a good deal of user-interface prototyping.

- In areas involving a low risk if the design was wrong, very little design elaboration was done. These areas included details of all of the help message options and all of the report-generation options, once the nature of these options had been established in some example instances.

A Detailed Design Go-Back: The UDF Tool

The Unit Development Folder (UDF) tool collects into an electronic "folder" all of the artifacts involved in the development of a single-programmer software unit (typically 500-1000 instructions): unit requirements, design, code, test cases, test results, and documentation. It also includes a management template for tracking the programmer's scheduled and actual completion of each artifact.

During the detailed design of the Unit Development Folder (UDF) tool, an alternative was considered to reuse portions of the Requirements Traceability Tool (RTT) to provide pointers to the requirements and preliminary design specifications of the unit being developed. This turned out to be an extremely attractive alternative, not only in avoiding duplicate software development, but also in surfacing several

issues involving many-to-many mappings between requirements, design, and code which had not been considered in designing the UDF tool. These led to a rethinking of the UDF tool requirements and preliminary design, which avoided a great deal of code rework that would have been necessary if the detailed design of the UDF tool had proceeded in a purely deductive, top-down fashion from the original UDF requirements specification. The resulting go-back led to a significantly different and more capable UDF tool, incorporating the RTT in its "users-hierarchy."

Spiral Model Features Illustrated by the Two Examples

From these two examples, we can see that the spiral approach:

- Fosters the development of specifications that are not necessarily uniform, exhaustive, or formal, in that they defer detailed elaboration of low risk software elements, and avoid unnecessary breakage in their design, until the high-risk elements of the design are stabilized.

- Incorporates prototyping as a risk-reduction option at any stage of development. In fact, prototyping and reuse risk analyses were often used in the process of going from detailed design into code.

- Accommodates go-backs to earlier stages of the spiral as more attractive alternatives are identified or as new risk issues need resolution.

3.5. Results of Using the Spiral Model

The resulting Software Productivity System developed and supported using the spiral model successfully avoided the risks identified, and achieved most of its objectives. The system has grown to include over 300 tools and over 1,300,000 instructions; 93% of the instructions were reused from previous project-developed, TRW-developed, or external software packages. All of the projects using the system have increased their productivity at least 50%; most have indeed doubled their productivity (as compared with cost estimation model predictions of their productivity using traditional methods).

However, one risk area was underestimated—the risk that projects with non-Unix target systems would not accept a Unix-based host system. Some projects accepted the host-target approach, but a good many did not for various reasons (customer constraints, zero-cost target machines). As a result, the system was less widely used on TRW projects than expected. This and other lessons learned have been incorporated into the spiral model approach to developing TRW's next-generation software development environment.

4. Spiral Model Advantages, Difficulties, and Implications

4.1. Spiral Model Advantages

The primary advantage of the spiral model is that its range of options allows it to accommodate the best features of existing software process models, while its risk-driven approach helps it to avoid most of their difficulties. In appropriate situations, the spiral model becomes equivalent to one of the existing process models. In other situations, it provides guidance on the best mix of existing approaches to be applied to a given project. The application of the spiral model to the TRW Software Productivity System discussed in Section 3 provides a good example of a risk-driven mix of specifying, prototyping, and evolutionary development.

The primary conditions under which the spiral model becomes equivalent to other main process models are summarized below.

- If a project has a low risk in such areas as getting the wrong user interface or not meeting stringent performance requirements; and it has a high risk if it loses budget and schedule predictability and control; then these risk considerations drive the spiral model into an equivalence to the waterfall model.

- If a software product's requirements are very stable (implying a low risk of expensive design and code breakage due to requirements changes during development); and if the presence of errors in the software product constitutes a high risk to the mission it serves; then these risk considerations drive the spiral model to resemble the two-leg model of precise specification and formal deductive program development.

- If a project has a low risk in such areas as losing budget and schedule predictability and control, encountering large-system integration problems, or coping with information sclerosis; and it has a high risk in such areas as getting the wrong user interface or user decision support requirements; then these risk considerations drive the spiral model into an equivalence to the evolutionary development model.

- If automated software generation capabilities are available, then the spiral model accommodates them either as options for rapid prototyping or for application of the transform model, depending on the risk considerations involved.

- If the high-risk elements of a project involve a mix of the risk items above, then the spiral approach will reflect an appropriate mix of the process models above. In doing so, its risk-avoidance features will generally avoid the difficulties of the other models.

In addition, the spiral model has a number of further advantages which are summarized below.

- *It accommodates strategies for developing program families, and for the reuse of existing software.* The steps involving the identification and evaluation of alternatives accommodate these options.

- *It accommodates preparation for life-cycle evolution, growth, and changes of the software product.* The major sources of product change are included in the product's objectives, and information-hiding approaches are included in the architectural design alternatives.

- *It provides a mechanism for incorporating software quality objectives into software product development.* This mechanism derives from the emphasis on identifying all types of objectives and constraints during each round of the spiral. The GOALS approach and software engineering goal structure in [Boehm, 1981; Chapter 3][17] provide a process and checklist for incorporating quality objectives.

- *It focuses on eliminating errors and unattractive alternatives early.* The risk-analysis, validation, and commitment steps cover these considerations.

- *It accommodates iterations, go-backs, and early termination of non-viable software projects.* The first two of these aspects were illustrated in the TRW-SPS example. The example also illustrated the overall objective of the spiral approach to start small, keep the spiral as tight as possible, and thus achieve the project's objectives with a minimum resource expenditure.

- *For each of the sources of project activity and resource expenditure, it answers the key question, "how much is enough?"* How much should a project do of requirements analysis, planning, configuration management, quality assurance, testing, formal verification, etc? Using the risk-driven approach, we can see that the answer is not the same for all projects, and that the appropriate level of effort is determined by the level of risk incurred by not doing enough.

- *It can support, and be supported by, advanced software development environments.* The process steps and their associated internal and external products can be treated as data base objects to be handled by an advanced object manager. Also, process and risk-management guidance for software developers can be incorporated into an evolving Knowledge Based Software Assistant or activity coordinator.

- *It does not involve separate approaches for software development and software enhancement (or "maintenance").* This aspect helps avoid the "second class citizen" status frequently associated with software maintenance. It also helps avoid many of the problems that currently ensue when high-risk enhancement efforts are approached in the same way as routine maintenance efforts.

- *It provides a viable framework for integrated hardware-software system development.* The focus on risk-management and on eliminating unattractive alternatives early and inexpensively is equally applicable to hardware and software.

- *On the other hand, it avoids forcing software development procedures into hardware development paradigms.* A good example of this is the review called "Critical Design Review," or CDR, which occurs after the detailed design is completed. For a hardware development risk profile, this review is indeed critical: as seen in Figure 2, it is the final review before the project begins to commit the bulk of its resources into producing hardware. From this standpoint, it is indeed critical to invest in an exhaustive, across-the-board review of the detailed design specifications before proceeding. For a software project, however, the risk profile is significantly different. Typically, in order to reduce the crucial factor of software development time, a software

project will work out detailed unit interfaces by the Preliminary Design Review (PDR), and then begin to commit the bulk of its resources to large numbers of people doing detailed design and code in parallel (see Figure 2). To interrupt this process with a single, large, across-the-board CDR is not only time-consuming and expensive, but also ineffective, as the inter-unit interface specifications were necessarily verified thoroughly at the PDR. Thus, the critical review for a software project is the PDR; the "detailed design review" function is performed much more cost-effectively by a program of individual design inspections or walkthroughs, followed as appropriate by an overall review of the major issues identified in the walkthroughs.

4.2. Spiral Model Difficulties

Although the full spiral model can be successfully applied in many situations, it still has some difficulties or challenges to address before it can be called a mature, universally applicable model. The three primary spiral model challenges are summarized below.

(1) *The spiral model currently works well on internal software developments like the TRW-SPS, but it needs fur-*

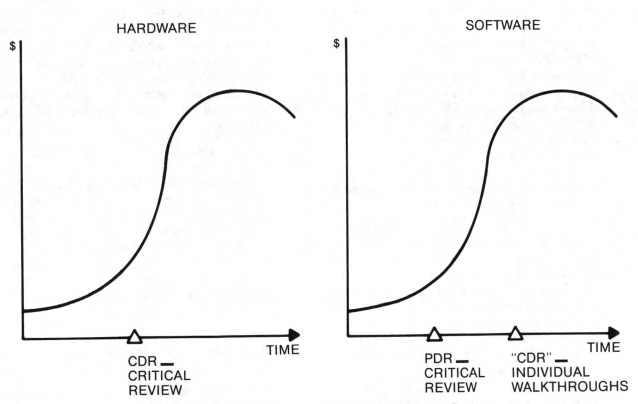

Figure 2: Risk-Oriented Management Refocuses Software Reviews onto Key Software Issues

ther work to match it to the world of contract software acquisition.

Internal software developments have a great deal of flexibility and freedom to accommodate stage-by-stage commitments, to defer commitments to specific options, to establish mini-spirals to resolve critical-path items, to adjust levels of effort, or to accommodate such practices as prototyping, evolutionary development, or design to cost. The world of contract software acquisition has a harder time achieving these degrees of flexibility and freedom without losing accountability and control.

Recently, a good deal of progress has been made in establishing more flexible contract mechanisms, such as the use of competitive front-end contracts for concept definition or prototype fly-offs; the use of level-of effort and award-fee contracts for evolutionary development; and the use of design-to-cost contracts. Although these have been generally successful, the procedures for using them still need to be worked out to the point that acquisition managers feel fully comfortable in using them.

(2) *The spiral model places a great deal of reliance on the ability of software developers to identify and manage sources of project risk.*

A good example is the spiral model's risk-driven specification, which carries high-risk elements down to a great deal of detail, and leaves low-risk elements to be elaborated in later stages, by which time there is less risk of breakage.

However, a team of inexperienced or low-balling developers may also produce a specification with a different pattern of variation in levels of detail: a great elaboration of detail for the well-understood, low-risk elements; and little elaboration of the poorly-understood, high-risk elements. Unless there is an insightful review of such a specification by experienced developer or acquisition personnel, this type of project will proceed to give an illusion of progress during a period in which it is actually heading for disaster.

Another concern is that a risk-driven specification will also be people-dependent. For example, a design may be produced by an expert, but may be implemented by non-experts. In this case, even though the expert does not need a great deal of detailed documentation, it is necessary for him to produce enough additional documentation to ensure that the non-experts will not go astray. Reviewers of the specification must be sensitive to these concerns as well.

With a conventional, document-driven approach, the requirement to carry all aspects of the specification to a uniform level of detail eliminates some potential problems, and creates a situation in which some aspects of reviews can be adequately carried out by inexperienced reviewers. But it also creates a large drain on the time of the scarce experts, who must dig for the critical issues within a large mass of non-critical detail. And further, if the high-risk elements have been glossed over by impressive-sounding references to poorly-understood capabilities (e.g., a new synchronization concept or a commercial DBMS), then there is an even greater risk of the conventional approach giving an illusion of progress in situations which are actually heading for disaster.

(3) *In general, the spiral model process steps need further elaboration to ensure that all of the participants in a software development are operating in a consistent context.*

Some examples are the need for more detailed definitions of the nature of spiral model specifications and milestones, the nature and objectives of spiral model reviews, and the nature of spiral model status indicators and cost-vs-progress tracking procedures. Another need is for guidelines and checklists to be used in identifying the most likely sources of project risk, and the most effective risk-resolution techniques for each source of risk.

It is currently feasible for highly experienced people to successfully use the spiral approach without these elaborations. But for large scale use in situations where people bring widely differing experience bases to the project, added levels of elaboration—such as have been accumulated over the years for document-driven approaches—are important in ensuring consistent interpretation and usage of the spiral approach across the project.

Efforts to apply and refine the spiral model have largely focussed on creating a discipline of software risk management, including techniques for risk identification, risk analysis, risk prioritization, risk management planning, and risk element tracking. An example of the results of this activity is the prioritized top-ten list of software risk items given in Figure 3. Another example is the risk management plan discussed in the next section. Other recent applications and extensions of the spiral model are presented in [Belz, 1986][18] and [Iivari, 1987].[19]

4.3. Spiral Model Implications: The Risk Management Plan

Even if an organization is not fully ready to adopt the entire spiral approach, there is one characteristic spiral model technique which can easily be adapted to any life-cycle model,

Figure 3: A Prioritized Top Ten List of Software Risk Items

Risk Item	Risk Management Techniques
1. Personnel shortfalls	— Staffing with top talent, job matching; teambuilding; morale building, cross-training; pre-scheduling key people.
2. Unrealistic schedules and budgets	— Detailed, multi-source cost and schedule estimation; design to cost; incremental development; software reuse; requirements scrubbing.
3. Developing the wrong software functions	— Organization analysis; mission analysis; ops-concept formulation; user surveys; prototyping; early users' manuals.
4. Developing the wrong user interface	— Task analysis; prototyping; scenarios.
5. Gold plating	— Requirements scrubbing; prototyping; cost-benefit analysis; design to cost.
6. Continuing stream of requirement changes	— High change threshold, information hiding; incremental development (defer changes to later increments).
7. Shortfalls in externally-furnished components	— Benchmarking; inspections; reference checking; compatibility analysis.
8. Shortfalls in externally-performed tasks	— Reference checking; pre-award audits; award-fee contracts; competitive design or prototyping; teambuilding.
9. Real-time performance shortfalls	— Simulation; benchmarking; modeling; prototyping; instrumentation; tuning.
10. Straining computer science capabilities	— Technical analysis; cost-benefit analysis; prototyping; reference checking.

and which can provide many of the benefits of the spiral approach. This is the *Risk Management Plan* summarized in Table 4. The Risk Management Plan basically ensures that each project make an early identification of its top risk items (the number 10 is not an absolute requirement), develop a plan for resolving the risk items, identify and plan to resolve new risk items as they surface, and highlight the project's progress vs. plans in monthly reviews.

The Risk Management Plan has been used successfully at TRW and other organizations, and has ensured an appropriate focus on early prototyping, simulation, benchmarking, key-person staffing measures, and other early risk-resolution techniques which have helped avoid many potential project "show-stoppers." The recent U.S. Department of Defense standard on software management, DoD-STD-2167, requires

that developers produce and use risk management plans, as does its counterpart Air Force regulation, AFR 800-14.

Table 4. Software Risk Management Plan

(1) Identify the project's top 10 risk items

(2) Present a plan for resolving each risk item

(3) Update list of top risk items, plan, and results monthly

(4) Highlight risk-item status in monthly project reviews

(5) Initiate appropriate corrective actions

5. Conclusions

(1) The risk-driven nature of the spiral model is more adaptable to the full range of software project situations than are the primarily document-driven approaches such as the waterfall model or the primarily code-driven approaches such as evolutionary development. It is particularly applicable to very large, complex, ambitious software systems.

(2) The spiral model has been quite successful in its largest application to date: the development and enhancement of the TRW SPS. Overall, the spiral approach was highly effective in achieving a high level of software support environment capability in a very short time, and in providing the flexibility necessary to accommodate a high dynamic range of technical alternatives and user objectives.

(3) The spiral model is not yet as fully elaborated as are more established models such as the waterfall model. Thus, although the spiral model can be successfully applied by software-experienced personnel, it needs further elaboration in such areas as contracting, specifications, milestones, reviews, status monitoring, and risk-area identification in order to be fully usable in all situations.

(4) Partial implementations of the spiral model such as the Risk Management Plan are compatible with most current process models, and are highly useful in helping projects to overcome their major sources of project risk.

Acknowledgments

I would like to thank Frank Belz, Lolo Penedo, George Spadaro, Bob Williams, Bob Balzer, Gillian Frewin, Peter Hamer, Manny Lehman, Lee Osterweil, Dave Parnas, Bill Riddle, Steve Squires, and Dick Thayer for their stimulating and insightful comments and discussions of earlier versions of this paper, and Nancy Donato for producing its several versions.

References

(1) H.D. Benington, "Production of Large Computer Programs," *Proc. ONR Symposium on Advanced Programming Methods for Digital Computers*, June 1956, pp. 15-27. Also available in *Annals of the History of Computing*, Oct. 1983, pp.350-361, and *Proceedings, ICSE 9*, IEEE-CS, 1987.

(2) W.W. Royce, "Managing the Development of Large Software Systems: Concepts and Techniques," *Proceedings, WESCON*, August 1970. Also available in *Proceedings, ICSE 9*, IEEE-CS, 1987.

(3) E.W. Dijkstra, "Notes on Structured Programming," Technische Hogeschool Eindhoven, Report No. EWD-248, April 1970. Also in O.J. Dahl, E.W. Dijkstra, and C.A.R. Hoare, *Structured Programming*, Academic Press, 1972.

(4) H.D. Mills, "Top-Down Programming in Large Systems," in *Debugging Techniques in Large Systems*, R. Ruskin (ed), Prentice-Hall, 1971, pp. 41-55.

(5) F.P. Brooks, *The Mythical Man-Month*, Addison-Wesley, 1975.

(6) B.W. Boehm, "Software Design and Structuring" in *Practical Strategies for Developing Large Software Systems*, E. Horowitz (ed), Addison-Wesley, 1975, pp. 103-128.

(7) B.W. Boehm, "Software Engineering," *IEEE Trans. Computers*, December 1976, pp. 1226-1241.

(8) J.R. Distaso, "Software Management—A Survey of the Practice in 1980." *IEEE Proceedings, Sept. 1980, pp. 1103-1119.*

(9) *D.L. Parnas, "Designing Software for Ease of Extension and Contraction," IEEE Trans. S/W Engr.*, March 1979, pp. 128-137.

(10) M.M. Lehman, "A Further Model of Coherent Programming Processes," *Proceedings, Software Process Workshop*, IEEE, Feb. 1984, pp.27-33.

(11) D.D. McCracken and M.A. Jackson, "Life Cycle Concept Considered Harmful," *Software Engineering Notes*, ACM, April 1982, pp. 29-32.

(12) R. Balzer, T.E. Cheatham, and C. Green, "Software Technology in the 1990's: Using a New Paradigm," *Computer*, Nov. 1983, pp. 39-45.

(13) D.A. Kolb, "On Management and the Learning Process," *MIT Sloan School Working Paper 652-73*, Cambridge, MA, 1973.

(14) B. Carlsson, P. Keane, and J.B. Martin, "R&D Organizations as Learning Systems," *Sloan Management Review*, Spring 1976, pp. 1-15.

(15) R. Fisher and W. Ury, *Getting to Yes*, Houghton Mifflin, 1981; Penguin Books, 1983.

(16) B.W. Boehm, M.H. Penedo, E.D. Stuckle, R.D. Williams, and A.B. Pyster, "A Software Development Environment for Improving Productivity," *Computer*, June 1984, pp. 30-44.

(17) B.W. Boehm, *Software Engineering Economics*, Prentice-Hall, 1981.

(18) F.C. Belz, "Applying the Spiral Model: Observations on Developing System Software in Ada," *Proceedings, 1986 Annual Conference on Ada Technology*, Atlanta, GA, 1986, pp. 57-66.

(19) J. Iivari, "A Hierarchical Spiral Model for the Software Process," *ACM Software Engineering Notes*, Jan. 1987, pp. 35-37.

Chapter 4: Planning a Software Engineering Project

1. Introduction to Chapter

Planning a software engineering project is defined as all the management activities that lead to the selection, among alternatives, of future courses of action for the project along with the program for carrying them out. Planning involves selecting the *objectives* and *goals* of the project and the *strate-* *gies, policies, programs,* and *procedures* for achieving them. "Planning is deciding in advance what to do, how to do it, when to do it, and who is to do it" [1].

Planning for a software engineering project can be partitioned into 10 general management activities (see Table 4.1). Each activity in the table is followed by its definition or an amplifying description.

I THOUGHT YOU WERE DOING THE PLANNING

Table 4.1: Planning Activities

Activity	Definition or Explanation
Set objectives or goals	— Determine objectives, activities, or desired outcome or results.
Develop strategies	— Decide major organizational goals and general program of action for reaching those goals.
Develop policies	— Make standing decisions on important recurring matters to provide a guide for decision making.
Determine courses of action	— Search for and examine different courses of action.
Make decisions	— Evaluate and select a course of action from among alternatives.
Set procedures and rules	— Establish methods, guides, and limits for accomplishing an activity.
Develop programs	— Establish policies, procedures, rules, tasks, schedules, and resources necessary to reach a goal or complete a course of action.
Forecast future situations	— Anticipate future events or make assumptions about the future; predict future results or expectations from courses of action.
Prepare budgets	— Assign or allocate costs or numbers to plan/program.
Document project plans	— Record decisions, courses of action, programs/plans, expected future situations, budget, and so on.

2. Overview of Chapter

The eleven papers in this chapter cover many aspects of planning a software engineering project. Planning or lack of planning is the major issue in software engineering development; it has given rise to more papers than all the other functions of managing a software development project combined.

The activities listed in Table 4.1 were used as an outline to identify a spectrum of papers on planning activities. These activities are discussed and illustrated in one or more of the following papers.

3. Description of Papers

The objectives or goals of a software engineering project can usually be found in the *software requirements specifications* and the *project management plans*. Usually we think of software requirements as being part of the software development process, rather than the management process. However, the objectives of a software engineering project are both technical and managerial. Without an accurate and detailed software requirements specification, the manager cannot possibly accurately schedule and estimate the cost of the project.

The Yeh, Zave, Conn, and Cole paper, "Software Requirements: New Directions and Perspectives," defines and discusses the following software engineering project objectives and requirements:

- Technical requirements (*functional requirements* and *non-functional requirements: performance, reliability, security,* and *operational constraints*).

- *Managerial requirements and constraints (development paradigms, size and cost, milestones* and review procedures, *acceptance criteria,* and so on).

- Mandatory (minimum), desirable, and optional requirements; *design-to-cost* consideration; and the application of *costs tradeoffs* for different design options.

- *User interface* and the application of pilot tests to determine user display requirements.

Note: only technical requirements should be documented in a software requirements specification [2]. Non-technical requirements belong in the project management plan (see Fairley's paper on "A Guide for Preparing Software Project Management Plans" in this chapter).

This paper also describes several models that can be used to represent requirement specifications including an informal description of PAISLey. Problems in determining software requirements are discussed and some solutions are proposed.

The second paper by Norm Howes is also about software requirements specifications and takes a unique approach to determining the project's objectives. Howes recommends preparing a users' manual as a substitute for the software requirements specifications as he did in this case study for a NASA application.

The next paper, by Miller, is an overview on planning a project and provides an excellent description on how to implement the plan (call a "program of action" in the management sciences; not to be confused with a "computer program"). He describes how to plan a generic project which could apply equally well to the development of a software engineering product. To Miller that project planning has essentially one purpose: to establish a foundation for execution and successful completion of the project. He discusses who is responsible for the plan, what the planning process is, what goes into a plan, and the planning document itself. The final part of the paper covers controlling the project according to the plan (an activity that will be discussed in Chapter 8).

The fourth paper is a series of slides on software development *policies* and *software engineering standards* prepared and presented by Ed Goldberg of TRW, Inc. for an early AIAA Software Management Conference. The slides describe a set of software engineering policies within the SEID division of TRW. These policies are generic to any large software development organization and therefore can be used as a model for other software development groups.

Managers must make decisions concerning possible courses of action. One of the activities of project management is the selection of the *methodologies* and *tools* necessary for developing the software system. The paper by David N. Card, "A Software Technology Evaluation Program," is one of the few available documents describing a method for selecting effective software engineering methodologies and tools. The reader should pay particular attention to the list of technologies under "Modern Programming Practices" and the list of review and management procedures listed under "Quality Assurance."

One of the major issues in software engineering today is called the *technology transfer gap*. The technology transfer gap, measured in years, can be defined as the time lapse between the development of a new product, tool or technique and its use by the consumers of that product, tool or technique. This technology transfer gap for software has been estimated to be on the order of 5-20 years [3] [4], with the longer periods of time being the rule rather than the exception. Ed Yourdon's presents "A Game Plan for Technology Transfer" for implementing new software development technologies in software development organizations which would reduce the technology transfer gap. The paper provides insight into problems encountered in trying to implement new techniques. In his game plan the trick is to incorporate new technology into the software development project without disrupting or threatening the success of the project. In conclusion, his paper makes recommendations on how to successfully transfer new technologies into a software project.

The seventh paper, by Cori, debates the necessity of having a master project schedule. He prescribes a method for defining project objectives, breaking down the work to be accomplished into manageable pieces, sequencing the work activities, and estimating activity duration (again part of management activity called "programs"). This paper also surveys and compares five scheduling techniques—*milestone chart, Gantt chart*, full wall scheduling, and *precedence networks (CPM and PERT)*.

One of the more effective planning tools in project management is the *work breakdown structure* (more commonly called a WBS). Tausworthe's "The Work Breakdown Structure in Software Project Management" presents an excellent description of the *process WBS* (in contrast to a *product WBS*) and ways it can be used by project management for project planning and control. The WBS is used to represent subprojects, tasks, subtasks, work packages, and so on. Tausworthe presents a checklist developed at the Jet Propulsion Laboratory for generating a WBS.

For a project manager to be able to "program" and budget a software project, he must understand how to estimate costs and schedules for a software engineering project. The next-to-last paper by Barry Boehm is an all-encompassing paper on software engineering economics and is patterned after his book *Software Engineering Economics* [5]. Boehm's paper identifies seven major software cost estimation techniques and lists the strengths and weaknesses of each. His paper also gives a short description of several software cost models: SDC cost model, TRW Wolverton model, Putnam SLIM model, Doty model, and RCA PRICE S model. A detailed description of the extremely popular COCOMO software cost estimation model is included. Also discussed are cost-benefit analysis, present value analysis, risk analysis, uncertainty, and the value of information.

To summarize this chapter, Dick Fairley provides "A Guide for Preparing Software Project Management Plans" which is based on the new proposed IEEE standard for a project management plans [6]. This paper delineates the contents of a software engineering project plan and can be used as a checklist for planning activities. As a famous philosopher once said, ''A plan in the mind of man is not a plan at all.''

References

1. H. Koontz and C. O'Donnell, *Principles of Management: An Analysis of Managerial Functions*, 5th ed., McGraw-Hill Book Company, NY, 1972.

2. ANSI/IEEE Std 830-1984, *IEEE Standard for ''Software Requirements Specifications,* IEEE, Inc., NY, 1984.

3. A.I. Wasserman and L.A. Belady, ''Software Engineering: The Turning Point,'' (from the ''The Oregon Report''), *Computer,* September 1978, pp. 30–39.

4. S.T. Redwine, Jr. and W.E. Riddle, ''Software Technology Maturation,'' *Proceedings of the 8th International Conference on Software Engineering,* IEEE Computer Society, 1985.

5. B.W. Boehm, *Software Engineering Economics,* Prentice-Hall, Inc., Englewood Cliff, NJ, 1981.

6. *IEEE Standard for Software Project Management Plans,* (Draft), P1058/D1, Computer Society of the IEEE, 1987.

Software Requirements: New Directions and Perspectives

Raymond T. Yeh
University of Maryland

Pamela Zave
Bell Laboratories

Alex Paul Conn
Digital Equipment Corporation

George E. Cole, Jr.
Johns Hopkins Hospital

24.1. INTRODUCTION

Statistics gathered during the past few years have produced an awareness of the enormous and alarming cost of maintaining large software systems. If the trend continues, the data-processing industry not only will become the most labor-intensive industry, but also will devote most of its productivity to maintaining old, ill-structured, and difficult-to-modify software.

Furthermore, it has been shown [1] that as the complexity (and entropy) of a system grow, the probability increases that any change will introduce additional errors. The result in each case is an increasingly unreliable system. Real danger is involved in the dependence of our society on such systems, as illustrated recently by false alarms triggered by software errors at the Strategic Command Center (reported in the *Washington Post*).

Although there are many reasons for the difficulty of maintaining software, lack of thorough attention to requirements analysis and specification, the earliest phase of software development, is a major one. For example, in two large command/control systems, 67 and 95%, respectively, of the software had to be rewritten after delivery because of mismatches with user requirements [2]. There are also many examples of total cancellation of projects because of lack of appropriate requirements and feasibility analyses. Some of the more expensive cases are the $56 million Univac-United Airlines reservation system and the $217 million Advanced Logistic System [3]. In general, it has been found that "design errors" (all errors made before implementation) range from 36 to 74% of the total error count [4]. These numbers are not the whole story, however; a design error takes from 1.5 to 3 times the effort of an implementation error to correct.

We have illustrated the importance of developing a good requirements methodology to control maintenance costs, but there are other equally pressing reasons. The requirements document has a unique role in the development of a software system: It is the basis for communication among customers, users, designers, and implementers of the system, and unless it represents an informed consensus of these groups, the project is not likely to be a success.

It must also carry the weight of contractual relationships between parties that sometimes become adversaries. In particular, the design and implementation must be validated against it.

The costs of neglecting these functions include lack of management control, inability to use top-down design or other software engineering techniques, user hostility, and lawsuits. In short, because the requirements phase comes so early in development, it has a tremendous impact on the quality (or lack thereof) of the development effort and the final product.

Current approaches to requirements engineering, unfortunately, are inadequate. Most of the available techniques concentrate on functional requirements and provide relatively weak structures for expressing them. They offer basically tools (primarily languages), rather than guidelines for analysis *or* specification.

In this paper, we suggest a systematic approach to obtaining software requirements, and point out the existence of available results from other fields such as data base management, artificial intelligence, and psychology that are of great relevance to the development of a good requirements document. We deal with all aspects of requirements documents and illustrate them with examples taken from an existing requirements document (see below). Because of space limitations, our discussion will be largely informal, but will guide the interested reader to more thorough presentations elsewhere.

The AFWET system (*Air Force Weapons Effectiveness Testing*, ultimately realized under the name *WESTE*) was an early real-time system that supported quantitative testing of U.S. military (conventional warfare) capability (see Figure 24.1). We describe it briefly here because its requirements document [5] is a plentiful source of bad examples and unsolved problems.

Weapons tests were military exercises involving such "test elements" as airplanes, ships, tanks, and ground defense positions (some playing the role of enemy forces) confined to a circle centered on Eglin Air Force Base in Florida. Test elements communicated

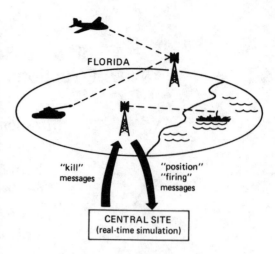

Figure 24.1. The AFWET system.

with a central site through standard military radio equipment, plus a contractor-supplied communications network.

During the test, moving elements would send periodic notifications of their positions to the central site. Mock firings of weapons would also cause messages to be sent, supplying all relevant parameters such as the direction of aim and so forth. The central system would simulate the battle in real time, determining which of the mock firings would have resulted in "kills." The results of the simulation were (1) used to display the course of the battle on graphics scopes for the benefit of officers in a control room, (2) dumped onto archival storage for later analysis, and (3) used to send "kill" notifications to "killed" test elements in the field. They would then react with a flashing light or loud noise and cease to participate in the battle.

24.2. CONCEPTUAL MODELING

In the early days of software development, machines were relatively small and so were systems. A program served in a well-understood, well-specified scientific domain, and thus could be written directly from a statement of need.

As we have moved to much larger systems and a variety of application domains, the need for precise specification of a system before implementation has increased. But the complexity of these systems demands an additional layer of understanding, a "buffer," between the real world and the requirements specification. This buffer allows an analyst to understand the problem before proposing a system to solve it—an understanding that can be achieved with an unassisted mental model if the problem is simple enough. For complex problems, a model must be constructed that is explicit and formal enough to be shared by a group of people. We call such problem models *conceptual models* because they are constructed at the level of human concept formulation.

One possible consequence of the lack of a conceptual model appears in the AFWET requirements:

Choice of major subsystems shall be the responsibility of the contractor; however, a typical range configuration may consist of the following subsystems.... Space Position Subsystem ... Data Subsystem ... Timing Subsystem ... Communication Subsystem ... Processor Subsystem ... Kill and Display Subsystem....

For lack of an approach to providing an introduction to, or overview of, the AFWET problem, the requirements writers had to present part of a design for the system!

If we accept the assumption that constructing a conceptual model is a necessary step in gaining understanding of large, complex problems, what do we model and how do we construct it?

We believe that conceptual modeling should be done "outside-in," beginning with the proposed system's environment and working inward toward the system. In many cases this will lead the analyst directly to the requirements, since the purpose of the system is to support a desirable mode of operation in the environment. This is particularly true when the project is to automate existing manual procedures, because then the computer system is a direct reflection of the current operations.

Other reasons for stressing understanding of the environment are that it will improve communication with customers and users (who are much more interested in their environment than your system) and because large applica-

tion programs are parts of their own environments [6]. But perhaps the most important reason of all, given the intrinsically evolutionary nature of large software systems [1], is that change in a system originates with change in the environment. By modeling the environment, the analyst can study potential changes, and possibly even provide a designer information that can be used during design so as to achieve modularity—the property whereby small changes in the environment cause correspondingly small changes in the system.

The overall structure of a conceptual model is shown in Figure 24.2. The environment consists of identifiable objects such as people, airplanes, terminals, forms and other types of data, and so forth. The states of these environment entities must be represented, as must the events (an agent makes a flight reservation, a machine overheats) that cause state changes. The target system can be similarly divided into states, and activities that interact with environmental events so as (ultimately) to influence them.

The model is structured by relationships and constraints on all these objects. "A is a subnet of B," "Helen and Bob are married," "faucet must be opened before water can flow," and so on, are simple examples of constraints and relationships, but new government regulations, hardware configuration changes, and a wide variety of other facts can be relevant.

To collect information on the environment, personal interviews and questionnaires are most often used. The actual modeling process can begin with either entities or events. When starting from an event, the information change

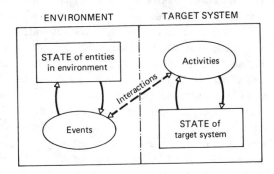

Figure 24.2. A conceptual model.

due to occurrence of that event must be reflected into the structure of the model. For example, a transaction "reservation request" from a remote terminal linked to an airline reservation system will change the available seats on a particular flight. Assuming such information is stored in a target system data base, this event will also trigger a system activity to change the data base. The state information is thus transmitted through the interaction between the system and its environment. Similarly, an analyst may start with entities from the environment to build up state information, and then consider changes to these entities so as to develop the structure of processes within the system. Interested readers are referred to Reference 7 for more details about information collection and to Reference 8 for more examples of conceptual modeling.

Note that the *outside-in* approach is neither *top-down* nor *bottom-up*—the model structure must be evolved in both directions. Top-down analysis is employed when an analyst asks an interviewee to elaborate on some previously identified feature of the environment, but a bottom-up approach is required to collect and integrate views of users in different parts of an organization.

The conceptual model is an important tool for understanding the requirements of a system, but it is *not* a requirements document. The latter, though derived from the model, has somewhat different properties, which will be the subject of the next section.

24.3. REQUIREMENTS DERIVATION

The conceptual model should be a rich, complex information structure—probably too rich and complex for the purposes of the software requirements document (SRD). For instance, a conceptual model of AFWET might include views of the system as seen by soldiers, officers, computer operators, and hardware maintenance personnel, and thus be highly redundant. It might also model more of the environment than is needed just to define the proposed system. This would be the case if the AFWET analysts were to decide (quite correctly!) that they need to understand the military background and purpose of the tests they are to in-

strument to assure themselves that the data they gather and display will be useful.

Thus the SRD is derived from the conceptual model by filtering and organizing, constantly aiming toward the "best-engineered" specification. Explicit goals for the SRD can be found by considering the thing it will be used for:

Many groups of people must communicate with each other through and about the SRD. Therefore it must be *understandable*.

In order to accommodate the evolutionary nature of large systems, the organization of SRD must be structured so that changes can be made with minimum effort. In a word, it must be *modifiable*.

Last but not least, the SRD is used to define the target system. To do this properly it should be *precise* (preferably formal), *unambiguous, complete* (a particularly important aspect of completeness being the role of the SRD in contractual obligations), *internally consistent,* and *minimal.* A minimal specification does not overconstrain the design of the system, which might exclude the best solutions to design problems.

As in most engineering situations involving multiple goals, the above properties cannot all be achieved in most situations. However, there does exist a set of mental tools and principles that can help the analyst to meet many of them.

The crucial issue here is the *decomposition of complexity,* also referred to as "separation of concerns," "divide and conquer" strategy, and so forth. For software development we can describe the goal of this method via two subgoals, namely, the *process goal* and the *product goal.* The process goal is to keep the process under our intellectual control at all times. The product goal is to organize the product in a fashion that allows others to comprehend the product by an amount of effort which is proportional to the size of the product. There are three powerful tools for decomposing complexity so as to achieve these goals (see Figure 24.3).

The first tool is the notion of *abstraction.* The use of abstraction allows us to suppress details and concentrate on essential properties. Thus, we refer to something as an abstraction

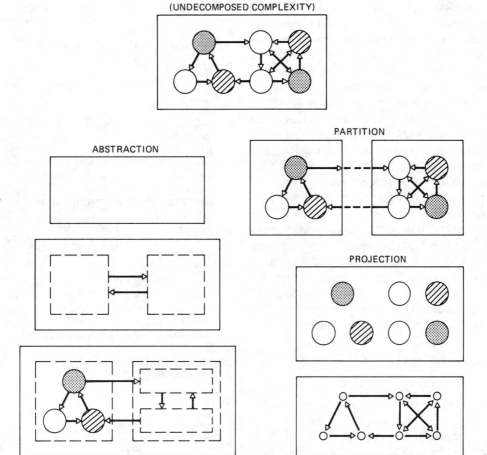

Figure 24.3. Three ways to decompose complexity.

if it represents several actual objects but is disassociated from any specific object. The use of abstraction forms natural hierarchies, allowing elaboration of more and more detail and hence providing intellectual control of the process.

The second tool is *partition,* that is, representing the whole as the sum of its parts. This tool allows us to concentrate on components or subsystems of the system one at a time. Partitioning makes systems modular. Note that if each partitioned component also has an abstraction hierarchy, then we have both a horizontal and a vertical decomposition of the system.

The third tool is *projection,* which enables us to understand a system from different viewpoints. A projection of a system represents the entire system, but with respect to only a subset of its properties; the perfect physical analogy

is an architectural drawing, which is a two-dimensional view of a three-dimensional building. The notion of a "view" of a data base [9] is another such example. Again, this tool allows us to separate particular facets of a system from the rest and therefore retain intellectual control.

Of course, any tool can be abused. In using the three structuring principles above, one must be guided by the principle of "information hiding" [10] and other observations about how specifications can be made coherent and flexible [11]. Arbitrary decompositions forced on system aspects that are too interdependent will cause more problems than they solve.

24.4. FUNCTIONAL REQUIREMENTS

Functional requirements describe what the target system *does,* and are clearly the heart of the SRD. Section 2 introduced the notion of an explicit model of the proposed system's environment as an important tool in requirements analysis (leading to the global model shown in Figure 24.2). From the viewpoint of functional requirements specification, there is an important additional advantage to having an explicit model of the environment: Since interactions between the environment and target system can then also be made explicit, it is much easier to specify the all-important environment/target system interface in an accurate, precise, understandable, and yet modifiable manner.

Thus the task of functional requirements specification is to find a formal representation for the detailed information needed to fill in Figure 24.2. The major challenge is complexity, and we will classify approaches to specification according to the primary dimension along which they decompose structure.

Data Models

Data-oriented models concentrate on specifying the *states* of Figure 24.2—the state of the target system will always be represented as a data structure, and the state of the environment can be modeled as such, even though the resulting data structure need never be implemented.

Research on data base problems has led to the recognition of abstract concepts that can be fruitfully used in data-oriented specifications of software systems of all kinds. We shall use the notation presented in Reference 12, a survey aimed at non-data-base specialists, to explain the most prominent data-structuring concepts.

At any moment, a data base or "data space" consists of a population of "individuals" or items. A data base modeling the environment of the AFWET system ("STATE of entities in environment" in Figure 24.2) could contain individuals representing test elements.

Individuals belong to (are instances of) types, and types can be subtypes of other types (obviously, an instance of a type is also an instance of all its supertypes). The type hierarchy for a data base is specified as part of the

Table 24.1. AFWET-Type Definition.

```
def TEST-ELEMENT:
    sub PLANE, SHIP, GROUND-DEFENSE-
        POSITION, TARGET
    com ROLE
    end
def PLANE:
    sub B-52G, F-4C
    com AIR-POSITION, WEAPONS
    end
def SHIP:
    com SURFACE-POSITION, WEAPONS
    end
def TANK:
    com SURFACE-POSITION, WEAPONS
    end
def GROUND-DEFENSE-POSITION:
    com SURFACE-POSITION, WEAPONS
    end
def TARGET:
    sub BRIDGE, DEPOT
    com SURFACE-POSITION
    end
def AIR-POSITION:
    com SURFACE-POSITION, ALTITUDE
    end
def BATTLEFIELD:
    com TEST-ELEMENT*
    end
def TEST:
    com FRAME*
    end
def FRAME:
    com TIME, TEST-ELEMENT*
    end
```

*The individual can have multiple components.

data base's *type definition*. Table 24.1, for instance, is a type definition for the real-time simulation portion of the AFWET system. It defines types using the syntax:

$$def \quad TYPE\text{-}NAME:$$

$$.$$
$$.$$
$$.$$

$$end,$$

and the types listed after the keyword *sub* are its subtypes. Thus an individual plane may be a member of types B-52G, PLANE, and TEST-ELEMENT. The use of types to structure data is referred to as *generalization*.

Individuals also have components that are

needed to describe them fully. Each component is identified with a type to which it must belong, and the proper components of individuals of certain types are listed after *com* in that type's definition. Thus a full description of an air position (an instance of type AIR-POSITION) requires a surface position and an altitude. Full description of a plane requires its air position and the weapons it is carrying. It also requires a role (friend or foe), a component that the PLANE type inherits from its supertype TEST-ELEMENT. It is clear that the component relation is also hierarchical, and its use to structure data is referred to as *aggregation.*

The state of the AFWET system (real-time simulation portion only) and its environment at any given time, is a data base consistent with this type definition (plus a great deal of read-only information, such as models of test-element motion and weapons threats, needed for simulation). There should be only one instance of type BATTLEFIELD, and its components represent the currently active test-elements (for elements marked by *, the individual can have multiple components of the designated type). Within the system, the state of the battlefield at a given time is represented by an instance of type FRAME, having as components a time and the test-elements that were active at that time. A full test is recorded in multiple frames. This is a particularly good example of what it means to reflect the structure of the environment within the system!

A data model must be interfaced with processing aspects of the system. At the very least, a set of primitive data manipulation operations should be enumerated, and these operations should be defined in terms of a first-order predicate language and the operations *create, destroy,* and *modify* applied to individuals in the data base. For instance, in the AFWET data base a simulated kill should *destroy* a test-element that is a component of the current battlefield. Once defined, these operations can be used as the interface between the data model and whatever higher-level processing model is preferred.

Data-oriented models, as the heart of requirements analysis and specification, have been very successful—especially in the domains of data processing and business information systems. Some good examples can be found in References 7, 13, and 14. The primary notion used there is the semantic net, a graphical formalism that was originally developed by artificial intelligence researchers for representing knowledge structures.

Data-Flow Processing Models

The most common model of processing used in conjunction with data-oriented models is the data-flow diagram, which simply names the major processing activities of the system and indicates which parts of the data model are inputs and outputs to each activity. If iterative refinement of the data-flow diagram is supported, and activities are defined (usually informally) in terms of data manipulation operations, a level of expressive power sufficient for many data-processing systems may be achieved.

The dataflow approach is central to SADT [15, 16], although there is additional emphasis on a methodology for team cooperation. The data-flow approach is supported with automated tools in PSL/PSA [17]. It can be extended with control information via Petri nets [18] or with resource synchronization [19].

The deficiencies of the data-flow model for specifying embedded (real-time) systems are apparent in the dataflow diagram for the AFWET system shown in Figure 24.4 (the "fight" function has been added to provide the "processing" that modifies the state of the environment). The global events and activities in this system are continuous, and are not activated by the appearance of a single input or any simple combination of inputs. At a lower level, they consist of complex combinations of pieces of computation that must occur asynchronously and in parallel. Data flow as a concept is simply not powerful enough to permit precise specification or effective decomposition of systems, such as embedded ones, in which concurrent and asynchronous operations occur at the requirements level.

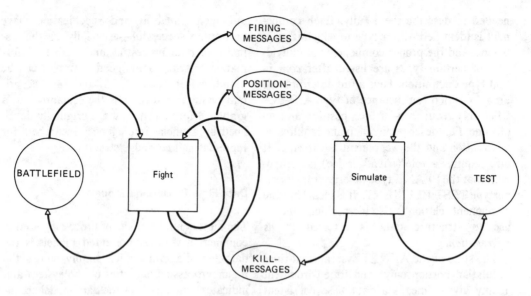

Figure 24.4. AFWET dataflow.

The Process Model

An approach that is better suited to specification of embedded systems emphasizes the "events" and "activities" portions of Figure 24.2. The central concept is the *process*, an autonomous computational unit that is understood to operate in parallel with, and interact asynchronously with, other processes. Processes have long been used as abstractions of concurrent activity within multiprogramming systems [20] and many recent articles have shown that they can be used to model data bases, monitors, functional modules, I/O devices, and presumably any other identifiable structure within a computing system [21, 22].

Formally, a process is just a "state space" (set of possible states) and a "successor relation" that maps predecessor states onto their possible successors. This simple concept is easily adapted to being a digital simulation of an object (person, machine, sensor, etc.) in the environment of a computer system.

The result of the generality of processes is that the requirements for a system can be specified by a set of asynchronously interacting processes, some of which represent objects in the environment and some of which represent objects in the target system. The environment of AFWET, for instance, becomes a set of processes, each one simulating a test element. All

processes respond to kill messages by becoming inactive. All processes representing test elements with weapons send firing messages whenever their internal, cyclic simulation algorithms decree that they have fired a weapon. All processes representing moving test elements periodically update their positions and send position messages to the central system. The result is an easily constructed, easily understood model with highly complex overall behavior; it is understandable simply because it is naturalistic, being made up of semiautonomous objects acting in parallel, just as the real world is.

Figure 24.5 shows an overall process-and-communication structure for the simulation portion of the AFWET system. The *test-element* processes are as described above. Processes representing radio towers put timestamps on the input messages and relay them to an *input-buffer* process. The *input-buffer* process collects into a batch all the messages relating to the period covered by a particular simulation step, waits until all messages from that period can reasonably be expected to have arrived, and then passes the batch to the *simulation* process. This simulator computes a new frame (and kill messages) from the old frame, the batch of messages, and its various mathematical models. Frames are passed on

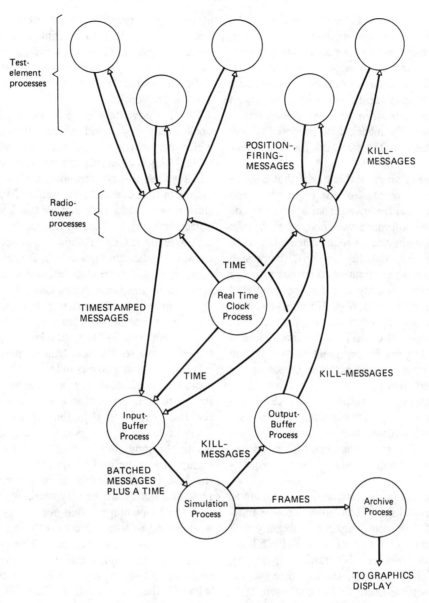

Figure 24.5. Processes of the AFWET system.

one by one to the rest of the system, where they are stored and otherwise used. Kill messages are relayed to the *test-element* processes via an *output-buffer* process and the *radio-tower* processes.

This has been an informal description of a formal requirements specification in PAISLey (Process-oriented, Applicative, Interpretable Specification Language [23–26]. PAISLey is a process-oriented language aimed at embedded systems. As the acronym indicates, its other major characteristics are that it is applicative and interpretable. The advantages of applicative languages are currently receiving well-deserved attention; recent results and trends are surveyed in Reference 27. The most important properties of applicative languages (for our purposes) are that they are precise and convenient vehicles for abstraction and that they are interpretable.

Interpretability carries with it many advantages. It means that the system-plus-environment model is executable and that it can be validated by testing—including demonstrations of behavior for customers, and performance simulations (if necessary). The advantages also continue throughout development since the environmental part of the model can be used as a *test bed* or *driver* during development, and the model of the proposed system can be used as the standard for acceptance testing.

The use of an excutable model that emphasizes the active parts of the required system can be termed the *operational* approach. The operational approach was first taken by the SREM system and its requirements language RSL [28, 29, and 30]. In RSL, processing paths from input stimulus to output response are specified directly and can be simulated for performance purposes. Stimulus-response paths are an important aspect of operational requirements, of course, but are incomplete in not including explicit representations of system states, internal synchronization, or potentially distributed environments.

PAISLey is more complete than RSL in including states, synchronization, and the system's environment, and it shows that the operational approach has some striking advantages for embedded system requirements.

One advantage is that the rigor of having to make a model that "runs" always proves to be a powerful influence against ambiguity and vagueness in requirements. In the AFWET example, for instance, the relationship among frames, input messages, and real time was arrived at after a great deal of confusion. It finally became clear that (1) simulation had to be oriented toward increments of time rather than toward events because the effect of a firing event may occur at any point during the entire interval that the bullet is still in the air, (2) the cost of backtracking would be prohibitive—once a computation was done it could not be undone by a late-arriving message, and (3) this meant that simulation time had to be enough behind real time so that all messages relating to a new frame could be assumed to have arrived when computation of the new frame began. Timestamps are put on messages at the radio towers because there is variable delay in the rest of the communication network, and the simulator must know accurately to which time a message refers (delay in the radio communications, being nearly constant, is not a problem).

Another advantage of operational specifications is that they provide natural structures to which performance requirements can be attached (this is especially important for embedded systems, given the prominence of performance in that domain). References 24 and 26 show how response time and feedback loop requirements can be specified formally, simply by attaching timing attributes to functions in the specification. In Figure 24.5, the timing requirements are more complex, but still representable in the same formalism. If g is the "granularity" of the simulation, that is, the increment of time between frames, then the successor function of the simulation process (which computes the next frame) must never take longer than g to evaluate. If the delay in radio communications is r, and the simulation time is to be no more than $r + d + g$ behind real time, then d must be the upper bound on delay in getting messages from the radio towers to the input buffer. Finally, if the timestamps are to be useful, the upper bound on the time it takes for any process to read the real-time clock must be very small.

A third advantage is that operational specifications make it possible to include resource requirements when necessary. Resource requirements are requirements that a particular resource or quantity of a resource be used. In AFWET the use of a time-multiplexed, fixed-delay radio communication link was a resource requirement,* imposed because that equipment was already owned and installed. PAISLey offers the generality of a complete model of computation, *including* asynchronous distributed computation. This means that no new system problem will surprise us with concepts unexpressible in the language.

Observations about performance and resources bring us to everyone's major reserva-

---

*Actually this is an inference from the requirements document, which is by no means clear on this point.

tion about operational requirements: Aren't these actually *design* specifications? Don't they say much more than should be said in the requirements? We believe that the answer is no, for the following reasons.

Extensive experience with requirements examples shows clearly that the essence of true design is *managing scarce resources to meet performance goals*. As long as a formalism does not force the specifier to make unnecessary decisions about performance and resources, then it is not forcing him to specify design rather than requirements. Fortunately, both applicative languages and the process model are excellent in this respect. For the "design-independence" of applicative languages, see References 31, 32; for the "design-independence" of processes, consider this very basic example: In Figure 24.5, we used as many processes to describe the central site as were logical and convenient. The design for this system will look quite different since it will probably have to deal with a scarce resource problem—only one processor. The designer will have to determine how a single processor can be multiplexed so as to implement, and meet the performance requirements of, all processes at the central site.

Another example of how the specification described by Figure 24.5 differs from a design

involves the real-time clock process, which "ticks" at regular intervals and can be read by other processes. It is not technically feasible to build a single global clock that can be read fast enough by a collection of remote sites. The design to meet this performance requirement will probably entail local clocks (which *can* be read fast enough) and a global synchronization protocol executed before each test begins.

The existence of resource requirements forces us to recognize two distinct meanings of design: from the "technical" viewpoint, it is managing resources to meet performance goals, but from the "administrative" (economic, political) viewpoint it is any property of the system that is not required to satisfy whoever is paying for it. From the technical viewpoint resource requirements are premature design decisions, but from the administrative viewpoint they are common and entirely legitimate requirements. They should be minimized, but can never be eliminated, and any requirements language that cannot handle them will be inadequate in many situations.

To summarize, operational structures do not overconstrain design unless they select a particular solution to a problem that has other feasible solutions. The AFWET example is rather extreme in that it involves quite a bit of what is technically design detail, but all the

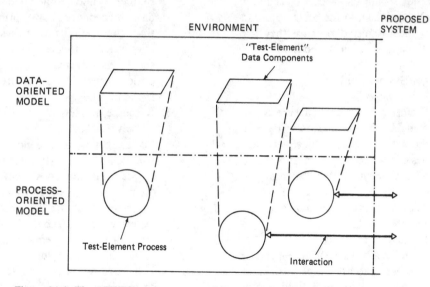

Figure 24.6. The AFWET environment model, projected onto process-oriented and data-oriented views.

"design" decisions were forced into requirements analysis by the customer's wishes or the technical infeasibility of other approaches.

A final, but important, property of any activity-oriented requirements language is its interface with data-oriented specifications. Different as Figure 24.5 may seem from the data model of Table 24.1, the two are actually quite compatible. The components of a test-element in the data model are exactly the same as the components of the state of a *test-element* process in the process model (see Figure 24.6)! This means that the process model and the data model can be viewed as *projections* of the same underlying model, which contains both, and the proposed system model supports a similar decomposition. Given the data *and* process complexity found in most large systems, compatibility between appropriate models for them cannot receive too much attention.

24.5. NONFUNCTIONAL REQUIREMENTS

Requirements other than functional ones have received very little attention, but may be an equally important part of the SRD. Since the state of the art is very far from having a comprehensive theory or methodology for these requirements, we present an annotated outline, intended to be used as a checklist of the various topics that should be at least considered, if not actually included, in the SRD. (Human factors have been omitted because they are discussed at length in the next section.)

I. Target System Constraints
  A. *Performance*
    Performance is defined here to include all factors that describe both the subjective and objective qualities of the target system. It is thus a measurement of the "success" of the target system, a constraint below which the system must not be allowed to fall.
    1. Real time
      In many systems, especially those that are embedded in or connected to specialized equipment, the real-time performance

is essentially a measurement of the success of the system. For example, in AFWET, if the system is not designed in some way to accept weapons firings in real time, then it is likely that some of the firings will be entirely missed and the validity of the mission compromised.
  2. Other time constraints
    Other time constraints refers to important relative timing considerations within the target system, which relate events to each other rather than to real time. These relationships would normally involve precedence but might also include information for choosing between competing activities based on some kind of priority system. In AFWET, for example, the computation of the lethality of a missile might not be carried out until the trajectory has been determined, and both the computations may be considered more important (of higher priority) than the movement of an unrelated tank, given a scarcity of computational resources. While detailed decisions on precedence or priority throughout the target system may be left to the designer, there should be a means for including critical constraints in this area in the requirements.
  3. Resource utilization
    Closely related to the rationale for assigning precedence constraints are the constraints on resource utilization. A system will often be built in which the computer resources are attached to expensive specialized equipment. Decisions on which equipment to service in which order may very well be directly related to the cost or importance of each item of specialized equipment, and

the performance of the system may very well be assessed in terms of the response to the needs of this equipment. The requirements thus should provide a means for specifying the handling of critical equipment and also for placing a constraint on the balanced or optimal use of the remaining resources in the system.

4. Accuracy, quality, comprehensiveness

Although timing and resource utilization are fundamental aspects of performance, other factors also characterize the target system performance. The accuracy of the detection and computation of data can be critical. In AFWET, two elements in combat must be accurately tracked for position, both by information that might be transmitted by the elements themselves or by appropriate external equipment, such as radar. This position information must be maintained at the same degree of precision during computations or the determination of a kill condition might be erroneous.

The quality of the target system can be an important requirement. For example, if a CRT display is fuzzy or distorted, then the relationships between elements might be incorrectly interpreted by viewing personnel. Akin to quality is the idea of comprehensiveness. If important data that could be displayed is never made available, or not presented when it could be a determining factor in a mission, the target system is performing at a less-than-optimal level. The requirements constrain the eventual design by identifying, at least in general terms, the degree of comprehensiveness desired. Designers can later figure out how to manipulate the data within the quality and human factors constraints.

B. *Reliability*

The reliability portion of the requirements outline has been adapted from the presentation in Reference 33, a study of multiprocessor systems. Reliability can be divided into two basic categories: availability of the physical equipment and integrity of the information. For requirements, the concern is about *failures* (noticeable events where the system violates its specifications) rather than *faults* (mechanical or algorithmic defects that will generate an error) [34] since the means by which the system maintains its specified level of reliability is a concern of the system developers, not those who write requirements. The purpose of defining and classifying the failures is so that constraints can be placed on the likelihood of such failures.

1. Availability

Failures that affect the availability of the system are, in general, ones that cause one or more devices to cease to function. Occasionally, a device will continue to operate, but at a reduced speed. If equipment ceases to function, we are not only interested in the duration of such failures, but also in their actual impact on the system. Today, it is much more common for critical components to be replicated and interconnected in such a manner that the target system continues to operate under a wide variety of failures. The requirements will have to be able to address the extent of degradation permissible under specified failures and the means with which the system copes with these problems (e.g., manual versus automatic reconfiguration). In a system such as AFWET, the ability to transmit critical information over more than one communication channel might be a requirement for dealing with a failure of one of those channels.

a. Definition and classification of failures that cause degraded functioning
b. Probability of each failure
c. Extent of degradation due to each failure (e.g., graceful degradation, reconfiguration, and self-repair)
d. Duration of each degradation

2. Integrity

Failures that affect the integrity of the system are those in which the computer is prevented from proceeding because loss of information precludes the computation of a valid result. When a failure does occur, the nature of the mission dictates the necessity of recovering outstanding requests or computations in progress. A requirement may specify the degree to which efforts should be taken to assure data integrity. In AFWET, trajectory and lethality computations should be completed without loss of information. On the other hand, an element that is not engaged in combat with another element might sustain a temporary loss of position without affecting the mission. The cost of recovering from every possible loss of state can be enormous with frequent rollback points causing a significant degradation in performance. The requirements might wisely place a limit on the cost of recovery by identifying states that are not critical enough to warrant a full roll-back-and-recovery exercise.

a. Definition and classification of failures that cause loss of state
b. Probability of each failure
c. Cost of recovery of state

C. *Security*

Most of security is arguably in the realm of design since it pertains to specific means by which the reliability of the system may be enhanced. However, there appear to be two areas in which security may be an appropriate requirement. The first is physical security, which may include, for example, all military standards for pressurized cable, disconnectable terminals, safes for storing classified tapes and disks, and even the criteria for destroying or reusing such storage media. The operational category includes any method that must be used to cipher, modularize, limit transmission or otherwise affect how or where sensitive information will be available. Note that the above physical considerations for reuse of tapes are in some ways part of the operational category since it is well known that disks, for example, even when erased or overwritten a dozen times, can be made to reveal their original (e.g., classified) information with specialized signal differentiating equipment.

1. Physical (e.g., gates, locks, safes, etc.)
2. Operational—protection of integrity of information

D. *Operating constraints*

1. Frequency and duration of use
Both the frequency and duration of use are not only important to know from a staffing and maintenance point of view, but also from the standpoint of available resources. If the computer equip-

ment is, for example, only used as part of the target system for a limited time period, it might be provided as a general facility at other times. Conversely, an already-existing facility may be adequate for supporting the needs of the target system. In a satellite probe, it might be very important to know that a computer module could be connected to some network and used for computational assistance when not operating in its primary capacity.

2. Control (e.g., remote, local, or not at all)

Control is another important operating constraint in many systems. An unmanned remote facility cannot be restarted by personnel if a failure occurs. Depending on the ability of personnel to reach the remote site, the equipment may need sophisticated automatic restart and even reconfiguration capabilities. Preventive maintenance may also not be possible in inaccessible locations such as in satellite or deep-sea probes. In addition, the proximity of the remote facility may affect the nature of interaction required since distant space probes experience significant transmission delays because of speed-of-light limitations.

3. Staffing requirements

E. *Physical constraints (e.g., size, weight, power requirements, temperature, humidity, portability, ruggedness)*

The physical constraints requirements are intended to include all factors relating to the physical placement of the equipment in the field. In the AFWET system, the nature of the pods connected to the wings of the aircraft placed lim-

its on the size, weight, power requirements, and ruggedness of the equipment that could be placed onto the pods. In some applications, even the camouflaging of the cabinets might be an important physical constraint.

II. System Development, Evolution and Maintenance

In many organizations, the plan for the development, evolution, and maintenance of the target is a separate document from the requirements since a development plan is considered to be a statement of how the requirements will be carried out. On the other hand, in many instances, large computer systems are requested and paid for by one group and developed and delivered by another. Constraints on the magnitude and cost of the development effort may very well be considered requirements to the group paying the bill. In this section, we discuss various categories relating to the life cycle plan for the target system.

A. *Kind of development*

The development of target systems can be divided into two gross categories: those efforts that are directed toward a single delivery date at which time the completed operational system will be furnished, and those efforts that plan to deliver working subsets of the requirements for evaluation in the field before embarking on a more complete version. The single full-scale effort is often itself iterative [35], but the early versions of such a system are not intended for use by the customer. Prototyping may be required in time-critical situations where delivering any kind of working system will fulfill an immediate need. Similarly, in state-of-the-art projects, careful analysis of a system shell may be needed to evaluate human factors and to clarify the requirements. Many software systems are almost always iterative. For example, operating systems are usually updated on a regular basis throughout their useful lives.

1. Single full-scale development
2. Iterative with prototyping

B. *Scale of effort*

The scale of effort is an essential factor in establishing requirements for the development of a target system. In iterative efforts, in which many prototypes or versions are envisioned, resources should be allocated for personnel, equipment, and overhead associated with the development of each version. When development time is included as a requirement, then an evaluation can be made assessing the feasibility of completing the stated goals within the proposed time frame. If an extended or advanced development is foreseen for one or more iterations, this information should also be incorporated into the requirements. Finally, each version should have a plan for delivery and installation. When equipment is to be installed in aircraft or naval vessels, delivery and installation may be a complex technical endeavor. And when numerous installations are already in the field, the requirements may need to call for special procedures for handling the complicated logistics of updating each installation. For each iteration:

1. Development time
2. Development resources
   a. Personnel
   b. Equipment
   c. Cost
3. Delivery and installation (e.g., packaging, shipment, assembly and test equipment)

C. *Methodology*

1. Quality control standards
   Methodology includes all the management techniques and procedures that assure the success of the project. Quality control is meant to address software as well as hardware, including the current ideas on top-down, structured, provable, modularized (and so on) software. Many organizations now include standardization enforcement software in their compilers and assemblers.

2. Milestones and review procedures (including feasibility studies)
   Milestones and review procedures track and evaluate partially completed systems. The milestone is an identifiable stage of completion, which can be used to determine whether parallel efforts are progressing on time with respect to one another. Review procedures are used by the developers themselves to assess the current progress of an effort. The contracting agency may request a feasibility study for implementing all or a portion of the entire system. In this case, a milestone might reflect the point at which the feasibility has been proven, thus enabling the initiation of serious subsystem design efforts.

3. Acceptance criteria (e.g., benchmarks)
   While a completed system is supposed to in all ways fulfill the requirements, the acceptance criteria identify specific tests and evaluation factors by which the developed system can be judged. Traditionally, the acceptance criteria are the "teeth" in the contract, against which disputes are settled. Since a target system can almost never be exhaustively tested, it is critical that the acceptance tests cover every significant combination of functions or

activities that the system is supposed to carry out successfully.

D. *Priority and changeability*

The priority and changeability category recognizes that requirements writers may need some way to incorporate flexibility into the requirements. It may be very important that some requirements be carried out, whereas others may represent "gold plating." When other constraints are considered, such as cost, size, training, development time, and so on, it may be necessary to drop some of the less critical requirements. A means for ranking requirements or associating some weighting factor to particular facets of a target system would be very useful. This ranking can follow Parnas's modularization based on the likelihood of change [36]. If a designer is to be expected to hide, in some modular organization, system decisions that could easily change, the information about what might change must be represented in the requirements. Along the same lines, if a general requirement could be satisfied by more than one entirely different solution, it might be necessary to be able to include detailed requirements for each of the solutions. For example, in AFWET, if the transmission of certain information could be satisfied either by ground cables or by microwave communication, the military specifications for each form of transmission would have to be included in the requirements.

1. Establishing relative importance of requirements
2. Identifying factors likely to change
   a. Ordering by changeability
   b. Identification of alternative requirements

E. *Maintenance*

The maintenance category here is specifically meant to exclude the evolutionary software activities that are often classified under "maintenance." The requirements are concerned with the system's breaking down and having to be brought back to working condition. For the software, the requirements might specify the staffing needed or a contractual agreement for fixing bugs. The document might list the kinds of programs or packages that will be supplied to fix bugs, and, in addition, what kinds of software will be embedded in the system (such as error logging or path counters) to aid in the discovery and tracing of errors. For hardware, it is necessary to know who will carry out both the preventive and repair-oriented maintenance. The requirements might need to spell out standards for a minimal set of test points at which the repairing individual can probe and assess the operation of the circuit.

1. Software
   a. Responsibility for fixing bugs
   b. Instrumentation (e.g., check points, audit trails, driver programs, simulators)
2. Hardware
   a. Frequency and duration of preventive maintenance
   b. Responsibility for repair of faults
   c. Test equipment and procedures (e.g., test points)

III. Economic Context of System Development

Very few projects are undertaken in which cost is no object. Even in extravagant programs, cost tradeoffs are seriously considered. However, satisfactory economic decisions are much more likely to be made if the cost goals and guidelines are spelled out in the requirements document.

A. *Cost tradeoffs*

Requirements for cost tradeoffs establish guidelines for determining whether existing equipment and software can be satisfactorily incorporated into the target system or whether a new effort is required. Very often this off-the-shelf equipment is not ideal and does not entirely satisfy the requirements in every respect. However, these cost-tradeoff requirements can be used effectively to overrule other requirements if the sacrifice is not too great. Some criteria are needed to indicate just how important the ready-made requirement is and what might be given up to fulfill it. It is important that the requirements convey the intended principles of cost tradeoffs. The military is, in many projects, using an approach that identifies a minimal set of capabilities to which desired features are added until a certain cost level is exceeded. The requirements must be able to convey just which functions are needed at any cost and which are add-ons. Note that some projects (e.g., computer toys or games) may be almost entirely a design-to-cost consideration. Even the nature of the functions may be relatively unimportant compared to the price at which it can be sold. Most projects fall between the two extremes, and the requirements must be able to indicate where the tradeoffs are to be made.

1. Utilization of existing technology versus development of new
   a. Hardware (e.g., CPUs, interfaces, peripheral equipment)
   b. Software (e.g., operating systems, compilers)
2. Primary objectives: design-to-cost versus design-to-function
   a. Established minimal requirements for designated levels of cost
   b. Relating alternate requirements with costs

B. *Cost of iterative system development*

Many projects are developed iteratively, whether or not the customer sees the intervening stages or prototypes. And almost all projects have milestones or baselines that indicate the achievement of some level of operation or functionality. Without cost limitations placed on these stages by the requirements, funds could be allocated to project phases in an unbalanced manner, starving, for example, later efforts due to disproportionate expenditures at the beginning of the project. In addition, if prototypes are to be delivered to the customer for interim use or evaluation, these costs should be addressed in the requirements.

1. Development cost of each prototype or milestone
2. Cost of delivery of prototype

C. *Cost of each instance of target system*

The development effort may be directed at producing many similar or identical target systems. Under these circumstances, the development costs will usually be amortized over the entire projected production run. Each instance of the target system in this case will have costs both from materials and from the applicable fraction of the development expenses. Any proposed evolutionary change to the target system after delivery will have to take into account the costs of updating each installation.

24.6. HUMAN FACTORS

Introduction

The psychological factors involved in software engineering are certainly one of the most neglected aspects of the entire discipline. Omission of such considerations from requirements analysis and specification may be a major reason for eventual user dissatisfaction with the delivered product. We conjecture that many of the human factors are of as much importance to the user as the so-called functional requirements. Thus, consideration of the psychological impacts, both of and on the user, in the requirements phase should have a substantial effect in helping to deliver software products that truly meet the needs of the user. Furthermore, an aggressive view of this facet of requirements should have an important impact on the lifetime cost of the entire project.

In the following sections we explore the nature and importance of human factors as related to the requirements of a project. We shall discuss the problems of communication between members of the user organization and software engineers, followed by specific human factors problems dealing with the target system's user interface. We then review some tools from psychology that may be used in attempting to solve some of these problems.

The Communication Problem

Many of the problems that originate early in requirements analysis can be attribted to lack of communication between the user community and the software engineers. There are several well-known communication problems. Ideas may be expressed in a vague or ambiguous manner, goals may be contradictory or incompletely formulated, and various users may have differing views of the desired system. Realization that these difficulties exist leads to the conclusion that good requirements analysis must depend upon intensive interaction with the user community at all authority levels, as well as feedback from the software engineers concerning their understanding of the desired system.

There are communication problems that cannot be solved simply by verbal communication, however, regardless of the amount of interaction and feedback involved. In this section we shall discuss the problem of novice versus expert knowledge, and the problem of tacit knowledge. These as-yet-unresearched prob-

lems may hold the key to developing systems that are well-engineered for humans.

When considering the members of the user community, we shall continue to use the word *user* in its broadest sense, including all of the members of a user organization who will have any degree of contact with the system at any time during its lifetime. This is certainly a broad class of users, with varying degrees of interest in the project, but we need not distinguish between them at this time.

Kaplan cites a rather disturbing example wherein the designer asks, "What do you want?", to which the user responds, "What have you got?" [37]. Although this is, or should be, an extreme example of initial interaction, it does point out some of the inherent difficulties in user/analyst dialogues. It also makes a strong case for the need to know the user [38]. This one principle is of major importance, for when the analyst truly knows the user (actually, users at all authority levels), then "What do you want?" will be be replaced with a whole series of ideas and questions with which meaningful discussion can begin.

It would be naive to think, however, that the analyst will find it easy to "get to know" the user. One major problem is that experts "see" quite differently from novices [37], as has been demonstrated in such famous studies as the one involving chess masters and novices [39]. In requirements analysis, the user is an expert in the application domain, the analyst is an expert in software engineering, and each is a novice in the domain of the other!

This phenomenon of seeing differently is partially explained by the compact and complex structure of the experts' knowledge. Experts have more points of entry into their semantic structures, and they form abstractions at a higher level than novices. This means that they have the ability to make use of a number of different representation schemes for mentally working with the same information. Thus, an expert might be able to make use of a picture, a sketch, a map, or even a cardboard model, whereas a novice might find the picture to be the only meaningful representation [40]. So we must conclude that the choice of model presentation is a critical factor to be considered when dealing with novice users. In general, the process of establishing a common domain of discourse should be the first matter of attention in a user/analyst dialogue. Also, this has to take place at all levels within the user organization because of the different views of the users.

We know that people, whatever their organizational status, have detailed and highly developed internal models of their working environments [37]. They understand what they do, how they accomplish their duties, and with whom or what they interact in their performance of daily tasks (we speak, of course, of people with a general level of work-related competence.) Regardless of their level of expertise, however, people know more than they can ever tell [41]. When this "tacit knowledge" concerns a desired software product, we are often at a loss as to how to bring forth this information. The problem is more than just a vagueness on the part of the user concerning desired functions for a proposed system because tacit knowledge is not describable by the user. Some tacit knowledge will always exist, but much can be brought out and made explicit.

Polanyi illustrates the existence of tacit knowledge with this example: We are all experts at recognizing familiar faces, yet how many features of a familiar face can you give specific details about? This is very difficult, even for faces with which you may be intimately familiar. Police artists, however, have developed methods that allow them to produce composite sketches of remarkable quality.

The idea of tacit knowledge is certainly not new. William James, in discussing what he called the "fringe" [42], said that

Every definite image in the mind is steeped and dyed in the free water that flows round it. With it goes the sense of its relations, near and remote, the dying echo of whence it came to us, the dawning sense of whither it is to lead. The significance, the value, of the image is all in the halo or the penumbra that surrounds and escorts it. . . .

Thus, we must probe, define, and refine this fringe in order to discover some of the tacit knowledge contained therein.

Since users are incapable of expressing their tacit knowledge, we should consider experimental techniques for revealing some of it. For now we simply note that people have an innate ability for nonverbal communication, primarily with themselves. People have the capacity to assume an "as if" stance [37]—they have the ability to assume roles and pretend. This means that one should expect to be able to produce worthwhile results from studies and experiments concerning human factors engineering. This has certainly proved to be the case in scientific investigations of programming languages [38, 43, 44, and 45]. We will have more to say on the subject of experimentation in the section on psychological tools.

In summary then, the apparent requirements will vary depending upon the view of the user. Regardless of his status within an organization, each user will have a well-developed internal model of the environment and his functions within it. Some of this information is readily available in the form of immediate needs (however vaguely they may be expressed), but some is tacit knowledge and may have to be determined experimentally.

The Target System's User Interface

In discussing the user interface requirements for a system, it is essential to differentiate between upper-echelon management and the end-user [14, 46]. Their views of the system are sure to be different. Management will be primarily concerned with the system's functional requirements, constraints, development schedule, and cost. The end-user, however, may take such factors as "correctness" for granted; he or she must work with the final product, and wants a system that provides a comfortable environment, not a hostile one.

The AFWET system requires displays, and so we will concentrate on displays as a good example of various user-interface issues. Luxenberg and Kuehn [47] note that

It is essential to display design that standard human factors requirements be satisfied. This covers a broad range of topics such as perception, comprehension, viewing environment, psychological factors, and operator comfort.

These issues are of great importance if the system is to be acceptable to the user community. Thus, in a requirements document it is not enough to simply specify that the display equipment will consist of certain kinds of devices, which is all that was done in the AFWET document. The details that seem to be most needed are given by Luxenberg and Kuehn and are shown in Table 24.2.

The information required in each of the table's categories and subcategories, however, is much more than just specifications in terms of certain absolutes or generalities—for instance, response time must be 3 seconds, or response must be real time. The requirements document should have proposals for testing the acceptability of various factors with the end-users. Thus, we are immediately led into the general area of testability and to the questions that naturally arise about what is or is not a testable requirement. If there is to be a display that queries a data base, for example, then the requirements for response time should also include either solid reasons for specifying a certain value or proposed experiments to determine what the needs of the end-user

Table 24.2. A Major Step in Display Design: Determination of Specifications.

A. Data Rates and Response Times
1. Updating response time
2. Rates of change of display data
3. Display access time
4. Display request rates
B. Amount of Data
1. Amount of display information
2. Number of display units
3. Display sizes
4. Audience size
C. Types of Display
1. Coding
2. Symbology
3. Display formats
D. Visibility
1. Luminance
2. Ambient lighting
3. Contrast
4. Resolution
E. Quality
1. Accuracy
2. Distortion
3. Flicker

really are and how the determination can be validated. It is necessary not only to verify what the needs are, but also to check that the final product meets them. This practice should be applied liberally to any parts of the specification that deal with the broad area of human factors.

Thus, requirements for AFWET should contain proposals for pilot studies of (1) the best symbology to use for the displays, (2) the qualities desired in such device specifics as contrast, resolution, and flicker, (3) the best means to display a kill. There should also be proposals to study whether or not the display needs to run "in real time," as stated in the AFWET document. Even a small difference in the amount of acceptable delay can make a tremendous difference to the system's designers, and it is all too easy to accept serious constraints on a user's word, without questioning the real need for them. It certainly seems plausible that observers could get as much information from delayed or replayed tests as from those seen in real time. In the AFWET case, probably the crucial factor is the extent to which the observers of the displays participate in the test as commanders, but this is nowhere mentioned in the requirements document.

Psychological Tools

Some of the problems of user/analyst interaction have been highlighted in the previous sections. We believe that aggressive work on the human factors of a project will not only help alleviate some of the inherent communication problems, but also provide a sound basis for a project that is manageable in terms of schedule, cost functionality, and human acceptability.

Besides the obvious need for much interaction and discussion in order for users and designers to speak a common language, what else can be done to help alleviate the communication problem? Winograd discusses three different domains of discourse and suggests that the terms used in the subject domain be those familiar to the user [48]. Other ideas presented by Kaplan [37] suggest that we can take advantage of users' abilities to assume roles, to mentally validate or reject "what if" conditions, and to become involved in the entire process of design. He suggests that simple models work better from the viewpoint of the user than do complicated or elaborate models. This confirms what we already know about expert versus novice knowledge structures. So, once a dialect has been established, the software engineer may begin planning experiments, pilot tests, and other interactions with actual end-users in an attempt to bring forth tacit knowledge that may play an integral role in the functioning of the desired product.

The early phases of requirements analysis should concentrate on dissolving the differences in the ways in which experts and novices see. Definitions (based upon the users' perspectives), intensive discussions, and notations should help make problem areas explicit, remove bias, and thus add to the understandings of both user and analyst. The use of models, quick prototypes, graphic aids, and other forms of nonverbal communication should be encouraged, since these give the user something that can be "indwelled" [41], that is, internalized. This process of indwelling is most important, for it is the only way to really know something. The "one picture is worth ten thousand words" idea may sound too simple, but the replacement of words by actions can give the user a better understanding of what is being developed. Thus, by having something to indwell, the user will have the ability to make a comparison with his internal model, which already exists. This could not be done, and certainly is not done, with any of the static, formal notations currently in use for the specification of requirements.

The use of models, and their associated tests with actual end-users, should become a part of the planned system development from the very beginning. These pilot tests must be used for a sufficient period of time to allow the user to get beyond any difficulties of novelty. They must also be repeated many times after there are no more learning problems, because the nature of "participant behavior" is characterized by the fact that the participant considers a number of hypotheses on each trial and can only reject some, but not all, of those that are not consistent with his internal models [49]. Further-

more, users can more readily reject undesirable qualities than affirm desirable ones, probably because many of the desirable properties are part of their tacit knowledge.

Finally, studies should be planned to further define and refine human needs. Brooks [50] states the advantages of behavioral/psychological studies, which are important here for two reasons. First, we can affirm or refute any behavioral assumptions that have been made. Second, such studies give quantitative information on the relative effectiveness of various techniques, thus giving us a solid basis for the selection of new tools, new features, and new areas of concern. Careful selection of the studies to be made can help reduce costs for the entire project by confirming at an early stage that any of a number of quality-control attempts are, or are not, successful. We should be most concerned with the ideas of simplicity, psychological acceptability, the "engineering out" of errors, and the bounds on human performance [38, 45, 51]. Scientific experimentation during the requirements phase can help assure that the developing product will meet any of a number of such goals, and at a lesser cost than if they are ignored until later in the project lifetime.

There may certainly be economic considerations and developmental time limitations to restrict the amount of experimentation involved in a particular project. Time constraints on the end-users may also be a factor. However, the nature of human factors is such that they are very amenable to a requirement that specifies that a study or experiment be used to further define some quality of the end-users' environment. The life-cycle of a project may easily be long enough so that, with good modularization of requirements, such studies can proceed in parallel with some of the other work.

Our section on human factors is intended, like the rest of this chapter, to serve as a checklist for topic inclusion. Many of the suggested areas should be cross-referenced with proposals, milestones, and experiments, as in the section on system development. Note that the issues raised in this section should follow from the broadest possible interpretation of human factors—we intend for the requirements to consider a wide range of psychological and physical factors, for instance, user acceptability, motivation, and the work environment.

We have been deliberately vague about the types of pilot tests, models, and other nonverbal communication tools the engineer may find of value. Much research needs to be done to discover what prototypes work best for the desired interaction between user and designer. Kaplan has performed some studies with architects and users, and his results indicate that simplicity helps avoid much confusion on the part of the user [37].

Another example concerns the use of the "operational" requirements specifications mentioned in Section 4. The requirements consist of an executable model of the proposed system interacting with its environment; this model could be exercised interactively to provide demonstrations to users. This is a promising direction since functional and performance requirements at all levels can be incorporated into the formal specification [23, 24]. The model could provide a basis for conducting many of the experiments proposed in the requirements document. The next question, however, is: How can system behaviors be communicated to the user? What tests of the system should be performed? How can the information be made suitable for indwelling by the user? These are issues relating to nonverbal communication that deserve immediate attention.

24.7. CONCLUSION

This report is by no means a complete survey of current knowledge on requirements. Some of the best-known approaches have been given short shrift (although they have already been widely reviewed). We have made no attempt to survey tools, even though it is apparent that automated data base facilities for requirements information, however primitive, may be tremendously helpful.

The significance of this chapter, in our view, is that we have included the "forgotten" areas of requirements: process-oriented as well as data-oriented requirements, nonfunctional as well as functional requirements, and human factors. We have stressed the newest and (to us) most promising approaches, over the familiar and (to us) inadequate ones.

We believe that the problem of deriving good requirements can be solved in three stages. The first concerns discovering, understanding, and describing informally the users' requirements (interpreting *user* in its broadest sense). The second involves constructing a conceptual model that integrates and consolidates different user views. The third consists of specifying a system to meet the requirements in an executable language, and validating that specification.

Specification languages, categorized on the basis of system types, fit some of these stages better than others. PAISLey is a good candidate for an executable specification language, but a structured data model expressed in terms of semantic nets many make the best all-around conceptual model. And for first-stage description of users' needs, application-specific, user-oriented languages are clearly called for. It is our belief that a general framework for such languages can be developed on the basis of a case-structured syntax. These are the directions which researchers will be pursuing in the near future.

ACKNOWLEDGMENTS

The research reported on here is partially supported by the U.S. Air Force under Contract AFOSR-77-3181B, and by the U.S. Army under Contract DASG60-80-C-0024.

REFERENCES

1. L. A. Belady and M. M. Lehman, "The Characteristics of Large Systems," in Peter Wegner (ed.), *Research Directions in Software Technology*, M.I.T. Press, Cambridge, Mass., 1979, pp. 106–138.

2. Barry W. Boehm, "Software and Its Impact: A Quantative Assessment," *Datamation* 19(May 1973):48–60.

3. Barry W. Boehm, *Software Engineering Economics*, Prentice Hall, Englewood Cliffs, N.J., 1981.

4. T. A. Thayer, "Understanding Software through Analysis of Empirical Data," TRW Software Series, TRW-SS-75-04, May 1975.

5. U.S. Air Force, "Air Force Weapons Effectiveness

Testing (AFWET) Instrumentation System," R&D Exhibit No. PGVE 64-40, Air Proving Ground Center, Eglin Air Force Base, Florida, 1965.

6. M. M. Lehman, "Programs, Life Cycles, and Laws of Software Evolution," *Proceedings of the IEEE 68,* (Sept. 1980):1060-1076.

7. Raymond T. Yeh, "Systematic Derivation of Software Requirements through Structured Analysis," *Computer Science SDBEG-15,* University of Texas at Austin, Sept. 1979.

8. Raymond T. Yeh and Pamela Zave, "Specifying Software Requirements," *Proceedings of the IEEE 68,* (Sept. 1980):1077-1085.

9. M. M. Astrahan, *et al.,* "System R: Relational Approach to Database Management," *ACM Transactions on Database Systems* 1(June 1976):97-137.

10. D. L. Parnas, "A Technique for Software Module Specification with Examples," *Communications of the ACM* 15(May 1972):330-336.

11. D. L. Parnas, "Designing Software for Ease of Extension and Contraction," *IEEE Transactions on Software Engineering* 5(March 1977):128-137.

12. John Miles Smith and Diane C. P. Smith, "A Data Base Approach to Software Specification," in W. E. Riddle and R. E. Fairley (eds.), *Software Development Tools,* Springer-Verlag, New York, 1980.

13. Nicholas Roussopoulous, "CSDL: A Conceptual Schema Definition Language for the Design of Data Base Applications," *IEEE Transactions on Software Engineering* 5(Sept. 1979):481-496.

14. Roland Mittermeir, "Requirements Analysis: Top Down or Bottom Up," TR DA 80/02/02, Institut Für Digitale Anlagen, Technische Universität Wien, Wien, Federal Republic of Germany, 1980.

15. Douglas Ross and Kenneth E. Schoman, Jr., "Structured Analysis for Requirements Definition," *IEEE Transactions on Software Engineering* 3(Jan. 1977):6-15.

16. Douglas Ross, "Structured Analysis (SA): A Language for Communicating Ideas," *IEEE Transactions on Software Engineering* 3(Jan. 1977):15-34.

17. D. Teichroew and E. A. Hershey III, "PSL/PSA: A Computer-Aided Technique for Structured Documentation and Analysis of Information Systems," *IEEE Transactions on Software Engineering* 3(Jan. 1977):41-43.

18. James L. Peterson, "Petri Nets," *Computing Surveys* 9(Sept. 1977):223-252.

19. M. Conner, "Process Synchronization by Behavior Controllers," Ph.D. thesis, Computer Science Department, University of Texas at Austin, 1979.

20. J. J. Horning and B. Randell, "Process Structuring," *Computing Surveys* 5(Jan. 1973):5-29.

21. C. A. R. Hoare, "Communicating Sequential Processes," *Communications of the ACM* 2(Aug. 1978):666-677.

22. Per Brinch Hansen, "Distributed Processes: A Concurrent Programming Concept," *Communications of the ACM* 21(Nov. 1978):934-941.

23. Pamela Zave, "A Comprehensive Approach to Requirements Problems," *Proceedings COMPSAC,* Chicago, Nov. 1979, pp. 117-122.

24. Pamela Zave, "Formal Specification of Complete and Consistent Performance Requirements," *Proceedings Texas Conference on Computing Systems,* Dallas, Tex., Nov. 1979, pp. 4B-18-4B-25.

25. Pamela Zave, "An Operational Approach to Requirements Specification for Embedded Systems," *IEEE Transactions on Software Engineering* 8(May 1982):250-269.

26. Pamela Zave and Raymond T. Yeh, "Executable Requirements for Embedded Systems." *Proceedings 5th Intl. Conf. on Software Engineering,* San Diego, Cal. (Mar. 1981): pp. 295-304.

27. Stephen W. Smoliar, "Applicative and Functional Programming," in C. R. Vick and C. V. Ramamoorthy (eds.), *Handbook of Software Engineering,* Van Nostrand Reinhold, New York, N. Y., this volume.

28. Mack Alford, "A Requirements Engineering Methodology for Real-Time Processing Requirements," *IEEE Transactions on Software Engineering* 3(Jan. 1977):60-69.

29. Thomas Bell, David Bixler, and Margaret Dyer, "An Extensible Approach to Computer-Aided Software Requirements Engineering," *IEEE Transactions on Software Engineering* 3(Jan. 1977):40-69.

30. Carl G. Davis and Charles R. Vick, "The Software Development System," *IEEE Transactions on Software Engineering* 3(Jan. 1977):69-84.

31. John Backus, "Can Programming Be Liberated From the von Neumann Style? A Functional Style and its Algebra of Programs," *Communications of the ACM* 21(Aug. 1978):613-641.

32. Stephen W. Smoliar, "Using Applicative Techniques to Design Distributed Systems," *Proceedings Specifications of Reliable Software Conference,* Cambridge, Mass., Apr. 1979, pp. 150-161.

33. A. K. Jones and P. Schwarz, "Experience Using Multiprocessor Systems—A Status Report," *Computing Surveys* 12(June 1980):121-165.

34. M. V. Zelkowitz, A. C. Shaw, and J. D. Gannon, *Principles of Software Engineering and Design,* Prentice-Hall, Englewood Cliffs, N.J., 1979, p. 8.

35. Alex Paul Conn, "Maintenance: A Key Element in Computer Requirements Definition," *Proceedings COMPSAC,* Chicago, Ill., Nov. 1980.

36. D. L. Parnas, "On the Criteria to be Used in Decomposing Systems into Modules," *Communications of the ACM* 15(Dec. 1972):1053-1058.

37. Stephen Kaplan, "Participation in the Design Process," in D. Stokes (ed.), *Psychological Perspectives on Environment and Behavior: Conceptual and Empirical Trends,* Plenum, New York, 1976.

38. Ben Schneiderman, "Human Factors Experiments in Designing Interactive Systems," *Computer* 12(Dec. 1979):9-20.

39. Herbert Simon, *The Sciences of the Artificial,* M.I.T. Press, Cambridge, Mass., 1970.

40. Mark David Weiser, "Program Slices: Formal, Psychological, and Practical Investigations of an Automatic Program Abstraction Model," Ph.D. thesis, University of Michigan, 1979.

41. Michael Polanyi, *The Tacit Dimension*, Anchor Books (Doubleday), New York, 1967, pp. 3–25.

42. William James, *Psychology: The Briefer Course*, Harper, 1892, pp. 30–37, 106–110.

43. Victor R. Basili and Robert Reiter, Jr., "An Investigation of Human Factors in Software Engineering," *Computer* 12(Dec. 1979):21–40.

44. H. E. Dunsmore and J. D. Gannon, "Data Referencing: An Empirical Investigation," *Computer* 12(Dec. 1979):50–59.

45. Ben Schneiderman, *Software Psychology: Human Factors in Computer and Information Systems*, Winthrop Publishers, Inc., 1980.

46. Roland Mittermeir, "Application of Database Design Concepts to Software Requirements Analysis," TR DA 79-11-01, Institute Für Digitale Anlagen, Technische Universität Wien, Wien, Federal Republic of Germany, 1979.

47. H. R. Luxenburg and R. L. Kuehn, *Display Systems Engineering*, McGraw-Hill, New York, 1968.

48. Terry Winograd, "Beyond Programming Languages," *Communications of the ACM* 12(July 1979):391–401.

49. Michael T. Rosner, *Cognition: An Introduction*, Scott, Foresman and Company, Glenview, 1975, pp. 61–92.

50. Ruven E. Brooks, "Studying Programmer Behavior Experimentally: The Problem of Proper Methodology," *Communications of the ACM* 23(Apr. 1980):207–213.

51. Ben Schneiderman and Richard Mayers, "Syntactics/Semantic Interactions in Programmer Behavior: A Model and Experimental Results," *Int. Journal of Computer and Information Sciences* 8(March 1979):219–238.

On Using the Users' Manual as the Requirements Specification

Norman R. Howes

Introduction

As almost everyone who has participated in defining, designing, coding, testing, or using a new computer system knows, writing the Users' Manual is one of the last things to be done, if not *the* last. The reason is that as computer systems are developed they tend to change along the way and consequently what the new system is *really* going to do and how it will behave in the hands of a user is not well understood until late in the development cycle. Elementary logic enables one to move from this observation to the conclusion that it is more efficient to write the Users' Manual at that stage in the development cycle when these questions are well understood, namely, near the end.

Also, almost everyone who has participated in the development of a computer system knows that for any software development effort to be successful a clear requirements specification should be developed at the beginning of the undertaking. On the other hand, the only document about the system the user is ever likely to understand (if indeed he can understand *that*) is the Users' Manual. In other words, most users never understand the requirements specification for the new systems they will be using. Often it is the case that the potential user of the new system is the one financing its development. In such cases it is common for them not to understand what they are buying.

Why is this the case? The way requirements specifications are usually developed is a group of "systems analysts" interview the potential users of the new system to determine what the system needs to do. Then after filtering this information (for feasibility, reliability, maintainability, etc., etc.) they produce a requirements specification. Requirements specifications tend to be very general. It is often difficult to determine *specifically* what the new system is going to do and usually *impossible* to determine what the user's interface to the system will be from the specification. Moreover, the wording of requirements specifications often uses technical jargon that is inaccessible to a potential user. Even such commonly used phrases are "user friendly" do not convey the same meaning to a nontechnical user as they do to a systems designer. Furthermore, using a formal requirements development method such as MIL-STD 490 or 2167 seems to do little to resolve this problem.

But why do the analysts produce requirements specifications that are so general or not accessible to users? This is a classic problem that is beyond the scope of this paper. Some specific examples of the problem are given in [HOW77]. Analysts defend generality in the requirements specifications on many grounds, most of which boil down to the fact that they don't want to make specific commitments early in the development cycle. Jules Schwartz [SCH75] says that development of the requirements specification "In many cases seems trivial, but it probably is the part of the process which leads to more failures than any other."

After the requirements specification is completed it is usually submitted to someone or some organization for review and acceptance. Usually the reviewing body is a "steering committee" or "users working group" or some similar organization. Almost always the reviewing body includes potential users. But these users usually do not understand the specification.

An investigation of why users don't demand specifications they can understand or of the politics of new system development that often cause them to adopt a "wait and see if it works" attitude is not the purpose of this paper. Its purpose is to investigate how the requirements specification *can* be made understandable to the potential users so the situation does not arise where the completed system is not utilized or is under-utilized. The author is familiar with several expensive failures where the new system never gained acceptance or was replaced by something else shortly, after it was finished.

Background

The design, implementation, and project management methodologies used on a large (over a million manhours) commercial software development effort were documented in [HOW82] and [HOW84]. The requirements specification development that preceded this effort was conducted in the manner described above and took more than a year to complete. Since the system was intended for international operation, small teams of the systems analysts made trips to remote locations all over the world to interview potential users at great cost to the customer. Upon return, the information gathered was analyzed, sifted, compared, consolidated, etc., and eight formidable volumes of requirements matrices and formal statements of requirements emerged in accordance with IBM's ISM methodology.

Later, a few of the participants in this undertaking were faced with developing a very similar system but this time on distributed personal computers rather than on a mainframe computer. Having been through a lengthy requirements definition phase on a similar project, it occurred to them that a significant manpower savings could be achieved if the requirements definition phase could be minimized on the current project. It was decided to write a Users' Manual *as if* the system to be developed already existed. Of course, a system was visualized that was similar to the one already developed. The Users' Manual was then presented to the potential users for review. Remarkably, the users seemed to understand what was being proposed. The Users' Manual was written like many of the user manuals for commercial PC software packages on the market today. Although this approach probably would not have been tried in other situations, at the time it seemed reasonable based on the experience gained from the previous project and its similarity to the previous project.

Recently, the requirements definition phase of the Space Station Data Management System (DMS), which is the space-based component of the Space Station Information System (SSIS), was undertaken using this method. The Space Station DMS consists of hardware, networks, and software to enable the various application subsystems on the Space Station to communicate with one another and the various services available to the Ada applications programmer to support distributed operations.

The requirements definition was carried out by a joint NASA/Lockheed working group. Requirements were developed with a view toward how they would be explained in the context of a users' manual. If requirements could not be stated clearly in this context, they were reworked until they could. Thereafter, the design and simulation of a system satisfying these requirements was done. A description of the simulation was given in [HOW86] and the Space Station DMS Users' Manual is [NAS86].

Because the users of the Space Station DMS will be Ada applications programmers, the user in this case is assumed to be very sophisticated. What the Users' Manual documents is a description of the services to be provided to the Ada programmer by the DMS, the format of the commands (utilities), the Ada types corresponding to the calling parameters, and the exceptions that are raised when the commands are not used correctly or the parameters are invalid. What follows is a case study of how this approach was used to define the requirements for the Space Station DMS Test Bed and how it was augmented with other techniques applicable to this specific project.

It turns out that this technique of using the users' manual as the vehicle for documenting requirements is not entirely new. After stumbling onto this technique in practice, it was pointed out to the author that something similar was documented in the literature at least once before [DON76]. Although somewhat different in spirit from what will be documented in this paper, it is none-the-less in the same vein.

Case Study

In March of 1985, as the result of previous related work, NASA gave Lockheed a Job Order to define the requirements for the Space Station DMS Test Bed. NASA convened a joint working group of NASA and Lockheed personnel to study what services would be needed by the applications programmer developing software for the various subsystems that are to be aboard the Station. The DMS is to provide those services that are common to all subsystems, such as the ability to communicate with one another over the network, to transfer files from one subsystem to another, etc.

The working group spent the first 120 days reviewing the documentation available relating to possible DMS requirements. This consisted of studies by various companies, consultants, working groups, university professors, etc. Most of these studies did not deal with what services the DMS needed to provide but rather statements of policy such as adhering to the ISO/OSI model, being technologically transparent, using token-passing buses, maintainability criteria, etc. Although this did not shed much light on requirements, it did serve to set boundries on the scope of the requirements.

During this period the working group classified and consolidated these policy statements to create a consistent baseline from which to work. It was the intent of the group that the requirements specification would adhere to this baseline policy statement (or at least not violate it). Thereafter, the working group undertook the definition of actual requirements. Since this was a broad undertaking, it was decided to tackle the problem one piece at a time. How to subdivide the overall task was a problem. Although it probably could have been handled in a variety of ways, the subdivision was based on the modern software engineering practice of *layering*.

Layering Requirements

It was conceived that the DMS software would be designed as a set of layers over the operating system of the subsystem computers. One of the statements in the baseline policy statement was that all the subsystems would be implemented on a Standard Data Processor (SDP). In other words, all core (as opposed to payload) subsystems on the Station will be implemented on computers having the same instruction set architecture (ISA). This will permit all core subsystem computers to use the same operating system. Further, these SDPs will be connected to the network via a standard network interface unit (NIU) that will also be a computer (possibly with the same ISA as the SDPs). The Network Operating System (NOS) component of the DMS will be in the NIUs. A diagram of the DMS together with the various subsystems is shown in Figure 1. The subsystem computers themselves are

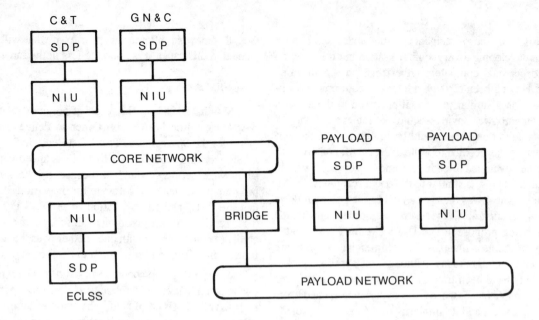

Figure 1

not considered to be a part of the DMS, nor is the application software that runs in them. The core and payload networks, the NIUs, and all of the DMS services software in the SDPs constitute the DMS.

It was envisioned that the lowest layer over the operating system would be the NOS so the working group decided to tackle these requirements first. After reviewing the anticipated needs of various core subsystems it was decided that both the ISO/OSI (International Standards Organization/Open Systems Interconnect) classes of message-handling services would be required, namely, a datagram service and a virtual circuit service.

Over the message-handling (datagram and virtual circuit) services, the Data Acquisition and Distribution Services and the File Management Services would be layered as shown in Figure 2. The DBMS would then be layered over the File Management Services. Note that this is not intended to imply that in the design phase the software would necessarily be designed this way. It was merely a way of thinking how it *might* be designed to assist in deciding what requirements needed to be defined first. As it turned out later when the software was designed, this layering scheme was actually used, but some of the layering proved to be too inefficient in operation to be practical for the high data rate requirements of the Station. A word of caution is in order at this point: Layering is not free! Although it is a boone for software maintainability, there is a performance price to pay.

For instance, it seemed reasonable to assume in the beginning that the File Management Service would require a virtual circuit capability for such things as file transfer, etc. but

it was not clear whether the File Management Services would require a datagram capability. In view of this it was decided to just assume the File Management Service would be layered over the NOS Services. Such combinations as layering the NOS over the File Management Services were not even considered as meaningful.

Using this layering model it was decided to develop the requirements in the order shown below:

(1) Datagram Services,

(2) Virtual Circuit Services,

(3) File Management Services,

(4) Database Management Services, and

(5) Data Acquisition and Distribution Services.

It was assumed this would be an iterative process in that requirements defined in a later category might cause modification of the requirements defined in an earlier category. That this was the case was confirmed as the requirements definition proceeded.

Rapid Prototyping

During the definition of requirements several questions arose as to the feasibility of various requirements. Although this is usually not a problem with defining requirements for most systems, the nature of the Space Station itself introduced requirements for services that were not known to exist in any other systems. For example, since Ada was designated the "language of choice" for the core subsystems on the

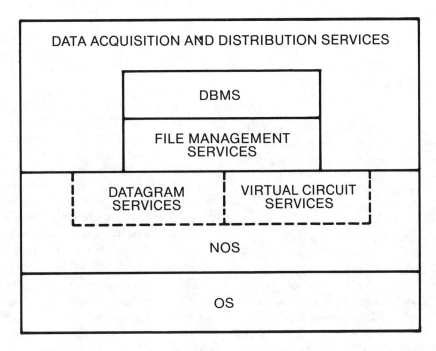

Figure 2

Station, and since the software development associated with it would dwarf most software developments, it was decided that communications requirements should be stated in terms of Ada objects rather than as protocols. With so much software to be developed, it was felt the Ada applications programmers would need all the help they could get.

Most communication networks, with which anyone has experience, use a protocol for transferring messages from one point to another. The application programmers must deal explicitly with transforming any data structures to be transmitted into the data structure of the protocol (which is often just a packet of bits or a string of ASCII characters) and then transforming it back at the other end. For the Space Station DMS, the applications programmer should not have to be concerned with translating Ada objects back and forth. Instead, the Ada applications programmer should be able to transmit Ada objects from one subsystem to another.

Stating this as a requirement is one thing but convincing ourselves that it is practical is another, especially when most of the members of the working group were only beginning to gain familiarity with Ada. To convince ourselves that some key requirements were feasible, it was decided that proof-of-concept programs should be written in Ada and tested to confirm the possibility of doing such things. This was done extensively with respect to the Data Acquisition and Distribution Services and the directory-building services of the File Management Services.

While this is not the ordinary usage of the term "rapid prototyping," such usage is in somewhat the same spirit as its conventional usage in the design phase of a project. The proof-of-concept programming also helped in refining the ideas behind the requirement. It is safe to say that in the areas where this "rapid prototyping" was done the requirements that emerged were an improvement over those originally proposed.

Simulation

After the requirements had been approved by NASA and published as the DMS Test Bed Users' Manual [NAS86], Lockheed was tasked by NASA to produce a simulation of the DMS services in Ada on a VAX in one of the NASA laboratories. Work on this simulation was completed in September 1986. During 1987, the actual Ada software implementation of the DMS services for the Space Station DMS Test Bed will be completed. The software design proceeded directly from the Users' Manual without the need for producing the conventional sort of requirements specification usually associated with software development. Furthermore, there is every indication that the potential users of the DMS services understand the requirements (Users' Manual).

The way the software design of the simulation proceeded from the Users' Manual is demonstrated in the following example. One of the first requirements documented was for an Ada application programmer to be able to send a message to another subsystem on one of the Space Station networks. It was decided that this should be accomplished by a utility (Ada procedure) named SEND. The user would call this service by issuing the command.

SEND (MESSAGE,ADDRESS);

where MESSAGE is the Ada object to be transmitted and ADDRESS its destination. Although this is not possible with most computer languages it is with Ada by making the SEND procedure part of a *generic* package and requiring the user of the SEND command to instantiate a copy of the package for each Ada object to be transmitted. Actually, MESSAGE is a record structure with a header field that tells the receiving subsystem what Ada object type is being transmitted as shown below:

```
type MESSAGE is
record
        HEADER: HEADER_TYPE;
        OBJECT: OBJECT_TYPE;
end record;
```

The definition of HEADER_TYPE and OBJECT_TYPE is not important to understand the example. In this way, we proceeded from the overall requirement, to the form of the command, to the types of the parameters used in the command, and, finally, to the exceptions that are raised (a feature of the Ada language) when the commands are used incorrectly.

Since each requirement is documented as a service (command) in the Users' Manual, it is a simple matter to write the Ada specification of the program unit to provide this service from its description in the Users' Manual. Some consideration needs to be given to which program units need to be grouped together into which packages and which data types need to be packaged together so the Ada scope and visibility rules are satisifed in a natural way. Then the package specifications can be written. After the package specifications are compiled (a check on completeness and consistency), the package bodies can be written.

Summary

As one might suppose, using the Users' Manual approach to requirements specification development can have a profound effect on the management of a software engineering project. It is natural to ask: What are the advantages and disadvantages of this approach? First, it appears to have the advantage of improving the representation of the objective of the project over conventional requirements specifications. It causes attention to be focused simultaneously on what is needed and in what mode it is needed. At any level of definition of system requirements, (i.e., at the highest level or for requirements definition of a subsystem of a larger system), it appears that an improvement in clarity can be achieved by documenting the requirements as if they were the Users' Manual for the system being developed.

This focusing of attention on the mode in which a service (requirement) is to be delivered has a tendency to streamline the requirements specification phase of a project. One of the reasons is that it has a tendency to rule out consideration of numerous hypothetical requirements in the light of practicality. Requirements have a tendency of spawning additional requirements. In the above example of the SEND command, if it is a requirement that the system provide a message transmission service, then perhaps it is the case that a user might have the occasion for sending the same message to multiple address. If so, then it may also be a requirement that a "multicast" capability is needed. In turn, if a multicast capability is needed, it might be nice if the user had the capability to assign a logical name to a list of addresses, and

then when a message was to be distributed to this list of addresses, the user could simply specify the logical name of the address list.

Later in the design phase, these "derived" requirements might be provided for by an additional command named MULTICAST that would make the logical name to address list assignment, and yet another command named BROADCAST that would broadcast a message to a list of addressees specified by this logical name. This, of course is but one way that such requirements could be implemented. But if during the requirements specification phase a Users' Manual is being developed, it is more likely that the systems analysts, while considering the mode in which these services are to be delivered, will discover that there is really no need for the additional MULTICAST and BROADCAST commands.

Instead, a multicast service can be built into the SEND command at virtually no extra cost. The ADDRESS parameter in the SEND command can be defined as a string of addresses, perhaps delimited by commas. If during the execution of a program, it is necessary to broadcast to a given list of addressees more than once, a programmer may wish to build a constant string consisting of the destination addresses. This constant string could then be used over and over in the SEND command. The end result is that the user has only one command to learn instead of three and the maintainers of the software have two less functions to maintain.

This example is one that actually occurred during the requirements specification for the DMS services for the Space Station. In retrospect, it is almost obvious that in this case, one command is better than three. But had the mode of delivering the service not been under consideration, three requirements rather than one integrated requirement may have emerged.

Another advantage for the state-of-the-art type project is that the requirements are stated in such a way that they can be simulated. This may be necessary when there are questions about the feasibility of providing services of a type that no known examples exist. Rapid prototyping can parallel the requirements specification development, thus providing yet other data points on the suitability of requirements.

Another advantage of the Users' manual approach is that it improves communication with the user/customer. The better the user understands exactly what is being specified, the better off the project manager will be in the long run. Not only will the risk of surprises to the user be reduced, but management controls of the type, which are strictly limited to improving the user's visibility that do not contribute either to the management of the project or to the quality of the product, are less likely to be installed.

Finally, this approach improves control of the project. As pointed out in the previous example, not only is clarity of the specification improved, but there is a natural flow of activity from the requirements specification into the high-level design of the system. Transition from the requirements phase of the project to the design phase has historically been a problem, especially when the requirements are developed by a different organization than the one responsible for the design and implementation.

Requirements traceability (for those projects that require such an activity) is facilitated by this approach. On large projects, it is often difficult to understand how certain design features relate back to the original requirements. Using this method, the design procedes in a natural way from the requirements. Software verification and validation criteria is easier to produce because of the more specific orientation of the requirements document.

The major disadvantage to using this technique at the present time is that it will be unfamiliar to the analysts that are to use it and to the potential user. People tend to be reluctant to use something they are unfamiliar with. If a system is being developed for a government customer, the question of how to fit this technique into the framework of MIL-STD 2167 may arise. Indeed, on the Space Station DMS project, it may become necessary to go back and develope a 2167 type specification in order to interface with other contractors that only know how to work in the MIL-STD 490 specification environment. These problems need to be dealt with and perhaps future uses of this approach will refine it to the point where there are no longer problems. And perhaps this paper will encourage others to try the approach and hopefully share their experience with the rest of us.

References

[DON76] W.S. Donelson, "Project Planning and Control," *Datamation*, June 1976.

[HOW86] N.R. Howes, "The TAVERNS Emulator: An Ada simulation of the Space Station Data Communications Network and software development environment," *Proceedings of the First International Symposium on Ada Applications for the NASA Space Station* Univ. of Houston, Clear Lake, Tex., June 1986.

[HOW84] N.R. Howes, Managing Software Development Projects for Maximum Productivity," *IEEE Transactions on Software Engineering*, Vol. SE-10, No. 1, pp. 27-35, January 1984.

[HOW82] N.R. Howes, Project Management Systems," *Information & Management*, Vol. 5, pp. 243-258, December 1982.

[HOW77] R. Howes and H.G. Hansen, Development of effective command and control systems," *Signal Magazine* (Jour. Armed Forces Commun. Electron. Assn.), pp. 44-48, February 1977.

[NAS86] Users' Manual for the Data Management System (DMS) Test Bed," NASA/JSC Document No. 22161, April 1986.

[SCH75] J.I. Schwartz, "Construction of Software, Problems and Practicalities," pp. 15-54, "Practical Strategies for Developing Large Software Systems" (a compilation of papers from the 1974 USC Seminar entitled *Modern Techniques for the Design and Construction of Reliable Software*), Addison-Wesley, Reading, Mass., 1975.

Article presents an exception-
oriented execution of a detailed
plan.

Reprinted with permission from *Journal of Systems Management*, Volume 29, Number 11, Issue 211, November 1978, pages 22-29. Copyright © 1978 by the Association for Systems Management.

Fundamentals of Project Management

BY WILLIAM B. MILLER

■ Project planning has essentially one purpose: establishing a foundation for execution of the plan and, therefore, successful completion of the project. The project plan is the game plan for the project. Other uses of the plan, such as communication, are important but secondary. Planning should be performed before work begins on project activities. It should include both general project planning and detailed planning for activities in the near future. Planning output should include:

—Definitions of project activities and required results.

—Estimates of work content of project activities, in terms of resources that could be used, such as mandays for people or processing hours for equipment.

—Activity schedules, with milestones and checkpoints for progress reviews.

—Specific assignments for personnel and other resources.

—Resource "loading" estimates (use of resources by time period) or budgets, for personnel, equipment, and other resources.

It is elementary that a plan should include this information. However, it has been my experience that many planners fail to include some of the information. Such a deficiency in plan is a harbinger of future problems.

Planning Responsibilities

Responsibilities for specific planning activities vary by project, but the fundamentals remain the same. They are:

1. The persons who are most knowledgeable about the project activities to be performed and the resources to be used should provide most of the input to the plan. Frequently these persons are the individuals who will be performing or directly supervising the activities. In other cases, they may be support technicians, such as engineers, who are experts on the tasks to be performed.

2. Project management has final responsibility for the plan and should direct its preparation. The plan must reflect their perspective. Often the persons who are most knowledgeable about the activities and resources will have a forest-and-trees perspective problem, which may lead them to be too optimistic or pessimistic about the time and resources required to perform activities (a well-known problem in systems projects).

A good plan should be largely the product of the knowledgeable workers and supervisors, or support technicians, with as few modifications as requested by management. Extensive participation or no participation by management is a sign of trouble because the resulting plan will, respectively, be based on desires rather than facts, or fail to reflect the experience and insights of management.

The Planning Process

The planning process is the sequence of events that produces a project plan. In a pragmatic sense, any sequence of events is acceptable if the resulting plan is acceptable. However, there are certain steps in the process that will be effective for most projects; these steps are the fundamentals.

1. First, project management and key worker and supervisory personnel should be selected, and their planning responsibilities should be defined.

178

2. A general project plan, consisting of the planning output described earlier, should be developed. This general plan should be reasonable and feasible, but detailed analysis to support it is not necessary. The content and structure of the plan will be described further in the next section.

3. Approvals for the general plan should be obtained. There is no point in proceeding with detailed planning if the plan in general terms is not acceptable, for example with regard to completion dates or resource requirements.

4. A detailed project plan should be developed. This plan should be complete in all details. All inconsistencies, resource loading problems, and conflicts should be eliminated. An example of such a situation is an unmanageable number of checkpoints occurring close together in time, perhaps in one day. This and other aspects of the detailed plan will be discussed later.

5. The general project plan should be revised to be consistent with the detailed plan. The general plan should be a summary of the detailed plan.

6. Approval of the detailed and revised general plans should be obtained. The total project plan, made up of the detailed and general plans, should be published.

These steps are essential in most projects. The number of iterations of one or more of them that is required to develop an acceptable plan may vary. Skipping steps or doing them in a radically different sequence is a violation of fundamentals that at best will be an inefficient way of producing a plan.

Specifics of the Plan

The purpose of the planning phase is to produce a plan with the components described earlier: activities, expected results, work content, schedules, resource assignments, and resource loads (budgets). The specific information content of the components must facilitate execution of the plan. This requirement leads to the following fundamentals:

1. The project must be subdivided into "chewable bites," a number of manageable activities, each with its own tangible end product. The activities' end products may collectively be the project's end product, or they may be intermediate stages in the generation of the project end product.

Activity and output definitions normally occur early in the planning phase. It has been my experience that they are a good indicator of how smoothly the remainder of the project will go. People who understand the value of defining precisely what is to be accomplished accept the other controls easily. On the other hand, people who prefer fuzzy or nonexistent definitions of what has to be done also reject budgets, schedules and other controls.

2. Each activity must be scheduled. Scheduling involves estimating the work content of an activity (e.g. man-days) which may vary by the specific resource used, assigning activities to resources (e.g., persons, pieces of equipment), and determining when each activity should be performed in order to meet the overall project deadline.

There are many scheduling techniques (network methods, for example). In the context of fundamentals, the following guidelines regarding selection of and output from the scheduling method should be observed:

—The scheduling method should be only as complex as is appropriate for the project at hand.

—"Back scheduling" methods, which schedule activities based on start dates of subsequent activities, are generally preferable to "forward scheduling" methods, which schedule activities to be completed when resources are available so long as the overall project deadline is retained. "Back scheduling" preserves the proper sequence of activities and avoids rework problems that may arise from completing activities earlier than necessary (rework is a real-world, not a theoretical, problem with "forward scheduling"). "Forward scheduling" has application, however, when scheduling information, such as work content estimates, may be unreliable or when resource scheduling is a significant concern.

—In the scheduling output, elapsed times of activities (completion date less start date) should be minimized. Multiple parallel assignments for personnel and other resources should be avoided. "One thing at a time" is a good rule. Obviously, it cannot always be observed. However, one of the most frequent scheduling mistakes is the scheduling of several activities to occur simultaneously and use the same resources, on the assumption that by some kind of magic each activity will receive its correct share of resources and be completed on time.

WILLIAM B. MILLER

Mr. Miller is a management consultant in the San Francisco office of Touche Ross & Co. He is a frequent contributor to professional journals and has authored other articles on various aspects of systems design and EDP management. He holds the CDP, a B.S. in Engineering, and an M.S. in Computer Science.

3. The schedule should include status points after completion of each activity or consumption of a certain amount of resources. If an activity is complex or critical, or its output is intended to be a polished product, status points during the activity, to assess progress, should be scheduled. Status points ensure that completion occurs as scheduled, with satisfactory quality. Tangible output should be emphasized; dealing with "percent complete" or subjective measures of progress can be dangerous. Status reviews require effort from project workers and management. Time for the status points must be planned, and responsibilities assigned.

4. Responsibility for each activity and resource consumption objective should be clear. When many people are assigned to an item, one should be in charge. The plan should include time for this person's administrative duties.

5. Recovery time and resources should be provided in the schedule. On a complex project, nobody is smart enough to plan it correctly at the outset. On any project, things can go wrong, such as people becoming ill. New, unforeseen activities will crop up; they always do and not all of them can be deferred. Recovery time can be provided implicitly, for example by not scheduling weekend work or overtime. It can be provided explicitly by leaving slack (unallocated) time or resources that would otherwise be available (during the normal 40-hour week, for example).

A trick that is often used by experienced Project Managers is to plan all activities to consume fewer resources than estimated, for example planning all activities to use 85% of estimated resource requirements. The remaining 15% becomes available as recovery resources that can be applied without exceeding the budget. This trick, of course, takes advantage of the fact that estimates are what their name states—estimates. Activity estimates will seldom be exactly accurate; they will be either high or low. In the absence of controls, the tendency is for only the low estimates and additional activities to be identified as the project progresses, causing budget overruns. On the activities where the estimates were high, work tends to expand to fill the budget. A good Project Manager will not allow that to happen and will bring such activities in under their budgets, at the 85% target or lower.

6. Resource "loading" or budgets—use of resources by time period—should be calculated for each resource employed on the project—people, equipment, money, etc. If the loading is inefficient, unrealistic, or does not meet project objectives, schedules and resource assignments should be adjusted in order to adjust the loading. When many resources are involved which are interchangeable except that activities' work contents depend on the specific resource used, this step may complicate planning because of many iterations of scheduling and loading calculations. The complexity is not a good reason for not performing the step. If it is not performed, the plan is sure to be deficient in some respect such as uneven equipment utilization or individuals scheduled for 60-hour weeks followed by 20-hour weeks.

The fundamentals apply to both general and detailed project planning. General planning should cover the life of the project at a macro level that is adequate for communication, resource commitments, upper management approvals, and integration with other projects. The general plan should include the same information as the detailed plan, but in summary form. Major activities, milestones and resource requirements should be specifically identified, but minor items should be lumped together.

The purpose of the detailed plan is control. The activities should be subdivided so far as is necessary to gain control. The fundamental rule is: an activity should be small enough that recovery will be easy if the activity is not completed as scheduled (which would be determined at the status point following the activity). A rule of thumb in many projects is that an activity should consume no more than 40 man-hours or 5 days elapsed time. Similarly, resource requirements should be subdivided, and status points for measurement of consumption should be scheduled such that excessive consumption would be identified while recovery was still possible. Planning and controlling at such a level of detail may not be popular with some people on the project. However, it is essential, and the situation is rare when controls can justifiably be abandoned in favor of goodwill.

The detailed plan should extend as far into the future as is feasible. One to three months probably is typical. Detailed planning should, therefore, be performed several times throughout the project, unless the project only covers a short time span for which the entire detailed plan can be developed at the beginning. In some cases, it may be a useful exercise to lay out the entire project in detail, but the purpose of such an exercise would be closer to the purpose of the general plan than to the purpose of the detailed plan. A detailed plan, against which progress will be measured rigorously, usually cannot be established more than a few weeks or months in advance of the activities to be performed.

A Project Manager without a plan is like a football team without a playbook, inventing plans during a game. However, I have seen some people try to operate that way. One company assigned a strategic planning project to a group of individuals from the planning function and gave them some general guidelines on what the plan should contain and who should have input to it. The planning person who managed the project did not put together a detailed plan and have it approved by the management who had given him his assignment. In fact, this individual appeared to believe that he was above such things as detailed planning, that they would have been a waste of his valuable time. His team produced a strategic plan that was good in many respects, but they overlooked a couple of matters that were important to corporate management, such as certain market analyses. The problems were corrected before the final plan was produced, but the project ended up requiring more money and time than had been budgeted.

Such failures have not been infrequent and will continue to be a problem so long as project situations exist. There is no evidence that projects are going to lose favor as a means of accomplishing business objectives. In fact, as Alvin Toffler predicted in *Future Shock*,[1] the project approach or "ad-hocracy" may continue to increase in popularity at the expense of traditional approaches that are ineffective in dealing quickly enough with new business problems arising at an ever-increasing rate. If business management is to cope with either today's projects or an increased volume of projects, as Toffler suggests, they simply must do better at using project management fundamentals such as thorough planning.

Planning Documentation

It should go without saying that the plan should be formally documented. However, a fundamental rule of documentation is that it should not be an end in itself, except as required for audit and archival purposes. Documentation is the basis for communication of the plan. It must be easy to understand. Charts and other visual aids are often appropriate. Frequently, the general plan and detailed plan should be separate documents because they communicate to different people.

For some kinds of projects, such as data processing projects, planning documentation may follow a standard format that reduces preparation time and is easily recognized by all parties involved. In other cases, the documentation may be unique and require explanation. Wherever possible, of course, proven documentation procedures should be used.

The documentation methodology should assist in developing the project plan. It should help in structuring the planning process. It may be an integral part of the planning. For example, with a network-structured plan, the development of the network and the plan may produce much of the documentation. If an automated system, such as a computerized scheduling system, provides planning assistance, adequate planning documentation may be normal output from the system.

Another fundamental is that the planning documentation should be useful in the execution phase of the project. Tracking project progress against anything other than the documented plan is inefficient and invites errors. This fundamental also provides a good cross-check on the content of the plan: anything that is to be measured during project execution should be spelled out in the plan, with anticipated results of the measurements. Conversely, there is no point in planning something if progress against the plan is not going to be measured. Planning and execution are opposite sides of the same coin.

Approval of the Plan

"Approval" should mean one thing: commitment. Approval of the plan should be obtained from two groups of people:
   —The people who must accept the schedule and provide the required resources.
   —The people who can cause the project to fail, by any means, fair or foul.
The two groups may or may not include the same persons.

The process of obtaining approvals should not be taken lightly. Clear, complete documentation of the plan is valuable. It is also important to remember that the people whose approval will be sought will not have lived closely with the planning process. The

[1]Alvin Toffler, *Future Shock*, Random House, Inc., 1970

persons presenting the plan must transmit on the receivers' wavelengths.

Sometimes approvals will not be immediately forthcoming. Depending on what the objections are to the plan, the options are to:

a. Modify the format and presentation to make the plan more understandable.

b. Apply more, fewer, or different resources to activities in order to change completion dates in the schedule.

c. Modify completion dates in order to affect resource usage (personnel, dollars, etc.).

d. Modify the scope of the project in order to affect completion dates or resource requirements.

e. Take a position that the plan as presented is necessary for successful completion of the project.

It is not possible to change one of the plan variables—activities and associated work content, schedules, and use of resources—without changing one or both of the others. (This does not imply that there are not several means of changing the components; for example, overtime may be an acceptable means for increasing resources in cases when hiring additional personnel may be unacceptable.) If such is possible, the plan has unnecessary slack in it. The only exception is an arbitrary management decision to eliminate recovery time from the schedule; this approach is rarely acceptable.

After the plan has been approved, it should be published with the approvals noted. The effect of the approval on the preparers of the plan and the individuals affected by the plan will be beneficial. In addition, the publication will usually have a positive effect on the persons who approved the plan, an effect that will tend to strengthen their commitments to it. It is difficult sometimes to know which effect is stronger or more important.

EXECUTION OF THE PLAN

Execution of the plan, of course, is what a project is all about. Control of the execution makes a project successful. Control is achieved by identifying and correcting things that are not proceeding according to the plan. Control actions include: monitoring progress of project activities, monitoring resource expenditures, monitoring overall project status, analysis of variances from plan, recovery of planning as required, and formal reporting of project status and recovery plans.

Control Responsibilities

In the final analysis, all control responsibilities rest with project management in the same way that the head coach and general manager bear overall responsibility for a football team's performance. On a day-to-day basis, responsibilities should be shared. The person (supervisor or worker) directly in charge of each activity or resource consumption objective in the plan should be responsible for monitoring progress, reporting status, and developing corrective action plans as required. If his (or her) part of the project gets into trouble, he has the first-line responsibility for getting it out of trouble.

Project management should be responsible for collecting status reports and corrective action plans. They should participate in the analysis of exceptions and recovery plans, and ensure that approved recovery plans are put into the formal control systems so that progress against the plans can be measured. They should prepare overall project reports and communicate project information to other management who need to be informed about the project.

The degree to which project management should participate in discussion of details is dependent upon the situation and the individuals involved. As far as I know, there is no valid guideline for such participation. There are good Project Managers who bore into many technical details, and there are equally good ones who rely totally on the process, the control system, and their administrative skills to attain their objectives.

Control Process

There are three steps in the control process, and these steps repeat throughout the life of a project.

1. Project status information—on activities and resource consumption—should be collected at points defined in the project plan. In addition, status information should be collected informally through a "grapevine" or "ear to the ground" process.

2. Recovery plans for exceptions to planned progress should be developed and approved by the responsible individuals.

3. The status reports and recovery plans should be published.

The repeating cycle of the three steps imposes order on the project. It creates a structure of the execution phase. A simple test of a project is whether a cycle of status determination, recovery planning and formal reporting has been established. If it has not, experience indicates that the project probably is not under control. If it has, the project may be under control, and you will have to look deeper, as described in the next section, to find out.

Guidelines for Status Reporting and Recovery Planning

Certain fundamental principles are applicable to the development of status reports and corrective action plans. Perhaps the most fundamental principle is that, for one reason or another, the project will not proceed as planned. Reasons normally include both faulty planning and faulty execution. This principle does not change the need for a plan, or course. Whether you are building a house or managing a project, you need a blueprint. The fact that the blueprint will prove to be inaccurate in some respects does not mean that you do not need it.

Given this fundamental principle and the objective of bringing the project in on schedule within budget, the remaining fundamentals are clear:

1. Identifying exceptions to plan as soon as possible after they occur is essential. Exception may involve resources or activities. They may involve either planned activities or resource usage, or totally new activities or resource requirements that were not foreseen during planning. The basic tool to identify exceptions should be the formal system, using status points in the plan. The status points, as you recall, were established at short enough intervals so that recovery would be possible if trouble were identified at the status points.

   The facts of life are that the formal system will sometimes be slow or inaccurate, for example because of pressure to report satisfactory progress. You should establish some informal contacts, a "grapevine" that will pick up project scuttlebutt and the like. Much of the information obtained in such a fashion will be useless, but occasionally a grain of truth will emerge. In addition to being an adjunct to the formal system for status reporting purposes, this is virtually the only way to identify potential problems when project progress to date has not been affected.

2. The response to identified problems must be quick and effective. Recovery plans must be prepared, analyzed, and approved rapidly. Problem review sessions should not be allowed to end without a plan to fix the problem or a specific assignment in that direction. Decision matters, especially those affecting the overall project schedule or budget, should be surfaced immediately to the level of management that can make the required decisions.

   Recovery planning usually includes making up activities that are behind schedule, adding new activities or resources, or reducing excessive resource consumption without changing activities' output. Sometimes activities must be redefined, however. A situation may develop in which accomplishing a planned activity will require far more resources than can be justified, and the proper action may be to eliminate the activity or reduce its scope. In such a case, the decision must be made quickly before more resources are wasted.

3. The response to problems should include procedures to reduce the chance of their recurrence or occurrence of other problems. Problems should be recorded on "Trouble Logs" and monitored until they are completely cleared up.

   Each recovery plan should be challenged with the question: what is being done differently that will cause the recovery plan to succeed where the original plan failed? The reason for each problem should be determined and positive action taken to prevent it from happening again. The impact of a problem on other items in the plan should be determined in order to avoid a domino effect. This may be easy or difficult, depending on the project and the tools being used. For example, a network system can be very useful in such an analysis.

4. Recovery planning should be thorough. Timeliness is usually more important in recovery planning than it was in the original Planning phase, but the process should be the same. Sometimes quick-and-dirty recovery planning may be required in order to get the project turned around, but it does not replace the need for thorough replanning when the necessary time becomes available.

One company that I know of got themselves into trouble by not following these fundamentals on a Material Requirements Planning (MRP) project. MRP is a computerized production and inventory control technique. It works by "exploding" production schedules into time-phased requirements for constituent components and material by using computerized bills of material and predetermined decision rules for stocking and inventory replenishment. The project manager had schedules for some project activities but not for some other activities that required the same people. In addition, his approach to recovery planning consisted only of eliciting commitments from his supervisors that they would catch up somehow. During the execution of the project, some activities were not accomplished as planned and some new activities arose. In my experience, this is normal on MRP projects. The first mistake in reacting to the exceptions was the inadequate recovery planning that relied on supervisors' commitments and their subsequent whipcracking over their subordinates. Rational analyses of the problems would have been more useful. When the pressure techniques failed, as they often do, it was recognized that certain activities' schedules would not be met. Because other schedules and personnel assignments had not been made, however, it was impossible to determine the effect of the slippages on the overall project schedule. Needless to say, there was a great deal of unpleasantness over the project manager's position that he was not going to meet his schedule but that he did not know how much he would be late.

Documentation

Documentation from the planning phase is the foundation for controlling the execution phase. Documentation from the execution phase provides continuous verification that the project is under control as it proceeds towards its conclusion. Documentation is the scoreboard that tells you if your team is winning.

The execution documentation should be based on the planning documentation, for ease of communication and to ensure that all essential information has been included. On many projects, the format that was appropriate for display of planned events, activities, and resource consumption will be equally appropriate for display of the actual occurrences. Sometimes, both planned and actual data can be displayed on the same document. This approach not only improves communication and understanding, but also assists in reducing the administrative burden of documentation. Automated systems may also help to reduce the amount of "administrivia" if many or all reports can be automatically generated from a simple set of input data.

Summary documentation during the execution phase should also parallel the planning documentation. It should be based on the general (macro level) plan produced during the planning phase. Execution documentation at a level different from either the general or the detailed plan is difficult to understand because there is nothing to which it can be related.

Documentation of exception conditions should clearly describe the planned condition, the actual condition, analysis of the problem and its impact, and the corrective action required or initiated. At its lowest level, dealing with specific exceptions such documentation can be directly useful in reacting to the conditions and solving the problems, as well as in communicating the situation to interested persons. When summarized and compared to a summary of the project plan, the documentation of exceptions should be the key indicator of project status to project management and other management. The information to

be summarized should be based on the elements of the plan. For example, if specific resource consumption objectives were planned, exceptions to the plan might be summarized in absolute value, compared to planned objectives in terms of percentage overrun or underrun, and extrapolated to end-of-project status.

Project management should at all times have an emotional or subjective impression of the status of the project. If this impression is not the same as the impression conveyed by the formal status reports, then something is amiss, and an investigation is warranted. Formal systems cannot entirely replace "gut feeling."

Recovery planning generally should be documented in the same way as the original planning phase. Recovery plans may be integrated into the overall project plan, using different notation to distinguish the recovery plans from the original plans. Recovery plans should not simply overlay the original plans, because of the potential loss of knowledge that recovery plans were necessary, which could lead to a false sense of security. It is seldom wise to bury the fact that replanning was required. It is also not appropriate to skip the approval process on recovery plans. They should be subjected to the same kinds of review as the original plan, possibly with increased attention to timeliness. The review may be less extensive if fewer resources are involved than in the original plan and no overall project delay is anticipated. If significant resources are involved or if a delay in the overall project schedule is anticipated, the review should be thorough, of course.

Conclusion

I have described what I believe are the fundamentals of project management, the rules that must be followed to get something done. The rules are summarized in Exhibit I, a Project Management Checklist.

Discussion of specific kinds of projects is beyond the scope of this article. For this reason, I have not dealt with issues such as how to select a scheduling or budgeting technique for a project, how to estimate work content of activities, how to determine the specific activities and resources to be controlled, or how to report progress on activities and resource consumption.

Discussion of personnel and environmental considerations is also beyond my scope here. When implementing the fundamentals, of course, the characteristics of the environment and the individuals who are involved must be considered. A technique that works on one project may be unnecessary or unsuccessful on another project that is identical except for the individuals or the environment. •jsm

PROJECT MANAGEMENT CHECKLIST

I. **Project Planning**

  A. Responsibilities

     1. Project workers, supervisors and support technicians were heavily involved in the planning.
     2. Project management directed preparation of the plan, provided their input to it, and accept responsibility for it.

  B. Process

     1. The General plan was approved prior to working on the Detailed plan.
     2. The Detailed plan was prepared, analyzed for reasonableness and feasibility, and modified as required. The General plan was modified to be consistent with the Detailed plan.
     3. The General and Detailed plans were formally approved and published.

  C. Specifics of the Plan

     1. Project activities and tangible output from each activity were defined.
     2. Work content of each activity was estimated.
     3. Each activity was scheduled and assigned to a resource; elapsed time of activities and multiple assignments to resources were minimized; responsibility for each item in the schedule is clear.
     4. Status points were included for measurement of activities' progress and resource consumption.
     5. Recovery time and resources were provided, either implicitly or explicitly.
     6. The plan was adjusted to obtain efficient and effective use of resources.
     7. The General plan covered all major items over the life of the project, and the Detailed plan covered all items in the near future.
     8. Status points in the Detailed plan were established such that recovery would not be difficult if problems were identified at the status points.

  D. Documentation

     1. Wherever possible, proven documentation procedures were used.
     2. All items (activities, resources) that were planned and are to be controlled during project execution were documented.

  E. Approvals

     1. Approvals of the plan were obtained from the persons who must support the plan or not oppose it in order for the project to be successful.

II. **Execution of the Plan**

  A. Responsibilities

     1. Project workers and supervisors have been monitoring progress, reporting status, and developing corrective action plans.
     2. Project management has carried out their responsibilities for analysis and approval of status reports and recovery plans, and for communication with upper management and other persons who are outside of day-to-day project activities.

  B. Process

     1. A structured process of status reporting, recovery planning, and publication of project progress reports was implemented.

  C. Implementation of Control Guidelines

     1. Formal and informal systems were implemented to identify exceptions to plan soon after they occurred or before they occurred.
     2. Response time to problems has been short; recovery plans have been prepared and approved quickly, and management has been available to make decisions.
     3. The response to problems has included analyses of why they occurred and positive actions to ensure that they or similar problems will not occur in the future.
     4. When problems have occurred, their impact on other items in the plan has been determined, and the other items have been replanned as required.
     5. Recovery planning has been thorough, based on the Planning fundamentals.

  D. Documentation

     1. The documentation procedures were designed to be consistent with the Planning documentation and to make use of it wherever possible.
     2. Detailed documentation of status, including exception conditions, has been developed and used in problem analysis and recovery planning. Summary documentation of project status and recovery plans has been prepared.
     3. Recovery planning documentation has preserved visibility of the original plan and the variance of the recovery plan from it.

  E. Approvals

     1. Approvals have been obtained for all changes to the original plan; the approval process was the same as for the original plan, with the depth of the review reflecting the significance of the changes.

EXHIBIT I

APPLYING CORPORATE SOFTWARE DEVELOPMENT POLICIES

E.A. Goldberg

December 6, 1977
January 27, 1978

SEID SOFTWARE DEVELOPMENT POLICIES OBJECTIVES

+ Provide Management Visibility
+ Reduce Software Development Risks
+ Identify and Work Problems Early
+ Provide Compatibility with New Trends in DoD Software
  Acquisition

SOFTWARE DEVELOPMENT POLICY APPLICABILITY

+ Applies to All New SEID Projects Developing Software
+ Applies to Both Deliverable and Non-Deliverable Software
+ Includes Formal Procedure for Requesting Deviations and
  Waivers
  - SEID General Manager Must Approve Deviations and
    Waivers for All Deliverable Software
  - Deviations Must Be Identified during Proposal Phase

WHAT'S NEW

+ Deviations and Waivers Must Be Formally Approved
  - Conformance to Good Standards and Practices Is No Longer
    the Exception but the Rule
+ Verification Required
  - Requirements Verification
  - Design Verification
+ Test-Related Activities
  - Test All Requirements
  - Perform Off-Nominal Testing
  - Determine Readiness for Acceptance Testing
+ New Planning Documentation
  - Software End-Product Acceptance Plan
  - Configuration Management Plan
  - Quality Assurance Plan

Reprinted with permission from *TRW, Defense and Space Systems Group*,
December 1977. Copyright © 1977 by TRW.

SEID SOFTWARE POLICY HIERARCHY

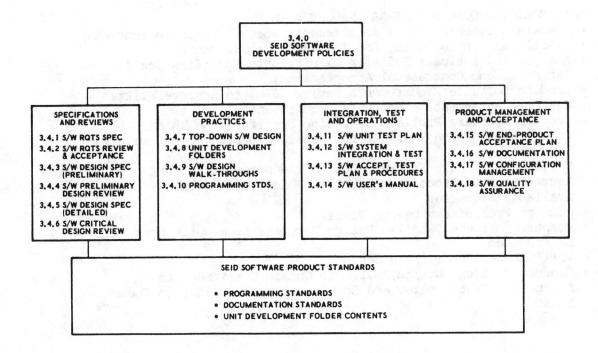

SEID POLICY OVER THE SOFTWARE LIFE CYCLE

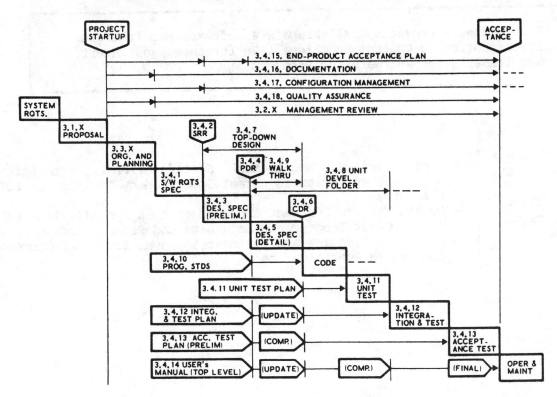

SPECIFICATIONS AND REVIEWS

SEID POLICY REQUIRES SOFTWARE PROJECTS TO
+ Prepare Written Software Requirements Specification to Control Functional, Performance, and Interface Requirements
+ Analyze and Evaluate Software Requirements Specification for Technical and Contractual Acceptability
+ Conduct Software Requirements Review (SRR) to Achieve Written Customer Agreement on Software Requirements
+ Prepare Software Preliminary Design Specification Which Establishes Design Baseline for Detailed Design of Software End Products
+ Verify Preliminary Software Design and Demonstrate That Aggregate Data Processing Resource Budgets Are within Total Available Resources
+ Conduct Preliminary Design Review
+ Prepare Software Detailed Design Document from Which Code Will Be Produced
+ Verify Detailed Software Design
+ Conduct Critical Design Review to Obtain Commitment to an Acceptance Test Program and Commitment to Proceed into Coding Phase

POLICY 3.4.1
SOFTWARE REQUIREMENTS SPECIFICATION

SIED Software Projects Shall Prepare a Software Requirements Specification to Control Functional, Performance, and Interface Requirements for Software End Products

---

This Policy Requires Project to

+ Produce Software Requirements Specification Prior to Software Requirements Review in Format Specified by Contract or SEID Standards
+ Obtain Written Customer Approval of this Specification as Basis for Computer Program and Data Base End Product Acceptance
+ Obtain Written TRW and Customer Approval for All Subsequent Changes to Specification

POLICY 3.4.2
SOFTWARE REQUIREMENTS REVIEW AND ACCEPTANCE

> SEID Software Projects Shall Conduct a Software Requirements
> Review (SRR) to Achieve Written Agreement with Customer on
> Provisions of Software Requirements Specification

This Policy
Requires
Project to

+ Prepare For SRR by:
  - Analyzing and Evaluating Software Requirements
    Specification for Technical and Contractual
    Acceptability
  - Developing Response to Each Problem Identified
    in Analysis or in Customer Review Comments
+ Conduct an SRR for TRW-Generated and Customer-Provided
  Requirements
  - Present Analysis Results; Describe Analysis
    Techniques
  - Address Issues and Problems
  - Document Agreements and Action Items and Obtain
    Project Manager and Customer Signature
  - Review Software End Product Acceptance Plan
+ Obtain Policy Waiver if Customer Will Not Approve
  Updated Software Requirements Specification

REQUIRED ANALYSIS TO PREPARE FOR SRR

+ Analyze Total Requirements Set for Completeness, Consistency,
  Testability, and Technical Feasibility from
  - Flow-Oriented Viewpoint
  - Functional Breakdown Viewpoint
+ Analyze Each Individual Requirement to Verify
  - Mandatory Requirements Are Clearly Distinguished from
    Design Goals and Options
  - Compatibility with System-Level Objectives
  - Technical Feasibility
  - Testability
  - Completeness
+ Analyze Total Requirements Set for Compatibility with
  Schedule, Funding, and Resources

POLICY 3.4.3
SOFTWARE DESIGN SPECIFICATION (PRELIMINARY)

> SEID Software Projects Shall Prepare a Preliminary
> Design Specification That Establishes the Design
> Baseline for Detailed Design of the Software
> End Products

This Policy Requires Project to

+ Produce Preliminary Design Specification
  Prior to Preliminary Design Review in Format
  Specified by Contract or SEID Standards
+ Demonstrate That Aggregate Data Processing
  Resource Budgets Are within Total Available
  Resources/Requirements
+ Establish Preliminary Design Specifications as
  Design Baseline after Preliminary Design Review

POLICY 3.4.4
SOFTWARE PRELIMINARY DESIGN REVIEW

> SEID Software Projects Shall Perform Design and Planning
> Activities Required to Establish a Preliminary Software
> Design Baseline and to Proceed into Detailed Design and
> Development

This Policy Requires Project to

+ Provide Reviewers with Specified Review Materials
+ Prepare for Preliminary Design Review (PDR) by:
  - Verifying the Preliminary Software Design
  - Reviewing Implementation Plans and Project/
    Performer Commitments
  - Identifying Technical and Contractual Issues,
    Including Non-Satisfied Requirements
+ Conduct PDR Which Addresses:
  - Design Overview, Identifying Software Structure, Design
    Rationale, Operation in System Environment, User Interface
  - Design Verification Results
  - Overview of Implementation and Test Plans
  - Technical and Contractual Issues
+ Document and Obtain Customer and TRW Written Approval on
  Disposition of Identified Technical and Contractual Issues,
  Agreements and Action Items

REVIEW MATERIALS REQUIRED PRIOR TO PDR

+ Preliminary Design Specification
+ Approved Software Requirements Specification (Including Interface Specifications)
+ Proposed Changes to Software Requirements Specification
+ Preliminary Users Manual
+ Preliminary Acceptance Test Plan
+ Preliminary Performance Estimates

REQUIRED PRELIMINARY DESIGN VERIFICATION ACTIVITIES

+ Verify:
  - Every Requirement Has Been Accounted for
  - Design Is Valid from Flow-Oriented and Functional Breakdown Points of View
  - Aggregate Design Budgets Satisfy Software Requirements Specification and Do Not Exceed Physical and Functional Limitations
+ Substantiate Software Design and Algorithm Selection through Engineering Analysis
+ Identify Design Approaches and Alternatives for High Risk Items

POLICY 3.4.5
SOFTWARE DESIGN SPECIFICATION (DETAILED)

> SEID Software Projects Shall Update and Expand the Preliminary Design Specification into a Detailed Design (Build-To) Specification from Which the Code Will Be Produced

This Policy Requires Project to

+ Produce Detailed Design Specification Prior to Critical Design Review in Format Specified by Contract or SEID Standards
+ Adhere to Basic Control Structures Allowed in Structured Programming
+ Update Detailed Design Specification after Integration Testing to Reflect As-Built Software

POLICY 3.4.6
SOFTWARE CRITICAL DESIGN REVIEW

SEID Software Projects Shall Conduct a Critical Design
Review to Gain Concurrence in the Adequacy of the Detailed
Software Design, and Obtain Commitment to Proceed into the
Coding Phase and Commitment to an Acceptance Test Program

This Policy
Requires
Project to

+ Provide Reviewers with Specified Review Materials
+ Prepare for Critical Design Review (CDR) by
  - Verifying Detailed Software Design
  - Reviewing Detailed Implementation and Test
    Plans and Project/Performer Commitments
  - Identifying Critical Issues, Including
    Unsatisfied Requirements
+ Conduct CDR Which Addresses
  - Design Overview Identifying Operation in System
    Environment; User Interface
  - Design Verification Results
  - Overview of Implementation and Test Plans
  - Technical and Contractual Issues
+ Document and Obtain Customer and TRW Written
  Approval on Disposition of All Identified Critical
  Issues, Agreements, and Action Items

REVIEW MATERIALS REQUIRED FOR CDR

+ Detailed Design Specification
+ Current Software Requirements Specification
  (Including Interface Specifications)
+ Proposed Changes to Software Requirements
  Specifications
+ Updated or Current Acceptance Test Plan
+ Design Evaluation or Trade Study Results
+ Updated Performance Estimates

EXAMPLES OR PROJECT MANAGER'S DISCRETIONARY AREAS

+ Documentation
  - Level of Detail and Size of Specifications
  - Number of Volumes and Relationship to Specific End Products
+ Degree of Formality
  - Preliminary Design Baseline
  - Detail Design Baseline
  - Associated Change Control Procedures
+ Use of Reqirements Specification or Design Specification
  Languages
+ Analysis Required for SRR, PDR, CDR
  - Could Be Full Scale System Simulation or Simple Hand Analysis
+ SRR, PDR, CDR
  - Presentation Format and Material Used
  - Duration

SEID POLICY OVER THE SOFTWARE LIFE CYCLE

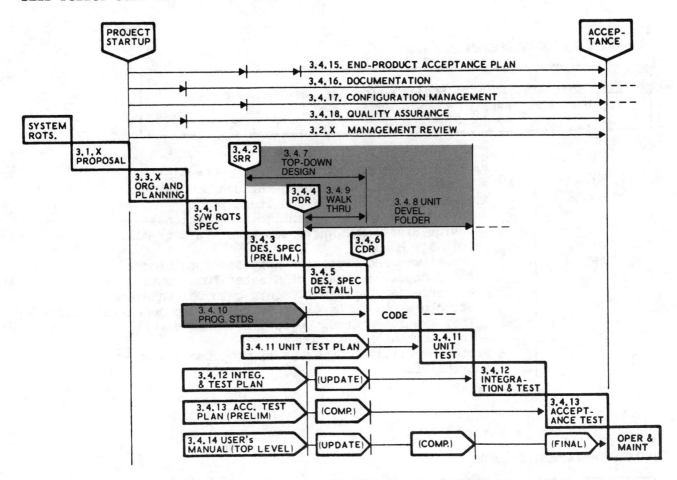

DEVELOPMENT PRACTICES

SEID Policy Requires Software Projects to

+ Perform Software Design Using a Top-Down Approach
+ Prepare and Maintain a Unit Development Folder (UDF) for Each
  Software Unit
+ Conduct Design Walk-Throughs at Unit Level as Design of Each
  Unit Completed
+ Use Programming Standards during Software Design, Code, and
  Maintenance Which Include:
  - Flowcharting Standards
  - Structured Programming Standards for All Higher Order
    Languages
  - Coding Standards
  - In-Line Commenting and Preface Text Standards

POLICY 3.4.7
TOP-DOWN SOFTWARE DESIGN

> SEID Software Projects Shall Design Software Using a
> Top-Down Approach

This Policy
Requires
Project to

+ Perform Design by Starting with Top-Level
  System Function, Proceeding through Downward
  Allocation, Evaluation, and Iteration
  - Initiate Design by Establishing Functional
    Design Hierarchy, Where Top-Level Is Over-All
    Software Mission
  - Break Down and Partition Software into Blocks
    for Successive Levels of Greater Functional Detail
  - Allocate and Map Requirements onto Design Hierarchy
  - Structure Lowest Level of Software Components So
    That Program Control Logic Can Implement All
    Input-Output Paths
+ Prototype Critical Lower-Level Components When
  Appropriate

POLICY 3.4.8
UNIT DEVELOPMENT FOLDERS

> SEID Software Projects Shall Prepare and Maintain a
> Unit Development Folder (UDF) for Each Software Unit

This Policy
Requires
Project to

+ Establish UDF's within One Month after PDR, Using
  Format Specified by Project or SEID Standards
+ Periodically Review UDF's to Assess Technical
  Adequacy and Schedule Compliance
+ Periodically Audit UDF's in Accordance with
  Quality Assurance Plan to Assess Compliance
  with Project Standards
+ Maintain UDF's until As-Built Software
  Documentation Is Baselined

UNIT DEVELOPMENT FOLDER COVER SHEET

PROGRAM NAME _____

UNIT NAME _____ CUSTODIAN _____

ROUTINES INCLUDED _____

SECTION NO.	DESCRIPTION	DUE DATE	DATE COMPLETED	ORIGINATOR	REVIEWER/ DATE
1	REQUIREMENTS				
2	DESIGN PRELIM: DESCRIPTION "CODE TO " "AS BUILT":				
3	FUNCTIONAL CAPABILITIES LIST				
4	UNIT CODE				
5	UNIT TEST PLAN				
6	TEST CASE RESULTS				
7	PROBLEM REPORTS				
8	NOTES				
9	REVIEWER'S COMMENTS				

POLICY 3.4.9
SOFTWARE DESIGN WALK-THROUGHS

> SIED Software Projects Shall Conduct Unit Design
> Walk-Throughs

This Policy
Requires
Project to

+ Conduct Design Walk-Throughs at Unit Level as
  Design of Each Unit Is Completed
  - One or More Individuals Other Than Originator
    Must Review (Designer/Programmer/Tester Desirable)
  - Originator Presents Design in Presence of Reviewers
  - Scope Includes Checks for
    * Design Responsiveness to Requirements
    * Design Completeness and Consistency
    * Flow of Data
    * Testability
    * Error Recovery Procedures
    * Modularity
+ Identify in Writing Problems Uncovered in Walk-Throughs

POLICY 3.4.10
PROGRAMMING STANDARDS

SEID Software Projects Shall Use Programming Standards
during Software Design, Code, and Maintenance

This Policy
Requires
Project to

+ Produce Project-Specific Programming Standards
  Document Prior to PDR Unless Programming Standards
  in "SEID Software Product Standards" Are Used
+ Conduct Periodic Audits of Design Documentation
  and Code in Accordance with Quality Assurance Plan
  to Assess Compliance with Programming Standards
+ Maintain Programming Standards Current during
  Software Design, Code, and Maintenance

SEID SOFTWARE PRODUCT STANDARDS

+ Complements Software Development Policies by Providing
  - Outlines of Documents Required by Policies
  - Minimum Contents for Unit Development Folders
  - Specific Programming Standards
    * Flow Charts
    * Structured Programming
    * Preface Commentary
    * Coding
+ Deviations
  - If Standards and Policy Affected, Policy Deviation Only
  - If Only Standards Affected, Standards Deviation Only
    * Approved by Project Manager and Project Review Authority

EXAMPLES OF PROJECT MANAGER'S DISCRETIONARY AREAS

+ Design Walk Throughs
  - Selection of Reviewers
  - Duration of Review
+ Problem/Corrective Action Disposition from Audits and
  Walk Throughs
+ Top-Down Coding and Other Good Practices
+ Level of Detail in UDF'S
  - Requirements
  - Detailed Design
  - Unit Test Plans
  - Unit Test Results
+ Use of Software Design Languages

SEID POLICY OVER THE SOFTWARE LIFE CYCLE

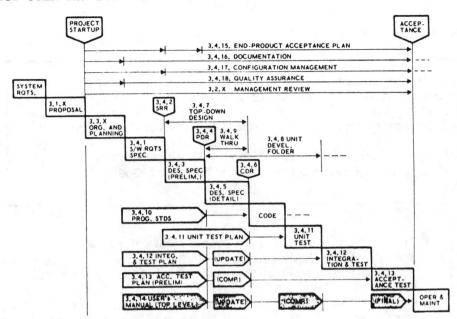

INTEGRATION, TEST, AND OPERATIONS

SEID Policy Requires Project to
+ Prepare an Overall Unit Test Plan Defining Testing Standards
  for Unit-Level Testing
+ Prepare Integration and Test Plans and Conduct Integration and
  Test Activities to
  - Integrate Software into Nominally Executing Production
  - Demonstrate Satisfaction of All Software Requirements
  - Demonstrate Software Operability over a Range of Conditions
+ Establish Software Test Baseline
+ Review Test Results and Readiness for Acceptance Tests
+ Prepare Acceptance Test Plans (and or Operator-Oriented
  Software) and Achieve Written Agreement for Customer Acceptance
+ Conduct Acceptance Test Program with Independent Test
  Organization
+ Produce a User's Manual Containing Instructions for Operating
  the Software

POLICY 3.4.11
SOFTWARE UNIT TEST PLAN

> SEID Software Projects Shall Prepare an Overall Unit
> Test Plan That Defines the Testing Standards for
> Unit-Level Testing

This Policy
Requires
Project to

+ Produce Unit Test Plan in Format Specified by
  Contract or SEID Standards
+ Review and Approve Unit Test Plan Prior to CDR
+ Does Not Contain Unit-Specific Test Cases—These
  Appear Only in UDF

POLICY 3.4.12
SOFTWARE SYSTEM INTEGRATION AND TEST

> SEID Software Projects Shall Plan for and Conduct Software
> Integration and Test Activities to Be Accomplished Prior to
> Acceptance Testing Which
> + Integrated Software Units into a Cohesive, Nominally Executing
>   Product
> + Demonstrate Satisfaction of All Software Requirements
> + Demonstrate Software Operability over a Range of Operating
>   Conditions

This Policy
Requires
Project to

+ Produce Integration and Test Plans in Format
  Specified by Contract or SEID Standards
+ Produce Plans within Two Months of PDR, Update Prior to
  CDR, and Update as Appropriate Prior to Test Initiation
+ Prepare Test Activity Network Showing Integration and Test
  Strategy in Terms of Test Event and Schedule Interdependencies
+ Design Tests to Exercise Software Throughout Anticipated Range
  of Operating Conditions
+ Employ Discrepancy Reporting System after Software Test
  Baseline Is Established
+ Review Test Planning and Preparation Activities Prior to Test
  Initiation
+ Review Test Results and Readiness for Acceptance Testing after
  Test Completion

POLICY 3.4.13
SOFTWARE ACCEPTANCE TEST PLAN AND PROCEDURES

> SEID Software Projects Shall Prepare an Acceptance Test Plan and
> Acceptance Test Procedures

This Policy
Requires
Project to

+ Produce Preliminary Acceptance Test Plan for PDR and Complete
  Acceptance Test Plan for CDR
+ Achieve Written Agreement with Customer That Execution of
  Defined Test Case in Manners Satisfying Acceptance Criteria,
  Will Result in Customer Acceptance
+ Obtain Written Approval by TRW and Customer for All Changes to
  Approved Plan
+ Produce Acceptance Test Procedures for Interactive or
  Operator-Oriented Software
+ Ensure Acceptance Test Program Is Directed by an Independent
  Project Test Organization Not Reporting to Development
  Organization

POLICY 3.4.14
SOFTWARE USER'S MANUAL

> SEID Software Projects Shall Produce a Software User's Manual
> Containing Instructions for Operating the Deliverable Software
> System

This Policy
Requires
Project to

+ Produce Software User's Manual in Format Specified in
  Contract or SEID Standards
  - Provide Top-Level Operational Description and
    Specification of Man/Machine Interfaces in PDR Version
  - Update User's Manual for CDR
  - Produce Complete Preliminary User's Manual Prior to Software
    Integration, for Use and Validation during Testing
  - Deliver Final User's Manual When Software Delivered to
    Customer

EXAMPLES OF PROJECT MANAGER'S DISCRETIONARY AREAS

+ Test Plans
  - Level Of Detail
  - Size
  - Number of Physical Volumes
+ Degree of Formality
  - Change Control
  - Discrepancy Reporting System
  - When to Establish Test Baseline
+ Specific Organization for Acceptance
  - Several Options Acceptable
+ Use of Test Data Folders and Other Good Test Practices

SEID POLICY OVER THE SOFTWARE LIFE CYCLE

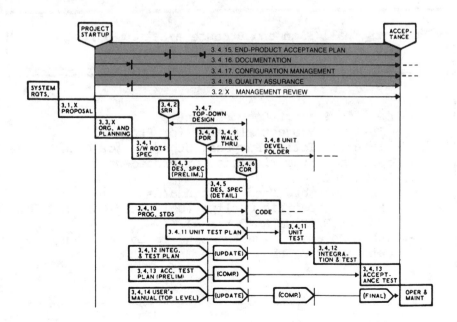

PRODUCT MANAGEMENT AND ACCEPTANCE

SEID Policy Requires Software Projects to

+ Produce a Software End-Product Acceptance Plan Covering All
  End-Products and Services Called for by Contract
+ Produce, at a Minimum, Mandatory Set of Documents Complying
  with Provisions of Contract and SEID Policy/Standards
+ Prepare a Configuration Management Plan and Perform
  Configuration Management Functions Required to Establish a
  Series of Baseline and Control Changes to Establish Baselines
+ Operate a Software Product Development Library
+ Prepare a Quality Assurance Plan and Perform Quality Assurance
  Functions Appropriate to Contract and Product

POLICY 3.4.15
SOFTWARE END-PRODUCT ACCEPTANCE PLAN

SEID Software Projects Shall Follow an Orderly Procedure,
Governed by a Written Plan, to Prepare for and Achieve Customer
Acceptance of All End-Products and Services Called for by Contact

---

This Policy
Requires
Project to

+ Produce a Software End-Product Acceptance Plan
  − Review Draft at SRR
  − Obtain Project and Customer Approval before End of PDR
+ Maintain a File of Acceptance-Related Data
+ Track Progress toward Acceptance (Per Plan)
+ Conduct an Acceptance Audit Near End of Contract Period

POLICY 3.4.16
SOFTWARE DOCUMENTATION

SEID Software Projects Shall Plan and Produce a Set of Software
Documents That Comply with the Contract and SEID Policies

This Policy
Requires
Project to

+ Identify Project Document Set
  − Early in Project Planning (or Proposal)
  − Identify Title, Purpose, Schedule for Each Document
+ Use Format from (in Order of Procedence)
  − Contract
  − SEID Software Product Standards
  − Project Specific Outline (Only When Contract/Standards
    Do Not Provide an Outline)
+ Choose Document Size and Binding to Suit Project/
  Customer/User Needs

MANDATORY DOCUMENTS

+ Software Requirements Specification	3.4.1	2.1
+ Software Design Specification	3.4.3 and	2.5
+ Software End-Product Acceptance Plan	3.4.15	2.2
+ Software Unit Test Plan	3.4.11	2.6
+ Software Integration and Test Plan	3.4.12	2.7
+ Software Acceptance Test Plan	3.4.13	2.8
+ Software User's Manual	3.4.14	2.9
+ Software Configuration Management Plan	3.4.17	2.4
+ Software Quality Assurance Plan	3.4.18	2.3

POLICY 3.4.17
SOFTWARE CONFIGURATION MANAGEMENT

SEID Software Projects Shall Perform Configuration
Management Functions Required to Establish a Series of
Baselines and Control Changes to Them

This Policy Requires Project to

+ Prepare a CM Plan, and Get It Approved, Prior to SRR, by
  – Project Manager
  – SEID PA Manager
+ Follow Approved CM Procedures for Issuance, Pretention,
  Change Control, Packaging, Delivery
+ Operate a Software Product Development Library

MINIMUM BASELINES

BASELINES	ESTABLISHED
REQUIREMENTS	AT SRR CLOSE-OUT
DESIGN	AT PDR CLOSE-OUT
TEST	DURING INTEGRATION AND TEST
PRODUCT	AT SOFTWARE ACCEPTANCE

POLICY 3.4.18
SOFTWARE QUALITY ASSURANCE

SEID Software Projects Shall Plan and Perform Quality
Assurance Functions Appropriate to Contract and Product

This Policy
Requires
Project to

+ Prepare a QA Plan
+ Get Plan Approved (within One Month of Project
  Startup) by
  - Project Manager
  - SEID PA Manager
+ Identify Person/Organization That Will Perform
  Project QA Functions
+ Provide for Periodic QA Audits
  - Relationship to Contract
  _ Relationship to Policies and Standards

EXAMPLES OF PROJECT MANAGER'S DISCRETIONARY AREAS

+ Document Size (Level of Detail) and Binding
  - Two-Page IOC May Suffice
  - Many Binding Options: Seperate Volumes Versus Sections
                              of a Comprehensive Project Plan
+ CM Task Definition, Activity Level, and Detailed Procedures
  Subject to
  - Minimum Tasks Specified in Contract/Policies
  - Plan Approval by SEID PA Manager
+ QA Task Definition, Activity Level, and Detailed Procedures,
  Subject to
  - Minimum Tasks Specified in Contract/Policies
  - Plan Approval by SEID PA Manager
+ Degree of Formality of CM and QA Controls

CUSTOMER BENEFITS

> We Can Now Guarantee Our Customers That They Will Get the
> Same Brand of Good Management Provided on Showcase Projects
>
> C.W. Besserer—March 1977

+ Customer Always Knows What He Is Getting
  - Requirements Are Documented and Baselined
  - End-Product Acceptance Plan Establishes What
    Will Be Delivered and When
  - Traceability Is Established from Requirements
    to Design to Test
  - Early Users' Manual Explain Man/Machine Interfaces
+ Customer Can Now Expect Certain Minimum Standards of Testing
  - Requirements and Design Are Verified Prior to Associated
    Review Point
  - All Requirements Are Tested
  - Software Is Exercised over Range of Off-Nominal Operating
    Conditions
  - Early Acceptance Test Plan Establishes Acceptance Criteria
  - An Independent Project Test Organization Directs Acceptance
    Test
+ Customer Achieves Assurance of Software Quality through
  Schedule Reviews
  - Customer Involvement in Reviews Encouraged
  - Formal Review Points at SRR, PDR, And CDR Establish
    Requirements and Design Baselines
  - Design Walk-Through Held to Catch Design Errors
  - Readiness Review for Acceptance Tests
  - Quality Assurance Audits Ensure Policies and Standards Being
    Followed (Review Requirements, Design, Documentation, Code,
    Testing, and Configuration Management)
+ Customer Receives Set of Documentation Appropriate to Customer/
  User/Project Needs
  - If Customer Format Not Specified Format of SEID Product
    Standard Used
  - UDF's Minimize Documentation Costs by Providing a Timely
    Accessible Collection of All Data Pertaining to a Unit
+ Customer Experiences Shorter Project Start-up Transients
  - Uniform Set of Policies and Standards Results in Ease of
    Personnel Transferability among Projects and in Minimal
    Personnel Retaining for New Projects
  - Universal Set of Programming Standards Avoids Need for
    Recreating Standards on Each New Project
  - Structured Programming and Top Down Design Results in More
    Uniform Software Development and Easier Software
    Maintainability

A software technology evaluation program

by **DAVID N CARD**

D.N. Card "A Software Technology Evaluation Program" Information and Software Technology, Volume 29, Number 6, July/August 1987. Copyright © 1987 by Butterworth Scientific and Co. (Publishers) Ltd.

Abstract: A wealth of potentially beneficial software engineering tools, practices, and techniques has emerged in the past few years. However, many of these innovations have never been empirically validated. The Software Engineering Laboratory (SEL), a cooperative project of the National Aeronautics and Space Administration, Computer Sciences Corporation, and the University of Maryland, conducts an extensive technology evaluation program. The SEL studies the production of FORTRAN software for spacecraft navigation systems. This paper summarizes the results of SEL investigations in the areas of design practices, coding techniques, test/ verification methods, and computer utilization. An earlier version of this paper appears in The Annals of XVIII Brazilian National Informatics Congress, *September 1985.*

Keywords: software engineering, software validation, programming languages.

Software provides an increasingly larger part of the functionality, and consequently the cost, of computer systems. For some large applications, the cost of the software component exceeds 75% of the total system cost. The ability to deliver reliable software on time at minimum cost has become essential to success in the computer industry. Software development organizations, therefore, have strong incentives to improve the software development process, principally by adopting new technology. In the context of this paper, the term 'technology' refers to tools, practices, and techniques applied by software developers.

Although many potentially beneficial software engineering tools, practices, and techniques have emerged in the past several years, many have never been empirically evaluated[1]. The difficulty of accurately measuring the software development process, in general, and technology use, in particular, accounts for much of the lack of

Computer Sciences Corporation, 8728 Colesville Rd, Silver Spring, MD 20910, USA

objective information in this area. Furthermore, the effectiveness of any technology may vary from one environment and application to another. This paper describes an ongoing technology evaluation program[2] conducted by the Software Engineering Laboratory (SEL) that is intended to resolve these issues, at least in part. The program attempts to implement a process engineering function in software development like that described by Agresti[3] and Card et al[4].

Software engineering laboratory

The SEL is a research project[2] sponsored by NASA and supported by Computer Sciences Corporation (CSC) and the University of Maryland (UM). The SEL studies software developed to support spacecraft flight dynamics applications at Goddard Space Flight Center. Figure 1 shows the organization of the SEL, which was established in 1977. Although most funding for SEL projects comes from NASA, both CSC and UM contribute resources to projects of special interest. The ongoing ADA project (see

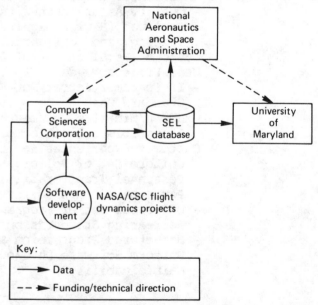

Figure 1. Software Engineering Laboratory (SEL)

 0950-5849/87/060291-10$03.00 © 1987 Butterworth & Co (Publishers) Ltd.

section on technology evaluation results) provides an example of this close cooperation.

The overall objective of the SEL is to understand the software development process in the flight dynamics environment and to identify the ways in which it can be altered to improve the quality and reduce the cost of the product. The SEL has monitored the development of more than 50 flight dynamics projects involving hundreds of programmers and analysts. In addition, the SEL conducts controlled experiments and other studies. The sources cited in the references provide detailed information about the results summarized here.

Flight dynamics software

The general class of spacecraft flight dynamics software studied by the SEL includes applications to support attitude determination/control, orbit adjustment, manoeuvre planning, and mission analysis for satellites in Earth orbit. The attitude ground support systems form a large and homogeneous group of software that has been studied extensively. Each system includes telemetry processor, data adjuster, and attitude computation subsystems as well as other necessary supporting functions.

Flight dynamics applications are developed in FORTRAN on IBM mainframe computers. System sizes range from 30 to 150 thousand source lines of code (85% FORTRAN). Reliability and response time requirements are moderate. That is, software failures do not immediately endanger the spacecraft; ground-based software does not exercise real-time control over the spacecraft. The fixed spacecraft launch data imposes a severe development time constraint. Acceptance testing must be completed two months before launch so that launch preparations can proceed on schedule. Table 1 summarizes some important characteristics of flight dynamics software development.

Table 1. Flight dynamics software

Project characteristics	average	high	low
Duration (months)	16	21	13
Effort (staff-years)	8	24	2
Size (1000 LOC)			
developed	57	142	22
delivered	62	159	33
Staff (full-time equivalent)			
average	5	11	2
peak	10	24	4
individuals	14	29	7
Application experience (years)			
managers	6	7	5
technical staff	4	5	3
Overall experience (years)			
managers	10	14	8
technical staff	9	11	7

Technology improvement approach

The SEL program of technology evaluation includes three steps:

- measurement
- evaluation
- transfer

Measurement establishes the baseline against which the effects of technologies can be compared. Next, technological innovations are attempted and their effects evaluated. After careful study, successful technologies are transferred to developers via guidelines, standards, and training.

Measurement

All engineering disciplines derive from principles of measurement and relationships among measures. Software engineering must develop such a measurement basis to become a true engineering discipline. Software engineering experts such as Boehm[5] (for cost estimation) and DeMarco[6] (for project control) are paying increased attention to the role of measurement in software development. Accurate measurement enables the establishment of performance baselines for comparing and estimating future projects. Also, innovations can be evaluated against the baseline.

The SEL developed a comprehensive data collection methodology[7] as the basis for its measurement activity. Measures collected include staffing, computer utilization, error reports, and product size/complexity measures, as well as the level of technology applied to each project. The SEL employs both questionnaires and automated methods of data collection. The collected data are assembled in a computerized database accessible to all SEL participants.

Because the software development process is complex and involves many different human and physical elements, many measures are needed to characterize it adequately. Examination of a model of software development, such as that shown in Figure 2, helps to define a comprehensive but nonoverlapping set of measures. This model includes the following components:

- Problem – statement of the information needs for which a software solution is desired.
- Personnel – software development team, managers, and supporting personnel.
- Process – practices, tools, and techniques employed by the personnel to develop the product; it proceeds in a series of steps (the software life cycle).
- Environment – physical and informational resources and constraints within which the personnel and process operate.

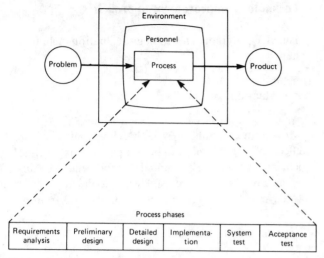

Figure 2. Software development model

- Product – software and documentation that solve the problem.

Measures are needed to characterize the principal attributes of these components before the relationships among the components can be determined. A complete set of measures constitutes a profile. Software development profiles form the baselines against which potential technology improvements are evaluated.

Evaluation

The process of identifying the costs and benefits associated with a technology is termed evaluation. Evaluation relies on the data collected by the measurement activity. Evaluators may follow one or more of three general approaches[8].

First, *case study*. This is an indepth comparison of two projects (one with new technology) or comparison of the new technology project to an established baseline.

Second, *multiproject variation*. This is a general measurement and analysis of varying levels of technology used in a large number of projects.

Third, a *controlled experiment*. This involves selection and control of subjects, tasks, methods, and environments in accordance with a predefined statistical design.

Even after assembling a substantial software engineering database, other obstacles to accurate technology evaluation remain, such as technologies which tend to be applied together; sample sizes tend to be small, and many nontechnology factors also affect the outcome of a software development project. Programmer performance (Figure 3) proved to be the most important factor with respect to both productivity and reliability. As noted by Boehm[5], these complications prohibit a simplistic statistical analysis and interpretation of the software development measures collected. Nevertheless, some trends in the data from SEL studies are clear.

Transfer

When the effectiveness of a technology has been demonstrated, the next step is to transfer it to software developers. The principal mechanisms used by the SEL to accomplish technology transfer include disseminating

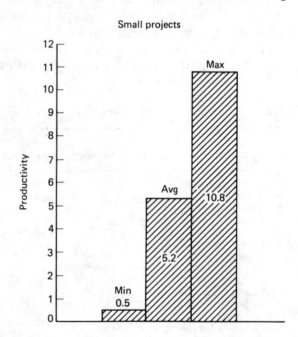

Notes: Large projects are greater than 20 000 source lines of code. Productivity is source lines per staff hour.

Figure 3. Programmer productivity variations

guidelines, developing tools, and conducting specialized training. The guidelines produced by the SEL cover management procedures[9], testing/verification[10], and programming practices[11]. Two important SEL-developed tools are the source code analyzer program[12], which has been distributed across the United States, and the configuration analysis tool[13], which is tailored to specific flight dynamics needs. The source code analyzer program counts operators, operands, decisions, statements, etc., in FORTRAN. Recent modifications by Harris Corporation and the Rome Air Development Center adapted it to analyze ADA code. Currently, SEL researchers are designing a training program for the ADA language[14] and appropriate design techniques.

Technology evaluation results

The SEL has extensively studied four software technology areas:

- design heuristics,
- programming practices,
- testing/verification,
- computer support/automation.

Although a great many other researchers have made significant contributions in these areas, this paper discusses only SEL results because of space limitations. Initial SEL studies focused on the implementation phase because most errors in the software occurred in that phase, even though it requires only one-third of the total effort (Figure 4). It thus appeared to be a leverage point[15] for process improvement. However, subsequent investigation showed that requirements errors were the most costly to correct, whereas design errors were much more

prevalent than first indicated. Ultimately, SEL efforts encompassed the entire life cycle.

Design heuristics

Modules are the basic units of design in the structured approach[16]. Design heuristics are rules and practices that specify how to design a good module. Those studied by the SEL include control coupling, data coupling, module size, and strength/cohesion. Figure 5 summarizes the results obtained with respect to fault rate. For example, 50% of high-strength modules were fault free while only 18% of low-strength modules were fault free. Specific conclusions are as follows:

- Module size was not a useful design criterion[17].
- High strength/cohesion promoted quality[17].
- Parameter coupling was not better than *common*[18].
- Smaller spans of control were generally better[18].

All design practices are not equally effective for all applications, environments, languages, etc. Furthermore, changes in computer hardware and software technology may affect the value of a practice[18]. For example, most negative conclusions about the value of *common* coupling were reached before *include* processors were widely available. Clearly, objective measurement is essential in making informed, current decisions about design strategies.

Programming practices

One group of individual technologies, referred to as modern programming practices, tends to be applied together. These technologies provide a flexible methodology

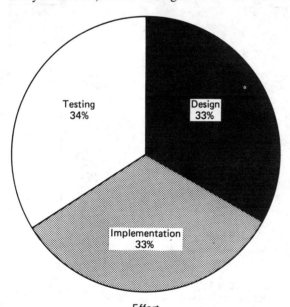

Effort

Figure 4. Origins of cost and errors

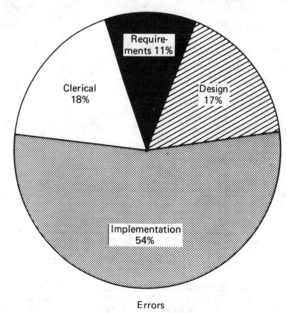

Errors

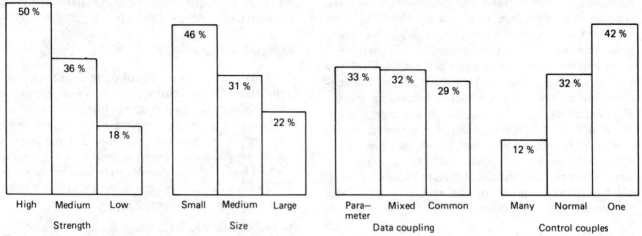

Figure 5. Design practices

for the (detailed) design, implementation, and verification of software. As practiced in the flight dynamics environment, the principal components are as follows:

- informal program design language,
- top-down development,
- structured programming,
- code reading,
- structured FORTRAN preprocessor or compiler.

These measures of individual technology use (1 = low use; 5 = high use) were combined to form a single index of overall structured programming use. Figure 6 shows the relationship of this index to error rate. The use of modern programming practices appears to be associated with a reduced error rate, with the principal contributor being the reading of structured code[19]. No significant correlation with development productivity was found. This implies that the reliability and maintainability benefits of modern programming practices are obtained at no additional cost in terms of development effort.

An experiment currently under way will compare the ADA and FORTRAN programming languages by implementing the same system twice, once in each language[20]. Figure 7 shows some early results from the ADA training

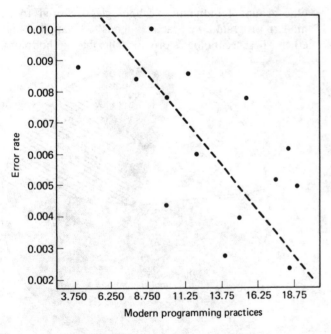

Notes: Error rate is errors per developed source line of code.
Modern programming practices is index combining six measures.
Correlation (r) = −0.64 (P < 0.05).

Figure 6. Effect of modern programming practices

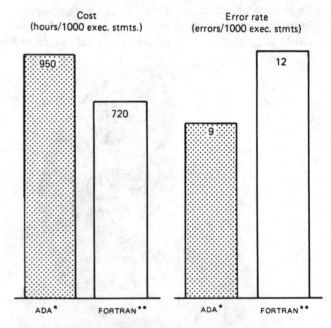

* Includes 5370 SLOC , 1402 exst.
does not include 570 training hours
** Based on flight dynamics projects

Figure 7. Software development in ADA

project conducted as part of this experiment. The cost and error rates for the ADA development lie within the 95% confidence interval for past FORTRAN projects.

Testing/verification

SEL investigations have encompassed both techniques and organizations for testing and verification. A recent study[21] compared the effectiveness of three verification techniques (Figure 8):

- code reading
- functional testing
- structural testing

In this controlled experiment, using professional programmers, code readers significantly outperformed both functional and structural testers in terms of the percent of errors detected and effort per error detected.

Quality assurance includes all review and management procedures undertaken to ensure the delivery of an effective and reliable product. The specific technologies studied by the SEL are as follows:

- requirements reviews
- design reviews
- design walkthroughs
- code walkthroughs
- test formalism
- test followthrough
- methodology reinforcement
- document quality assurance
- development standards
- code configuration control
- code library (PANVALET)
- configuration analysis tool

For the analysis described here, the individual measures of technology use were combined to form a single index of overall quality assurance activity (percentage of technologies used). Figure 9 shows the relationship of this index to error rate. Quality assurance activity appears to be associated with a reduced error rate[19]. No significant correlation with development productivity was found. This implies that the reliability benefits of quality assurance are obtained at no additional cost in terms of development effort. Moreover, a cost savings should be realized during maintenance.

Independent verification and validation (IV and V) is an approach to software quality assurance in which each product of the development team is assessed by an independent team. The major functions of an IV and V team are to ensure that the product of each phase of the software life cycle is consistent with the product of the previous phase (i.e. verification). Also an IV and V team ensures that the product of each phase accurately responds to the original system requirements (i.e., validation). Some of the claimed benefits of IV and V are as follows:

- Earlier detection of errors,
- More complete detection of errors,
- Improved visibility to management.

The SEL compared performance measures from two projects to which IV and V was applied with two similar non-IV and V projects[22]. Figure 10 shows that IV and V appeared to increase development cost without reducing the error rate. However, a subjective assessment indicated that visibility to management did increase.

Computer support and automation

Another major factor in software development is the computing environment. Special changes to this environ-

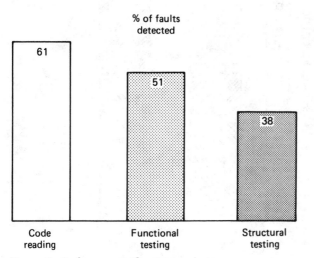

Figure 8. Software verification techniques

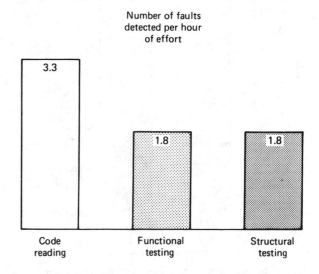

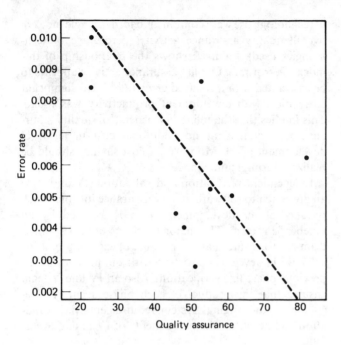

Notes: Error rate is errors per developed source line of code.
Quality assurance is index combining 12 measures.
Correlation (r) = −0.60 (P < 0.05).

Figure 9. Effect of quality assurance

ment usually cannot be made to conform to the needs of any single project. Nevertheless, it can have a strong effect on the development process[19]. Initially, the flight dynamics computing environment only provided the programmer with facilities for editing, compiling, linking, and testing source code. Figure 11 shows that most of this resource is expended during implementation and test.

A recent SEL study showed that extensive computer use is associated with low productivity[19]. Heavy computer users may not spend enough time desk checking and planning their work before jumping into code and test. However, another recent study[23] indicated that computer support, through software tools, for design and planning activities, not previously provided, can increase the overall productivity and reliability of the software development process. Figure 12 shows the reaction of users to two workstation demonstration systems[24]; the response was overwhelmingly favourable. Current SEL research efforts focus on expert systems for management and programming support environments. However, these projects are still in their early stages.

Conclusion

SEL experience demonstrates that the software development process in a specific environment can be improved

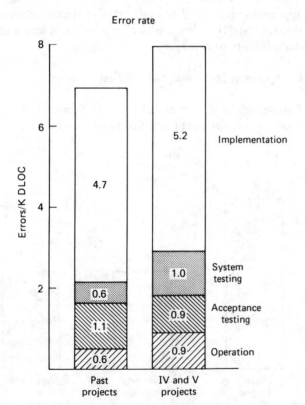

Figure 10. Independent verification and validation

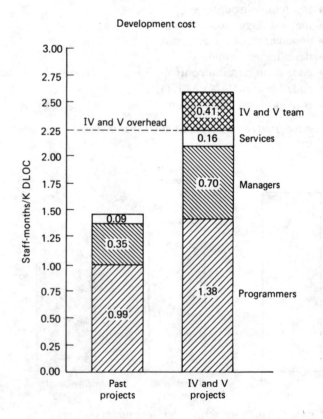

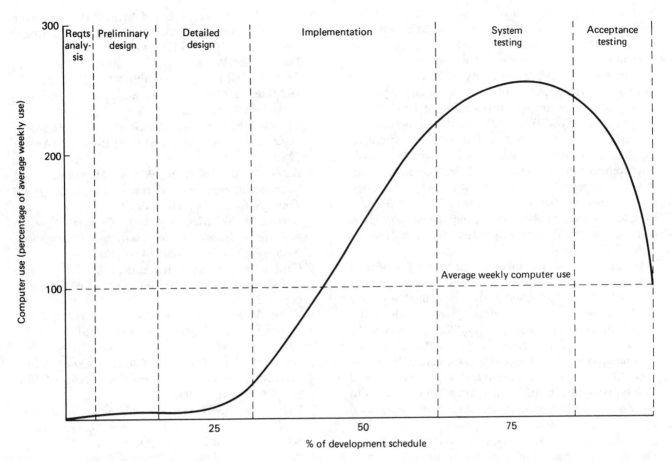

Figure 11. Computer utilization profile

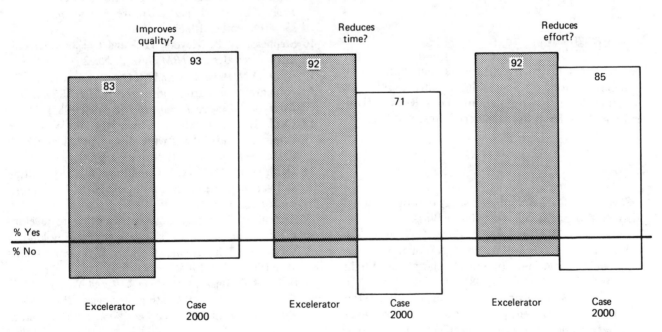

Figure 12. Design workstations

by a systematic program of measurement, technology evaluation, and transfer. Other similar organizations can also apply the lessons learned by the SEL. First, the use of appropriate design, programming, and verification practices increases software reliability without noticeably increasing development cost. Second, a formal program of quality assurance also improves software reliability at little or no net cost. While many modern programming concepts are firmly established in software engineering practice, formal quality assurance procedures are only now coming into widespread use. Third, intensive computer use appears to be associated with low productivity. Programmers who spend a lot of time at the terminal tend to be less productive. Additional computer support alone does not necessarily increase productivity. It must be the right kind of support.

In summary, these results suggest that a formal and conscientious method of software development yields a more reliable product. On the other hand, methods alone do not appear to improve development productivity; automation is needed too. It is very difficult to reduce the cost of *developing* a software product, although a more reliable product should require less subsequent maintenance. Methods and tools are synergistic; computer and tool support must be integrated into a formal process to be effective. SEL experience indicates that progress toward productivity and quality improvement is evolutionary rather than revolutionary. It proceeds in small steps. Despite technological advances, the major factor in both productivity and reliability continues to be personnel capability and performance (see Figure 4)[25].

Acknowledgment

The author would like to recognize the contributions of F E McGarry (Goddard Space Flight Center), G T Page (Computer Sciences Corporation), and V R Basili (University of Maryland) to the material presented here.

References

1 Sheil, B A 'The psychological study of programming' *ACM Computing Surveys* (March 1981)
2 Card, D N, McGarry, F E, Page, G T *et al The Software Engineering Laboratory*, National Aeronautics and Space Administration/Goddard Space Flight Center (NASA/GSFC) SEL-81-104 (February 1982)
3 Agresti, W W 'Applying industrial engineering to the software development process' *Proc. IEEE Computer Society Twenty-Third Int. Conf.* (September 1981)
4 Card, D N, Clark, T L and Berg, R A 'Improving software quality and productivity' *Info. and Software Technol.* Vol 29 No 5 (1987) pp 235–241
5 Boehm, B W *Software Engineering Economics* Prentice-Hall Englewood Cliffs NJ, USA (1981)
6 DeMarco, T *Controlling Software Projects* Yourdon Press New York, USA (1982)
7 Church, V E, Card, D N, McGarry, F E *et al Guide to Data Collection* NASA/GSFC SEL-81-101 (August 1982)
8 Basili, V R, Selby, R W and Hutchens, D H 'Experimentation in software engineering' *IEEE Trans. Software Eng.* (July 1986)
9 Agresti, W W, McGarry, F E, Card, D N, *et al Manager's Handbook for Software Development*, NASA/GSFC SEL-81-205 (April 1984)
10 Card, D N, Edwards, E and Antle, C *Software Testing and Verification* NASA/GSFC SEL-85-005 (December 1985)
11 Wood, R *Programmer's Handbook for Flight Dynamics Software Development* NASA/GSFC, SEL-86-001 (March 1986)
12 Decker, W J and Taylor, W A *FORTRAN Static Source Code Analyzer Program User's Guide*, NASA/GSFC SEL-78-202 (April 1985)
13 Decker, W J and Taylor, W A *Configuration Analysis Tool System Description and User's Guide* NASA/GSFC SEL-80-104 (December 1982)
14 Basili, V R 'Analysis of software development in ADA' *Proc. Ninth Annual Software Engineering Workshop* NASA/GSFC SEL-84-004 (November 1984)
15 McGarry, F E 'Software engineering leverage factors' *Proc. Eleventh Annual Software Engineering Workshop* (December 1986)
16 Stephens, W P, Meyers, G J and Constantine, L L 'Structured design' *IBM Syst. J.* No 2 (1974)
17 Card, D N, Page, G T and McGarry, F E 'Criteria for software modularization' *Proc. IEEE Eighth Int. Conf. on Software Engineering* (August 1985)
18 Card, D N, Church, V E and Agresti, W W 'An empirical study of software design practices' *IEEE Trans. Software Eng.* (February 1986)
19 Card, D N, McGarry, F E and Page, G T 'Evaluating software engineering technologies' *IEEE Trans. Software Eng.* (July 1987)
20 Agresti, W W 'Measuring ADA as a software development technology in the software engineering laboratory' *Proc. Tenth Annual Software Engineering Workshop* (December 1985)
21 Selby, R W, Basili, V R, Page, G T and McGarry, F E 'Evaluating software testing strategies' *Proc. Ninth Annual Software Engineering Workshop* (November 1984)

22 **Page, G T, McGarry, F E and Card, D N** 'A practical experience with independent verification and validation' *Proc. Eighth Int. Computer Software and Applications Conf.* (November 1984)

23 **McGarry, F E, Valett, J D and Hall, D L** 'Measuring the impact of computer resource quality on the software development process and product' *Proc. Hawaiian Int. Conf. on System Sciences* (January 1985)

24 **Koerner, K, Mital, R, Card, D N and Maione A** 'An Evaluation of Programmer/Analyst Workstations' *Proc. Ninth Annual Software Engineering Workshop* NASA/GSFC SEL-84-004 (November 1984)

25 **McGarry, F E** 'Measuring Software Technology' *Proc. Seventh Annual Software Engineering Workshop* NASA/GSFC SEL-82-007 (December 1982) □

A Game Plan for Technology Transfer

Edward Yourdon

Yourdon Inc., a subsidiary of DeVy Inc.
1501 Broadway
New York, NY 10036

Introduction

A software development project is usually a part of an overall *systems* development project, whose purpose is to deliver new or improved functionality to a community of end users. The new system, with its highly visible "high-tech" technology, is often a source of concern to some of the end users, who ask: How will this new technology affect me? Will it help me do my job better, or will it actually be a hindrance? Do I have any choice in using this new technology, or is it being forced on me from above?

Ironically, participants in the software development project often ask the same questions of themselves as they build the system—for they often find that they themselves are required to use new and unfamiliar technology to build their system. Examples abound:

- New hardware, new terminals, etc.
- New programming languages—e.g., Ada, 4th generation languages, and Prolog.
- New database management systems, telecommunications systems, etc.
- New productivity tools: application generators, CASE (Computer Assisted Software Engineering) workstations, etc.
- New project management methodologies.
- New application areas—e.g., factory automation, which incorporates the new MAP technologies.
- New software paradigms—e.g., heuristic programming techniques, inference engines and other examples from the AI and expert systems fields.

Indeed, the only software development projects that commonly avoid these problems are maintenance projects and "software factory" projects where the same work is done repetitively.

Sometimes the new technology is a minor and insignificant part of the software development project. But when the new technology is a major component of the project—and especially when it is perceived as a *critical* component—a number of problems can occur. For instance: Because the technology is new, the available in-house development staff usually needs training. This can present logistical and budgetary problems, as well as complicating the project schedule. As a result, some organizations avoid doing *any* training in the new technology; others will spend only enough money to train the project leader, who is then expected to pass the newly learned (and usually imperfectly learned) material, by word of mouth or by photocopying of course materials, to the rest of his project team. Only rarely does the organization invest the time and money to ensure that *all* of the project team members are properly trained to use the new technology.

Depending on the circumstances, there may be "political resistance" to the use of the new technology. Any of the following groups might object: the members of the project team; the project manager, or peers of the project manager; higher levels of management; members of the quality assurance department, members of the internal auditing department, members of the training department or DP standards department, etc.; and/or external auditors.

The reasons for such political resistance are myriad, and the reader can almost certainly supply his own list. Among the more common examples of resistance are the "not invented here" syndrome, the statement that "This is not the right time to try a new technology," and "We've always done things our own way, and it's always worked."

Furthermore, the new technology may be perceived as "the straw that breaks the camel's back. Some software projects have enough other problems (unrealistic schedules, uncooperative users, inexperienced management or staff, etc.) that the addition of a new, unfamiliar technology is "the last straw." The irony is that the new technology is often brought in in an attempt to solve those other project problems—e.g., "There's no way we can develop all of this software in time using COBOL, so we'll bring in a new fourth-generation language."

Worse, if the software development project is perceived as a failure, the new technology associated with the project may be blamed for the failure. Whether the blame is justified or not, it sometimes leads to a political decision (often accompanied by a great deal of emotion) to "throw the baby out with the bath water": to throw out the new technology and outlaw its use on subsequent projects.

And then, of course, there is the danger that the new technology doesn't work! For example, the project team might decide to use a fourth generation programming language, only to discover later that it runs 10 times or 100 times less efficiently than the conventional third generation languages; or the project team might use a new programmer workstation that doesn't work at all; or it might pick a database management system that has serious interface problems with the vendor's telecommunications system. Or it might fall victim to "vaporware": new technology that looks promising, but does not actually exist when the project team needs it.

But in my experience, project failures associated with new technology have more often been the result of "technology transfer" issues of the kind described above than failures in the technology itself. Technology is not perfect, to be sure; and the promises made by vendors of technology often exceed, by an order of magnitude, what can actually be delivered. But these failings of technology are overshadowed, time and again, by the failure of the project team and the project manager to properly assess and use the technology.

General Advice on New Technology

Sometimes the problem is not the new technology, but inappropriate use of the new technology. The most common example of this is a desire on the part of the project team (or, sometimes, the project leader) to turn a *development* project into a *research* project in an attempt to experiment with and explore new technology. If the project team is far removed from the end-user (geographically, politically, spiritually, etc.) and if it does not understand the "bottom-line" business objectives that led to the request for a new system in the first place, then it will be very easy for them to fall into this trap. And since the end user is not in a position to know whether new software development technology is necessary (he has enough trouble dealing with the technological impact of the new system), it is often up to the project manager to ensure that the project team does not fritter away its time and energy (and risk the success of the project) playing with technology for the sake of technology.

Another common problem is that of *multiple* new technologies being introduced *simultaneously* into a project—e.g., a new programming language *plus* a new database management system *plus* a new project management methodology. In addition to exacerbating the problems that would have been experienced with any one new technology, there is another problem: incompatibility between the various new technologies. Sometimes the incompatibility is entirely technical in nature—e.g., the new programming language is incompatible with the new new database management system,

or the new programmer workstation is incompatible with the data dictionary that the rest of the organization uses—but more often, the incompatibility is one of terms, definitions and semantics. For example, the terms and definitions associated with a new project management methodology (Spectrum, Method/1, etc.) may be incompatible with the new software engineering approach (e.g., the Jackson technique, the Warnier-Orr technique, or the Yourdon technique).

Finally, there is the problem of *imposed* technology—i.e., the case where neither the project team nor the project manager has any desire to use a new technology, but is forced to do so by higher levels of management; outside or external standards; the organization's standards department; and/or the end user (who may have inherited the new technology from somewhere else).

Externally imposed technology (or anything else *new* that is externally imposed) is a real problem for the project manager: if it succeeds, he will get no credit; if it fails, he will get all of the blame. The most important thing for the project manager, in my experience, is to be sure that he and the rest of his project team present a common, unified front to the rest of the organization. They can actively oppose the new technology; they can grudgingly accept it; they can announce an enthusiastic, "devil-may-care" attitude of adopting the new technology. But whatever they do, the project team (the individual programmers, analysts, and other team members) should be singing the same tune as the project manager. This requires a great deal of trust and communication between the project manager and the project team members; lacking that communication, such externally imposed new technology can act as a wedge that will drive the team apart from the manager.

A Game Plan for Technology Transfer

From the comments above, one might conclude that it would be better not to use new technology in a software development project. But this is not realistic or practical, of course: there are a number of reasons—both good and bad— for implementing new technology. The trick is to incorporate new technology into the software development project without disrupting or threatening the success of the project. Having watched several software devleopment projects go through this experience, I have found the following techniques to be of great help:

Make sure all interested parties know why the new technology is being used. It is important for the project manager to explain to his subordinates, his peers, and his higher-level managers why the new technology is being used; if appropriate, the project manager should also be prepared to explain the risks and the benefits of the new technology. Support from higher levels of management is also important: programmers and systems analysts will be reluctant to use a new technology if they sense that managers two or three levels above them are fundamentally disinterested in it or opposed to it.

Provide appropriate training before the project team uses the new technology. Though this suggestion should be an obvious one, I am constantly surprised by how often it is ignored. The project team is often given (a) no training, or (b) training six months before they have a chance to use the technology, or (c) training six months after they have begun using the new technology, or (d) superficial and inadequate training.

Try to use the new technology on a prototype or pilot project before using it on a "real" project. A pilot project in some other part of the software development organization can provide invaluable experience about the new technology; it can also provide one or more internal "consultants" who can offer assistance to the project team. If this is not possible (and it is usually beyond the control of the project manager to arrange such pilot projects), then the project manager should consider using the new technology to build a subset, or a prototype, of the overall system that his project team is working on. For example, a three- to six-month "mini-project" could be formed to build a small piece of the overall system with the new technology—in order to gain "hands-on" experience that will prove invaluable for the overall project that might continue on for another two to three years. One of the advantages of this approach is that it allows the organization to develop its own *customized* "user's manual" to show all of the project members how to use the new technology. Sometimes this user's manual can take the form of a standard textbook, or set of training materials; more often, though it will an edited amalgam of several different textbooks, illustrated with examples that are pertinent to the organization.

Get outside technical assistance throughout the project. External consulting assistance may appear expensive, but it usually represents a very minor part of the overall project budget—and it is an incredibly cheap form of "insurance" when using new, complex technology that could threaten the success of the project. The consulting assistance can be provided by the vendor of the new technology, if appropriate, or can be obtained from other outside organizations. In some cases, the consulting can be provided from other groups within the organization; however, my experience has been that such consulting is generally not successful if it is provided by the organization's training department or standards department. In any case, the technical support or consulting assistance should be budgeted explicitly, so that it will not be considered a "luxury" to be discarded at the first available moment.

Give the project team a forum for voicing their concerns and problems. In almost every case, the project team will run into problems as they begin to use the technology. Even if the problems are not catastrophic, the project team will feel a certain amount of frustration and resentment—and if they are made to feel that their concerns are not legitimate, there is a significant danger that they will, to whatever extent possible, avoid using the new technology. (If the new technology is a new mainframe computer, they may not be able to avoid it at all, aside from the extreme action of quitting; but if the new technology is something "soft" like a new project management methodology or a new software engineering discipline, it may be very easy to stop using it.) Periodic "gripe" sessions—perhaps including the vendor of the new technology, and with the consultants mentioned above—are a good way for the project team to let off steam, as well as a good way for the project manager to get an early warning of potentially serious problems.

Use common sense, on a case-by-case basis, to determine exceptions to the use of the new technology. A new technology may have been adopted on the assumption that it will be universally appropriate for the project—but as the real work of the project gets underway, it may become evident that the new technology isn't appropriate in certain areas. For example, the project team may have decided to use a new fourth generation language for their software development work; it may be discovered midway through the project that a more conventional third-generation language—even (ugh!) assembler—is necessary for certain parts of the system where throughput and efficiency are important. Such decisions need to be made on a case-by-case basis, and they should be made by the project manager (who, in turn, may have to consult with outside auditors, higher levels of management, etc.) rather than by the software developers themselves.

Avoid paralysis. In the extreme case, the project team can become thoroughly overwhelmed by the new technology and gradually end up spending all of its time (a) trying to understand the new technology, (b) arguing about the merits of the new technology, or (c) trying to make it work. For example, a project team using structured analysis for the first time will sometimes experience "analysis paralysis," and the project manager will find that the entire team is spending all of its time arguing about whether they are correctly following the procedures of structured analysis that they have read in a textbook. The project manager must watch for this paralysis and force the team to move on—either by making hard, unilateral decisions on his own, or by making use of the consulting assistance described earlier to answer questions about the new technology.

Summary

In any technological field—especially the field of computer software—it is easy to become overly enamored with technology issues. Those who develop software systems are quite accustomed to the cultural resistance that is shown by the end users for whom the system is built; software developers often complain that end users don't "appreciate" the elegance or sophistication of the system.

The irony is that this same group of software developers has its own cultural resistance to new technology. Over and over again, we have seen that the technology itself advances more quickly than the ability (or willingness) of the end user population (which in this case means software developers) to adapt to it.

It has been observed that it took the military community seventy-five years to change from the technology of muskets to the technology of rifles. A software development manager who is not sensitive to technology transfer problems runs the risk of experiencing the same kind of delay!

Fundamentals of Master Scheduling for the Project Manager

Kent A. Cori
Donohue & Associates, Inc.

Reprinted with permission from *Project Management Journal*, June 1985
pages 78-89. Copyright © 1985 by Project Management Institute.

The role of the project manager is to effectivel. schedule, allocate, use, and replace resources to achieve specified project goals. One of his or her primary project tasks is to schedule and budget the activities and resources (people, materials, and equipment) so that resources are available when needed, activities are completed in the correct order, and the project objective is reached in a cost effective and efficient manner. The project Master Schedule is one of the most formidable tools available to the project manager in performing his or her duties.

We will address the importance of planning to the project manager and survey the techniques that can be employed for scheduling a typical project. The role of the project manager, preparation of the project Master Schedule and project budget, scheduling and budgeting considerations and computer applications will be discussed. In addition, five popular scheduling techniques will be described and compared.

Functions Of The Project Manager

A project consists of a set of well defined, related tasks culminating in a major output and requiring an extensive period of time to complete. Projects may be unique, such as custom designing manufacturing machinery, or require outputs that are so large or time consuming that they have to be produced one at a time, such as construction of a highway interchange. Project management is the process of facilitating the performance of others to attain the project objective.

Project management can be categorized into four separate functional areas. These are planning, organizing, directing, and controlling.

These areas and the activities which comprise each are shown in Figure 1. Note that project management revolves on the hub of decision making which in turn revolves around information.

Preparing The Project Master Schedule

The major output of the planning process is the project Master Schedule. This is a graphic presentation of all project related activities necessary to produce required output. The project Master Schedule and the thought process behind it are the keys to a successful project. They allow the project manager to effectively coordinate and facilitate the efforts of the entire project team for the life of the project. This schedule is dynamic in that it will undoubtedly be modified as the project proceeds and unanticipated changes in scope, logic, or timing are required.

Without the Master Schedule, effective project control would be virtually impossible. Directing the project team would be extremely difficult if individual tasks have not been identified and the interrelationships among them defined. Control of the overall project is based on periodically monitoring progress and comparing the results to the Master Schedule. If the Master Schedule does not exist, it is impossible to accurately estimate project status. One of the project manager's primary administrative responsibilities is to complete the project within budget. Projects which are not completed within the time frame established by the Master Schedule almost invariably exceed planned costs.

Many project managers are reluctant to prepare a project plan. The most common complaint is that planning takes too much time and costs too much money. What these project managers do not realize is that because planning is a means of preventive action in that it requires anticipation of potential future difficulties, the long-term payoff is far greater than the short-term cost. Another objection is that it is too tedious. Planning is an iterative process requiring mental activity rather than action. This barrier is a result of the fact that most project managers perceive themselves as "doers," not "thinkers." Finally, ego affects the project

Figure 1
Project Management Cycle

manager's attitude toward planning. Many feel that they can handle any eventuality and prefer to "shoot from the hip." Unfortunately, this adversely affects their overall performances which in turn reduces the effectiveness of their project teams.

For a schedule to be effective, it must possess several major characteristics. It must be:

- Understandable by those who must use it;
- Sufficiently detailed to provide a basis for measurement and control of project progress;
- Capable of highlighting critical tasks;
- Flexible, easily modified and updated;
- Based upon reliable time estimates;
- Conform to available resources; and
- Compatible with plans for other projects that share these same resources.

The project manager must be aware from the outset of the scheduling process that many factors must be considered in preparation of the project Master Schedule. Some of the major factors that may affect the project schedule are the project objectives, demands of other projects, resource requirements and constraints, and individual capabilities of team members. The range of competing factors is usually so extensive

that the whole process of planning must be regarded somewhat as an intuitive art. The job of the project manager is to replace intuition with scientific reasoning to as great a degree as possible. This is done by employing a number of different techniques in a logical sequence that is designed to eliminate one variable at a time.

Seven separate steps are necessary for the development of any project Master Schedule. These steps must always be undertaken in the proper sequence, although the amount of attention devoted to each and the methods used to complete each step are dependent upon the size, complexity, and duration of the project. The seven steps are:

1. Defining the project objectives.
2. Breaking down the work to be accomplished.
3. Sequencing the project activities.
4. Estimating the activity durations and costs.
5. Reconciling the project Master Schedule with project time constraints.
6. Reconciling the project Master Schedule with resource constraints.
7. Reviewing the schedule.

Defining Project Objectives

The primary responsibility of the project manager is to ensure that the end product meets the client's requirements; therefore, the first scheduling task of the project manager is to clarify project objectives by translating them into quantifiable terms. A project objective is a statement specifying the results to be achieved. These statements form the foundation for the entire planning process, including development of the Master Schedule.

The project objectives will be reviewed frequently throughout the project. They will be referred to at the onset of the project to identify the project team's responsibilities. During the project, they will be reviewed to identify changes that fall outside the original project scope. At the project's conclusion, they will be reviewed to help the project manager perform an objective postmortum review of the project.

A well defined project objective has several characteristics. The objective will be:

1. Attainable — The objective identifies a target which can be reasonably achieved given the project's time and resource constraints. If the objective is set too high, credibility is destroyed because the sense of shortfall is greater than the sense of accomplishment.

2. Definitive — It spells out in concrete terms what is to be achieved and to what degree. The results to be attained are clearly defined. Only those objectives related to project or organizational goals are included. Routine project activities must not be mistaken for objectives.
3. Quantifiable — It specifies a yardstick for completion which can be identified by all concerned, especially those responsible for its achievement. The establishment of measurable objectives is mandatory so that performance can be compared to a standard.
4. Specific Duration — It defines the time parameters within which the task is to be achieved. This is also necessary for evaluation of project progress.

Breaking Down The Work To Be Accomplished

Once well thought out project objectives are developed, the project manager can move on to producing a work breakdown structure (WBS) of activities to be performed. The WBS is nothing more or less than a checklist of the work that must be accomplished to meet the project objectives. A WBS is prepared through a very structured approach; general work is broken down into smaller, more specialized work. Major project work packages are first identified. The tasks necessary to produce these work packages can then be defined. These tasks can be further segmented into subtasks. Finally, the activities necessary for completion of these subtasks are listed.

The WBS lists the major project outputs and those departments or individuals primarily responsible for their completion. The WBS is a tool used by the project manager to become intimately familiar with the scope of the project.

This enhances his or her ability to monitor *all* the work in progress. This systematic approach also helps prevent the omission of critical tasks or activities. In any large project something will be forgotten; however, by using this approach the number of omissions will be greatly reduced. The WBS is also useful in developing budgets for each discipline or department.

Sequencing The Work Activities

It is obvious that production of the Master Schedule involves identifying the interrelationships among activities. This, in turn, influences the sequence in which they are to be accomplished.

For very simple projects, the use of milestones or a Gantt chart is often sufficient. These charts provide a clear display of the time scale involved, but do not illustrate the interrelationships among the various activities. A Gantt chart is also very useful for estimating the relationship between work load and time. A relatively recent development in this area is full wall scheduling. Under this method, members of the project team all have input into the project Master Schedule.

Unfortunately, the use of milestones, a Gantt chart, or full wall scheduling as the only means for scheduling medium to large scale projects is usually not adequate. The interdependence among activities is a critical factor in the management of even a moderately complex project. In this instance, a precedence network analysis approach can be an extremely effective management tool. This approach utilizes a graphic technique to clearly illustrate activity interrelationships and sequence. The two best known techniques are CPM (Critical Path Method) and PERT (Program Evaluation and Review Technique). Precedence network scheduling techniques display a project in graphic form and relate its component activities in such a way as to focus attention on those which are crucial to the project's completion. Precedence networks can be drawn to a time scale to facilitate resource allocation and budgeting.

A more detailed discussion and comparison of the various scheduling techniques is presented later in this article.

Estimating Activity Durations And Costs

Once the individual activities have been defined and the sequence in which they are to occur has been identified, it is necessary to make an estimate of the amount of time that must elapse between the start and completion of each activity. These estimates are not based directly on the work content in man-hours, but solely upon the calendar time required to complete the activity. Such estimates are typically based on the experience of the scheduler with similar projects. Normal delays must be included.

The estimation of activity duration is related to the costs for that activity. It is usually more expensive to "crash" or complete an activity in an unusually short period of time. This directly affects project cost.

Neither overall project timing constraints nor resource limitations are directly considered at this stage. These will be considered in subsequent steps.

Reconciling The Master Schedule With Available Project Timing Constraints

This step has three main objectives:

1. To determine the anticipated duration of the entire project.
2. To identify those activities which play a critical part in contributing to the overall project duration. These are the activities that, together, form the critical path of a precedence network diagram.
3. To quantify the amount of float possessed by all noncritical activities.

The first of these objectives can be achieved by any of the major scheduling techniques. However, to achieve the remaining two objectives requires the use of some form of a precedence network analysis technique.

If this time analysis predicts a project duration longer than originally desired, it is necessary to review and perhaps revise the network. It may be possible to reduce some activity duration estimates, although this must never be done without a good reason. A more fruitful approach usually lies in examining the structure of the network itself, in rearranging it so that some activities can be started earlier in relation to others.

For all but the very simplest projects, the use of a computer is necessary to carry out the time analysis of the network and the subsequent resource allocation.

Reconciling The Master Schedule With Available Resources

Once the overall project time constraints are met, allocation of resources can be considered. If a firm happens to be short of work with a large reserve of resources waiting to be employed, then it would be theoretically possible to complete a project without worry about resource allocations at all. Each task or activity could simply be started as soon as possible, dependent only upon the sequencing restrictions defined in the network diagram. Resources scheduled on this unlimited basis form a load pattern called a resource aggregation.

These resource aggregation patterns are characteristically very uneven. They display sharp peaks and troughs in the day-to-day demand for each type of resource (equipment, materials, labor). This state of affairs is undesirable partly because the peaks are likely to exceed the quantity of resources available and also because an uneven usage of resources is typically uneconomical. Steps must be taken to smooth out the work load. This is the process of resource allocation or resource leveling. It is achieved by adjusting the scheduled starting dates for some noncritical activities which would otherwise occur during peak loading periods. The project manager endeavors to produce a smooth pattern of resource demand without delaying the completion of the project. This is done by revising the schedule within the network logic and project timing constraints already identified, and the amount of float possessed by each noncritical activity. If any activity has to be delayed beyond this calculated float, the project duration will be extended with consequences.

Projected costs must also be reconciled with the budget. It may be necessary to increase the duration of selected activities or eliminate them entirely to reduce costs in order to meet the budget.

Reviewing The Schedule

Once the schedule is complete, the project manager should audit it to determine whether it is realistic. Reasonable criteria should have been applied in the generation of activity budgets and durations. The completed network plan makes clear the effects of the factors influencing the scheduling and budgeting process. The effects of technical and management reviews, vacations, conflicts or resource constraints should be apparent, for example.

The project manager must remember that planning is an evolutionary process. The results of this audit may necessitate additional revisions to the schedule. The project manager should also review the assumptions that went into the development of the schedule. Times to complete activities are often based on the questionable assumption that a particular resource, such as a particular piece of equipment, will be available at a given point in time. Sometimes activity durations are based on greater-than-regular work week performance by some employees. This is always a dangerous assumption. Although this may be required as the project progresses, it is seldom reasonable to base a schedule on this assumption at the beginning of a project. In addition, the project manager should ensure that the necessary flexibility is available in the schedule to accommodate unanticipated project delays, such as inclement weather.

Survey Of Five Scheduling Techniques

As previously discussed, five of the major scheduling approaches are the milestone, Gantt, full wall scheduling, CPM, and PERT techniques. A detailed presentation of the mechanics for each of these scheduling techniques is beyond the scope of this article. Several authors (e.g., [2] [3] [4] [5] [7] [9]) have published detailed descriptions of the formats, conventions and procedures to be followed in preparing the various types of schedules. However, it is imperative that the project manager understand the purpose, advantages and disadvantages of each of these scheduling techniques; therefore, a general discussion and comparison of each follows.

The Milestone Chart

The milestone chart is the simplest scheduling method. This method is best applied to small projects being performed by only a few people because it does not exhibit the interrelationships among the activities. This approach has also been used to summarize complex schedules containing many tasks.

The advantages of the milestone chart are the ease and minimal cost of preparation. The disadvantage is that a milestone chart shows only completion dates. This may result in uncertainty over activity start dates and interrelationships for all but very simple projects. Comparing the actual completion dates with the target completion dates provides only a general indication of overall schedule status. This approach does not provide sufficient feedback to the project manager for control of even moderately complex projects.

The Gantt Chart

The Gantt or bar chart is frequently used for smaller projects (less than 25 activities) and overcomes some of the disadvantages of milestone charts. This type of schedule is perhaps the most widely used scheduling technique. Many people find it easier to understand a Gantt chart than a precedence network.

Although it is not possible to show the interdependence among activities on the Gantt chart, it is easier to show possible overlapping of activities than with either a CPM or PERT network. In many cases, CPM and PERT networks are translated directly onto a Gantt calendar chart. The Gantt chart can then be used to estimate resource and budget requirements versus time. This is done by identifying the amount of resources or budget needed per unit of time for each activity and calculating the total for all activities occurring during a specified time period.

Full Wall Scheduling

A technique known as "full wall scheduling" has been used successfully by several firms in recent years.

A large wall on which vertical lines are drawn five inches apart and horizontal lines spaced three inches apart is required. The spaces between each pair of vertical lines represent one work week. The horizontal lines serve to separate the members of the project team. This method generally works best for projects with more than 25 but fewer than 100 tasks, and with a project team of three to ten people.

The project manager first develops a preliminary milestone schedule and list of project tasks, identifying who is responsible for each task. Each task is written on two index cards. The first card is labeled "start" and the second card is labeled "finish." Each team member is then given the appropriate cards.

The entire project team is assembled in the room where the scheduling wall is located. Each person begins by tacking each card onto the wall under a week they select. As the scheduling proceeds, tasks may be divided into subtasks or better defined as required. Additional tasks not anticipated by the project manager are also added at this stage. The arrangement of the cards will be continually modified until all participants are satisfied that the necessary constraints and activity interrelationships have been addressed and the project schedule is attainable. The project manager then makes a record drawing of the full wall schedule and distributes it to the project team members.

The major advantage of the full wall scheduling procedure is the high degree of interaction that takes place during the scheduling meeting. Conflicts can be identified early, discussed and resolved. It also forces the project team members to make a firm commitment to the project manager on their assigned activities very early in the project.

A disadvantage of the full wall scheduling technique is that it requires all parties to meet for the scheduling activity. Firms with multiple offices may face logistics problems. Also, getting a large project team together for a relatively long period of time can be difficult. However, if the project manager thoroughly develops the task outline and milestone schedule prior to the meeting, and efficiently directs the proceedings during the scheduling meeting, the time required for the actual activity can be minimized.

A second major disadvantage of this method is that it does not clearly show the interrelationships of tasks or the critical path as do the precedence methods of scheduling, although these interrelationships must be identified in order to develop the schedule. Because changes that occur during the project often require revision of the original project Master Schedule, the project manager must rely on his or her memory to reconstruct the interrelationships. This is seldom feasible for medium to large size projects.

Precedence Networks

The most popular forms of the precedence network are the Critical Path Method (CPM), the Program Evaluation and Review Technique (PERT), and their variants. Scheduling by means of a precedence network is a dynamic process in which subdivisions, modifications, additions or deletions of activities may be made at any point in time. Initial development of the network requires that the project be thoroughly defined and thought out. The network diagram clearly and precisely communicates the plan of action to the project team and the client.

A project is most amenable to these techniques if:
- It has well defined activities.
- Activities may be started, stopped, and conducted separately within a given sequence.
- Activities interrelate with other activities.
- Activities are ordered in that they must follow each other in a given sequence.
- An activity, once started, must continue without interruption until completion.

The network is a graphic model portraying the sequential relationships between key events in a project and showing the plan of action. CPM and PERT identify the critical path, which is the longest sequence of connected activities through the network. This critical path serves as the basis for planning and controlling a project.

To expedite or "fast-track" a project, it is necessary only to speed up those activities on the critical path. Without knowledge of the critical path activities, the project manager would have to fast-track all activities, resulting in wasted resources. This approach also allows the project manager to identify those activities which are not critical. If unavoidable delays in the overall project occur, the project manager can delay these activities if desired to reduce unwarranted resource demand.

Because changes in the project scope and timing requirements typically occur as the project proceeds, the critical path identified at the outset of the project may not ultimately determine the overall project duration. Often, some activity that was not originally on the critical path is delayed to such an extent that the entire project is prolonged, creating a new critical path. The project manager must continually monitor those activities which have a high delay potential and have very little float as well as those on the critical path. The more complicated the project, the more "near-critical" activities and paths will exist. The project manager must assess the impacts of significant project changes on these activities as well as those on the critical path to be assured that a new critical path has not been formed.

The differences between CPM and PERT are not fundamental, but merely one of viewpoint. The first basic difference is that CPM emphasizes activities while PERT is event oriented. On a CPM chart, events would not be symbolized, rather arrows representing each activity would connect to each other at nodes. In a PERT chart, events are specifically designated and emphasized by their placement in boxes. Arrows connecting the boxes have no specific identification. The advantage of a PERT event oriented chart is that the events can be considered milestones. These milestones can be spelled out in contracts or reports to facilitate managerial control.

The second major difference between the two techniques is the fact that PERT permits explicit treatment of probability for its time estimates while CPM does not. This distinction reflects PERT's origin and scheduling advanced development projects that are characterized by high degrees of uncertainty and CPM's origin in the scheduling of fairly routine plant maintenance activities. In general, CPM is used by construction and other industries where the project includes well defined activities with a low level of uncertainty. PERT is more likely to be used where research development and design form significant parts of the project resulting in relatively high levels of uncertainty.

The PERT technique acknowledges the effects of probability by including estimates of the minimum, most likely, and maximum periods of time required to complete an activity. The expected time for each activity is then calculated by taking an average of these three estimates. Some authors [3] [4] [6] [9] give the most likely time estimate a higher weight to reflect its greater probability of occurrence. However, the overall project duration is not significantly different using either approach.

Many managers have found that such efforts are not necessary and result in an overly complicated planning process. This often leads to reluctance to accept the basic idea of network planning, to the disadvantage of the project. Many project managers simply use the most likely time estimate for each activity duration. The decision whether to use CPM or PERT and whether to use a single or multiple activity duration estimates is most often based on personal preference.

Recently developed variations of the CPM and PERT techniques have allowed these approaches to be used for estimating, monitoring and controlling project resource requirements and costs. This is done by plotting the network on a time scale (x-axis) and inputting anticipated costs and resource requirements for each activity. This then enables projection of costs and resource needs for a specified time period without the intermediate step of translating the network into a bar chart format.

There are several rules of thumb to be used in developing either a CPM or PERT network:

1. The network should have a minimum of about 20 events. A Gantt chart is usually more appropriate for projects smaller than this.
2. Networks that are not computerized should usually be limited to those with fewer than 100 events; 300 events is a practical upper limit. Computerized networks of as many as 12,500 activities have been used on large construction projects although 1000 to 2000 is more common. Networks for non-construction types of projects are frequently much smaller. The project manager must realize that the greater the number of activities used in the network, the more difficult the network becomes to encompass and update.
3. Project characteristics that justify the use of a large number of descriptive activities or events are:
   - Very critical
   - High risk or uncertainty
   - Involvement of many people or organizations
   - Technical complexity
   - Activity at diverse geographic locations

Comparison Of The Five Scheduling Techniques

Each of the five scheduling techniques discussed has inherent strengths and weaknesses. These strengths and weaknesses are summarized in Table 1.

The type of scheduling technique to be used for a project should be selected on a case-by-case basis. Table 2 rates each of the techniques with regard to some of the more important selection criteria.

Computerization Of Scheduling Techniques

Small projects can be analyzed manually but the use of computer analysis offers many advantages for even moderately complex projects. The use of a computer permits not only the resource allocation of single projects, but also the simultaneous consideration of all activities from the total range of projects being handled within an entire firm, so that the computer schedules the firm's complete resources. Provided that the networks for all projects have been sensibly constructed, multi-project scheduling by computer tends to produce working schedules that remain valid for the life of each project, and need little or no revision as work proceeds.

Computer software packages are available which will plot the network, illustrate the critical path, identify the available float for each activity, project resource and budget requirements, and summarize the results in conveniently tabulated reports. These packages can handle any number of projects at one time, making them suitable for scheduling the firm's total operations. Many of these packages can be used for all three types of scheduling techniques.

Examples of currently available software packages that can handle projects with up to 5000 activities and yet still be run on microcomputers are: PMS-II by North American Mica, Inc.; PERTMASTER by Westminster Software, Inc.; CPM/PERT by Elite Software; and TRAC LINE by TRAC LINE Software, Inc. These packages typically cost $500-$1500. Several of these also include resource allocation subroutines.

There are also software packages that can handle extremely large projects that are suitable for large mainframe computers. These include: PAC I, II and III by AGS Management Systems, Inc.; PMC2 by M. Bryce & Associates, Inc.; and CRAM by Environmental Services, Incorporated. These systems can cost $10,000 or more.

Summary

The planning stage is a critical aspect of any project. During this stage, the project manager defines the project objectives, identifies the activities necessary to complete the project, estimates the level of resources and amount of time necessary to complete the project, and establishes the framework for management control of the project. The project Master Schedule is one of the major planning and control tools available to the project manager. In order to prepare an effective project Master Schedule, it is necessary to follow a structured approach. Several commonly accepted scheduling techniques are available to the project manager. Each has its inherent advantages and disadvantages. Each can be used singly or in conjunction with other scheduling techniques and each can be computerized. The information contained in this article should be sufficient to convince the project manager of the importance of preparing a project Master Schedule and provide the basis for selection and development of the most appropriate technique or techniques for his or her next project.

References

1. Badawy, M.K., *Developing Managerial Skills in Engineers and Scientists*. New York: Van Nostrand Reinhold Company, 1982.
2. Burstein, D. A System to Keep Projects on Budget, on Schedule. *Consulting Engineer*, July, 1983, 69-72.
3. Burstein, D., & Stasiowski, F., *Project Management for the Design Professional*. London: Architectural Press, Ltd., 1982.
4. Chase, R.B., & Aquilano, N.J. Production and Operations Management: A Life Cycle Approach. *Production and Operations Management: A Life Cycle Approach*. Homewood, IL: Richard D. Irwin, Inc., 1981.
5. Ivancevich, J.M., Donnelly, J.H. Jr., & Gibson, J.L. *Managing for Performance*. Plano, TX: Business Publications Inc., 1983.
6. Knutson, J.R. *How to be a Successful Project Manager*. Boston, MA: Education for Management, Inc., 1980.
7. Lock, D. (ed.) *Engineers Handbook of Management Techniques*. Epping, Essex, England: Gower Press, Limited, 1973.
8. O'Brien, J.J., & Zilly, R.G., *Contractor's Management Handbook*. New York, NY: McGraw-Hill Book Company, 1971.
9. Spiegle, E. *The Engineer as Manager*. Seattle, WA: Battelle, Inc., 1983.
10. Spirer, H.F., & Symons, G.E. *Successful Management of Civil Engineering Projects*. Larchmont, NY: MGI Management Institute, Inc., 1979.

Kent Cori, P.E., is the Public Works Engineering Department Manager for the consulting engineering firm of Donohue & Associates, Inc. at their Milwaukee, Wisconsin Division Office. Mr. Cori has his B.S. Civil and Environmental Engineering, University of Wisconsin, Madison and his M.B.A., University of Wisconsin, Whitewater.

* * *

Table 1
Comparison of Scheduling Techniques

MILESTONE TECHNIQUE

Criteria	Strengths	Weaknesses
Applicability	Only small errors in measurement are likely to occur if activity durations are short.	No explicit technique for depicting interrelationships.
Reliability	Simplicity of system affords some reliability.	Frequently unreliable because judgment of estimator may change over time. Numerous estimates in a large project, each with some unreliability, may lead to errors in judging status.
Implementation	Easiest of all systems because it is well understood.	Difficult to implement for the control of operations where time standards do not ordinarily exist and must be developed.
Simulation Capabilities	———————	No significant capability.

Criteria	Strengths	Weaknesses
Updating Status	Easy to update periodically. Not necessary to use computer.	
Flexibility	————	Poor accommodation of frequent logic changes.
Cost	Data gathering, processing and display relatively inexpensive.	The chart tends to be inflexible. Program changes require new charts.

GANTT TECHNIQUE

Criteria	Strengths	Weaknesses
Applicability	Only small errors in measurement are likely to occur if activity durations are short.	No explicit technique for depicting interrelationships.
Reliability	Single duration estimate for each activity avoids errors due to over-complexity.	Frequently unreliable because judgment of estimator may change over time. Numerous estimates in a large project, each with some unreliability, may lead to errors in judging status.
Implementation	Easiest of all systems in some respects because it is well understood.	Quite difficult to implement for the control of operations where time standards do not ordinarily exist and must be developed.
Simulation Capabilities	————	No significant capability.
Updating Status	Easy to update graphs periodically if no major program changes. Not necessary to use computer.	May have to redo graphs because of inability to update current charts.
Flexibility	Can also be used for estimating resource requirements.	If significant logic changes occur frequently, numerous charts must be completely reconstructed.
Cost	Data gathering and processing relatively inexpensive. Display can be inexpensive if existing graphs can be updated and if inexpensive materials are used.	The graph tends to be inflexible. Program changes require new graphs, which are time consuming and costly. Expensive display devices are frequently used.

FULL WALL TECHNIQUE

Criteria	Strengths	Weaknesses
Applicability	Accurately depicts work sequence.	No explicit representation of activity interrelationships. Can not be easily computerized.

Reliability	Single duration estimate for each activity avoids errors due to over-complexity. Input from project team members often eliminates errors and problems at the outset.	Numerous estimates in a large project, each with some unreliability, may lead to significant errors in judging overall project status.
Implementation	Graphic display of work sequence and early discussion of project is desired by project managers. Easily explained and understood.	Time requirements and logistics problems are difficult to overcome.
Simulation Capabilities	_____	No significant capability.
Updating Status	Moderate capability. Activities are clearly identified and time estimates can be obtained as needed.	Usually requires redrawing schedule. Often difficult to update because activity interrelationships are not explicitly shown.
Flexibility	Schedule can be changed to reflect scope changes. Can be used to estimate resource requirements.	Schedules for even moderately complex projects become complicated.
Cost	Can reduce overall project costs through better planning and control.	More man-hours are required than in any other system; hence this approach is often the most costly.

CPM TECHNIQUE

Criteria	Strengths	Weaknesses
Applicability	Accurately depicts work sequence and interrelationships among activities.	No formula is provided to estimate probable time to completion; consequently, the technique is as valid as the estimator. The margin of error is generally less on projects with little uncertainty.
Reliability	Single duration estimate for each activity avoids errors due to over-complexity.	Numerous estimates in a large project, each with some unreliability, may lead to significant errors in judging overall project status.
Implementation	Graphic display of work sequence and activity interrelationships is desired by managers of complex projects.	Relatively difficult to explain to those unused to approach. Complexity of schedule may intimidate clients.
Simulation Capabilities	Excellent for simulating alternative plans if computerized, especially when coupled with time-cost-resource aspects.	Requires computer for all but very small projects.
Updating Status	Good capability. Activities are clearly identified and time estimates can be obtained as needed.	Schedules for even moderately complex projects require use of computer.

Flexibility	Portions of the network can be easily changed to reflect scope changes if computerized. Can be used to estimate resource requirements if plotted on time scale.	Schedules for even moderately complex projects require use of computer.
Cost	Can reduce overall project costs significantly through better planning and control.	Considerable data are required to use CPM as both a planning and status reporting tool and a computer is almost invariably required. Therefore, the cost outlay can be fairly extensive.

PERT TECHNIQUE

Criteria	Strengths	Weaknesses
Applicability	PERT, like CPM, is capable of depicting work sequence. The use of three time estimates should make it more accurate than any other technique.	Overly complex for small projects.
Reliability	Probabilistic duration estimates may be more accurate than single estimate.	Securing three duration estimates for each activity requires more information which could introduce additional error.
Implementation	Graphic display of sequence and event interrelationships is desired by managers of complex projects.	The complete PERT system is quite complex, and therefore, difficult to implement. May intimidate first time users and clients.
Simulation Capabilities	Excellent for simulating alternative plans if computerized, especially when coupled with time-cost-resource aspects.	Requires computer for all but very small projects.
Updating Status	Events are clearly identified and elapsed times can be obtained as needed.	Estimation of activity durations is quite time consuming, and calculation of expected times requires use of a computer.
Flexibility	As the project changes over time, the network and new time estimates can be readily adjusted to reflect changes. Can be used to estimate resource requirements if plotted on time scale.	Schedules for even moderately complex projects require use of computer.
Cost	Can reduce overall project costs significantly through better planning and control.	More data and more computation are required than in any other system; hence the system is very costly.

Table 2
Selecting a Scheduling Technique

Criteria	Milestone	Gantt	Full Wall	CPM	PERT
Activities versus Events Oriented	Event	Activity	Event	Activity	Event
Suitability for Large Projects	Poor	Poor	Fair	Excellent	Excellent
Suitability for Small Projects	Good	Good	Poor	Poor	Poor
Degree of Control	Very Low	Low	Moderate	High	Highest
Acceptance by Unsophisticated Users	Best	Excellent	Good	Fair	Poor
Ease of Assembly	Easiest	Easy	Hardest	Hard	Harder
Degree of Flexibility	Lowest	Low	Moderate	High	Highest
Ease of Manual Calculation	Easiest	Easy	Moderate	Hard	Hardest
Accuracy of Projections	Fair	Fair	High	Higher	Highest
Cost to Prepare and Maintain	Lowest	Low	Highest	High	Higher
Vague Project Scope	Poorest	Poor	Fair	Good	Excellent
Complex Project Logic	Poorest	Poor	Better	Excellent	Excellent
Critical Completion Date	Fair	Fair	Good	Good	Excellent
Frequent Progress Check Required	Good	Good	Good	Fair	Hard
Frequent Updating Required	Easiest	Easy	Hardest	Hard	Harder
Frequent Logic Changes Required	Poor	Poor	Poor	Fair	Fair
Appeal to Client	Good	Good	Excellent	Excellent	Excellent

The Work Breakdown Structure in Software Project Management*

Robert C. Tausworthe

Jet Propulsion Laboratory

Reprinted with permission from *The Journal of Systems and Software*, *1*, pages 181-186. Copyright © 1980 by Elsevier/ North Holland, Inc.

The work breakdown structure (WBS) is a vehicle for breaking an engineering project down into subproject, tasks, subtasks, work packages, and so on. It is an important planning tool which links objectives with resources and activities in a logical framework. It becomes an important status monitor during the actual implementation as the completions of subtasks are measured against the project plan. Whereas the WBS has been widely used in many other engineering applications, it has seemingly only rarely been formally applied to software projects, for various reasons. Recent successes with software project WBSs, however, have clearly indicated that the technique can be applied and have shown the benefits of such a tool in management of these projects.

This paper advocates and summarizes the use of the WBS in software implementation projects. It also identifies some of the problems people have had generating software WBSs, and the need for standard checklists of items to be included.

INTRODUCTION

If one were to be given the task of writing a program, such as that structurally illustrated in Figure 1, in which the target language instruction set was not intended to be executed by some dumb computer, but, instead, by intelligent human beings, then one might be thought to have an easier job than colleagues who write their programs for machines. However, a little reflection will show that this job is much more difficult

for a number of reasons, among which are ambiguities in the English language and a multitude of human factors [1]. However, such a program, often named the PLAN (Figure 2), is an essential part of almost every industrial project slated for success.

One of the difficulties in writing this program is the supplying of enough detail so as to be executable without allowing ambiguity. Another is getting the right controls into the program so that the programees perform as stated in the PLAN. Still another is making the PLAN complete, with all contingencies covered and a proper response to each supplied. One final problem of note here is making the plan bug-free, or reliable, so that once execution starts, if everything proceeds according to the PLAN, there is no need to deviate.

Programmers well-schooled in modern techniques [2] would approach the writing of this PLAN in a structured way, using top–down design methodology, modular development, stepwise refinement, hierarchic layering of detail, structurally sound constructions, and semantically definite documentation. Such an approach would tend to bring a measure of organization to the PLAN, understandability to its documentation, and reliability to its execution. If created in this way, the resulting format of the PLAN work tasks would have the attributes of what is known in the engineering industry as a "work breakdown structure" [3], structurally illustrated in Figure 3.

The work breakdown structure (WBS) is an enumeration of all work activities in hierarchic refinements of detail, which organizes work to be done into short, manageable tasks with quantifiable inputs, outputs, schedules, and assigned responsibilities. It may be used for project budgeting of time and resources down to the individual task level, and, later, as a basis for progress reporting relative to meaningful management milestones. A software management plan based

---

*The work reported in this paper was carried out at the Jet Propulsion Laboratory of the California Institute of Technology under contract NAS 7-100, sponsored by the National Aeronautics and Space Administration.

Address correspondence to Robert C. Tausworthe, Jet Propulsion Laboratory, 4800 Oak Grove Drive, Pasadena, California 91103.

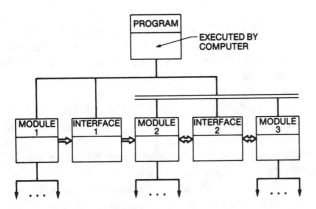

Figure 1. The modular hierarchy of a program.

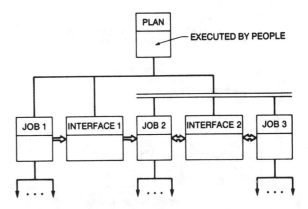

Figure 3. The work breakdown structure (WBS).

on a WBS contains the necessary tools to estimate costs and schedules accurately and to provide visibility and control during production.

Such a plan may be structured to evaluate technical accomplishments on the basis of task and activity progress. Schedules and PERT/CPM [4] networks may be built upon technical activities in terms of task milestones (i.e., accomplishments, outputs, and other quantifiable work elements). Projected versus actual task progress can be reviewed by technical audit and by progress reviews on a regular (say, monthly or biweekly) basis. Formal project design reviews are major checkpoints in this measurement system.

But knowing modern programming theory does little good if one does not also have the programming experience to which to apply it. Similarly, the knowledge of what a WBS is, what its goals are, what its benefits are, and what its structure is supposed to be like, does not necessarily instruct one in how to apply that knowledge toward developing a WBS for a particular project.

In the following sections of this paper, I shall review some of the characteristics and benefits of the

WBS and discuss how these can be developed and applied in software implementation projects. This material will be oriented principally toward new-software production tasks, although many of the concepts will be applicable also to continuing maintenance and operations tasks.

THE WORK BREAKDOWN STRUCTURE

The goals assumed here for generating the WBS are to identify work tasks, needed resources, implementation constraints, and so on, to that level of detail which yields the accuracy stipulated in the original PLAN, and to provide the means for early calibration of this accuracy and corrective replanning, if required, during the actual implementation.

How refined should this WBS be? Let me answer this question by showing how the WBS and schedule projection accuracy are interrelated.

If a project has identified a certain number of equal-effort "unit" milestones to be achieved during the course of implementation, then the mere number of such milestones achieved by a certain date is an indicator of the progress toward that goal. A graph of accumulated milestones as a function of time, sometimes called a "rate chart," permits certain predictions to be made about the future completion date rather handily and with quantifiable accuracy, especially if the milestones are chosen properly. Figure 4 shows a rate chart of a hypothetical software project.

Let it be supposed that it is known a priori, as a result of generating the WBS, that a project will be completed after M milestones have been met. These milestones correspond to all the tasks that have to be accomplished, and can be accomplished once and for all (i.e., some later activity does not reopen an already completed task; if one does, it can be accommodated by making M larger to include all such milestones as

Figure 2. The PLAN is a people program.

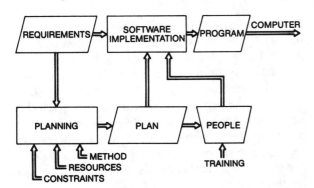

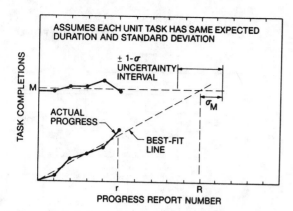

Figure 4. Conceptual progress rate chart.

separate events). The number M, of course, may not be precisely known from the first, and any uncertainty in M is certainly going to affect the accuracy of estimated completion date. Such uncertainties can be factored in as secondary effects later, when needed for refinement of accuracy.

Now, let it be further supposed that it has been possible to refine the overall task into these M milestones in such a way that each task is believed to require about the same amount of effort and duration to accomplish (Figure 5). Viewed at regular intervals (e.g., biweekly or monthly). a plot of the cumulative numbers of milestones reported as having been completed should rise linearly [5] until project completion.

More quantitatively, let m be the average number of tasks actually completed during each reporting period, and let σ be the standard deviation of the actual number of milestones completed each reporting period about this mean value (the values of m and σ are presumed to be constant over the project duration). The value of m is a reflection of the team average pro-

Figure 5. The unit task.

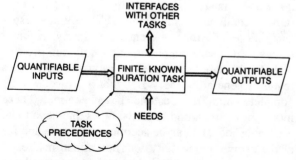

- SIZED FOR A SINGLE INDIVIDUAL

- NO FURTHER BREAKDOWN INTO SUBTASKS

ductivity and σ is a measure of the ability to estimate their production rate. Both attest to team effectiveness: first, in their ability to produce and, second, in their ability to create a work plan that adequately accounts for their time.

By design, the mean behavior of the milestone completion status is linear, a straight line from the origin with slope m. The project should require M/m reporting periods to complete, which time, of course, should not depend on whether a WBS was made (I am discounting, in this discussion, whether WBS generation increases or decreases productivity). Thus, M/m should be a constant value, relatively speaking. If M is made large, tasks are smaller and shorter, so proportionately more of them are completed each reporting period. The project schedule will, in fact, assume some productivity or mean accomplishment rate, but an actual performance value will generally be unknown until progress can be monitored for some period of time.

However, although the numbers M and σ may not affect team productivity, they do directly influence the effectiveness with which a project can monitor its progress and predict its future accomplishments. Generation of a WBS, of course, gives (or estimates) the parameter M. Monitoring the completion of milestones provides estimates for m and σ. From these, projections of the end date and calculations for the accuracy of this prediction can be made. Based on such information, the project can then divert or reallocate resources to take corrective action, should progress not be deemed suitable.

In this simplified model, a least-square-error straight-line fit through the cumulative milestone progress over the first r reports (of an expected $R=M/m$ reports) at regular ΔT intervals will predict the time required to reach the final milestone. It will also provide an estimate of m and σ. The normalized predicted completion date may be expected to deviate from the projected value (as a one-sigma event) by no more than [5]

$$\sigma_M \leq 1.48 \, \sigma_1 \, (R/rM)^{1/2}$$

within first-order effects. The value $\sigma_1 = \sigma/m^{1/2}$ represents the normalized standard deviation of an individual task milestone (it is limited to values of less than unity in the underlying model), and σ_M represents the deviation in time to reach milestone M.

The bound permits the specification of WBS characteristics that enable accurate early predictions of future progress. High overall accuracy depends on a combination of low σ_1 and large M. One may compensate for inaccurate appraisals of productivity only by generating a very detailed WBS.

As an example, suppose that a 10% end-date prediction accuracy is required (i.e., $\sigma_M = 0.1$) by the end of the first quarter ($r/R = 0.25$) of a project. Then, as shown in Figure 6, the trade-off figure is $M/\sigma_1^2 = 876$. Hence, if the WBS is highly uncertain ($\sigma_1 = 1$), that WBS should contain 876 unit milestones. If the project is confident that it can hold more closely to its average productivity (and has most contingencies provided for) with $\sigma_1 = 0.5$, then it needs only about 220 milestones. A 1-person-year project with biweekly reporting, one milestone per report (26 milestones in all), must demonstrate a $\sigma_1 = 0.17$ level of task prediction accuracy.

It is therefore both necessary and important to generate a detailed WBS rather carefully and to monitor milestone achievements relative to this WBS very faithfully, if accuracy in predicting the future progress of a project is of great importance.

REASONABLE SCHEDULE ACCURACY

A project engineer on a 2-year, 10-person task may perhaps be able to manage as many as 876 subtasks, each formally assigned and reported on. That amounts to about one subtask completion per week from each of the other nine workers; but the generation of the descriptions for the 876 tasks will require considerable effort. Moreover, it is unlikely that such a detailed plan would have a σ as large as one week; if the project engineer is able to break the work accurately into 876 week-long subtasks, task deviations can probably be estimated to well within a week.

The ability of the project engineer (or planning staff) to generate a clear and accurate WBS will determine the level to which the WBS must be taken. Greater accuracy of the work breakdown definition produces greater understanding and clarity of the actions necessary to complete task objectives. If the work is understood, readily identified, and achievable

as discerned, the confidence of reaching the objectives is high. Thus, the further the subtask descriptions become refined, the better the estimator is able to assess the individual subtask durations and uncertainties. Refinement ceases when the appropriate M/σ_1^2 is reached.

Practically speaking, a work plan with tasks shorter than 1 week in duration will usually require too much planning and management overhead to be worthwhile. On the other hand, a work plan with tasks longer than 1 or 2 weeks will probably suffer from a large σ_1. Thus, a breakdown into 1- or 2-week subtasks is probably the most reasonable target for planning purposes.

A work year consists of about 47 actual weeks of work (excluding vacation, holidays, sick leave, etc.). Therefore, a project of w workers can reasonably accommodate only about $47w/d$ tasks per year (including management tasks) each of duration d weeks; spread over y years, the total number of milestones can reach $M = 47wy/d$, so that the practical accuracy limit one may reasonably expect at the one-quarter point in a project ($r/R = 0.25$) is about

$$\sigma_M \leqslant 0.432\sigma_1(d/wy)^{1/2}.$$

Note that accuracy is related to the total person-year effort in a project, other things being equal. A 3-person-year project completing 1 task per person-week can expect to have $\sigma_M \leqslant 0.216\sigma_1$. With a $\sigma_1 = 0.4$ (± 2 days per weekly task), the end-date estimation accuracy is within 10%.

GENERATING THE WBS

There is no mystery about making a WBS. People do it all the time, although they seldom call the result a WBS. Most of the things we do, in fact, are probably first organized in our heads, and for small undertakings, most of the time that works out well. For more complex undertakings, especially those involving other people, it becomes necessary to plan, organize, document, and review more formally.

The general algorithm for generating a WBS is even fairly simple to state. It goes something like this:

1. Start with the project statement of work, and put this TASK on top of the "working stack."
2. Consider the TASK at the top of the working stack. Define technical performance objectives, end-item objectives, reliability and quality objectives, schedule constraints, and other factors, as appropriate; inputs and materials required for starting the task; accomplishments and outputs that signal the completion of the task; known prec-

Figure 6. WBS unit milestones and variance ratio.

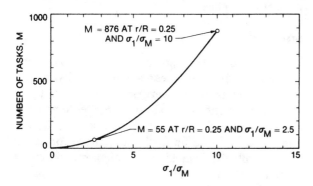

edent tasks or milestones; known interfacing tasks; and resources required, if known. Determine whether this task can be accomplished within the duration (or cost) accuracy goal.

3. If the goal is achieved, skip to the next step; otherwise, partition the current TASK into a small number of comprehensive component subtasks. Include interfacing tasks and tasks whose output is a decision regarding substructuring of other subtasks. Mark the current TASK as a "milestone," pull its description off the working stack, push it onto the "finished stack," and push each of the subtask descriptions onto the working stack.

4. Repeat from step 2 until the working stack is empty.

5. Sequence through all items from the "finished" stack and accumulate durations (costs) into the proper milestones.

The steps in this algorithm are not always simple to perform and cannot always be done correctly the first time or without sometimes referring to items already put into the "finished" list. The process is one of creation and thus requires judgment, experience, identification of alternatives, trade-offs, decisions, and iteration. This last is required since, as the project statement of work is refined, eventually the implementation of the program itself appears as one of the subtasks to be refined. When this subtask is detailed into component parts, the work descriptions begin to follow the influences of the program architecture, organizational matters, chronological constraints, work locations, and "whatever makes sense."

Therefore, the formation of the WBS, the detailed planning, and the architectural design activity are all mutually supportive. The architecture indicates how to structure the tasks, and the WBS goals tell when the architectural phase of activity has proceeded far enough. Scheduling makes use of the WBS as a tool and in turn influences the WBS generation by resolving resource conflicts.

There are many subtasks in a software project, however, that are not connected with the architecture directly, such as requirements analysis, project administration and management, and preparations for demonstration and delivery. The structure of these subtasks, being independent of the program architecture, can be made fairly standard within a given organization for all software productions. However, since there is no automatic or closed-loop means to guarantee that all the planning factors needed in the WBS actually get put into it, a standard WBS checklist can be a significant boon to proper software project planning, to decrease the likelihood of something "dropping through the cracks."

STANDARD WBS CHECKLIST

Previous experience [6] at the Jet Propulsion Laboratory with WBS methodology has permitted moderately large software implementation projects to detect schedule maladies and to control project completions within about 6% of originally scheduled dates and costs. The WBSs were formed by individuals with extensive software experience, overseen by an expert manager. None of the software individuals had ever made a WBS before, and the manager had never tried one on a software project. Together, with much travail, they assembled ad hoc items into a workable system.

A candidate standard WBS outline and checklist is currently being assembled and evaluated within the Deep Space Network (DSN) at the Jet Propulsion Laboratory. This standard WBS checklist includes many factors gained from previous successes and contains items to avert some of the identified shortcomings. Table 1 shows the upper-level structure of this WBS checklist. Detailed task descriptions are also in the process of documentation and evaluation. A short application guidebook is planned, to instruct cognizant individuals in the method, approach, and practice.

Such a checklist and guidebook, together with useful automated WBS entry, update, processing, and report generation aids, impose standards on software projects that are intended to facilitate the project management activity and make it more effective. Initial scheduling and downstream rescheduling of subtasks are aided by a WBS data base that contains precedence relationships, durations, costs, resource requirements, resource availability, and similar constraints on each subtask. PERT and critical-path methods (CPM) are applied directly to the WBS database, resulting in a preliminary schedule. Alterations of this schedule are then effected by editing the WBS via additional constraints recorded into the data base. Actual production progress is measured by marking milestone completions. These are then plotted into a rate chart and all significant milestones are projected to a best-estimate completion date.

PROBLEMS

The WBS is a well-known, effective project engineering tool. It has not been applied to software projects as often as to hardware and construction, probably because the planning and architectural design tasks in software have not always been sufficiently integrated as to be mutually supportive for several reasons: all of the management, support, and miscellaneous tasks were seldom fully identifiable and de-

Table 1. SOFTWARE IMPLEMENTATION PROJECT: Outline of Detailed Work Breakdown Structure

1. ANALYZE SOFTWARE REQUIREMENTS
   1.1 Understand functional and software requirements
   1.2 Identify missing, vague, ambiguous, and conflicting requirements
   1.3 Clarify stated requirements
   1.4 Verify that stated requirements fulfill requestor's goals
   1.5 Assess technology for supplying required software
   1.6 Propose alternate requirements or capability
   1.7 Document revised requirements
2. DEVELOP SOFTWARE ARCHITECTURE
   2.1 Determine architectural approach
   2.2 Develop external functional architecture
   2.3 Develop software internal architecture
   2.4 Assess architected solution vs. requirements
   2.5 Revise architecture and/or renegotiate requirements
   2.6 Document architecture and/or changed requirements
3. DEVELOP EXTERNAL FUNCTIONAL SPECIFICATION
   3.1 Define functional specification standards and conventions
   3.2 Formalize external environment and interface specifications
   3.3 Refine, formalize, and document the architected external operational view of the software
   3.4 Define functional acceptance tests
   3.5 Verify compliance of the external view with requirements
4. PRODUCE AND DELIVER SOFTWARE ITEMS
   4.1 Define programming, test and verification, QA, and documentation standards and conventions
   4.2 Formalize internal environment and interface specifications
   4.3 Obtain support tools
   4.4 Refine and formalize the internal design
   4.5 Define testing specifications to demonstrate required performance
   4.6 Define QA specifications
   4.7 Code and check the program
   4.8 Demonstrate acceptability and deliver software
5. PREPARE FOR SOFTWARE SUSTAINING AND OPERATIONS
   5.1 Train cognizant sustaining and maintenance personnel
   5.2 Train cognizant operations personnel
   5.3 Deliver sustaining tools and materials
   5.4 Deliver all software and data deliverables to operations
   5.5 Install the software and data into its operational environment
   5.6 Prepare consulting agreement between implementation and operations
6. PERFORM PROJECT MANAGEMENT FUNCTIONS
   6.1 Define project goals and objectives
   6.2 Scope and plan the project
   6.3 Administrate the implementation
   6.4 Evaluate performance and product
   6.5 Terminate the project

tailable during the planning phase; because separation of work into manageable packets quite often requires design decisions properly a part of the detailed design phase; because a basis for estimating subtask durations, costs, and other constraints has not existed or been known; and because software managers have not been trained in WBS methodology. Modern software engineering studies of phenomenology and methodology are beginning to close the gaps, however.

The existence of useful tools and methods does not ensure their acceptance; nor does their acceptance ensure project success. Plans and controls are essential project aids but unfortunately do not guarantee success either. The WBS is a planning, monitor, and control tool whose potential for successful application within a software project has been demonstrated. However, further research and demonstrations are necessary before a WBS-oriented software planning and control methodology and system are as well integrated into the software industry as structured programming has only recently become. Fortunately, many organizations and individuals are sensitive enough to the software management crisis of past years that headway is being made [7].

Happily, the solutions will almost certainly not be unique, but will range over limits that accommodate management and programming styles, organizational structures, levels of skill, areas of expertise, cost and end-date constraints, and human and technical factors.

REFERENCES

1. I. Avots, Why Does Project Management Fail? *California Management Review* XII (1), 77–82, Fall 1969.
2. Robert C. Tausworthe, *Standardized Development of Computer Software,* Prentice-Hall, Englewood Cliffs, N.J., 1977.
3. V. G. Hajek, *Management of Engineering Projects,* McGraw-Hill, New York, 1977.
4. DoD and NASA Guide, PERT/COST, Office of The Secretary of Defense and NASA, Washington, D.C., June, 1962.
5. Robert C. Tausworthe, Stochastic Models for Software Project Management, Deep Space Network Progress Report No. 42–37, Jet Propulsion Laboratory, Pasadena, California, February 1977, pp. 118–126.
6. M. McKenzie and A. P. Irvine, Evaluation of the DSN Software Methodology, Deep Space Network Progress Report No. 42–46, Jet Propulsion Laboratory, Pasadena, California, August, 1978.
7. M. M. Lehman et. al., *Software Phenomenology,* working papers of The Software Life Cycle Management Workshop, U.S. Army Institute for Research in Management Information and Computer Science, Atlanta, Georgia, August 1977.

Despite claims to the contrary, no accurate method exists to predict time and manpower needed to develop a software system.

MAKING SOFTWARE DEVELOPMENT ESTIMATES "GOOD"

by Andrew B. Ferrentino

A software system was estimated to require 30,000 lines of source code and an 18-month development period. Six weeks before the scheduled delivery date, it was reported to be progressing according to plan. Two weeks before the scheduled delivery, project management reported that the estimated size of the system had been revised to over 100,000 lines of code. Delivery would be delayed at least one year. Sound familiar?

There are many reasons for such a disaster. One reason, possibly characteristic of most such projects, is the manner of interpretation and use of estimation by the project management. The problem begins with the failure to recognize the difference between estimation parameters, such as system size (measured in lines of source code), and the product of the development process, namely the system itself. When this distinction is lost, development progress is measured in terms of lines of code generated rather than the more concrete notion of functions fully implemented. Project progress, then, is measured as:

$$\frac{L_G}{L_E} \times 100\%$$

where L_G is lines of source code generated to date and L_E is total lines of source code originally estimated.

Applying this progress measure in the context of the horror story cited above, the following analysis might plausibly explain what happened. Six weeks before scheduled delivery, the number of lines of source code was 29,000, thus

$$\frac{L_G}{L_E} \times 100\% = \frac{29,000}{30,000} = 97\%$$

Project management may then have concluded that they were right on schedule even though many of the programmers on the project knew that, based on real progress, the end was nowhere in sight. The real progress is measured on the basis of the implemented, tested and documented functions, irrespective of the original estimate of system size.

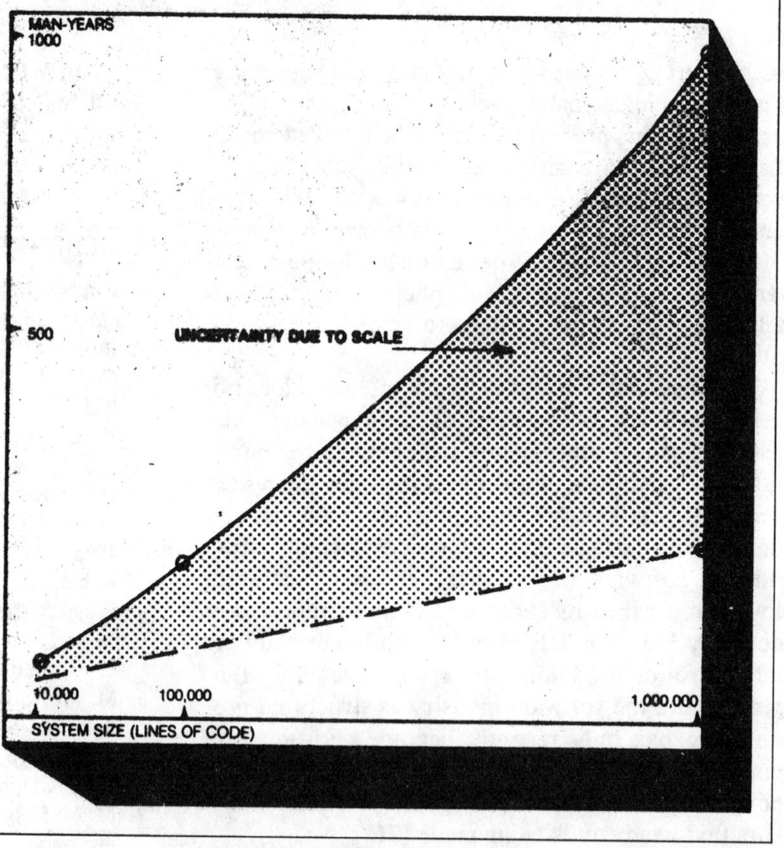

CHARTS BY CYNTHIA STODDARD

FIG. 1

THE EFFECT OF SCALE

If we could accurately predict the size of the system at the start of the project, lines of code generated would be an accurate measure of project progress. However:

1. Accurate estimation is not attainable in the current state of software engineering.

2. Some of the management pitfalls ensue from assuming that accurate estimation is possible.

3. There is a management approach to software development that can increase our success rate.

In essence, estimation is an educated guess at the time and manpower needed to develop a system. Although this guess can be quantified through analysis or statistics, it is still a guess. Despite claims to the contrary, there is no method to accurately predict the time and manpower needed to develop a software system. The parameters we use to compute our estimates, e.g., system scale, error removal, programmer productivity, and requirements stability vary enormously.

SEPTEMBER 1981

Cost of error removal can vary widely, from as little as 5% to 10% to as much as 50% to 60% of total development cost.

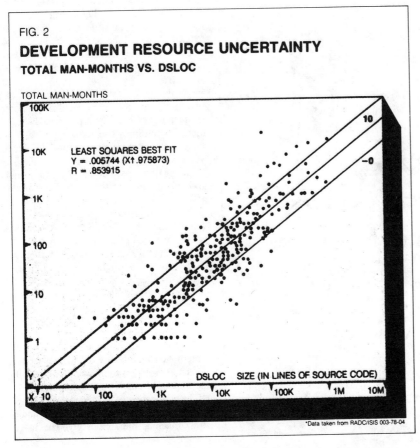

FIG. 2

DEVELOPMENT RESOURCE UNCERTAINTY
TOTAL MAN-MONTHS VS. DSLOC

*Data taken from RADC/ISIS 003-78-04

If the requirements for a software system are well defined at the start of the development cycle and remain fixed throughout, the development resources should be much smaller than if the requirements are ill-defined or continually changing. Unfortunately, the latter is usually a fact of life. Good techniques for managing change are required if development costs are to be minimized.

One downfall of development projects is management that thinks requirements can be fixed at the start and kept constant. We had the unfortunate experience of being part of a project on which several million dollars were expended but which never progressed beyond the requirements phase. In this case, the customer was not willing to proceed with design until the "complete" requirements were specified. Because of the complexity of the problem, this was impractical and led to the failure of the project. With large systems (especially pioneers) requirements can rarely be fixed at the start. There is a continual learning process that causes change.

Requirements widely affect the development resources. If the development project team cannot effectively manage changing requirements, resource utilization will be unpredictable.

Fig. 2 shows actual development project statistics indicative of variability.* For 100,000 lines of code systems, note that the development resources vary from approximately 100 to 10,000 man-months—two orders of magnitude. It is difficult to assert that accurate estimation of development resources is plausible in the face of this data. In fact, we can do better than the range shown because the data represents projects of varying characteristics. When these characteristics are taken into account, then a statistically valid range can be derived for similar projects. But this is possible only in a *statistical* sense, i.e., when dealing with averages. When focusing on a specific project anything can happen, including complete failure.

EFFECTS OF SCALE

As the size of a system increases, the resources required to develop the system do not increase linearly. Rather, they may increase exponentially, as shown in Fig. 1. The more people required to do the job, the greater the required interaction. The number of possible interactions increases in a squared relation with the number of people, i.e., with N people, there are $(N^2 - N)/2$ possible interactions. To manage these interactions, personnel must be increased.

If it were possible to eliminate the added interactions, the number of people required might increase only linearly with system size. The use of good design principles, such as decomposition, can result in designs where small task groups can independently develop parts of the system. The design of the system, then, and the degree to which the organization can be structured to mirror the design decomposition, can result in substantial resource savings. The cross-hatched area of Fig. 1, represents the variability associated with system scale.

The cost of error removal can vary widely. Error removal costs can be as little as 5% to 10% or as much as 50% to 60% of the total development cost. One factor determining the cost of error removal is the degree to which system testing is used. If system testing is the sole means of error removal the cost will be high, as most errors are introduced early in the development process and the cost of removing an error increases the longer it remains undetected.

The most difficult aspect is individual programmer variability. Many controlled experiments have tried to gauge this variable, and although the quantitative results differ, they are all consistent in demonstrating great variation from one individual to another. Below are typical ranges of variation from a representative sampling of programmers working on identical problems:

CODING TIME	25:1
ERROR REMOVAL TIME	26:1
Size (lines of code)	5:1

Despite this tremendous variation we tend to treat one programmer like another in estimating resources. To get the most productivity from a group, individual strengths must be identified and matched to the work. Because this is impractical for most projects, average productivity figures must be used in estimation. This introduces a large margin of uncertainty.

HINDSIGHT ESTIMATE

The size of a system may have been estimated to be 80,000 lines of code but the completed system contained 175,000 lines of code. Was the original estimate no good? In hindsight one can say what the "correct" estimate should have been, but this is another way of saying that one can make an accurate estimate. The following anecdote shows that even in hindsight there is no correct estimate.

A system development job was bid and won for a fixed price of $250,000. After contract award the winning company learned that the next lowest bid was $1.2 million. An audit was immediately called and the professional audit team reported that indeed the system would cost over $1 million to develop.

Because optimizing programmer productivity is often impractical, average productivity figures must be used in estimation.

"Terrific references, but I'll give it to you straight—being an advanced systems technologist does not qualify you to be a second baseman."

©DATAMATION

To salvage the effort, a small, experienced team was assigned to the job. It endeavored to use all the best software engineering practices and management controls to develop a good design, control change, and reduce the impact of error. The system was developed for $300,000.

Now, in hindsight, which was the correct estimate: $250,000, $300,000 or $1.2 million? If the audit had never been performed but the team still managed to do it for $300,000, would the project have been considered a success? Or could the job have been done for $100,000? Or was it really a success after all?

None of the above statements are "correct," for a different team using different techniques may have performed the job for $1.5 million. The same team with the same techniques may have done the job for $600,000 if it had made a bad design decision requiring later correction. We can't make good estimates, but we can make estimates good.

It is imperative, then, to manage development projects in order to make estimates good. To accomplish this, a combination of management and software engineering techniques must be brought to bear, such as:
● Well-defined milestones: specification complete, coding complete, unit test complete, etc. must be used as the means to measure software development progress against budget expended.
● The concept of software development in increments (or releases) of increasing functions will provide a framework for controlling the impact of changing requirements.
● The application of advanced designed techniques such as information hiding and abstract machine hierarchies give rise to good designs.
● Verification techniques such as formal walkthroughs and informal proof techniques help to identify errors soon after they are introduced.   ✳

Andrew B. Ferrentino, vice president of Lesko/Fox Associates, Washington, D.C. management consultants, has had over 15 years' experience in the analysis, design, implementation, and management of communications/computer-based systems.

Software Engineering Economics

BARRY W. BOEHM

Abstract—This paper summarizes the current state of the art and recent trends in software engineering economics. It provides an overview of economic analysis techniques and their applicability to software engineering and management. It surveys the field of software cost estimation, including the major estimation techniques available, the state of the art in algorithmic cost models, and the outstanding research issues in software cost estimation.

Index Terms—Computer programming costs, cost models, management decision aids, software cost estimation, software economics, software engineering, software management.

I. INTRODUCTION

Definitions

The dictionary defines "economics" as "a social science concerned chiefly with description and analysis of the production, distribution, and consumption of goods and services." Here is another definition of economics which I think is more helpful in explaining how economics relates to software engineering.

Economics is the study of how people make decisions in resource-limited situations.

This definition of economics fits the major branches of classical economics very well.

Macroeconomics is the study of how people make decisions in resource-limited situations on a national or global scale. It deals with the effects of decisions that national leaders make on such issues as tax rates, interest rates, foreign and trade policy.

Microeconomics is the study of how people make decisions in resource-limited situations on a more personal scale. It deals with the decisions that individuals and organizations make on such issues as how much insurance to buy, which word processor to buy, or what prices to charge for their products or services.

Economics and Software Engineering Management

If we look at the discipline of software engineering, we see that the microeconomics branch of economics deals more with the types of decisions we need to make as software engineers or managers.

Clearly, we deal with limited resources. There is never enough time or money to cover all the good features we would like to put into our software products. And even in these days of cheap hardware and virtual memory, our more significant software products must always operate within a world of limited computer power and main memory. If you have been in the software engineering field for any length of time, I am sure

you can think of a number of decision situations in which you had to determine some key software product feature as a function of some limiting critical resource.

Throughout the software life cycle,[1] there are many decision situations involving limited resources in which software engineering economics techniques provide useful assistance. To provide a feel for the nature of these economic decision issues, an example is given below for each of the major phases in the software life cycle.

- *Feasibility Phase:* How much should we invest in information system analyses (user questionnaires and interviews, current-system analysis, workload characterizations, simulations, scenarios, prototypes) in order that we converge on an appropriate definition and concept of operation for the system we plan to implement?

- *Plans and Requirements Phase:* How rigorously should we specify requirements? How much should we invest in requirements validation activities (automated completeness, consistency, and traceability checks, analytic models, simulations, prototypes) before proceeding to design and develop a software system?

- *Product Design Phase:* Should we organize the software to make it possible to use a complex piece of existing software which generally but not completely meets our requirements?

- *Programming Phase:* Given a choice between three data storage and retrieval schemes which are primarily execution time-efficient, storage-efficient, and easy-to-modify, respectively; which of these should we choose to implement?

- *Integration and Test Phase:* How much testing and formal verification should we perform on a product before releasing it to users?

- *Maintenance Phase:* Given an extensive list of suggested product improvements, which ones should we implement first?

- *Phaseout:* Given an aging, hard-to-modify software product, should we replace it with a new product, restructure it, or leave it alone?

Outline of This Paper

The economics field has evolved a number of techniques (cost-benefit analysis, present value analysis, risk analysis, etc.)

---

[1] Economic principles underlie the overall structure of the software life cycle, and its primary refinements of prototyping, incremental development, and advancemanship. The primary economic driver of the life-cycle structure is the significantly increasing cost of making a software change or fixing a software problem, as a function of the phase in which the change or fix is made. See [11, ch. 4].

Manuscript received April 26, 1983; revised June 28, 1983.

The author is with the Software Information Systems Division, TRW Defense Systems Group, Redondo Beach, CA 90278.

Reprinted from *IEEE Transactions on Software Engineering*, Volume SE-10, Number 1, January 1984, pages 4-21. Copyright © 1984 by The Institute of Electrical and Electronics Engineers, Inc.

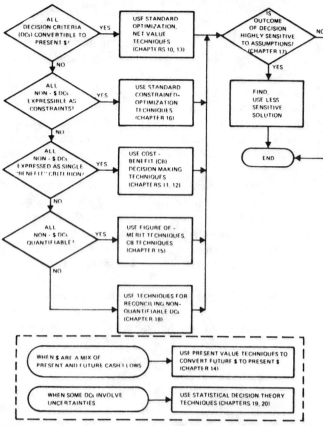

MASTER KEY
TO SOFTWARE ENGINEERING ECONOMICS
DECISION ANALYSIS TECHNIQUES

Fig. 1. Master key to software engineering economics decision analysis techniques.

for dealing with decision issues such as the ones above. Section II of this paper provides an overview of these techniques and their applicability to software engineering.

One critical problem which underlies all applications of economic techniques to software engineering is the problem of estimating software costs. Section III contains three major sections which summarize this field:

III-A: Major Software Cost Estimation Techniques

III-B: Algorithmic Models for Software Cost Estimation

III-C: Outstanding Research Issues in Software Cost Estimation.

Section IV concludes by summarizing the major benefits of software engineering economics, and commenting on the major challenges awaiting the field.

II. SOFTWARE ENGINEERING ECONOMICS ANALYSIS TECHNIQUES

Overview of Relevant Techniques

The microeconomics field provides a number of techniques for dealing with software life-cycle decision issues such as the ones given in the previous section. Fig. 1 presents an overall master key to these techniques and when to use them.[2]

---

[2] The chapter numbers in Fig. 1 refer to the chapters in [11], in which those techniques are discussed in further detail.

As indicated in Fig. 1, standard optimization techniques can be used when we can find a single quantity such as dollars (or pounds, yen, cruzeiros, etc.) to serve as a "universal solvent" into which all of our decision variables can be converted. Or, if the nondollar objectives can be expressed as constraints (system availability must be at least 98 percent; throughput must be at least 150 transactions per second), then standard constrained optimization techniques can be used. And if cash flows occur at different times, then present-value techniques can be used to normalize them to a common point in time.

More frequently, some of the resulting benefits from the software system are not expressible in dollars. In such situations, one alternative solution will not necessarily dominate another solution.

An example situation is shown in Fig. 2, which compares the cost and benefits (here, in terms of throughput in transactions per second) of two alternative approaches to developing an operating system for a transaction processing system.

- *Option A:* Accept an available operating system. This will require only $80K in software costs, but will achieve a peak performance of 120 transactions per second, using five $10K minicomputer processors, because of a high multiprocessor overhead factor.

- *Option B:* Build a new operating system. This system would be more efficient and would support a higher peak throughput, but would require $180K in software costs.

The cost-versus-performance curve for these two options are shown in Fig. 2. Here, neither option dominates the other, and various cost-benefit decision-making techniques (maximum profit margin, cost/benefit ratio, return on investments, etc.) must be used to choose between Options A and B.

In general, software engineering decision problems are even more complex than Fig. 2, as Options A and B will have several important criteria on which they differ (e.g., robustness, ease of tuning, ease of change, functional capability). If these criteria are quantifiable, then some type of figure of merit can be defined to support a comparative analysis of the preferability of one option over another. If some of the criteria are unquantifiable (user goodwill, programmer morale, etc.), then some techniques for comparing unquantifiable criteria need to be used. As indicated in Fig. 1, techniques for each of these situations are available, and discussed in [11].

Analyzing Risk, Uncertainty, and the Value of Information

In software engineering, our decision issues are generally even more complex than those discussed above. This is because the outcome of many of our options cannot be determined in advance. For example, building an operating system with a significantly lower multiprocessor overhead may be achievable, but on the other hand, it may not. In such circumstances, we are faced with a problem of *decision making under uncertainty*, with a considerable *risk* of an undesired outcome.

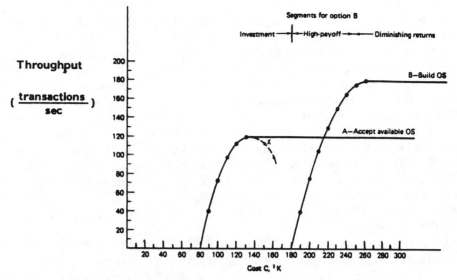

Fig. 2. Cost-effectiveness comparison, transaction processing system options.

The main economic analysis techniques available to support us in resolving such problems are the following.

1) Techniques for decision making under complete uncertainty, such as the maximax rule, the maximin rule, and the Laplace rule [38]. These techniques are generally inadequate for practical software engineering decisions.

2) Expected-value techniques, in which we estimate the probabilities of occurrence of each outcome (successful or unsuccessful development of the new operating system) and complete the expected payoff of each option:

$$EV = \text{Prob(success)} * \text{Payoff(successful OS)}$$
$$+ \text{Prob(failure)} * \text{Payoff(unsuccessful OS)}.$$

These techniques are better than decision making under complete uncertainty, but they still involve a great deal of risk if the Prob(failure) is considerably higher than our estimate of it.

3) Techniques in which we reduce uncertainty by *buying information*. For example, *prototyping* is a way of buying information to reduce our uncertainty about the likely success or failure of a multiprocessor operating system; by developing a rapid prototype of its high-risk elements, we can get a clearer picture of our likelihood of successfully developing the full operating system.

In general, prototyping and other options for buying information[3] are most valuable aids for software engineering decisions. However, they always raise the following question: "how much information-buying is enough?"

In principle, this question can be answered via statistical decision theory techniques involving the use of Bayes' Law, which allows us to calculate the expected payoff from a software project as a function of our level of investment in a prototype

[3] Other examples of options for buying information to support software engineering decisions include feasibility studies, user surveys, simulation, testing, and mathematical program verification techniques.

or other information-buying option. (Some examples of the use of Bayes' Law to estimate the appropriate level of investment in a prototype are given in [11, ch. 20].)

In practice, the use of Bayes' Law involves the estimation of a number of conditional probabilities which are not easy to estimate accurately. However, the Bayes' Law approach can be translated into a number of *value-of-information guidelines*, or conditions under which it makes good sense to decide on investing in more information before committing ourselves to a particular course of action.

Condition 1: There exist attractive alternatives whose payoff varies greatly, depending on some critical states of nature. If not, we can commit ourselves to one of the attractive alternatives with no risk of significant loss.

Condition 2: The critical states of nature have an appreciable probability of occurring. If not, we can again commit ourselves without major risk. For situations with extremely high variations in payoff, the appreciable probability level is lower than in situations with smaller variations in payoff.

Condition 3: The investigations have a high probability of accurately identifying the occurrence of the critical states of nature. If not, the investigations will not do much to reduce our risk of loss due to making the wrong decision.

Condition 4: The required cost and schedule of the investigations do not overly curtail their net value. It does us little good to obtain results which cost more than they can save us, or which arrive too late to help us make a decision.

Condition 5: There exist significant side benefits derived from performing the investigations. Again, we may be able to justify an investigation solely on the basis of its value in training, team-building, customer relations, or design validation.

Some Pitfalls Avoided by Using the Value-of-Information Approach

The guideline conditions provided by the value-of-information approach provide us with a perspective which helps us avoid some serious software engineering pitfalls. The pitfalls below are expressed in terms of some frequently expressed but faulty pieces of software engineering advice.

Pitfall 1: Always use a simulation to investigate the feasibility of complex realtime software. Simulations are often extremely valuable in such situations. However, there have been a good many simulations developed which were largely an expensive waste of effort, frequently under conditions that would have been picked up by the guidelines above. Some have been relatively useless because, once they were built, nobody could tell whether a given set of inputs was realistic or not (picked up by Condition 3). Some have been taken so long to develop that they produced their first results the week after the proposal was sent out, or after the key design review was completed (picked up by Condition 4).

Pitfall 2: Always build the software twice. The guidelines indicate that the prototype (or build-it-twice) approach is often valuable, but not in all situations. Some prototypes have been built of software whose aspects were all straightforward and familiar, in which case nothing much was learned by building them (picked up by Conditions 1 and 2).

Pitfall 3: Build the software purely top-down. When interpreted too literally, the top-down approach does not concern itself with the design of low level modules until the higher levels have been fully developed. If an adverse state of nature makes such a low level module (automatically forecast sales volume, automatically discriminate one type of aircraft from another) impossible to develop, the subsequent redesign will generally require the expensive rework of much of the higher level design and code. Conditions 1 and 2 warn us to temper our top-down approach with a thorough top-to-bottom software risk analysis during the requirements and product design phases.

Pitfall 4: Every piece of code should be proved correct. Correctness proving is still an expensive way to get information on the fault-freedom of software, although it strongly satisfies Condition 3 by giving a very high assurance of a program's correctness. Conditions 1 and 2 recommend that proof techniques be used in situations where the operational cost of a software fault is very large, that is, loss of life, compromised national security, major financial losses. But if the operational cost of a software fault is small, the added information on fault-freedom provided by the proof will not be worth the investment (Condition 4).

Pitfall 5: Nominal-case testing is sufficient. This pitfall is just the opposite of Pitfall 4. If the operational cost of potential software faults is large, it is highly imprudent not to perform off-nominal testing.

Summary: The Economic Value of Information

Let us step back a bit from these guidelines and pitfalls. Put simply, we are saying that, as software engineers:

"It is often worth paying for information because it helps us make better decisions."

If we look at the statement in a broader context, we can see that it is the primary reason why the software engineering field exists. It is what practically all of our software customers say when they decide to acquire one of our products: that it is worth paying for a management information system, a weather forecasting system, an air traffic control system, an inventory control system, etc., because it helps them make better decisions.

Usually, software engineers are *producers* of management information to be consumed by other people, but during the software life cycle we must also be *consumers* of management information to support our own decisions. As we come to appreciate the factors which make it attractive for us to pay for processed information which helps *us* make better decisions as software engineers, we will get a better appreciation for what our customers and users are looking for in the information processing systems we develop for *them*.

III. Software Cost Estimation

Introduction

All of the software engineering economics decision analysis techniques discussed above are only as good as the input data we can provide for them. For software decisions, the most critical and difficult of these inputs to provide are estimates of the cost of a proposed software project. In this section, we will summarize:

1) the major software cost estimation techniques available, and their relative strengths and difficulties;
2) algorithmic models for software cost estimation;
3) outstanding research issues in software cost estimation.

A. Major Software Cost Estimation Techniques

Table I summarizes the relative strengths and difficulties of the major software cost estimation methods in use today.

1) *Algorithmic Models:* These methods provide one or more algorithms which produce a software cost estimate as a function of a number of variables which are considered to be the major cost drivers.

2) *Expert Judgment:* This method involves consulting one or more experts, perhaps with the aid of an expert-consensus mechanism such as the Delphi technique.

3) *Analogy:* This method involves reasoning by analogy with one or more completed projects to relate their actual costs to an estimate of the cost of a similar new project.

4) *Parkinson:* A Parkinson principle ("work expands to fill the available volume") is invoked to equate the cost estimate to the available resources.

5) *Price-to-Win:* Here, the cost estimate is equated to the price believed necessary to win the job (or the schedule believed necessary to be first in the market with a new product, etc.).

6) *Top-Down:* An overall cost estimate for the project is derived from global properties of the software product. The total cost is then split up among the various components.

7) *Bottom-Up:* Each component of the software job is separately estimated, and the results aggregated to produce an estimate for the overall job.

The main conclusions that we can draw from Table I are the following.

- None of the alternatives is better than the others from all aspects.

- The Parkinson and price-to-win methods are unacceptable and do not produce satisfactory cost estimates.

242

TABLE I
STRENGTHS AND WEAKNESSES OF SOFTWARE COST-ESTIMATION METHODS

Method	Strengths	Weaknesses
Algorithmic model	• Objective, repeatable, analyzable formula • Efficient, good for sensitivity analysis • Objectively calibrated to experience	• Subjective inputs • Assessment of exceptional circumstances • Calibrated to past, not future
Expert judgment	• Assessment of representativeness, interactions, exceptional circumstances	• No better than participants • Biases, incomplete recall
Analogy	• Based on representative experience	• Representativeness of experience
Parkinson Price to win	• Correlates with some experience • Often gets the contract	• Reinforces poor practice • Generally produces large overruns
Top-down	• System level focus • Efficient	• Less detailed basis • Less stable
Bottom-up	• More detailed basis • More stable • Fosters individual commitment	• May overlook system level costs • Requires more effort

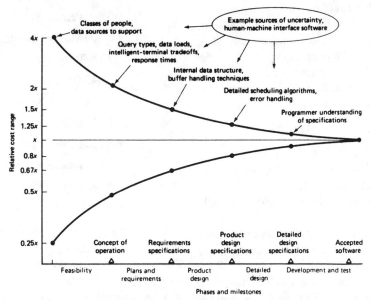

Fig. 3. Software cost estimation accuracy versus phase.

• The strengths and weaknesses of the other techniques are complementary (particularly the algorithmic models versus expert judgment and top-down versus bottom-up).

• Thus, in practice, we should use combinations of the above techniques, compare their results, and iterate on them where they differ.

Fundamental Limitations of Software Cost Estimation Techniques

Whatever the strengths of a software cost estimation technique, there is really no way we can expect the technique to compensate for our lack of definition or understanding of the software job to be done. Until a software specification is fully defined, it actually represents a range of software products, and a corresponding range of software development costs.

This fundamental limitation of software cost estimation technology is illustrated in Fig. 3, which shows the accuracy within which software cost estimates can be made, as a function of the software life-cycle phase (the horizontal axis), or of the level of knowledge we have of what the software is intended to do. This level of uncertainty is illustrated in Fig. 3

with respect to a human–machine interface component of the software.

When we first begin to evaluate alternative concepts for a new software application, the relative range of our software cost estimates is roughly a factor of four on either the high or low side.[4] This range stems from the wide range of uncertainty we have at this time about the actual nature of the product. For the human–machine interface component, for example, we do not know at this time what classes of people (clerks, computer specialists, middle managers, etc.) or what classes of data (raw or pre-edited, numerical or text, digital or analog) the system will have to support. Until we pin down such uncertainties, a factor of four in either direction is not surprising as a range of estimates.

The above uncertainties are indeed pinned down once we complete the feasibility phase and settle on a particular concept of operation. At this stage, the range of our estimates diminishes to a factor of two in either direction. This range is

---

4 These ranges have been determined subjectively, and are intended to represent 80 percent confidence limits, that is, "within a factor of four on either side, 80 percent of the time."

243

reasonable because we still have not pinned down such issues as the specific types of user query to be supported, or the specific functions to be performed within the microprocessor in the intelligent terminal. These issues will be resolved by the time we have developed a software requirements specification, at which point, we will be able to estimate the software costs within a factor of 1.5 in either direction.

By the time we complete and validate a product design specification, we will have resolved such issues as the internal data structure of the software product and the specific techniques for handling the buffers between the terminal microprocessor and the central processors on one side, and between the microprocessor and the display driver on the other. At this point, our software estimate should be accurate to within a factor of 1.25, the discrepancies being caused by some remaining sources of uncertainty such as the specific algorithms to be used for task scheduling, error handling, abort processing, and the like. These will be resolved by the end of the detailed design phase, but there will still be a residual uncertainty about 10 percent based on how well the programmers really understand the specifications to which they are to code. (This factor also includes such consideration as personnel turnover uncertainties during the development and test phases.)

B. Algorithmic Models for Software Cost Estimation

Algorithmic Cost Models: Early Development

Since the earliest days of the software field, people have been trying to develop algorithmic models to estimate software costs. The earliest attempts were simple rules of thumb, such as:

- on a large project, each software performer will provide an average of one checked-out instruction per man-hour (or roughly 150 instructions per man-month);
- each software maintenance person can maintain four boxes of cards (a box of cards held 2000 cards, or roughly 2000 instructions in those days of few comment cards).

Somewhat later, some projects began collecting quantitative data on the effort involved in developing a software product, and its distribution across the software life cycle. One of the earliest of these analyses was documented in 1956 in [8]. It indicated that, for very large operational software products on the order of 100 000 delivered source instructions (100 KDSI), that the overall productivity was more like 64 DSI/man-month, that another 100 KDSI of support-software would be required; that about 15 000 pages of documentation would be produced and 3000 hours of computer time consumed; and that the distribution of effort would be as follows:

Program Specs:	10 percent
Coding Specs:	30 percent
Coding:	10 percent
Parameter Testing:	20 percent
Assembly Testing:	30 percent

with an additional 30 percent required to produce operational specs for the system. Unfortunately, such data did not become well known, and many subsequent software projects went through a painful process of rediscovering them.

During the late 1950's and early 1960's, relatively little progress was made in software cost estimation, while the frequency and magnitude of software cost overruns was becoming critical to many large systems employing computers. In 1964, the U.S. Air Force contracted with System Development Corporation for a landmark project in the software cost estimation field. This project collected 104 attributes of 169 software projects and treated them to extensive statistical analysis. One result was the 1965 SDC cost model [41] which was the best possible statistical 13-parameter linear estimation model for the sample data:

$$MM = -33.63$$
$$+9.15 \text{ (Lack of Requirements) (0-2)}$$
$$+10.73 \text{ (Stability of Design) (0-3)}$$
$$+0.51 \text{ (Percent Math Instructions)}$$
$$+0.46 \text{ (Percent Storage/Retrieval Instructions)}$$
$$+0.40 \text{ (Number of Subprograms)}$$
$$+7.28 \text{ (Programming Language) (0-1)}$$
$$-21.45 \text{ (Business Application) (0-1)}$$
$$+13.53 \text{ (Stand-Alone Program) (0.1)}$$
$$+12.35 \text{ (First Program on Computer) (0-1)}$$
$$+58.82 \text{ (Concurrent Hardware Development) (0-1)}$$
$$+30.61 \text{ (Random Access Device Used) (0-1)}$$
$$+29.55 \text{ (Difference Host, Target Hardware) (0-1)}$$
$$+0.54 \text{ (Number of Personnel Trips)}$$
$$-25.20 \text{ (Developed by Military Organization) (0-1).}$$

The numbers in parentheses refer to ratings to be made by the estimator.

When applied to its database of 169 projects, this model produced a mean estimate of 40 MM and a standard deviation of 62 MM; not a very accurate predictor. Further, the application of the model is counterintuitive; a project with all zero ratings is estimated at minus 33 MM; changing language from a higher order language to assembly language adds 7 MM, independent of project size. The most conclusive result from the SDC study was that there were too many nonlinear aspects of software development for a linear cost-estimation model to work very well.

Still, the SDC effort provided a valuable base of information and insight for cost estimation and future models. Its cumulative distribution of productivity for 169 projects was a valuable aid for producing or checking cost estimates. The estimation rules of thumb for various phases and activities have been very helpful, and the data have been a major foundation for some subsequent cost models.

In the late 1960's and early 1970's, a number of cost models were developed which worked reasonably well for a certain restricted range of projects to which they were calibrated. Some of the more notable examples of such models are those described in [3], [54], [57].

The essence of the TRW Wolverton model [57] is shown in Fig. 4, which shows a number of curves of software cost per object instruction as a function of relative degree of difficulty

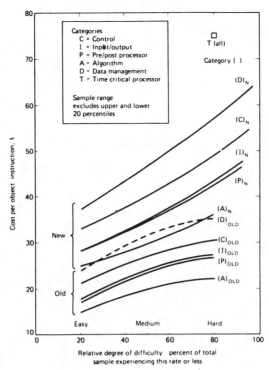

Fig. 4. TRW Wolverton model: Cost per object instruction versus relative degree of difficulty.

(0 to 100), novelty of the application (new or old), and type of project. The best use of the model involves breaking the software into components and estimating their cost individually. This, a 1000 object-instruction module of new data management software of medium (50 percent) difficulty would be costed at $46/instruction, or $46 000.

This model is well-calibrated to a class of near-real-time government command and control projects, but is less accurate for some other classes of projects. In addition, the model provides a good breakdown of project effort by phase and activity.

In the late 1970's, several software cost estimation models were developed which established a significant advance in the state of the art. These included the Putnam SLIM Model [44], the Doty Model [27], the RCA PRICE S model [22], the COCOMO model [11], the IBM-FSD model [53], the Boeing model [9], and a series of models developed by GRC [15]. A summary of these models, and the earlier SDC and Wolverton models, is shown in Table II, in terms of the size, program, computer, personnel, and project attributes used by each model to determine software costs. The first four of these models are discussed below.

The Putnam SLIM Model [44], [45]

The Putnam SLIM Model is a commercially available (from Quantitative Software Management, Inc.) software product based on Putnam's analysis of the software life cycle in terms of the Rayleigh distribution of project personnel level versus time. The basic effort macro-estimation model used in SLIM is

$$S_s = C_k K^{1/3} t_d^{4/3}$$

where

S_s = number of delivered source instructions
K = life-cycle effort in man-years
t_d = development time in years
C_k = a "technology constant."

Values of C_k typically range between 610 and 57 314. The current version of SLIM allows one to calibrate C_k to past projects or to past projects or to estimate it as a function of a project's use of modern programming practices, hardware constraints, personnel experience, interactive development, and other factors. The required development effort, DE, is estimated as roughly 40 percent of the life-cycle effort for large systems. For smaller systems, the percentage varies as a function of system size.

The SLIM model includes a number of useful extensions to estimate such quantities as manpower distribution, cash flow, major-milestone schedules, reliability levels, computer time, and documentation costs.

The most controversial aspect of the SLIM model is its tradeoff relationship between development effort K and between development time t_d. For a software product of a given size, the SLIM software equation above gives

$$K = \frac{\text{constant}}{t_d^4} .$$

For example, this relationship says that one can cut the cost of a software project in half, simply by increasing its development time by 19 percent (e.g., from 10 months to 12 months). Fig. 5 shows how the SLIM tradeoff relationship com-

TABLE II
FACTORS USED IN VARIOUS COST MODELS

GROUP	FACTOR	SDC, 1965	TRW, 1972	PUTNAM, SLIM	DOTY	RCA, PRICE S	IBM	BOEING, 1977	GRC, 1979	COCOMO	SOFCOST	DSN	JENSEN
SIZE ATTRIBUTES	SOURCE INSTRUCTIONS			X	X		X	X		X	X	X	X
	OBJECT INSTRUCTIONS	X	X		X	X							
	NUMBER OF ROUTINES	X				X					X		
	NUMBER OF DATA ITEMS						X			X	X		
	NUMBER OF OUTPUT FORMATS								X			X	
	DOCUMENTATION				X		X				X		X
	NUMBER OF PERSONNEL			X			X	X			X		X
PROGRAM ATTRIBUTES	TYPE	X	X	X	X	X	X	X			X		
	COMPLEXITY		X	X		X	X			X	X	X	X
	LANGUAGE	X		X				X	X		X	X	
	REUSE			X		X		X	X	X	X	X	X
	REQUIRED RELIABILITY			X		X				X	X		X
	DISPLAY REQUIREMENTS				X						X		X
COMPUTER ATTRIBUTES	TIME CONSTRAINT		X	X	X	X	X	X		X	X	X	X
	STORAGE CONSTRAINT			X	X	X	X			X	X	X	X
	HARDWARE CONFIGURATION	X				X							
	CONCURRENT HARDWARE DEVELOPMENT	X			X	X	X			X	X	X	X
	INTERFACING EQUIPMENT, S/W										X	X	
PERSONNEL ATTRIBUTES	PERSONNEL CAPABILITY			X		X	X			X	X	X	X
	PERSONNEL CONTINUITY						X				X		
	HARDWARE EXPERIENCE	X		X	X	X	X		X	X	X	X	X
	APPLICATIONS EXPERIENCE		X	X		X	X	X	X	X	X	X	X
	LANGUAGE EXPERIENCE			X		X	X		X	X	X	X	X
PROJECT ATTRIBUTES	TOOLS AND TECHNIQUES			X		X	X	X		X	X	X	X
	CUSTOMER INTERFACE	X					X				X	X	
	REQUIREMENTS DEFINITION	X			X		X				X	X	X
	REQUIREMENTS VOLATILITY	X			X	X	X		X	X	X	X	X
	SCHEDULE			X		X				X	X	X	X
	SECURITY						X				X	X	
	COMPUTER ACCESS			X	X		X	X		X	X	X	X
	TRAVEL/REHOSTING/MULTI-SITE	X			X	X				X	X	X	X
	SUPPORT SOFTWARE MATURITY									X		X	
CALIBRATION FACTOR				X		X				X			
EFFORT EQUATION	$MM_{NOM} = C(DSI)^X$, X =		1.0		1.047		0.91	1.0		1.05-1.2		1.0	1.2
SCHEDULE EQUATION	$t_D = C(MM)^X$, X =						0.35			0.32-0.38		0.356	0.333

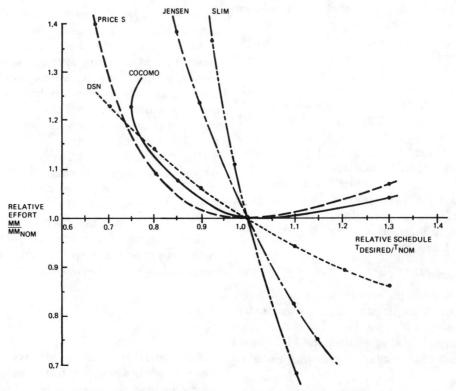

Fig. 5.   Comparative effort-schedule tradeoff relationships.

TABLE III
DOTY MODEL FOR SMALL PROGRAMS*

$$MM = 2.060 \, I^{1.047} \prod_{j=1}^{j=14} f_j$$

Factor	f_j	Yes	No
Special display	f_1	1.11	1.00
Detailed definition of operational requirements	f_2	1.00	1.11
Change to operational requirements	f_3	1.05	1.00
Real-time operation	f_4	1.33	1.00
CPU memory constraint	f_5	1.43	1.00
CPU time constraint	f_6	1.33	1.00
First software developed on CPU	f_7	1.92	1.00
Concurrent development of ADP hardware	f_8	1.82	1.00
Timeshare versus batch processing, in development	f_9	0.83	1.00
Developer using computer at another facility	f_{10}	1.43	1.00
Development at operational site	f_{11}	1.39	1.00
Development computer different than target computer	f_{12}	1.25	1.00
Development at more than one site	f_{13}	1.25	1.00
Programmer access to computer	f_{14}	Limited Unlimited	1.00 0.90

* Less than 10,000 source instructions

pares with those of other models; see [11, ch. 27] for further discussion of this issue.

On balance, the SLIM approach has provided a number of useful insights into software cost estimation, such as the Rayleigh-curve distribution for one-shot software efforts, the explicit treatment of estimation risk and uncertainty, and the cube-root relationship defining the minimum development time achievable for a project requiring a given amount of effort.

The Doty Model [27]

This model is the result of an extensive data analysis activity, including many of the data points from the SDC sample. A number of models of similar form were developed for different application areas. As an example, the model for general application is

$$MM = 5.288 \, (KDSI)^{1.047}, \quad \text{for } KDSI \geqslant 10$$

$$MM = 2.060 \, (KDSI)^{1.047} \left(\prod_{j=1}^{14} f_j \right), \quad \text{for } KDSI < 10.$$

The effort multipliers f_i are shown in Table III. This model has a much more appropriate functional form than the SDC model, but it has some problems with stability, as it exhibits a discontinuity at KDSI = 10, and produces widely varying estimates via the f factors (answering "yes" to "first software developed on CPU" adds 92 percent to the estimated cost).

The RCA PRICE S Model [22]

PRICE S is a commercially available (from RCA, Inc.) macro cost-estimation model developed primarily for embedded system applications. It has improved steadily with experience; earlier versions with a widely varying subjective complexity factor have been replaced by versions in which a number of computer, personnel, and project attributes are used to modulate the complexity rating.

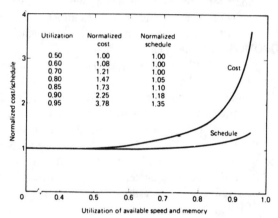

Fig. 6.   RCA PRICE S model: Effect of hardware constraints.

PRICE S has extended a number of cost-estimating relationships developed in the early 1970's such as the hardware constraint function shown in Fig. 6 [10]. It was primarily developed to handle military software projects, but now also includes rating levels to cover business applications.

PRICE S also provides a wide range of useful outputs on gross phase and activity distributions analyses, and monthly project cost-schedule-expected progress forecasts. Price S uses a two-parameter beta distribution rather than a Rayleigh curve to calculate development effort distribution versus calendar time.

PRICE S has recently added a software life-cycle support cost estimation capability called PRICE SL [34]. It involves the definition of three categories of support activities.

• *Growth:* The estimator specifies the amount of code to be added to the product. PRICE SL then uses its standard techniques to estimate the resulting life-cycle-effort distribution.

• *Enhancement:* PRICE SL estimates the fraction of the existing product which will be modified (the estimator may provide his own fraction), and uses its standard techniques to estimate the resulting life-cycle effort distribution.

• *Maintenance:* The estimator provides a parameter indicating the quality level of the developed code. PRICE SL uses this to estimate the effort required to eliminate remaining errors.

The COnstructive COst MOdel (COCOMO) [11]

The primary motivation for the COCOMO model has been to help people understand the cost consequences of the decisions they will make in commissioning, developing, and supporting a software product. Besides providing a software cost estimation capability, COCOMO therefore provides a great deal of material which explains exactly what costs the model is estimating, and why it comes up with the estimates it does. Further, it provides capabilities for sensitivity analysis and tradeoff analysis of many of the common software engineering decision issues.

COCOMO is actually a hierarchy of three increasingly detailed models which range from a single macro-estimation scaling model as a function of product size to a micro-estimation model with a three-level work breakdown structure and a set of phase-sensitive multipliers for each cost driver attribute. To provide a reasonably concise example of a current state of the art cost estimation model, the intermediate level of COCOMO is described below.

Intermediate COCOMO estimates the cost of a proposed software product in the following way.

1) A nominal development effort is estimated as a function of the product's size in delivered source instructions in thousands (KDSI) and the project's development mode.

2) A set of effort multipliers are determined from the product's ratings on a set of 15 cost driver attributes.

3) The estimated development effort is obtained by multiplying the nominal effort estimate by all of the product's effort multipliers.

4) Additional factors can be used to determine dollar costs, development schedules, phase and activity distributions, computer costs, annual maintenance costs, and other elements from the development effort estimate.

Step 1—Nominal Effort Estimation: First, Table IV is used to determine the project's development mode. Organic-mode projects typically come from stable, familiar, forgiving, relatively unconstrained environments, and were found in the COCOMO data analysis of 63 projects have a different scaling equation from the more ambitious, unfamiliar, unforgiving, tightly constrained embedded mode. The resulting scaling equations for each mode are given in Table V; these are used to determine the nominal development effort for the project in man-months as a function of the project's size in KDSI and the project's development mode.

For example, suppose we are estimating the cost to develop the microprocessor-based communications processing software for a highly ambitious new electronic funds transfer network with high reliability, performance, development schedule, and interface requirements. From Table IV, we determine that these characteristics best fit the profile of an embedded-mode project.

We next estimate the size of the product as 10 000 delivered

TABLE IV
COCOMO SOFTWARE DEVELOPMENT MODES

Feature	Mode		
	Organic	Semidetached	Embedded
Organizational understanding of product objectives	Thorough	Considerable	General
Experience in working with related software systems	Extensive	Considerable	Moderate
Need for software conformance with pre-established requirements	Basic	Considerable	Full
Need for software conformance with external interface specifications	Basic	Considerable	Full
Concurrent development of associated new hardware and operational procedures	Some	Moderate	Extensive
Need for innovative data processing architectures, algorithms	Minimal	Some	Considerable
Premium on early completion	Low	Medium	High
Product size range	<50 KDSI	<300 KDSI	All sizes
Examples	Batch data reduction	Most transaction processing systems	Large, complex transaction processing systems
	Scientific models	New OS, DBMS	
	Business models	Ambitious inventory, production control	Ambitious, very large OS
	Familiar OS, compiler	Simple command-control	Avionics
	Simple inventory, production control		Ambitious command-control

TABLE V
COCOMO NOMINAL EFFORT AND SCHEDULE EQUATIONS

DEVELOPMENT MODE	NOMINAL EFFORT	SCHEDULE
Organic	$(MM)_{NOM} = 3.2(KDSI)^{1.05}$	$TDEV = 2.5(MM_{DEV})^{0.38}$
Semidetached	$(MM)_{NOM} = 3.0(KDSI)^{1.12}$	$TDEV = 2.5(MM_{DEV})^{0.35}$
Embedded	$(MM)_{NOM} = 2.8(KDSI)^{1.20}$	$TDEV = 2.5(MM_{DEV})^{0.32}$

(KDSI = thousands of delivered source instructions)

source instructions, or 10 KDSI. From Table V, we then determine that the nominal development effort for this Embedded-mode project is

$$2.8(10)^{1.20} = 44 \text{ man-months (MM)}.$$

Step 2—Determine Effort Multipliers: Each of the 15 cost driver attributes in COCOMO has a rating scale and a set of effort multipliers which indicate by how much the nominal effort estimate must be multiplied to account for the project's having to work at its rating level for the attribute.

These cost driver attributes and their corresponding effort multipliers are shown in Table VI. The summary rating scales for each cost driver attribute are shown in Table VII, except for the complexity rating scale which is shown in Table VIII (expanded rating scales for the other attributes are provided in [11]).

The results of applying these tables to our microprocessor communications software example are shown in Table IX. The effect of a software fault in the electronic fund transfer system could be a serious financial loss; therefore, the project's RELY rating from Table VII is High. Then, from Table VI, the effort multiplier for achieving a High level of required reliability is 1.15, or 15 percent more effort than it would take to develop the software to a nominal level of required reliability.

TABLE VI

INTERMEDIATE COCOMO SOFTWARE DEVELOPMENT EFFORT
MULTIPLIERS

Cost Drivers	Ratings					
	Very Low	Low	Nominal	High	Very High	Extra High
Product Attributes						
RELY Required software reliability	.75	.88	1.00	1.15	1.40	
DATA Data base size		.94	1.00	1.08	1.16	
CPLX Product complexity	.70	.85	1.00	1.15	1.30	1.65
Computer Attributes						
TIME Execution time constraint			1.00	1.11	1.30	1.66
STOR Main storage constraint			1.00	1.06	1.21	1.56
VIRT Virtual machine volatility*		.87	1.00	1.15	1.30	
TURN Computer turnaround time		.87	1.00	1.07	1.15	
Personnel Attributes						
ACAP Analyst capability	1.46	1.19	1.00	.86	.71	
AEXP Applications experience	1.29	1.13	1.00	.91	.82	
PCAP Programmer capability	1.42	1.17	1.00	.86	.70	
VEXP Virtual machine experience*	1.21	1.10	1.00	.90		
LEXP Programming language experience	1.14	1.07	1.00	.95		
Project Attributes						
MODP Use of modern programming practices	1.24	1.10	1.00	.91	.82	
TOOL Use of software tools	1.24	1.10	1.00	.91	.83	
SCED Required development schedule	1.23	1.08	1.00	1.04	1.10	

* For a given software product, the underlying virtual machine is the complex of hardware and software (OS, DBMS, etc.) it calls on to accomplish its tasks

TABLE VII

COCOMO SOFTWARE COST DRIVER RATINGS

Cost Driver	Ratings					
	Very Low	Low	Nominal	High	Very High	Extra High
Product attributes						
RELY	Effect: slight inconvenience	Low, easily recoverable losses	Moderate, recoverable losses	High financial loss	Risk to human life	
DATA		$\frac{\text{DB bytes}}{\text{Prog. DSI}} < 10$	$10 \leqslant \frac{D}{P} < 100$	$100 \leqslant \frac{D}{P} < 1000$	$\frac{D}{P} \geqslant 1000$	
CPLX	See Table 8					
Computer attributes						
TIME			≤ 50% use of available execution time	70%	85%	95%
STOR			≤ 50% use of available storage	70%	85%	95%
VIRT		Major change every 12 months Minor: 1 month	Major: 6 months Minor: 2 weeks	Major: 2 months Minor: 1 week	Major: 2 weeks Minor: 2 days	
TURN		Interactive	Average turnaround <4 hours	4–12 hours	>12 hours	
Personnel attributes						
ACAP	15th percentile*	35th percentile	55th percentile	75th percentile	90th percentile	
AEXP	≤4 months experience	1 year	3 years	6 years	12 years	
PCAP	15th percentile*	35th percentile	55th percentile	75th percentile	90th percentile	
VEXP	≤1 month experience	4 months	1 year	3 years		
LEXP	≤1 month experience	4 months	1 year	3 years		
Project attributes						
MODP	No use	Beginning use	Some use	General use	Routine use	
TOOL	Basic microprocessor tools	Basic mini tools	Basic midi/maxi tools	Strong maxi programming, test tools	Add requirements, design, management, documentation tools	
SCED	75% of nominal	85%	100%	130%	160%	

* Team rating criteria: analysis (programming) ability, efficiency, ability to communicate and cooperate

TABLE VIII
COCOMO MODULE COMPLEXITY RATINGS VERSUS TYPE OF
MODULE

Rating	Control Operations	Computational Operations	Device-dependent Operations	Data Management Operations
Very low	Straightline code with a few non-nested SP$^\alpha$ operators: DOs, CASEs, IFTHENELSEs. Simple predicates	Evaluation of simple expressions: e.g., $A = B + C \cdot (D - E)$	Simple read, write statements with simple formats	Simple arrays in main memory
Low	Straightforward nesting of SP operators. Mostly simple predicates	Evaluation of moderate-level expressions, e.g., $D = SQRT(B^{**}2-4.^\cdot A^\cdot C)$	No cognizance needed of particular processor or I/O device characteristics. I/O done at GET/PUT level. No cognizance of overlap	Single file subsetting with no data structure changes, no edits, no intermediate files
Nominal	Mostly simple nesting. Some intermodule control. Decision tables	Use of standard math and statistical routines. Basic matrix/vector operations	I/O processing includes device selection, status checking and error processing	Multi-file input and single file output. Simple structural changes, simple edits
High	Highly nested SP operators with many compound predicates. Queue and stack control. Considerable intermodule control.	Basic numerical analysis: multivariate interpolation, ordinary differential equations. Basic truncation, roundoff concerns	Operations at physical I/O level (physical storage address translations; seeks, reads, etc). Optimized I/O overlap	Special purpose subroutines activated by data stream contents. Complex data restructuring at record level
Very high	Reentrant and recursive coding. Fixed-priority interrupt handling	Difficult but structured N.A.: near-singular matrix equations, partial differential equations	Routines for interrupt diagnosis, servicing, masking. Communication line handling	A generalized, parameter-driven file structuring routine. File building, command processing, search optimization
Extra high	Multiple resource scheduling with dynamically changing priorities. Microcode-level control	Difficult and unstructured N.A.: highly accurate analysis of noisy, stochastic data	Device timing-dependent coding, micro-programmed operations	Highly coupled, dynamic relational structures. Natural language data management

αSP = structured programming

Cost Driver	Situation	Rating	Effort Multiplier
RELY	Serious financial consequences of software faults	High	1.15
DATA	20,000 bytes	Low	0.94
CPLX	Communications processing	Very High	1.30
TIME	Will use 70% of available time	High	1.11
STOR	45K of 64K store (70%)	High	1.06
VIRT	Based on commercial microprocessor hardware	Nominal	1.00
TURN	Two-hour average turnaround time	Nominal	1.00
ACAP	Good senior analysts	High	0.86
AEXP	Three years	Nominal	1.00
PCAP	Good senior programmers	High	0.86
VEXP	Six months	Low	1.10
LEXP	Twelve months	Nominal	1.00
MODP	Most techniques in use over one year	High	0.91
TOOL	At basic minicomputer tool level	Low	1.10
SCED	Nine months	Nominal	1.00
	Effort adjustment factor (product of effort multipliers)		1.35

The effort multipliers for the other cost driver attributes are obtained similarly, except for the Complexity attribute, which is obtained via Table VIII. Here, we first determine that communications processing is best classified under device-dependent operations (column 3 in Table VIII). From this column, we determine that communication line handling typically has a complexity rating of Very High; from Table VI, then, we determine that its corresponding effort multiplier is 1.30.

Step 3—Estimate Development Effort: We then compute the estimated development effort for the microprocessor communications software as the nominal development effort (44 MM) times the product of the effort multipliers for the 15 cost driver attributes in Table IX (1.35, in Table IX). The resulting estimated effort for the project is then

(44 MM) (1.35) = 59 MM.

Step 4—Estimate Related Project Factors: COCOMO has additional cost estimating relationships for computing the resulting dollar cost of the project and for the breakdown of cost and effort by life-cycle phase (requirements, design, etc.) and by type of project activity (programming, test planning, management, etc.). Further relationships support the estimation of the project's schedule and its phase distribution. For example, the recommended development schedule can be obtained from the estimated development man-months via the embedded-mode schedule equation in Table V:

$$T_{DEV} = 2.5(59)^{0.32} = 9 \text{ months}.$$

As mentioned above, COCOMO also supports the most common types of sensitivity analysis and tradeoff analysis involved in scoping a software project. For example, from Tables VI and VII, we can see that providing the software developers with an interactive computer access capability (Low turnaround time) reduces the TURN effort multiplier from 1.00 to 0.87, and thus reduces the estimated project effort from 59 MM to

(59 MM) (0.87) = 51 MM.

The COCOMO model has been validated with respect to a sample of 63 projects representing a wide variety of business, scientific, systems, real-time, and support software projects. For this sample, Intermediate COCOMO estimates come within 20 percent of the actuals about 68 percent of the time (see Fig. 7). Since the residuals roughly follow a normal distribution, this is equivalent to a standard deviation of roughly 20 percent of the project actuals. This level of accuracy is representative of the current state of the art in software cost models. One can do somewhat better with the aid of a calibration coefficient (also a COCOMO option), or within a limited applications context, but it is difficult to improve significantly on this level of accuracy while the accuracy of software data collection remains in the "±20 percent" range.

A Pascal version of COCOMO is available for a nominal distribution charge from the Wang Institute, under the name WICOMO [18].

Recent Software Cost Estimation Models

Most of the recent software cost estimation models tend to follow the Doty and COCOMO models in having a nominal

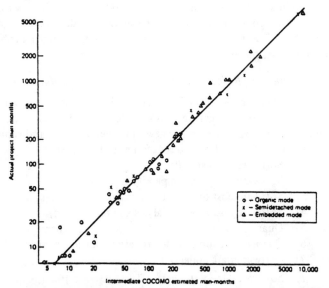

Fig. 7. Intermediate COCOMO estimates versus project actuals.

scaling equation of the form $MM_{NOM} = c(KDSI)^x$ and a set of multiplicative effort adjustment factors determined by a number of cost driver attribute ratings. Some of them use the Rayleigh curve approach to estimate distribution across the software life-cycle, but most use a more conservative effort/schedule tradeoff relation than the SLIM model. These aspects have been summarized for the various models in Table II and Fig. 5.

The Bailey-Basili meta-model [4] derived the scaling equation

$$MM_{NOM} = 3.5 + 0.73 (KDSI)^{1.16}$$

and used two additional cost driver attributes (methodology level and complexity) to model the development effort of 18 projects in the NASA-Goddard Software Engineering Laboratory to within a standard deviation of 15 percent. Its accuracy for other project situations has not been determined.

The Grumman SOFCOST Model [19] uses a similar but unpublished nominal effort scaling equation, modified by 30 multiplicative cost driver variables rated on a scale of 0 to 10. Table II includes a summary of these variables.

The Tausworthe Deep Space Network (DSN) model [50] uses a linear scaling equation ($MM_{NOM} = a(KDSI)^{1.0}$) and a similar set of cost driver attributes, also summarized in Table II. It also has a well-considered approach for determining the equivalent KDSI involved in adapting existing software within a new product. It uses the Rayleigh curve to determine the phase distribution of effort, but uses a considerably more conservative version of the SLIM effort-schedule tradeoff relationship (see Fig. 5).

The Jensen model [30], [31] is a commercially available model with a similar nominal scaling equation, and a set of cost driver attributes very similar to the Doty and COCOMO models (but with different effort multiplier ranges); see Table II. Some of the multiplier ranges in the Jensen model vary as functions of other factors; e.g., increasing access to computer resources widens the multiplier ranges on such cost drivers as personnel capability and use of software tools. It uses the Rayleigh curve for effort distribution, and a somewhat more conservative effort-schedule tradeoff relation than SLIM (see Fig. 5). As with the other commercial models, the Jensen model produces a number of useful outputs on resource expenditure rates, probability distributions on costs and schedules, etc.

C. Outstanding Research Issues in Software Cost Estimation

Although a good deal of progress has been made in software cost estimation, a great deal remains to be done. This section updates the state-of-the-art review published in [11], and summarizes the outstanding issues needing further research:
1) Software size estimation;
2) Software size and complexity metrics;
3) Software cost driver attributes and their effects;
4) Software cost model analysis and refinement;
5) Quantitative models of software project dynamics;
6) Quantitative models of software life-cycle evolution;
7) Software data collection.

1) Software Size Estimation: The biggest difficulty in using today's algorithmic software cost models is the problem of providing sound sizing estimates. Virtually every model requires an estimate of the number of source or object instructions to be developed, and this is an extremely difficult quantity to determine in advance. It would be most useful to have some formula for determining the size of a software product in terms of quantities known early in the software life cycle, such as the number and/or size of the files, input formats, reports, displays, requirements specification elements, or design specification elements.

Some useful steps in this direction are the function-point approach in [2] and the sizing estimation model of [29], both of which have given reasonably good results for small-to-medium sized business programs within a single data processing organization. Another more general approach is given by DeMarco in [17]. It has the advantage of basing its sizing estimates on the properties of specifications developed in conformance with DeMarco's paradigm models for software specifications and designs: number of functional primitives, data elements, input elements, output elements, states, transitions between states, relations, modules, data tokens, control tokens, etc. To date, however, there has been relatively little calibration of the formulas to project data. A recent IBM study [14] shows some correlation between the number of variables defined in a state-machine design representation and the product size in source instructions.

Although some useful results can be obtained on the software sizing problem, one should not expect too much. A wide range of functionality can be implemented beneath any given specification element or I/O element, leading to a wide range of sizes (recall the uncertainty ranges of this nature in Fig. 3). For example, two experiments, involving the use of several teams developing a software program to the same overall functional specification, yielded size ranges of factors of 3 to 5 between programs (see Table X).

The primary implication of this situation for practical software sizing and cost estimation is that *there is no royal road to software sizing.* This is no magic formula that will provide an easy and accurate substitute for the process of thinking through and fully understanding the nature of the software product to be developed. There are still a number of useful

TABLE X
SIZE RANGES OF SOFTWARE PRODUCTS PERFORMING SAME FUNCTION

Experiment	Product	No. of Teams	Size Range (source-instr.)
Weinberg & Schulman [55]	Simultaneous linear equations	6	33–165
Boehm, Gray, & Seewaldt [13]	Interactive cost model	7	1514–4606

things that one can do to improve the situation, including the following.
- Use techniques which explicitly recognize the ranges of variability in software sizing. The PERT estimation technique [56] is a good example.
- Understand the primary sources of bias in software sizing estimates. See [11, ch. 21].
- Develop and use a corporate memory on the nature and size of previous software products.

2) Software Size and Complexity Metrics: Delivered source instructions (DSI) can be faulted for being too low-level a metric for use in early sizing estimation. On the other hand, DSI can also be faulted for being too high-level a metric for precise software cost estimation. Various complexity metrics have been formulated to more accurately capture the relative information content of a program's instructions, such as the Halstead Software Science metrics [24], or to capture the relative control complexity of a program, such as the metrics formulated by McCabe in [39]. A number of variations of these metrics have been developed; a good recent survey of them is given in [26].

However, these metrics have yet to exhibit any practical superiority to DSI as a predictor of the relative effort required to develop software. Most recent studies [48], [32] show a reasonable correlation between these complexity metrics and development effort, but no better a correlation than that between DSI and development effort.

Further, the recent [25] analysis of the software science results indicates that many of the published software science "successes" were not as successful as they were previously considered. It indicates that much of the apparent agreement between software science formulas and project data was due to factors overlooked in the data analysis: inconsistent definitions and interpretations of software science quantities, unrealistic or inconsistent assumptions about the nature of the projects analyzed, overinterpretation of the significance of statistical measures such as the correlation coefficient, and lack of investigation of alternative explanations for the data. The software science use of psychological concepts such as the Stroud number have also been seriously questioned in [16].

The overall strengths and difficulties of software science are summarized in [47]. Despite the difficulties, some of the software science metrics have been useful in such areas as identifying error-prone modules. In general, there is a strong intuitive argument that more definitive complexity metrics will eventually serve as better bases for definitive software cost estimation than will DSI. Thus, the area continues to be an attractive one for further research.

3) Software Cost Driver Attributes and Their Effects: Most of the software cost models discussed above contain a selection of cost driver attributes and a set of coefficients, functions, or tables representing the effect of the attribute on software cost (see Table II). Chapters 24–28 of [11] contain summaries of the research to date on about 20 of the most significant cost driver attributes, plus statements of nearly 100 outstanding research issues in the area.

Since the publication of [11] in 1981, a few new results have appeared. Lawrence [35] provides an analysis of 278 business data processing programs which indicate a fairly uniform development rate in procedure lines of code per hour, some significant effects on programming rate due to batch turnaround time and level of experience, and relatively little effect due to use of interactive operation and modern programming practices (due, perhaps, to the relatively repetitive nature of the software jobs sampled). Okada and Azuma [42] analyzed 30 CAD/CAM programs and found some significant effects due to type of software, complexity, personnel skill level, and requirements volatility.

4) Software Cost Model Analysis and Refinement: The most useful comparative analysis of software cost models to date is the Thibodeau [52] study performed for the U.S. Air Force. This study compared the results of several models (the Wolverton, Doty, PRICE S, and SLIM models discussed earlier, plus models from the Boeing, SDC, Tecolote, and Aerospace corporations) with respect to 45 project data points from three sources.

Some generally useful comparative results were obtained, but the results were not definitive, as models were evaluated with respect to larger and smaller subsets of the data. Not too surprisingly, the best results were generally obtained using models with calibration coefficients against data sets with few points. In general, the study concluded that the models with calibration coefficients achieved better results, but that none of the models evaluated were sufficiently accurate to be used as a definitive Air Force software cost estimation model.

Some further comparative analyses are currently being conducted by various organizations, using the database of 63 software projects in [11], but to date none of these have been published.

In general, such evaluations play a useful role in model refinement. As certain models are found to be inaccurate in certain situations, efforts are made to determine the causes, and to refine the model to eliminate the sources of inaccuracy.

Relatively less activity has been devoted to the formulation, evaluation, and refinement of models to cover the effects of more advanced methods of software development (prototyping, incremental development, use of application generators, etc.) or to estimate other software-related life-cycle costs (conversion, maintenance, installation, training, etc.). An exception is the excellent work on software conversion cost estimation performed by the Federal Conversion Support Center [28]. An extensive model to estimate avionics software support costs using a weighted-multiplier technique has recently been developed [49]. Also, some initial experimental results have been obtained on the quantitative impact of prototyping in [13] and on the impact of very high level nonprocedural languages in [58]. In both studies, projects using prototyping and VHLL's were completed with significantly less effort.

5) Quantitative Models of Software Project Dynamics: Current software cost estimation models are limited in their ability to represent the internal dynamics of a software project, and to estimate how the project's phase distribution of effort and schedule will be affected by environmental or project management factors. For example, it would be valuable to have a model which would accurately predict the effort and schedule distribution effects of investing in more thorough design verification, of pursuing an incremental development strategy, of varying the staffing rate or experience mix, of reducing module size, etc.

Some current models assume a universal effort distribution, such as the Rayleigh curve [44] or the activity distributions in [57], which are assumed to hold for any type of project situation. Somewhat more realistic, but still limited are models with phase-sensitive effort multipliers such as PRICE S [22] and Detailed COCOMO [11].

Recently, some more realistic models of software project dynamics have begun to appear, although to date none of them have been calibrated to software project data. The Phister phase-by-phase model in [43] estimates the effort and schedule required to design, code, and test a software product as a function of such variables as the staffing level during each phase, the size of the average module to be developed, and such factors as interpersonal communications overhead rates and error detection rates. The Abdel Hamid–Madnick model [1], based on Forrester's System Dynamics world-view, estimates the time distribution of effort, schedule, and residual defects as a function of such factors as staffing rates, experience mix, training rates, personnel turnover, defect introduction rates, and initial estimation errors. Tausworthe [51] derives and calibrates alternative versions of the SLIM effort-schedule tradeoff relationship, using an intercommunication-overhead model of project dynamics. Some other recent models of software project dynamics are the Mitre SWAP model and the Duclos [21] total software life-cycle model.

6) Quantitative Models of Software Life-Cycle Evolution: Although most of the software effort is devoted to the software maintenance (or life-cycle support) phase, only a few significant results have been obtained to date in formulating quantitative models of the software life-cycle evolution process. Some basic studies by Belady and Lehman analyzed data on several projects and derived a set of fairly general "laws of program evolution" [7], [37]. For example, the first of these laws states:

> "A program that is used and that as an implementation of its specification reflects some other reality, undergoes continual change or becomes progressively less useful. The change or decay process continues until it is judged more cost effective to replace the system with a re-created version."

Some general quantitative support for these laws was obtained in several studies during the 1970's, and in more recent studies such as [33]. However, efforts to refine these general laws into a set of testable hypotheses have met with mixed results. For example, the Lawrence [36] statistical analysis of the Belady-Lahman data showed that the data supported an even stronger form of the first law ("systems grow in size over their useful life"); that one of the laws could not be formulated precisely enough to be tested by the data; and that the other three laws did not lead to hypotheses that were supported by the data.

However, it is likely that variant hypotheses can be found that are supported by the data (for example, the operating system data supports some of the hypotheses better than does the applications data). Further research is needed to clarify this important area.

7) Software Data Collection: A fundamental limitation to significant progress in software cost estimation is the lack of unambiguous, widely-used standard definitions for software data. For example, if an organization reports its "software development man-months," do these include the effort devoted to requirements analysis, to training, to secretaries, to quality assurance, to technical writers, to uncompensated overtime? Depending on one's interpretations, one can easily cause variations of over 20 percent (and often over a factor of 2) in the meaning of reported "software development man-months" between organizations (and similarly for "delivered instructions," "complexity," "storage constraint," etc.) Given such uncertainties in the ground data, it is not surprising that software cost estimation models cannot do much better than "within 20 percent of the actuals, 70 percent of the time."

Some progress towards clear software data definitions has been made. The IBM FSD database used in [53] was carefully collected using thorough data definitions, but the detailed data and definitions are not generally available. The NASA-Goddard Software Engineering Laboratory database [5], [6], [40] and the COCOMO database [11] provide both clear data definitions and an associated project database which are available for general use (and reasonably compatible). The recent Mitre SARE report [59] provides a good set of data definitions.

But there is still no commitment across organizations to establish and use a set of clear and uniform software data definitions. Until this happens, our progress in developing more precise software cost estimation methods will be severely limited.

IV. SOFTWARE ENGINEERING ECONOMICS BENEFITS AND CHALLENGES

This final section summarizes the benefits to software engineering and software management provided by a software engineering economics perspective in general and by software cost estimation technology in particular. It concludes with some observations on the major challenges awaiting the field.

Benefits of a Software Engineering Economics Perspective

The major benefit of an economic perspective on software engineering is that it provides a balanced view of candidate software engineering solutions, and an evaluation framework which takes account not only of the programming aspects of a situation, but also of the human problems of providing the best possible information processing service within a resource-limited environment. Thus, for example, the software engineering economics approach does not say, "we should use

these structured structures because they are mathematically elegant" or "because they run like the wind" or "because they are part of the structured revolution." Instead, it says "we should use these structured structures because they provide people with more benefits in relation to their costs than do other approaches." And besides the framework, of course, it also provides the techniques which help us to arrive at this conclusion.

Benefits of Software Cost Estimation Technology

The major benefit of a good software cost estimation model is that it provides a clear and consistent universe of discourse within which to address a good many of the software engineering issues which arise throughout the software life cycle. It can help people get together to discuss such issues as the following.

• Which and how many features should we put into the software product?

• Which features should we put in first?

• How much hardware should we acquire to support the software product's development, operation, and maintenance?

• How much money and how much calendar time should we allow for software development?

• How much of the product should we adapt from existing software?

• How much should we invest in tools and training?

Further, a well-defined software cost estimation model can help avoid the frequent misinterpretations, underestimates, overexpectations, and outright buy-ins which still plague the software field. In a good cost-estimation model, there is no way of reducing the estimated software cost without changing some objectively verifiable property of the software project. This does not make it impossible to create an unachievable buy-in, but it significantly raises the threshold of credibility.

A related benefit of software cost estimation technology is that it provides a powerful set of insights on how a software organization can improve its productivity. Many of a software cost model's cost-driver attributes are management controllables: use of software tools and modern programming practices, personnel capability and experience, available computer speed, memory, and turnaround time, software reuse. The cost model helps us determine how to adjust these management controllables to increase productivity, and further provides an estimate of how much of a productivity increase we are likely to achieve with a given level of investment. For more information on this topic, see [11, ch. 33], [12] and the recent plan for the U.S. Department of Defense Software Initiative [20].

Finally, software cost estimation technology provides an absolutely essential foundation for software project planning and control. Unless a software project has clear definitions of its key milestones and realistic estimates of the time and money it will take to achieve them, there is no way that a project manager can tell whether his project is under control or not. A good set of cost and schedule estimates can provide realistic data for the PERT charts, work breakdown structures, manpower schedules, earned value increments, etc., necessary to establish management visibility and control.

Note that this opportunity to improve management visibility and control requires a complementary management commitment to define and control the reporting of data on software progress and expenditures. The resulting data are therefore worth collecting simply for their management value in comparing plans versus achievements, but they can serve another valuable function as well: they provide a continuing stream of calibration data for evolving a more accurate and refined software cost estimation models.

Software Engineering Economics Challenges

The opportunity to improve software project management decision making through improved software cost estimation, planning, data collection, and control brings us back full-circle to the original objectives of software engineering economics: to provide a better quantitative understanding of how software people make decisions in resource-limited situations.

The more clearly we as software engineers can understand the quantitative and economic aspects of our decision situations, the more quickly we can progress from a pure seat-of-the-pants approach on software decisions to a more rational approach which puts all of the human and economic decision variables into clear perspective. Once these decision situations are more clearly illuminated, we can then study them in more detail to address the deeper challenge: achieving a quantitative understanding of how people work together in the software engineering process.

Given the rather scattered and imprecise data currently available in the software engineering field, it is remarkable how much progress has been made on the software cost estimation problem so far. But, there is not much further we can go until better data becomes available. The software field cannot hope to have its Kepler or its Newton until it has had its army of Tycho Brahes, carefully preparing the well-defined observational data from which a deeper set of scientific insights may be derived.

REFERENCES

[1] T. K. Abdel-Hamid and S. E. Madnick, "A model of software project management dynamics," in *Proc. IEEE COMPSAC 82*, Nov. 1982, pp. 539–554.

[2] A. J. Albrecht, "Measuring Application Development Productivity," in *SHARE-GUIDE*, 1979, pp. 83–92.

[3] J. D. Aron, "Estimating resources for large programming systems." NATO Sci. Committee, Rome, Italy, Oct. 1969.

[4] J. J. Bailey and V. R. Basili, "A meta-model for software development resource expenditures," in *Proc. 5th Int. Conf. Software Eng.*, IEEE/ACM/NBS, Mar. 1981, pp. 107–116.

[5] V. R. Basili, "Tutorial on models and metrics for software and engineering," IEEE Cat. EHO-167-7, Oct. 1980.

[6] V. R. Basili and D. M. Weiss, "A methodology for collecting valid software engineering data," Univ. Maryland Technol. Rep. TR-1235, Dec. 1982.

[7] L. A. Belady and M. M. Lehman, "Characteristics of large systems," in *Research Directions in Software Technology*, P. Wegner, Ed. Cambridge, MA: MIT Press, 1979.

[8] H. D. Benington, "Production of large computer programs," in *Proc. ONR Symp. Advanced Programming Methods for Digital Computers*, June 1956, pp. 15–27.

[9] R. K. D. Black, R. P. Curnow, R. Katz, and M. D. Gray, "BCS software production data," Boeing Comput. Services, Inc., Final Tech. Rep., RADC-TR-77-116, NTIS AD-A039852, Mar. 1977.

[10] B. W. Boehm, "Software and its impact: A quantitative assessment," *Datamation*, pp. 48–59, May 1973.

[11] ——, *Software Engineering Economics*. Englewood Cliffs, NJ: Prentice-Hall, 1981.

[12] B. W. Boehm, J. F. Elwell, A. B. Pyster, E. D. Stuckle, and R. D. Williams, "The TRW software productivity system," in *Proc. IEEE 6th Int. Conf. Software Eng.*, Sept. 1982.

[13] B. W. Boehm, T. E. Gray, and T. Seewaldt, "Prototyping vs. specifying: A multi-project experiment," *IEEE Trans. Software Eng.*, to be published.

[14] R. N. Britcher and J. E. Gaffney, "Estimates of software size from state machine designs," in *Proc. NASA-Goddard Software Eng. Workshop*, Dec. 1982.

[15] W. M. Carriere and R. Thibodeau, "Development of a logistics software cost estimating technique for foreign military sales," General Res. Corp., Rep. CR-3-839, June 1979.

[16] N. S. Coulter, "Software science and cognitive psychology," *IEEE Trans. Software Eng.*, pp. 166–171, Mar. 1983.

[17] T. DeMarco, *Controlling Software Projects*. New York: Yourdon, 1982.

[18] M. Demshki, D. Ligett, B. Linn, G. McCluskey, and R. Miller, "Wang Institute cost model (WICOMO) tool user's manual," Wang Inst. Graduate Studies, Tyngsboro, MA, June 1982.

[19] H. F. Dircks, "SOFCOST: Grumman's software cost eliminating model," in *IEEE NAECON 1981*, May 1981.

[20] L. E. Druffel, "Strategy for DoD software initiative," RADC/DACS, Griffiss AFB, NY, Oct. 1982.

[21] L. C. Duclos, "Simulation model for the life-cycle of a software product: A quality assurance approach," Ph.D. dissertation, Dep. Industrial and Syst. Eng., Univ. Southern California, Dec. 1982.

[22] F. R. Freiman and R. D. Park, "PRICE software model—Version 3: An overview," in *Proc. IEEE-PINY Workshop on Quantitative Software Models*, IEEE Cat. TH0067-9, Oct. 1979, pp. 32–41.

[23] R. Goldberg and H. Lorin, *The Economics of Information Processing*. New York: Wiley, 1982.

[24] M. H. Halstead, *Elements of Software Science*. New York: Elsevier, 1977.

[25] P. G. Hamer and G. D. Frewin, "M. H. Halstead's software science—A critical examination," in *Proc. IEEE 6th Int. Conf. Software Eng.*, Sept. 1982, pp. 197–205.

[26] W. Harrison, K. Magel, R. Kluczney, and A. DeKock, "Applying software complexity metrics to program maintenance," *Computer*, pp. 65–79, Sept. 1982.

[27] J. R. Herd, J. N. Postak, W. E. Russell, and K. R. Stewart, "Software cost estimation study—Study results," Doty Associates, Inc., Rockville, MD, Final Tech. Rep. RADC-TR-77-220, vol. 1 (of two), June 1977.

[28] C. Houtz and T. Buschbach, "Review and analysis of conversion cost-estimating techniques," GSA Federal Conversion Support Center, Falls Church, VA, Rep. GSA/FCSC-81/001, Mar. 1981.

[29] M. Itakura and A. Takayanagi, " A model for estimating program size and its evaluation," in *Proc. IEEE 6th Software Eng.*, Sept. 1982, pp. 104–109.

[30] R. W. Jensen, "An improved macrolevel software development resource estimation model," in *Proc. 5th ISPA Conf.*, Apr. 1983, pp. 88–92.

[31] R. W. Jensen and S. Lucas, "Sensitivity analysis of the Jensen software model," in *Proc. 5th ISPA Conf.*, Apr. 1983, pp. 384–389.

[32] B. A. Kitchenham, "Measures of programming complexity," *ICL Tech. J.*, pp. 298–316, May 1981.

[33] ——, "Systems evolution dynamics of VME/B," *ICL Tech. J.*, pp. 43–57, May 1982.

[34] W. W. Kuhn, "A software lifecycle case study using the PRICE model," in *Proc. IEEE NAECON*, May 1982.

[35] M. J. Lawrence, "Programming methodology, organizational environment, and programming productivity," *J. Syst. Software*, pp. 257–270, Sept. 1981.

[36] ——, "An examination of evolution dynamics," in *Proc. IEEE 6th Int. Conf. Software Eng.*, Sept. 1982, pp. 188–196.

[37] M. M. Lehman, "Programs, life cycles, and laws of software evolution," *Proc. IEEE*, pp. 1060–1076, Sept. 1980.

[38] R. D. Luce and H. Raiffa, *Games and Decisions*. New York: Wiley, 1957.

[39] T. J. McCabe, "A complexity measure," *IEEE Trans. Software Eng.*, pp. 308–320, Dec. 1976.

[40] F. E. McGarry, "Measuring software development technology: What have we learned in six years," in *Proc. NASA-Goddard Software Eng. Workshop*, Dec. 1982.

[41] E. A. Nelson, "Management handbook for the estimation of computer programming costs," Syst. Develop. Corp., AD-A648750, Oct. 31, 1966.

[42] M. Okada and M. Azuma, "Software development estimation study—A model from CAD/CAM system development experiences," in *Proc. IEEE COMPSAC 82*, Nov. 1982, pp. 555–564.

[43] M. Phister, Jr., "A model of the software development process," *J. Syst. Software*, pp. 237–256, Sept. 1981.

[44] L. H. Putnam, "A general empirical solution to the macro software sizing and estimating problem," *IEEE Trans. Software Eng.*, pp. 345–361, July 1978.

[45] L. H. Putnam and A. Fitzsimmons, "Estimating software costs," *Datamation*, pp. 189–198, Sept. 1979; continued in *Datamation*, pp. 171–178, Oct. 1979 and pp. 137–140, Nov. 1979.

[46] L.H. Putnam, "The real economics of software development," in *The Economics of Information Processing*, R. Goldberg and H. Lorin. New York: Wiley, 1982.

[47] V. Y. Shen, S. D. Conte, and H. E. Dunsmore, "Software science revisited: A critical analysis of the theory and its empirical support," *IEEE Trans. Software Eng.*, pp. 155–165, Mar. 1983.

[48] T. Sunohara, A. Takano, K. Uehara, and T. Ohkawa, "Program complexity measure for software development management," in *Proc. IEEE 5th Int. Conf. Software Eng.*, Mar. 1981, pp. 100–106.

[49] SYSCON Corp., "Avionics software support cost model," USAF Avionics Lab., AFWAL-TR-1173, Feb. 1, 1983.

[50] R. C. Tausworthe, "Deep space network software cost estimation model," Jet Propulsion Lab., Pasadena, CA, 1981.

[51] ——, "Staffing implications of software productivity models," in *Proc. 7th Annu. Software Eng. Workshop*, NASA/Goddard, Greenbelt, MD, Dec. 1982.

[52] R. Thibodeau, "An evaluation of software cost estimating models," General Res. Corp., Rep. T10-2670, Apr. 1981.

[53] C. E. Walston and C. P. Felix, "A method of programming measurement and estimation," *IBM Syst. J.*, vol. 16, no. 1, pp. 54–73, 1977.

[54] G. F. Weinwurm, Ed., *On the Management of Computer Programming*. New York: Auerbach, 1970.

[55] G. M. Weinberg and E. L. Schulman, "Goals and performance in computer programming," *Human Factors*, vol. 16, no. 1, pp. 70–77, 1974.

[56] J. D. Wiest and F. K. Levy, *A Management Guide to PERT/CPM*. Englewood Cliffs, NJ: Prentice-Hall, 1977.

[57] R. W. Wolverton, "The cost of developing large-scale software," *IEEE Trans. Comput.*, pp. 615–636, June 1974.

[58] E. Harel and E. R. McLean, "The effects of using a nonprocedural computer language on programmer productivity," UCLA Inform. Sci. Working Paper 3-83, Nov. 1982.

[59] R. L. Dumas, "Final report: Software acquisition resource expenditure (SARE) data collection methodology," MITRE Corp., MTR 9031, Sept. 1983.

Barry W. Boehm received the B.A. degree in mathematics from Harvard University, Cambridge, MA, in 1957 and the M.A. and Ph.D. degrees from the University of California, Los Angeles, in 1961 and 1964, respectively.

From 1978 to 1979 he was a Visiting Professor of Computer Science at the University of Southern California. He is currently a Visiting Professor at the University of California, Los Angeles, and Chief Engineer of TRW's Software Information Systems Division. He was previously Head of the Information Sciences Department at The Rand Corporation, and Director of the 1971 Air Force CCIP-85 study. His responsibilities at TRW include direction of TRW's internal software R&D program, of contract software technology projects, of the TRW software development policy and standards program, of the TRW Software Cost Methodology Program, and the TRW Software Productivity Program. His most recent book is *Software Engineering Economics*, by Prentice-Hall.

Dr. Boehm is a member of the IEEE Computer Society and the Association for Computing Machinery, and an Associate Fellow of the American Institute of Aeronautics and Astronautics.

A Guide for Preparing Software Project Management Plans

Richard E. Fairley
George Mason University

1: Introduction

This guide describes the structure and contents of software project management plans (SPMP). It identifies those essential elements that should appear, and optional elements that may appear, in all SPMPs. The guide is intended to assist a project manager, software engineer, or student in the selection, organization, and presentation of planning information needed by managers, customers, system engineers, software engineers, and members of a software project team.

This guide is primarily concerned with management plans for software projects; however, it can be used to plan any project for developing or modifying systems that include computers, other hardware, software, people, and procedures. If the guide is used to prepare the plan for a total system, the resulting plan should be called a *system* project management plan.

The guide is generic in nature; it can be applied to commercial, scientific, or military software projects, both real-time and batch-oriented. Applicability of the guide is not restricted by the size, complexity, or criticality of the software product. The guide can be used to produce a SPMP for any segment of a product lifecycle, including (part or all of) the initial product development effort, a major product enhancement, or ongoing maintenance activities.

This document does not provide any guidance for development of customer requirements, nor does it recommend any particular product development strategy, design methodology, tool, or technique. However, this guide does require that the technical methods used on a project be specified in the SPMP for that project.

The remainder of this guide is organized as follows: Section 2 provides an introduction to the concepts and terminology of software project planning; Section 3 provides an overview of software project management plans; Section 4 presents a detailed description of the various components of a project plan; and the Appendix contains definitions of terms used throughout this document.

2: Concepts and Terminology of Software Project Planning

A *software project* encompasses all of the technical and managerial efforts required to deliver to a *customer* a product (a set of products) that satisfies the terms of the *project agreement*. These project efforts must be planned, initiated, monitored, and controlled to ensure adherence to schedule, budget, and quality criteria. An informal discussion of this viewpoint follows. Precise definitions of the italicized terms used throughout this discussion are provided in the Appendix.

A *software project* has a specific duration, consumes resources, and produces tangible *work products*. Some of the work products are delivered to the customer; these are the *project deliverables*. The customer is the individual or organization that specifies the product requirements and accepts delivery of the resulting *project deliverables*. The term "customer," as used here, is not meant to imply a financial transaction between the developer and the customer.

The project agreement is a document, or set of documents, that defines the scope, duration, cost, and deliverables for the project. A project agreement typically takes the form of a contract, a statement of work, a systems engineering specification, a user requirements specification, a business plan, or a project charter. Specifications for the project deliverables should include the exact items, quantities, delivery dates, and delivery locations required to satisfy the terms of the project agreement. The project deliverables may be self-contained or they may be part of a larger system.

From the manager's point of view, the various efforts required to complete a software project can be categorized as project *functions, activities,* and *tasks*. A task is the smallest unit of management accountability; it is thus the atomic unit of planning and tracking for a software project. Tasks have finite durations, consume resources, and produce tangible results (typically a document or a code module) that can be assessed according to some predetermined acceptance criteria.

The exact nature of the work to be done in completing a task is specified in a *work package*, which typically consists of a package name, a description of the work to be done, the preconditions for initiating the task, the estimated duration of the task, required resources (e.g., numbers and types of personnel, machines, software tools, travel, secretarial support), the work products to be produced, the acceptance criteria for the work products, the risks, and the completion criteria for the task.

A task is successfully completed when the completion criteria for the task are satisfied; the completion criteria include (and may be identical to) the acceptance criteria for the work products produced by the task. A work product might be (some part of) the *project plan*, or the functional requirements, or a design document, a source code module, test plans, users' manual, meeting minutes, memos, schedules, budgets, or problem reports.

The appropriate size for a task is somewhat problematic. During initial project planning, tasks are by necessity large units of work. Because tasks are the atomic units of management planning and control, large tasks must be decomposed to sizes that permit adequate monitoring of the project. It may be impossible to decompose these large tasks without thorough analysis and some preliminary design work on the product, but eventually each task must be decomposed so that a well-defined work assignment exists for each worker assigned to each task. On the other hand, a task should be large enough to avoid micro-management of the project and to allow some autonomy on the part of the task workers.

The proper size for a task depends on the nature of the work to be done, the confidence of the manager that the task can be completed on schedule and within budget, and the criticality of the task to the overall success of the project. A typical level of task decomposition is for each task to provide a job assignment for one or two workers for a duration of one week to one month.

Related tasks are usually grouped into hierarchical sets of activities and functions. An activity is a major unit of work (e.g., preliminary design and integration testing) that culminates in achievement of a major *project milestone*. A project function is an activity that spans the entire duration of the project (e.g., configuration management or quality assurance). Activities and functions can have subactivities; tasks are (and must be) the lowest-level elements in the hierarchy. The grouping of related tasks into functions and activities imposes a hierarchial structure on a project that allows separation of concerns and provides a rationale for organizing the project team. The hierarchical relationships among activities, functions, and tasks are often depicted using a work breakdown structure.

In addition to hierarchical relations, activities and tasks (work elements) also have precedence relations. Typically, a work element cannot be initiated until other work elements have been completed, and a completed work element may be a precondition to the initiation of other work elements. Precedence relations can be depicted using precedence charts, PERT charts, and critical path charts.

Completed activities and tasks result in project milestones. A task should not have externally visible milestones, other than task completion; such a composite task should be treated as a project activity and the original tasks should become the subtasks of the activity. The hierarchical and precedence relations among tasks must be planned, tracked, and reorganized as evolving circumstances may dictate.

A project milestone is a scheduled event used to measure progress (e.g., successful preliminary design review or integration testing completed). Achievement of a milestone usually results in one or more *baselines*, which are work products that have been formally reviewed and accepted. Baselined work products are placed under change control and can only be changed through formal change control procedures. A baseline (e.g., design document or test plan) often forms the basis for further work.

A *process model* for a software project depicts the relationships of the project functions, activities, and tasks to the milestones, baselines, reviews, and flow of work products. Examples of process models include the waterfall model, the spiral model, the incremental model, and the functional model. The process model for a software project must explicitly incorporate project initiation and project termination activities.

3: An Overview of Software Project Management Plans

The software project management plan (SPMP) is the controlling document for a software project. It specifies the technical and managerial approaches to be used in developing a software product or the software component of a larger product. Related plans for the project (e.g., configuration management, quality assurance, validation and verification) are considered to be part of the SPMP and they must be incorporated, either directly or by reference, in the SPMP. The plan must specify the managerial and technical functions, activities, and tasks in sufficient detail to ensure that the resulting software product will satisfy the needs, software requirements, and contractual agreements of the project.

The SPMP is the companion document to the statement of customer requirements. In practice, development of the initial version and subsequent updates of these two documents must proceed in parallel, with iterations, tradeoffs, and checks for consistency being made between the documents. Typically, parts (sometimes all) of these documents are incorporated into the project agreement.

A SPMP is the project manager's statement of understanding with the development organization and the project team members. The project agreement (which includes some or all of the SPMP) forms the statement of understanding between the project manager and the customer. Initial development and periodic updating of the SPMP is thus the manager's tool for establishing and maintaining communication with the customer, the development organization, and the project team members.

The format of a SPMP is presented in Table 1. The various sections and subsections of a SPMP should be ordered in the prescribed sequence; however, initial development and subsequent updating of the SPMP need not proceed in the indicated sequence. As indicated in Table 1, the essential elements of a SPMP are:

0. A title page, a revision sheet that contains the history of updates to the SPMP, a preface that describes the scope and purpose of the SPMP, a table of contents, and lists of figures and tables.

1. An introductory section that describes the project and the SPMP. Items to be included in the Introduction are a brief overview of the project; a list of project deliverables; plans for producing both scheduled and unscheduled updates to the SPMP; reference materials for the SPMP; and definitions, acronyms, and abbreviations used throughout the document.

2. A section that describes organizational aspects of the project. Items to be included are the process model for the project; the internal organizational structure of the project; the interfaces between the project and other organizational entities; and the major areas of functional responsibilities for the project.

3. A section that describes the management processes used to conduct the project. Items of importance include objectives and priorities for the project; risk management procedures; the monitoring and controlling mechanisms to be used; and the staffing plan.

4. A section describing the technical processes to be used in the project. Issues of importance include the technical methods, tools, and techniques to be utilized; the software documentation plan; and plans for the project support functions, such as configuration management, quality assurance, and verification and validation.

5. A section describing the work elements, schedule, and budget. Items to be included in this section include a description of the work packages; dependencies among work packages; resource requirements for the project; allocation of the budget and schedule to the various work elements; and a project schedule.

Certain other components may be included in additional sections of the SPMP or distributed throughout the SPMP as appropriate. Additional areas of importance on a particular project might include a training plan for product users, a system installation plan, or a product maintenance plan.

An index of the key terms and acronyms used throughout the SPMP is recommended to improve usability of the SPMP. Appendices can be used to provide supporting details that would detract from the SPMP if included in the body of the SPMP.

Table 1: Format of a Software Project Management Plan

Title Page
Revision Sheet
Preface
Table of Contents
List of Figures
List of Tables

1. Introduction
1.1 Project Overview
1.2 Project Deliverables
1.3 Evolution of the SPMP
1.4 Reference Materials
1.5 Definitions and Acronyms

2. Project Organization
2.1 Process Model
2.2 Organizational Structure
2.3 Organizational Boundaries and Interfaces
2.4 Project Responsibilities

3. Managerial Process
3.1 Management Objectives and Priorities
3.2 Assumptions, Dependencies, and Constraints
3.3 Risk Management
3.4 Monitoring and Controlling Mechanisms
3.5 Staffing Plan

4. Technical Process
4.1 Methods, Tools, and Techniques
4.2 Software Documentation
4.3 Project Support Functions

5. Work Elements, Schedule, and Budget
5.1 Work Packages
5.2 Dependencies
5.3 Resource Requirements
5.4 Budget and Resource Allocation
5.5 Schedule

Additional Components
Index
Appendices

4: Detailed Description of Software Project Management Plans

This section of the guide describes each of the essential elements in a software project management plan. This presentation follows the format presented in Table 1.

4.0: Front Matter

The front matter of a SPMP consists of the title page, revision sheet, preface, table of contents, and indexes for the figures and tables contained in the SPMP.

The Title Page should contain a title and a revision notice sufficient to uniquely identify the document. A separate revision sheet should contain the version number of the current document, the date of release, approval signature(s), a list of pages that have been changed in the current version of the plan, and a list of version numbers and dates of release for all previous versions of the SPMP.

The Preface should describe the purpose of the SPMP, indicate the scope of activities covered by the SPMP, and identify the intended audience for the SPMP.

The Table of Contents and the Lists of Figures and Tables should provide the titles and page numbers for section headings, subsection headings, and figures and tables.

4.1: Introduction (Section 1 of the SPMP)

This section of the SPMP contains the project overview, project deliverables, plan of evolution for the SPMP, references, and definitions and acronyms.

4.1.1: Project Overview

The Project Overview provides an executive summary of the software project. It contains a description of the project, a product summary, and a summary of the essential elements of the SPMP.

The project description should state the reasons for the project, the scope of activities encompassed by the project, and the expected outcome of the project.

The product summary should be a brief overview (1 to 2 pages) of the product to be delivered. The summary should identify by name the software product(s) to be delivered (e.g., Host DBMS, R2 Operating System, AJAX Scheduling Program, etc.), briefly explain the objectives and benefits of the product, and present the major functional and performance capabilities of the product (and what the product will not do, if important). The product summary should be consistent with similar statements in the project agreement (requirements specifications, contract, statement of work). This product summary should not replace, override, augment, or in any way be construed as an official statement of product requirements or contractual obligations.

The remainder of the Project Overview should summarize the essential elements of the SPMP, including the major work activities and work products, the major project milestones, the required resources, and the master schedule and budget.

4.1.2: Project Deliverables

The subsection that contains Project Deliverables should list all of the items to be delivered to the customer, the delivery dates, delivery locations, and quantities required to satisfy the terms of the project agreement. This list of deliverables should not be construed as an official statement of project requirements. Reference to the project agreement, which contains the official product requirements and list of deliverables, should be provided in this section of the SPMP.

4.1.3: Evolution of the SPMP

The subsection on Evolution of the SPMP should describe plans for producing both scheduled and unscheduled updates to the SPMP. Methods of disseminating the updates should be specified. Mechanisms for placing the initial version of the SPMP under change control, and mechanisms for controlling changes to subsequent versions of the SPMP, should be described.

4.1.4: Reference Materials

The subsection on Reference Materials should provide a complete list of documents and other sources of information referenced in the SPMP. Each referenced document should be identified by title, report number (if applicable), date, author, and publishing organization. Other sources of information, such as electronic files, should be identified in an unambiguous manner using identifiers that include date and version number. The reference materials should also include any standards, policies, procedures, or guidelines that apply to the project. Any deviations from these controlling documents should be identified and justifications for the deviations provided.

4.1.5: Definitions and Acronyms

The subsection on Definitions and Acronyms should provide definitions of terms, acronyms, and abbreviations required to properly interpret the SPMP. The definitions may be provided by reference to one or more appendices in the SPMP, or by reference to other documents.

4.2: Project Organization (Section 2 of the SPMP)

This section of the SPMP specifies the process model for the project, describes the organizational structure of the project, identifies the organizational interfaces between the project and other organizational entities, and defines areas of project responsibilities.

4.2.1: Process Model

The Process Model for a project defines the relationships of the project functions, activities, and tasks to the major milestones, baselines, reviews, work products, project deliverables, and sign-offs that span the duration of the project. Process models are usually defined using a combination of graphical and textual notations. The process model should include project initiation and termination phases.

4.2.2: Organizational Structure

The subsection on Organizational Structure describes the internal management structure of the project. Graphical devices such as organizational charts, matrix diagrams, and work breakdown structures can be used to depict the organizational structure of a software project.

4.2.3: Organizational Boundaries and Interfaces

The subsection on Organizational Boundaries and Interfaces describes the administrative and managerial boundaries between the project and other entities such as the parent organization, the customer organization, subcontracted organizations, and other organizational entities that interact with the project. In addition, this section should specify the administrative and managerial interfaces between the project and the project support functions (e.g., configuration management, quality assurance, and validation and verification).

4.2.4: Project Responsibilities

The subsection on Project Responsibilities should identify and state the nature of each major function and activity of the project, and identify the individuals who are responsible for those functions and activities. Examples of functions and activities that might be identified include, but are not limited to: project management, configuration management, quality assurance, product design, implementation, integration testing, facilities maintenance, and publications. A functional responsibility matrix should be used to depict project responsibilities.

4.3: Managerial Process (Section 3 of the SPMP)

This section of the SPMP presents the project objectives and priorities; lists the assumptions, dependencies, and constraints for the project; describes the risk management procedures; specifies monitoring and controlling mechanisms for the project; and describes the staffing plan.

4.3.1: Management Objectives and Priorities

The Management Objectives and Priorities subsection states the philosophy, goals, and priorities for the project. Topics to be specified might include, but are not limited to: the frequency and mechanisms of reporting on quality and productivity; the relative priorities among requirements, schedule, and budget; a statement of intent to reuse existing software; crisis management procedures to be followed; and plans for professional development of project staff members.

4.3.2: Assumptions, Dependencies, and Constraints

This subsection describes the Assumptions, Dependencies, and Constraints for the project. Assumptions are the fundamental conditions that must hold for the project to succeed; for example, it is assumed that the customer will provide increased funding for the project during the second year of development. Dependencies are conditions external to the project that must be true in order for the project to proceed as

planned; for example, meeting the performance requirements is dependent upon successful development of a faster microprocessor by the hardware group. Constraints are environmental conditions that the software product must satisfy; for example, the resulting product must operate on a given machine in a fixed memory partition of a given size.

4.3.3: Risk Management

Risk Management is concerned with identifying, assessing, tracking, and contingency planning for the risk factors associated with the project. Risks to be considered include contractual risks, technological risks, risks due to the size and complexity of the product, risks in personnel acquisition and retention, and risks in achieving customer acceptance of the product. Risk factors can be identified by examining the Assumptions, Dependencies, and Constraints in Section 3.2 of the SPMP.

4.3.4: Monitoring and Controlling Mechanisms

The subsection on Monitoring and Controlling Mechanisms defines the reporting mechanisms, report formats, information flows, review and audit mechanisms, and other tools and techniques to be used in collecting, analyzing, and reporting information on product quality, project schedule, expenditures, productivity, and progress. Monitoring and controlling should occur at the level of the work packages associated with the project tasks. Thus, the project tasks should be decomposed to a level that is sufficient to provide adequate monitoring of the project. The relationship of the monitoring and controlling mechanisms to the project support functions such as configuration management and quality assurance should be defined in this subsection of the SPMP.

4.3.5: Staffing Plan

The Staffing Plan identifies the personnel needs for the project and describes methods for meeting those needs. Items to be specified in this subsection include the required skills, number of people by skill (and skill level), starting time and duration of need, and the methods to be used in obtaining, training, retaining, and phasing out the required personnel. The allocation and scheduling of personnel to the various project tasks are specified in Sections 5.4 and 5.5 of the SPMP.

4.4: Technical Process (Section 4 of the SPMP)

This section of the SPMP specifies the technical methods, tools, and techniques to be used on the project; the software documentation plan; and the project support functions.

4.4.1: Methods, Tools, and Techniques

The subsection on Methods, Tools, and Techniques specifies (either directly or by reference to another plan which is part of the SPMP) the computing system(s), development methodology(s), team structure(s), programming language(s), and other notations, tools, techniques, and methods to be used to specify, design, build, test, integrate, document, deliver, modify, and maintain the project deliverables. Not all projects are concerned with all of these technical activities; this subsection of the SPMP should address all of those activities encompassed by the project.

This subsection should also contain (either directly or by reference) the standards, guidelines, policies, and procedures that govern development and/or modification of the work products and project deliverables. Deviations from prescribed standards, guidelines, policies,and procedures should be documented in this section of the SPMP.

4.4.2: Software Documentation

The Software Documentation plan is contained in this subsection of the SPMP, either directly or by reference to another document. The documentation plan should specify the documentation requirements for the project and the milestones, baselines, reviews, and sign-offs for documentation, as well as the task definitions, work packages, schedules, and resources needed to implement the plan. The individuals responsible for preparing and implementing the documentation plan should be identified in Section 2.4 of the SPMP (Functional Responsibilities) and the resource requirements, schedule, and budget for documentation should be incorporated into Section 5 of the SPMP.

4.4.3: Project Support Functions

The subsection on Project Support Functions should describe plans for support functions such as quality assurance, configuration management, validation and verification, facilities maintenance, and publications. The exact numbers and types of support functions to be specified are dependent on the nature of the software project and the environment in which the project is conducted; thus, the exact number of subsections in this section will depend on the particular circumstances. Justification for omitting quality assurance and configuration management plans (if omitted) should be documented in this section.

The plans for project support functions can be incorporated directly into the SPMP or by reference to other plans. These plans should be developed to a level of detail consistent with the other sections of the SPMP, and the functional responsibilities, resource requirements, schedule, and budget for the support functions should be incorporated into Section 2.4 and Section 5 of the SPMP.

4.5: Work Elements, Schedule, and Budget (Section 5 of the SPMP)

This section of the SPMP specifies the work packages and the dependencies among work packages (both hierarchical and precedence), the resource requirements, budget and resource allocation, and schedule for the project—all at the level of work packages.

4.5.1: Work Packages

This subsection specifies the Work Packages for the software project. Work packages are associated with project tasks and are used to specify task details. The attributes of a work package include (but are not limited to) the package name, a description of the work to be done, the preconditions for initiating the task, estimated duration of the task, required resources (e.g., personnel, skills, machine access, software tools, travel, secretarial support), the work products to be produced, the acceptance criteria for the work products, the risks, and the completion criteria for the task.

Each work package should be uniquely identified using a systematic numbering scheme. In addition, the hierarchical relationships among project functions, activities, and tasks should be presented in the form of a work breakdown structure. The systematic numbering scheme for identifying work packages should be keyed to the hierarchical groupings in the work breakdown structure.

Appropriate sizing of tasks and their associated work packages is discussed in Section 2 of this guide.

4.5.2: Dependencies

Dependencies specify the precedence relations among project functions, activities, and tasks in order to account for the dependencies of these work elements on external events and the ordering that must be preserved among the work elements. Techniques such as precedence charts, PERT charts, and critical path charts can be used to indicate dependencies. These graphical devices illustrate those work elements that can proceed in parallel, those that must occur in serial fashion, and the various project milestones.

4.5.3: Resource Requirements

The subsection on Resource Requirements provides an estimate of the resources needed to conduct the project. Resources to be accounted for include, but are not limited to, personnel, computer time, support software, computing hardware, special-purpose hardware, office and laboratory facilities, travel, and resources required to maintain the project resources. Loading charts can be used to provide graphical depictions of the various resource requirements as functions of time throughout the project.

4.5.4: Budget and Resource Allocation

The Budget and Resource subsection of the SPMP indicates the allocation of budget and resources to the various project functions, activities, and tasks. A systematic numbering scheme can be used to establish cost accounting centers for the project. Resource Gantt charts can be used to determine resource clashes and perform resource leveling. An earned value scheme can be used to allocate budget and resources to project work elements, and to track expenditures and resource utilization.

4.5.5: Schedule

The Schedule subsection provides the schedule for the various project functions, activities, and tasks taking into account the precedence relations among the work elements, the required milestone dates, and the resource constraints. Schedules should be expressed in calendar dates, rather than in time increments relative to a key project milestone.

4.6: Additional Components (Section 6 of the SPMP)

Certain additional components may be required in the SPMP to account for special circumstances. Typical additional components include subcontractor management plans, security considerations, independent verification and validation plans, training plans (for project members and/or product users), hardware procurement plans, facilities plans, installation plan, data conversion plan, system transition plan, or the product maintenance plan. If present, the additional subsections of the SPMP must be developed in a format and to a level of detail consistent with the other sections of the SPMP.

4.7: Back Matter

The back matter consists of information that improves the utility and usability of the SPMP. Typical items in the back matter include an index of key terms and acronyms; appendixes that contain useful information which is unsuitable for the body of the SPMP (detailed personnel lists, details of cost estimates, detailed work breakdown structures, etc.); notes, which are supplementary information that the reader may want to know; and a glossary of terms that might be too large to be placed in the body of the SPMP.

References

The following documents contain information that may be useful in preparing a software project management plan:

ANSI/IEEE Std 729-1983, *IEEE Standard Glossary of Software Engineering Terminology*, IEEE, Inc., New York, 1983.

ANSI/IEEE Std 730-1984, *IEEE Standard for Software Quality Assurance Plans*, IEEE, Inc., New York, 1984.

ANSI/IEEE Std 828-1983, *IEEE Standard for Software Configuration Management Plans*, IEEE, Inc., New York, 1983.

ANSI/IEEE Std 829-1983, *IEEE Standard for Software Test Documentation*, IEEE, Inc., New York, 1983.

ANSI/IEEE Std 830-1984, *IEEE Guide for Software Requirements Specifications*, IEEE, Inc., New York, 1984.

Appendix

Definitions

Activity. A major unit of work to be completed in achieving the objectives of a *software project*. An activity has precise starting and ending dates, incorporates a set of *tasks* to be completed, consumes resources, and produces tangible results. An activity may contain other activities in a hierarchical manner; however, the lowest level activities in the hierarchy must have task descendents. Dependencies often exist among activities and tasks, so that completion of one activity or task may provide necessary preconditions for initiation of subsequent activities and tasks.

Baseline. A work product that has been formally reviewed and agreed upon and that can be changed only through formal change control procedures. Baselines often provide the basis for further work.

Customer. An individual or organization that provides the product specifications and formally accepts the *project deliverables*. The customer may be internal or external to the parent organization of the project. A financial transaction between customer and developer is not necessarily implied.

Document. A data medium, electronic or paper, and the data recorded on it.

Documentation. (1) A collection of documents on a given subject. (2) Any written or pictorial information describing, defining, specifying, reporting, or certifying activities, requirements, procedures, or results.

Function. An *activity* or set of activities that spans the entire duration of a software project. Examples of project functions include project management, configuration management, quality assurance, and project cost accounting. Functions may be decomposed into subfunctions and activities.

Milestone. A scheduled event that is used to measure progress. An individual project member or manager is identified and held accountable for achieving the milestone on time and within budget. Examples of major milestones include a customer or managerial sign-off, issuance of a specification, completion of system integration, and product delivery. Minor milestones might include baselining a software module or completing a chapter of the users' manual.

Process model. A model of a *software project* that depicts the relationships of the project *functions, activities,* and *tasks* to the major *milestones, baselines, reviews, work products, project deliverables,* and sign-offs (both customer and managerial) that span the project. A process model must include project initiation and project termination activities. A software project may span only a segment of the *software product lifecycle;* in this case, the process model spans a sub-interval of the product lifecycle.

Project agreement. A document or set of documents agreed to by the developer and the *customer* that specifies the scope, objectives, assumptions, management interfaces, risks, staffing plan, resource requirements, cost estimate, schedule, resource and budget allocations, *project deliverables,* and acceptance criteria for the project. Documents in a project agreement may include some or all of the following: a contract, a statement of work, system engineering specifications, user requirements specifications, functional specifications, a business plan, or a project charter.

Project deliverables. The items to be delivered to the customer, including quantities, delivery dates, and delivery locations, as specified in the *project agreement.* The project deliverables may include some or all of, but are not limited to, the following: customer requirements, functional specifications, design documentation, source code, object code, users' manuals, principles of operation, installation instructions, training aids, product development tools, and maintenance procedures. Project deliverables may be self-contained or may be part of a larger system.

Review. A meeting at which a work product, or a set of work products, is presented to project personnel, managers, users, customers, or other interested parties for comment or approval.

Software product. Computer software and the related documents and documentation that are developed or modified for delivery to a *customer.*

Software product lifecycle. The set of all events and endeavors that occur within the birth-to-death cycle of a *software product.*

Software project. The set of all *activities, functions,* and *tasks,* both technical and managerial, required to satisfy the terms and conditions of the *project agreement.* A software project has specific starting and ending dates, consumes resources, and has the goal of producing a product or set of products that satisfies the project requirements, as specified in the project agreement. A software project may be self-contained or may be part of a larger project. In some cases, a software project may span many years and consist of numerous subprojects, each being a well-defined and self-contained software project having *project deliverables.*

Software project management. The process of planning, organizing, staffing, monitoring, controlling, and leading a *software project.*

Software project management plan. The controlling document for managing a software project. A software project management plan defines the technical and managerial *functions, activities,* and *tasks* necessary to satisfy the requirements of a software project, as defined in the *project agreement.*

Task. The smallest unit of work subject to management accountability. A task must be small enough to allow adequate planning and tracking of the project, but large enough to avoid micro-management. The specification of work to be accomplished in completing a task is documented in a *work package.* Related tasks are usually grouped to form *functions* and *activities.*

Work package. A specification of the work to be accomplished in completing a project *task.* A work package specifies the objectives of the work, the staffing requirements, the expected duration, the resources to be used, the results to be produced, the acceptance criteria for the *work products,* the name of the responsible individual, and any special considerations for the work.

Work product. Any *document, documentation,* or other tangible item that results from working on a project *function, activity,* or *task.* Examples of work products include the project plan, functional requirements, design documents, source code, test plans, meeting minutes, schedules, budgets, and problem reports. Some subset of the work products will form the set of *project deliverables.*

Chapter 5: Organizing a Software Engineering Project

1. Introduction to Chapter

Organizing a software engineering project is defined as all the management activities that result in the design of a formal structure of software engineering tasks and relationships between these tasks. Organizing involves determining and itemizing the activities required to achieve the objects of the software development project, grouping of these activities into logical groups, and determining the relationships within and between the groups. It also involves assignment of each groups of activity to an organizational entity and the delegation of responsibility and authority to the organizational entity to carry out the assignment.

Organizing a software engineering project can be partitioned into six general management activities (see Table 5.1). Each activity in the table is followed by its definition or an amplifying description.

IT'S YOUR WEEK
TO GET
ORGANIZED

RUSH

Table 5.1

Activity	Definition or Explanation
Identify and group required tasks	— Define, size, and group tasks to be done.
Select and establish organizational structures	— Define or select structures necessary to accomplish required duties and tasks and to control, coordinate, and communicate among these duties and tasks.
Create organizational positions	— Establish title, duties, scope, and relationships for each position.
Define responsibilities and authority	— Define responsibilities for each position and the authority to be granted for the accomplishment of those responsibilities.
Establish position qualifications	— Define qualifications for persons to fill each position.
Document organizational structures	— Record organizational structure, assignment of responsibility and authority, position descriptions, and so on.

2. Overview of Chapter

The five papers in this chapter discuss the various aspects of organizing a software engineering project. The activities listed in Table 5.1 were used as an outline for the purpose of identifying quality papers related to organizing activities. All papers here deal with identifying general software engineering tasks and the organizational structures needed to accomplish them.

The three papers by Fife, Youker, and Mantei provide criteria for selecting the appropriate organizational structures for the software product and process.

The paper by Middleton emphasizes the need to identify the different responsibilities and authority between *functional* and *project organizations* and briefly defines the qualifications of a project manager. Mantei's paper identifies three different types of software engineering teams along with the appropriate positional responsibilities and authority.

Both Stuckenbruck and Youker indicate the need for top management to give a clear project charter (document) for the matrix organization in defining responsibilities and authority for the project manager as well as the role of the functional departments. Youker points out the need to have a matrix strategic plan to keep from overloading the functional departments.

3. Description of Papers

The first paper, by Dennis Fife, was written especially for this tutorial. It defines and describes five alternative organizational forms for software projects and six criteria (factors) to consider in choosing a project organization. Each of the five organizations are described according to their objective and mission, authority and work breakdown, and reporting and communication capabilities. The paper demonstrates that each software engineering life-cycle phase tends to favor one organizational structure over another, for example a matrix organization is best for the requirements phase while a project organization is best for the detailed design phase.

Fife's paper goes on to identify some broad organizational positions for each organizational type, the responsibilities and authority connected with them, and personnel growth.

The paper by C.J. Middleton discusses "How to Set Up a Project Organization." He explains the purpose in establishing project organizations, four different project types, and the problems in dividing up the work between the newly created *project organizations* and the older established *functional organizations*. Also discussed are the costs of project organizations and the possible temporary or permanent effects of project organizations on the companies using them.

This is an older paper written when project organizational structures were receiving maximum attention (particularly in the aerospace industry) and before the matrix organizational structure became popular. Middleton's inter nix structure is really a matrix organization. His series of organizational structures are very similar to the project structures in Youker's paper, also reprinted in this chapter.

Middleton identifies ten management activities that an effective project must be responsible for. He further discusses the major problems in allocating various project tasks between the functional and project organizations—an issue that is still very much alive today. A small part of Middleton's paper is devoted to staffing a software engineering project; a subject discussed in the next chapter.

The next paper, by Stuckenbruck, is a definitive description of the application of the *matrix organization* to a project. He sometimes refers to the matrix organization as the *two-boss organization* and defines it as a "multidisciplinary team whose members are drawn from various line or functional units of the hierarchical organization." Stuckenbruck also lists eight advantages and ten disadvantages of using the matrix organization. He points out that the matrix approach is frequently a readily available scapegoat for other organizational problems such as poor planning and inadequate control. The author devotes considerable time discussing how to make the matrix organization work. Stuckenbruck believes there is a need to achieve a *balance of power* between the matrix and functional organizations.

The fourth paper is a well-known paper from the *Project Management Quarterly* by Robert Youker, "Organizational Alternatives for Project Management." This paper stipulates that there are really only two project organizations, project and functional, and that the various degrees of mixing of these two techniques are what we call a "matrix" organization (see Figure 8 in Youker's paper). The author also discusses how to make matrix organizational structures work.

(The *Project Management Quarterly* (now called *Project Management Journal*) is a publication of the Project Management Institute. Individuals interested in finding out more about the Institute can contact them at PO Box 43, Drexel Hill, PA 19026.)

The fifth paper, by Mantei, is a modern-day classic. The paper analyzes and discusses the various programming team structures and the effect these structures have on programming tasks. The team structures analyzed are the *chief programmer team*, the *egoless programming team*, and the *controlled-decentralized team*. (The controlled-decentralized team structure is more frequently called the hierarchical or project team structure.) This paper also describes seven salient properties of programming tasks and compares the performance of each team structure against these properties.

How to Know a Well-Organized Software Project When You Find One

Dennis W. Fife
2500 Woodcutter Ct.
Reston, VA 22091

Here's an easy memory test: have you ever worked on a poorly organized project? Commonplace humor tells us that most people immediately would say yes. Some even would say they can't remember working on one that was *well* organized!

A new project's organization sometimes solidifies quickly, but more often remains vague or obviously temporary for a while. A transient organization may cause many perceived problems, but holding off decisions gives start-up uncertainties time to dissipate. A lasting organization can be set up once contract and budget negotiations are finished, personnel are onboard, and roles and tasks are clarified. Personal or social factors, such as the ambition or obstinacy of some key person or animosity between certain people, may weigh heavily in the final step. But, an organization should be planned deliberately to suit a project's characteristics, such as duration, and staff size and skills mix.

Most people prefer to work within an organization with well-defined roles, responsibilities, and communication avenues, as in a classical organization chart or manual. A defined organization tells people what they are supposed to do, what others do, and how they do it together.

But, formal organization is impersonal, and limited in its scope or timeliness. So, the ongoing effort customarily called management provides day-to-day guidance, working methods, and the personal touch of motivating and nurturing individuals. In theory, management reinforces the formal organization structure and gives it practical effect. In practice, management may undermine organization or render it irrelevant, either by action or inaction. Then of course you find power centers that are not predicted or shown by the organization chart, accompanied by a degree of chaos, individual frustration, and misdirected or redundant effort.

Organization and management of software projects haven't been of the highest concern for the profession, judging from Thayer's survey to pinpoint major issues [1]. The Chief Programmer Team concept [2] and software psychology [3] brought attention to this area a while ago, without gaining widespread acceptance, it seems. Still, Thayer's respondents chose project communications as among major issues.

Explaining this ambivalence is not essential here. Glaser [4] has well-phrased ideas about it. Compared to the technical problems of software production, management or organizational issues rightfully pale as a profession-wide concern. But, take an individual or personal viewpoint. To succeed consistently in job situations, you cannot ignore the management environment. Doing so just abets any upper level mismanagement that could hinder your performance. If your managers are foundering, you ought to intervene to help solve organizational, management, or other project problems. So, responsible technicians need to appreciate good organizational and management strategy for software projects.

This paper presents five alternative organizational forms for software projects, and analyzes how each typically works, and whether this suits software activities. The analysis draws partly on project management theory but largely on practical software development experience. Matters of management style and individual personalities or behavior patterns are secondary, if discussed at all. These mostly uncontrollable factors often operate independently of an organizational structure and, in the extreme, can overwhelm any perceived purpose or advantage of a formal organization. Though intriguing, they ought to be treated in a more effective genre, say a novel or personal memoir.

Criteria for Organizing a Project

Brief highlighting of factors to consider in choosing a project organization may help to appreciate the five forms as they are introduced. In an overall sense, only one thing matters: the organization should conduct the project effectively. Looking at what this involves leads to factors and questions such as these:

Providing the required resources and staff skills. How do organizations differ in making resources, including personnel, available? What constraints or time lags may apply?

Directing project effort effectively. Does an organization have adequate management and supervisory capability to optimize productivity and to cope with unforeseen problems?

Are specific task goals easily planned and agreed by responsible staff and supervisors?

Meeting review and communication requirements. Is an organization efficient and timely in assimilating the necessary progress information for reporting? Is it convenient to meet the unexpected client needs for progress or other information? Can daily project communication needs be met easily?

Giving a suitable context of work style and methods. Is the typical working approach of an organization suited to the nature of the project's deliverable system and development technology? Will its conventional operating methods fit the project?

Achieving stability required for client and staff confidence. Does the organization convey an adequate aura of stability to reassure staff and clients of continued progress and acceptable results? Would project termination or redirection offer smoother adjustments for clients or staff?

Offering personnel motivation and career growth. Is the organization conducive to staff development and growth opportunities?

Organizational Forms

General management theory [5] defines three typical organizational patterns for projects, called respectively the Functional, Matrix, and Project Organizations. Two more are apparent candidates for software projects. The fourth, called the Application Organization, particularly applies with software products. A fifth form arises because the Matrix Organization can operate in two very different ways. As will be seen, the Application and Functional Organizations conventionally handle multiple projects, while Matrix and Project Organizations exist to carry out only one project.

Each organization approaches basic project decisions differently. The basic decisions, rather than routine, ongoing management activity, produce the sharpest comparisons and receive the most attention here. They include: delineating an objective or mission; developing a work breakdown structure; selecting people and assigning them to roles; delegating authority; and designating reporting and communication channels.

The discussions below compare a single software development or maintenance group operating in one of the organizational forms and conducting one or more projects. The term "group" refers to the assigned people, under any of the organizational forms, while the term "manager" refers to the position that has direct authority over the group. The common expresssion "top management" refers to the group manager's collective supervision, from immediately above on up to the highest level.

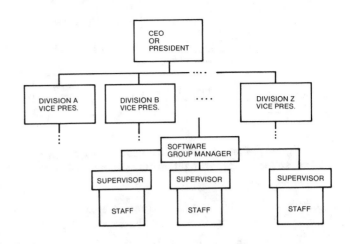

Figure 1: The enterprise context for analyzing the organization of a software development group at department level.

Within the management hierarchy of its parent enterprise, the group is taken to include the first two levels of supervision. The group manager is the higher and his or her subordinate unit supervisors are the lower, or first level of supervision. This means the group is comparable to a conventional department or branch, as depicted in Figure 1. Making this restriction focuses analysis on the working level impact and the immediate effect of organization on technical progress.

However, the enterprise organization chart, when traced from the top executive position to the lowest level unit, usually would show a succession of different organizational patterns at each level. How these patterns should be chosen for software development, or the broad question of how to organize all software development across an enterprise, falls beyond the scope of this paper. There is no direct analysis of how a large company or the Federal government, for instance, should organize all of its software development.

Application Organization

The familiar structure of many large businesses, offering various products or services to regional or national markets, represents an Application Organization on an enterprise level. The subordinate major divisions of the enterprise have names indicating either a distinct product line or customer application, the basis of missions assigned by top management. A manufacturing company with major units called the Commercial Division, the Power Division, and the Defense Systems Division serves as one example. The frequent choice

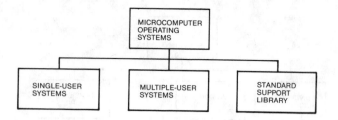

Figure 2: Example of an Application Organization, a software department organized by deliverable products.

of organizing a business by geographic area is a sizing or profitability decision, irrelevant to the analysis intended here.

Objective and mission. An Application Organization fits a group with expertise in producing self-standing products of certain types. It is most suitable for a commercial software group involved in development, maintenance, and customer support. This type of organization sharply focuses on the deliverable results and limits of a group's mission. It especially aids profit-centered management and strong customer support.

In software development, different types of software, such as Operating Systems or Business Applications, as in Figure 2, constitute the names and missions of subordinate units in an Application Organization. Its set of product specialties strictly delineates the organization's mission, and evolution or expansion into other products areas is a major organizational change.

Subordinate units operate self-sufficiently most of the time. New projects are identified with an established product type, perhaps imperfectly, and assigned to the unit with that mission. The subordinate group takes complete responsibility for the project.

Authority and work breakdown. An Application Organization carries out a number of projects, not just one. The group manager is the project manager for all of them. He or she ultimately makes the crucial project decisions, such as resource allocation, delivery dates, and product configuration choices. The group manager as a result also serves as the negotiating authority with customers.

The group manager commonly delegates certain authority to subordinate supervisors for individual projects, retaining review or approval rights over their decisions. Through direction of subordinates, the group manager leads or influences the formulation of the work breakdown, assignments to individual workers, selection of personnel, etc., for each project.

Permanent personnel usually comprise the resources available to meet project needs. Under stress, the enterprise may release a few others for temporary reassignment to the group. The manager also can move personnel between subordinate units to accommodate a particular project, though disturbing existing personnel relationships may create problems too. Acquiring more staff normally means a permanent decision,

made with a cautious estimate of the future workload. Thus, personnel arrangements may take time to finalize, and this organization cannot easily accommodate a rapidly growing project.

In summary, an Application Organization represents a traditional hierarchical organization, but one with clearly visible product objectives. It is well adapted for long-term, stable efforts, and provides effective motivation for a diversified group devoted to a few products.

Reporting and Communication. Reporting to top management and communicating with customers follow straightforward traditional patterns. Usually one subordinate unit manager is involved, reporting to the group manager, who in turn reports only to his or her designated supervisor. Customers interact with the group manager, or on limited issues, with a subordinate. Responsibilities are as clear as they ever are, and serious problems can be taken up the management chain for assistance or resolution.

Functional Organization

A Functional Organization is one formed around technical expertise or discipline, or a narrow set of work methods. A Sales group, an Applied Mathematics group, a Programming group, or a System Analysis group represents a Functional Organization. Functional Organization dominates many technology-oriented enterprises, because it serves well to develop skills, morale, and synergistic productivity among people of like talents and background.

Objective and mission. A Functional Organization has many similarities to an Application Organization. For example, it also normally conducts multiple projects. Distinctions between the two, however, are not subtle. Basically, a Functional Organization is a service-oriented group, not a product group. Its customary projects predominantly require the singular expertise of the group, rather than a broad range of experience and skills. A Functional Organization typically has much less diversity in personnel skills than an Application Organization. For example, a software testing group, as a Functional Organization, has a narrower range of skills, but at greater depth, than an Application Organization that also includes testing specialists for its product work. Figure 3 depicts a Functional Organization for a programming group.

Authority and work breakdown. A major distinction between Functional and Application Organizations occurs in handling projects. A Functional Organization, having narrow skills and purposes for its subordinate groups, typically cannot conduct a full development project entirely within just one of its groups. This forces a choice on top management: create a different organization for such a project, or make the project fit the existing organization. Under the latter, managers break the project down and schedule it by skills required. This results in a phased project, handed off from

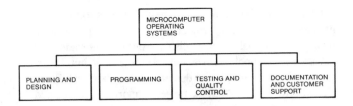

Figure 3: Example of a Functional Organization, a software department organized by expertise or discipline.

one subordinate unit to another when each phase finishes. Since this seldom happens perfectly, two or more units may be involved jointly for a time, with responsibility shared between the relevant managers. The group manager, having ultimate responsibility, has to arbitrate differences and ensure good coordination between subordinate supervisors to keep a project moving ahead. In practice, subordinate units must collaborate on software projects extensively, in contrast to an Application Organization.

Because the group manager and subordinates direct several projects, they direct any one as a part-time effort, and occasionally a shared effort. If a project is important and is in trouble, it presumably gets good attention from the managers, but only occasional attention when it appears to be going well. As in the Application Organization, immediate supervisors make individual work assignments, subject to the guidance of the group manager. Individual workers have roles based on their expertise or discipline.

As in the Application Organization, available resources are limited as a practical matter to those in the group. Acquiring more people normally means permanent committments, not made quickly. Moreover, in this regard, functional specialization poses special difficulties. Sometimes, group members tend to take an elitist view of their expertise. If tolerated, this can severely inhibit quick hiring of new personnel. Also, the support staff needed for a full-scale project, having skills quite different than the mainstream group, are difficult to place organizationally, both short and long term.

Reporting and communication. In a Functional Organization, project reporting and communication falls unalterably on the group manager, because of shared and part-time responsibilities spreading within the group. Conflicts or discrepancies are resolved by the group manager for presentation to higher management or customers. Otherwise, the organization communicates within the enterprise according to a traditional hierarchical pattern, as done in an Application Organization.

Matrix Organization

The Matrix Organization may be the most easily remembered organizational type, because its name portrays its operation so well. It is widely practiced in technology enterprises, especially aerospace and large systems companies. It gives a picturesque name to a commonplace problem-solving approach, the company task force.

Objective and mission. A Matrix Organization is devoted to a specific project. As you may know already, it establishes a project group by drawing on personnel, particularly specialists, from many places in an enterprise, without displacing them from their "home" organization. A project leader or manager is assigned from one unit, and project staff assembled of full or part-time personnel from various units of the enterprise. Top management collaborates to select the manager and staff, and may elect a steering or review committee of higher managers to guide the project as well (See Figure 4.) This approach particularly suits a project that may be very uncertain or short-lived, yet needs the skills of hard-to-find specialists. This typifies Department of Defense contracts and proposal efforts, and explains why defense contractors lead in using the Matrix Organization.

Authority and work breakdown. Two degrees of matrix management can be recognized, reflecting the authority and sometimes the charisma of the project leader. A Strong Matrix Organization emerges when the project leader gains the roles of principal authority in customer negotiations and budget authority in allocating project funds for the participating personnel. This strong measure of control allows the project leader to dominate any review committee, acquire personnel as desired, and focus the project goals to advantages he or she perceives in the enterprise. Control of real money (that is, separate additional funding as opposed to

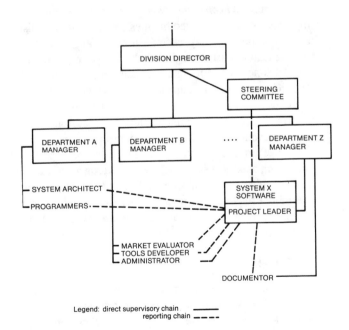

Figure 4: Example of a Matrix Organization, a project group assembled of part-time staff from many departments.

"shell" or "soft" funding from each participant's home unit budget) is the key to achieving a Strong Matrix operation.

A Weak Matrix Organization, on the other hand, has the project leader in the limited role of team coordinator and spokesperson to higher management. Typically, a steering committee or one executive retains any budget authority and serves as negotiator with the customer. In cases where a Weak Matrix occurs naturally, such as a company task force pursuing an internal study, there is no real money budget and often no identifiable customer other than the steering committee.

A Strong Matrix Organization operates much like a Project Organization (see below). The major difference centers on the committment of personnel. A Matrix Organization typically has few full-time, dedicated people—until it grows large and stable. The staff works part-time, and has other obligations back in their home units or with other projects. The staff works only to fulfill clearly defined tasks and milestones, and their participation is negotiated from specific tasks needing their expertise.

Consensus and frequent negotiation are the hallmarks of a matrix approach. The reason is evident especially in the Weak Matrix form, where the leader's authority may be transient and conceded by peers, rather than delegated by superiors. Compromise marks the work breakdown and personnel assignments, often with less than the optimum results. The project leader may have to assume personally any unaccepted but essential assignments, especially for quick reaction.

Reporting and communication. Because of part-time staffing, possibly compounded by physical separation in distant offices, reporting may become a signficant burden. The project leader must contend with the competing assignments of part-time staff in monitoring their progress versus plan, and reporting to the customer and higher management. Voluntary, close cooperation is crucial to success in the matrix approach. Communication with customers, and usually even with upper management of the enterprise, is a joint effort because the leader relies on the expertise of the principal project staff. However, a Strong Matrix Organization reduces such difficulties, because the project leader has more effective control, and either can force desired performance from participants, or replace them with more responsive personnel.

Project Organization

A Project Organization is a permanent group formed exclusively to carry out a single, long-term project. It typically fits within an enterprise on a par with other conventional departments (but may compare to higher or lower level units, depending on project size). It has its own full-time staff. Its manager acts with a broad range of independent authority on technical, management, and financial matters, and is the principal negotiator with the client or customer.

Objective and mission. A Project Organization gives the greatest visibility to a project within an enterprise. A top management decision to establish a Project Organization indicates various conclusions about the project. It implies that project size and complexity demand focused and tightly controlled effort. It says that the project importance merits dedicated resources and the same organizational stature as well established activities. It suggests expanding activity and opportunity, and so connotes that future growth is expected in the organization's mission.

Authority and work breakdown. Typically, the manager establishes a formal structure within a Project Organization by delegating prescribed responsibilities to subordinate supervisors or administrators. In many cases, the internal organization is an Application Organization paralleling the component structure of the end product, but with certain supporting functional units as well. That is, subordinate units typically take major product subsystems as their missions, but depend on functional groups such as configuration management or testing to assist them, as seen in Figure 5. Now, note that the Chief Programmer concept describes a Project Organization, but argues for minimal delegation of responsibility in order to ensure single-point control of system design. For a single-project technical organization, the single-point control theme is highly pertinent, even if implementation of the Chief Programmer concept is not. The manager of a Project Organization must closely direct technical control, to coordinate products of subordinate groups, ensure interface compatibility, harmonize schedules, etc.

Reporting and communication. The reporting difficulties of Matrix and Functional Organizations disappear with a Project Organization. Conventional hierarchical reporting applies. Large projects with numerous tasks may generate tedious reporting, but standards and computer-aided project control can offset much of this burden. Dual reporting obligations of the project manager, to top management and to customers, surely are elevated because of project importance, if a Project Organization is warranted.

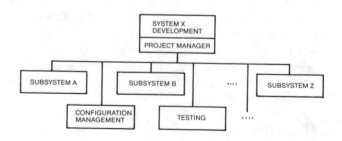

Figure 5: Example of a Project Organization, a development group organized into component and functional units.

Practical Implementations

The five forms above do not fully cover the possible spectrum of organizational types. The distinctions among the five fall into three categories. The first is whether one or multiple projects are performed. The second is whether a single project's work is done part-time or full-time by most personnel, especially the group manager. The third is whether the group is organized internally by function, by products, or by both criteria. An example of an omitted case is a functional organization that is set up to perform only one project. It is hard to imagine a realistic case of software development where this would be a practical, lasting choice, though it certainly could represent the history of a prematurely terminated project.

Of course, any form of organization may result when top managers pursue ulterior motives unrelated to organizational purposes. Such motives might include disguising a group when its purpose is unacceptable to top management or would create conflict, or disabling a group in order to justify disbanding it. The collateral impact on personnel in such circumstances is usually profound. Clearly these are cases where personality studies reveal far more than management analyses.

Technical groups observed in practice may appear to incorporate subordinate units of two or more of the forms described above. Such an organization simply may be one at a higher level in the parent enterprise than discussed here. Otherwise, it is explainable as either a compromise because the preferred organization was unattainable for personnel or political reasons, or else a temporary pattern that will soon evolve into the preferred form. For example, a Functional Organization might be forced to take on a full-scale software product development, which is not suitable for its basic purpose. To minimize difficulties such as subdividing the project across subordinate units, the manager may set up a new unit as a Project Organization, reassigning personnel to staff it. If the project fully succeeds and grows, the project unit should emerge as a separate Project Organization of equal standing as its parent. If not, the personnel will be assigned back to their original units, and the project unit disbanded without disturbing the parent's original structure. Regardless, the immediate decision introduces another hierarchical level of management, and the analysis herein applies to the newly formed Project Organization.

Evaluations

The above discussion defining organizational types already has suggested factors for comparing them, such as purpose and major advantages. A very specific assessment would require the context of a real project and enterprise. To help readers do that, having such context, general insights can be developed from the factors suggested earlier for choosing an organization. Figure 6 shows a comparative table for selected project needs implied by such factors. Its length makes it impractical to discuss here. Instead, a more concise example is drawn from three of the earlier factors.

First, the organization has to help in effective direction of the project effort. Second, the organization should be effective and stable over, say, a period of some months. That is, long-term effectiveness should outweigh the short-term, in some measure. Third, an organization should offer career growth opportunity for more capable people, so that they are encouraged to remain, rather than leave.

The first two can be addressed together in terms of the conventional pattern of so-called life cycle phases. There is widespread understanding of the project effort in each phase. What is the most effective software organization for each phase, and what do these answers portend for organizational stability?

Career growth opportunities should be judged for both managerial and technical opportunities. Managerial growth usually means greater responsibility, such as the opportunity to manage projects or to have more authority in doing so. Technical growth can be viewed as the opportunity to develop and practice innovative software development methods or tools. Does any organizational type stand out in supporting or encouraging such career growth objectives?

The comments to follow offer one view on these two questions, and lead to a final recommendation on organizing software projects over their life cycle.

Life Cycle Aspects

The effort of each life cycle phase tends to favor one organization over another, and as argued here, the evolution from one phase to another can be smooth and without serious compromises or instability.

Requirements analysis. Project effort in this phase concerns communicating with end users and understanding the customer's business and viewpoint. Often it requires a marketing outlook, to draw out the customer by exploring state-of-the-art possibilities and cost-benefit factors. The need for a variety of personnel skills, including knowledge of customer's operations, and typical project start-up uncertainty, suggests the Matrix Organization as the most effective initial choice. The Project Organization appears unfavorable because of its longer set-up time, which probably would provide less in personnel resources than needed early in a project. But, a more important and pertinent reason is the requirements uncertainty. A stable basis for internally setting up a Project Organization usually is missing at this early phase.

Preliminary/conceptual design. This phase requires technical creativity bolstered by a strong sense of practicality and the state of the art. Here, now and more so in the future,

Figure 6: Comparison of Organizations for Meeting Project Needs

Legend: H—highly suitable; P—possibly suitable; L—least suitable.

Project Need or Goal	Application	Relative Strength of Each Organizational Form			
		Functional	Weak Matrix	Strong Matrix	Project
Deliver a plan or analysis	P	P	H	P	L
Deliver a product design	H	H	L	H	H
Deliver a fully tested product	H	L	L	P	H
Give dedicated leadership	L	L	P	H	H
Interact strongly with customer	P	L	L	H	H
Staff-up quickly	P	P	P	L	L
Gain diverse skills	P	L	H	H	P
Serve long duration	P	L	L	P	H
Exploit complex technology	P	P	P	H	H
Endure high risk	P	P	H	H	L
Manage large staff	L	L	L	H	H
Train new staff	P	H	P	H	H
Recruit new staff	P	L	L	P	H

designers employ sophisticated tools and formal design disciplines. Competing design ideas are assessed and winnowed down. This stresses single-point control as espoused in the Chief Programmer concept. A Strong Matrix Organization appears most effective as an evolutionary step from the prior phase, giving stronger technical control while retaining the staffing flexibility of the Matrix approach.

Detailed design. Starting from the architecture produced by the prior phase, this one develops detailed programming specifications for building the intended system. Early effort in this phase may include rapid prototyping tasks. Test planning and related validation tasks, as well as devising standards and tools, must reach conclusion. At this phase of effort, all parties are committed to producing a deliverable system. A Project Organization, primarily based on a subsystem or component breakdown but with functionally organized support units, has greatest potential effectiveness. It provides dedicated staffing, streamlined reporting, and strong control of specialized working units necessary to this phase.

Implementation and testing. This phase concentrates on programming and corrective redesign activities. But validation and verification (with testing as its major aspect) and configuration management, initially as support efforts, become the primary tasks at its conclusion. The Project Organization recommended for the preceding phase continues to be the most effective choice for organizing the development group. The primary reasons are its dedicated staffing and single-point control, along with its flexibility to accommodate product and functionally oriented groups in one organization.

Maintenance and operation. After delivery of a completed working system, the customer typically assumes the maintenance and future redesign responsibilities. Unless the system has many residual problems or is a predominant factor in the customer's business, a Project Organization is not appropriate for the small and narrow scope of maintenance. Given that other software maintenance tasks exist also, organizing the computer software personnel as an Application or Functional Organization is a natural decision. The choice between these two hinges on the overall scale of the customer's information system resources. A business with few systems can use its computer personnel more effectively in a Functional Organization. But as computer usage proliferates, requiring expertise and steady effort on many packages, an Application Organization becomes more effective among the alternatives.

Conclusion. The above broad view of each project phase identifies a preferred evolution for a software development organization. As a project begins, a Matrix Organization serves best for quickly involving various technical experts and advisors on user needs to define the requirements and future system concept. In fact, innovative approaches to project formulation, such as the Demosophia and normative group technique [6], imply use of this organization. For later intensive design and implementation efforts, a Project Organization stands out as best for accomplishing single-point control and concentrating resources on system components. Upon delivery of a well-working system, an Application Organization is the most typical home for conducting product-oriented maintenance.

Assessing organizational stability can exclude the Maintenance phase if a separate user organization will do it. In that case, the organizational transitions accompanying the life cycle phases seem natural and minimal if the above evolution is followed. The Matrix Organization serves as a model precursor of the Project Organization, allowing part-time support to fit into roles that will evolve to full-time assignments as the project matures. Internal organizational changes will appear as natural adjustments to technical development.

An unavoidable and possibly abrupt transition occurs on entering the Maintenance phase, if a development project has been conducted by software personnel of the user organization. Its Project Organization will be disbanded, some staff will go on to new development projects, while others will take on maintenance assignments, including the newly delivered system. This is an easily expected change, and can be easily planned in gradual steps. Also, since an aura of success attends it, it can have a positive benefit to morale. It is a small cost to accept in order to gain the advantages of better organization during the major project effort.

Personnel Growth

The evolution recommended above also provides a clear growth opportunity for management-oriented personnel. A Matrix Organization is clearly transient, but formed on a new basis and for a special purpose compared to established groups in the enterprise. It offers new leadership roles to be filled. Most interested people would see good prospects for new contributions and individual recognition. Those missing the incentive probably are too loyal or committed to their home unit or other projects, and wouldn't be persuaded by another organizational approach. Further evolution to the Project Organization extends the management opportunities by raising the group stature and offering more supervisory responsibilities.

Technical personnel, on the other hand, seek advancement through opportunities that will enhance their skills and experience, such as: rapid prototyping, formal design methods, new programming languages and tools, real-time requirements, etc. Of course, system requirements, not organizational approach, raise these technical challenges. The pertinent question on organization is, then, given that an interesting challenge exists, what organization affords the best opportunity to pursue and learn the most from it? Practicing technical innovations across a project of some size suggests having functional units devoted to the skills or tools involved. This provides synergism among the specialists, and a concentrated resource to help apply the tools or methods to the entire project effort. But as already argued, a Functional Organization is very difficult to sustain throughout a full-scale development project. An Application Organization diffuses expertise among subsystem or component-oriented groups. The organizational evolution recommended earlier seems most workable also for technical opportunities. In the initial Matrix Organization, one or more specialists can establish the innovations involved, train other project members, and foster their approach in the project's development. In the transition to a Project Organization, pertinent functional units can perform alongside the product or component units as necessary to provide resources and carry out the technical mandate. Individual technicians then have an excellent opportunity to associate with like-minded peers and gain stature for their expertise in an application setting.

Conclusion

For most established software groups, traditionally organized along Functional or Application lines, a major new development project should be an occasion for organizational innovation. A clearly prefered evolution is to begin with a Matrix Organization for the project, and as project requirements crystallize and management committment solidifies, change to Project Organization with full-time staffing and leadership.

Technicians need to be vigilant about organizational dynamics. Functional Organization, though traditional for consultants and preferred by technicians accordingly, is not practical for full-scale development because of limited flexibility and management difficulty.

References

[1] R. H. Thayer, A. Pyster, and R. C. Wood, "Validating Solutions to Major Problems in Software Engineering Project Management," *Computer*, 15, 65–77, August 1982.

[2] F. T. Baker, "Chief Programmer Team Management of Production Programming," *IBM Systems Journal*, 1, 56–73, 1972.

[3] G. Weinburg, *The Psychology of Computer Programming*, Van Nostrand/Rheinhold, New York, 1971.

[4] G. Glaser, "Managing Projects in the Computer Industry," *Computer*, October 1984, 45–53.

[5] R. Youker, "Organizational Alternatives for Project Managers," *AMA Management Review*, 66, 46–53, November 1977.

[6] J. Warfield, "Some Laws and Principles of Design," Annual Meeting of the General Systems Research Society, 1985.

• Lessons to be learned from the experience of those companies that assign major tasks to special units rather than to functional departments.

How to Set Up a Project Organization

By C. J. Middleton

❪ Lockheed Aircraft Corporation uses project management at its Puget Sound shipbuilding facility for new ship contracts and conversion contracts. Functional departments do the work, but project managers see to it that assigned projects are completed on schedule, within budget, and in conformance with specifications.

❪ Avco Corporation assigns project managers at its Research and Advanced Development Division to two types of activities: space systems and ballistic missile reentry systems. Project managers maintain total program control, assisted by a staff of technical, administration, and functional department personnel.

❪ General Dynamics Corporation established a project organization at the Fort Worth Division for accomplishing the F-111A and F-111B aircraft programs. At the same time management beefed up the B-58 bomber project organization. Why? To ensure proper managerial attention and support in providing spare parts and services for B-58's already delivered or to be delivered to the customer.

❪ Three companies — The Boeing Company, Douglas Aircraft Company, and Lockheed — set up extensive project organizations for their competition for the C5A transport aircraft program. Large numbers of employees were hired, transferred, or borrowed from other jobs to devote full time to the competition effort. When Lockheed won the award, the other companies disbanded their project organizations.

These examples show that companies are finding it advantageous to establish project organizations for handling such special assignments as developing a new product, building a factory, and investigating departures from their traditional business.

This article explains the aims of management in setting up project units, the varieties of forms they have taken, the problems of dividing assignments with functional segments of companies, and the techniques of forming the work force. It also discusses the costs of project organizations and the possible temporary or lasting effects of these organizations on companies.

Criteria for Use

Typically, a project organization is responsible for completing an assigned objective on schedule, within cost and profit goals, and to established standards. The objective is usually one requiring special management attention and emphasis for a long period of time. Projects lasting only a few weeks or months, however, can be accomplished with a minimum of disruption by teams or task forces. A team or task force borrows employees from existing company organizations, but jobs are not held open elsewhere in a company for project organization personnel.

Generally, the project approach can be effectively applied to a one-time undertaking that is:

• Definable in terms of a specific goal.

• Infrequent, unique, or unfamiliar to the present organization.

• Complex with respect to interdependence of detail task accomplishment.

Advantages and Disadvantages of the Project Management Approach

How well have companies using project organizations met their objectives? To get some insight on this question, I made a mail survey of aerospace companies and received 47 responses. The main advantages and the extent to which companies agree on them are listed in FIGURE I. Other benefits reported by some companies include:

1. Better project visibility and focus on results.
2. Improved coordination among company divisions doing work on the project.
3. Higher morale and better mission orientation for employees working on the project.
4. Accelerated development of managers due to breadth of project responsibilities.

FIGURE I. MAJOR ADVANTAGES

Advantages	Percent of respondents
Better control of the project	92%
Better customer relations	80
Shorter product development time	40
Lower program costs	30
Improved quality and reliability	26
Higher profit margins	24
Better control over program security	13

FIGURE II. MAJOR DISADVANTAGES

Disadvantages	Percent of respondents
More complex internal operations	51%
Inconsistency in application of company policy	32
Lower utilization of personnel	13
Higher program costs	13
More difficult to manage	13
Lower profit margins	2

Not all of the results have been advantageous, however. Some aerospace companies have had difficulty using project organizations. The main disadvantages reported are listed in FIGURE II. Several companies reported other disadvantages from their own experience. These include:

1. Tendency for functional groups to neglect their job and let the project organization do everything.
2. Too much shifting of personnel from project to project due to priorities.
3. Duplication of functional skills in the project organization.

In evaluating the results of the survey, it appears that a company taking the project organization approach can be reasonably certain that it will improve controls and customer relations (if this is a factor), but internal operations will be more complex.

• Critical to the company because of the threat of loss or serious penalty.[1]

The one-time undertaking often involves a new product, where the emphasis is on research, development, testing, and production. Although such an effort is mainly developmental, the project manager cannot ignore the ultimate marketability of his product any more than a product manager can ignore the development of products which he is marketing.

Important Role

The traditional functional form of organization is based on the premise that there will be a continuous flow of products or services, with substantial similarity in the performed tasks. Functional organizations often cannot accomplish unusually complex or markedly different projects because of these conditions:

▶ No one in a functional organization besides the company or division manager is entirely responsible for project costs and profits. Functional department executives are concerned only with doing specialized work within budget.

▶ Functional departments often are jealous of their prerogatives, and fight to promote and preserve their specialties rather than work toward a unified project objective.

▶ The total perspective of a project is lost among functional departments. They can be guilty of "tunnel vision" — that is, a concern for only their own portions of the task without regard for

[1] See John M. Stewart, "Making Project Management Work," Business Horizons, Fall 1965, p. 54.

the impact of their actions on the company and on the project.

▶ More and faster decision making is required on a new project, and it is slowed by passing interdepartmental problems to the top through all levels of functional departments. This process often delays important project decisions or prevents them from being made.

▶ Functional departments performing repetitive tasks often lack the flexibility and responsiveness necessary to cope with new and rapidly changing project requirements.

The project organization can provide the arrangement, emphasis, and control necessary to counteract any weaknesses, functional or otherwise, that could impair successful completion of the project.

Wide Responsibility

To be able to wield total control, a project organization must be responsible for:

1. *Product Definition* — Define or direct the definition of products to be developed in terms of hardware, software, and services, including standards for performance, quality, reliability, and maintainability.

2. *Task and Funds Control* — Assign tasks and allocate funds to all groups performing the tasks and/or procuring hardware and services for the project.

3. *Make-or-Buy Decisions* — Coordinate analyses of company capabilities, capacities, and efficiencies, and make final decisions on whether the company supplies or buys hardware and services for the project. Participate in selection of major sources.

4. *Scheduling* — Develop master project schedules and coordinate schedule requirements with affected company organizations, associate subcontractors, and customers.

5. *Project Status* — Establish status-reporting systems and continuously monitor project expenditures, schedules, task completions, cost to complete, and deliveries.

6. *Identification and Solution of Problem* — Identify problems significant to project success and initiate action to solve them.

7. *Project Change Control* — Approve and exercise control over all project changes, including design changes.

8. *Associate or Subcontract Control* — Have control of major subcontractors involved in team arrangements on major tasks.

9. *Customer and Public Relations* — Serve as the outside contact for the project.

10. *Market Potentials* — Maintain awareness of customer attitudes, customer desires, and any other factors which could affect the project. Develop plans for logical follow-up action, potential or new applications, or new versions of the project hardware or services.

All of the above controls are required for a product design-development effort. Not all of them are needed for other types of projects, but all essential controls must be in the hands of the project organization if it is wholly accountable for results.

Organization Table

The size of an organization needed to exercise project control can vary from one person to several thousand employees organized by departments, sections, and groups. In all cases, however, management must appoint one person as the project head.

Kinds of Project Units

The organization structure and the elements needed for project control are governed by the desires of top management and by company and project circumstances:

◖ An *individual* project organization consists of only one person — the project manager. He exercises project control through the functional departments performing all the work on the project. No activities or personnel (except clerical support) report directly to him.

◖ In a *staff* project organization, the project manager is provided a staff to exercise control through activities such as scheduling, task and funds supervision, and change control, and to carry out any functions unique to the project, like testing or site activation. Functional departments still perform the primary tasks of engineering, procurement, and manufacturing.

◖ An *intermix* project organization is established when some of the primary functions are removed from functional departments and are assigned to report directly to the project manager, along with staff functions.

◖ Under an *aggregate* organization, all departments and activities required to accomplish a project report directly to the project manager.

A project organization can change radically in form during its lifetime. For example:

One aerospace company formed an individual project organization, supported by a team of representatives borrowed from functional departments, during the proposal stage. After the company received the contract award, it created an intermix organization which included engineering and manufacturing for the development phase. After starting the production phase, the company reduced the group to a staff-type for production and all follow-on contracts.

A project organization can also be the beginning of an organization cycle. The project may become a long-term or permanent effort that eventually becomes a program or branch organization. The latter in turn may become separated from the parent organization and be established as a full-fledged product division, functionally organized. Then management may create a series of new project organizations within the new product division, starting the cycle over again.

Supervisory Limits

Large unit size, particularly in the cases of intermix or aggregate groups, may cause the manager to lose personal control over the project, forcing him to rely more on formal organization and procedures. With a staff of 100 or more, he must create a formal structure with written outlines of responsibility. Except in the case of the aggregate project unit, the project manager must rely on support and services from functional organizations. His degree of authority and his relationship to functional departments therefore are critical and must be spelled out to ensure successful use of the concept.

The extent of delegated authority has been established by different companies in different ways. For instance:

(1) Project managers in Company A are authorized to direct any department or division to take whatever action is necessary to maintain good program performance, ensure the timely delivery of reliable, qualified products to customers, and encourage follow-on business. Each department performing work on a project appoints a representative who is responsible to the project manager for work done in the department. The project manager is head of an individual project organization and can prescribe to functional departments only what is required on the project and when. How the task is performed remains under the departments' supervision.

(2) The project organization exercises overall management of the XXX weapons system for the president of Company B. It translates customer requirements into task definition and assigns the tasks to functional organizations. While no line authority extends from the project manager into the functional departments, he monitors their performance. The functional departments appoint sections or individuals to discharge their responsibilities under XXX project management control. When a new function must be created in order to fulfill unique project requirements, the function is established in the project management unit only if it is not feasible to do it within an existing functional department. This project manager is head of a staff project organization and exercises more authority than the project manager of Company A.

(3) A project of major scope is placed in a division of Company C under the direction of a project manager, who reports to the president. The project manager brings together and directs all of the division's functions and resources required for successful completion of the project. The division's functional departments transfer their functions and personnel to the project when it can be done logically, practically, and economically. Those operations that cannot continue in a divided condition remain in the division's functional departments, although the departments still furnish the required services. This is an example of the intermix project organization, and the project manager here has more authority than the project manager from Company B.

Some companies have found that a project manager can adequately control a project — even though none of the organizations working on the project reports directly to him — if he controls the money, sets the schedules, and defines the performance criteria. When the project is on schedule, within cost and profit objectives, and advancing well, everyone is satisfied. If problems arise, the project manager can identify the functional persons who are responsible and make sure they take corrective action — if higher management backs him.

Functional Response. Other companies have found that the need for departments reporting directly to the project manager depends on the effectiveness, responsiveness, and attitude of the functional organizations. For example:

The engineering department in a West Coast aerospace company had a reputation for its expeditious and efficient product designs that met performance specifications. Company management decided that little could be gained by forming an engineering department within the project organization. So the company located the engineering groups near the project manager to shorten lines of communication on product definition, change control, and customer technical coordination. The project manager experienced no difficulty in maintaining project control.

In many companies the project manager's authority is defined in an organization description, but in practice it may be something else. Then he exercises only the limited authority he can acquire by his own devices. Sometimes the project organization has been created at the request of the customer. Functional unit supervisors often dislike the project concept, partly because it superimposes the project manager and his organization on a functional structure that has existed for many years. Most of the managerial know-how and experience is in functional departments, and their supervisors often have difficulty in adjusting to becoming service organizations for the project and relinquishing some of the authority they previously enjoyed.

There are no definite ground rules for determining the extent of project management authority. It must be decided by each company after consideration of project requirements and organizational and managerial strengths. Whatever approach is used, top management can avoid problems by:

1. Delineating the extent of the project manager's authority over the project and in his dealings with functional organizations.

2. Supporting the project manager to enable him to exercise his authority.

Otherwise, the program will be impeded as project managers and functional group managers engage in muscle-flexing and infighting to see who really runs the show.

Task Allocation

Dividing functions between project and functional organizations when a staff or intermix project group is being formed poses a number of problems. An important factor to be considered is whether leaving the functional unit intact is necessary to maintain company capability. Obviously, some operations, such as machine shops, laboratories, electronic data processing, and accounting, cannot be sensibly divided. An attempt to encompass such activities in the project would create enormous facility or operating problems, and increase project costs significantly.

A better understanding of the problem can be gained by considering the experience of one Southwest aerospace company. Its management wanted to establish certain procurement functions in the project organization, with the object of combining all the elements that affect cost, schedule, and performance in the unit. The company thought it had found a solution in assigning to the project organization the responsibility of procuring major systems and equipment items, while leaving procurement of raw stock and standard hardware to the functional organization. This, however, only settled the issue of who did the buying; it left unanswered which organization would perform other necessary functions. An analysis indicated that it was also necessary to identify those units which would:

• Determine the quantities and source of hardware to be procured.

• Receive and stock shipments from vendors.

• Issue and control inventories in support of manufacturing and customer service activities.

• Procure repair parts and spares to support manufacturing and customer deliveries.

• Conduct pricing, estimating, and make-or-buy analyses on potential procurements.

• Process and negotiate repair of purchased recoverable parts and systems.

• Package and ship items to be delivered or repaired.

One aircraft company with several projects going on at the same time attempted to avoid dividing functions and yet create an intermix project organization. Management ordered the engineering department to report to the project organization having the greatest task while it continued to provide service to the other projects. This scheme is objectionable because it —

. . . causes major priority problems, except in cases where a company has only one very large project and one or more very small ones;

. . . forces the manager of the largest project to worry about serving other smaller projects, thus defeating the purpose of the project organization.

Some management practitioners have proposed that the project manager be permitted to take his business outside the company if he is dissatisfied with the quality of work of a functional organization on the project. Most companies, however, would hesitate to grant their project managers so much authority. For one reason, the work of the functional unit in question may be necessary to the company's future. Also, a decision by one project manager to subcontract a task could seriously impair work on other projects by upsetting task loads and causing loss of critical skills. Furthermore, providing facilities and skills to complete existing projects and compete for future ones remains the responsibility of functional departments. Decisions of this kind should be made by the company president, to protect the long-range interests of the company.

Personnel Matters

The project manager is often selected during the proposal phase of an undertaking. In those instances, he plays a major role in determining the project organization's functions and responsibilities. In other cases, top management makes these decisions after the project is initiated, then names the project manager. His first task, and one of his most important tasks, is selecting — and getting — the personnel needed to accomplish the job.

Manager's Qualities

It is, of course, essential that the project manager have superior leadership ability. He must have administrative experience in engineering and manufacturing. And he must be skilled in planning, budgeting, scheduling, and other control techniques.[2] A weak project manager cannot be made strong and effective by creating additional controls or a top-heavy project organization structure.

Sometimes a functional executive is designated project manager in addition to his normal duties. In such cases, he must have time available to devote to the project, and care must be taken so that the project does not conflict with his functional responsibilities. Otherwise, the project will suffer from lack of attention or biased decision making.

It must be kept in mind that veteran functional managers cannot be expected to accept direction readily from some lesser executive who is suddenly promoted to project manager. Top management can avoid this problem by:

√ Selecting a man who already has a high position of responsibility, or placing him high enough in the organization.

[2] For a full discussion of his role, see Paul O. Gaddis, "The Project Manager," HBR May–June 1959, p. 89.

√ Assigning him a title as important-sounding as those of functional unit managers.

√ Supporting him in his dealings with functional managers.

If the project manager is expected to exercise project control over the functional departments, then he must report to the same level as the department managers, or higher.

Staffing the Unit

Usually the manpower for a project organization comes from functional departments or from other project organizations which are phasing out. The project manager often encounters difficulty, however, in getting the people he wants, because:

1. Several projects may be competing for talent at the same time, and there may not be enough to go around.

2. Functional department executives may be unwilling to make the requested personnel available.

3. The selected employees may be unwilling to transfer.

One project manager found that publicizing his project, mixing in professional societies, and inviting important people to inspect his project were successful techniques for attracting and holding personnel. This indirect approach, however, is more likely to be necessary in attracting talent from other companies in more glamorous industries.

Within a company, the direct approach, in which the project manager discusses his requirements with the functional organization head who has the talent, usually solves the problem. In companies with several ongoing projects, where there are shortages of talent or a particular talent cannot be applied full-time to one project, the best solution may be to leave the talent in a central functional organization to serve all projects.

Hesitant Employees. One of the most serious problems that the project manager may face is the reluctance of employees to join a project organization because they fear that at the completion of the job their employment may be terminated, or they may be transferred to other, less desirable jobs. An employee with a record of good progress and an established reputation in a functional department is likely to turn down an offer to join a project unit; he may be influenced by functional executives' often-held view that the establishment of a project organization is a reflection of inadequate performance on their part. In short, an employee may feel that in leaving the relative stability and security of a functional group he will have burned his bridges behind him and have no "home" to return to at the conclusion of the project.

Another factor affecting an employee's decision is the division of responsibilities between a functional organization and its counterpart in the project organization. A survey conducted by the Aerospace Industries Association revealed that when part of the procurement function has been placed in a project, the functional organization has retained either complete control or partial control of personnel selection and placement, coordination of salary grades, and coordination of salary increases.[3] The employee who becomes a part of the project organization in this circumstance finds that the project manager has little or no control over pay increases and promotions.

Management can do a number of things to encourage employees to transfer to project organizations. For instance, salary increases can be offered to employees as inducements to accept the risks involved. Furthermore, a number of promotional opportunities will usually result from forming a project organization, since additional management structure is being created. The company can make special efforts to relocate personnel phasing out of existing project organizations, and thereby create an atmosphere of security. (Incidentally, if a project manager does not look after his staff during phase-out of a project, he may not get them back on another project.) The use of financial incentives and a policy of "taking care" of people could, however, increase cost excessively.

In many cases, the excitement and glamor of a project with some promise of longevity is all that is needed to attract the personnel required. If the project manager is unable to complete his staffing within the company, he may want to seek talent outside the company.

Cost Considerations

The cost of a project organization varies, of course, according to its size, extent of new facilities and equipment needed, and its duration, among other factors. How much cost control a project manager has, or should have, is some-

times difficult to determine. Here are some aspects of cost worthy of consideration.

Greater Efficiency

Added cost from reduced manpower utilization is incurred when functions counterpart to those in the project organization continue to exist in the functional groups or in other project units. Dividing the work will cause loss of efficiency, particularly when it involves functions such as program planning, budgeting, and contracts administration, where the task to be accomplished is harder to identify and the performance is harder to measure. (Some companies, to their chagrin, have suffered unwarranted cost resulting from failure to reduce manpower levels in functional units when tasks are transferred to the project group.)

While increases in costs from reduced manpower utilization, from added management, and from expanded facilities probably cannot be avoided, they are likely to be small compared to other project costs. In any case, they may be offset by reduced costs in procurement, engineering, tooling, and manufacturing. For example, one survey of aerospace companies revealed that inclusion of the procurement function in a project organization results in improved performance sufficient to offset the usually higher operating costs.[4] Another survey, which dealt only with the engineering function, reported that 8 out of 19 large companies found that contract overruns had decreased or were eliminated by incorporating the function in project units.[5]

Since it is doubtful whether any company ever has managed identical projects under functional and project forms of organization, a company often finds it difficult to determine the effects on costs from use of the project approach. Nearly always, however, companies find they are exercising better cost control. They are applying more management to the project; tasks and budgets are better defined, changes more rigidly controlled, performance more closely watched; and management initiates action sooner to prevent or correct problems.

[3] *Summary of Project vs. Functional Organization Survey*, a report prepared by the Materials Procurement Committee, Aerospace Industries Association, February 1963.
[4] Aerospace Industries Association, op. cit.
[5] General Dynamics/Astronautics, *Impact of a Project Structured Organization on Administrative Matters*, Eighth Engineering Administrative Conference (San Diego, California, June 1, 1963).

EXHIBIT I. BREAKDOWN OF COSTS FOR PROJECT AND EXTENT CONTROLLED BY
PROJECT ORGANIZATION IN COMPANY Y

AREA OF COST		PERCENT OF DOLLARS SPENT	PERCENT OF DOLLARS UNDER DIRECT CONTROL OF PROJECT ORGANIZATION
SUBCONTRACTED TASK		50%	50%
PURCHASED PARTS AND MATERIALS		10	0
DIRECT LABOR (INPLANT)	ENGINEERING	6	4
	MANUFACTURING	8	4
	TOOLING	4	0
	OTHER	2	1
INDIRECT LABOR AND OVERHEAD (INPLANT)		20	4
TOTAL		100%	63%

Managerial Controls

While cost control is a key part of managerial supervision of a project, it is not always necessary for the project manager to oversee all expenditures directly. For example:

Company X did not try to give the project manager direct control over costs; instead it established a staff-type project organization. The project manager had control over funds allocation on all matters except burden costs outside the project organization. The various functional departments were incrementally funded for the task in current periods, and the project manager watched project progress to ensure task accomplishment in accordance with funds allocation. The project manager reallocated funds for task changes, but let the functional unit managers worry about controlling costs within the funds allocated. This system worked well for Company X.

Putting all feasible cost matters under the control of the manager while maintaining other project objectives does not always turn out as envisioned. In one situation:

Company Y gave the project manager as much direct control over costs as possible, while trying to minimize the cost of the project. It established an intermix project organization containing the unique, control, and primary functions that could be divided economically without undue loss of efficiency or without incurring large facility expense. For example, the project manager had total responsibility for subcontract management, but procurement of sheet metal and standard parts was left in the functional material organization. Engineering design was transferred to the project organization, but research laboratories, drawing, and other services were still performed on a centralized basis by the functional units. Other key functions were similarly divided.

After this arrangement was in operation a while, Company Y analyzed its costs and found them to be categorized as shown in EXHIBIT I. All its efforts to give the project manager cost supervision had resulted in giving him control over only 63% of the total. Without direct control over subcontracting, he would have exercised control over only 13% of total project costs.

Effects on Company

However a company operates its project organizations, they are bound to affect the company while the units are carrying on their missions and even after they have been disbanded.

Maintaining Capability

An undesirable impact on company capabilities may result from using project organizations, because of these factors:

• Project priorities and competition for talent may interrupt the stability of the organization and interfere with its long-range interests by upsetting the traditional business of functional organizations.

• Long-range planning may suffer as the company gets more involved in meeting schedules and fulfilling the requirements of temporary projects.

• Shifting people from project to project may disrupt the training of new employees and specialists, thereby hindering their growth and development within their fields of specialization.

• Lessons learned on one project may not be communicated to other projects. One executive who was transferring from a project being phased out to a new project found the same mistakes being made that he had encountered on his former assignment three years earlier. He felt that the problem resulted from splitting normal functional responsibilities among project organizations and from not having enough qualified, experienced employees to spread among all organizations.

An individual-type project organization has of course the least impact on developing and maintaining company capability. The functional departments are doing the work; the resources and skills they develop on one project can be applied to current and succeeding projects.

In a staff-type project organization, however, the problem of maintaining capability may arise. Unique functions, such as site construction and testing, have no permanent impact, since the groups created for these tasks are usually disbanded at the conclusion of the task or project. Primary tasks, such as engineering, procurement, and manufacturing, are not affected, since they are accomplished by the functional organizations. Some of the project support functions, however, such as financial control, contract administration, program planning, and customer coordination, are performed by the staff-type project organization as control activities. When these functions are divided among several project organizations or between project organizations and functional departments, there is some danger of losing efficiency — not having enough talent or the right talent on a particular project — and losing the capability at the end of phase-out of the project.

The same problem, with greater magnitude, has been experienced by intermix and aggregate project organizations, since primary functions such as engineering, procurement, and manufacturing are also assigned to the project organizations.

Structural Changes

A predictable result of using the project approach is the addition of organization structure and management positions. Thus:

One aerospace company, Company Z, compared its organization and management structure as it existed before it began forming projects units with the structure that existed afterward. The results are shown in EXHIBIT II. The number of departments had increased from 65 to 106, while total employment remained practically the same. The number of employees for every supervisor had dropped from 13.4 to 12.8. The company con-

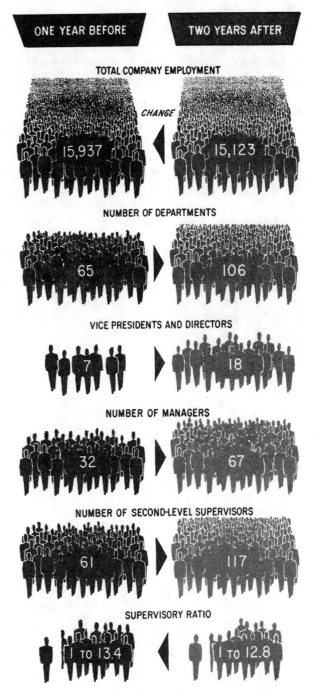

EXHIBIT II. MANAGEMENT STRUCTURE CHANGES IN COMPANY Z FROM PROJECT ORGANIZATIONS

ONE YEAR BEFORE   TWO YEARS AFTER

TOTAL COMPANY EMPLOYMENT
CHANGE
15,937   15,123

NUMBER OF DEPARTMENTS
65   106

VICE PRESIDENTS AND DIRECTORS
7   18

NUMBER OF MANAGERS
32   67

NUMBER OF SECOND-LEVEL SUPERVISORS
61   117

SUPERVISORY RATIO
1 TO 13.4   1 TO 12.8

cluded that a major cause of this change was the project groups.

Company Z uncovered proof of its conclusion when it counted the number of second-level and higher management positions. It found it had 11 more vice presidents and directors, 35 more managers, and 56 more second-level supervisors. Although the company attributed part of this growth to an upgrading of titles, the effect of the project organizations was the creation of 60 more management positions.

Conclusion

Before establishing a project organization, a company should assess the nature of the job and its requirements. Then the company should evaluate its existing structure to pinpoint any organizational weaknesses that might inhibit successful accomplishment of the project. The project organization should be assigned any functions needed to compensate for known or probable organizational deficiencies. The scale of project organization is determined by the kind and scope of the organization functions assigned to it. Naturally a company should set up the minimal project structure necessary. Individual and staff project units can provide the emphasis and control needed for most missions, without the problems and disadvantages inherent in dividing primary functions. Intermix

and aggregate project organizations are required rarely, and only for extremely critical and complex projects.

Neither the role of the project manager nor that of the functional manager can be permitted to dominate in a company using the project method. Functional organizations must perform tasks and services in support of project management. Project management must recognize the responsibility of functional organizations for developing and maintaining company capabilities. Top management must resolve conflicts between them to protect the company's best interest.

Functional organization specialization is the most efficient way to manufacture quantities of products in most industries. Project organizations are temporary and should complement or supplement functional departments. They should not replace functional organizations because functional specialization in areas such as engineering, manufacturing, and procurement is essential for the preservation and perpetuation of industrial capabilities.

Creation of a project organization will not automatically ensure successful accomplishment of an assigned objective. It is not a panacea for overcoming all functional organization weaknesses. But it can be a great asset to those companies which possess the acumen to exploit its strengths.

The Matrix Organization

LINN C. STUCKENBRUCK
University of Southern California

Ed. note: The Southern California Chapter of the Project Management Institute has been working on a book project for approximately one year. The title of the book will be The Implementation of Project Management, *and it has been designed as an aid to the newly appointed project manager, who says, "Now what do I do?" The project plan is to have the book ready for sale at the 1979 International Seminar/Symposium at Atlanta. The following paper is a representative chapter from the book.*

What Is A Matrix Organization?

A matrix organization is defined as one in which there is dual or multiple managerial accountability and responsibility. However, the term matrix means quite different things to different people and in different industries (1)(5). In a matrix there are usually two chains of command, one along functional lines and the other along project, product, or client lines. Other chains of command such as geographic location are also possible.

The matrix organizational form may vary from one in which the project manager holds a very strong managerial position to one in which he plays only a coordinating role. To illustrate the organizational principles, a matrix will be considered first in which there is a balance of power between the project and functional managers. It must be recognized that such a balanced situation, considered by some authorities to be ideal, probably seldom occurs in practice.

The Two-Boss Matrix

In a balanced matrix organization various people in the organization have two bosses (figure 1). This represents an abandonment of the age-old management concept, "Thou shalt have but one boss above thee." None of the reporting relationships shown in figure 1 are dotted-line relationships. Solid- and dotted-line relationships have various interpretations depending upon local management custom. However, solid lines normally connect managers with their direct subordinates, the man above being the boss. Dotted lines are usually used to indicate staff relationships or reporting relationships of lesser importance. The project manager in the matrix organization is not a staff man nor does he normally have less authority than the functional managers reporting on the same level. Neither can the relationships shown in figure 1 be simply described by such terms as "he reports to the functional manager only for technical direction," or "he reports to the project office for budgetary and schedule control." Such descriptions are inadequate to describe how the matrix organization really works because in reality, not just on paper, the project personnel do have two bosses.

Implicit in the definition of the matrix organization is the recognition that the project is temporary whereas the functional departments are more permanent. Although all organizations are temporary in that they are con-

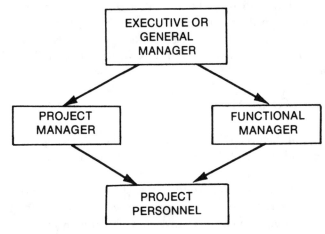

Figure 1: The basic unit of the matrix organization.

stantly changing, the matrix is designed to be temporary and a particular organizational structure lasts only for the finite life of the project.

Why the Matrix?

The matrix developed as a natural evolution of organizational structures in answer to a very definite real-world need. The need was for an organizational form capable of managing the recent very large and very complex programs, projects, and problems, and for managing limited resources. The conventional hierarchical management organization could not cope with the added complexity and the enormous amount of information that had to be processed, and conventional management theory was of little help in solving these new and unique problems.

Most management theorists predicted that the lack of any clear-cut single line of responsibility and authority would result in managerial ineffectiveness. There is no evidence to indicate that multiple authority and role conflict lead to ineffectiveness (16).

The primary reason for adopting the matrix in a large organization can be pinpointed in the fact that functions and skills are fragmented throughout the organizational structure. Individual functional departments have great difficulty in solving very large problems because of a failure to view the total system and a tendency to suboptimize or solve the problem within their particular discipline. According to an old aerospace cliche, "An engineer attacks *every* problem as if it had an engineering solution." How few of today's big civil and social problems have purely technical solutions?

Since it was found to be impractical to fragment the problem and have the various functional organizations work only on their portion of the problem, "microcompanies" were formed (21). This represented the development of the pure project organization. It was very rapidly realized that this alternative was not only very unwieldly but had many disadvantages with respect to efficient functional operations. The matrix was the next logical development.

Growth of the Matrix

As problems and projects have become more complex, the inadequacy of the hierarchical organizational structure became apparent. At the same time, the necessity for designing the organization around the task to be performed was realized. Fortunately, varied but more complex organizational alternatives have become available. The present management philosophy is that there is no "one best way" for all projects to organize. Rather there

are many alternatives from which to select a specific project. Among these alternatives are various forms of the matrix.

A formalized matrix form of organization was first developed and documented in the United States aerospace industry where it evolved during the growth of the large, complex projects of the 1950s and 1960s. If a project was very large, it usually became a pure project organization in which all of the functions and resources necessary to accomplish the objectives of the project were put in a single hierarchical organization. This alternative worked very well if the project or program was very large, and if the government customer was similarly organized, and if the customer not only insisted on such an organization but was willing to pay for its added expense.

However, the aerospace industry found that it had many more projects which were not particularly large, but were exceedingly complex, and therefore not conveniently handled within a single discipline. Today, it is rare to find a real-world problem that is unidisciplinary. In addition, top management still felt a strong need to have a single source of information and a single point of responsibility for each project or program. Some form of project management was obviously needed, and not being willing to bear the expense of making each project a little empire of its own, the matrix was a natural evolution in management thinking. The term "matrix" began to be applied to organizations at this time, and as indicated by Davis and Lawrence, "It probably seemed like a fitting term for mathematically trained engineers in that industry to apply to the gridlike structure that was evolving . . ." (10).

The Matrix Organization

It has been recognized that the matrix organizational structure has applications far beyond that of project (program or product) management (12). However, in this discussion the matrix will only be considered from the viewpoint of its most highly developed application — that of project management.

The term "matrix project organization" refers to a multidisciplinary team whose members are drawn from various line or functional units of the heirarchical organization. The organization so developed is temporary in nature, since it is built around the project or specific task to be done rather than on organizational functions. The matrix is thus built up as a team of personnel drawn from both the project and the functional or disciplinary organizations. In other words a project organization is superimposed on the conventional functional hierarchical organization.

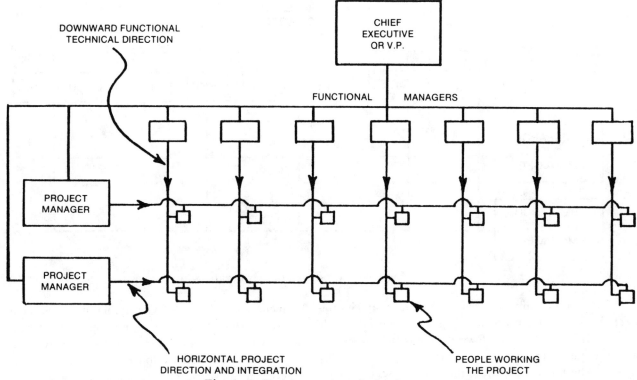

Figure 2. Simple matrix organization

The matrix in its simplest form is shown diagramatically in figure 2, indicating how the matrix received its name.

The matrix shown in figure 2 represents a general organizational structure. To be more specific, engineering, research, product and construction matrix organizations are shown in figures 3, 4, 5, and 6 respectively.

The matrix is thus a multi-dimensional structure that tries to maximize the strengths and minimize the weaknesses of both the project and the functional structures (25).

Does the Matrix Work?

No specific organizational form can be guaranteed to work at all times, or to improve productive output. However, it can be said that some organizational forms have a better chance of working than others, particularly if they are designed to meet the needs of project work. As previously indicated, the matrix meets a number of well-defined needs. The principal need is for an organizational structure that can handle the great complexity of a multidisciplinary effort.

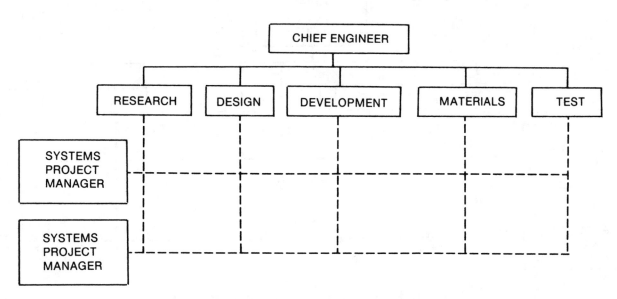

Figure 3. An engineering matrix organization

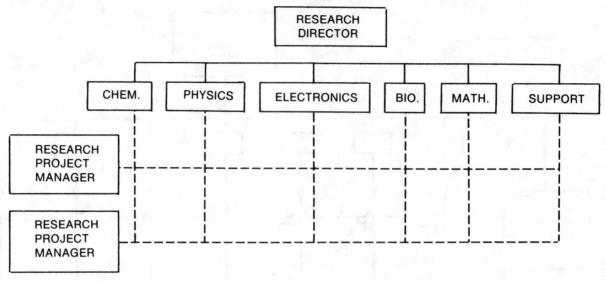

Figure 4. A research matrix organization

If the multidisciplinary need is really there, and if project management is necessary, then the matrix is a viable organizational solution. However, the matrix is a complex organizational form and will not automatically work. The number of things that can go wrong is endless, but the most usual reason for failure of the matrix results from either foot-dragging or downright sabotage on the part of functional management and even by lower level supervision. As indicated in the previous discussion of project management, it is necessary to assure that the matrix will work by thoroughly selling the concept to top management and to all involved functional management. If everyone involved in the matrix is "a believer," and every effort is expended to make it work, the matrix will work and will result in outstanding project accomplish-

ment. As indicated previously, if only takes one uncooperative disciplinary manager dragging his feet to make the whole project fail. However, active, enthusiastic, and aggressive support by top management will counteract even the most recalcitrant functional manager.

Advantages of the Matrix

The matrix organization has many advantages which far outweigh its principal disadvantage of complexity. Among the more universally accepted advantages of the matrix which go beyond the advantages of project management in general are the following (2)(22):

- *Project Objectives Clear* — Project objectives will not only be highly visible through the project office, but

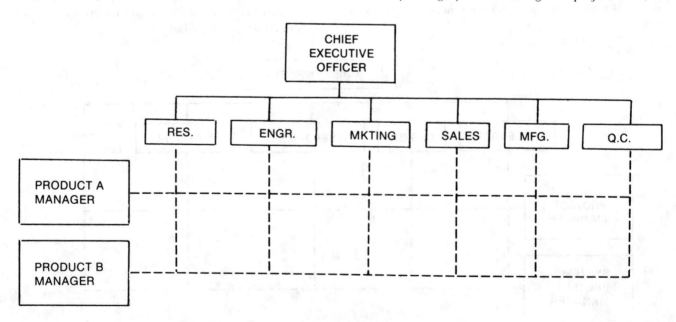

Figure 5. A product industry matrix organization

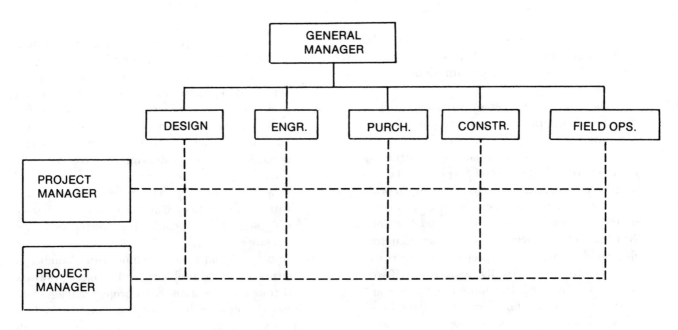

Figure 6. A construction industry matrix organization

will also be balanced with the objectives of the functional organization.

- *Project Integration* — There is a clear and workable mechanism for achieving project integration of subsystems and work packages across functional departmental lines. Coordination across functional lines can easily be achieved.

- *Efficient Use of Resources* — The maximum efficient utilization can be made of scarce company resources. It is the most efficient use of manpower since personnel can be used only part-time if desired, and can be shared between projects. It is the most efficient use of facilities, machinery, equipment, and other resources since these resources can be shared between or among projects. Allocation of scarce resources can be negotiated between project and functional management, or corporate priorities may be established. The matrix is therefore less expensive than an equivalent pure project organization.

- *Information Flow* — Information dissemination should be very effective since there is provision for both horizontal and vertical flow. Horizontal flow provides for project systems information to flow from functional unit to functional unit. Vertical flow provides for detailed disciplinary information to flow from project to project, and to various levels of management. Information of use to other projects is not locked up within a single project.

- *Retention of Disciplinary Teams* — Teams of functional experts and specialists are kept together even though

projects come and go. Therefore technology and know-how is not lost when a project is completed. Specialists like to work with other specialists in the same discipline, and they will be better able to continually exchange ideas and information. As a result, when teams of functional specialists work together, a synergistic effect occurs, resulting in increased innovation and productive output, even though individually they may be working on different projects.

- *High Morale* — Morale problems occur less frequently since the worker in the matrix responds first to the morale-building experience of working on a successful project resulting in visible achievements. This will be true whether the achievement is a ballistic missile, an aircraft, a power plant, or the introduction of a new soap into the marketplace. Secondly, worker morale is normally higher when they can work with their fellow specialists. Thirdly, by retaining his functional "home," the specialist may have a clearer career progression up the functional ladder. On the other hand, if he finds that his talents and interests are multidisciplinary, he can set his career objectives toward the project office.

- *Development of Project Managers* — The matrix is an excellent training ground for prospective project managers since promising candidates can easily be spotted in the multidisciplinary project environment. A common occurrence would be the transfer of a person who had demonstrated the ability to work across functional departmental lines to the project office as an assistant project manager. His career progression would then be to project manager, which is an excellent path leading to top management.

- *Project Shutdown* — In a matrix organization project termination is not the traumatic and painful event that it can be in a pure project organization. It is not uncommon for a large aerospace or construction project to have several thousand people working in a pure project organization. What do you do with several thousand people when the project is completed? Large layoffs are almost unavoidable since only a relatively few people can be relocated unless major buildups in another project are occurring. Matrix projects are normally smaller with fewer people overall involved. In addition, the people are spread across a whole functional organization and each department has only a few people to relocate.

Problems of the Matrix

The matrix organization does have some disadvantages and problems, but they need not be considered insurmountable. Knowing what problems may occur is "half the battle" in overcoming them. The following disadvantages are inherent in the matrix organization:

- *Two Bosses* — The major disadvantage is that the personnel on the project are working for two bosses. In any type of conflict situation a person could easily become "the man in the middle." Further problems of conflict can be caused by project personnel playing one boss against the other.
- *Complexity* — The matrix organization is inherently more complex than either a functional or a pure project organization, since it is the superimposition of one on the other. This complexity shows itself in the following problems:
  - *Difficulties in Monitoring and Controlling* — Complexity results from the number of managers and personnel involved and from the number of people that must be kept informed. Fortunately, modern computer techniques have helped to keep this problem under control, but basically it's still a "people" problem.
  - *Complex Information Flow* — This is a problem only because there are so many people and organizational units involved. Both the project and functional managers must be certain that they have touched bases with each other for any major decisions in their areas of responsibility.
  - *Fast Reaction Difficult* — The project manager is sometimes faced with a problem of achieving fast reaction times, primarily since there are so many people to be consulted. The project manager in

the matrix ususally does not have strong vested authority, therefore considerable negotiation is necessary. Project management was primarily conceived to prevent this problem, but it can be a problem if the management system keeps the project manager from making any decisions without consultation with functional and top management. If the matrix is working, the problem won't occur.

- *Conflicting Guidance* — The more complex organization with two lines of authority always increases the possibility of conflicting instructions and guidance.
- *Priorities* — A matrix organization with a number of projects faces real problems with project priorities and resource allocation. Each project manager will obviously consider his project to have the highest priority. Similarly, each functional manager will consider that the allocation of resources and priorities within his department is his own business. As a result, the decisions involving project priorities and often the allocation of resources must be made at a high level. This often puts an undue and unwelcome load on the top executive officer in the matrix. This problem has led to the use of a manager of projects, or a super project manager in some organizations. His principal functions would be to consult with higher levels of management to assure equitable allocation of resources and to periodically reassess project priorities. This effort can be extremely valuable in reducing conflict and anxiety within the matrix.
- *Management Goals* — There is a constant, although often unperceived, struggle in balancing the goals and objectives of project and functional management. A strong project manager may place undue emphasis on time and cost constraints, while a functional manager may concentrate on technical excellence at the expense of schedules. Top management must assure that a careful balance of the goals of both project and functional management is maintained.
- *Potential for Conflict* — As discussed in a later section of this chapter, whenever there are two project managers competing for resources, there is potential for conflict. This conflict may evidence itself primarily as a struggle for power. However, it also may evidence itself by backbiting, foot-dragging and project sabotage. Conflict and competition may also be constructive as an aid to achieving high performance; however, it cannot be allowed to degenerate to personal antagonism and discord. In project work conflict is inevitable; keeping it constructive is the

problem in matrix management.

- *Effects of Conflict on Management* — Since conflict and stress are inherent in the matrix organization, considerable attention must be given to the individuals who will function as both project and functional managers. Individuals vary greatly in their ability to function effectively under stress. Conflict, particularly the role conflict typical of the two-boss situation, can produce stress, anxiety, and reduced job satisfaction. Considerable attention must be directed toward assuring that prospective managers have a high tolerance for conflict situations.

Davis and Lawrence have discussed the problems of the matrix which they term matrix pathologies (11). They list and discuss the following problems: power struggles, anarchy, groupitis, collapse during economic crunch, excessive overhead, decision strangulation, sinking, layering, and navel gazing. They indicate that many of these difficulties occur in more conventional organizations, but that the matrix seems somewhat more vulnerable to these particular ailments.

They indicate that power struggles are inevitable in a matrix because it is different from the traditionally structured hierarchy. In the matrix, power struggles are a logical derivative of the ambiguity and shared power that has been built purposefully into the design. Corporations will find it exceedingly difficult to prevent power struggles from developing, but they must prevent them from reaching destructive lengths.

Anarchy is defined as a company quite literally coming apart at the seams during a period of stress. As the authors admit, this is an unlikely occurrence, and the more explicit the organizational agreements are the less likely it is to occur.

Groupitis refers to confusing matrix behavior with group decision making. The matrix does not require that all business decisions be hammered out in group meetings. Group decision making should be done as often as necessary, and as little as possible.

Collapse during economic crunch refers to the frequently noted fact that matrix organizations seem to blossom during periods of rapid growth and prosperity, and to be buffeted and/or cast away during periods of economic decline. It seems natural that during periods of crisis, top management thinks that the organization needs a firmer hand and reinstitutes the authoritarian structure. "There is no more time for organizational toys and tinkering. The matrix is done in." Thus the matrix is the readily available scapegoat for other organizational problems such as poor planning and inadequate control.

One of the concerns of organizations first encountering the matrix is that it is too costly since it appears, on the surface, to double up on management by adding another chain of command. It is true that initially overhead costs do rise, but as the matrix matures, these overhead costs decrease and productivity gains appear.

It is suggested that moving into a matrix can lead to the strangulation of the decision process. "Will all bold initiatives be watered down by too many cooks?" Three possible situations can arise: (1) the necessity for constant clearing of all issues with the functional managers, (2) escalation of conflict caused by constant referral of problems up the dual chain of command, and (3) some managers feel that every decision must be a crisp, unilateral decision, therefore they will be very uncomfortable and ineffective in a matrix organization.

Sinking refers to the observation that there seems to be some difficulty in keeping the matrix viable at the corporate or institutional level, and a corresponding tendency for it to sink down to lower levels in the organization where it survives and thrives. This phenomena may be indicative of top management not understanding the matrix or the matrix may just be finding its proper place.

Layering is defined as a phenomena in which matrices within matrices are found. By itself, layering may not be a problem, but it sometimes creates more problems than it solves because the unnecessary complexity may be more of a burden than it is worth.

Navel gazing refers to the tendency to become absorbed in the organization's internal relations at the expense of the world outside the organization, particularly to clients. This concentration on the internal workings of the organization is most likely to occur in the early phases of a matrix when new behaviors have to be learned.

Making the Matrix Work

After examining the disadvantages and problems of working in a matrix organization, one may view the problems as insurmountable. How then does a company get this complex organizational form to function? Its successful operation, like that of any management organization, depends almost entirely on actions and activities of the various people involved. First, top management must give real and immediate support to the matrix, including a clear project charter. This charter should state the purpose of the project and spell out the responsibilities and authority of the project manager. In addition it should indicate to the fullest extent possible his relationships with the functional managers involved in the project.

Functional management must modify much of their managerial thinking and their usual operational procedures and activities in order to make the matrix work.

This may mean a considerable change in the way they determine their priorities. It may be a considerable shock to functional management to find that their priorities must change, and that the project comes first. Project management must realize that they get their job accomplished primarily through the process of negotiation, and that they should become negotiation experts. If all major decisions are made with the concurrence of the involved functional managers, the project manager finds himself in a very strong position in insisting that the decision be carried out and that the desired goals be accomplished. In addition, the project personnel must be able to adapt to the two-boss situation which can be a traumatic experience when first encountered.

Who Is the Real Boss?

Whenever the two-boss situation is encountered, the logical question that can be asked is: who is the real boss? Theoretically it should be possible to divide the authority and responsibility more or less equally between the project and functional managers. However, there is no agreement among the experts as to whether a balance of power is necessary or even desirable.

Even if there is a balance of power, the question of who is the real boss may depend on other factors. For instance, the line or discipline manager is usually perceived as the real boss by the employees in a matrix organization. This is a natural situation since the discipline manager represents "home base" — the disciplinary home to which the employee returns after the project is completed. In addition, the disciplinary manager normally carries the most weight when it comes to performance evaluations and promotions. However, there are usually some employees who relate so strongly to the overall project, that they perceive the project manager to be the real boss. So perhaps there is no one real boss, rather there is a continually shifting balance of power (29).

Balance of Power

At the heart of the operation of the matrix is the balance of power. Theoretically, it should be possible to divide the authority and responsibility more or less equally between the project and functional managers, however to do so is difficult and seldom occurs. It has been attempted to clearly delineate the authority and responsibilities of both project and functional management so as to assure a balance of power. Such a delineation has been presented by one management author (7) who has divided the responsibilities as shown in table 1.

Table 1. Delineation of Responsibilities

Project Manager's Responsibilities
1. What is to be done?
2. When will the task be done?
3. Why will the task be done?
4. How much money is available to do the task?
5. How well has the total project been done?

Functional Manager's Responsibilities
1. How will the task be done?
2. Where will the task be done?
3. Who will do the task?
4. How well has the functional input been integrated into the project?

Another way of stating the roles is: the project manager is responsible for the overall integration of the total project system and the functional manager is responsible for technical direction in his discipline.

The so-called responsibility chart has been proposed as a useful device in defining jurisdictional areas of management (17)(20). A simplified example of a responsibility chart is show in table 2. Such a chart is probably more meaningful than organization charts or job descriptions, particularly is it is filled in during a meeting of all concerned managers resulting in agreement on the job responsibilities. This process results in potential conflicts being confronted early, before specific problems arise.

Table 2. Example of a Responsibility Chart
Source: Ref. 17, p. 171.

Actors \ Decisions	Laboratory Manager	General Manager	Project Manager	Marketing Manager	Controller
Change in Budget					
Allocate Manpower					
Change in Design Specification					
Change in Schedule					

R = Responsible
A = Approve
C = Consult
I = Inform

Certainly such a delineation indicates where the major responsibilities lie, but it cannot guarantee a balance of power. In fact, there are many reasons why it is almost impossible to have a truly "equal" balance of power between functional and project management. Not the least of these reasons is the fact that we are dealing with people, and all people, including managers, are different. Managers have differing personalities and differing management styles. Some management styles depend on the persuasive abilities of the manager while others depend on or tend to fall back on strong support from top management. In addition, power is a fluctuating and constantly changing condition that cannot be static even if one so desired (23).

The breakdown of responsibilities shown in table 1 and table 2, although useful in planning and decision making, is highly simplistic. What conscientious, knowledgeable project manager would not get personally involved in "how will the task be done?" His project schedule and "when will the task be done?" responsibilities do not allow him the luxury of sitting back and waiting for functional management to make every technical decision. He must ensure that technical decisions are made on schedule. He then must review the key technical decisions and challenge them if necessary. As project integrator, he has the overriding responsibility for evaluating *every* key project decision to determine how it interfaces with the other project tasks, and with his schedule and budget. The project manager therefore must get involved and influence every project action and as a last resort he always has appeal rights or veto power — for the good of the project. The project manager even gets involved in "who will do the task?" After all, the highest achievers and most innovative personnel in the discipline organizations will be highly sought after, and the project managers will seek to obtain only the very best people for their projects.

On the other hand, what good functional manager will not get deeply involved in the details of "what, when and for how much money?" He has a strong personal interest in these details since his organization has to perform the tasks spelled out in the project schedules and budgets. He must assure that the task is realistically priced and technically feasible. The responsibilities listed in table 1 can therefore only be used as indicators as to where the major responsibilities lie.

Since the project, program or product is usually a very important part of a company's activities, the project manager is a *very* important person. He is the one who puts the company in a position where it can make more profit, or lose money.

Therefore, in terms of the balance of power, it would seem that the project manager would always have the scale of power tipped in his direction, particularly with the firm support of top management. Not necessarily so!

In fact, not usually so, at least in a matrix organization. In a pure project organization, there is no question as to who holds the power. But in a matrix organization the functional manager has powerful forces on his side. As previously pointed out, the functional manager is normally perceived by project personnel to be the real boss. This is often inevitable since functional management is part of the unchanging ladder in the management hierarchy and is therefore perceived to be "permanent" by the employees. After all, the functional organization represents "home-base" to which project personnel expect to return after the completion of the project.

Very strong top-management support for the project manager is necessary to get the matrix to work, and even very strong support will not guarantee project success. However, the matrix will not work without it. The project manager must get the job done by every means at his disposal even though he may not be perceived as the real boss. He can always appeal to higher authority, however such actions must be kept to a minimum or top management may view the project manager as ineffective.

The Project/Functional Interface

The secret of the successfully functioning matrix can thus be seen to be not just a pure balance of power, but more a function of the type of interface relationships between the project and individual functional managers. Every project decision and action must be negotiated across this interface. This interface is a natural conflict situation since many of the goals and objectives of project and functional management are different. Depending on the personality and dedication of the respective managers, this interface relationship can be one of smooth-working cooperation or bitter conflict. A domineering personality or power play is not the answer. The overpowering manager may win the local skirmish, but usually manages sooner or later to alienate everyone working on the project. Cooperation and negotiation are the keys to successful decision making across the project/functional interface. Arbitrary and one-sided decisions by either the project or functional manager can only lead to or intensify the potential for conflict. Unfortunately for the project manager, he can accomplish little by himself, and must depend on the cooperation and support of the functional managers. That old definition of successful management — "one who gets things done by working through others" — is essential for successful project management in the matrix organization.

The project manager in a matrix organization has two very important interfaces — with top management and with functional management. A good working relationship with and ready access to top management is essential for resolving big problems and removing obstacles. A good working relationship with functional management will ensure that most problems are resolved at their level and will not have to go to top management. The conventional matrix model (figure 1) does not adequately emphasize these most important relationships. Obviously, neither the project manager nor the functional managers can sit in their offices and give orders. The various managers must be communicating with each other on at least a daily basis, and usually more often. Therefore a more adequate organizational model is shown in figure 7, which shows the managerial relationships as double-ended arrows, indicating that the relationships are two-way streets. Consultation, cooperation, and constant support are particularly necessary on the part of the project and functional managers. These are very important relationships, keys to the success of any matrix organization, and must be carefully nurtured and actively promoted by top management and by both project and functional management.

The difficulties that occur at the project/functional interface are emphasized if the salient differences between the role of the project manager and the traditional functional manager are analyzed. Such an analysis has been made by Cleland (7) and indicated that

"while these differences are possibly more theoretical than actual, differences do exist, and they affect the manager's modus operandi and philosophy." Both project and functional management must work to achieve activity harmony in spite of these conflicting objectives and roles. The matrix organization actually is a method of deliberately utilizing conflict to get a better job done. The project team must be more concerned with solving the problem rather than with *who* solves it. Teamwork and problem solving must be emphasized rather than role definition.

Achieving a Balance of Power

Achieving a balance of power between project and functional management may in many cases be a desirable goal. Certainly it should be a way of minimizing potential power struggles and unnecessary conflicts. There is no certain way to assure that there is a balance of power, and it is probably seldom really achieved. However, it can be approached by assuming that the project manager has the full support of top management and that he reports at a high enough level in the management hierarchy.

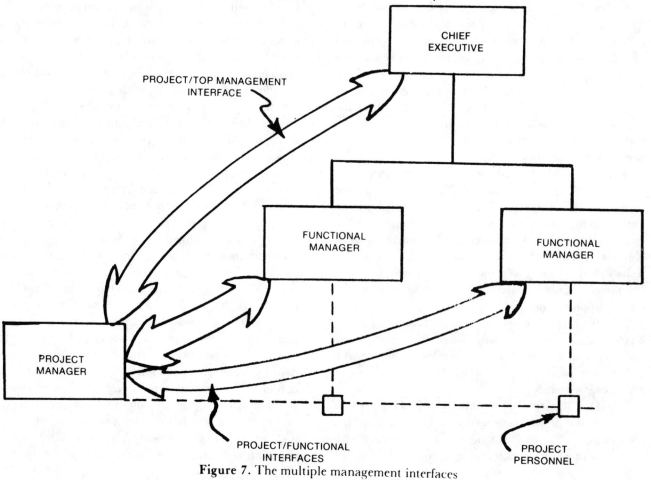

Figure 7. The multiple management interfaces

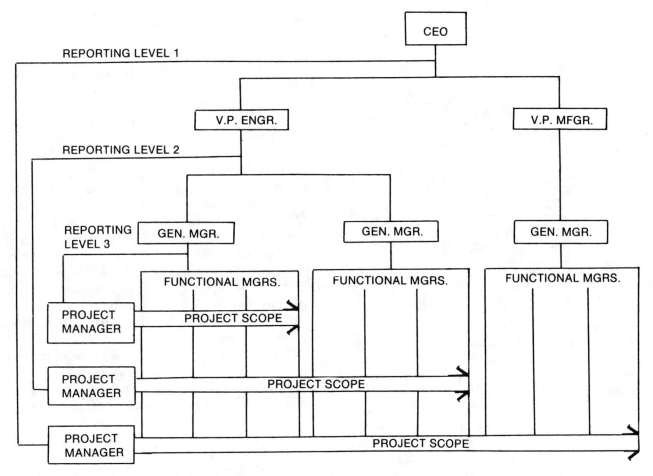

Figure 8. Project management reporting levels

How High Should Project Management Report?

It is not just a question of balance of power, but does the project manager have sufficient clout to be effective? For the most part, the project manager's clout is a direct function of the level at which he reports in the hierarchical organization. If he is to be effective, the project manager must be on at least an equal level with the highest level of functional management that he must deal with. As indicated in figure 8, there can be a considerable difference in reporting level depending whether the project is confined to a single department or spreads across the entire company's activities. This optimum reporting level will change during the life of a project as the effort progresses from basic research to the manufacture of a product.

Strong vs. Weak Matrix

In many situations it may not be desirable to have a balance of power. For instance, a project may be so important to the company, or the budget and schedule so tight that top management feels that the project manager

must be in a very strong position. Or perhaps the project manager feels that he must tilt the organizational balance of power in his favor to obtain better project performance. For instance, construction management has found from experience that a strong project office is often necessary to achieve good project performance (3). On the other hand, top management may feel that functional management needs more backing. In either case, the balance of power can be tilted in either direction by changing any one or any combination of the following three factors:

- *The administrative relationship.* — The levels at which the project and involved functional managers report, and the backing which they receive from top management.
- *The physical relationship.* — The physical distances between the various people involved in the project
- *The time spent on the project.* — The amount of time spent on the project by the respective managers

These three factors can be used to describe whether the matrix is strong or weak. The strong matrix is one in which the balance of power is definitely on the side of project management. This can be shown by the model in

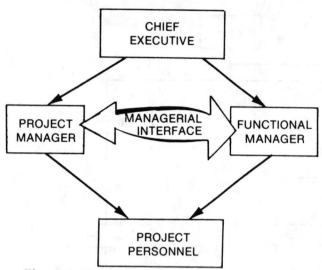

Figure 9. The balance of power in a strong matrix

figure 9. A weak matrix has been described by project managers as one in which the balance of power tilts decisively in the direction of line or functional management. Many organizations have thus, for various reasons including the inability to make the two-boss system work, modified the matrix by shifting the balance of power. Galbraith has described the managerial alternatives as a continuum ranging from pure project to functional (figure 10) (13)(17). The matrix falls in the middle of the continuum, and can range from very weak to very strong depending on the relative balance of power.

It is easy to see how the administrative relationships can be used to create a strong matrix. The higher the project manager reports in the hierarchical organization, and the more visible support he gets from top management, the more likely it is that the matrix will be strong. The physical relationship would involve actually split-

ting the project personnel away from their physical reporting relationship with their functional managers. One approach would be to put the entire project team together in the same room, away from their functional bosses. This would seem to be very desirable on the part of most project managers, but would have some disadvantages in regard to utilization of functional facilities and interaction with other functional personnel. The approach of putting all the project personnel together has been described as a tight matrix, whereas the situation of widely-separated project personnel has been described as a loose matrix.

The organizational alternatives have also been described in terms of the percentage of the organizational personnel who are full-time members of the project team (25). In this manner, the various organizational structures can be described as a continuum where the three organizational forms (functional, project, and matrix) are a continuum ranging from functional on one end and pure project on the other (figure 3, chapter 4). In a functional organization, there is no one on the project team, and in a pure project organization, essentially everybody is on the project team. The matrix falls in between, and includes a variety of organizational alternatives ranging from a weak to a strong matrix. A weak matrix is described as having only a part-time coordinator whereas a strong matrix has a project office containing such project functions as systems engineering, cost analysis, scheduling, and planning.

Summary

The matrix organizational structure has had a great influence on project management. The matrix evolved to fill a need for an organization capable of dealing with great project size and complexity. The result was increased organizational complexity. However, it has greatly added to the versatility and effectiveness of project management. The matrix has permitted project management to be effective not only for very large projects but small projects as well, and has been extremely valuable for solving multidisciplinary problems.

The matrix organizational form is only desirable if there is a real need for its added complexity. Not only is it not for everyone, but it cannot be guaranteed to work. It will only work if the entire organization, from top management to the project personnel, are thoroughly "sold" on the matrix concept. There are many reasons why the matrix will not work, but failure to lay the groundwork and fully prepare the organization is the principle reason for failure. The matrix will function and result in very improved project productivity if top

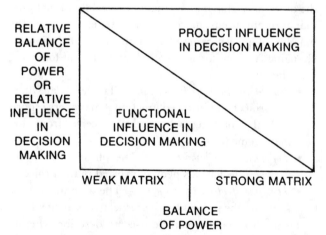

Figure 10. The balance of power in weak and strong matrices

management gives its unwavering support and if functional management and the project personnel accept the matrix as a "way of life" which can only be of great advantage to the company in improving output and profit.

REFERENCES

1. Archibald, Russell D., *Managing High-Technology Programs and Projects.* New York: John Wiley & Sons, 1976, pp. 14–15.
2. Blake, Stewart P., *Managing for Responsive Research and Development.* San Francisco: W. H. Freeman and Co., 1978, p. 176.
3. Caspe, Marc S., "An Overview of Project Management and Project Management Services," *Project Management Quarterly* VII: 4, December 1976, pp. 30–39.
4. Cleland, David I. and William R. King, *Systems, Organizations, Analysis, Management: A Book of Readings.* New York: McGraw-Hill Book Company, 1969, pp. 281–290.
5. Cleland, David I. and William R. King, *Management: A Systems Approach.* New York: McGraw-Hill Book Company, 1972, pp. 337–362.
6. Cleland, David I. and William R. King, *Systems Analysis and Project Management*, Second Edition. New York: McGraw-Hill Book Company, 1975, pp. 183–202.
7. Cleland, David I. and William R. King, *Systems Analysis*, p. 237.
8. Cleland, David I., "Understanding Project Authority," *Business Horizons* Spring 1966, p. 231.
9. Davis, Stanley M. "Two Models of Organization: Unity of Command versus Balance of Power," *Sloan Management Review* Fall 1974, pp. 29–40.
10. Davis, Stanley M. and Paul R. Lawrence, *Matrix.* Reading, Mass.: Addison-Wesley Publishing Company, 1977, p. 3.
11. Davis, Stanley M. and Paul R. Lawrence, *Matrix*, pp. 129–144.
12. Davis, Stanley M. and Paul R. Lawrence, *Matrix*, pp. 155–192.
13. Galbraith, Jay R., "Matrix Organization Designs," *Business Horizons* February 1971, pp. 29–40.
14. Galbraith, Jay R., ed., *Matrix Organizations: Organization Design for High Technology.* Cambridge, Mass.: MIT Press, 1971.
15. Galbraith, Jay R., *Designing Complex Organizations.* Reading, Mass.: Addison-Wesley Publishing Company, 1974.
16. Galbraith, Jay R., *Organizational Design.* Reading, Mass.: Addison-Wesley Publishing Company, 1977, p. 167.
17. Galbraith, Jay R., *Organizational Design*, p. 171.
18. Grinnell, Sherman K. and Howard P. Apple, "When Two Bosses Are Better Than One," *Machine Design* January 9, 1975, pp. 84–87.
19. Mee, John F., "Ideational Items: Matrix Organization," *Business Horizons* Summer 1964, pp. 70–72. (Reprinted in Cleland and King, *Systems, Organizations, Analysis, Management: A Book of Readings*, pp. 23–25.)
20. Melcher, R., "Roles and Relationships: Clarifying the Manager's Job," *Personnel* May–June 1967. (Reprinted in Caspe, "An Overview of Project Management and Project Management Services," pp. 365–371.)
21. Miller, J. Wade, Jr. and Robert J. Wolf, "The 'Micro-Company,'" *Personnel* July–August 1968, pp. 35–42.
22. Middleton, C. J., "How to Set Up a Project Organization," *Harvard Business Review* March–April 1967, pp. 73–82.
23. Sayles, Leonard R., "Matrix Management: The Structure with a Future," *Organizational Dynamics* Autumn 1976, pp. 2–17.
24. Tytler, Kathryn, "Making Matrix Management Work — And When And Why It's Worth The Effort." *Training* October 1975, pp. 78–82.
25. Youker, Robert B., "Organizational Alternatives for Project Management," *Project Management Quarterly* VIII: 1, March 1977, pp. 18–24. (Reprinted in *Management Review*, November 1967, pp. 46–52.)

Organization alternatives for project managers

There is no one perfect organizational structure for managing projects and similar temporary organizations. But you can—and should—assess the feasibility of the various alternatives.

ROBERT YOUKER

*Economic Development Institute
World Bank*

Robert Youker *is a lecturer in EDI's Industry and Public Utilities Courses Division and director of the Agri-Industry Course. Formerly president of Planalog Management Systems, a managing consulting firm, Mr. Youker has also acted as deputy director of the Division of Private and International Organizations of the Peace Corps.*

This article is adapted from Project Management Quarterly, *Vol. VIII, No. 1, by permission of Project Management Institute, P.O. Box 43, Drexel Hill, Pennsylvania 19026.*

MANAGEMENT REVIEW

IN THE PAST TEN YEARS interest has grown in techniques and approaches for management of temporary projects (in contrast to ongoing operations). There has been an explosion of literature dealing with these techniques and strategies, and more recently, we have seen the beginnings of organized academic research on various aspects of project management.

However, in discussions and in the literature we still seem to be confused about the exact meaning of some terms. This is particularly true in the area of alternative approaches for the management of projects.

Functional organizations

The most prevalent organizational structure in the world today is the basic hierarchical structure (Figure 1). This is the standard pyramid with top management at the top of the chart and middle and lower management spreading out down the pyramid. The organization is usually broken down into different functional units, such as engineering, research, accounting, and administration.

The hierarchical structure was originally based on such management theories as specialization, line and staff relations, authority and responsibility, and span of control. According to the doctrine of specialization, the major functional subunits are staffed by such disciplines as engineering and accounting. It is considered easier to manage specialists if they are grouped together and if the department head has training and experience in that particular discipline.

The strength of the functional organization is in its centralization of similar resources. For example, the engineering department provides a secure and comfortable organizational arrangement with well-defined career paths for a young engineer. Mutual support is provided by physical proximity.

The functional organization also has a number of weaknesses. When it is involved in multiple projects, conflicts invariably arise over the relative priorities of these projects in the competition for resources. Also, the functional department based on a technical specialty often places more emphasis on its own specialty than on the goals of the project. Lack of moti-

Reprinted with permission from *Project Management Journal*, Volume VIII, Number 1, March 1977, pages 18-24. Copyright © 1977 by Project Management Institute.

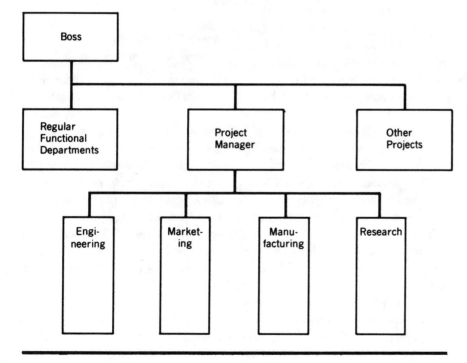

**Figure 1
Functional Organization**

Boss

VP
Engineering
x

VP
Finance
x

VP
x
Research

VP
Marketing
x

VP
Manufacturing
x

**Figure 2
Projectized Organization**

Boss

Regular Functional Departments

Project Manager

Other Projects

Engineering

Marketing

Manufacturing

Research

vation and inertia are other problems.

However, many companies use the functional organization for their project work as well as their standard operations. The world is a complicated place. In addition to discipline and function, other nuclei for organizational structures include products, technologies, customers, and geographic location.

Project organizations

The opposite of the hierarchical, functional organization is the single-purpose project or vertical organization. In a projectized organization, all the resources necessary to attain a specific objective are separated from the regular functional structure and set up as a self-contained unit headed by a project manager. The project manager is given considerable authority over the project and may acquire resources from either inside or outside the overall organization. All personnel on the project are under the direct authority of the project manager for the duration of the project.

In effect, a large organization sets up a smaller, temporary, special-purpose structure with a specific objective. It is interesting to note that the internal structure of the project organization is functional, that is, that the project team is divided into various functional areas (Figure 2).

Note that the term here is "project organization," not "project management." You can manage projects with all three types of organizational structure. The advantages of the project organization come from the singleness of purpose and the unity of command. An esprit de corps is developed through the clear under-

NOVEMBER 1977

standing of, and focus on, the single objective. Informal communication is effective in a close-knit team, and the project manager has all the necessary resources under his direct control.

The project organization, however, is not a perfect solution to all project management problems, as some have suggested. Setting up a new, highly visible temporary structure upsets the regular organization. Facilities are duplicated and resources are used inefficiently. Another serious problem is the question of job security upon termination of the temporary project. Personnel often lose their "home" in the functional structure while they are off working on a project.

The functional, hierarchical organization is organized around technical inputs, such as engineering and marketing. The project organization is a single-purpose structure organized around project outputs, such as a new dam or a new product. Both of these are unidimensional structures in a multidimensional world. The problem in each is to get a proper balance between the long-term objective of functional departments in building technical expertise and the short-term objectives of the project.

Matrix organizations

The matrix organization is a multidimensional structure that tries to maximize the strengths and minimize the weaknesses of both the project and the functional structures. It combines the standard vertical hierarchical structure with a superimposed lateral or horizontal structure of a project coordinator (Figure 3).

The major benefits of the matrix organization are the balancing of ob-

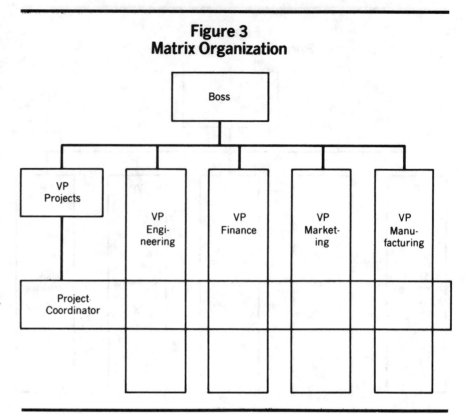

**Figure 3
Matrix Organization**

jectives, the coordination across functional department lines, and the visibility of the project objectives through the project coordinator's office. The major disadvantage is that the man in the middle is working for two bosses. Vertically, he reports to his functional department head. Horizontally, he reports to the project coordinator or project manager. In a conflict situation he can be caught in the middle.

The project manager often feels that he has little authority with regard to the functional departments. On the other hand, the functional department head often feels that the project coordinator is interfering in his territory.

The solution to this problem is to define the roles, responsibility, and authority of each of the actors clearly. The project coordinator specifies

what is to be done and the functional department is responsible for how it is done (Figure 4).

Criteria for selecting an organizational structure

In the field of management, zealots like to say that their particular model is best. Neophytes want a simple and unambiguous answer. Experienced and thoughtful observers, however, know that no one particular approach is perfect for all situations. The current vogue in management literature is the contingency model. This theory states that the best solution is contingent upon the key factors in the environment in which the solution will have to operate.

The same is true for the choice of an organizational structure. What we need, then, is a list of key factors that

Figure 4
Matrix Organization Relationship
of Project Management to Functional Management

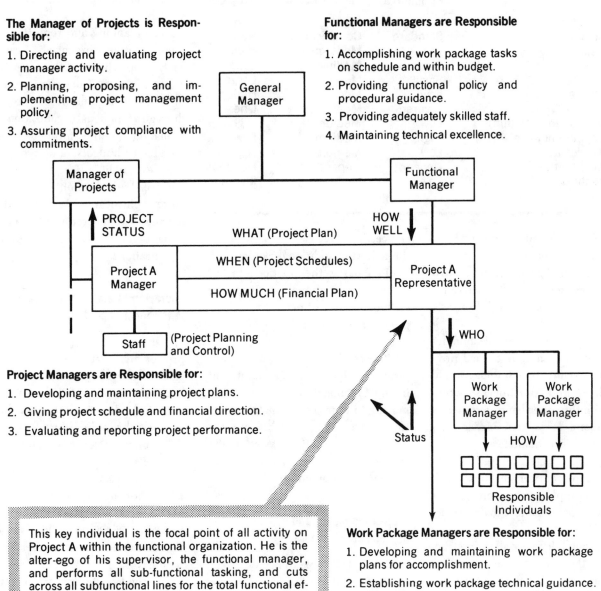

The Manager of Projects is Responsible for:

1. Directing and evaluating project manager activity.
2. Planning, proposing, and implementing project management policy.
3. Assuring project compliance with commitments.

Functional Managers are Responsible for:

1. Accomplishing work package tasks on schedule and within budget.
2. Providing functional policy and procedural guidance.
3. Providing adequately skilled staff.
4. Maintaining technical excellence.

General Manager

Manager of Projects

Functional Manager

PROJECT STATUS

WHAT (Project Plan)

HOW WELL

Project A Manager

WHEN (Project Schedules)

HOW MUCH (Financial Plan)

Project A Representative

Staff (Project Planning and Control)

WHO

Status

Work Package Manager

Work Package Manager

HOW

Responsible Individuals

Project Managers are Responsible for:

1. Developing and maintaining project plans.
2. Giving project schedule and financial direction.
3. Evaluating and reporting project performance.

This key individual is the focal point of all activity on Project A within the functional organization. He is the alter-ego of his supervisor, the functional manager, and performs all sub-functional tasking, and cuts across all subfunctional lines for the total functional effort on Project A. He actively plans and controls organization's efforts on the project.

Work Package Managers are Responsible for:

1. Developing and maintaining work package plans for accomplishment.
2. Establishing work package technical guidance.
3. Establishing work package detailed schedule and operating budgets.
4. Controlling and reporting work package performance.

Adapted from **Management: A Systems Approach,** by Cleland and King, McGraw-Hill Book Co., 1972, p. 347.

NOVEMBER 1977

Figure 5
Criteria for Organization Design Decisions

	Functional	Favors Matrix	Project
Uncertainty	Low	High	High
Technology	Standard	Complicated	New
Complexity	Low	Medium	High
Duration	Short	Medium	Long
Size	Small	Medium	Large
Importance	Low	Medium	High
Customer	Diverse	Medium	One
Interdependency (Within)	Low	Medium	High
Interdependency (Between)	High	Medium	Low
Time Criticality	Low	Medium	High
Resource Criticality	Depends	Depends	Depends
Differentiation	Low	High	Medium

will help us to choose the right organizational structure for the given conditions on a specific project with a given organization and a particular environment. A set of such factors is listed in Figure 5.

For example, an organization developing many new but small projects with standard technology would most likely find a functional structure best. On the other hand, a company with a long, large, complex, and important project should favor the project organizational structure. A firm in the pharmaceutical business with many complicated technologies would probably go to a matrix structure.

It is possible to use all three structures in the same company on different projects. All three structures might also be used on the same project at different levels—for example, an overall matrix structure for the project with a functional substructure in engineering and a project organization in another functional subarea.

Before we can make a final choice, however, we must consider the following additional factors:

1. What is the relationship between organizational design, the skills of the project manager, and the project planning and reporting system?

2. Are there ways we can improve coordination and commitment in the functional structure without moving to a project or matrix structure?

3. What variations exist in the matrix structure and what are the advantages of each variation?

Project managers and organizational design

It is not possible to decide on the organizational design without also deciding whom to select as the project manager and what kind of design you want for the planning and reporting systems. These decisions are closely interrelated. For example, a successful project organization requires a project manager with the broad skills of a general manager. He must combine technical knowledge of the subject matter with management abilities before he can lead the entire project team. It makes no sense to select a project organization form if such a project manager is not available.

The planning and reporting system in a project organization can be fairly simple because the team is in close proximity. The opposite is true in the management of projects through a functional organization. Information in the form of plans, schedules, budgets, and reports is the key medium for integrating a functional organization. Therefore, a more sophisticated planning and reporting system is required in a functional organization than in a project organization.

Improving lateral communications in the functional structure

Organizations typically turn to a project organization or a matrix organization because the normal functional structure has failed on a series of projects. It is not necessary, however, to "throw the baby out with the bath water." Before giving up on the functional organization, analyze the real problems and see if steps can be taken short of reorganization. Some results of a reorganization may be favorable, but other unintended but logical consequences are certain to be unfavorable.

Methods of lateral or horizontal communication need to be developed across functional department boundaries. Alternative approaches for lateral communication include:

1. Such procedures as plans, budgets, schedules, and review meetings.

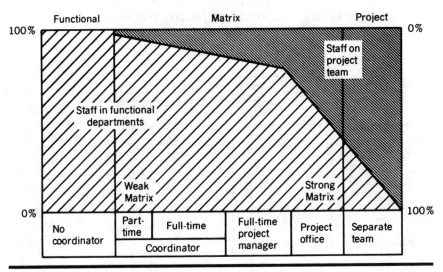

Figure 6
Organizational Continuum

2. Direct contact between managers.

3. Informal liaison roles.

4. Teams.

These are integrating mechanisms short of the establishment of a matrix organization. They help to break down the barriers that seem to separate different disciplines, departments, and geographic locations.

Weak to strong matrix—a continuum

The three major organizational forms—functional, matrix, and project—may be presented as a continuum ranging from functional at one end to project at the other end (Figure 6). The matrix form falls in between and includes a wide variety of structures, from a weak matrix near functional to a strong matrix near project. The continuum in Figure 6 is based on the percentage of personnel who work in their own functional department versus the percentage of personnel who are full-time members of the project team. Note that in a functional or-

ganization the project team has no personnel of its own. The dividing line between functional and matrix is the point at which an individual is appointed with part-time responsibility for coordination across functional department lines.

The bottom line of Figure 6 shows that a weak matrix has a part-time coordinator. The matrix gets stronger as you move from full-time coordinator to full-time project manager and finally to a project office that includes such personnel as systems engineers, cost analysts, and schedule analysts. The difference between a coordinator and a manager is the difference between mere integration and actual decision-making.

On the far right we have the project organization. Ordinarily, there is a clear distinction between a strong matrix in which most of the work is still being performed in the functional departments and a project organization in which the majority of the personnel are on the project team.

It is rare for a project organization

to have all the personnel on its team. Usually some functions, such as accounting or maintenance, would still be performed by the functional structure.

Some persons have taken issue with the use of the term "strong matrix." They say that a strong matrix comes from an even balance of power between the functional departments and the project office. That may be true in some instances, but not always. Strong and weak are not used in the sense of good and bad. Rather, they refer to the relative size and power of the integrative function in the matrix.

Measuring authority:
Functional vs. project staff

Another way to differentiate between a strong matrix and a weak matrix is to analyze the relative degree of power between the functional departments and the project staff. We could construct another continuum with function on the left and project on the right. For a given project we would decide where the power rests on the continuum for decisions over project objectives, budgets, cost control, quality, time schedule, resources, personnel selection, and liaison with top management. On any given project the power will be strongly functional for some factors and strongly project for others. However, a profile line can be drawn from top to bottom that would indicate whether the trend is to the left (weak) or to the right (strong).

Making matrix management work

Matrix management is a controversial concept. Some people have

NOVEMBER 1977

had bad experiences operating in a matrix. Others have had a great deal of success. It does require careful definition of authority and responsibility as well as strenuous efforts toward coordination and diplomacy. The matrix is basically a balance of power between the goals of the functional structure and of a specific project.

Overloaded functional departments

One key problem with matrix organizations is that they tend to overload the functional departments with work. If a functional department makes a commitment to work more man-hours on projects than it has available, conflicts over priorities between projects are inevitable. This problem can be alleviated, if not solved, by better planning.

A matrix organization will not work effectively unless a matrix strategic plan setting priorities on objectives and a matrix budget allocating resources also exist. For example, in Figure 7, the project manager for Project A will add horizontally across functional departments to get his total budget. In a similar manner, the vice-president of manufacturing must add vertically across all the projects for which he has committed funds and resources as well as his strictly departmental efforts. The matrix budget must add up to 100 percent in both directions. The usual picture is that the functional departments are overcommitted and show required man-hours of perhaps 120 percent of actual man-hours available. When this happens, politics and disappointment become inevitable.

The golden rule in matrix management states, "He who has the gold

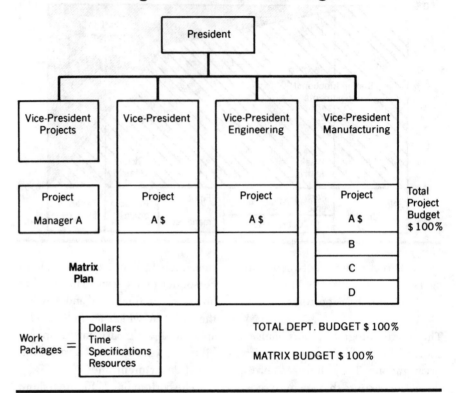

Figure 7
Matrix Organization and Matrix Budget

makes the rules." If a project manager does not control the budget, he can only beg for handouts from the functional departments. A matrix budget assigns resources to the project manager for purchases from the functional departments. Making up such a budget takes careful work during long-range and annual planning. Regular updating of the matrix plan and budget are also necessary.

Survival techniques in the matrix

A common picture of the project coordinator in a matrix organization is of a frustrated diplomat struggling to cajole the functional departments into performing the work on schedule and within budget. His po-

sition is difficult, but the following approaches can help:

1. It is important to have a charter from top management defining responsibilities and authority for the project manager as well as the role of the functional departments.

2. The project coordinator or manager must anticipate conflicts in the matrix. Conflict is inevitable with dual authority, but it can be constructively channeled.

3. Since conflict is inevitable, it is important to take positive steps to develop teamwork. Regular lunches or social gatherings help to foster a team spirit. In recent years, the behavioral sciences have developed a number of specific techniques for alleviating or using conflict effectively.

Training programs for matrix managers should include experiences with such techniques.

4. The project coordinator's main power comes from the approved objectives, plans, and budgets for the project. Use these documents to hold departments to their commitments.

5. It is vital that the functional department heads be committed to the plans and schedules for the project as well as the lower-level task leaders. Functional managers should review and sign off on these documents.

6. It is usually best to avoid direct conflict with the functional department heads. The matrix manager should use his boss when a situation threatens to get out of hand.

7. It is important to remember that the project coordinator is concerned with "what" is to be done, not "how." Use a management-by-objectives approach and do not supervise the functional departments (Figure 4) too closely.

8. Many of the problems of matrix management flow from the uncertainty inherent in the project environment. By definition, a project is, to some extent, a "new" effort. Careful and continuous planning can help reduce uncertainty.

No one perfect organizational structure for managing projects exists. The functional, the project, and the different matrix structures all have strengths and weaknesses. The final choice should come after weighing various factors in the nature of the task, the needs of the organization, and the environment of the project.

The functional structure will work for many projects in many organizations, especially if lateral communications can be improved through integrating mechanisms and procedures short of hiring a matrix coordinator.

When a matrix approach is chosen, the entire organization must put a good deal of effort into it to make it work. In particular, the project coordinator or project manager in the matrix must be carefully chosen and trained. His interpersonal skills are more important than his technical knowledge.

In many situations, a project organization may appear to be the simplest solution from the viewpoint of the project manager. However, the functional managers or top management may not find it to be the best long-range or most strategic decision. •

COMPUTING
PRACTICES

"The Effect of Programming Team Structures on Programming Tasks" by M. Mantei from *Communications of the ACM,* Volume 24, Number 3, March 1981, pages 106-113. Copyright © 1981, Association for Computing Machinery, Inc., reprinted by permission.

The Effect of Programming Team Structures on Programming Tasks

Marilyn Mantei
The University of Michigan

1. Introduction

Two philosophies for organizing programming teams have achieved a moderate amount of popularity, if not utilization, in the data processing field. These are the egoless programming team proposed by Weinberg [28] and the chief programmer team proposed by Mills [18] and implemented by Baker [1]. In Weinberg's structure, the decision-making authority is diffused throughout project membership; in Baker's team, it belongs to the chief programmer. Communication exchanges are decentralized in Weinberg's team and centralized in the chief programmer organization. Neither structure is totally

SUMMARY: The literature recognizes two group structures for managing programming projects: Baker's chief programmer team and Weinberg's egoless team. Although each structure's success in project management can be demonstrated, this success is clearly dependent on the type of programming task undertaken. Here, for the purposes of comparison, a third project organization which lies between the other two in its communication patterns and dissemination of decision-making authority is presented. Recommendations are given for selecting one of the three team organizations depending on the task to be performed.

Key words and phrases: chief programmer team, project management, software engineering, group dynamics, programming team structures
CR Categories: 3.50, 4.6
Author's address: M. Mantei, Graduate School of Business Administration, The University of Michigan, Ann Arbor, MI 48109.
© 1981 ACM 0001-0782/81/0300–0106 75¢.

decentralized, democratic, centralized, or autocratic, but both Weinberg and Baker present arguments on why their methods will lead to superior project performance. Baker's project succeeds with a specific, difficult, and highly structured task. Weinberg's recommendations have no specific task in mind.

Research conducted in small group dynamics [7, 23, 27] suggests that a decision to use either team structure is not clear-cut and that there are strong task dependencies associated with each group's performance. The next two sections an-

alyze Weinberg and Baker's organizations. In Section 4, a third, commonly encountered team organization is presented for the purposes of comparison. The fifth section conducts this comparison, recommending which of the three structures should be selected for a given property of a programming task.

2. An Analysis of Weinberg's Team Structure

Weinberg is a promoter of the egoless programming concept. His teams are groups of ten or fewer

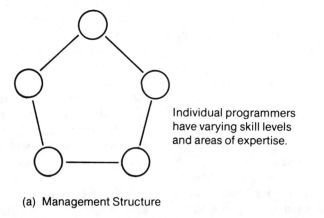

Individual programmers have varying skill levels and areas of expertise.

(a) Management Structure

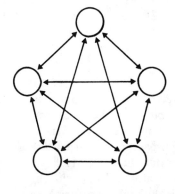

(b) Communication Channels

Fig. 1. Egoless Team Structure. Authority is dispersed and communication linkages decentralized.

programmers who exchange their code with other team members for error examination. In addition to code exchanges, goals are set by group consensus. Group leadership is a rotating function, becoming the responsibility of the individual with the abilities that are currently needed. Figure 1(a) illustrates the basic management structure of an egoless team; Figure 1(b) shows the communication exchanges that occur within this structure. The team proposed by Weinberg is acknowledged to be mythical in light of today's organization practices, but Weinberg feels that it is the appropriate organization for the best qualitative and quantitative code generation. Using the factors of amount of code produced, of time to produce code, and of error freeness to gauge programming performance, some task-related problems occur with Weinberg's team structure.

Bavelas [3] and Leavitt [14], in their experiments on centralized and decentralized group problem-solving behavior, found that decentralized groups take more time and generate twice as many communications as centralized groups. This suggests that a Weinberg group would function well in long-term continuing projects without time constraints (such as program maintenance). It would not, however, adequately perform a rush programming project.

A second weakness of Wein-

berg's proposal is the *risky shift phenomena* [5]. Groups engage in riskier behavior than individuals, both because of the dispersion of failure and the high value associated with risk taking in Western culture. In the case of a group programming team, decisions to attempt riskier solutions to a software problem or to establish high risk deadlines would be more easily made. In a software project with a tight deadline or a crucial customer, a group decision might cause the project to fail.

The democratic team structure works best when the problem is difficult. When the problem is simple, performance is better in an autocratic highly structured group [12]. Ironically, democratic groups attempt to become more autocratic as task difficulty increases. In the decentralized group, the additional communication which aided in solving the difficult problem is superfluous; it interferes with the simple problem solution. Tasks such as report generation and payroll programming fall into the category of simple tasks—for these, a Weinberg group is least efficient.

The decentralized group is lauded for its open communication channels. They allow the dissemination of programming information to all participants via informal channels. By virtue of code exchanges and open communication, Weinberg concludes that the product will be

superior. March and Simon [16] point out that hierarchical structures are built to limit the flow of information, because of the human mind's limited processing capabilities. In the decentralized groups, as investigated by Bavelas, although twice as many communications were exchanged as in centralized groups, the groups often failed to finish their task. Similarly, individuals within a nonstructured programming group may be unable to organize project information effectively and many suffer from information overload. The structure and limited flow associated with hierarchical control may be assets to information assimilation.

Decentralized groups exhibit greater conformity than centralized groups [11]; they enforce a uniformity of behavior and punish deviations from the norm [20]. This is good if it results in quality documentation and coding practices, but it may hurt experimental software development or the production of novel ideas.

Despite the pressure to conform and an apparent lack of information organization, decentralized groups exhibit the greatest job satisfaction [23]. For long projects hurt by high turnover rates, job satisfaction is a major concern. Job satisfaction is also important for healthy relationships with the public or a customer— if indeed this is a necessary element of the programming project.

In summary, Weinberg's decentralized democratic group does not perform well in tasks with time constraints, simple solutions, large information exchange requirements, or unusual approaches. A difficult task of considerable duration which demands personal interaction with the customer is optimal for a Weinberg team.

3. An Analysis of Baker's Team Structure

Baker describes the use of a highly structured programming team to develop a complex on-line information retrieval system for the New York Times Data Bank; the team is a three-person unit. It consists of a *chief programmer*, who manages a *senior level programmer* and a *program librarian*. Additional programmers and analysts are added to the team on a temporary basis to meet specific project needs. Figure 2(a) illustrates the structure of the chief programmer team; the communication channels are shown in Figure 2(b).

The chief programmer manages all technical aspects of the project, reporting horizontally to a project manager who performs the administrative work. Program design and assignment are initiated at the top level of the team. Communication occurs through a programming library system, which contains up-to-date information on all code developed. The program librarian maintains the library and performs clerical support for the project. Rigid program standards are upheld by the chief programmer.

The Baker team is a centralized autocratic structure in which problem solutions and goal decisions are made at the top level. The task which the team undertakes is well-defined, but large and complex. Definite time constraints exist. Baker concludes that this compact highly structured team led to the successful completion of the project and that it has general applicability.

Several weaknesses exist in Baker's argument. Shaw [21] finds that a centralized communication network is more vulnerable to saturation at the top level. Information from all lower modes in this structure flows upward to the parent mode. Baker's team was intentionally small and worked with a highly structured system for managing project information; both these factors were critical to the success of the project. A third, equally important factor was the team leader's ability to handle project communication. This ability is closely related to the leader's software expertise. A less experienced leader or a more complex problem might have changed the project's success, even with staffing constraints and information management. Yourdon [29] points out that the effective chief programmer is a rare individual and indicates that most so-called chief programmer teams are headed by someone who is unlikely to adequately handle the communication complexity.

Centralized groups exhibit low morale [3]; this, in turn, leads to dissatisfaction and poor group cohesiveness. Members of highly cohesive groups communicate with each other to a greater extent than members of groups with low cohesion [15]. With a clearly defined problem that is split into distinct modules, this lack of communication will have little impact, but an ill-defined problem with many interfaces would suffer in a chief programmer team environment. The two software modules (the interface systems) on this project which might have served as indicators of this communication condition are, as a matter of fact, developed as a joint effort between the chief programmer and another team member.

Communication in a status hierarchy tends to be directed upward; its content is more positive than that of any communication directed downward [27]. In a tricky, difficult programming task, this favorable one-way flow of communication denies the group leader access to a better solution or, at least, an indication of problems in the current solution. Decentralized groups generate more and better solutions to problems than individuals working alone [25]—such as a chief programmer. The major basis for the success

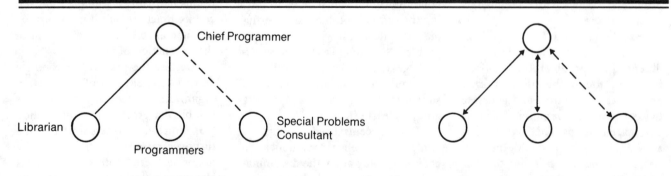

Librarian   Programmers   Chief Programmer   Special Problems Consultant

(a) Management Structure   (b) Communication Channels

Fig. 2. Chief Programmer Team Structure. Authority is vested in the chief programmer and communication is centralized to this individual.

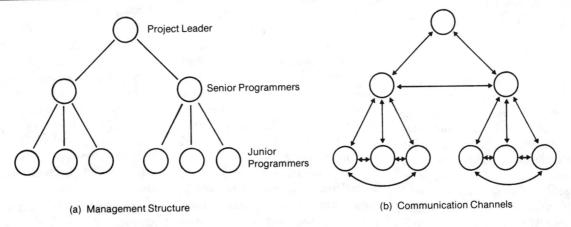

(a) Management Structure   (b) Communication Channels

Fig. 3. Controlled Decentralized Team Structure. Authority is vested in the project leader and senior programmers, but communication at each level of the management hierarchy is decentralized.

of the New York Times Data Bank project was the team's ability to meet the delivery date. A centralized structure completes tasks more quickly than any decentralized form of control [14], but perhaps a more creative solution might have resulted from a different approach. Proponents of good software management stress concern for the software life cycle [8, 9, 13]. This implies that consideration be given not only to project completion schedules but to the software's usability, cost to the customer, and modifiability.

In summary, communication exists to a much lesser degree in centralized groups and is directed toward the manager. Both difficult tasks requiring multiple inputs for solution and unstructured tasks requiring substantial cooperation fare poorly in this kind of communication environment. Group morale and, thus, goal motivation are low in such a hierarchical structure. A simple, well-structured programming task with rigid completion deadlines and little individual interface with the client is perfect for the chief programmer team.

4. An Analysis of a Controlled Decentralized Team Structure

In practice, programming team structures vary considerably. Most take on some form of organization that draws from both Weinberg's egoless team and Baker's chief programmer team. A third, frequently used organization which we will call the controlled decentralized (CD) team is described in this section.

The controlled decentralized team has a project leader who governs a group of senior programmers. Each senior programmer, in turn, manages a group of junior programmers. Figure 3(a) illustrates the organization of this group; Figure 3(b) indicates the flow of communication that takes place in this type of group structure.

Metzger [17] describes this organization as a reasonable management approach. He makes two recommendations: First, he suggests that intermediate levels of management are preferable to requiring all senior programmers to report to the project leader and, second, he recommends that the programming groups be partitioned not according to code module assigned, but in terms of the type of role played in the project, e.g., test, maintenance, etc. Shneiderman [24] lists this structure as the most probable type of project organization. Like Yourdon [29], he suggests that the individual subgroups in the project participate in structured walkthroughs and code exchanges in the manner of Weinberg's egoless teams.

The CD team possesses control over the goal selection and decision-making aspects of the Baker team and the decentralized communication aspects of the Weinberg team. Setting project goals and dividing work among the groups are the tasks of the project leader. More detailed control over the project's functions is assigned to the senior programmers. Within each programming subgroup, the organization is decentralized. Problem solving is a group activity as is checking for code errors. Each group leader serves as the sole recipient or gatekeeper of project information for the subgroup and acts as a liaison with the leaders of the other groups. The communication and control problems of the egoless and chief programmer teams do not disappear in a CD structure but occur in the subgroups of the controlled decentralized team that correspond to the Weinberg and Baker teams: Thus, the properties of the subtask allocated to any of the subgroups interact, in a similar fashion, with the subgroup structure.

The decentralized subgroups of the CD team work poorly with highly structured or simple tasks. Group solutions are best directed at difficult problems. Much of the creative and difficult part of programming is planning the design and partitioning the work. In the CD structure this work is completed by the project leader. The senior programmers then take on their portion of the task and develop a group solution. Ironically, when the task is most difficult, the team structure is least effective. A poll of programming managers and academics indicated that the area they believed needed the most attention in software engineering was the planning and design stage [26], the work carried out by the CD team project leader.

With small problems, the CD team is unnecessary since its very structure presumes the existence of a larger project. As Brooks [6] points out, even though adding individuals to a project increases the communication problems and, thus, the effectiveness of the project's members, it is still necessary to have large teams for those programming tasks which are so large they could not be accomplished in a reasonable length of time by a few programmers.

Although control over projects is exercised from above, the group problem-solving approach at lower levels will take longer, and projects will be more likely to fall behind in meeting deadlines. The structure of the CD team would tend to centralize the egoless programming subgroups. Because of the senior programmer's gatekeeper role, he or she would emerge as an informal leader in group sessions. This, in turn, would lower individual satisfaction with the project and generate the ensuing problems of a high job turnover rate and group socialization difficulties. Because of this strong tendency toward centralization, shorter projects are best for the CD structure.

A controlled decentralized team is an effective error-purge mechanism. The code walkthroughs and group input at the code generation level will filter out many errors. Code generated in this fashion is more reliable than code coming from a chief programmer team operation.

Programming tasks that are not easily subdivided suffer in a CD team. Note in Figure 3(b) that communication between groups occurs at the senior programmer level. Projects requiring micro-decision communication about code interfaces cannot expect this communication to be conveyed effectively through a liaison person functioning at a macro level in the project.

In summary, the controlled decentralized team will work best for large projects which are reasonably straightforward and short-lived. Such teams can be expected to produce highly reliable code but not necessarily on time or in a friendly manner. They are ill-suited for long-term researchlike projects.

Team Structure and Programming Task Relationships

This section describes seven salient properties of programming tasks and compares the performance of each team structure discussed in relationship to these task properties. The relevant properties are:

(1) *Difficulty*. The program required to solve the problem can be complex, consisting of many decision points and data interfaces, or it may be a simple decision tree. Distributed processing systems and projects with severe core or rapid response time constraints fall into the *difficult* category. Much of the scientific programming would come under the *simple* category heading.

(2) *Size*. Programs may range from ten to hundreds of thousands of lines of code for any given project.

(3) *Duration*. The lifetime of the programming team varies. Maintenance teams have a long lifetime; one-shot project teams have a short lifetime.

(4) *Modularity*. If a task can be completely compartmentalized into subtasks, it is highly modular. Most programming problems can be split into subtasks, but the amount of communication required between the subtasks determines their modularity rating. A tape system for payroll reports is a highly modular task.

A data management system for the same purpose has a low degree of modularity.

(5) *Reliability*. Some tasks such as patient monitoring systems have severe failure penalties, while other tasks, such as natural language processing experiments, need not be as reliable, although working programs are always desirable. The reliability measure depends on the social, financial, and psychological requirements of the task.

(6) *Time*. How much time is required for task completion? Is the time adequate or is there time pressure? The penalty for not meeting a deadline strongly affects this measure.

(7) *Sociability*. Some programming tasks require considerable communication with the user or with other technical personnel, such as engineers or mathematicians, while other tasks involve interaction with the team alone. Computer center consulting groups that develop user aids have higher sociability requirements than groups programming their own set of software tools.

Throughout this paper, the labels egoless programming team and chief programmer team have prevailed. For the purposes of comparison, these terms have been changed to names reflecting the decision-making authority and communication structure of the teams. The three teams are:

1. Democratic Decentralized (DD). This group is like Weinberg's proposed team; it has no leaders, but appoints task coordinators for short durations. Decisions on problem solutions and goal direction are made by group consensus. Communication among members is horizontal.

2. Controlled Decentralized (CD). The CD group has a leader who coordinates tasks. Secondary management positions exist below that of the leader. Problem solving remains a group activity but partitioning the problem among groups is a task of the leader. Communication is decentralized in the subgroups and centralized along the control hierarchy.

Table I. Recommended Team Structures for Programming Task Features.

Group Structures	Difficulty		Size		Duration		Modularity		Reliability		Time Required		Sociability	
	High	Low	Large	Small	Short	Long	High	Low	High	Low	Strict	Lax	High	Low
Democratic Decentralized	X			X	X		X		X			X	X	
Controlled Decentralized		X	X		X		X		X			X		X
Controlled Centralized		X	X		X		X			X	X			X

3. Controlled Centralized (CC). This group is like Baker's team. Both problem solving and goal directions are generated by the team leader. Communication is vertical along the path of control.

The expected interaction of each of these team structures with the factors governing program tasks can be drawn from experimental research on small group dynamics. To assess performance quality, team structures are assumed to be evaluated on the quality of generated code and the time in which the code generation was completed.

Table I lists recommended group structures for each task variable. Under the category *task difficulty*, simple problems are best performed by a centralized structure which completes tasks faster. Decentralization works best for difficult problems. Groups are found to generate more and better solutions than individuals. Unfortunately, the CD team is centralized precisely where the problem is difficult. The DD team is the best solution for difficult problems. For simpler programming tasks, a CC or CD structure is recommended.

As programming tasks increase in size, the amount of cooperation required among group members increases. Group performance is negatively correlated with the cooperation requirements of a task. As tasks become *very large*, the DD group is no longer viable because of its cooperation requirements. CC and CD groups can be effectively regrouped into smaller structures to handle the task. When the task size requires a smaller number of programmers, the DD group performs better because of its high level of communication. For *very small* tasks, the CC group is best because it does not require the additional communication of democratic groups; but then, a group is unnecessary. An individual will do.

The duration of the task interacts with group morale. Short tasks may not require high group morale, whereas long tasks will suffer from high personnel turnover if morale is low. DD groups have high morale and high job satisfaction. This should be the preferred group structure for ongoing tasks. The CC and CD groups are effective for short-term tasks.

If task modularity is low, the DD group performs best because of its higher volume of communication. Cooperative (read DD) groups have higher orderliness scores than competitive (read CC) groups [10]. This orderliness is essential for maintaining the interfaces of a low modularity task. Nondirective leadership has been found to be most effective when a task has a high multiplicity of solutions. Directive leadership is best for tasks with low multiplicity solution choices [22]. A DD group can be characterized as having nondirective leadership, CC and CD groups as having directive leadership. High modularity tasks have a low multiplicity of solutions, and thus the CD and CC groups can be expected to exhibit the best performance given such tasks.

CC and CD groups perform well when confronted with high reliability requirement problems. Decentralized groups have been found to make less errors and produce better solutions to problems. A CC group is more error-prone and probably should never be used for projects in which relatively simple errors can result in disaster.

A decentralized group takes longer to complete a problem than a centralized group. If tasks have severe time constraints, a CC team is best. When time is not crucial, the low motivation of CC groups can interfere with task completion. Therefore, the more democratic groups are preferred, with the DD structure being the best choice.

If a task requires high sociability, the DD team structure is best. Groups learn faster than individuals (such as the team leaders of CC groups). Therefore, a DD group would understand a user's interface problem in a shorter period of time. DD groups are higher in social interaction and morale than CD or CC groups. These traits will enhance their social relationships with the task contacts.

6. Conclusion

Many programming task features interact with each other, e.g., a large project is often a difficult one. Group structures that are effective for one aspect of a task may be totally wrong for another. In selecting a team structure, it is important to use a decision-making algorithm to prioritize, weight, or combine the crucial task variables.

Little experimental work on programming team and task interaction has been carried out. Basili and Reiter [2] found relationships between the size of a programming group and several software metrics. They also found cost differential behavior arising from the software development approach taken, with structured techniques being notably cheaper. Only one programming task was performed by the experimental groups. Weinberg's suggestions on group organization are anecdotal and Baker's conclusions are confounded by the team personnel and the programming methods selected.

Most of the research on group problem-solving behavior was conducted in a laboratory setting with students and tasks of short duration. A problem exists in trying to apply these conclusions to the external work environment. In particular, programming tasks generally involve an entirely different time span than laboratory experiments. Becker [4] scathingly criticizes these "cage" experiments. Rogers [19] suggests substituting network analysis field work to understand the effects of group structures.

None of these task/structure recommendations have been tested in a software development environment. Despite all these shortcomings, the application of a body of research on group dynamics to the organization of personnel on a programming project is a step forward from the hit-and-miss guessing that is the current state of the art.

References

1. Baker, F.T. Chief programmer team management of production programming. *IBM Syst. J. 1* (1972), 57–73. Baker presents a case history of a program project management organization, the chief programmer team. This compact management strategy coupled with top-down program development methods achieves above average success in terms of productivity and error-free code.

2. Basili, V.R., and Reiter, R.W., Jr. The investigation of human factors in software development. *Comptr. 12*, 12 (Dec. 1979), 21–38. This paper examines the impact of a programming team's size and program development approach, disciplined or ad hoc, on the software product. The disciplined method resulted in major savings in development efficiency and smaller groups built larger code modules.

3. Bavelas, A. Communication patterns in task-oriented groups. *J. Acoustical Soc. America 22* (1950), 725–730. Bavelas describes an experiment in which the communication structures of a circle, wheel, and chain were imposed on small groups by the physical arrangement of cubicles and message slots. Each structure was then measured for its problem-solving efficiency.

4. Becker, H. Vitalizing sociological theory. *Amer. Sociological Rev. 19* (1954), 377–388. Becker refers to the small group laboratory studies as "cage studies" and recommends their use by sociological theorists only for an awareness of such studies' limiting conditions.

5. Bem, D.J., Wallace, M.A., and Kogen, N. Group decision making under risk of adversive consequences. *J. Personality and Social Psychol. 1* (1965), 453–460. This paper demonstrates, in a context of adversive consequences (loss of money, induced nausea, etc.), that unanimous group decisions concerning matters of risk shift toward greater risk-taking than individual decisions. Moreover, the authors provide evidence that the underlying process for the risky shift is a diffusion of the responsibility among group members.

6. Brooks, F.P., Jr. *The Mythical Man-Month: Essays on Software Engineering*. Addison-Wesley, Reading, Mass., 1975. This work is a lyrical, enjoyable, and sage discussion of the problems and pitfalls that beset a mammoth software project—developing the IBM 360 operating system.

7. Cartwright, D., and Zander, D., Eds. *Group Dynamics: Research and Theory*. 3rd edition, Harper and Row, N.Y., 1968. This serves as an excellent compendium of the spurt of group dynamics research activity in the late 1950s which laid the groundwork for what we know about group behavior today.

8. Cave, W.C., and Salisbury, A.B. Controlling the software life cycle—The project management task. *IEEE Trans. Soft. Engr. SE-4*, 4 (July 1978), 326–334. This paper describes project management methods for controlling the life cycle of large software systems distributed to multiple users. It emphasizes responding to user satisfaction and user requirements and suggests methods to establish and maintain control in an extended dynamic environment.

9. De Roze, B.C., and Nyman, T.H. The software life cycle—A management and technological challenge in the department of defense. *IEEE Trans. Soft. Engr. SE-4*, 4 (July 1978), 309–318. De Roze and Nyman describe the software life cycle management policy and practices that have been established by the Department of Defense for improving the software development process.

10. Deutsch, M. The effects of cooperation and competition upon group process. *Human Relations 2* (1949), 129–152, 199–231. Deutsch describes an experiment which establishes two forms of group relationships, cooperative and competitive. Besides better communication, increased orderliness and higher productivity result when the cooperative group relationship exists.

11. Goldberg, S.C. Influence and leadership as a function of group structure. *J. Abnormal and Social Psychol. 51* (1955), 119–122. The experiment described in this paper compares group influence on group members in three organization structures: a star, a fork, and a chain. Individuals holding central positions were influenced less than other group members.

12. Guetzkow, H., and Simon, H.A. The impact of certain communication nets upon organization and performance in task-oriented groups. *Mgmt. Sci. 1* (1955), 233–250. The authors establish three communication structures: all-channel, wheel, and circle; they then examine their effect on solving a relatively simple communication problem. The restrictions of the wheel organization aided the solution process, whereas those of the circle hindered it. The lack of restrictions in the all-channel case also hurt the solution process.

13. Jensen, R.W., and Tonies, C.C., Eds. *Software Engineering*. Prentice–Hall, Englewood Cliffs, N.J., 1979. Here, several breakdowns of what constitutes a software life cycle are presented. The authors indicate that if the customer-use phase is included in this breakdown, the time spent on the code development constitutes a relatively small portion of the project.

14. Leavitt, H.J. Some effects of certain communication patterns on group performance. *J. Abnormal and Social Psychol. 46* (1951), 38–50. Leavitt compares problem-solving effectiveness in both wheel and circle communication structures. The wheel structure was faster but the circle structure accounted for fewer errors.

15. Lott, A.J., and Lott, B.E. Group cohesiveness, communication level, and conformity. *J. Abnormal and Social Psychol. 62* (1961), 408–412. This paper describes an experiment in which groups were scored on cohesiveness and then tallied for the amount of communication generated in a discussion session. Highly cohesive groups communicated more.

16. March, J.G., and Simon, H.A. *Organizations*. Wiley, New York, 1958. March and Simon focus on the members of formal organizations as rational men. From this, they point out that the basic features of organizational structure and function derive from characteristics of the human problem-solving process and rational choice.

17. Metzger, P.W. *Managing a Programming Project*. Prentice–Hall, Englewood Cliffs, N.J., 1973. Metzger suggests a project organization constrained in terms of the types of tasks that are undertaken in the development of a software system. He goes on to describe how these tasks should be managed via this hierarchical arrangement.

18. Mills, H.D. Chief programmer teams: Principles and procedures. IBM Rep. FSC 71–5108, IBM Fed. Syst. Div., Gaithersburg, Md., 1971. Mills suggests that the large team approach to programming projects could eventually be replaced by smaller, tightly organized and functionally specialized teams led by a chief programmer.

19. Rogers, E.M., and Agarwala-Rogers, R. *Communication in Organizations*. Free Press, N.Y., 1976. The basic research on group structures in small group network communication is summarized and critiqued in a thoroughly readable manner.

20. Schachter, S. Deviation, rejection and communication. *J. Abnormal and Social Psy-*

chol. 46 (1951), 190–207. This article describes an experiment in which three group members were paid to respectively 1) deviate from, 2) follow, and 3) change over to the group position taken on an issue. Groups with high cohesiveness scores produced greater rejection only of the deviant individual.

21. Shaw, M.E. Some effects of unequal distribution of information upon group performance in various communication nets. *J. Abnormal and Social Psychol.* 49 (1954), 547–553. In this paper, the amount of independence and, thus, individual satisfaction are examined in various group structures. Low centralization in groups led to member satisfaction.

22. Shaw, M.E., and Blum, J.M. Effects of leadership styles upon performance as a function of task structure. *J. Personality and Social Psychol.* 3 (1966), 238–242. Shaw and Blum describe an experiment in which they manipulated the leadership of two groups to be nondirective or directive. Given three tasks of varying solution multiplicity, directive leadership performed best with low multiplicity tasks.

23. Shaw, M.E. *Group Dynamics: The Psychology of Small Group Behavior.* McGraw-Hill, N.Y., 1971.

24. Shneiderman, B. *Software Psychology.* Winthrop, Cambridge, Mass., 1980. Shneiderman discusses the good and bad points of the Weinberg and Baker teams and a third conventional team. He notes that an egoless team may be difficult to maintain and a competent chief programmer hard to find, concluding that the currently existing conventional organization has strong chances for successful projects—especially with a competent manager.

25. Taylor, D.W., and Faust, W.L. Twenty questions: Efficiency of problem solving as a function of the size of the group. *J. Experimental Psychol.* 44 (1952), 360–363. Taylor compares individual problem-solving to group problem-solving in a game of 20 questions. Even after several days of practice, groups of two and four individuals asked less questions to discover an answer than sole participants.

26. Thayer, R.H., Pyster, A., and Wood, R.C. The challenge of software engineering project management. *Comptr. 13,* 8 (Aug. 1980), 51–59. The three authors report on a survey of software project management experts who were asked to indicate the most important issues facing software engineering. The structure of programming projects was rated as unimportant; planning received the highest ratings.

27. Thibaut, J.W., and Kelley, H.H. *The Social Psychology of Groups.* Wiley, N.Y., 1959. The second section of this book presents a general theory for group formation and group dynamics—in particular, the status systems within groups, conformity requirements, group goal setting behaviors, and the roles played by individuals within the group. In all, not light reading for the nonsociologist.

28. Weinberg, G. *The Psychology of Computer Programming.* Van Nostrand Reinhold, N.Y., 1971. Weinberg provides homilies, advice, and some wisdom about the psychological considerations of the programming process. It is here that he suggests the egoless approach to programming and discusses its potential advantages—Weinberg is short on supportive research, but the book is fun to read.

29. Yourdon, E. *Managing the Structured Technique.* Prentice-Hall, Englewood Cliffs, N.J., 1976. Yourdon discusses the chief programmer team and Weinberg's egoless debugging techniques in a complete scenario for project management. He labels the chief programmer team impractical because of the dearth of true chief programmers.

Chapter 6: Staffing a Software Engineering Project

1. Introduction to Chapter

Staffing a software engineering project is defined as all the management activities that involve manning and keeping manned the positions which were established by the organizational structure. This includes selecting candidates for positions, training or otherwise developing both candidates and incumbents to accomplish their tasks effectively, appraising and compensating the incumbents, and terminating the incumbent when the organizational structure position or incumbent is no longer needed.

Staffing for a software engineering project can be partitioned into eight general management activities (see Table 6.1). Each activity in the table is followed by its definition or an amplifying description.

Table 6.1: Staffing Activities

Activity	Definition or Explanation
Fill organizational positions	— Select, recruit, or promote qualified people for each position.
Assimilate newly assigned personnel	— Orient and familiarize new people with the organization, facilities, and tasks to be done.
Educate or train personnel	— Make up deficiencies in position qualifications through training and education.
Provide for general development	— Improve knowledge, attitudes, and skills.
Evaluate and appraise personnel	— Evaluate and record the quality and quantity of assigned work.
Compensate	— Give wages, bonuses, benefits, or other financial remuneration.
Terminate assignments	— Transfer or separate redundant personnel.
Document staffing decisions	— Record staffing decisions, training requirements and plans, appraisal records, and so on.

2. Overview of Chapter

The five papers of Chapter 6 address the correct staffing and training for a software engineering project. The management activities listed in Table 6.1 were used as an outline for the purpose of identifying papers on staffing activities.

The paper by Zawacki discusses *recruiting* to fill organizational positions. McGill's paper discuss corporate software engineering *training* as an alternative to hiring when quality software engineers are not available. Bartol and Martin point out that software personnel *turnover* is unavoidable and that computer people terminate their jobs for a variety of reasons. Moneysmith deals with the annual performance evaluation and appraisal.

3. Description of Papers

The first paper by Zawacki, is interestingly entitled, "How to Pick Eagles," i.e., how to go about picking promising recruits for the *data processing* task. The author feels that the interview and selection process should be geared to matching a person's growth needs to job scope. He points out that if an interviewer selects only high-quality people when not all the jobs are high-quality some of the software engineers hired will end up with low job satisfaction and, more important, low productivity.

Zawacki itemizes those items that appear to influence an interviewer in the selection process. He also discusses the reasons for these biases. Zawacki provides an interview guideline for people interested in selecting the best people for the job.

The second paper, by Sackman, Erikson, and Grant, entitled "Exploratory Experimental Studies Comparing Online and Offline Programming Performance" is another paper on software engineering that has stood the test of time. The experimental results reported include the often quoted statistic, "The capabilities of individual programmers can vary as much as 26 to 1." The reason for including this paper is to demonstrate to project managers that the proper or improper selection (staffing) of software engineers or programmers for a project can cause a very large swing in *software productivity*.

The next paper in this set affirms education as one answer to the software engineering shortage. McGill presents an interesting perspective on the in-house training of software engineers. He points out that new computer science graduates are often not trained to begin work as either a programmer or software engineer building large-scale software systems. He points out that many experienced employees with technical degrees make good software engineers. McGill recommends that each company conduct its own courses in software engineering. He presents a case study done on a six-month software engineering course which was conducted by a large aerospace firm.

The fourth paper, by Bartol and Martin, addresses the management problems associated with turnover of the data processing staff. The authors indicate that all turnover isn't bad. A change in staff can bring in new ideas and get rid of unproductive people. Management has the responsibility of terminating the unproductive people and keeping the productive ones.

The last paper, with the unusual title of "I'm OK—and You're Not," is a short, two-page paper by Moneysmith addressing the problem of evaluating employees. Moneysmith makes several good points concerning the right way and the wrong way to evaluate your employees.

HOW TO PICK EAGLES

by Robert A. Zawacki

While speaking recently at an Amdahl users group, I was asked the following question: "Have you ever published anything on how to select the right people for dp jobs?" I had just finished reading Ken Follett's best-selling book, *On Wings of Eagles* (William Morrow and Co. Inc., New York, 1983), and was fascinated by the author's frequent descriptions of how Electronic Data Systems selected "eagles," or promising recruits. This made me reflect on what I knew about interviewing and selecting the right dp person for the job.

What is your objective during the selection process? I assume it is to match people with dp jobs. I recommend a review of the following framework before beginning the selection process.

The objective during the selection process is to match a person's growth need strength (*GNS*) with a job's scope task or motivating potential score (*MPS*). *GNS* is an individual's need to grow, to develop beyond the present point, to be stretched and challenged by the job. The scope of the job can range from high to low. A high-scope task in dp is development, while a low-scope task is mounting tapes in operations. During the interview, the interviewer is attempting to select high-*GNS* people for high scope jobs (see cell 1 in Fig. 1) and conversely to select lower *GNS* people for lower-scope jobs (cell 4, Fig. 1).

During the interview, the interviewer is attempting to match people and jobs and to minimize the mismatches in cells 2 and 3 (also Fig. 1).

An interviewer who selects only high-*GNS* people may end up with a flock of eagles who are assigned to jobs that are lower in scope because high-scope jobs are scarce. This mismatch soon results in lower job satisfaction and productivity once the learning phase is over.

All available research indicates that the ability of a dp manager to predict how a future employee will perform, based upon a one-hour interview, is very low. Yet most managers have great confidence in their predictive ability based upon impressions formed in a brief interview. An industrial psychologist, Abraham K. Korman, in his book, *Industrial and Organizational Psychology* (Prentice-Hall, Englewood Cliffs, N.J., 1971), summarizes what influences a manager's judgment in the selection situation:

• Interviewers tend to develop a stereotype of a good candidate and then seem to match applicants with stereotypes.

• Biases are established early in the interview.

• During an interview in which the applicant is accepted, the interviewer talks more and in a more favorable tone than in an interview in which the applicant is rejected.

• Interviewers are influenced more by unfavorable than by favorable information.

• Seeing negative candidates before positive candidates will result in a greater number of favorable acceptances than the other way around.

• There are reliable and consistent individual differences among interviewers in their perceptions of the applicants they see as acceptable.

• Factual written data seem to be more important than physical appearance in determining judgments; this increases with the interviewing experience.

In *Applied Psychology in Personnel Management* (Reston Publishing Co., Reston, Va., 1982), Wayne F. Cascio updated Korman's summary with these additional conclusions:

• Early impressions are crystallized after a mean interview time of only four minutes.

• The ability of a candidate to respond concisely, to answer questions fully, to state personal opinions when relevant, and to keep to the subject at hand appears to be crucial to obtaining a favorable employment decision.

• Interviewers benefit very little from day-to-day interviewing experience.

• An interviewer who begins an interview with an unfavorable expectancy may tend to give an applicant less credit for past accomplishments and ultimately may be more likely to decide that the applicant is unacceptable.

• Interviews must be structured.

SO WHY THE VARIANCE?

Why is there a discrepancy between a manager's belief about his or her predictive ability and the research results? There appear to be two main reasons for this mismatch of effectiveness. First, interviewees tend to give sociably desirable answers to the interviewer. Assume a systems analyst desperately wants a job at the Hartford Insurance Group because her husband was recently transferred to Hartford. She can prepare for the interview by studying the company's financial reports, familiarize herself with its products, equipment, and even talk to other systems analysts at the company. In a one-hour interview, the odds are in her favor that she will get the job.

Second, the interviewer's biases are formed by a poor research methodology. In the example above, assume the interviewer interviews five people for the systems analysis job—a high-scope job. After interviewing each candidate, the interviewer selects the person who was rated the highest. This person joins the company and is an above-average employee for the next two or three years. The interviewer's impressions about his predictive ability are reinforced because he sees the positive results of his interview. What the interviewer does not know is how the other four would have performed. They may even be superior to the person hired.

There are three types of interviews: structured or patterned, nondirective, and problem interviews. In the problem interview, a project or situation is given to the applicant. A group interview where job-related questions are asked is an exmple of this type of interview. The major shortcoming of the problem interview is that it can be perceived by the applicant as a stress interview. When an interview is perceived as stressful, a programmer (who has employment options), may say, "If that is the way they treat their people, who would want to work there?"

The major shortcoming of the nondirective interview is that some dp managers believe they have an innate talent for selecting good people and they "wing it" during the interview. Being able to talk a good game does not necessarily ensure success with an interview. All applicants must be asked the same questions for comparisons to be valid. Because of the shortcomings of other methods, we therefore recommend the patterned or structured interview.

Patterned interview guidelines.

1. Preparing for the interview.

　　a. Arrange for a comfortable physical environment.

　　b. Get away from the telephone and interruptions.

　　c. Clear your mind and review these guidelines.

　　d. Write down four or five open-ended questions that will help you evaluate a candidate's growth potential, strengths, and other attributes.

　　e. Review the position description and determine the scope of the job (*MPS*). Determine the cell in Fig. 1 that you are attempting to fill through the interview.

　　f. Review the candidate's résumé.

2. Structuring the interview.

　　a. Use multiple interviewers; this increases the predictive validity.

　　b. Keep short notes.

　　c. Ask each candidate the same core questions.

3. Conducting the interview.

　　a. The opening minutes of the interview are critical because both candidate and interviewer are forming impressions.

　　b. Greet the candidate in a friendly manner.

　　c. Establish rapport and trust by discussing a common point of interest. Determine this from the candidate's résumé.

　　d. Be aware of your facial expressions. Talk in a relaxed manner and attempt to smile.

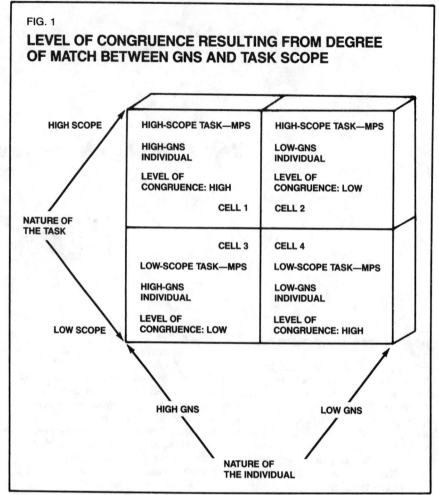

FIG. 1

LEVEL OF CONGRUENCE RESULTING FROM DEGREE OF MATCH BETWEEN GNS AND TASK SCOPE

HIGH SCOPE

HIGH-SCOPE TASK—MPS
HIGH-GNS INDIVIDUAL
LEVEL OF CONGRUENCE: HIGH
CELL 1

HIGH-SCOPE TASK—MPS
LOW-GNS INDIVIDUAL
LEVEL OF CONGRUENCE: LOW
CELL 2

NATURE OF THE TASK

CELL 3
LOW-SCOPE TASK—MPS
HIGH-GNS INDIVIDUAL
LEVEL OF CONGRUENCE: LOW

CELL 4
LOW-SCOPE TASK—MPS
LOW-GNS INDIVIDUAL
LEVEL OF CONGRUENCE: HIGH

LOW SCOPE

HIGH GNS　　　　LOW GNS

NATURE OF THE INDIVIDUAL

　　e. Try to conduct the interview face-to-face. Do not have a desk or table between yourself and the candidate.

　　f. Start with a broad general question to relax the applicant. Then proceed to more specific questions.

　　g. Ask open-ended questions that permit the applicant to do at least 50% of the talking. For example, a poor question would be "Did you graduate from college?" A better way to word it would be, "Please tell me about your college courses and experiences."

　　h. Give positive strokes to the candidate when possible: "You completed a very complex and innovative project while working at *xyz* Corp."

　　i. Use pauses to your advantage to keep the applicant talking.

　　j. Bring the interview to a polite close. Observe time limits and gently remind the candidate that you are out of time.

　　k. End the interview by telling the candidate the time schedule for hiring and when and who will get back to her.

　　l. Escort the candidate to the next interviewer and thank him for his time and interest.

4. After the Interview.

　　a. Record the interview while answers to questions and impressions are fresh in your mind.

　　b. Schedule a meeting with other interviewers to compare and discuss all candidates.

　　c. Send a follow-up letter to the selected candidate and to any unsuccessful candidates. I recommend a personal letter from a dp manager rather than a general letter from a personnel specialist. How the unsuccessful candidates are "cooled out" is critical. Beside considerations of common decency, it must be remembered rejected applicants may be a source for future employment needs, and a company's image is affected by how candidates are treated.

While the personal interview has low predictive validity, most dp managers still want to meet and see candidates rather than leaving that process to personnel. By following these guidelines, the accuracy of the interview process can be improved. That, in turn, will contribute to the overall effectiveness of the dp department.

Robert A. Zawacki is a principal in the consulting firm, Couger/Zawacki and Associates, Colorado Springs, where he has been studying and consulting on the human side of dp for the past nine years. His most recent book is *Supervisory Management,* Harper & Row, New York, 1984.

Operating Systems

B. RANDELL, Editor

"Exploratory Experimental Studies Comparing Online and Offline Programming Performance" by H. Sackman, W.J. Erikson, and E.E. Grant from *Communications of the ACM*, Volume 11, Number 1, January 1968, pages 3-11. Copyright © 1968, Association for Computing Machinery, Inc., reprinted by permission.

Exploratory Experimental Studies Comparing Online and Offline Programming Performance

H. SACKMAN, W. J. ERIKSON, AND E. E. GRANT
System Development Corporation
Santa Monica, California

Two exploratory experiments were conducted at System Development Corporation to compare debugging performance of programmers working under conditions of online and offline access to a computer. These are the first known studies that measure programmers' performance under controlled conditions for standard tasks.

Statistically significant results of both experiments indicated faster debugging under online conditions, but perhaps the most important practical finding involves the striking individual differences in programmer performance. Methodological problems encountered in designing and conducting these experiments are described; limitations of the findings are pointed out; hypotheses are presented to account for results; and suggestions are made for further research.

KEY WORDS AND PHRASES: online vs. offline performance, programmer/computer communication, programming experimental-empirical studies, programming cost effectiveness, programming performance, debugging effectiveness, time sharing vs. batch processing, factor analysis application, programmer trainee performance, basic programming knowledge test, experienced programmer study, analysis of variance, programmer individual differences
CR CATEGORIES: 2.40

Introduction

Computer programming is a multibillion dollar industry. Major resources are being expended on the development of new programming languages, new software techniques, and improved means for man-computer communications. As computer power grows and computer hardware costs go down because of the advancing computer technology, the human costs of computer programming continue to rise and one day will probably greatly exceed hardware costs.

This research was sponsored by the Advanced Research Projects Agency Information Processing Techniques Office and was monitored by the Electronic Systems Division, Air Force Systems Command, under contract F 1962867C0004, Information Processing Techniques, with the System Development Corporation.

Amid all these portents of the dominating role that computer programming will play in the emerging computer scene, one would expect that computer programming would be the object of intensive applied scientific study. This is not the case. There is, in fact, an applied scientific *lag* in the study of computer programmers and computer programming—a widening and critical lag that threatens the industry and the profession with the great waste that inevitably accompanies the absence of systematic and established methods and findings and their substitution by anecdotal opinion, vested interests, and provincialism.

The problem of the applied scientific lag in computer programming is strikingly highlighted in the field of online versus offline programming. The spectacular increase in the number of time-shared computing systems over the last few years has raised a critical issue for many, if not most, managers of computing facilities. Should they or should they not convert from a batch-processing operation, or from some other form of noninteractive information processing, to time-shared operations? Spirited controversy has been generated at professional meetings, in the literature, and at grass roots, but virtually no experimental comparisons have been made to test and evaluate these competing alternatives objectively under controlled conditions. Except for related studies by Gold 1967 [4], and by Schatzoff, Tsao, and Wiig 1967 [11], the two experimental studies reported in this paper are, to our knowledge, the first on this central issue to have appeared. They illustrate the problems and pitfalls in doing applied experimental work in computer programming. They spell out some of the key dimensions of the scientific lag in computer programming, and they provide some useful guidelines for future work.

Time-sharing systems, because of requirements for expanded hardware and more extensive software, are generally more expensive than closed-shop systems using the same central computer. Time-sharing advocates think that such systems more than pay for themselves in convenience to the user, in more rapid program development, and in manpower savings. It appears that most programmers who have worked with both time-sharing and closed-shop systems are enthusiastic about the online way of life.

Time sharing, however, has its critics. Their arguments are often directed at the efficiency of time sharing; that is, at how much of the computational power of the machine is actually used for productive data processing as opposed to how much is devoted to relatively nonproductive functions (program swapping, idle time, etc.). These critics (see Patrick 1963 [8], Emerson 1962 [2], and Macdonald 1965 [7]) claim that the efficiency of time-sharing systems is questionable when compared to modern closed-shop methods, or with economical small computers. Since online systems are presumably more expensive than offline systems, there is little justification for their use except in those situations where online access is mandatory for system operations (for example, in realtime command and control systems). Time-sharing advocates respond to these charges by saying that, even if time sharing is more costly with regard to hardware and operating efficiency, the savings in programmer man-hours and in the time required to produce working programs more than offset such increased costs. The critics, however, do not concede this point either. Many believe that programmers grow lazy and adopt careless and inefficient work habits under time sharing. In fact, they claim that instead of improving, programmer performance is likely to deteriorate.

The two exploratory studies summarized here are found in Grant and Sackman 1966 [5] and in Erikson 1966 [3]. The original studies should be consulted for technical details that are beyond the scope of this paper. They were performed by the System Development Corporation for the Advanced Research Projects Agency of the Department of Defense. The first study is concerned with online versus offline debugging performance for a group of twelve experienced programmers (average of seven years' experience). The second investigation involved nine programmer trainees in a comparison of interactive versus noninteractive program debugging. The highlights of each study are discussed in turn, and the composite results are interpreted in the concluding section. For easier reference, the first experiment is described as the "Experienced Programmer" study, and the second as the "Programmer Trainee" study.

The two experiments were conducted using the SDC Time-Sharing System (TSS) under the normal online condition and simulated offline or noninteractive conditions. TSS is a general purpose system (see Schwartz, Coffman, and Weissman 1964 [14], and Schwartz and Weissman 1967 [15]) similar in many respects to the Project MAC system (see Scherr 1966 [12]) at the Massachusetts Institute of Technology. Schwartz 1965 [13] has characterized this class of time-sharing system as providing four important properties to the user: "instantaneous" response, independent operation for each user, essentially simultaneous operation for several users, and general purpose capability.

TSS utilizes an IBM AN/FSQ-32 computer. The following is a general description of its operation. User programs are stored on magnetic tape or in disk file memory. When a user wishes to operate his program, he goes to one of several teletype consoles; these consoles are direct input/output devices to the Q-32. He instructs the computer, through the teletype, to load and activate his program. The system then loads the program either from the

disk file or from magnetic tape into active storage (drum memory). All currently operating programs are stored on drum memory and are transferred, one at a time, in turn, into core memory for processing. Under TSS scheduling control, each program is processed for a short amount of time (usually a fraction of a second) and is then replaced in active storage to await its next turn. A program is transferred to core only if it requires processing; otherwise it is passed up for that turn. Thus, a user may spend as much time as he needs thinking about what to do next without wasting the computational time of the machine. Although a time-sharing system processes programs sequentially and discontinuously, it gives users the illusion of simultaneity and continuity because of its high speed.

1. Experienced Programmer Study

1.1 Experimental Design

The design used in this experiment is illustrated in Figure 1.

	Online		Offline	
GROUP I	Algebra	(6)	Maze	(6)
GROUP II	Maze	(6)	Algebra	(6)
Totals		(12)		(12)

Fig. 1. Experimental design for the experienced programmer study

The 2 × 2 Latin-square design with repeated measures for this experiment should be interpreted as follows. Two experimental groups were employed with six subjects in each; the two experimental treatments were online and offline program debugging; and the Algebra and Maze problems were the two types of programs that were coded and debugged. Repeated measures were employed in that each subject, serving as his own control, solved one problem task under online conditions and the other under offline conditions. Note in Figure 1 that each of the two program problems appears once, and only once, in each row and column to meet the requirements of the 2 × 2 Latin-square. Subjects were assigned to the two groups at random, and problem order and online/offline order were counterbalanced.

The statistical treatment for this design involves an analysis of variance to test for the significance of mean differences between the online and offline conditions and between the Algebra and Maze problems. There are two analyses of variance, corresponding to the two criterion measures—one for programmer man-hours spent in debugging and the other for central processor time. A leading advantage of the Latin-square design for this experiment is that each analysis of variance incorporates a total of 24 measurements. This configuration permits maximum pooled sample size and high statistical efficiency in the analysis of the results—especially desirable features in view of the small subject samples that were used.

1.2 METHOD

A number of problems were encountered in the design and conduct of this experiment. Many are illustrative of problems in experimenting with operational computer systems, and many stemmed from lack of experimental precedent in this area. Key problems are described below.

1.2.1 Online and Offline Conditions.
Defining the online condition posed no problems. Programmers debugging online were simply instructed to use TSS in the normal fashion. All the standard features of the system were available to them for debugging. Defining the offline condition proved more difficult. It was desired to provide a controlled and uniform turnaround time for the offline condition. It was further desired that this turnaround time be short enough so that subjects could be released to their regular jobs and the experiment completed in a reasonable amount of time; on the other hand, the turnaround time had to be long enough to constitute a significant delay. The compromise reached was two hours—considerably shorter than most offline systems and yet long enough so that most of the programmer-subjects complained about the delay.

It was decided to simulate an offline system using TSS and the Q-32 by requiring the programmer to submit a work request to a member of the experimental staff to have his program operated. The work request contained specific instructions from the programmer on the procedures to be followed in running the program—essentially the same approach used in closed-shop computer facilities. Strictly speaking, then, this experiment was a comparison between online and *simulated* offline operations.

Each programmer was required to code his own program using his own logic and to rely on the specificity of the problem requirements for comparable programs. Program coding procedures were independent of debugging conditions; i.e., regardless of the condition imposed for checkout—online or offline—all programmers coded offline. Programmers primarily wrote their programs in JTS (JOVIAL Time-Sharing—a procedure-oriented language for time sharing).

1.2.2 Experimental Problems.
Two program problem statements were designed for the experiment. One problem required the subjects to write a program to interpret teletype-inserted, algebraic equations. Each equation involved a single dependent variable. The program was required to compute the value of the dependent variable, given teletype-inserted values for the independent variables, and to check for specific kinds of errors in teletype input. All programmers were referred to a published source (Samelson and Bauer 1960 [10]) for a suggested workable logic to solve the problem. Programs written to solve this problem were referred to as Algebra programs.

The other problem called for writing a program to find the one and only path through a 20 × 20 cell maze. The programs were required to print out the designators of the cells constituting the path. Each cell was represented as an entry in a 400-item table, and each entry contained information on the directions in which movement was possible from the cell. These programs were referred to as Maze programs.

1.2.3 Performance Measures.
Debugging time was considered to begin when the programmer had coded and compiled a program with no serious format errors detected by the compiler. Debugging was considered finished when the subject's program was able to process, without errors, a standard set of test inputs. Two basic criterion measures were collected for comparing online and offline debugging—programmer man-hours and central processor (CPU) time.

Man-hours for debugging were actual hours spent on the problem by the programmer (including turnaround time). Hours were carefully recorded by close personal observation of each programmer by the experimental staff in conjunction with a daily time log kept by the subjects. Discrepancies between observed time and reported time were resolved by tactful interviewing. TSS keeps its own accounting records on user activity; these records provided accurate measures of the central processor time used by each subject. The recorded CPU time included program execute time, some system overhead time, and times for dumping the contents of program or system registers.

A variety of additional measures was obtained in the course of the experiment to provide control data, and to obtain additional indices of programmer performance. Control measures included: TSS experience, general programming experience (excluding TSS experience), type of programming language used (JTS or machine language), and the number of computer runs submitted by each subject in the offline condition. Additional programmer performance measures included: man-hours spent on each program until a successful pass was made through the compiler (called coding time), program size in machine instructions, program running time for a successful pass through the test data, and scores on the Basic Programming Knowledge Test (BPKT)—a paper-and-pencil test developed by Berger, et al., 1966 [1] at the University of Southern California.

1.3 RESULTS

1.3.1 Criterion Performance.
Table I shows the means and standard deviations for the two criterion variables, debug man-hours and CPU time. These raw score values show a consistent and substantial superiority for online debug man-hours, from 50 percent to 300 percent faster than the offline condition. CPU time shows a reverse trend; the offline condition consistently required about 30 percent less CPU time than the online mode. The standard deviations are comparatively large in all cases, reflecting extensive individual differences. Are these results statistically significant with such small samples?

Table II shows three types of analysis of variance applied to the Latin-square experimental design. The first is a straightforward analysis of raw scores. The second is

TABLE I. EXPERIENCED PROGRAMMER PERFORMANCE

DEBUG MAN-HOURS

	Algebra		Maze	
	Online	Offline	Online	Offline
Mean	34.5	50.2	4.0	12.3
SD	30.5	58.9	4.3	8.7

CPU TIME (sec)

	Algebra		Maze	
	Online	Offline	Online	Offline
Mean	1266	907	229	191
SD	473	1067	175	136

TABLE II. COMPARATIVE RESULTS OF THREE ANALYSES OF VARIANCE

Performance measures	Significance levels		
	Raw Scores	Square root	Square root with covariance
1. DEBUG MAN-HOURS			
Online vs. Offline	None	.10	.025
Algebra vs. Maze	.025	.001	.10
2. CPU TIME			
Online vs. Offline	None	None	None
Algebra vs. Maze	None	.001	.05

TABLE III. RANGE OF INDIVIDUAL DIFFERENCES IN PROGRAMMING PERFORMANCE

Performance measure	Poorest score	Best score	Ratio
1. Debug hours Algebra	170	6	28:1
2. Debug hours Maze	26	1	26:1
3. CPU time Algebra (sec)	3075	370	8:1
4. CPU time Maze (sec)	541	50	11:1
5. Code hours Algebra	111	7	16:1
6. Code hours Maze	50	2	25:1
7. Program size Algebra	6137	1050	6:1
8. Program size Maze	3287	651	5:1
9. Run time Algebra (sec)	7.9	1.6	5:1
10. Run time Maze (sec)	8.0	.6	13:1

an analysis of square root transformed scores to obtain more normal distributions. The third is also an analysis of variance on the square root scores but with the covariance associated with programmer coding skill parceled out statistically; that is, individuals were effectively equated on coding skill so that online/offline differences could be tested more directly.

These applications resulted in six analyses of variance (three for each criterion measure) as shown in Table II. The columns in Table II represent the three kinds of analysis of variance; the rows show the two criterion measures. For each analysis of variance, tests for mean differences compared online versus offline performance and Algebra versus Maze differences. The entries in the cells show the level of statistical significance found for these two main effects for each of the six analyses of variance.

The results in Table II reveal key findings for this experiment. The first row shows results for online versus offline performance as measured by debug man-hours. The raw score analysis of variance shows no significant differences. The analysis on square root transformed scores shows a 10 percent level of significance in favor of online performance. The last analysis of variance, with covariance, on square root scores, shows statistically significant differences in favor of the online condition at the .025 level. This progressive trend toward more clearcut mean differences for shorter debug man-hours with online performance reflects the increasing statistical control over individual differences in the three types of analyses. In contrast to debug man-hours, no significant trend is indicated for online versus offline conditions for CPU time. If real differences do exist along the lines indicated in Table I for more CPU time in the online mode, these differences were not strong enough to show statistical significance with these small samples and with the large individual differences between programmers, even with the square root and covariance transformations.

The results for Algebra versus Maze differences were not surprising. The Algebra task was obviously a longer and harder problem than the Maze task, as indicated by all the performance measures. The fairly consistent significant differences between Algebra and Maze scores shown in Table II reflect the differential effects of the three tests of analysis of variance, and, in particular, point up the greater sensitivity of the square root transformations over the original raw scores in demonstrating significant problem differences.

1.3.2 *Individual Differences.* The observed ranges of individual differences are listed in Table III for the ten performance variables measured in this study. The ratio between highest and lowest values is also shown.

Table III points up the very large individual differences, typically by an order of magnitude, for most performance variables. To paraphrase a nursery rhyme:

> When a programmer is good,
> He is very, very good,
> But when he is bad,
> He is horrid.

The "horrid" portion of the performance frequency distribution is the long tail at the high end, the positively skewed part which shows that one poor performer can consume as much time or cost as 5, 10, or 20 good ones. Validated techniques to detect and weed out these poor performers could result in vast savings in time, effort, and cost.

To obtain further information on these striking individual differences, an exploratory factor analysis was conducted on the intercorrelations of 15 performance and control variables in the experimental data. Coupled with visual inspection of the empirical correlation matrix, the main results were:

a. A substantial performance factor designated as "programming speed," associated with faster coding and debugging, less CPU time, and the use of a higher order language.

b. A well-defined "program economy" factor marked by shorter and faster running programs, associated to some extent with greater programming experience and with the use of machine language rather than higher order language.

This concludes the description of the method and results of the first study. The second study on programmer trainees follows.

2. Programmer Trainee Study

2.1 Experimental Design

A 2×2 Latin-square design was also used in this experiment. With this design, as shown in Figure 2, the Sort Routine problem was solved by Group I (consisting of four subjects) in the noninteractive mode and by Group II (consisting of the other five subjects) in the interactive mode. Similarly, the second problem, a Cube Puzzle, was worked by Group I in the interactive mode and by Group II in the noninteractive mode.

	Interactive	Noninteractive
GROUP I (4)	Cube Puzzle	Sort Routine
GROUP II (5)	Sort Routine	Cube Puzzle
Total	9 Subjects	

Fig. 2. Experimental design for the programmer trainee study

Analysis of variance was used to test the significance of the differences between the mean values of the two test conditions (interactive and noninteractive) and the two problems. The first (test conditions) was the central experimental inquiry, and the other was of interest from the point of view of control.

2.2 Method

Nine programmer trainees were randomly divided into two groups of four and five each. One group coded and debugged the first problem interactively while the other group did the same problem in a noninteractive mode. The two groups switched computer system type for the second problem. All subjects used Tint (Kennedy 1965 [6]) for both problems. (Tint is a dialect of Jovial that is used interpretively with TSS.)

2.2.1 *Interactive and Noninteractive Conditions.* "Interactive," for this experiment, meant the use of TSS and the Tint language with all of its associated aids. No restrictions in the use of this language were placed upon the subjects.

The noninteractive condition was the same as the interactive except that the subjects were required to quit after every attempted execution. The subjects ran their own programs under close supervision to assure that they were not inadvertently running their jobs in an interactive manner. If a member of the noninteractive group immediately saw his error and if there were no other members of the noninteractive group waiting for a teletype, then, after he quit, he was allowed to log in again without any waiting period. Waiting time for an available console in the noninteractive mode fluctuated greatly but typically involved minutes rather than hours.

2.2.2 *Experimental Problems.* The two experimental tasks were relatively simple problems that were normally given to students by the training staff. The first involved writing a numerical sort routine, and the second required finding the arrangement of four specially marked cubes that met a given condition. The second problem was more difficult than the first, but neither required more than five days of elapsed time for a solution by any subject. The subjects worked at each problem until they were able to produce a correct solution with a run of their program.

2.2.3 *Performance Measures.* CPU time, automatically recorded for each trainee, and programmer man-hours spent debugging the problem, recorded by individual work logs, were the two major measures of performance. Debugging was assumed to begin when a subject logged in for the first time, that is, after he had finished coding his program at his desk and was ready for initial runs to check and test his program.

2.3 Results

2.3.1 *Criterion Performance.* A summary of the results of this experiment is shown in Table IV. Analysis of variance showed the difference between the raw score mean values of debug hours for the interactive and the noninteractive conditions to be significant at the .13 level. The difference between the two experimental conditions for mean values of CPU seconds was significant at the .08 level. In both cases, better performance (faster solutions) was obtained under the interactive mode. In the previous experiment, the use of square root transformed scores and the use of coding hours as a covariate allowed better statistical control over the differences between individual subjects. No such result was found in this experiment.

If each of the subjects could be directly compared to himself as he worked with each of the systems, the problem of matching subjects or subject groups and the need for extensive statistical analysis could be eliminated. Unfortunately, it is not meaningful to have the same subject code and debug the same problem twice; and it is extremely difficult to develop different problems that are at the same level of difficulty. One possible solution to this problem would be to use some measure of problem difficulty as a normalizing factor. It should be recognized that the use of any normalizing factor can introduce problems in analysis and interpretation. It was decided to use one of the more popular of such measures, namely, the number of instructions in the program. CPU time per instruction and debug man-hours per instruction were compared on the two problems for each subject for the interactive and noninteractive conditions. The results showed that the interactive subjects had significantly lower values on both compute seconds per instruction (.01 level) and debug hours per instruction (.06 level).

TABLE IV. PROGRAMMER TRAINEE
PERFORMANCE

DEBUG MAN-HOURS

	Sort Routine		Cube Puzzle	
	Interactive	Noninteractive	Interactive	Noninteractive
Mean	0.71	4.7	9.2	13.6
SD	0.66	3.5	4.2	7.0

CPU TIME (sec)

	Sort routine		Cube puzzle	
	Interactive	Noninteractive	Interactive	Noninteractive
Mean	11.1	109.1	290.2	875.3
SD	9.9	65.6	213.0	392.6

2.3.2 *Individual Differences.* One of the key findings of the previous study was that there were large individual differences between programmers. Because of differences in sampling and scale factors, coefficients of variation were computed to compare individual differences in both studies. (The coefficient of variation is expressed as a percentage; it is equal to the standard deviation divided by the mean, multiplied by 100.) The overall results showed that coefficients of variation for debug man-hours and CPU time in this experiment were only 16 percent smaller than coefficients of variation in the experienced programmer study (median values of 66 percent and 82 percent, respectively). These observed differences may be attributable, in part, to the greater difficulty level of the problems in the experienced programmer study, and to the much greater range of programming experience between subjects which tended to magnify individual programmer differences.

In an attempt to determine if there are measures of skill that can be used as a preliminary screening tool to equalize groups, data were gathered on the subject's grades in the SDC programmer training class, and as mentioned earlier, they were also given the Basic Programming Knowledge Test (BPKT). Correlations between all experimental measures, adjusted scores, grades, and the BPKT results were determined. Except for some spurious part-whole correlations, the results showed no consistent correlation between performance measures and the various grades and test scores. The most interesting result of this exploratory analysis, however, was that class grades and BPKT scores showed substantial intercorrelations. This is especially notable when only the first of the two BPKT scores is considered. These correlations ranged between .64 and .83 for Part I of the BPKT; two out of these four correlations are at the 5 percent level and one exceeds the 1 percent level of significance even for these small samples. This implies that the BPKT is measuring the same kinds of skills that are measured in trainee class performance. It should also be noted that neither class grades nor BPKT scores would have provided useful predictions of trainee performance in the test situation that was used in this experiment. This observation may be

interpreted three basic ways: first, that the BPKT and class grades are valid and that the problems do not represent general programming tasks; second, that the problems are valid, but that the BPKT and class grades are not indicative of working programmer performance; or third, that interrelations between the BPKT and class grades do in fact exist with respect to programming performance, but that the intercorrelations are only low to moderate, which cannot be detected by the very small samples used in these experiments. The results of these studies are ambiguous with respect to these three hypotheses; further investigation is required to determine whether one or any combination of them will hold.

3. Interpretation

Before drawing any conclusions from the results, consider the scope of the two studies. Each dealt with a small number of subjects—performance measures were marked by large error variance and wide-ranging individual differences, which made statistical inference difficult and risky. The subject skill range was considerable, from programmer trainees in one study to highly experienced research and development programmers in the other. The programming languages included one machine language and two subsets of JOVIAL, a higher order language. In both experiments TSS served as the online or interactive condition whereas the offline or noninteractive mode had to be simulated on TSS according to specified rules. Only one facility was used for both experiments—TSS. The problems ranged from the conceptually simple tasks administered to the programmer trainees to the much more difficult problems given to the experienced programmers. The representativeness of these problems for programming tasks is unknown. The point of this thumbnail sketch of the two studies is simply to emphasize their tentative, exploratory nature—at best they cover a highly circumscribed set of online and offline programming behaviors.

The interpretation of the results is discussed under three broad areas, corresponding to three leading objectives of these two studies: comparison of online and offline programming performance, analysis of individual differences in programming proficiency, and implications of the methodology and findings for future research.

3.1 ONLINE VS. OFFLINE PROGRAMMING PERFORMANCE

On the basis of the concrete results of these experiments, the online conditions resulted in substantially and, by and large, significantly better performance for debug man-hours than the offline conditions. The crucial questions are: to what extent may these results be generalized to other computing facilities; to other programmers; to varying levels of turnaround time; and to other types of programming problems? Provisional answers to these four questions highlight problem areas requiring further research.

The online/offline comparisons were made in a time-shared computing facility in which the online condition was the natural operational mode, whereas offline conditions had to be simulated. It might be argued that in analogous experiments, conducted with a batch-processing facility, with real offline conditions and simulated online conditions, the results might be reversed. One way to neutralize this methodological bias is to conduct an experiment in a hybrid facility that uses both time-sharing and batch-processing procedures on the same computer so that neither has to be simulated. Another approach is to compare facilities matched on type of computer, programming languages, compilers, and other tools for coding and debugging, but different in online and offline operations. It might also be argued that the use of new and different programming languages, methods, and tools might lead to entirely different results.

The generalization of these results to other programmers essentially boils down to the representativeness of the experimental samples with regard to an objective and well-defined criterion population. A universally accepted classification scheme for programmers does not exist, nor are there accepted norms with regard to biographical, educational and job experience data.

In certain respects, the differences between online and offline performance hinge on the length and variability of turnaround time. The critical experimental question is not whether one mode is superior to the other mode, since, all other things equal, offline facilities with long turnaround times consume more elapsed programming time than either online facilities or offline facilities with short turnaround times. The critical comparison is with online versus offline operations that have short response times. The data from the experienced programmer study suggest the possibility that, as offline turnaround time approaches zero, the performance differential between the two modes with regard to debug man-hours tends to disappear. The programmer trainee study, however, tends to refute this hypothesis since the mean performance advantage of the interactive mode was considerably larger than waiting time for computer availability. Other experimental studies need to be conducted to determine whether online systems offer a man-hour performance advantage above and beyond the elimination of turnaround time in converting from offline to online operations.

The last of the four considerations crucial to any generalization of the experimental findings—type of programming problem—presents a baffling obstacle. How does an investigator select a "typical" programming problem or set of problems? No suitable classification of computing systems exists, let alone a classification of types of programs. Scientific versus business, online versus offline, automated versus semiautomated, realtime versus non-realtime—these and many other tags for computer systems and computer programs are much too gross to provide systematic classification. In the absence of a systematic classification of computer programs with respect to underlying skills, programming techniques and applications, all that can be done is to extend the selection of experimental problems to cover a broader spectrum of programming activity.

In the preceding discussion we have been primarily concerned with consistent findings on debug man-hours for both experiments. The opposite findings in both studies with regard to CPU time require some comment. The results of the programmer trainee study seem to indicate that online programming permits the programmer to solve his problem in a direct, uninterrupted manner, which results not only in less human time but also less CPU time. The programmer does not have to "warm up" and remember his problem in all its details if he has access to the computer whenever he needs it. In contrast, the apparent reduction of CPU time in the experienced programmer study under the offline condition suggests an opposing hypothesis; that is, perhaps there is a deliberate tradeoff, on the part of the programmer, to use more machine time in an exploratory trial-and-error manner in order to reduce his own time and effort in solving his problem. The results of these two studies are ambiguous with respect to these opposing hypotheses. One or both of them may be true to different degrees under different conditions. Then again, perhaps these explanations are too crude to account for complex problem-solving in programming tasks. More definitive research is needed.

3.2 Individual Differences

These studies revealed large individual differences between high and low performers, often by an order of magnitude. It is apparent from the spread of the data that very substantial savings can be effected by successfully detecting low performers. Techniques measuring individual programming skills should be vigorously pursued, tested and evaluated, and developed on a broad front for the growing variety of programming jobs.

These two studies suggest that such paper-and-pencil tests may work best in predicting the performance of programmer trainees and relatively inexperienced programmers. The observed pattern was one of substantive correlations of BPKT test scores with programmer trainee class grades but of no detectable correlation with experienced programmer performance. These tentative findings on our small samples are consistent with internal validation data for the BPKT. The test discriminates best between low experience levels and fails to discriminate significantly among highest experience levels. This situation suggests that general programming skill may dominate early training and initial on-the-job experience, but that such skill is progressively transformed and displaced by more specialized skills with increasing experience.

If programmers show such large performance differences, even larger and more striking differences may be expected in general user performance levels with the advent of information utilities (such as large networks of time-shared computing facilities with a broad range of information services available to the general public). The computer science community has not recognized (let alone faced up to) the problem of anticipating and dealing with very large individual differences in performing tasks involving man-computer communications for the general public.

In an attempt to explain the results of both studies in regard to individual differences and to offer a framework for future analyses of individual differences in programmer skills, a differentiation hypothesis is offered, as follows: when programmers are first exposed to and indoctrinated in the use of computers, and during their early experience with computers, a general factor of programmer proficiency is held to account for a large proportion of observed individual differences. However, with the advent of diversified and extended experience, the general programming skill factor differentiates into separate and relatively independent factors related to specialized experience.

From a broader and longer range perspective, the trend in computer science and technology is toward more diversified computers, programming languages, and computer applications. This general trend toward increasing variety is likely to require an equivalent diversification of human skills to program such systems. A pluralistic hypothesis, such as the suggested differentiation hypothesis, seems more appropriate to anticipate and deal with this type of technological evolution, not only for programmers, but for the general user of computing facilities.

3.3 FUTURE RESEARCH

These studies began with a rather straightforward objective—the comparison of online and offline programmer debugging performance under controlled conditions. But in order to deal with the online/offline comparison, it became necessary to consider many other factors related to man-machine performance. For example, it was necessary to look into the characteristics and correlates of individual differences. We had to recognize that there was no objective way to assess the representativeness of the various experimental problems for data processing in general. The results were constrained to a single computing facility normally using online operations. The debugging criterion measures showed relationships with other performance, experience, and control variables that demanded at least preliminary explanations. Programming languages had to be accounted for in the interpretation of the results. The original conception of a direct statistical comparison between online and offline performance had to give way to multivariate statistical analysis in order to interpret the results in a more meaningful context.

In short, our efforts to measure online/offline programming differences in an objective manner were severely constrained by the lack of substantive scientific information on computer programming performance—constrained by the applied scientific lag in computer programming, which brings us back to the opening theme. This lag is not localized to computer programming; it stems from a more fundamental experimental lag in the general study of man-computer communications. The case for this assertion involves a critical analysis of the status and direction of computer science which is beyond the scope of this article; this analysis is presented elsewhere (Sackman 1967 [9]). In view of these various considerations, it is recommended that future experimental comparisons of online and offline programming performance be conducted within the broad framework of programmer performance and not as a simple dichotomy existing in a separate data-processing world of its own. It is far more difficult and laborious to construct a scientific scaffold for the man-machine components and characteristics of programmer performance than it is to try to concentrate exclusively on a rigorous comparison of online and offline programming.

Eight broad areas for further research are indicated:

a. Development of empirical, normative data on computing system performance with respect to type of application, man-machine environment, and types of computer programs in relation to leading tasks in object systems.

b. Comparative experimental studies of computer facility performance, such as online, offline, and hybrid installations, systematically permuted against broad classes of program languages (machine-oriented, procedure-oriented, and problem-oriented languages), and representative classes of programming tasks.

c. Development of cost-effectiveness models for computing facilities, incorporating man and machine elements, with greater emphasis on empirically validated measures of effectiveness and less emphasis on abstract models than has been the case in the past.

d. Programmer job and task analysis based on representative sampling of programmer activities, leading toward the development of empirically validated and updated job classification procedures.

e. Systematic collection, analysis, and evaluation of the empirical characteristics, correlates, and variation associated with individual performance differences for programmers, including analysis of team effectiveness and team differences.

f. Development of a variety of paper-and-pencil tests, such as the Basic Programming Knowledge Test, for assessment of general and specific programmer skills in relation to representative, normative populations.

g. Detailed case histories on the genesis and course of programmer problem-solving, the frequency and nature of human and machine errors in the problem-solving process, the role of machine feedback and reinforcement in programmer behavior, and the delineation of critical programmer decision points in the life cycle of the design, development and installation of computer programs.

h. And finally, integration of the above findings into the broader arena of man-computer communication for the general user.

More powerful applied research on programmer performance, including experimental comparisons of online and offline programming, will require the development in depth of basic concepts and procedures for the field as a whole—a development that can only be achieved by a concerted effort to bridge the scientific gap between knowledge and application.

REFERENCES

1. BERGER, RAYMOND M., ET AL. Computer personnel selection and criterion development: III. The basic programming knowledge test. U. of S. California, Los Angeles, June 1966.
2. EMERSON, MARVIN. The "small" computer versus time-shared systems. *Comput. Autom.*, Sept. 1965.
3. ERIKSON, WARREN J. A pilot study of interactive versus non-interactive debugging. TM-3296, System Development Corporation, Santa Monica, Calif., Dec. 13, 1966.
4. GOLD, M. M. Methodological for evaluating time-shared computer usage. Doctoral dissertation, Alfred P. Sloan School of Management, M.I.T., 1967.
5. GRANT, E. E., AND SACKMAN, H. An exploratory investigation of programmer performance under online and offline conditions. SP-2581, System Development Corp., Santa Monica, Calif., Sept. 2, 1966.
6. KENNEDY, PHYLLIS R. TINT users guide. TM-1933/00/03, Syst. Develop. Corp., Santa Monica, Calif., July. 1965.
7. MACDONALD, NEIL. A time shared computer system—the disadvantages. *Comput. Autom.* (Sept. 1965).
8. PATRICK, R. L. So you want to go online? *Datamation 9*, 10 (Oct. 1963), 25–27.
9. SACKMAN, H. *Computers, System Science, and Evolving Society*, John Wiley & Sons, New York, (in press) 1967.
10. SAMELSON, K., AND BAUER, F. Sequential formula translation. *Comm. ACM 3* (Feb. 1960), 76–83.
11. SCHATZOFF, M., TSAO, R., AND WIIG, R. An experimental comparison of time sharing and batch processing. *Comm. ACM 10* (May 1967), 261–265.
12. SCHERR, A. L. Time sharing measurement. *Datamation 12*, 4 (April 1966), 22–26.
13. SCHWARTZ, J. I. Observations on time shared systems. Proc. ACM 20th Nat. Conf., 1965, pp. 525–542.
14. ——, COFFMAN, E. G., AND WEISSMAN, C. A general purpose time sharing system. Proc. AFIPS 1964 Spring Joint Comp. Conf., Vol. 25, pp. 397–411.
15. ——, AND WEISSMAN, C. The SDC time sharing system revisited. Proc. ACM 22nd Nat. Conf., 1967, pp. 263–271.

The Software Engineering Shortage: A Third Choice

JAMES P. McGILL

Reprinted from *IEEE Transactions on Software Engineering*, Volume SE-10, Number 1, January 1984, pages 42-49. Copyright © 1984 by The Institute of Electrical and Electronics Engineers, Inc.

Abstract—As interest in the concepts and methods of software engineering increases, many companies, particularly in aerospace, find it difficult to acquire software developers with the desired skills. The option of full-time, company-based training is discussed with suggestions for implementation. Lessons learned from the actual implementation of such a program are discussed along with possible directions for future evolution.

Index Terms—DSDD, industrial training, software engineering, software life cycle.

SEVERAL books and magazine articles have appeared in recent years chronicling the recognition of a "software crisis" in the late 1960's and subsequent attempts to deal with it [1]. Essentially, the crisis referred to the fact that as large development projects, involving both hardware and software, began to be undertaken, it was discovered that the hardware was often delivered in working condition while the software was either not delivered or required extensive reworking upon delivery. The reaction to this problem was a careful examination of typical software development techniques, which led to the discovery that they were generally chaotic and abetted a more fundamental problem, the inability of humans to communicate effectively with one another. The result has been the emergence of several modern methodologies all designed to overcome the communication problem by stressing requirements analysis, modular design, structured programming, and other procedures that promote a clear understanding of the problem and a disciplined, thoroughly documented approach to a solution.

The gradual shift from haphazard development to the methodical engineering of software has led to the emergence of a new type of engineer, the *Software Engineer* [2]. A software engineer may be defined as an individual who is skilled in the application of sound, established engineering and management principles to the analysis, design, construction, and maintenance of software and its associated documentation. Despite the inescapably logical arguments which can be made for the modular techniques, industry has been slow to incorporate or even recognize the need for them or those who practice them. This situation is now changing [3].

The Department of Defense, too often the recipient of poorly developed software, is becoming aggressive in its support of the newer techniques of software development and management. Those industries, such as aerospace, which interface heavily with the DoD, are becoming very interested in hiring software engineers. The need for these professionals has been recognized.

Manuscript received December 1, 1982.

The author is with the Lockheed Missiles and Space Company, Inc., Department 62-M4, Building 581, P. O. Box 504, Sunnyvale, CA 94086.

A SHORTAGE OF SOFTWARE ENGINEERS

The services of software engineers who understand the software development cycle and the tools and methods applicable to each phase of that cycle, are being sought nationwide. Unfortunately, the supply of such persons is quite small. Papers have appeared proposing model undergraduate and graduate curricula for degrees in software engineering [4], [5]. A handful of universities have begun to experiment with such curricula. Indeed, Seattle University and the Wang Institute have just recently awarded the nation's first master's degrees in software engineering. But the supply of new graduates benefiting from these programs does not come close to satisfying the current demand. Therefore, a company seeking the services of a software engineer frequently is left with two choices:

1) assuming that no software engineering graduates are available, it can hire someone with a degree in computer science, mathematics, electrical engineering, other technical discipline, and let that person learn the software development life cycle through on-the-job experience, perhaps supplemented by seminars; or

2) the company can attempt to lure established software engineers away from other companies.

Neither of these solutions is satisfactory. A new graduate lacking experience in large-scale software development will require a break-in period which could last months or years before s/he become productive. During this period, the individual's contributions to the effort could actually be detrimental if not strictly controlled.

Robbing Peter to pay Paul is also no solution. It merely shifts the problem to another company. The industry-wide problem remains.

A THIRD CHOICE

There is a third alternative, however. By establishing a program for cross training some of their own experienced engineers in the disciplines of software engineering, companies could create a continuous source of such talent. The goal of such a program would be to produce software development specialists trained in the recognized foundation areas of computer science, management techniques, communication skills, problem solving, and design theory [6]. A large company undertaking such a program enjoys significant advantages over universities. These include the following.

• Once committed, the company typically has more financial resources to devote to the program.

• The company can reasonably expect selected candidates to be more mature, motivated, and experienced than college students.

• The company typically has experienced software development personnel. Such persons can make excellent lecturers on software development topics.

• The company environment provides a unique opportunity for research into the effectiveness of new methods of software development. Feedback from such monitoring can quickly be incorporated into the company training program. Universities would require much longer to react to such feedback.

• The training may be slanted directly toward specific company needs, further reducing the break-in period after graduation from the program.

Ideally, graduates should be immediately useful and productive upon joining their respective development projects. The students selected for the program should, therefore, not be newly hired college graduates (although a modified program for new hires is certainly feasible). They should already have some familiarity with the company. They should have a record of demonstrated competence in computer related technical disciplines (math, physics, programming).

Pursuant to this goal of immediate postgraduate productivity, the training program must expose students to a variety of subjects. Defense contractors, for example, typically find themselves developing software of a highly technical nature. The training program, in such a company, might be obliged to include courses in mathematics, systems engineering, and physics. The desirability, in any company, to complement disciplined, modular program design with similarly disciplined coding techniques implies the need for familiarity with the concepts of structured programming. Competent instruction in Pascal or Ada[1] would fill this need. In any case, the heart of such a program will be the software engineering course.

The choice of the subject matter of the courses, their durations, and objectives will, naturally, reflect the overall gram goals constrained by time, budget, and other resources. The technical courses should provide the background to enable students to understand the nature of a typical company software system development problem. The programming course should imbue the student with an appreciation of the inherent value of modular programming as well as provide him with the tool. The software engineering course must introduce the student to the concept of solving a problem by breaking it up into smaller, simpler problems (i.e., analysis). The student should learn the value of developing a detailed logical design prior to writing any code. S/he should develop an appreciation for the problems of software project management through the study of such concepts as the software system development life cycle, its associated documentation, quality assurance, configuration mangement, software testing, design reviews, etc. This understanding of the management implications of project development should make the student more amenable to *being* managed.

Instructors for all courses should be experienced and highly trained (probably masters level) in their respective subjects. Software engineering instruction poses unique problems. There are few experts in the subject and they spend a lot of time disagreeing on many issues. The software engineering instructor should, ideally, be an experienced software project manager who has become educated in the modern techniques of software development. Since such persons will be hard to come by, an acceptable compromise is a qualified (advanced technical degree) employee with a few years of company software development experience and the motivation to quickly become expert in modern methods of software project development and management.

There are several methods other than the usual instructor lecture which could be effective in a software engineering course. Many of the management topics could be effectively addressed by experienced company personnel acting as guest lecturers. There are excellent video tape courses available on software engineering. There are also several companies offering seminars on various related subjects.[2] While these are expensive, they are also quite informative and, in a well-planned program, could be cost effective. A crucial adjunct to lectures is "hands-on" experience. The students should be required to participate in the analysis, design, documentation, and management of a typical company software development effort. The requirement that such development be a team effort is important. A lack of understanding of the necessity of and problems associated with a team development effort appears to be a major weakness of the typical new college graduate.

The choice of a suitable class project presents some problems. A major lesson to be learned from such a project concerns the amount of paperwork associated with it and an appreciation, from a managerial point of view, of the necessity for this documentation in a large project. The choice of a small project which might be completed in, say, a few months hardly justifies the required amount of documentation. On the other hand, a more typical problem might have to be abbreviated to the point of becoming totally unrealistic and, therefore, of limited benefit. A solution is to choose a problem of moderate size (perhaps a one or two year life cycle) and only concentrate on the conceptual and development phases. After all, it has been pointed out that errors committed in these phases are typically not discovered until after coding has been completed and are the most costly to fix [7].

Student work on the problem should be held as closely as possible to the realities of work on a typical company project. The students should be exposed to the same types of tools, reviews, audits, walkthroughs, etc. that are documented in the standards and practices of the company. In particular, every student should be required to give oral presentations before experienced software engineers and managers who are unafraid to ask probing questions or reveal design weaknesses. Students should also be exposed to management decisions and dilemmas.

IMPLEMENTATION

It is clear that the training program implied by the above paragraphs is a lengthy one. It is unrealistic to plan it as a program of part-time study. It is, instead, clearly a full-time program lasting several months. The student would retain company employment and full salary while participating. The company would, if necessary, handle the placement of students upon graduation.

---

1 Ada is a registered trademark of the U.S. Department of Defense.

2 Integrated Computer Systems and Yourdon, Inc., for example.

The facilities required for implementation of the implied program are actually rather modest. Floor and office space will be required to support a group of, perhaps, six full-time instructors, a senior instructor/coordinator, an administrator, and clerical personnel. Thus, a total initial staff of around ten persons is implied. A classroom equipped with chalk boards, screen, overhead projector, a video tape machine and large enough to seat the class comfortably is required. There should be computer facilities available for the students supporting whatever language is being taught. Smaller meeting rooms will be needed for individual project teams. The classroom may be used for the oral presentations if it is large enough. If not, such a meeting room will be required. An extensive reference library will be desirable. Word processing and/or secretarial support will be necessary to handle the required documentation associated with the class project. Textbooks, course notes, video courses, microprocessors, and other training aids would be provided by the company. Financial support should be available to keep instructors informed of current happenings in academia, government acquisitions, and industry by encouraging attendance and participation in state-of-the-art seminars and short courses.

The potential benefits of such a program are obvious. The availability of a steady supply of software engineers will partially satisfy a company need. In addition, the knowledge that such training exists may well prove an inducement in attracting and retaining new talent. The methods and standards taught in the training program can eventually establish themselves throughout the company. The training program, as it matures, will be in a position to monitor the success or failure of specific techniques. Such research would not only be of tremendous benefit to the parent company but to the software development industry in general.

A clear problem with the proposed program is the fact that it involves a considerable investment and, therefore, firm executive support. Such support may be hard to win without a proven track record to back up claims of potential benefits. Such a complete track record does not yet exist. However, at least one large aerospace company, Lockheed Missiles and Space Company, Inc., Sunnyvale, CA, has instituted such a program. It is now five years old. The remainder of this article will be devoted to a description of this program and lessons learned.

THE DSDD PROGRAM

The program, which has been active since late 1978, is known as *Extra Prime Skills—A Data Systems Design and Development (DSDD) Training Program*. It was established to help fill the recognized company need for software engineers and to provide an alternate career path for some of its employees, primarily scientists and engineers. Employees with a technical degree or equivalent background and at least a year of continuous employment with the company are eligible to apply. Applicants are interviewed by DSDD management. Characteristics which the interviewers look for are genuine interest in a career in software development with the company, willingness to accept the implied work load, and the ability to work well in, and contribute to, a group effort. A class of 25 students is chosen from the applicants. Two such classes

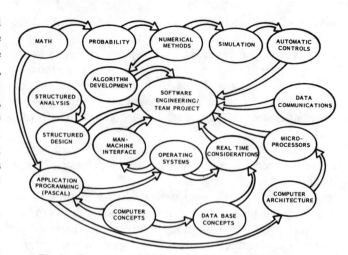
Fig. 1. Support relationships of the various DSDD courses.

are graduated each year. Students are required to attend classes full time, 7:30 until 4:00, Monday through Friday, for the full six months of the program. They have no other company related duties during this time. They continue to receive their normal salaries during the full training period.

A typical student day consists of four to six hours of lecture and two to four hours of study time which may be used for working on homework, computer programs, or the class project. Experience has shown that the forty hours per week on site must typically be augmented by ten to twenty hours, or more, of additional work on the student's own time. Individual classes are taught in blocks ranging from one to six weeks, two hours per day. The exception is the software engineering block which runs continuously throughout the entire six months. Courses consist of lectures by instructors, guest lecturers from within the company, professionals on video tape, and outside consultants who conduct seminars on specific topics. Students are required to complete homework assignments, including computer programs, and take periodic examinations in the various courses. Textbooks and/or lecture notes, at no expense to the student, are provided for each course.

Since most of the software developed within the company is of a highly technical nature, DSDD students receive courses in mathematics and engineering disciplines as well as those in software development. Not surprisingly, the software engineering course is the heart of the program. All other courses support it either directly or indirectly. The relationship of the courses to one another is depicted in Fig. 1.

Fig. 2 illustrates a typical DSDD schedule.

The staff required to support this effort currently consists of five instructors, one senior instructor/coordinator, one administrator, and one secretary. Typical instructor backgrounds include mathematics, computer science, electrical engineering, and other technical fields. A candidate for an instructor position is expected to have a degree (preferably advanced) in a technical discipline. S/he is expected to have experience in the subjects to be taught as well as some general teaching experience. Each instructor is assigned to teach courses amounting to roughly 100 hours of in-class time per six months. During the periods when the instructors are not participating in daily instruction, they are encouraged to at-

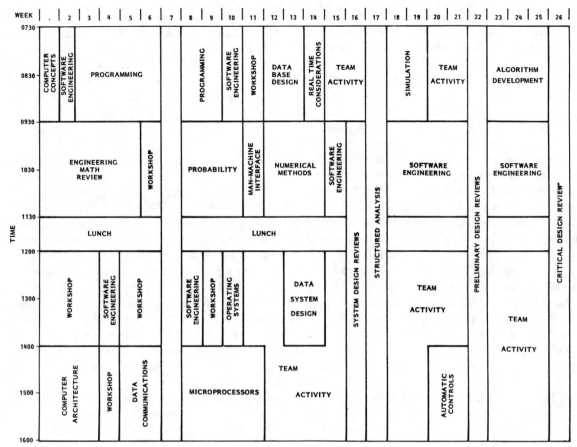

Fig. 2. Typical 26-week DSDD course schedule.

tend other lectures and seminars for the purpose of increasing the breadth and depth of their backgrounds. Sufficient travel money is budgeted to allow each instructor to attend several seminars each year.

Instructors are encouraged, in particular, to keep their respective courses current. This is especially important in a subject such as software engineering which continues to evolve rapidly. The DSDD software engineering course has matured considerably in the last four years. Instruction currently combines lectures, both live and on video tape, special seminars and a lengthy class project.

THE DSDD SOFTWARE ENGINEERING COURSE

Topics covered in the software engineering lectures include a brief history of software development and the "software crisis," requirements analysis, software design, software testing, quality assurance, configuration management, the development life cycle, DoD procurement procedures, and the associated documentation.

The class project involves developing the application software to control the operation of a Wind Energy Generation System (WEGS) which is to provide electricity to a number of consumer areas. The students are provided with initial documentation specifying the requirements of the system from which are to be extracted those requirements which might properly be allocated to software. They are also provided with detailed requirements regarding the documents which they will prepare and deliver to the "customer."

The initial work consists of analyzing the system require-

ments and preparing for a formal presentation at which these requirements are reviewed for clarity and completeness and any proposed changes may be presented. This initial presentation is a System Requirements Review (SRR) and is held before a "customer team" made up of experienced company software developers and managers who are selected for this activity. This initial work is done under the supervision of a student committee selected by the staff. The successful completion of the SRR results in the establishment of an initial, agreed-to, or "baselined," set of system requirements from which subsequent work may proceed. Since instruction is heavily slanted toward software development for the DoD, the SRR and all other reviews, as well as all the documentation, are prepared and presented in accordance with the appropriate military standards. Since the SRR is conducted fairly early in the training program (after approximately six weeks) the presentations are typically naive. Emphasis is placed on presentation style, conduct of the review, and a demonstrated understanding of the nature of the problem. The students are also required to address how they intend to manage the development of the proposed software. Many questions are asked by the customer team for the purpose of pointing out areas where more attention is needed and where expressed ideas are clearly infeasible.

A typical SRR lasts about two hours. The subsequent reviews generally take longer. After SRR, the student committee is dissolved and the entire class is divided up into five 5-person teams. The teams and their respective chairpersons are appointed by the staff. The members of the original

333

student committee are disbursed among the five teams and are not, generally, permitted to act as chairpersons of their respective teams. This gives others a chance to be exposed to the problems of management. The new teams proceed, competitively, to develop a top-level partitioning of the problem and to allocate the baselined requirements appropriately. The results of each team's analysis are presented at a System Design Review (SDR). At the review, each team is required to present its top-level breakdown of the problem into roughly autonomous subproblems, each of which will ultimately evolve into a manageable piece of software called a Computer Program Configuration Item (CPCI). The proposed allocation of requirements to CPCI's is also presented.

In addition, each team is required to develop supporting documentation. This documentation consists of an allocation document detailing the allocation of the software requirements to the proposed CPCI's, a Computer Program Development Plan (CPDP) detailing how development of the software will be managed, and an Interface Management Document (IMD) which serves as a repository for detailed definitions of data and control items crossing interfaces between pieces of software, between software and hardware, and between software and humans. This implies a total of 15 documents from the 5 teams to be reviewed by the staff and customer team prior to the SDR. Since a typical SDR lasts around three hours, three days are generally set aside for the completion of all five of them. After the completion of the last SDR, one team's design and management approach is chosen as the one exhibiting the "least risk" and that approach is then adopted by the entire class for the remainder of the program. The selected team is designated the "integrating contractor" responsible for coordinating the activities of the other four teams. Each team, at SDR, is expected to address potential problems of this upcoming management activity and present its plan for ensuring a smoothly coordinated, post-SDR development effort. The students generally exhibit, during this management portion of the SDR, a greatly improved understanding of, and appreciation for, the problems and benefits of a team effort.

After SDR, the class has approximately 5 weeks to prepare for their Preliminary Design Review (PDR). The PDR generally consists of presentations by each team on its assigned CPCI. By PDR, each CPCI will have been further broken down into functional components with previously existing and newly derived requirements allocated appropriately. The integrating contractor generally addresses matters of management, perceived areas of risk, requested baseline changes, etc. The PDR generally requires one to two days to complete. The teams are required to produce development specifications in accordance with the appropriate military standard. The integrating contractor is responsible for updating the CPDP and the IMD. After the PDR is completed, one CPCI is selected and the class works on converting the functional analysis into a physical design. The functions of the CPCI are gathered into functionally cohesive Computer Program Components (CPC). The results of this effort are the subject of the final review.

The last month is spent preparing for the final review. This is the Critical Design Review (CDR). It typically requires one day and, therefore, is often held the day before graduation.

By this time, the teams have developed the CPC's of the selected CPCI to a codable level. The required documentation is a Product Specification, which describes the physical implementation of the preceding analysis, an updated CPDP and an updated IMD. By CDR, the students have generally become quite comfortable in their role as contractor and typically conduct a very professional review.

THE CUSTOMER TEAM

The role of the customer team in the reviews is crucial. They rely on their experience and knowledge of the class project to help them judge the quality of the reviews. Severe and unremitting criticism has produced an early defeatist attitude which has seriously degraded the value of subsequent instruction. On the other hand, conducting reviews before a realistic customer is probably the most valuable experience of the entire program. The customer team, therefore, "plays its role" by asking penetrating questions, requesting action items, and openly commenting about design or management features which they find troublesome. The proper mix has not been easy to find and requires iteration. But it is too important to ignore. The customer team has generally been experienced in all phases of software development, including software management, and most have attended several actual reviews with typical company customers and, in some instances, have actual customer experience. At least one team member has repeated this experience with every class to date. This has had the benefit of providing continuity in customer attitudes and role-playing. It has also been found beneficial to have former students on the customer teams. The comments of graduates are typically of special interest to the students.

AN EVALUATION

The program, as described in the above paragraphs, clearly represents a major commitment on the part of the company. The annual budget for DSDD is approaching 1.5 million dollars. This is, of course, overhead money and, therefore, clearly implies that DSDD enjoys the support of the highest levels of management. The continued existence and evolution of DSDD reflects the conviction that the work being done is both important and successful.

The ability of any such program to evolve is, of course, one of its most important characteristics. DSDD courses are constantly being modified as instructors find better ways to teach specific areas. In addition, surveys are sent out periodically to former students and their managers. These surveys provide some feedback on student performance and the usefulness of the current courses offered. They have revealed areas of strength and weakness. Fig. 3 and Table I summarize a statistical breakdown of recent survey responses.

Of primary concern is how immediately useful a typical student is after leaving the program to join an existing development project. The data collected so far are too scant and immature to support any firm conclusions. However, at least one manager is on record as having observed that his DSDD graduates seem to have roughly a two year head start over new college graduates with technical degrees. In addition, they are very stable employees. In an environment of high mobility and turnover [9], less than 5 percent of all DSDD graduates have

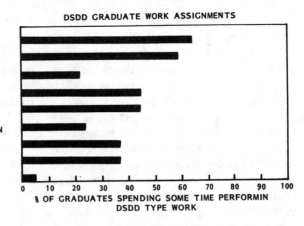

DSDD GRADUATE WORK ASSIGNMENTS

JOB CATEGORY

A. DATA SYSTEMS CONCEPT DESIGNER
B. SOFTWARE DESIGN SPECIALIST
C. COMPUTATIONAL HARDWARE
D. SOFTWARE DEVELOPMENT SPECIALIST
E. DATA SYSTEM INTEGRATION & TEST
F. DATA SYSTEM OPERATION
G. CONFIGURATION CONTROL & DOCUMENTATION SPECIALIST
H. OTHER
I. NONE OF THE ABOVE

% OF GRADUATES SPENDING SOME TIME PERFORMIN DSDD TYPE WORK

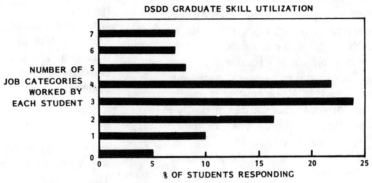

DSDD GRADUATE SKILL UTILIZATION

NUMBER OF
JOB CATEGORIES
WORKED BY
EACH STUDENT

% OF STUDENTS RESPONDING

Fig. 3. Summary of survey data on DSDD graduate utilization by job category.

TABLE I
SUMMARY OF SURVEY RESPONSES

	Utilization			
Subject	Never	Seldom	On Occasion	Often
Calculus	56%	27%	13%	4%
Probability	49	36	10	6
Control Theory	55	25	14	6
Data Communications	24	21	31	23
FORTRAN Programming	43	24	21	11
PASCAL Programming	66	15	13	6
Numerical Analysis	64	21	14	0
Data Base Concepts	17	21	39	24
Simulation	48	30	16	7
Algorithm Development	34	35	21	10
Technical Writing	10	3	30	57
Software Engineering	12	8	28	50
Structured Analysis	8	18	37	37
Structured Design/Programming	17	18	31	34
Real Time Consideration	20	31	27	22
Microprocessors	29	32	25	14
Operating Systems	20	27	37	17
Decision Analysis	26	26	35	13
Display Sys/Man-Mach. Interface	24	13	32	30

Did you enjoy DSDD? Yes 96%   No 4%   Would you do it again?
Yes 90%   No 10%

If you are doing programming, was the DSDD training an aid in producing programs. Yes 85%   No 15%

What programming language is the basis of the work you are doing and did DSDD aid you in that work.   (78 responses)

ATLAS 6%, PASCAL 9%, FORTRAN 36%, Assembly 18%, Basic 10%, Machine 3%, Cobol 12%, Jovial 1%, CBE 1%, PL/M 1%, JCL 3%.

Was H/W training an aid? Yes 84%   No 16%

Were you able to easily integrate into the organization to which you were assigned? Yes 81%   No 19%   (If no, please comment)

left the company. This is even more significant in light of the fact that there is no postgraduate company service requirement.

The DSDD graduates serve the important function of carrying their knowledge to their respective projects. This has two benefits. First, it immediately provides dissemination of new and useful information to co-workers who did not have the opportunity to attend classes. Second, the knowledge and documentation that is making its way into the field may slowly establish consistent standards and methods of software development throughout the company. The students, furthermore, are not just "software people." The technical courses enable them to converse with professional scientists and engineers in technical terms, thereby reducing the hazards of misunderstanding which generally plague human communication. In short, DSDD has evolved into a strong, successful program.

More important than obvious successes, however, are the areas of possible weakness which are found. Identification and elimination of these will guarantee continued improvement in the program. Some of these areas will now be addressed.

The DSDD mathematics courses have included reviews, lasting three to six weeks, of the calculus, statistics and probability, and numerical methods. These courses are viewed as essential to the objectives of the program. However, because of differences in the backgrounds of the students, the level of enthusiasm for these courses varies widely. Part of the solution to this problem lies in the careful selection of in-class examples and homework problems which clearly illustrate the relevance of these courses.

The student project is designed with two specific goals in mind. First, it is complex enough to require a team effort and, therefore, a realistic management effort. Thus, it gives students exposure to the methods and problems associated with software development and software project management. Second, it involves a problem requiring some technical sophistication on the part of the students and, hence, allows application of some of the skills developed in other courses. But the class project suffers from the obvious constraints of time and resources. It was pointed out earlier that the project should be of sufficient complexity to justify the required documentation. The project satisfies this requirement. As a result, only part of its total life cycle is ever addressed. The students only take the project as far as CDR which precedes actual coding. Thus, the students develop detailed modules which will never be coded, test plans which will never be implemented, etc. In addition, certain time-consuming aspects of the project have been short circuited by allowing the students to make some simplifying assumptions. While these unrealistic elements do not negate the tremendous worth of the project, they have the potential to lessen its impact. This problem is diminishing with each class, however, as minor adjustments are continually made to infuse the project with more realism.

Former students complain of a resistance to change on the part of their co-workers and managers. Management feedback tends to substantiate this. Many existing managers are only too aware of the software crisis and the difficulty in managing a software development project. They are understandably wary of new techniques in a field where cost and budget overruns are common, especially in the absence of detailed data showing predictable increases in productivity linked to these methods. Such data will be forthcoming eventually. Until that time, it must be recognized that managerial pragmatism is proper and will be overcome only slowly as the techniques prove themselves and evolve to fit the manager's respective contexts. As the hard evidence accumulates, however, it may be assumed that the drive toward universal acceptance will greatly accelerate. The students are, therefore, urged to adapt and use the ideas of requirements analysis, modularity, clear and disciplined documentation, etc. in their own work. In this way, the required track record will be slowly established. Continuing efforts by the DoD to effect better system design approaches will also, no doubt, prod managers to be open to new techniques.

The company assumes the responsibility of placing new DSDD graduates. DSDD policy in this area is set by a guiding board of directors. Every attempt is made to match graduates with open slots in such a way that student desires and company requirements are met. Obviously, there is never a set of 25 perfect matches. Postgraduate surveys have contained complaints in this regard. Efforts to improve the placement process are continuing. The current placement effort begins with the initial candidate screening interview. The prospective student's responses and résumé are used to gauge his/her special areas of interest. The candidate is also informed that the initial postgraduate placement may not be precisely what was desired. Monitoring and counseling of students and monitoring of company needs continues throughout the six months of classes. This effort has greatly reduced the number and nature of the complaints.

The inherent subjectivity of a topic like software engineering can lead to frustration on the part of the students and the instructor. The customer team expresses certain opinions during the reviews, guest lecturers express different views,

and the instructor may end up presenting a third. While all the expressed viewpoints have several common denominators, the students often become concerned over the inability of anyone to point out one specific "right answer" to questions of management, testing, quality assurance, etc. This frustration is mirrored in the instructor who perceives the problem but is unable to fully alleviate it. It is necessary for the instructor to constantly remind the students that there are no "right" answers, merely "less risky" ones as indicated by evidence compiled from previous projects. The purpose of the course is to present methods, not solutions.

Conclusions

The objective of DSDD is to alleviate the software engineering shortage at LMSC by providing experienced engineers with the opportunity to redirect their careers toward software. The feasibility of such a program has now been amply demonstrated. The program is recommended to other companies currently experiencing a shortage of experienced software engineers.

Directions of Future Growth

One thing seems clear. The need for DSDD and the necessary support are likely to continue into the foreseeable future. This, of course, implies further growth and evolution. Areas of expansion which are already being actively pursued include the development of abbreviated courses to be offered to a spectrum of employees ranging from managers to new hires. The subject matter will be similar to that of the six month course but greatly compressed. Managers are being offered overview courses in the concepts of requirements analysis, logical design, structured coding, testing, documentation, etc. The purpose of such courses is to acquaint managers with the tools and methodology in which DSDD students are trained and suggest proper ways to use these students after graduation. New hires will be offered orientation training before they arrive at their designated organizations. This training will consist of lectures and short exercises in software engineering subjects, programming, and technical disciplines. Other directions of growth include the following.

- Establishment of improved lines of communication to and from active projects for the purpose of assessing student performance and gathering data on the impact of the new techniques.

- Improvement of existing teaching methods through incorporation of new equipment such as personal computers and simulation hardware/software.

- Establishment of lines of communication and cooperation with local universities for the purpose of exchanging ideas, data, students, and instructors.

- Replacement of the current Pascal programming instruction with a course in Ada.

References

[1] H. D. Mills, "Software development," *IEEE Trans. Software Eng.*, vol. SE-2, pp. 265–273, Dec. 1976.
[2] J. Fagenbaum, "A new breed: The software engineer," *IEEE Spectrum*, pp. 62–66, Sept. 1981.
[3] J. W. Plummer, "Extra prime skills," *Military Electron./Counter-

measures, p. 29, Dec. 1978.

[4] R. W. Jensen and C. C. Tonies, *Software Engineering.* Englewood Cliffs, NJ: Prentice-Hall, 1979.

[5] R. W. Jensen, C. C. Tonies, and W. I. Fletcher, "A proposed 4-year software engineeering curriculum," *SIGCSE Bull.,* vol. 10, pp. 84–92, Aug. 1978.

[6] P. Freeman, A. I. Wasserman, and R. Fairley, "Essential elements of software engineering education," in *Proc. Int. Conf. Software Eng.,* 1976, pp. 116–122.

[7] B. W. Boehm, "Software engineering," *IEEE Trans. Comput.,* vol. C-25, pp. 1226–1241, Dec. 1976.

[8] C. D. Labelle, K. Shaw, and L. J. Hellenack, "Solving the turnover problem," *Datamation,* pp. 144–152, Apr. 1980.

James P. McGill received the B.S. degree in mathematics from the University of Maryland, College Park, in 1970 and the M.S. degree in applied mathematics from the University of Nevada, Reno, in 1977.

He undertook additional graduate study in numerical methods from the University of California, Davis, from 1977 to 1979. He joined Lockheed in 1979 after finishing his graduate study and a tour of duty as a Naval Intelligence Officer. After two years of developing simulation software in support of ballistic missile defense research, he joined the DSDD program and became the software engineering instructor.

Managing the
Consequences of DP
Turnover: A Human
Resources Planning
Perspective

Kathryn M. Bartol
University of Maryland

David C. Martin
American University

Abstract

This paper argues that there are both postiive and negative consequences associated
with turnover in the data processing field. In order to maximize the positive consequences, data processing managers must analyze employees in terms of a quality-
replaceability matrix. This matrix helps to determine what further managerial actions
are necessary in order to have appropriate human resources to meet the data processing
needs of the organization.

High turnover has become endemic to the data processing field. Willoughby (1977) has
estimated that annual turnover in the data processing field ranged between 15 and 20
percent during the 1960's, declined to about 5 percent in the early 1970's, and began
to rise again by the end of the decade. A 1979 Datamation study (McLaughlin, 1979)
showed the rate of DP personnel turnover to be about 28 percent annually. Even in the
midst of the recent economic recession, Gray (1982) estimated DP turnover at 15 pecent
annually.

While the persistent high levels of turnover among data processing personnel have been
widely discussed (e.g., Cherlin, 1981; Gray, 1982; and McLaughlin, 1979), the turnover
statistics have mainly been viewed in terms of their negative implications. Indeed,
there are a number of potentially negative results associated with high personnel
turnover. However, recent research suggests that turnover may also have positive
results (Mobley, 1982; Steers and Mowday, 1981; Staw, 1980). The purpose of this paper
is to assess what DP managers can do to manage turnover in such a way that the positive
effects are maximized and the negative effects are minimized.

In any discussion of managing turnover, it must be recognized that some turnover is
unavoidable. Obvious examples of unavoidable turnover are retirements, promotions, and
seasonal help. Employees also leave organizations for a number of personal reasons,
such as job transfer of spouse or relocation necessitated by family illness, which
are largely beyond the control of the manager. Successfully managing turnover requires
the manager to concentrate his or her efforts on turnover that the manager has a high
probability of influencing. Hence this paper discusses turnover that is potentially
avoidable through appropriate managerial action.

Consequences of Turnover

Effectively managing turnover requires a consideration of both the negative and positive
consequences of turnover. Only after weighing the pros and cons of turnover, can managers effectively manage their human resources.

"Managing the Consequences of DP Turnover: A Human Resources Planning Perspective" by K.M. Bartol and D.C. Martin from Proceedings of the
20th ACM Computer Personnel Research Conference, 1983, pages 79-86.
Copyright © 1983, Association for Computing Machinery, Inc., reprinted
by permission.

Negative Consequences

Negative consequences generally receive the most attention when considering the effects of turnover. We outline some of the major negative consequences of turnover applicable to the data processing function.

Major Project Disruption. The loss of key personnel during software development can seriously delay and even permanently impair important projects. During the systems design phase, for example, the resignation of heavily involved personnel may result in significant losses of vital undocumented information and necessitate the recollection of data related to systems parameters and requirements (Lasden, 1980). During the programming, testing, and implementation phases, losses of key personnel can over-burden other project participants, cause the project to fall behind schedule, lead to schedule and cost overruns, and increase the probability of errors in the final system.

Other Performance Related Disruptions. Major performance disruptions can also occur with the loss of important personnel who are working in areas other than major systems development. For example, the loss of personnel who perform maintenance on complex systems may cause delays in implementing needed changes. Furthermore, inexperienced replacements may unwittingly make changes that lead to serious output errors which may or may not be recognized immediately. Similar arguments can be made for the potential disruptive effects of resignations in other areas such as management or systems programming.

Loss of Strategic Opportunities. Turnover of critical personnel can sometimes cause organizations to postpone or cancel projects which can enhance their position relative to competitors and/or increase profits (Mobley, 1982). For example, a turnover-caused postponement of a project to link a major parts supplier with its customers may enable a competitor to make market inroads (Barret and Konsynski, 1983).

Recruitment and Selection Costs. Although the monetary costs associated with recruitment and selection are widely recognized, there has been little systematic research documenting actual costs. Recruitment involves such costs as advertising, employment agency fees, travel costs associated with campus visits or recruitment at computer related associations, entertainment costs for prospective recruits, administrative costs, and even bounty payments to present employees for recommending new prospects (Cherlin, 1981; McLaughlin, 1979; Sloane, 1983). Selection involves such costs as reference checks, interviewing, testing, further travel and entertainment costs for prospective employees, and related administrative costs (Mobley, 1979).

Training and Development Costs. Even if the individual possesses the needed technical skills, there is a learning curve involved until the individual becomes familiar with the organization. McLaughlin (1979) notes that it frequently takes six to eighteen months for a new recruit in the data processing field to reach a reasonable productivity level. Without even considering the salary being paid to the new recruit, initial training costs can involve orientation, the time of a trainer, and disruptions of productivity among others as they try to orient the newcomer. Based on an informal survey, Acker (1981) estimates that the cost of recruiting, relocating, and the first three months of training is likely to run in the range of $6,000 to $10,000 per new hire. However, this figure appears to be rather conservative if one considers the true costs of replacing a good performer with experience in the organization.

Decline in Morale. Personnel leaving an organization can frequently cause morale problems, particularly if the person is perceived as leaving due to poor conditions. Remaining employees may view the person leaving as getting ahead and they themselves may be induced to think about searching for a new organization. In addition, the loss of a key person on a project and the ensuing work difficulties may discourage those who remain. Finally, an individual leaving may have serious detrimental effects on a cohesive work group, at least in the short run (Staw, 1980).

Positive Consequences

Not all consequences of turnover are negative. Increasingly the positive aspects of turnover are being studied by researchers (e.g., Mobley, 1982; Dalton, Todor, and Krackhardt, 1982). There are several potentially positive consequences of turnover that are particularly applicable to the data processing field.

Increased Performance. One positive possibility is that relatively poor performers will leave and be replaced by better performers (Muchinsky and Morrow, 1980). Where this occurs, there can be a net gain in productivity, especially in the long run.

Salary and Benefit Cost Savings. Higher levels of turnover normally produce a work force with less longevity. A relatively junior work force is much less costly to the organization in the form of regular pay, overtime pay, FICA, costs, pensions, and length of vacations. Dalton and Todor (1982) suggest that considerable cost savings can be realized by accepting a higher turnover rate in an organization and that the savings could be maximized by hiring new people who have the requisite skills to replace more senior employees who are at the top of the pay scale. In many situations in the data processing area, however, the loss of valuable experience can outweigh cost savings.

Innovation and Adaptability. New employees frequently bring with them technological expertise and experience gained elsewhere. This infusion of new knowledge and ideas is important in helping an organization remain innovative. Turnover can also help facilitate changes in staffing patterns to reflect new needs. For example, many data processing organizations now require individuals with advanced technical knowledge in data communications. The increasing availability of software packages could also change the necessary configurations of talent needed in the future. Thus turnover can enable organizations to adapt more quickly to changing environments.

Increased Internal Mobility. Particularly when more senior employees leave, the turnover opens up promotional possibilities for high performing, lower level staff (Staw, 1980). These opportunities may be crucial for retaining newer promising employees. LaBelle, Shaw, and Hellenack (1980) have argued for the importance of career ladders and promotional possibilities in the data processing field.

Increased Morale. When poor performers or individuals who tend to create distructive conflict leave, the result can be increased morale. For example, the removal of an individual who misses deadlines, does inferior work, and delays projects can be a boost to others on the project and make those who are performing well feel more equitably treated. Bartol (1983) found that individuals who viewed their organizations as rewarding professional behavior were less likely to turnover. Turnover of individuals who do not engage in professional behaviors may help to enhance perceptions that the organization does indeed value high quality work.

Decrease in Other Withdrawal Behaviors. Mobley (1982) has noted that individuals who are unhappy with a particular organization may not leave the organization, but may engage in other forms of withdrawal such as absenteeism, poor quality work, and even sabotage. Sabotage is a particularly difficult problem for the data processing field, because the damage which can be done by an individual employee through programming changes and security breaches is greater than with most jobs. It frequently is better if disgruntled employees leave an organization before withdrawal behaviors become acute.

Quality-Replacement Matrix

Negative and positive consequences of turnover are normally viewed in terms of their cumulative effects on an organization. e.g., high turnover is costly or low turnover does not provide enough new ideas, fresh views, and stimulation. Yet, when one considers actually managing turnover, the perspective must shift to turnover as an individual phenomenon. Decisions concerning whether or not an individual remains with an organization are usually a product of the forces to remain versus the forces to leave as they impact on a particular person (Vroom, 1964). Thus, turnover must be managed as it applies to individuals and their specific situations.

The goal of the organization is to retain those individuals who are high quality employees in terms of job skills and particularly those who are difficult to replace (Dalton, Todor, and Krackhardt, 1982). Similarly, those employees of inferior quality who are easily replaced should be terminated as soon as possible. Organizations, therefore, normally give unusual weight to the quality and replaceability of an individual when assessing an individual's net worth to the organization. These factors are paramount when considering those issues which normally lead to retaining a person in the organization, e.g., pay recognition, job autonomy, training, and participation in decision making.

The prime outcomes of the quality and replaceability issues as they relate to turnover are indicated in Figure 1. All employees in an organization can be classified into one of the four categories shown.

Replaceability

	Difficult	Easy
High Quality (Potential) **Low**	I Disfunctional Turnover	II Functionality Depends on Costs
	IV Short Run Dysfunctional/ Long Run Functional	III Functional Turnover

Figure 1 The Quality-Replaceability Matrix

Figure 1 suggests that high quality employees are assets to the organization and that, if they are difficult to replace, turnover among this group (Category I) is very dis-functional for the organization. A systems analyst who does high quality work and also is familiar with the organization is an example of an individual who would fall into Category I. On the other hand, those high quality employees who are relatively easy to replace (Category II) may or may not become costly turnovers to the organization. An example of an individual in Category II would be a high quality keypunch operator. In some cases it could be cost effective from an economic, psychological, and organizational health standpoint to replace an individual from this group. In other instances, costs associated with the turnover of an individual in this group may be prohibitive, even though replacements are readily available. Thus organizations have some choice when dealing with individuals in this category and their actions should be dictated by the costs associated with the decision. However, serious consideration should be given to the quality of performance rendered by the person. It is possible that an individual in this group (Category II) who performs well may become even more valuable with a small investment in training. Even though the final decision concerning what the organization would do to preclude or induce turnover is one of choice, it is likely that for people in this group (Category II) the organization will take actions which would result in the person remaining.

However, in contrast to this group of employees, those who are regarded as low quality and difficult to replace (Category IV) also represent a choice for the organization. A maintenance programmer who is slow and frequently makes errors before finally making necessary changes may know a system very well and, therefore, be difficult to replace in the short run. Because such individuals are difficult to replace, it may be some time before a new person hired can adequately perform the job. This could result in some short term problems for the organization. Yet if a suitable replacement is eventually selected, the losses associated with the turnover may be attenuated over time and the long term result could be quite positive. This type of scenario is usually both time and resource dependent. Yet because individuals in Category IV are low quality employees, even though they are difficult to replace, the organization should view them as being there by the choice of the organization and as individuals that may be terminated or leave at some future time.

The last group of individuals indicated in Figure 1 is that which includes the low quality employees who are easily replaced. An example here would be a programmer who has not kept up technically and who accomplishes very little on the job. This is the group (Category III) which most organizations want to terminate as soon as possible. Departures of Category III individuals will improve the efficiency and overall health of the organization. This is functional turnover--it is the proper releasing or terminating of individuals who do not meet the norms of the organization. It is normally good both for the organization and the individual, at least in the long run. However, some firms have policies which permit termination only in the most severe situations.

Thus effective management of the turnover process is an extremely critical function. Data processing managers who wish to be staffed adequately for future challenges and opportunities must devote considerable attention to managing turnover.

Turnover Management Process

There are several basic steps involved in managing turnover. Each of these steps is outlined below.

Categorizing Employees

Employees must be evaluated in view of their potential value to the organization. Many issues must be considered when making such an evaluation. These include not only levels of current performance, but also the degree to which they could master the necessary skills required to perform their current jobs, their demonstrated capabilities and desires to assume additional responsibility, their abilities to work with others, their abilities to manage, and ultimately their abilities to extend the organizational image to the desired audience. Based on these and other considerations germane to the specific organization, employees should be evaluated and subsequently assigned to one of the categories (retain, choose likely to retain, choose likely to release, and release the employee) indicated in Figure 2.

Replaceability

	Difficult	Easy
High	I Retain	II Choose - Likely To Retain
Quality (Potential) Low	IV Choose - Likely to Release	III Release

Figure 2 - Personnel Management Objectives

for Each Category of Employee

Determining Personnel Actions to be Accomplished

Subsequent to determining the category into which employees fall, personnel actions appropriate for that group of individuals should be initiated. These should be of assistance to both the individual and the organization as both should benefit from this review. The goal of these actions should be to manage the careers of employees in such a manner as to make them so valuable to the organization that they are regarded as a Category I (retain) employee. Where they are not now performing satisfactorily and apparently will not perform to the standards of the organization, they should become candidates for Category III (release). Typically the personnel actions which should be considered for employees in each of the respective quadrants are as follows (See Figure 2):

Category I (Retain). These are the organization's most valued employees. They must be challenged and supported, as their contributions are essential to the success of the organization. They should be trained to the maximum extent possible, not only in a technical area, but also in the broader aspects of operating the organization, to include management training when appropriate. These employees should be prepared for positions of increasing responsibility, assuming they desire to be promoted in the organization.

Bartol and Martin (1982) have argued that the quality of personnel will become even more important in the future than in the past because the role of data processing is changing. Data processing personnel need to be more heavily involved in helping to develop and implement data processing related aspects of an organization's strategic plan. To increasingly fulfill this role in the future will require not only technical skills, but also greater knowledge of the business of the organization.

Where possible, jobs for individuals in Category I should be enriched to include additional functions (Couger and Zawacki, 1980). Job enrichment normally includes the assignment of planning and budgetary control to the individual while focusing on the total responsibility for a given function (e.g., an entire system). The group of individuals may also be rotated between jobs to gain additional skills, experience, and exposure to other facets of the organization (Wallace & Szilagyi, 1982). Special efforts must be made to retain this group of individuals, to include adequate compensation, recognition of work, sponsorship of work initiatives, participation in appropriate decision making sessions, and encouragement to expand their functions.

Category II (Choose, Likely to Retain). This group of individuals includes some of the most dependable employees in the organization. They have demonstrated that they can perform satisfactorily. They are people who have potential with the organization, yet are currently lacking or have not yet indicated that they have certain skills which would make them valuable assets to the organization. The organization can help employees in this group. Skill training can be provided, individuals can be rotated to other jobs to gain experience and insight, there can be some participation in the decision making which concerns their specific work, and they can be given projects which include a high degree of personal identity for them. However, the primary orientation of the career development actions for this group must be on technical and business skill acquisition and recognition through such means as promotions, which are contingent on becoming totally proficient in a given area. In those areas where there are an abundance of people qualified to perform a specific job, the primary emphasis for increasing the value of the person to the firm should be on learning and perfecting skills which are concerned with the next higher level of job which is normally a function which integrates several skills.

Category III (Release the Employee). This group of individuals does not fit the norms of the organization. For any number of reasons (e.g., poor performance, absenteeism, lack of motivation, the person does possess adequate skills but does not have the motivation required to reach the minimum level of proficiency expected of a person in a particular job), the members of this group have not succeeded and are not expected to be able to meet the requirements of the organization. They should not receive additional training or be recipients of any other nonrequired organizational benefits. Depending on the specific individual circumstances, they should be given as much consideration as possible in assisting them find employment. However, the involuntary separation policy of some organization may preclude immediate dismissal of an individual except for extremely serious acts or omissions. Many factors, such as longevity, quality of performance during their careers with the organization, stress of the function, and circumstances under which the act was committed or omitted, are considered prior to arriving at a decision concerning the fate of the employee. However, in those cases where it is beneficial that the employee be separated but organizational policy precludes such action, the employee should probably be managed in a manner similar to those in Category IV.

Category IV (Choose-Like to Release). These employees constitute a work force composed of questionable worth to the organization. They are characterized as being generally unreliable, undependable, requiring an unusual amount of supervision, and of marginal efficiency. Yet their output contributes to the overall production of the organization. Normally there would be a short term decrease in the firm's ability to meet its obligations if a person from this group left the organization. Yet the current prognosis for members of this group is that they will eventually leave the organization or the organization will choose to release them. Thus in a sense, they are in a state of movement toward either voluntary or involuntary separation. Organizations must decide whether or not these indiviudals could be trained and subsequently become the type of employee that should be retained (Category I). Perhaps a skill or behavioral training course could assist in reorienting the individual toward a more rewarding career both for him/herself and the organization. This should be the goal of the organization whenever possible. The actions by the organization must be very carefully considered as training is costly and must be viewed by individuals as a medium by which they could become valuable assets. Training, in those cases, should not be perceived as a reward for previous actions, but instead as a means of salvaging employees who otherwise may become turnover statistics. Where an organization's policy is to "retain and retrain" whereever possible (versus terminating the employee), training should be given to individuals who are viewed as belonging in Category III. The goal here would be eventual reclassification to Category II or I.

Planning Individual Career Development Actions

Specific actions, such as training, job rotation, promotion, or termination should be arranged for the individuals concerned, whenever possible, and included in the organizational budget. Planned action is particularly important because in many cases job opportunities will depend on vacancies which in most organizations are fairly predictable. Yet most replacement actions include some form of training which must arranged and funded. Thus, these significant individual actions must be programmed into the overall annual personnel management program and deliberatley executed in order to provide the skills required by the organization at the time they are needed.

Developing Replacement Tables

In order to ensure that qualified people are available when required, specific actions must be taken by the organization to prepare them to perform specific jobs. This can be accomplished using several strategies. One of the most prevalent strategies used by organizations today is that of preparing a replacement table. This table lists each significant, normally highly skilled or supervisory, function, as well as the incumbent and the person who could be expected to replace the incumbent. The state of preparedness of the identified replacement is also indicated as well as actions which are to be taken to increase the ability of this individual to do the job. Replacement charts force supervisors to identify that training and experience necessary for individuals who are to prepared to assume certain positions. As such, these tables play a key role in the career development of many members of the organization.

Conducting Periodic Reviews

Both organizations and indivduals change. Thus an individual may have been classified into a given category, but after a period of time following the completion of training, job rotation or other means of career enhancement, or even perhaps some unsatisfactory performance, the individual should be reevaluated. In some situations, a segment of the work force may improve significantly during a period of time and all members therein may be reclassified depending on their contribution to the group effort. However, the necessity for a periodic reevaluation is clear if the system is to be responsive to the needs of the organization. The timing of the reevaluation is a function of the character of the work environment and the demands of the indiviudals in the work force. Extremely dynamic work environments and highly complex jobs usually dictate more frequent evaluations, perhaps every ninety to one hundred and eighty days. Whereas more stable environments and well defined jobs are normally reevaluated less frequently, perhaps once a year. The reevaluation process then becomes the first step in succeeding personnel actions affecting the individual. Thus career development actions are planned, programmed and executed based on updated evaluations of employees.

Summary

There are both positive and negative consequences associated with turnover. In order to maximize the positive consequences, management must be proactive in ensuring that the proper personnel actions are planned, funded, and implemented. Only through the use of an effective turnover management process will data processing functions have the appropriate human resources to meet the needs of their organizations. Without such human resources, the tremendous potential for strategic utilization of computers will be lost to many organizations.

References

Acker, S. R. Turning around turnover. Data Management, March, 1981, 44-56.

Barrett, S., & Konsynski, B. Inter-organization information sharing systems. Management Information Systems Quarterly, December, 1982, Special Issue, 93-105.

Bartol, K. M. Turnover among DP personnel: A casual analysis. Communications of the ACM, in press.

Bartol, K. M., & Martin, D.C. Managing information systems personnel: A review of literature and managerial implications. Management Information Systems Quarterly, December, 1982, Special Issue, 49-70.

Cherlin, M. The toll of turnover. Datamation, 1981, 27, 4, 209-212.

Dalton, D. R., & Todor, W. D. Turnover: A lucrative hard dollar phenomenon. Academy of Management Review, 1982, 7, 212-218.

Gray, S. B. 1981 DP salary survey. Datamation, 1982, 28, 11, 114-123.

LaBelle, C. D., Shaw, K., & Hellenack, L. J. Solving the turnover problem. Datamation, 1980, 26, 4, 144-148.

Lasden, M. Recycling displaced dissastisfied pros. Computer Decisions, 1980, 12, 1, 36-48.

McLaughlin, R. A. The old bugagoo, turnover. Datamation, 1979, 25, 11, 97-101.

Mobley, W. H. Some unanswered questions in turnover and withdrawal research. Academy of Management Review, 1981, 7, 111-116.

Mobley, W. H. Employee turnover: Causes, consequences, and control. Reading, Ma.: Addison-Wesley Publishing Co., 1982.

Muchinsky, P. M., & Morrow, P. C. A multi-disciplinary model of voluntary turnover. Journal of Vocational Behavior, 1980, 17, 263-290.

Sloane, A. A. Personnel - Managing Human Resources. Englewood Cliffs, NJ: Prentice Hall, Inc., 1983.

Staw, B. M. The consequences of turnover. Journal of Occupational Behaviour, 1980, 1, 253-273.

Steers, R. M., & Mowday, R. T. Employee turnover and the post decision accomodation process. In B. M. Staw and L. L. Cummings (Eds.), Research in Organizational Behavior. Greenwich, Conn.: JAI Press, 1981.

Vroom, V. H. Work and motivation. New York: Wiley, 1964.

Wallace, M. J., & Szilagyi, A. D. Managing behavior in organizations. Glenview, Ill.: Scott Foresman and Company, 1982.

Willoughby, T.C. Computing personnel turnover: A review of the literature. Computer Personnel, Autumn, 1977, 7, 11-13.

I'm OK—and You're Not

The annual performance review is a harrowing experience for both the employee and the boss.

BY MARIE MONEYSMITH

It doesn't matter which side of the desk you're sitting on: Employee evaluations can cause even the most stouthearted to shrink from the encounter. For the employee under review it's an understandably tense experience—something akin to awaiting a tax audit. Much less considered, but equally acute, is the anxiety level of the executive delivering the verdict.

"It's very seldom that I run into a manager who says she enjoys giving reviews," says Myrt W. Webb, a Los Angeles-based performance management consultant with 30 years' experience. "That's basically because the review is so negatively oriented. It's a confrontational kind of thing, a punishment, and a negative reinforcer."

A perfect example of this is the experience of Kaye B., a public relations director, who still recalls the first review she ever gave. "The employee was a woman who had an abrasive personality when she was in a *good* mood," she explains. "She'd been in the department longer than I had and was older, too. I was so intimidated by the thought of confronting her with any criticism that I put the review off for three months, knowing that it held up her raise. By the time I faced her, she was furious: She told me I was incompetent and unfit to be a director. We spent an hour shooting the criticism back and forth. If I knew then what I know now, I would have caught her off guard by talking about some of her good points instead of launching into a full-scale attack."

The negative nature of the review is complicated by the fact that what seems like a simple enough task is really a highly sensitive undertaking. "Most people have no training at all in

Marie Moneysmith last wrote for SAVVY *about job boredom (February 1984).*

evaluation, and they don't feel comfortable with it," explains Charles Leo, a Sherman Oaks, California-based seminar leader and a specialist in performance evaluation systems. "Consequently, they avoid the review. They may not do it and say they did. Or they may not confront unsatisfactory behavior at all and say only good things—which doesn't help anyone."

"As it is usually done, the performance review probably does more harm than good," adds Webb. "One study found that 84 percent of the performance reviews examined had resulted in an ego-deflating experience for the employee, the reviewer or both."

Fortunately, this situation can be improved. Here are some suggestions:

Make employee evaluations an ongoing process. First and foremost, an employer should never accumulate a list of things done wrong during the year and then dump it on the employee during the review. Instead, practice giving reviews on a day-to-day basis. "Get used to telling your employees they're doing something inappropriate *when* they're doing it, not six months later," Leo advises. "The review should be a formal recap of what you've already discussed with the employee."

Evaluate behavior, not personality: Karen K., a marketing executive with a major food distributor, still remembers the review she had seven years ago, when she was criticized for not being more ambitious. "I was so flabbergasted, I couldn't even respond," she recalls. "Not one word was said about my performance, which, as it turned out, was fine. The entire review was based on my supervisor's idea that I was too complacent."

"The biggest problem managers have is a tendency to identify an employee by what she *is* instead of what she *does*," explains Webb. "Employees are afraid of being told they lack initiative, because that's perceived as a character flaw, and it's frightening. But if you point out to them that they only fulfilled 80 percent of the sales quota, they can accept that and deal with it."

An excellent tool that helps in this area is an agreed-upon description of what is expected from the employee. "Everyone needs to know from day one what constitutes an acceptable job, and also what is considered above-acceptable work," explains Cathy Kachur, faculty member of the University of California at San Diego, San Diego State, and National University business extension schools. "Without those standards you can't evaluate effectively."

Be candid. Granted, it's not easy to look someone in the eye and tell her where she needs to improve. But doing anything less shortchanges your employee *and* you. "It's a disservice to lie to the person or to shade the truth and then write something else behind her back," says Leo. "Never lead someone to think she's doing a perfect job when she's not."

Lynn F., a traffic manager in an ad agency, recalls a traumatic dismissal from a job where she had received a favorable review only weeks before.

"My supervisor said everything was fine, and three weeks later I was fired. It made me extremely wary of being told I was doing well," she says. "I was like Chicken Little for the next few years. No matter what I was accomplishing I kept expecting the sky to fall."

One tactic that helps in being candid is to avoid accusatory language. Statements like "You're not being very professional about following through on projects" are hard to accept. But when the same basic idea is restated as "Let's talk about why that report fell through the cracks and what we can do about it," it becomes more palatable.

Be specific. There's nothing worse than telling someone she needs to improve without explaining precisely what, how, and why. Criticizing someone for being slow is not an effective way to evaluate behavior. But pointing out to an employee that she regularly misses important weekly deadlines and then helping her to look at the causes of that lateness and what can be done about them is. "Discuss the implications and consequences of what the person is doing," says Leo. "Let her know right where she stands if the behavior is improved, and if it's not, what the outcome might be."

Critique and compliment. Praise is one the most powerful motivators there is. The person under review should be reminded of her strengths as well as of her weaknesses. "It is crucial that you concentrate on the things the person has done well, because

they're what you want more of," Webb stresses. "The more you focus on those things, the more the employee will tend to bring those about."

Again, specifics are in order. Instead of "You're doing fine," let employees know that they have an exceptional ability to handle customers or a talent for taking charge in difficult situations.

Don't be afraid of dialogue. One common mistake when it comes to evaluations is using the "get it over with" approach. "The manager calls the employee in, reads a laundry list of areas to work on, and announces that the meeting is over," says Leo. "As a result, the employee is left reeling. You must give meetings like this enough time for a decent dialogue between the two of you. And minimize interruptions, because it puts someone off if you're taking phone calls. You should be there for the person, to solicit and to listen to her responses." For the same reason, you should hold the review in territory where you feel comfortable (your office or a conference room), not in a restaurant or in the employee's office, where you're likely to become distracted from the purpose of the review.

A couple of other points: Try turning the tables occasionally. "Every so often, check in with your employees," suggests Leo. "Ask them what you are doing as a manager that helps them— and what you're doing that doesn't. But don't do it during the review or right afterward, because it looks like

you're being apologetic or condescending."

If the traditional review is something you're having a hard time dealing with right now, Webb offers another tactic. "Let the employee score herself on how she honestly feels she has performed over the last six months or so. Then the two of you can discuss the scorecard.

"The first time managers do this," Webb continues, "they are afraid the employees will judge themselves excellent in every category. But the surprising thing is that most people are far more critical of their behavior than someone else would be. It sounds dubious, but this method has been used for some time now, and it turns out that the premise is valid. Managers report that they don't mind doing performance reviews with this system."

Finally, come to terms with the fact that an evaluation is a difficult process and you may never feel completely comfortable doing it. The important thing is that it gets results. Jeannette F. has been a supervisor in a large accounting firm for twelve years and has completed dozens of reviews. "My palms don't sweat as much, and my voice doesn't crack like it did the first time," she says. "That's because I've seen people respond to realistic, constructive, fair criticism, and become better employees. And I know now that even though it can be uncomfortable, in the long run, everyone benefits from an honest evaluation."

Chapter 7: Directing a Software Engineering Project

1. Introduction to Chapter

Directing a software engineering project is defined as all the management activities that deal with guiding and motivating employees to follow the plan. Once employees are trained and oriented, the manager has a continuing responsibility for monitoring their assignments, guiding them towards improved performance, and motivating them to perform to the best of their abilities.

Directing a software engineering project can be partitioned into nine general management activities (see Table 7.1). Each activity in the table is followed by its definition or an amplifying description.

MY NEEDS HAVE BEEN SATISFIED, TEDDY—YOU DIRECT THE CHARGE

San Juan Hill

Table 7.1: Directing Activities

Activity	Definition or Explanation
Provide leadership	— Induce subordinates to accomplish their assignments with enthusiasm and confidence.
Supervise personnel	— Give assigned personnel day-to-day instructions, guidance, and discipline to fulfill their assigned duties.
Delegate authority	— Give authority and discretion to act and expend resources to subordinates.
Motivate personnel	— Persuade and induce personnel to take desired action.
Coordinate activities	— Integrate activities in the most effective and efficient combinations.
Facilitate communications	— Insure free flow of correct information.
Resolve conflicts	— Encourage differences of opinion and resolve resulting conflicts.
Manage changes	— Stimulate creativity and innovation in achieving goals.
Document directing decisions	— Document decisions involving delegation of authority, communication and coordinations procedures and policies, and so on.

2. Overview of Chapter

This chapter contains six short papers on directing and motivating. The activities listed in Table 7.1 were used as an outline for the purpose of identifying papers on directing activities.

The paper by Boyatzis discusses leadership through the use of power. The paper by Raudsepp is an excellent paper on one of the most effective tools of management: the delegation of authority.

Fitz-enz's paper discusses what motivates managers and data processors. Powell and Posner propose that the most powerful motivating forces are excitement and commitment while the paper by Couger discusses quality circles as a means to facilitate communications.

The final document by Kirchof and Adams gives an overview of conflict management for project managers.

3. Description of Papers

The initial paper, by Boyatzis, is on *leadership* and the effective use of power. Power is defined as the ability of one person to influence another. This paper discusses the various types of power and power bases. It states that managers and leaders have the ability and authority to influence other people and that along with this authority comes the responsibility to be more aware of their power and use it effectively. Boyatzis believes that there are five key attributes which determine the quality of an individual's leadership ability.

Raudsepp's paper, "Delegate Your Way to Success," elaborates on one of the most valuable tools in the manager's toolbox: the ability to *delegate authority* and resources to another individual in order to accomplish the organization's objectives. The author defines delegation of authority as the passing on, by one person to another, of the accountability for a given task. He reports that "a manager who delegates with intelligence and consistent follow-up can accomplish far more than the manager who hugs to his (or her) bosom the tasks his subordinates should be doing." He also gives a list of reasons why managers do <u>not</u> delegate authority and demonstrates how that can be avoided.

The third paper, by Jac Fitz-enz, takes a look at what it takes to motivate a data processor. The author has collected statistics comparing the importance of motivational factors between programmer-analysts, project leaders, and managers. The results are compared to Hertzberg's results of the 1960s.

The fourth paper, by Powell and Posner, talks about using staff excitement and commitment as keys to project success. The paper begins with an interesting scenario in which a typical pre-employment interview is conducted to determine if the person being interviewed would be right for the given project. The manager must make the project goals the worker's goals. This paper also provides five lessons and corresponding payoffs the project manager could employ to motivate people to become more excited and committed to a project.

The next paper, by Couger, discusses *quality circles* and how to adapt them to American data processing organizations. Couger points out that data processing personnel and data processing managers have a low need for social interaction and communication and therefore require special training and practice before they can become effective in using quality circles.

The last paper by Kirchof and Adams is the first chapter from a monograph, *Conflict Management for Project Managers*, published by the Project Management Institute. This short overview states that conflicts will exist in all project environments. As the authors state, "severe conflict is the rule in projects where participants are 'loaned' to the project and thus must report to two bosses, namely their functional managers for evaluation and career development, and the matrix project manager for task assignment and work direction." Since conflict is natural it must be managed and used to benefit both the project and the organization. (The complete monograph can be obtained from the Project Management Institute, PO Box 43, Drexel Hill, PA 19026.)

350

Leadership: The Effective Use of Power

Richard E. Boyatzis[1]

Introduction

Managers and leaders of all kinds are in positions of relatively high ability to influence other people. With this ability comes a responsibility to use power effectively and to be more aware of the process of influencing others.

Pause and think about what words and images come to mind in connection with the idea of power—words like *dictator* or *force,* images like *war* or *riots,* i.e., words and images with bad connotations. But power is not bad. If you can separate the use of power from the goals of power, you can see that the goals may be "good" or "bad," but the exercise is neither. Yet, the use of power can be judged; it can be found to be effective or ineffective. When people react to power as something "bad," they are usually saying either that the use of power was ineffective, or that the goals of power were questionable. In this paper we are concerned with the effectiveness of power, specifically power in a work-organization setting.

There are five key dimensions which determine the quality of an individual's leadership ability. An effective leader is one who can:

1. Make other people feel strong, help them to feel that they have the ability to influence their future and their environment;

2. build others' trust in the leader;

3. structure cooperative relationships rather than competitive relationships;

4. resolve conflicts by mutual confrontation of issues rather than by avoidance or forcing a particular solution, and

5. stimulate and promote goal-oriented thinking and behavior.

Power is the ability of one person to influence another. You can, for instance, give a person advice, offer him a job, or threaten to reduce his salary; however, a more subtle concept of influence than this is involved in that person's *reaction to you.* "Influence" occurs when he respects you, likes you, or desires to be like you and thereby opens the door to some control over him. Two psychologists, John French and Bertram Raven, have identified five types of power: reward power, coercive power, identification power, expert power, and legitimate power. When you influence someone, you are using one or more of these types of power. Before we turn to a discussion of the expression of leadership ability in the five ways we just mentioned, let us look briefly at the sources of power.

Reward Power

Reward power is based on one person's perception of another's ability to reward him. It increases in direct proportion to the amount of rewards a person sees another as controlling. Within an organizational setting, giving someone a raise or bonus, promoting him to a job with more responsibility, expanding his budget—these are highly visible uses of reward power to influence a person to do a better job for the organization; stopping by someone's work place just to say good morning is a more indirect use and, again, depends on his perception of your ability to provide whatever he considers as a tangible reward.

Coercive Power

Coercive power is based on one person's perception of another's ability to punish him. The strength of coercive power is proportional—not necessarily to the ability to punish but to the degree to which he perceives ability to punish. Where perception of this ability is faulty, some tension is likely until his perception and reality are in closer accord. A reprimand for not submitting a report on time, scorn for mistakes, denying a raise or promotion—these are examples of coercive power used to force performance of job activities closer to the stated standards. Let us add that withholding a promised reward or a standard reward of some sort is also a use of coercive power.

Expert Power

The total "amount" of knowledge is being increased by new technologies and communication advances; at least as important as this growth pattern in the *content* is the growth trends in our *awareness* of the complexities in our social and physical environments. As populations increase, new forms of relationships (and more of them) come into being so that men are more interdependent and at the same time are (or should be) more willing to deal with change and ambiguity. In this kind of situation (our situation, right now, 1970's) the traditional recourse to hierarchical authority can be dysfunctional and the recourse to expert authority, whether formally recognized in an organization structure or not, can pay off.

1. Richard E. Boyatzis is Director of Organizational Development for McBer and Company. Originally published in *Management of Personal Quarterly,* Bureau of Industrial Relations, University of Michigan, 1971. Reprinted with the author's permission.

Expert power is based, then, in one person's perception that another's expertise, knowledge and approach can offer him a payoff he can't achieve another way.

Identification Power

Identification power follows from one's perception of similarity between himself and another, or his desire to be like another. The Horatio Alger stories (or Mickey Rooney's Andy Hardy series) influenced American youth to work hard; the ability of these models to influence youth was based on identification power: many youths had the same economically poor childhood, possibly even touched also with temptations to break the law. Executives who are respected and well liked derive their power from many sources—but their identification power should not be underplayed; many people are willing to be influenced by people whom they feel are friends and can be trusted at a personal level.

Legitimate Power

Legitimate power stems from three sources: shared value, acceptance of social structure, or the sanction of a legitimizing agent. In a manufacturing company, a foreman assigns work to line workers. They do the work because they accept the management structure of the company which makes it legitimate for the foreman to assign work. When a person influences another, he is using one or more of these types of power. Let us now examine what effects each of these types of power, when used by a leader, or manager, has on his subordinates.

Making People Feel Strong

An effective leader makes other people feel strong. He helps them to gain an ability to influence their future and their environment. When a person feels strong, he enjoys his work, feels personally involved, and is motivated to continue and improve work. This is because a person who feels strong is more aware of his surroundings; he feels that he is able to direct his life and wants to gain as much information about life potentials as possible. An ineffective leader makes other people feel weak. When a person feels weak, he is not in control of his fate; he works to the extent that others tell him to work. He feels no sense of pride in his occupational accomplishments.

In working with several plant facilities of a large manufacturing company, I found one plant director who made the managers working in his plant feel strong and another director who made his managers feel weak. The director of plant A felt that he had to know what was happening in all parts of the plant at all times. He insisted on having all managers file weekly reports of operations. Decisions concerning personnel and changes in operating procedures had to have his approval. Any problems were supposed to be brought to his attention immediately. The director of plant B had monthly staff meetings with the managers in his plant. He asked them to take part in setting the production goals for their units. He wanted them to obtain his approval only for major changes in operating procedures, and gave them most of the responsibility for their units. He told them to feel free to ask for his help on any matters.

The managers working for the director of plant A did what they were told because the director used reward and coercive power to influence them. He used his source of legitimate power as a reminder to the managers that he could punish them if they did not follow his instructions. He treated them as if they were weak, and they felt weak in their organization.

The managers working for the director of plant B had control over what they did. They eagerly accepted responsibility for their activities. The director of plant B based most of his influence on expert power, (an expert in administration and their type of manufacturing). He asked the managers to see him as a resource for help. By collectively setting goals with the managers and maintaining a warm, friendly attitude, the director was able to base his influence on identification power rather than depending on the reward and coercive power that was a part of his position. The managers in his plant felt strong and enjoyed their work. The production records of the two plants were similar, while the level of job satisfaction of the employees was different. Plant A had a high rate of turnover at the managerial level. There was a sense of urgency in the organization which caused tension. The director imposed an attitude of "Hurry up and do the work, or else" in the plant. The managers in plant B were satisfied with their work. They felt a personal challenge that resulted in their working diligently and creatively. They had a tendency to treat their subordinates in the same honest and friendly manner as the director treated them.

For a manager to base his influence primarily on his ability to reward or punish an employee, he must create a climate in which he maintains control of evaluations and the dispensation of rewards. The workers are dependent on the manager for all recognition of accomplishment or quality work; this makes people feel powerless. Managers who explain how they judge quality work to their subordinates and enter evaluation discussion sessions with their employees are helping their subordinates to feel responsible for their own work. Their influence becomes based on shared values of quality work and self appraisal, or their expertise in evaluating the work, at the same time their subordinates feel strong.

Building Trust in the Leader

An effective leader makes his subordinates feel that they are part of the organization and share an involvement in the company's operations. If they have concern for each other as human beings and trust each other, they can work more efficiently for the group because it *needs* their contribution, and because they don't have to waste time worrying about what others are going to do to them.

The manager of a research and development department of an electronics company was not concerned with building trust. He held regular staff meetings for the members of the department during which they discussed their work and periodically he would meet with each project group to discuss their progress. The engineers accomplished their assignments, but with little creativity in their solutions to problems. Interviewing several of the engineers made it apparent that they were reluctant to come up with new ideas because they felt that the manager would take the credit with top management. They felt he handled assignments in a purely political manner. When asked what they thought his major occupational goal was, they responded bitterly "To get ahead in this company."

The manager *was* fighting a political battle with other departments of the company for funding. He wanted to expand the research staff (pay higher salaries) and attempt several new projects. In dealing with his subordinates, he tried to show his concern for the quality of their work and their job satisfaction, but something was missing. The engineers responded to the manager's requests only because of his ability to punish or reward them. Although he believed it was important to be an effective manager, he had not based his influence on types of power that would inspire trust. The engineers did not feel a part of the company and were not aware of the goals of the research department, and therefore, suspected the manager of using the group for his own needs. What could he have done to build the necessary trust in him and commitment to the company? Had he clarified the goals of the department and explained how he thought the group could contribute to the goals of the company, the engineers could have seen how his actions related to their common goals, not just his personal goals. By sharing the proceedings of the corporate management meetings he attended, he could have highlighted for the engineers the obstacles the department was facing. Being more open generally than he was would have led to an increase in trust. The manager's ability to influence his subordinates would have been based on identification and expert power rather than reward and coercive power: identification power because the engineers would have felt that he was concerned about them as individuals, expert power because by communicating to them the intricacies of being a manager, he would allow them to see that he had special abilities as an administrator.

Cooperating to Achieve Common Goals

An effective leader structures the relationships among his subordinates so that they cooperate to achieve the shared goals of the department, and so that they cooperate with other departments to achieve the company's goal. When a competition is created, ostensibly one party wins and one party loses. But even the winner loses, if he loses the trust or respect of those he was competing with. An effective manager will have his subordinates working with each other to accomplish their own objectives. People working together are more able to accomplish their personal goals than when operating alone.

An executive who structures a competition between managers to build an incentive runs a high risk. By structuring the situation so that one wins and others lose, one manager's incentive to work has increased slightly (at least during the competition, it might slack by the time that he is enjoying the fruits of winning) and the others lose incentive. The results may represent an aggregate loss of incentive.

A manager's influence is based in part on his legitimate power in the organization. If he tends to structure competitive relationships within his department, his subordinates will be dependent on him for rewards (winning) and punishment (losing); if he structures cooperative relationships, his subordinates will be less dependent on him (if at all) for the rewards of cooperating, and he will be able to establish his influence on more effective bases—the bases of identification power and expert power.

Confronting Conflicts Instead of Running Away

An effective leader handles conflict by confronting it with his subordinates. He does not avoid the issues by denying the problem exists, by forcing his solution without consulting the other individuals involved, or by smoothing over the problem ("It isn't too bad; we'll get it licked"). He knows he cannot solve a problem by running away from it.

One morning, the president of XYZ, inc. received a call from his vice president of marketing who said that production had not fulfilled its commitment to meet a deadline for the promotion of a new product, and that the V.P. for production had admitted that the commodity would not be ready for another two months. The president asked him to be in his office at one o'clock that afternoon; they could settle the issue at that time. He also called the V.P. of production and all other vice presidents that might be involved and asked them to attend. The meeting started with heated words between the vice presidents each blaming someone else for the delay. The president quieted everyone to say that there were two goals for the meeting: first, they had to decide what would happen now in terms of maintaining good client relationships; second, they would discover what actions caused the delay and correct procedures so that it would not occur a second time. He stressed the fact that they were at the meeting to correct errors, not to affix blame and punish someone for a mistake.

The questions concerning what to do next were quickly settled. As the discussions about what caused the delay began, each person moved to the edge of his seat, ready to defend his past actions. The president asked for a historical rundown of the development of the new product and the production schedule. As each point was made, the president was careful to check to see if there was a challenge to the information. If someone disagreed, he asked the group to arrive at a consensus as to what really happened. Although the meeting took three hours, the vice presidents began to work together. By mutually confronting differences of perception as to what had occurred, they arrived at an accurate picture of the incidents leading to the delay. Some of the problems which contributed to the delay were intentional expressions of disapproval for other vice presidents. Once these disagreements were faced openly, they could understand each other's position and come to agreement.

The president, in this case, based his initial ability to influence the vice presidents on his expert power as an administrator, although he also utilized his legitimate power as the executive of the company to call the meeting. Once the meeting began, he moved beyond a reliance on legitimate power to influence the process of the meeting by emphasizing that the purpose of meeting was to correct the situation and by not affixing blame or punishing people—in other words, he eliminated the expectation of his use of reward or coercive power in the meeting to leave the way open for his expert authority to hold sway.

Coaching Goal-Oriented Behavior

An effective leader/manager helps his subordinates by cooperating to set meaningful goals. People work more diligently and efficiently when they have a verbalized description, not just some vague "understanding" or generalized expectations of where they are going. When a person sets a goal, he starts to think of his means, how he intends to achieve that goal. When a manager sets goals unilaterally for his subordinates, he is taking responsibility for their actions, he is basing his influence on reward and coercive power. He must allow his subordinates to participate in setting their goals so they can feel responsible for actions, and he thereby shows a trust in their capabilities and a concern for hearing their opinions and ideas. His ability to influence his subordinates is then based on legitimate power to some extent and on identification power to a greater extent.

Where Do You Stand?

Feeling powerless is a major cause of tension in organizations, for it hinders organizational performance. The ineffective use of power leaves people with the feeling that one person or a small group of people run their lives. This paper has examined five characteristics which facilitate the effective use of power.

If these ideas sound interesting (even if you do not totally agree with them), you may want to examine how your subordinates perceive your exercice of influence and your behavior on the five characteristics discussed. In talking to them, listen for statements or concerns they might have about gaining power or keeping power they now have. Are they defensive about work decisions they have made when you ask about them? Do they make decisions without checking with you? Do they come to you with new ideas? Do they ask for your opinion on their failures as well as their successes? Do they feel that they have some control over seeing their performance goals? Do they feel that their part of the organization is in a state of continual conflict with another part of the organization?

Asking you subordinates how they feel about your exercise of influence may lead to some rewarding discussion. It certainly will be an effective use of power.

DELEGATE YOUR WAY TO SUCCESS

by Eugene Raudsepp

Most managers accept the premise that the best way to get their work done is to make optimum use of subordinates. Yet most managers admit, when pressed, that they don't delegate as much as they should.

The problem is probably more emotional than procedural. Effective delegation is, admittedly, one of the most difficult managerial tasks. It depends on the finely woven interrelationship between the manager, subordinates, and top management. It depends on the type of company and its goals. It also depends heavily on trust and confidence. But the biggest problem is that many managers, as they climb the executive ladder, continue to feel that if they want a job done right, they have to do it themselves.

A manager who delegates with intelligence and consistent follow-up can accomplish far more than the manager who hugs to his (or her) bosom the tasks his subordinates should be doing. The manager should devote most of his time and energies to planning, supervising, and delegating. That way, he'll contribute more than he might even from a superlative job on tasks that

---

The author is president of Princeton Creative Research, Inc., Princeton, NJ, and is author of the books Creative Growth Games *and* More Creative Growth Games.

Reprinted from *Computer & Communications Decisions* March 1981, pages 157-158, 163-164. Copyright © 1981, Hayden/VNU.

Delegation

his subordinates might not do quite as well. Inadequate delegation limits a manager's effectiveness because he gets bogged down in detail. Carried to its logical extreme, nondelegation can bring operations almost to a standstill.

When a manager delegates successfully, he changes his role from a performer to a trainer, motivator, and evaluator. Through delegation, he develops initiative and self-starting ability in his subordinates. He broadens them on their jobs, increases production, and improves morale. Most employees strive to live up to what is expected of them. They are willing and eager to face challenges, knowing that they are expected to deliver.

What is delegation?

Delegation is simply the passing on, by one person to another, of responsibility for a given task. But effective delegation involves a great deal more.

Delegation is not the abdication of responsibility; it is a continuing process. The manager should always be available to give advice and assistance when needed. He should make sure that needed resources are available, check performance at agreed-upon dates, and generally remain involved as advisor, leader, and sharer of responsibility. He should keep checks and controls on every task he delegates. The degree and kind of control varies, of course, with each subordinate. Some subordinates resent overcontrol and do a good job without frequent checking. Others need the security of formalized periodic reports on their assignments. Either way, there's no excuse for suddenly discovering that a subordinate is not handling his assignment properly.

Effective delegation requires patience and an initial investment of time. "I could have done the job myself twice over for all the time I spent explaining the work to him," is a frequently voiced excuse for not delegating. This may be true, especially with new subordinates. But the time expended is bound to pay off

According to author Eugene Raudsepp, it is important for managers to instruct subordinates to accomplish certain results, rather than to perform certain activities.

in the long run.

Delegation should not be viewed as an opportunity to get rid of unpleasant jobs or those in which the manager is not proficient. Also, it's a mistake to delegate too many meaningless or "make-work" jobs, especially during slack periods. This is a transparent maneuver—one that could lead the subordinate to look on all future delegated tasks as unimportant.

Helps employees develop

Ideally, delegation should help a subordinate develop not only his skills but also his judgment. He must understand what kinds of decisions he has the authority to make. If his authority to make decisions is too restricted, he will infer a lack of confidence in his ability to handle responsibility. If a subordinate is to be held accountable, he or she must have responsibility and authority with a minimum of interference. Effective delegation includes the right to make decisions and mistakes.

Delegation requires meticulous planning, particularly if complex or difficult projects are involved. It entails establishing priorities, setting objectives, and deciding how the project should be accomplished and

by whom, how long it should take, and how well it should be done. This type of planning isn't easy, and some managers tend to avoid it.

There are dozens of reasons why managers do not delegate. Those given here are the most common—but they can be avoided.

Lack of confidence in subordinates. Fearing unsatisfactory results, a manager may reason that a subordinate's judgment might be faulty, or that he will not follow through on his chores. He may feel that the subordinate is too young to command the respect and cooperation of older workers.

Such a manager feels that he must keep track of every detail to get a job done right. He may be a perfectionist who sets high personal standards of performance. He is often tempted to perform a job himself, feeling that he can do the work better and more quickly than his subordinates. Such an attitude must be shunned unless the lack of confidence in a subordinate is based on past experience.

Lack of self-confidence. Many managers, especially those recently promoted or hired, feel insecure in their jobs and in their relationship with their superiors, peers, and subordinates. They may feel overwhelmed by their new duties and responsibilities. As a result, they regress to the pleasant and familiar security and routine of the work they did before they became managers.

Poor definition of duties. A manager must have a clear understanding of his responsibilities and authority. Obviously, he can delegate only those responsibilities that have been assigned to him. If he is unsure of the nature of his own job, he can hardly be expected to delegate properly.

Aversion to risk-taking. Delegation involves making calculated risks. Even with clear communication and instructions, proper controls, and trained subordinates, something will eventually go wrong.

Fear of subordinates as competitors. This frequently leads to open and excessive criticism of a

Delegation

subordinate's work, thwarting or playing down his achievements, pitting him against another subordinate to put him in a bad light, ignoring or side-tracking his suggestions and ideas, and concealing his talent or misusing it in low-skill jobs.

An inflated self-image. Some managers believe that they are the pivot upon which all their department's operations turn. This type of manager, as a rule, checks on all details himself. He makes all the decisions, and considers his way of doing things the only right one. He goes to great pains to hire people who reinforce his image of himself. To protect his "kingpin" posture, he makes certain, through selective communication, that only he gets the big picture of what is going on.

The effect that the "indispensable" manager has on his subordinates can be devastating. He fosters only dependence. Whatever self-confidence and individuality his subordinates may have had are soon obliterated; they become automatons who follow only directions and never initiate ideas of their own. Eventually, stronger subordinates become restive. They realize that their growth potential is severely stunted and that the only wise course of action is to resign and go on to someplace where they can grow.

Equating action with productivity. A manager may be hyperactive. Such a person is often afraid that delegation might leave him with nothing to do. Quite commonly, a hyperactive manager complains constantly about overwork, and subordinates have a difficult time getting to see him.

Fear of appearing lazy. Delegation might be construed, by both superiors and subordinates, as trying to avoid working. This can be a sensitive point. A manager, particularly a new one, or one who is unsure of his own talents, can also feel that it is a sign of weakness to need subordinates' help to keep up with workloads.

Poor example. A common reason a manager does not delegate is that his superior did not delegate. The reasoning is "If my boss got to where he is with his style of leadership, why shouldn't I copy him?"

Many young or newly promoted managers who have been held back by their own superiors in the past do not delegate because they want to keep the reins in their own hands, as a protective device.

Analyzing subordinates

A prime requisite for effective delegation is a comprehensive inventory of subordinates' capabilities: skills, qualifications, experience, special talents, interests, motivations, attitude, potential, and limitations.

Such analyses, which should include meetings with subordinates to get their own estimation of their abilities and aspirations, enables the manager to decide to which subordinates he can delegate immediately, and which need further coaching and experience.

Here are a few facts to make delegation easier for all concerned:
● Be sure you and your supervisor agree on what your job is. Take all the initiative you can without encroaching on others' rights. A narrow definition of your job restricts you.

● Be sure your subordinates understand what you expect them to do. The simplest way to delegate is to tell your subordinates what authority you reserve for yourself. It may help to list matters you want discussed with you before any action is taken.
● Prepare written policies your subordinates can use to guide their decisions. A soundly conceived and clearly understood set of policies lets subordinates make decisions and take action with confidence.
● Be humble enough to admit that someone else may be able to do the job as well as you can.

● Make as many subordinates as possible directly responsible to you.

This will help you communicate, make decisions, take action, and exercise control.
● Make subordinates responsible for accomplishing results rather than activities. Once the expected results are spelled out, the subordinate should be able to choose methods he will use in accomplishing them.
● Reward those who get things done. Subordinates will accept responsibility and actively participate in accomplishing objectives only if they feel that rewards go to those who perform. The rewards for being right must always be greater than the penalties for being wrong.
● Distinguish between rush jobs and the less immediate but more important things you have to do; spend more time on the important tasks than the trivial ones.

Self-questioning can ease the decision of what and how much to delegate:
● How important is the decision? Are the stakes so high that a mistake cannot be tolerated? If so, the matter probably cannot be delegated successfully.
● Even though you are more competent than your subordinate, are you as close to the problem? Is your decision more apt to be right?
● Does your failure to delegate mean that you are not giving adequate attention to other more important parts of your job?
● Does your failure to delegate mean you are not developing your subordinates? Are they capable of being developed? If not, can they be transferred or replaced?
● What do top managers really expect of you? Are they measuring you principally by results, so that your decisions must be right? Do they really expect you to develop people?

The art of delegation is a difficult one to learn, but it's a vital management skill. If you do it right, you'll improve employees' morale, get more work done, and ease the burden on yourself. □

How Much Is Enough?

You can get a good idea of whether you are delegating as much as you should by answering the following questions. The more "Yes" answers you give, the more likely it is that you're not delegating enough.

- Do you often work overtime?
- Do you take work home evenings and on weekends?
- Is your pile of unfinished work increasing?
- Do you find that daily operations are so time-consuming that you have little time left over for planning and other important matters?
- Do you feel you have to have close control of every detail to have the job done right?
- Do you frequently find yourself bogged down, trying to cope with the morass of small details?
- Do you frequently have to postpone long-range projects?
- Are you harassed by frequent unexpected emergencies in your department?
- Is a good part of your working day spent on tasks your subordinates could do?
- Do you lack confidence and respect for your subordinates' abilities to shoulder more responsibilities?
- Do you understand what your responsibilities and authority are?

- Do you find yourself irritable and complaining when the work of your group doesn't live up to expectations?
- Do you find that your subordinates never show any initiative?
- Are friction and low morale characteristic of your work group?
- Do your subordinates defer all decisions on problems to you?
- Are policies to guide your subordinates in making decisions ambiguous?
- Do you instruct your subordinates to perform certain activities, rather than to accomplish certain results?
- Have subordinates stopped coming to you to present their ideas?
- Do operations slow down considerably when you are away from your job?
- Do you feel that you're abdicating your role as a manager if you have to ask your subordinates' assistance in order to complete your projects?
- After delegating a project, do you breathe down the subordinate's neck?
- Do you believe that your status and the salary you earn automatically mean that you have to be overworked?

Excitement And Commitment: Keys To Project Success

Gary N. Powell
University of Connecticut
Barry Z. Posner
University of Santa Clara

In *The Soul of a New Machine,* the Pulitzer Prize-winning account of the design of a new computer by a special project group at Data General, Tracy Kidder describes the rituals which the company used to get people excited and committed to the project. Almost every member of the project team passed through the initiation rite called "signing up." By signing up for the project, a person agreed to do whatever was necessary for the project to succeed. This could mean forsaking of family, friends, hobbies, and all vestiges of a non-work life until the project was completed. (When, of course, a new round of getting people signed up would be started again for the next project.)

The reasons behind the signing-up ritual for the company are simple. When workers have made this kind of commitment to a project, they are no longer coerced to work on it. Instead, they have volunteered.

Signing up began with the hiring of new recruits for the project. (Old hands who had been through the signing up process before were dealt with differently.) Applications were reviewed for indications that the applicant may or may not be inclined to sign up. For example, one man who listed "family life" as his main avocation was judged to be giving a sign that he may not be willing to sign up and was turned away. When an application provoked initially favorable reactions, the applicant was invited for an interview.

The following passage describes how Carl Alsing, one of the project managers, would conduct a typical interview. Alsing's thoughts during the interview are in parentheses.

Alsing would ask the young engineer, "What do you want to do?"

Exactly what the candidate said—whether he (most applicants were male) was interested in one aspect of computers or another—didn't matter. Indeed, Alsing didn't care if a recruit showed no special fondness for computers; and the fact that

an engineer had one of his own and liked to play with it did not argue for him.

If the recruit seemed to say in reply, "Well, I'm just out of grad school and I'm looking at a lot of possibilities and I'm not sure what field I want to get into yet," then Alsing would usually find a polite way to abbreviate the interview. But if the recruit said, for instance, "I'm really interested in computer design," then Alsing would prod. The ideal interview would proceed in the following fashion.

"What interests you about that?"

"I want to build one," says the recruit.

(That's what I want to hear," thinks Alsing. "Now I want to find out if he means it.")

"What makes you think you can build a major computer?" asks Alsing.

"Hey," says the recruit, "no offense, but I've used some of the machines you guys have built. I think I can do a better job."

("West and I have a story that we tell about Eagle machine. But I want to hear this guy tell me part of that story first. If he does, if there's some fire in his eyes—I say 'in his eyes', because I don't know where it is, if it's there, it's there—but if he's a little cocky and I think we probably want this person, then I tell him our story.")

"Well," says Alsing, "we're building this machine that's way out in front in technology. We're gonna design all new hardware and tools." ("I'm trying to give him a sense of 'Hey, you've finally found in a big company a place where people are really doing the next thing.'") "Do you like the sound of that?" asks Alsing.

"Oh, yeah," says the recruit.

("Now I tell him the bad news.")

"It's gonna be tough," says Alsing. "If we hired you, you'd be working with a bunch of cynics and egotists and it'd be hard to keep up with them."

"That doesn't scare me," says the recruit.

"There's a lot of fast people in this group," Alsing goes on. "it's gonna be a real hard job with a lot of long hours. And I mean long hours."

"No," says the recruit, in words more or less like these. "That's what I want to do, get in on the ground floor of a new architecture. I want to do a big machine. I want to be where the action is."

"Well," says Alsing, pulling a long face. "We can only let in the best of this year's graduates. We've already let in some awfully fast people. We'll have to let you know."

("We tell him that we only let in the best. Then we let him in.") [6]

Data General went to great lengths to get an unusually high degree of commitment to the computer design project, and for the most part they succeeded. You will not always get this kind of commitment to a project, and furthermore you may not need it to as great an extent. However, you will need to make sure that your project team is *behind* the project, all working in the same direction to achieve the project's goals rather than *in front of* the project, acting as a roadblock to progress. For this to be accomplished, people need a lot more than goals and objectives laid out before them and being told what to do. They need to feel like they are participating in an exciting venture, guided by a *shared vision* of how their joint efforts will make them successful.

The Shared Vision as a Key to Excellence

McKinsey & Company, a management consulting firm, recently conducted a study of American companies which were judged to be excellent in performance. In their best-selling report of the study, *In Search of Excellence,* Thomas Peters and Robert Waterman, Jr. found eight basic practices to be characteristic of successfully managed companies. In consulting the practice which might be most important, they said:

Let us suppose that we were asked for one all-purpose bit of advice for management, the truth that we were able to distill from the excellent companies research. We might be tempted to reply, "Figure out your value system. Decide what your company *stands for* [9]."

Excellent companies have clearly articulated beliefs about how they intend to run their businesses, which lead to a shared vision among employees that adherence to these beliefs will bring them success. For Caterpillar Tractor, the core belief is "24-hour parts service anywhere in the world," reflecting a high commitment to the prompt meeting of customer needs. At DuPont, the credo "better things for better living through chemistry" demonstrates a belief that product innovation is most important. The slogan "IBM means service" expresses the high customer service orientation of that company [5]. These phrases may sound like instant cliches, suitable for hanging on office walls or bulletin boards but not much else. Yet, to the contrary, they act as powerful motivating devices for thousands of employees in these companies as expressions for core beliefs.

Project managers can also promote shared visions among project team members. At Data General, the shared vision was to design a state-of-the-art computer. For a new sports-oriented cable television channel, the shared vision among program planners could be to broadcast a majority of the games of local teams ("The *best* coverage of local sports is on CABL"); to cover an eclectic range of sports such as on ABC-TV's Wide World of Sports, which pursued this vision with great success for many years ("See *all* the sports on CABL"); or to achieve excellence in technical coverage of sports ("Sports are *better* on CABL").

All of the above alternatives are plausible goals for the project teams involved. However, we have not yet identified what turns ordinary goals into shared visions which contribute to the success of the project. In other words, we need to address the question:

How can employees be stimulated to identify with project goals to the extent that they expend extra effort to achieve the goals?

This question can be answered in two ways. One way is to describe what project managers can do to promote the forming of shared visions. (The signing up ritual of Data General provides us an initial clue as to what may work.) The other way is to describe what people are looking for in their jobs that leads them to commit themselves to project goals. Since every management strategy ultimately is based on understanding of people, let us first examine why people do what they do on the job, or what motivates their work-related behavior. Then we will discuss how project managers can put this knowledge to use.

Why People Do What They Do

Management theories which attempt to explain why

people do what they do have gone through several stages of evolution. Before the twentieth century, there was no collection of thought called "management theory" at all. Nonetheless, management took place and people occasionally wrote down their thoughts about how to get others to go along with their wishes. For example, the Italian statesman Machiavelli wrote in *The Prince,* published in 1532, on whether it was better for a prince to be loved or feared:

> The reply is, that one ought to be both feared and loved, but as it is difficult for the two to go together, it is much safer to be feared than loved. Men have less scruple in offending one who makes himself loved than one who makes himself feared; for love is held by a chain of obligation which, men being selfish, is broken whenever it serves their purpose; but fear is maintained by a dread of punishment which never fails [7].

Not surprisingly, the term Machiavellianism has been handed down over the years to refer to political opportunism and denial of the relevance of morality in political affairs.

One of the first people to write explicitly about management was Frederick Taylor, who argued that management should be made into an exact science. Taylor was the grandfather of the time and motion study approach to management. He argued that, for management to be doing its job, work should be broken down into discrete, highly programmed segments which could be performed repetitively without variation by different workers. Max Weber complemented Taylor's theories by advocating that bureaucracy, or management by set rules and procedures, was the best form of organization. Thus the Taylor-Weber "rational" school of thought, which prevailed from about 1900 to 1930, was primarily concerned with rules about such issues as division of labor and optimum spans of control (numbers of people who should be working for a given manager). If they were speaking to today's project managers, Taylor and Weber would stress the establishment of distinct tasks for project team members, with assigned times and specified procedures by which the efforts of team members would be coordinated. The same would apply for managerial jobs if there were more than one project being managed.

An important challenge to this approach made by Elton Mayo ushered in the next stage of management thought. Mayo started out in the Taylor tradition by conducting experiments on the effects of various workplace characteristics on worker productivity at a Western Electric plant in Hawthorne, New Jersey. When the lighting was turned up for one experimental group of workers, productivity went up also. When the lighting was turned back down so that the effects of other factors could be tested, productivity went up again! Mayo concluded that the amount of attention paid to employees was an important influence on worker productivity [10]. The Hawthorne experiments prompted what was called the "human relations" school of thought, which prevailed from about 1930 to 1960. Speaking to project managers, Mayo would emphasize the establishment of open communications between themselves and project team members, so that employees would feel that management was concerned for them and cared that their needs were met.

In the early 1950's, Abraham Maslow extended the human relations approach to a "human potential" movement. Maslow proposed a hierarchy of human needs, ranging from the "lower order" needs of food, shelter, and economic security through "middle order" needs for social relationships and ego satisfaction up to the pinnacle of self-actualization needs, which could only be satisfied when all other needs were satisfied first. To Maslow, the healthy person was one who was operating at the top of the hierarchy—creative, autonomous, and virtually independent of others [8]. (Douglas McGregor's "Theory X versus Theory Y" promoted essentially the same view of human potential.)

Maslow's theory was basically self-oriented, in that it seemed to propose that people can best be self-fulfilled when they stand alone, rather than when they work in conjunction with others. As such, although it was developed two decades earlier, it provided perfect justification for what Tom Wolfe called the "me decade" of the 1970's. Daniel Yankelovich, in his early 1980's study of American attitudes and values over several decades, questioned this orientation. He identified the desire in people to *identify with* and *commit themselves* to something more than just satisfaction of their own needs. According to Yankelovich, individuals today are looking for something to believe in which is larger than themselves and which embraces other people besides themselves [12]. His exhortation to project managers would be to provide the opportunity for individuals to satisfy these needs by promoting visions of success and fulfillment which require coordinated effort and can be shared with other people.

We have reviewed several theorists' views of why people do what they do. The rational approach of Taylor and Weber stressed employees' presumed desires for predictability in their jobs and being told what to do. It basically regarded workers as similar to industrial machinery, with assigned tasks that were designed and regulated by others. The human relations approach of Mayo emphasized individuals' desires for being on the receiving end of managerial attention, satisfying their needs for social interaction and ego gratification. The human potential approach of Maslow regarded these previous approaches as addressing lower order and middle order needs, respectively; once these needs were satisfied, individuals were expected to pursue the higher order need of self-fulfillment or self-actualization. Maslow's theory focused on the "self" aspect of self-fulfillment. What can be called the "fulfillment with others" approach of Yankelovich focused on the needs for individuals to share in an experience of commitment with other people.

As you have probably noticed, the progression in these theories has been towards the shared visions approach which McKinsey & Company found characteristic of excellent American companies. Little mention is made in the rational or human relations approaches of the satisfaction and excitement which can come from visions of organizational success which are shared with other employees. However, Yankelovich incorporates elements of both of these approaches. He suggests that employees need guidance in coordinating their efforts, but that they also need to be encouraged to identify with a shared vision of how success can be achieved.

Now that we have a better understanding of the needs which motivate today's workers, let us look at what project managers can do to meet these needs.

Using People's Intelligence

The personal computer business was a major growth industry in the early 1980's. More than 150 competitors were fighting to carve out a niche for themselves in the rapidly changing market where demand was doubling every year. Technological advances which improved the state of the art and enabled computers to be assembled at lower costs were commonplace. IBM was a late-comer to the personal computer business, belatedly introducing its entry in August, 1981, at a time when Tandy (Radio Shack) and Apple Computer, Inc. were fighting for the market lead. Only two years later, *Business Week* announced that the battle for market supremacy was over and that the winner was IBM. The company once known solely for its large main-frame computers had taken over 26% of the annual market for personal computers in 1983 and was expected to

account for half of the world market in 1985 [3].

Texas Instruments (TI) had pioneered the home computer market four years previously and was focusing on the market for smaller, non-business oriented computers in 1983. However, its home computer operation lost a stunning $183 million in the second quarter of 1983, causing TI to report its first quarterly loss ever. Whereas, on April 21, 1983, the president of TI had predicted that 1983 would be a significantly *better* year than 1982, a June 10 news release predicted that 1983 would be a significantly *poorer* year for the company than 1982 [4].

What caused these differences in fortunes for the two companies? A large part of the answer lies in how project teams were created and managed. IBM set up the task force responsible for what was to become the company's personal computer (PC) as an independent business unit, not subject to the same rules which required most of its product design teams to account for their every move. As one of the PC designers put it, "If you're going to compete with five men in a garage, you have to do something different." What IBM did differently was to grant the team considerable autonomy to make its own decisions, as if it was a small business in itself rather than submerged in a larger company. As a result, some of the decisions made were contrary to IBM's traditional practices. For example, instead of using IBM-manufactured circuitry, the PC used a microprocessor made by another manufacturer as its heart. Upon granting the project team full responsibility for the design of the computer, IBM was delighted to find that a highly successful product which challenged the conventional company wisdom emerged.

At Texas Instruments, project management was a different story altogether. The company had been considered excellent according to McKinsey & Company's criteria. Peters and Waterman reported in *In Search of Excellence* that, according to TI Chairman Mark Shepherd, Jr., TI had a "fluid, project-oriented environment." However, in 1983, *Business Week* found that TI was operating more by a top-down, autocratic approach to decision-making than by placing responsibility in autonomous project teams. Project managers were demoralized when their proposals for product development, capital expenditures, and marketing strategy were consistently overruled at higher levels. Hence, the company was slow to recognize and respond to changes in the minicomputer market, suffered significant losses and eventually abandoned the market entirely.

What was the difference between the IBM and the TI approaches to the computer business? The major difference was that IBM was granting its project teams the freedom to make full use of people's intelligence. Project teams had relatively few constraints placed on the decisions they could make. They did not have *complete* latitude—for example, the team given the task to design a personal computer would not have lasted very long if it decided instead to design a new main-frame computer which could compete directly with IBM's existing product line. Instead, the team was given a fairly broad goal to be achieved (design a personal computer) with little further direction as to how to achieve it. In contrast, TI was *not* making full use of the intelligence of project team members. The company was setting performance goals to be achieved but was giving people little freedom to decide how they would go about achieving the goals. The end results of these two opposite approaches were high performance and morale at IBM, and low performance and morale at TI.

Many other examples can be cited to demonstrate that, to be successful, companies and project teams are organizing their efforts to make use of people's intelligence. The recent emphasis on quality circles, which has been borrowed from Japanese management, stems from the recognition that employees on the line often have good ideas about how to improve productivity which managers do not have. At higher levels, General Motors has been totally revamping the way it develops new cars, by centering experimental operations on "companies within a company" with the power to coordinate new car projects from design to marketing; this approach is replacing the older, design by committee approach in which responsibilities were divided among five divisions [2]. Even American Telephone & Telegraph Co., which recently underwent the divestiture of its 22 Bell operating companies, is recognizing the need to have more autonomous project groups to compete in the rapidly changing telecommunications industry.

In short, project teams achieve the best results when people have the chance to contribute their own ideas to the project and, when possible, responsibility for making important decisions based on their jobs. These conditions give project team members the opportunity to experience the fulfillment in their ideas with others which Yankelovich identified as a critical motivator for today's workers.

Of course, these conditions do not *guarantee* project success. When project team members are given the chance to use their collective intelligence, they may misread the market they are trying to penetrate, underestimate the demands of the task they are trying to accomplish, or commit any of a host of other possible errors which subtract from the success of the project. However, if project team members appear to have the necessary skills, aptitudes, and experience to make intelligent decisions, they are best motivated, and their talents are best taken advantage of, when they are given the chance to rise or fall based on their own decisions and efforts.

Rewarding Positive Behavior

So far, we have argued that considerable autonomy and responsibility should be granted to project teams and distributed among project team members in order to get best results. We have not yet said anything, though, about how project managers should respond to employees' performance, good or bad, as the project is being completed. For this, we need to introduce another critical aspect of getting people excited and committed—the rewarding of positive behavior.

B.F. Skinner observed that positive reinforcement of behavior, or the provision of rewards for jobs well done, contributes to the behavior being repeated. On the other hand, negative reinforcement of behavior, or the threat of punishment for jobs poorly done, discourages the behavior but does not necessarily contribute to someone's engaging in the desired behavior [11]. For example, criticizing telephone directory assistance operators when their average times per customer call are high could encourage operators to cut off requests for information prematurely rather than to be more efficient in their conveying of the necessary information.

Some companies have taken the notion of rewarding positive behavior and expanded it into elaborate systems of rites, rituals, and ceremonies. Mary Kay Cosmetics conducts "seminars" for salespeople at its Dallas headquarters which are actually reward-giving extravaganzas. On different awards nights, employees identified as heroes parade across the stage in bright red jackets to tell stories about how they achieved success in the Mary Kay traditions. Gifts of cars, diamonds, mink coats, etc., are given to top salespeople. The culmination of the extravaganza comes with the crowning of Queens (supersaleswomen) in each product category.

Another company presents plaques called "Attaboys" to reward outstanding individual performance. When an "Attaboy" is to be presented, the worker's manager rings a bell and all employees in the area drop whatever they are doing to witness the presentation of the plaque. When someone has received five "Attaboys," they are eligible for a "Gotcha" which is personally signed by the head of the company's U.S. operations [5]. In the same vein, the Los Angeles Dodgers baseball team instituted a "Mr. Potato Head" award during its 1983 season which was given to the best performer after every ballgame. The award lightened the clubhouse atmosphere as well as rewarded good performance and was seen to contribute to the team's winning of its division that year.

Such ceremonies border on the silly side, for sure. However, they provide the opportunity for people to laugh at themselves, which is always healthy. More importantly, they provide rewards for positive behavior which, as Skinner noted, almost always increase the probability that similar behavior will occur in the future.

Some people make the mistake of assuming that the only kind of reward employees will respond to is monetary. Although increased salary or bonuses certainly are appreciated, people's need for and liking of rewards extends much further. Verbal recognition of performance in front of one's peers, and visible manifestations of awards such as certificates, plaques, and other tangible gifts also serve as powerful rewards for people. They also provide a way of encouraging *shared* visions of success far more than individual monetary rewards. Project managers who are always looking for ways of rewarding positive behavior, thereby helping employees to share some of the psychological benefits of seeing themselves as winners, will contribute in an important way to the success of their projects.

When to Start

It is desirable that the building of commitment to the project take place as soon as possible. In the case of new recruits to be assigned to the project, this means at the time of hiring. (Recall how the signing up ritual was incorporated by Data General into its employment interviews for new computer engineers.) For people who already are employees, this means early in the planning stage of the project. The intelligence of project teams can be utilized best if their ideas are included in the plans for the project as well as the project's execution. Hence, the members of IBM's personal computer product development team were basically told to go and design a personal computer, while being left to develop whatever plans they needed for their work by themselves.

If employees are excited and committed to the project at its onset, they will be primed to give their utmost to the project throughout its duration. Then the job for the project manager becomes not to coerce employees into performing, but instead to act as a facilitator helping them in their efforts to produce a high quality output for the project on or in advance of schedule. Efforts to build a sense of commitment to the project among project team members in its early stages will most certainly pay off in the long run.

Lessons for the Project Manager

The lessons (and payoffs) for the project manager in getting people excited and committed are many:

1. *Create exciting possibilities* by giving project managers the BIG picture and by promoting the meaningfulness of their efforts. People need to know, at the onset, not only *what* they are trying to accomplish but for *whom* and *why*. To do otherwise is to foster the alienation and apathy of "it's just another job" or, to borrow from Gertrude Stein, "a job is like a job is like a job is like a job." Remember the ancient Greek tale of Sisyphus, who was condemned to spend eternity pushing a boulder up the mountainside. Upon arriving at the top, the boulder tumbled down the mountainside and Sisyphus began his lonely task again.

2. *Inspiring the shared vision* results from creating exciting possibilities. As Wayne Rosing, the design engineer on Apple's LISA project, put it, "It was a dream. And the dream was the major force behind all our efforts." Inspiration is fostered by the project manager's clarity of focus *and* perspective. The schedule, however important it is, is only the means to an end—the end must be worthy of our efforts. Or as Don Quixote Qidte, the man of LaMancha, told his project team, "It's a quest...to follow a dream." When there are shared goals the project team members are likely to be highly committed, loyal, productive, willing to put in long hours, and less hassled and tense.

3. *Increase visibility* of the project team's efforts. Part of the magic behind scheduling documents is that they are public and make visible the member's commitment. They also provide information about critical interdependencies, without which there is little incentive to cooperate or feel a shared sense of

responsibility and fate. Visibility may be the force which holds most major religions together as congregants are asked to "believe." Project managers need to "get religion" for their team by making visibile and public the project team members' efforts for one another.

4. *Empower participants* to be effective by utilizing their intelligence and natural drive. After all, do you really know any healthy person who tries to be ineffective (even though at times even the best of us will fail)? Empowering others requires giving them the resources and authority necessary to make things happen. Many successful project managers discover that this does not result in a zero-sum game. On the contrary, as one senior project manager exclaimed, "Since I've started giving it [power] away, I've never had so much authority." This premise has been well tested: Effective managers find that empowering others — sharing their power and responsibility — results in more committed and responsible subordinates. Putting power in the hands of others is like investing money in a savings account: It is guaranteed to pay interest.

5. *Spread the Attaboys around* is another successful investment strategy for project managers. In our seminars we have never heard project team members say they were "thanked enough" by their managers. Among the many purposes that milestones serve should be marking time for celebration! Whether it is one hop at a time, like for Don Bennett, the first amputee to climb (hop) to the top of Mt. Rainer (14,400 feet high) or Neil Armstrong's "one small step for a man, one giant step for mankind," the result is the same: People want to be effective, people want to be noticed, and they want to be appreciated. One key characteristic of the excellent companies research is their respect for the individual and their almost childlike exuberance for hoopla around accomplishment. In the words of the *One Minute Manager,* "Find something they're doing right, and praise it right away."[1] Spreading the good word about the accomplishments of your project team members is likely to increase their visibility and to enhance their own power and reputation. Some of the credit will inevitably find its way back to their project manager and his/her ability to get people excited and committed.

There is an irony in all of this, however. Project managers who understand these lessons and adroitly apply these principles are not likely to remain very long as managers of their current projects if they work in a hierarchical organization. Instead, they are likely to be promoted to project manager positions with even larger responsibilities. Excitement and commitment, keys to *project* success, are also keys to *project manager* success!

References

1. Blanchard, K. & Johnson, S. *The One Minute Manager.* New York: Morrow, 1982.
2. GM Overhauls the Way New Cars Take Shape. *Business Week,* September 19, 1983, 114Q-114R.
3. How the PC Project Changed the Way IBM Thinks. *Business Week,* October 3, 1983, 86, 90.
4. Texas Instruments Cleans Up Its Act. *Business Week,* September 19, 1983, 56-61.
5. Deal, T.E. & Kennedy, A.A. *Corporate Cultures: The Rites and Rituals of Corporate Life.* Reading, MA: Addison-Wesley, 1982.
6. Kidder, T. *The Soul of a New Machine.* New York: Avon Books, 1981, 65-66.
7. Machiavelli, N. *The Prince.* New York: New American Library, 1952, 90.
8. Maslow, A.A. *Motivation and Personality.* New York: Harper & Row, 1954.
9. Peters, T.J. & Waterman, R.H., Jr. *In Search of Excellence: Lessons from America's Best-Run Companies.* New York: Harper & Row, 1982, 278.
10. Roethlisberger, F.J. & Dickson, W.J. *Management and the Worker.* Cambridge, MA: Harvard University Press, 1939.
11. Skinner, B.F. *Beyond Freedom and Dignity.* New York: Knopf, 1971.
12. Yankelovich, D. *New Rules: Searching for Self-Fulfillment in a World Turned Upside Down.* New York: Random House, 1981.

Dr. Gary N. Powell is an Associate Professor of Management and Organization at the University of Connecticut. He has published over 30 articles in professional journals and made over 50 presentations at professional meetings. In addition to project management, Dr. Powell's current research interests include leadership, power, recruitment, organizational change, and women and men in management.

Dr. Barry Z. Posner is an Associate Professor of Management at the Graduate Schools of Business and Administration, University of Santa Clara. He has published over 40 articles in a variety of professional journals, has recently completed two books for the American Management Association, and has planned and participated in management development programs for several major organizations. In addition to project management, Dr. Posner's training programs include leadership, motivation, group dynamics, conflict management, team building, and communications.

***

He spends his time conversing with a big black box.

WHO IS THE DP PROFESSIONAL?

by Jac Fitz-enz

The average programmer is excessively independent—sometimes to a point of mild paranoia. He is often eccentric, slightly neurotic, and he borders upon a limited schizophrenia.
D.H. Brandon

Statements such as this one by D.H. Brandon, president of Brandon Consulting Group, Inc. of New York City, and a long time lecturer on data processing management topics, have served to stimulate investigations into the nature of the data processing professional.

A legend has developed around the mysterious creature who inhabits a large, air-conditioned room and spends his time conversing with a big, black box. Some people claim he is a genius, too bright for the common person to comprehend. Others say he is a recluse who is only capable of communicating with a box. Most accounts of his personality and behavior are inferences built on top of speculations. Solid data concerning his nature is hard to find.

Many managers and researchers have formed the opinion that programmers, as an occupational group, are rather unusual individuals compared with people who select other careers. They supposedly are willing to work in isolation, wish to avoid interaction and possible confrontation with others including direct supervisors, prefer minimal structure and routine, and are motivated primarily by achievement rather than external rewards, status, or approval of others.

In the data processing environment, so much happens so fast that training data processing personnel to be better managers usually takes a priority far behind technological concerns. If we will but find the time to teach our managers something about why people behave as they do, to train them in better communication methods and to show them how to structure work so that personal drives can be unshackled, we could obtain an increase in productivity far surpassing what the latest piece of hardware or software can give us.

We conducted research in a dozen companies in the western United States during the latter part of 1977 to attempt to find out something about the dp pro's motivation to work and his desires for communicating with the organization that employs him. Data was gathered using a survey questionnaire designed and pretested for the specific project. Some 1,500 subjects in several industries, occupations, and job levels responded to the questionnaire.

Any study of motivation must proceed from the premise that motivation is an inherent trait. We talk about motivating employees. This is not possible. In reality, all a manager can do is provide a setting which allows an individual to satisfy his internal drives. As we reviewed our data it became apparent that this is a personality truism.

During the 1960s, Fred Herzberg directed a motivational research project which lead to his now popular two-factor theory of motivation. It claims that basic motivational elements can be split into two categories labeled "hygienes" or "dissatisfiers" and "motivators" or "satisfiers." Herzberg identified eleven hygienes: Salary, Possibility for Growth, Interpersonal Relations with Subordinates, Status, Interpersonal Relations with Superiors, Interpersonal Relations with Peers, Technical Supervision, Company Policy and Procedures, Working Conditions, Noninterference with Personal Life, and Job Security. These, he said, are aspects of the job which must be maintained at an essentially positive level before motivation can flourish.

His motivators or satisfiers number five: Achievement, Recognition, the Work Itself, Responsibility, and Advancement.

Herzberg's theory has been widely publicized. Because it is currently the most widely referenced theory in industrial training, we chose to correlate our findings with his.

Table 1 is a comparison of Herzberg's rankings with those of our subjects.

There are similarities and differences. Responsibility, which ranked fourth in the Herzberg results, dropped to seventh in our study. When we cut the data by Job Level, a reason for the shift surfaced.

Fig. 1 presents a cross section of the responses from programmer/analysts, project leaders, and managers.

While managers ranked Responsibility first and project leaders (PL's) ranked it fourth, programmer/analysts (P/A's) ranked it ninth. For the P/A's, Responsibility fell far below what are normally considered lower level hygiene factors. Even Personal Life topped Responsibility. This finding brought up some tantalizing questions.

If P/A's do not want the responsibility that goes with their work, it may suggest that they are copping out. Does it mean that they are approaching their jobs from a purely self-centered direction? Does it mean that they do not want to be accountable for their results? Of the first five Herzberg factors, four can be viewed as essentially ego-centered. Responsibility is the only factor Herzberg found to have an organizational orientation. Achievement, Recognition, Advancement, and the content of the Work Itself all supply the individual with personal satisfaction. Although having necessary responsibility to carry out the job is also ego-reinforcing, it has the corresponding element of obligation to the organization. Did the respondents rank it low because they took it as a given? Probably not. If that were so, it would follow that PL's and managers who rose from a programmer level should also take it for granted.

Men chose work itself as the greatest motivator. Women chose it fifth.

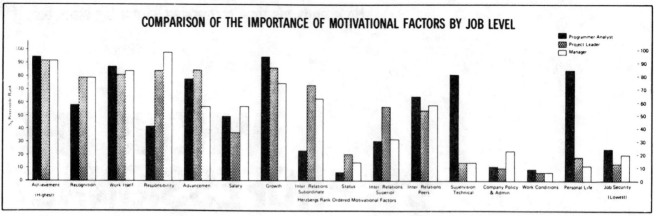

Fig. 1. Rankings of motivational factors are compared for programmer/analysts, project leaders, and managers.

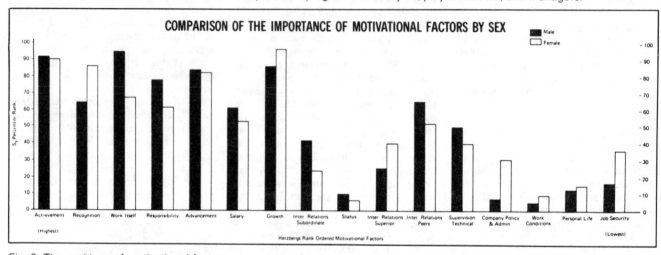

Fig. 2. The rankings of motivational factors are compared by sex.

RANK ORDER COMPARISON OF FIRST LEVEL FACTORS

Herzberg Results	Study Results
1. Achievement	1. Achievement
2. Recognition	2. Possibility for growth
3. Work itself	3. Work itself
4. Responsibility	4. Recognition
5. Advancement	5. Advancement
6. Salary	6. Supervision, technical
7. Possibility for growth	7. Responsibility
8. Interpersonal relations, subordinate	8. Interpersonal relations, peers
9. Status	9. Interpersonal relations, subordinate
10. Interpersonal relations, superior	10. Salary
11. Interpersonal relations, peers	11. Personal life
12. Supervision, technical	12. Interpersonal relations, superior
13. Company policy & admin.	13. Job security
14. Working conditions	14. Status
15. Personal life	15. Company policy & admin.
16. Job security	16. Working conditions

Table 1. Results of the 1960s Fred Herzberg study are compared with those of the author's study.

GENERATION GAP

Subsequent to the survey, follow-up interviews were held with a number of programmers to elicit a reason for this difference. The interviews were not very illuminating. No seemingly sensible alternatives to the self-centered theory were given. As a result, we are stuck with one of two speculations. First, indeed the generation gap does exist. Today's younger workers may not value Responsibility the same way that Herzberg's subjects in the 1960s did. The second possibility is equally provocative. There may be something in the way the programmer's job is structured that robs him of a sense of responsibility and hence a desire for it. If that is the case, dp managers have a major problem on their hands. At this time, the finding leaves us perplexed and calls for further investigation.

When the data was subdivided by sex, as shown in Fig. 2, other peculiarities appeared.

Men chose the Work Itself as the greatest motivator and placed it in the 93rd percentile. Women chose it fifth in the 68th percentile. Conversely, the women placed Recognition third in the

368

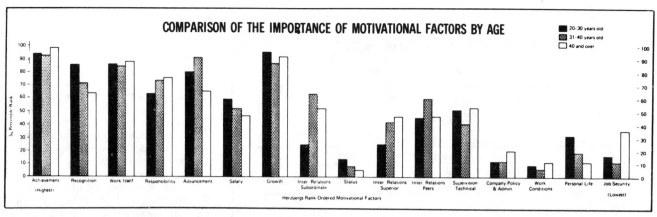

Fig. 3. The rankings of motivational factors are compared by age.

86th percentile; while men ranked it seventh in the 65th percentile.

Finally, the age breakdown in Fig. 3 brings out an interesting point. As age increased, the importance of Salary decreased almost in a straight line from 59th to 52nd to 46th percentile, and from seventh to ninth to eleventh in rank order. This result supports another popular conception of human motivation. Abraham Maslow proposed a theory in the '50s which placed needs in a hierarchy from basic survival through safety, social, and ego needs, to complete human fulfillment which he labeled self-actualization. He claimed that as one level of need is satisfied it is supplanted by a higher level need. In this case, as individuals aged and presumably made more money, thus satisfying survival and safety needs, salary became less motivating while need for personal growth and interpersonal relationships strengthened.

There are a number of other interesting variances overall from Herzberg's theory. The more we dissect the data, the more we can see that while there are basic similarities in the motivational patterns of people, individual differences do pertain. It is apparent that, to some degree, dp professionals have motivational drives which do not fully correspond to other occupational groups. The implication for management is that in order to have motivated employees, supervisors must understand and bear with individual needs. The monolithic notion that "people are all alike" simply is not supportable.

We also surveyed our subjects' attitudes toward organizational communication. We asked them to rank order, in terms of importance to them, organizational topics in which they were most interested. We also asked them to choose for each topic the source which they most and least preferred to have deliver the information. Table 2 shows the rank order of interest by job level, sex, and age.

Without exception, Job Performance and Career Opportunity information have been ranked first and second, well above all other topics. Personnel programs, such as salary and benefit information, usually rank third, closely followed by Company Profit performance and Changes in the work or organization of the unit. The remaining topics are of considerably less interest.

In this instance, overall changes ranked third, slightly ahead of Personnel information. Our guess is that since most dp departments are rapidly growing and changing organizations, this topic is of unusually high interest. In more stable units such as Accounting or Purchasing, change is not as prevalent. Profit information dropped from fourth to fifth in the ranking, and the degree of interest dropped off quite sharply.

Given the above, we would expect that the greatest effort would be being made to communicate information on performance and opportunity. Yet all evidence shows undeniably that organizations do their poorest jobs on these topics. A review of the literature over the past 20 years consistently shows cor-

PERSONAL INTEREST OPTIONS

Rank ordered	Job Level			Sex		Age		
	Percentile Rank			Percentile Rank		Percentile Rank		
Interests	Programmer/ Analyst	Project Leader	Manager	Male	Female	20-30	31-40	40+
1. Current job performance	90	85	92	92	99	95	90	92
2. Future career opportunities	87	89	82	89	94	92	86	78
3. Changes in organization & activities of dept.	63	63	62	62	71	66	57	61
4. Changes in personnel policies	55	53	45	44	46	49	50	61
5. Corporate profit performance	29	26	47	23	24	19	42	37
6. Company operating policies and procedures	24	37	21	15	22	31	29	23
7. General company activities	7	5	6	1	10	9	5	6

Table 2. Personal interest options are ranked by job level, sex, and age group.

We should spend more time helping supervisors become good communicators.

MOST PREFERRED COMMUNICATIONS SOURCE

Source options: A Immediate Supervisor (one level up)
B Senior DP Executive
C Senior Executive outside of DP
D Senior Staff Specialist

Topic	Job Level			Sex		Age		
	Programmer/ Analyst	Project Leader	Manager	Male	Female	20-30	31-40	40+
1. Current job performance	A	A	A	A	A	A	A	A
2. Future career opportunities	B	B	A	B	A	B	B	A
3. Changes in organization & activities of dept.	A	A	A	A	A	A	A	A
4. Changes in personnel policies	A	A	A	A	A	A	A	C
5. Corporate profit performance	C	C	C	C	C	C	C	C
6. Company operating policies and procedures	C	B	A	A	B	A	B	C
7. General company activities	A	A	A	A	A	A	A	A

Table 3. Most-preferred communications sources are ranked by job level, sex, and age group.

porate failure in coming up with a satisfactory performance appraisal system. Career counseling programs have received slightly less attention and no more success. The greatest gains in improving employee attitudes and morale are probably to be found in concentrating our efforts to effectively communicate this information.

The data on communication sources displayed in Table 3 is equally clear-cut.

ON THE SPOT The supervisor is unquestionably the person on the spot. Our early research was based on the assumption that while the immediate supervisor would be looked to for performance evaluation, other sources would be preferred for other topics. This was not and is not the case. Most often the supervisor appears as the most preferred source. Never is he chosen as the least preferred. On four to six topics out of seven, the supervisor is chosen first. The supervisor is better known, usually more trusted, and more capable of translating and interpreting for the subordinate the probable effect of most information.

Other research has shown that a supervisor has a great deal of influence on the general morale of his subordinates. More than any other individual, and more than other such potent forces as the company itself, the supervisor is the critical element. Hence, it is obvious we should spend more time helping supervisors become good communicators. They are important in both positive and negative situations. First, they are the most sought after communicators when it comes to telling the company story. Second, they can be the deciding force when there is individual or group discomfort.

Again, the opportunity is before us. We can achieve the greatest gains by training supervisors at all levels to communicate better. Conversely, we have the most to lose by continuing to ignore the current deficiency.

Charles Andrew, speaking at a recent conference of Production and Inventory Control Specialists, said:

"Successful implementation of an edp system has to start with a valid, realistic management theory—a balancing of the operations orientation with some practical thoughts from the behavioralists."

Gerald Weinberg, in his book on the application of psychology to computer programming, goes even further by noting that personality is displayed in everything we do or say. In particular he asserts, it is reflected in programming efforts. Weinberg believes that the personality of the programmer is observable in the manner in which he approaches the task and the product that results from his labor.

Our study attempted to determine some of the needs and communications desires of people in the business of data processing. When applied at this particular point in the rapid evolution of information processing, we feel it has particular significance.

The study has shown that while data processing professionals display some idiosyncracies, they have much in common with other people. A basic knowledge of human behavior can help us perceive and cope with the attitudes, interest, needs, and values of our employees. We must keep in mind that no matter how sophisticated our technology becomes, we will always have to rely on human beings to design, build, sell, install, service, and use it. Efficient and effective performance of these tasks is directly dependent on our ability to understand and manage these people. ❈

JAC FITZ-ENZ

Dr. Fitz-enz is director of industrial relations for Four-Phase Systems, Inc. in Cupertino, California. Prior to this he was vice president of organization development for Imperial Bank, in Los Angeles. He has published articles on personnel, training, and psychological subjects and has consulted with a variety of organizations. Dr. Fitz-enz received his Ph.D. in communications and industrial relations from the Univ. of Southern California, M.A. from San Francisco State, and B.A. from Notre Dame.

CIRCULAR SOLUTIONS

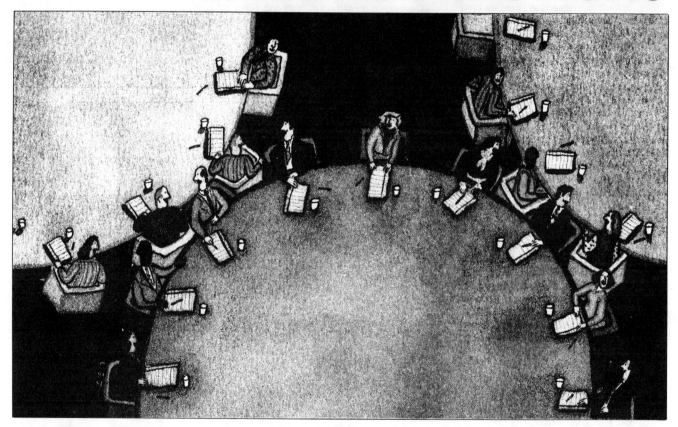

ILLUSTRATION LONNI SUE JOHNSON

by J. Daniel Couger

The quality circle—a team of eight to 10 volunteers who meet regularly to identify and solve problems—is perhaps the most transferable of the management techniques that have helped bring Japan to economic prominence. It is also one of the most beneficial: the Japanese Ministry of International Trade and Industry (MITI) attributes savings of $25 billion since 1963 to the use of the quality circle (QC).

These two facts would seem to bode well for the use of QC techniques on this side of the Pacific. Success with quality circles, however, has not been as widespread here as one might expect. Consider the comments of the head of all dp activities for a large West Coast bank: "The quality circle is just anoth-

er name for the task force approach to problem solving. Every so often our profession must come up with a new label to rejuvenate an old problem-solving approach."

Quality circles are not productive in this man's organization and the reason is clear. He doesn't understand the technique and hasn't trained his personnel in the special procedures necessary for an effective program. On the other hand, organizations that train their people well and implement their QC programs properly are realizing significant benefits, including a return on investment of around 6 to 1—about double that of traditional task force techniques. So although there are potential problems for dp shops that use quality circles, the rewards are equally real. A bit of history should shed some light on both.

Most people are aware of the political

influence of General Douglas MacArthur, commander of the U.S. occupation of Japan; not as many people are aware of his influence on the Japanese economic recovery. One area where MacArthur aided Japanese industry was in statistical quality control (SQC). He arranged for a U.S. expert in SQC, Dr. Edward W. Deming, to be a consultant to Japanese industry in improving the quality of its products. In 1951, the Union of Japanese Scientists and Engineers (JUSE) honored him by creating the annual Deming awards, the highest honor an individual or firm can receive in the field of quality (see Sud Ingle's *Quality Circles Master Guide*, 1982, Prentice-Hall Inc.; Englewood Cliffs, N.J.).

Deming's successor in "aid to Japan" was Dr. Joseph M. Juran. In 1952 Deming introduced Juran to K. Koyanagi, the founder of JUSE after World War II. Koyanagi extended an invitation to Juran to lecture in Japan. Two years later, Juran spent two months in Japan lecturing on the subject "Management of Quality Control," and subsequently returned to lecture about eight more times. Juran's approach to quality involved management, not just engineers and quality control personnel, and formed a basis for the quality circle program that emerged several years later. From that background evolved the work of Dr. Kaoru Ishikawa, a professor at the University of Tokyo, and board member of JUSE. Ishikawa is generally credited with formalizing the quality circle technique as it is used today in Japan.

The data on American use of quality circles substantiate my assertion that cultural differences are minimal in the use of this technique, compared to other successful Japanese management practices. According to the IAQC (International Association of Quality Circles), over 1,000 U.S. companies are using the quality circle technique, with over 10,000 circles in operation.

The growth has been exponential. The first American publication on the subject was Juran's 1967 article, "The Quality Circle Phenomenon." In 1968 JUSE sponsored a visit to the U.S. by a QC team that was invited to speak in a number of U.S. firms. Nevertheless, it was not until 1974 that the first U.S. quality circle program was installed at Lockheed Corp.'s Missile and Space Division, Sunnyvale, Calif. Lockheed employees Wayne Reiker and Donald Dewar were the principals in that successful installation. Lockheed credited the QC technique with saving over $72 Million. Table I lists typical QC projects at Lockheed as well as two high-return projects at American Airlines. These and other projects established the ROI norm of 6 to 1 for quality circle projects.

FIRST QC USE IN DP

It is only fair to the reader to reveal my own bias toward quality circles. Although I am primarily a computer scientist, One of my doctorate fields was behavioral science. In addition to membership in IAQC, I've had close interaction with both Japanese managers and nonmanagers through 12 years of teaching in the Japan-America Institute of Management Science. My conclusions are based on those interactions along with two other sources: a telephone survey of managers and QCfacilitators and a review of the published literature on quality circles.

IAQC has released a bibliography with over 100 entries on quality curcles.[1] Not one of those publications describes QC use in the

[1]To obtain a copy of Kathleen Terry's "A Bibliography on Quality Circles," contact IAQC, P.O. Box 30635, Midwest City, OK 73140.

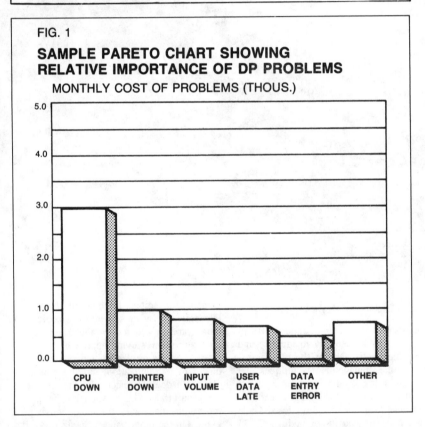

TABLE I

DOLLAR SAVINGS OF SOME TYPICAL QC APPLICATIONS

Lockheed Corporation

• Improved styles and types of test boxes	$ 65,600
• Recommended spray-coating PC boards instead of flow-coating them (reduced defects)	380,000
• Developed process to desolder and remove hybrids from PC boards without damage to hybrids	388,000
• Implemented "buddy check" systems; this systematized team effort in assembling cables substantially reduced the number of errors	54,000
• Developed a method of applying silver solder to triaxial cables, thereby reducing the number of cable rejects	6,250

American Airlines

• Analyzed reconditioning hand grinders—saved man-hours and money versus using old ones	115,000
• Redesigned shop area to eliminate $50 per hour downtime on machinery and provided supervisory office space on shop floor	250,000

FIG. 1

SAMPLE PARETO CHART SHOWING RELATIVE IMPORTANCE OF DP PROBLEMS

MONTHLY COST OF PROBLEMS (THOUS.)

computer field. Nor could IAQC identify QC use in computer departments; all they have is a list of computer manufacturers who had installed quality circles. Therefore, I began a telephone survey by calling the manufacturers. I found that Hewlett-Packard and IBM had installed a few circles in data processing departments. These references led to others, and during the next two months I called over 60 companies and identified QC use in 32 dp departments.

The survey revealed mixed results in the use of quality circles in dp, as the following quotes illustrate.

Con: "It is almost impossible to input those [Japanese] techniques to pull U.S. businesses and dp shops out of a productivity rut," according to Henry Nanjo, a Japanese American, director of dp for the City of San Francisco. "Quality circles were a disaster in our organization," reported a QC facilitator (who asked that his name not be published) in

One bank's data entry quality circle redesigned the batching approach for data entry jobs and saved $40,000 per year.

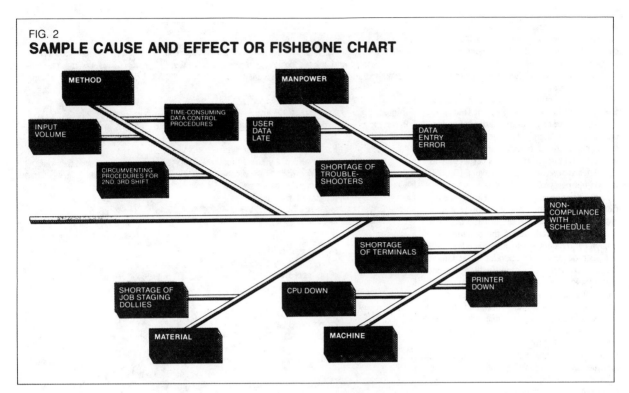

FIG. 2
SAMPLE CAUSE AND EFFECT OR FISHBONE CHART

a large dp organization in St. Louis.

Pro: "We've realized many benefits from our 15 quality circles," says Paul Karr, QC facilitator in the computer area of Boeing Wichita. "While many benefits are less tangible, such as improved employee attitude and morale, others were quite tangible. We saved over $100,000 on one project alone."

To understand the reasons for these conflicting results, it is necessary to consider the QC program in detail. The 11 guidelines for quality circles are:

1. The team consists of a regular work unit and its supervisor.
2. Participation is voluntary.
3. Team meetings are held once a week, for one hour.
4. Team members are trained in problem solving, including communications and behavioral techniques and analytical techniques.
5. One team member serves as facilitator and is trained in special techniques for that purpose.
6. The team selects the problems it wishes to resolve.
7. Problems are prioritized and analyzed.
8. Solutions are developed, along with implementation recommendations.
9. A control system for tracking results is designed.
10. A formal presentation is made to management.

11. The team has primary responsibility for implementation of its recommended solutions.

The tools used in steps seven and eight (analysis and resolution of the problem) include some techniques normally used in dp and others new to dp. They are:

1. Data gathering. Taking samples, and other data collection techniques.
2. Data representation. Use of Pareto charts. Pareto is the European scholar who in the 19th century developed a charting method to attract attention to the narrow distribution of wealth. Pareto analysis differentiates the important from the less important problems or problem characteristics. A histogram is plotted, where each column represents a different problem. The height of the columns indicates the relative importance of the problems. Columns are plotted in descending order, from left to right, and problems on the left are attacked initially because that's where the biggest payoff is. Fig. 1 shows a Pareto chart for several dp problems.
3. Stratification. Data are separated into two or more groups, to be examined separately. This approach enables the problem to be divided into smaller, more easily solved subproblems.
4. Scatter diagrams. Scatter diagrams will identify any relationship between variables. Data on different variables are plotted on one graph, to determine if some connection exists.

5. Cause and effect diagrams. The cause and effect technique facilitates identification of the true cause or causes of a problem. The effect (problem) is stated on the right-hand side of the chart. All of the possible causes are listed to the left. A cause and effect analysis diagram resembles a fish skeleton and is occasionally referred to as a fishbone diagram. Fig. 2 is a cause and effect chart for a typical dp problem.
6. Brainstorming. The brainstorming technique employs group or collective creativity. QC use of this procedure specifics stressing quantity of ideas; avoiding evaluation of ideas until a subsequent session; and, after the initial surge of group response, asking participants to submit one more idea per turn.
7. Control charts. Control charts depict control limits around the standard. They track results over a period of time. Control charts are updated on a regular basis so the QC team can monitor progress toward a solution.

The survey results showed that companies that used the guidelines and analytical techniques achieved positive results.

BENEFITS OF THE QC APPROACH One proof of the value of the QC approach is its application to a perpetual dp problem—documentation. First, it is surprising that quality circles would choose to work on this problem. Few people enjoy documentation; most consider it

Dp managers have a low need for social interaction and therefore require special training and practice in team-building activities.

nonchallenging and time-consuming. Second, it is surprising how many of the initial quality circles in a dp department put this problem high on their priority list for solution. This trend alone should demonstrate the value of the QC.

An example of positive results is the Boeing-Wichita QC activity. Their first quality circle chose to develop standards for documenting old systems. Their second QC chose to mechanize the documentation of new systems. An average of two hours per week was saved per analyst, resulting in over $100,000 in savings per year.

Other examples of QC benefits identified in the telephone survey include a data entry quality circle at Bank of America, San Francisco, that redesigned the batching approach for data entry jobs and saved $40,000 per year. A computer operator QC at Union Bank, Los Angeles, identified equipment that could be discontinued, and saved $35,000 a year in leasing costs. A data entry QC at the same company designed an improved timekeeping system that reduced staff cost by $35,000 per year. A distributed systems QC at Packaging Corp. of America, Evanston, Ill., designed a new disk allocation scheme that saved $25,000 in the acquisition of additional disk capacity. (Respectively, these companies are now running 15, 5, 21, and 3 quality circles.)

Dp organizations that deviated from the guidelines listed previously had far less success with quality circles. Reasons for failure include:

- *Inadequate preparation.* The QC approach appears easier to implement than it really is. The guidelines are straightforward and the analytical tools are easy to learn. As a result, the tendency is to bypass formal training. Three days of training for circle leaders and facilitators and eight hours of training for circle participants is the norm for companies with good results.
- *Involuntary participation.* Although few organizations openly violate the QC principle of voluntary participation, some managers implicitly pressure their subordinates to participate.
- *Application on inappropriate problem.* Some problems are not within the purview of quality circles. Company policies, supervisory personality issues, salary issues, and union/management issues are examples of problems that should be excluded from QC consideration. On the other hand, quality of work life (QWL) issues are most appropriate, despite absence of quantitative benefits. Quality circles have tackled QWL problems as momentous as the overall working environment and as mundane as the potholes in the parking lot.
- *Application in an unhealthy organization.* In companies where general dissent or unrest

A QUALITY CIRCLE IN ACTION

The following describes the formation of a quality circle and its subsequent activities through completion of the pilot study.

Kickoff minus 9 weeks:	Top-level manager reads DATAMATION article on benefits of quality circles. He reproduces copies for each member who attends the weekly managerial staff meeting. At the meeting he requests that they be prepared to discuss the subject the following week.
Kickoff minus 8 weeks:	Managers discuss pros and cons of quality circle concept, agree to begin program. Steering committee is appointed (two managers, two nonsupervisory employees) and charged with responsibility of presenting an action plan the following week.
Kickoff minus 7 weeks:	Steering committee reports to managerial staff meeting, recommending pilot quality circle in a unit with supervisory support and a good candidate for the facilitator role.
Kickoff minus 6 weeks:	Supervisor and facilitator attend three-day quality circle training session (available from a variety of sources). Upon their return, an announcement is made on the formation of pilot quality circle with request for volunteers.
Kickoff minus 4 weeks:	Supervisor and facilitator begin training quality circle team two hours per week for four weeks.
Kickoff:	Pilot quality circle develops list of possible projects. A high-visibility, short-term project is selected to enable the pilot program to be evaluated within three months.
Kickoff plus 4 weeks:	Team gathers data, develops Pareto charts, scatter diagrams, and cause and effect charts.
Kickoff plus 5 weeks:	Team brainstorms solutions, selects most appropriate approach, assigns responsibilities for developing solution.
Kickoff plus 8 weeks:	Over next three weeks, team develops solution.
Kickoff plus 9 weeks:	Team prepares proposal to submit for management approval.
Kickoff plus 10 weeks:	Team makes formal presentation to top management, obtains approval to implement solution.
Kickoff plus 14 weeks:	Over next four weeks, team implements solution. Method to track benefits is derived.

Although the pilot study is a low-risk approach, it forestalls widespread benefits for almost one year. The schedule is tight; nevertheless, it consumes almost five months. By the time the second round of circles begins producing results, approximately one year has lapsed from the time of the initial management discussion. This may have been appropriate for the companies who were the first to use the QC technique in dp, but today sufficient experience exists to question the need for a pilot study. If the 11 guidelines are carefully followed in QC implementation, there is little risk of failure.

But there are alternative approaches for the management that feels uncomfortable without a pilot study. The multiplexing technique employs several pilot studies in parallel, e.g., one in operations, one in applications programming, and one in the systems software group. With the overlapping approach, instead of using sequential processing (waiting until the pilot study is completed), subsequent circles are started as soon as the advantages and problems of initiating a circle are ascertained. The cycle stealing method requires meeting twice per week or for several hours instead of one hour per week in order to complete the pilot study much sooner.

A variation of these approaches is to start several circles simultaneously in one department where there is considerable interest from both managers and subordinates. Although all areas within dp are appropriate for QC application, the best marketing strategy is to begin where interest in the concept is highest.

A QC run by a facilitator instead of a unit supervisor produces poor results.

exists due to major managerial or budget/schedule problems, QCs have produced few benefits. Examples are federal agencies where huge budget reductions are occurring. QC emphasis by management in these organizations is perceived by the workers primarily as an attempt to reduce labor cost.

● *Lack of management support.* Few QC programs have been successful as a grass roots movement. As in most other successful practices, top-down commitment is required.

These mistakes are not peculiar to dp; the literature shows they apply to any organization. The dp survey, however, revealed one problem unique to this field. It is not unusual, in dp organizations where the QC approach produces minimal results, to find the quality circle being run by the facilitator instead of the unit supervisor. In many of the poorly producing circles, the supervisor no longer—or only infrequently—attends circle meetings. In other cases, the facilitator has been in charge from the outset.

This may surprise QC facilitators and supervisors in other parts of the company, but it simply reinforces earlier research by Dr. Robert Zawacki and myself that identified the low need for social interaction of dp management. Our studies of over 2,000 dp managers (at three levels) revealed that their need for social interaction is significantly lower than that of their peers in other parts of the firm.

We should not ignore the calamitous consequences of this abnormality in QC practice. With their low proclivity for interaction, dp supervisors need training and practice in team-building activities to a much greater ex-

tent than their counterparts in other areas of the firm. Yet, when they get the opportunity to acquire these important skills through active participation in the quality circle, dp supervisors are inclined to delegate the responsibility to the team facilitator.

Facilitators typically have a high need for social interaction. They are naturally inclined to acquire in-depth knowledge of the behavioral tools taught in the QC training sessions. First-line supervisors have strong technical skills and are naturally inclined to acquire in-depth knowledge of the technical tools taught in the QC training sessions.

TWO TYPES MAKES A GOOD TEAM Therefore, these two types make a good team for implementing the pilot quality circle. The supervisor (team leader) performs the project management function and the facilitator ensures that team members are communicating well. The supervisor improves his behavioral knowledge through observing the facilitator's good behavior skills. By the end of the first project, the supervisor has improved his behavioral skills and starts to perform a greater share of the facilitative role. The facilitator then assumes a coordinating function for a number of circles and conducts most of the training of new circles.

Another variation in dp application of quality circles is to place less emphasis on cost and benefit measurement. QC practice in other parts of the company places high emphasis on "before and after" comparisons. By contrast, the dp organizations that have

established sound measurement approaches are few and far between. As cited earlier, a few progressive organizations have established measurement systems, resulting in the 6 to 1 ROI guideline.

Many dp departments using the QC program are convinced of its value even though they have not emphasized cost/benefit analysis. Their view on use of QCs is illustrated by the comment of Bill Raymond, a QC facilitator in the Health Services Division of McDonnell-Douglas in St. Louis: "We began in 1980 with three circles and now have 12; it's obvious to management and everyone else that the circles have been very beneficial." Jim Shunk, a QC facilitator for Hewlett-Packard, Cupertino, reports a similar attitude in his company: "There is management philosophy and management support for QC at HP and not high priority for cost/benefit analysis."

Unlike the "zero defects" program that originated during the earliest manned space flights, the quality circle program is not designed to "psyche us up" but rather to provide a highly proceduralized approach for improvement in quality and productivity. The QC approach uses a special set of analytical techniques to examine a problem, a special set of group dynamics techniques to generate creative solutions, and finally, a set of evaluative techniques to compare alternatives. The group must convince management of the value of its solution, and then take charge of its implementation.

Quality circles have proved quite beneficial to data processing organizations that have adhered to QC guidelines and utilized QC analytical techniques. But despite the 6 to 1 ROI potential, the greatest benefit of quality circles may not be quantifiable. It is the opportunity for low-social-need supervisors to learn to interact more effectively with subordinates. Improving the mutual problem-solving capability of supervisors and subordinates, through the vehicle of the quality circle, may be the most important return on investment.

Perhaps the delay in adopting QC programs is due to the lack of publications on its applicability to the dp department. It is hoped that this paper will encourage discussion and use of quality circles in our field. ✱

FAMOUS QUOTES BY ROCKS

IGNEOUS IS BLISS.

T.O. SYLVESTER

J. Daniel Couger is Distinguished Professor of Computer and Management Science at the University of Colorado. His national studies of key motivational factors resulted in motivation norms for 15 jobs in the computer field. He and his coresearcher, Robert Zawacki, have over 15 publications on the subject, including their book *Motivation and Management of Computer Personnel* (Wiley Interscience, 1980).

CARTOON BY T.O. SYLVESTER

Conflict Management for Project Managers

by John R. Adams
Nicki S. Kirchof

Department of Management
School of Business
Western Carolina University
Cullowhee, North Carolina 28723

Published By:

PROJECT MANAGEMENT INSTITUTE
Drexel Hill, Pennsylvania 19026

First Printing: Oct. 1982
Second Printing: Feb. 1986

PREFACE

The project manager, by the nature of the work, must understand at least the rudiments of a wide variety of specialized fields if the project is to be successfully completed. Efforts to control the project to achieve specified cost, schedule, and performance targets, for example, lead the project manager deeply into the development of management information systems. An understanding of the engineering specialties which underlie the project is widely publicized as a requirement for an effective project manager. Contract management and negotiation skills are other fields in which the project manager must perform as the project progresses through its life cycle. Perhaps an even more critical skill requirement lies in the area of conflict management.

In most cases, those who become project managers begin their careers in one or more of the technical specialities which underlie the particular project of which they are in charge. Typically, because of their excellent performance of the technical work in their speciality, they are promoted into the ranks of project management. In general, their technical skill can be assumed. For a major project, however, the new job also requires consummate skill in managing human interrelationships in a highly conflict-prone environment. Conflicts *will* exist in all project environments. Severe conflict is the rule in projects where participants are "loaned" to the project and thus must report to two bosses, namely their functional manager for evaluation and career development, and the project manager for task assignment and work direction. In such conflict-prone situations, a failure on the part of the project manager to recognize and carefully manage the details of the conflict situation can easily lead to a total collapse of the project team.

Conflict is natural to all human organizations and can lead to many beneficial results for both the project and the project manager. To achieve these results, the project manager must be able to recognize and categorize the conflict situation, and then select from among the several strategies available — the conflict management approach that will resolve the issue with favorable results for the project. The purposes of this monograph are to (1) review the concepts of conflict and conflict management as they apply in the project environment; (2) summarize the conflict management methods available to the project manager and indicate the situations in which each might be most appropriately used; and (3) integrate these two purposes into an analysis of two-party conflict, indicating the probable results of a conflict situation between two parties when each uses varying modes of conflict management. Throughout the monograph, materials are carefully selected to be of value to the project manager from the viewpoint of the project manager.

The project manager, both the neophyte and the scarred veteran of many project wars, will find this monograph a useful summary and an excellent primer for conflict management. It is not intended that this monograph be an exhaustive or comprehensive coverage of conflict management theory. Rather, it is a selective presentation of the essentials of conflict management which are typically needed and used in the project management environment. The monograph is designed to be concise yet readable, usable either as an initial introduction or as a refresher in this field for the project manager. A periodic review of this monograph is likely to make us all more effective project managers.

CONFLICT IN ORGANIZATIONS

One of the primary, underlying reasons conflict exists in organizations today is the tremendous amount of change that has occurred in the workplace in recent years. In order to survive in today's environment, organizations need to adapt rapidly to change. "The Industrial Revolution was characterized by the development of the factory system of production,"[1] which led to the division of labor and our modern, large-scale bureaucracy. Production systems were established to produce goods in the "most efficient" manner, and a change in that system was allowed only after extensive testing proved that the new method provided important and measurable improvements in efficiency. In this environment, change occurred very slowly. Organizations were highly structured and roles were clearly defined. In the past thirty years, however, there has been a revolution in popular concepts of organization which has led to the development of new organizational structures. This revolution has occurred primarily as a response to a rapidly changing environment which demanded dynamic organizations that could adapt to change. Some factors which have led to this "dynamic" environment are technological advances, new concepts of education, increased leisure time, and major societal concerns over environmental and energy issues.[2] Because of automation and other technological changes, new types of managerial occupations have developed along with changes in supervisor/subordinate relationships (Ritzer, 1977). The revolution in education has led to an abundance of educated people and positive implications for the professionals, but negative implications for the semi-skilled worker. Increased leisure time is an outgrowth of technological advances and the increase in the percentage of educated people. These changes lead to conflict as people disagree on how organizations should adapt and as they see the results of that adaptation benefiting or hurting their status and prospects.

Another basic cause of conflict which stems from the change that now seems to constantly surround organizations is the incongruence of goals and objectives of the organization's employees. Typically, the organization's goals and objectives are formulated by top management along with the purposes, values, and missions pursued by the organization. Employees have to abide by these goals and objectives to remain loyal to and employed by the firm. However, the firm's goals and objectives may differ markedly from the individual employee's personal goals and objectives, a situation which can cause extensive conflicts. Fifty years ago, the classical management organization, as shown in Figure 1, was found to be satisfactory for control of the organization's activities.[3] Conflicts were at a minimum, since employees were able to set and pursue long-range objectives consistent with those of the organization.[4]

The increased rate of change demanded a more dynamic organization. Projects and project terms were developed to deal with, manage, and create change. The goals of individuals and organizations became even more incongruent as the projectized organizational structure evolved (Figure 2). The organization structure became even more complex. Project managers and functional managers competed for authority. "Because the individual

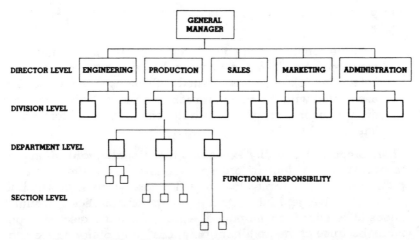

Figure 1. The Traditional Management Structure

Source: Harold Kerzner, *Project Management: A Systems Approach to Planning Scheduling and Controlling*. New York: Van Nostrand Reinhold Company, 1979, p. 42.

performing the work is now caught in a web of authority relationships, additional conflicts came about because functional managers were forced to share their authority with the project manager".[5] Therefore, inconsistent goals between supervisors and subordinates, as well as between individuals and organizations, existed in the projectized environment also, but for different reasons than those of the traditional organization.

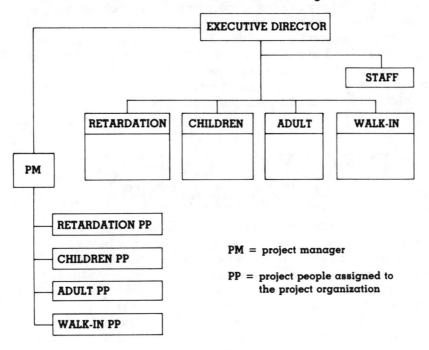

Figure 2. Projectized Form of Organization

Source: John R. Adams, Stephen C. Barndt and Martin D. Martin, *Managing by Project Management*, Dayton, Ohio, Universal Technology Corporation , 1979, p. 45.

These factors of change and incongruent goals evident in the individual/organization and the supervisor/subordinate relationships found within the project lead to high levels of conflict. Thus, the project organization is a major center of conflict. As Butler states:

> . . . the conflict specifically associated with project management may be classified into two broad, partly overlapping categories: (a) conflict associated with change; and (b) conflict associated with the concentration of professionals of diverse disciplines in a more or less autonomous group effort which has limited life.[6]

Therefore, conflict readily exists in a traditional organization and is even more evident in projects. Conflict is inevitable in organizations " . . . because they have limited means with which to satisfy the divergent interests of their various publics."[7] Conflict needs to be effectively managed, especially in a project environment, because of the imminent time, cost, and performance constraints imposed on the project effort. The primary responsibility for conflict management in the project lies with the project manager. If the project is to be successful, the project manager must cope with conflict and develop profitable resolutions.

Conflict management is a critical issue for the project manager, for uncontrolled conflict can literally tear the project apart. The purpose of this monograph is to provide the theoretical and practical understanding of conflict and its management needed to enable the project manager to successfully deal with the project's conflict problems. A view of conflict management with an emphasis on the project manager's role is developed. First, the theory of conflict management is reviewed. Second, conflict as it applies specifically in project organizations is analyzed and reviewed. Third, the relationship between the project manager and conflict management is examined. The role of the project manager is then reviewed in relation to power, the five modes of conflict resolution, and the project manager's ability to influence people toward less destructive conflict. Finally, an approach to conflict resolution for the project manager is provided.

THEORY OF CONFLICT MANAGEMENT

Conflict is generally defined as "a clash between hostile or opposing elements or ideas."[8] As applied to human behavior, it is a disagreement between individuals which can vary from a mild disagreement to a win/lose, emotion-packed confrontation. There are two basic, but opposing, views of conflict, the traditional and the modern (see Figure 3). The traditional view sees conflict as being primarily negative. In this view, conflict is caused by troublemakers; it is bad; and it should be avoided. The manager who views conflict in this way avoids admitting that it exists, keeps it under cover, and tries to suppress it. The contemporary view sees conflict in a more positive light. According to this view, conflict is inevitable. It is a natural result of change and is frequently beneficial to the manager if properly managed. In particular, an atmosphere of tension, and hence conflict, is essential in any organization committed to developing or working with new ideas, for innovation is simply the process of bringing together differing ideas and perspectives into a new and different synthesis. This latter view is much more realistic in modern organizations. In today's environment, conflict is inevitable because of the various competing unit objectives, personal goals, uses for resources, and

TRADITIONAL VIEW	CONTEMPORARY VIEW
• Caused by Trouble-Makers	• Inevitable between Humans
• Bad	• Often Beneficial
• Should be Avoided	• Natural Result of Change
• Must be Suppressed	• Can and Should Be Managed

Figure 3. What Is Conflict?

divergent viewpoints that exist and must be integrated toward the organization's objectives. It is how the individual manager views and deals with conflict that makes it constructive or destructive for the organization. From the author's perspective, the primary aim is to manage conflict constructively to achieve the organization's goals. In order to do this, it is necessary to understand the conditions leading to conflict, the potential results of conflict, and the various methods of dealing with conflict in an organizational setting.

In his book, *Interpersonal Conflict Resolution*, Alan C. Filley develops nine conditions which predispose an organization toward conflict (see Table 1).[9]

Table 1
Antecedent Conditions Leading to Conflict

1. Ambiguous Jurisdictions
2. Conflict of Interest
3. Communication Barriers
4. Dependence on One Party
5. Differentiation in Organization
6. Association of the Parties
7. Need for Consensus
8. Behavior Regulations
9. Unresolved Prior Conflicts

These antecedent conditions for conflict do not exist separately in any organization. It is the extent to which they exist in combination which creates the conditions for conflict. All of them may exist within a single organization at one time. As stated earlier, conflict is a disagreement among individuals. These antecedent conditions simply set the stage for personal disagreement.

The first antecedent condition is called "ambiguous jurisdictions." This situation occurs when two or more parties have related responsibilities, but their work boundaries and role definitions are unclear. This type of occurrence can be found frequently in both the projectized and the matrix organizational structures because both use the "two-boss concept." "Conflict of interest," the second condition leading to conflict, exists when two or more parties want to achieve different or inconsistent goals and desires relative to each other from their association with the organization. For example, the engineer may wish to build his reputation by association with a unique and advanced design, while the manager may be more concerned with completing the job on schedule and at low cost using a standard design. "Communication barriers" is the third condition of conflict. Communication difficulties create misunderstandings and inhibit their resolution by blocking efforts to explain the needs, viewpoints, and actions of those involved in the organization. When there is a "dependence on one party," there tends to be a situation of conflict because one person is dependent on the other to provide needed resources. "Differentiation in organization" exists when different sub-units of the organization are responsible for different tasks. This exists in all organizations. However, in modern organizations dealing with today's complex technologies, there tends to be large numbers of both horizontal and vertical divisions of tasks, creating many specialized groups with their own languages, acronyms, goals, and perspectives. "Association of the parties" is the sixth condition leading to conflict. When people *must* associate together and make joint decisions, conflicts can occur. This situation is especially prevalent when different technical groups have to work together with a variety of management groups. In this case, there may be little of the common ground needed for agreement found in the association. The "need for consensus" follows closely "association of the parties" as a condition leading to conflict. These two conditions are very similar in that, again, people *must* work together. But, when a need for consensus exists, people *must* willingly agree among themselves. There is no decision maker available able or willing to select among several alternatives and enforce the selected solution. When several people from different backgrounds, having different goals, must freely agree on a course of action, the conflict generated can be extremely protracted and difficult to manage. The eighth condition leading to conflict is called "behavior regulations." When the individual's behavior must be regulated closely, as in situations involving high levels of safety and security concerns, high levels of conflict frequently exist as individuals resist the tight boundaries placed on their actions. Their views of what is necessary may differ markedly from that of the organization, and the regulation of activities may inhibit the ease of accomplishing work. As a result, high levels of frustration may exist leading to extensive conflict. Finally, "unresolved prior conflicts" tend to build up and create an atmosphere of tension, which can lead to still more and more intense conflicts. In many cases, the longer conflicts last without a satisfactory resolution being developed, the more severe they become. The use of raw power to "settle" conflicts may also generate more intense conflict at a later time. If one party is unwilling to resolve a conflict, those people involved are likely to generate more difficulties until they may become totally unable to work together. Thus, a failure to manage and deal with conflicts largely guarantees that the manager's job will become more difficult in the future.

These nine antecedent conditions of conflict exist in every organization at all times to a greater or lesser extent. They tend to be more apparent in the project and matrix forms of organization because these organizational structures are frequently used to create change using modern, advanced technology in highly complex and uncertain situations. When these conditions are found, it is up to the project manager to avoid potential destructive results of conflict by controlling and channeling it into areas that can prove beneficial to the project.

Destructive conflict can be highly detrimental to the organization and can significantly alter its productivity. It can drastically hamper the decision making process, making it long, complex, and difficult. Conflict can also cause the formation of competing coalitions within the organization, thus reducing employee commitment to the organizational goals. In essence, destructive conflict can lead to a number of devisive, frustrating distractions which degrade the effort normally applied toward organizational goals.

In order to avoid these destructive consequences, the manager must channel the conflict in such a way that it is either resolved or used for constructive purposes. There are a number of positive results to be derived from conflict. One of these is the "diffusion of more serious conflict."[10] Games, for example, can be used to control the attitudes of people. Games provide a competitive situation which has entertainment value and can provide tension release to the parties involved.[11] Such conflict processes, which have acceptable resolution procedures already established, can function as preventive measures against more destructive outcomes. Similarly, systems which provide for participation by the members of an organization in decision making, while positively associated with the number of minor disputes between parties, are negatively associated with the number of major incidents which occur between members of the organization (Corwin, 1969).[12] Therefore, closeness among organization members is a means of channeling aggressive behavior and tends to result in disagreements which, in turn, reduce the likelihood of major fights and disruptions. Another positive value of conflict is the "stimulation of a search for new facts or resolutions."[13] When two parties who respect each other are involved in a disagreement, the process can sometimes lead to a clarification of facts. Conflict can also stimulate the search for new methods or solutions. "When parties are in conflict about which of two alternatives to accept, their disagreement may stimulate a search for another solution mutually acceptable to both."[14] In both cases, the conflict needs to be managed to keep attention on the facts of the situation and to keep the emotional content low.

An "increase in group cohesion and performance"[15] is another potential value of conflict. Conflict situations between two or more groups are likely to increase both the cohesiveness and the performance of the groups in question. In this situation, however, the effects of conflict must be divided into two periods: during the conflict itself, and after a winner and loser have been determined. During the conflict, there is extremely high loyalty to the group associated with willingness to conform to group attitudes and ideas. Little effort is made to understand the opponent, and the opponent's position is evaluated negatively. The level of effort allocated to the group effort is increased. Therefore, in this sense, competition is valuable as a stimulus to work groups. However, when conflicts end, the situation changes. The leader of the winning group gains status. This person's influence tends to continue and be extended. The leader of the losing group, however, loses status and tends to be blamed for the loss. The group atmosphere also changes. There exists a high level of tension, a desire to avoid problems, an intense desire to do better, and highly competitive feelings in the losing group. These factors decrease in the winning group and are replaced by a feeling of accomplishment and satisfaction.[16] The losing group will tend to try harder next time and the winning group will tend to relax. Therefore, during the conflict, there is an increase in group cohesion and performance in both groups. These attitudes can decrease in both groups once the conflict is resolved, but they decrease for different reasons. "The measure of power or ability"[17] is the fourth value of conflict. Conflict can provide a fairly accurate method of measurement. Through conflictive situations, the relative power between two parties may be identified. "Coercion, control, and suppression requires clear superiority of power of one party over another, whereas problem solving requires an equalization of power among the parties.[18] Suppression of one party by another can therefore be avoided by creating an approximately equal power balance, and this approach usually leads to the use of problem solving methods to resolve disagreements.

The potential results of conflict described above demonstrate that the results of conflict are not necessarily all bad. In fact, conflict is neither good nor bad but can have both positive and negative results for the organization. It really depends on the atmosphere created by the manager as he manages the conflict situations in his organization. Destructive results of conflict, however, need to be avoided by careful and detailed conflict management.

From a management perspective, there are five distinct methods for dealing with conflict (see Figure 4). The project manager must carefully select the appropriate mode for handling conflict within his organization so that an atmosphere conducive to constructive results is developed. The five modes, smoothing, withdrawing, compromise, forcing, and problem solving, are defined and viewed in light of their general effectiveness in this section.[19] Later, they are analyzed and reviewed in depth in relation to the project manager's role. *Smoothing* is defined as "deemphasizing differences and emphasizing commonalities over conflictual issues."[20] Smoothing keeps the atmosphere friendly; but if used too frequently or as the main or only method of dealing with conflict, the conflicts will never be faced. *Withdrawal* can be defined as "retreating from actual or potential disagreements and conflict situations."[21] This method is appropriate only in certain situations, for example, when a "cooling off" period is needed to gain perspective on the conflict situation. Both smoothing and withdrawal are delaying, ignoring tactics which will not resolve the conflict but will temporarily slow the situation down. Note that, if the conflict is not dealt with and resolved in the long run, future conflict will be more severe and intense. *Compromising*, "considering various issues, bargaining, and searching for solutions which attempt to bring some degree of satisfaction to the conflicting parties,"[22] is a situation where neither party can win, but each may get some degree of satisfaction out of the situation. A compromise *does* hurt; both parties must give up something that is important to them, but compromise *does* usually provide some acceptable form of a resolution. Forcing and problem solving also provide resolutions. *Forcing* is "exerting one's viewpoint at the potential expense of another party, characterized by a win-lose situation.[23] That is, one party wins while the other loses. Forcing can increase conflicts later as antagonisms build up among the parties involved. It should therefore generally be used by the project manager as a last resort. *Problem solving* (or confrontation) is a mode where the disagreement is addressed directly. It is a process where conflict is treated as a problem. That is, the problem is defined, information is collected, alternatives are developed and analyzed, and the most appropriate alternative is selected in a typical problem solving technique. This method is considered theoretically to be the best way of dealing with conflict because both parties can be fully satisfied if they can work together to find a solution that meets both of their needs. It is a time-consuming process, however, and it requires that both parties desire to solve the problem and are willing to work together toward a mutually agreeable solution. If a solution is needed quickly or immediately, however, the problem solving approach simply cannot work.

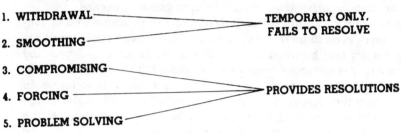

1. WITHDRAWAL ——————————— TEMPORARY ONLY, FAILS TO RESOLVE
2. SMOOTHING
3. COMPROMISING
4. FORCING ——————————— PROVIDES RESOLUTIONS
5. PROBLEM SOLVING

PROJECT MANAGER MUST CAREFULLY SELECT THE APPROPRIATE MODE.

Figure 4. Five Conflict Management Modes

Of the five basic modes, some are more conducive to certain situations than others. Problem solving is considered the "best" mode since it can lead to innovative results capable of satisfying all parties. It does not work in all situations, however, especially when time is critical. Smoothing and withdrawing are delaying actions which cannot resolve the issue. Forcing provides a rapid solution but may make the conflict more intense in the long run. Compromise provides a resolution but rarely satisfies anyone. So, again, it is up to the project manager to identify the type and source of the conflict, evaluate the situation objectively, and select one of the conflict handling modes to solve the issue. In other words, the project manager must *manage* the conflict situation.

There are other methods the project manager can use in handling conflict. These differ from the five modes of conflict in that they relate more specifically to personal styles of handling conflict. Filley identifies these five styles of handling conflict as:

> high concern for personal goals and low concern for relationships (win-lose); low concern for personal goals and high concern for relationships (yield-lose); low concern for personal goals and low concern for relationships (lose, leave); moderate concern for personal goals and moderate concern for relationships (compromise style); and high concern for personal goals and high concern for relationships (integrative style).[24]

These essentially "one party" styles of conflict resolution can be related to the five modes as seen in Figure 5. With these relationships in mind, an examination of these personal styles follows. The win-lose style is the "tough battler" who seeks to meet his goals at all costs.[25] The yield-lose style is the friendly helper, "who overvalues maintenance of relationships with others and undervalues achievement of his own goals."[26] The lose-leave style person sees conflict as "a hopeless, useless, and punishing experience."[27] The compromise style person will try to find a position where each side can end up with something. Finally, the integrative style person seeks to satisfy his own goals as well as the goals of others.[28] He is the problem solver. Like the five modes reviewed earlier, the problem solving and compromise-oriented styles (integrative and compromise) are the most successful styles. The win-lose style, yield-lose style, and lose-leave styles would not be effective because of their extremes. The compromise style and integrative style must be evident in a successful project organization. The first three styles (win-lose, yield-lose, lose-leave) would ultimately lead to project failure, while the last two (compromise, integrative) would lead to project success.

In summary, conflict is inevitable in an organization and is usually considered to be a disagreement among two or more parties. The results can be good or bad for the organization, depending upon how the manager manages the conflict. The antecedent conditions for conflict provide a guideline for managers to follow in predicting the type and intensity of conflict likely to exist in the organization. Destructive conflict can be very detrimental to the organization, and it is the manager's responsibility to control and channel the conflict process for constructive results. The five methods of dealing with conflict and their general effectiveness give project managers some tools with which to manage conflict in their project environments.

		Concern for	
		Personal Goals	Relationships
Force	Win-lose	High	Low
Smooth	Yield-lose	Low	High
Withdraw	Lose-leave	Low	Low
Compromise	Compromise	Medium	Medium
Problem Solver	Integrative	High	High

Figure 5. Styles of Conflict Resolution

FOOTNOTES

1. George Ritzer, *Working: Conflict and Change.* Englewood Cliffs, N.J.: Prentice-Hall, Inc., 1977, p. 8.
2. Ibid., p. 40.
3. Harold Kerzner, *Project Management: A Systems Approach to Planning Scheduling and Controlling.* New York: Van Nostrand Reinhold Company, 1979, p. 42.
4. Ibid., p. 42.
5. Ibid., p. 48.
6. Arthur G. Butler Jr., "Project Management: A Study in Organizational Conflict," *Academy of Management Journal.* March 1973, p. 89.

7. Ibid., p. 86.
8. David B. Guralink, editor, *Webster's New World Dictionary.* Cleveland: William Collins and World Publishing Co., Inc., 1947, p. 298.
9. Alan C. Filley, *Interpersonal Conflict Resolution.* Glenview, Illinois: Scott, Foresman and Company, 1975, p. 4.
10. Ibid.
11. Ibid.
12. Ibid., p. 5.
13. Ibid.
14. Ibid.
15. Ibid., p. 6.
16. Ibid., p. 7.
17. Ibid.
18. Ibid.
19. See R.R. Blake and J.S. Mouton, *The Managerial Grid.* Houston: Gulf Publishing Company, 1964 and application by Hans J. Thamhain and David L. Wilemon, "Conflict Management in Project Life Cycles," *Sloan Management Review*, Vol. 16, No. 3, Spring 1973, pp. 31-50.
20. Hans J. Thamhain and David L. Wilemon, "Conflict Management in Project-Oriented Work Environments," *Proceedings of the Sixth Annual Seminar/Symposium.* Drexel Hill, Pennsylvania: Proceedings of the PMI, 1974, p. 3.
21. Ibid., p. 87.
22. Ibid.
23. Ibid.
24. Filley, p. 51.
25. Ibid.
26. Ibid.
27. Ibid., p. 52.
28. Ibid.

ABOUT THE AUTHORS

Dr. John R. Adams is the Director for Educational Services of the Project Management Institute (PMI), and an Associate Professor of Organization and Management at Western Carolina University, Cullowhee, North Carolina. A very active member of PMI since 1972, he is a past associate editor of the Project Management Journal (PMJ), journal of the Institute; a Past President of the Ohio Chapter of PMI; Project Manager and Instructor for the Weekend Workshops, conducted in conjunction with the Annual PMI International Symposium/Seminar; and a frequent contributor of papers to both the PMJ and the Annual PMI Symposium/Seminar. Dr. Adams holds the Ph.D. degree in Business Administration from Syracuse University, a Master of Science in Management from Florida State University, and a Bachelor of Science in Electrical Engineering from the University of New Hampshire. He has held a number of responsible project manager positions in the U.S. aerospace program, and has directed a number of large research programs for a major U.S. Air Force research laboratory.

Nicki S. Kirchof is an Associate for Educational Services of the Project Management Institute (PMI), and a Graduate Research Assistant at Western Carolina University, Cullowhee, North Carolina. An expert in both written and spoken German, she has performed extensive research in the field of project management emphasizing its international and educational aspects. She is co-editor of *A Decade of Project Management*, a PMI book of selected readings from the 1970's *Project Management Quarterly*, and is an author of several articles on project and matrix management. She addressed an INTERNET Symposium on adapting project management to a specific organization's needs. Ms. Kirchof completed the Master of Business Administration Degree from Western Carolina University early in 1983, and has pursued her career in internationally-oriented project management.

Chapter 8: Controlling a Software Engineering Project

1. Introduction to Chapter

Controlling a software engineering project is defined as all the management activities that ensure that actual work goes according to plan. It measures performance against goals and plans, reveals when and where deviation exists, and, by putting in motion actions to correct deviations, helps ensure accomplishment of plans.

Controlling a software engineering project can be partitioned into six general management activities (see Table 8.1). Each activity in the table is followed by its definition or an amplifying description.

YOUR JOB, HEINZ—KEEP DESIGN ERRORS UNDER CONTROL

Table 8.1: Controlling Activities

Activity	Definition or Explanation
Develop standards of performance	— Set conditions or measurements that will exist when tasks are correctly done.
Establish monitoring and reporting systems	— Determine necessary data, who will receive it, and when they will receive it.
Measure results	— Determine accomplishments of, or extent of deviation from, goals and standards.
Initiate corrective actions	— Reinforce standards, adjust goals, or replan.
Reward and discipline	— Praise, remunerate, and discipline applicable personnel.
Document controlling methods	— Document the standards, methods of reporting and control, bonus plans et al., decision points, and so on.

2. Overview of Chapter

The nine papers in this chapter all have to do with controlling a software engineering project. The activities listed in Table 8.1 were used as an outline for the purpose of identifying papers on controlling activities.

Ferrentino has written a short paper on the problems in controlling a software engineering project when cost and schedule estimates are based on estimating the lines of deliverable code. Buckley provides a procedure for establishing software engineering standards in an industrial organization.

The following papers concentrate on measuring, reporting on, and correcting the software engineering *process:*

- Unit Development Folders by Frank Ingrassia provides an up-to-date method for the management control of a software development unit or team.
- The paper by Weinberg and Freedman discusses the establishing of a reporting system by which *project status* can be reported.
- Walter's paper sets forth procedures by which a software development project can be audited.
- Howes' paper relies on the earned-value method of measuring progress as a means of controlling the software engineering process.
- Roger Gould provides a self-assessment questionnaire for the evaluation of a software development process.

The following papers concentrate on measuring, reporting on, and controlling the software engineering *product:*

- The paper by Weinberg and Freedman also discusses the establishing of a reporting system by which *technical status* can be reported.
- Fagan's updated paper on inspection systems furnishes a means for providing control of the quality of the software engineering products.
- The paper by Bersoff on configuration management provides a means of controlling both software and software documentation as it is developed.

3. Description of Papers

The paper by Andrew Ferrentino concerns both the difficulties in estimating the correct cost and schedule for a software development project and the difficulties in bringing a system in on time and within cost. The paper questions the current approach in determining the current status of a project by comparing the number of lines of code completed to the number of lines of code estimated. He points out that an incompatibility exists when the original estimate was made using lines of code and it is software functionality that is delivered. Ferrentino believes that "we can't make good estimates but we can make estimates good." He also argues that a combination of good software engineering and project management practices will enable us to deliver a software engineering project on time and within cost.

The next paper is by Fletcher Buckley who developed the first IEEE Software Engineering Standard. Buckley has written this paper on *software engineering standards* especially for this tutorial. He tells how to place software engineering standards in a software development environment—something equivalent to waving a red flag at an enraged bull. Emphasis is placed on a practical implementation using proven techniques. Buckley's unique writing style makes for interesting reading.

The third paper, by Weinberg and Freedman, discusses formal technical review procedures, each applicable to particular types of technical material and to the particular mix of the review committee. Additional information on the subject can be found in their book, *Handbook of Walkthroughs, Inspections, and Technical Reviews* [1]. As the title indicates, different types of reviews both formal and informal are analyzed and compared with emphasis on the managerial and

---

1. D.P. Freedman and G.M. Weinberg, *Handbook of Walkthroughs, Inspections, and Technical Reviews*, 3rd ed., Little, Brown and Company, Boston, 1982.

technical roles. (Note: Weinberg is generally credited with furthering the concept of the walkthrough through his "egoless programming team" and "egoless technical reviews." He says however that the term "walkthrough" goes back well before his time.)

"The Unit Development Folder (UDF): A Ten-Year Perspective," by Frank Ingrassia, the originator of the UDF, is an update for this tutorial of his landmark paper on *Unit Development Folders*. The Unit Development Folder (UDF) concept is one of today's most widely used software engineering management control techniques. This is the first update of the original paper, and it incorporates the changes in the uses of the UDF since its conception and introduction in 1977.

Note: The unit development folder is sometime call a software development file folder or a software engineering notebook.

The fifth paper, entitled "Advances in Software Inspections," by Michael Fagan is also an update. Michael Fagan, the originator of the inspection system, presents new studies and experiences that enhance the use of the inspection process. The inspection system is a static testing technique used to verify that software meets its requirements. Fagan reports the inspections usually detect more defects in the product, at lower cost, than does machine testing. (The inspection system is very similar to a walkthrough.) Examples of these benefits are cited followed by a description of the inspection process.

In the next paper, Ed Bersoff defines *configuration management* as the discipline of identifying the configuration of a system at discrete points in time for the purpose of systematically controlling changes to the configuration and maintaining the integrity and traceability of the configuration throughout the system life cycle. Configuration management keeps track of the various artifacts developed during the lifetime of a software project through *identifying, controlling, auditing,* and *status accounting the various software development products.*

Bersoff reminds us that controlling code is not enough; the documentation that enables us to use and operate the code must also be controlled. This paper also provides a lengthy description of the *program support library (PSL).* Bersoff discusses the major problems involved in deciding how to properly manage the software configuration: too much control is cumbersome; too little control invites disaster.

Another paper, by Gene Walters, is entitled "Investigative Audits for Controlling Software Development." It is a detailed, procedural document on precisely how to conduct a *investigative audit,* how an *audit team* should function, the questions it should ask of the development group, and how to draw the proper conclusions. Walters, an experienced auditor of software projects, uses the case study approach to describe an investigative audit. Walters updated an earlier paper on this subject just for this tutorial.

The next paper by Norm Howes, entitled "Managing Software Development Projects for Maximum Productivity," presents a method for scheduling, costing, and controlling projects both large and small. The paper places emphasis on the *earned value method* of controlling a software development project by comparing budgeted, earned, and actual hours used in developing a software system. A case study is used for an example.

The last paper in this chapter is a self-assessment procedure which project managers can use to measure their knowledge about software engineering project management. The assessment procedure presents thirty questions with possible answers and references.

Criteria For Controlling Projects According To Plan[1]

Hans J. Thamhain
Worcester Polytechnic Institute

David L. Wilemon
Syracuse University

Introduction

Few project managers would argue the need for controlling their projects according to established plans. The challenge is to apply the available tools and techniques effectively. That is, to manage the effort by leading the multifunctional personnel toward the agreed-on objectives within the given time and resource constraints. Even the most experienced practitioners often find it difficult to control programs in spite of apparent detail in the plan, personnel involvement, and even commitment. As summarized in Table 1, effective program management is a function of properly defining the work, budgets and schedules and then monitoring progress. Equally importantly, it is related to the ability to keep personnel involved and interested in the work, obtain and refuel commitment from the team as well as from upper management, and to resolve some of the enormous complexities on the technical, human and organizational side.

Responding to this interest, a field study was initiated to investigate the practices of project managers regarding their project control experiences. Specifically, the study investigates:

1. Type of project control problems experienced by project managers.
2. Project management practices and performance.
3. Criteria for effective project control.

Method Of Investigation

Data were collected over a period of three years from a sample of over 400 project leaders in predominantly technical undertakings, such as electronics, petrochemical, construction, and pharmaceutical projects. The

Table 1

Challenges of Managing Projects According to Plan

Rank	Challenge	Frequency (Mentioned by % of PM's)
1	Coping with End-Date Driven Schedules	85%
2	Coping with Resource Limitations	83%
3	Communicating Effectively among Task Groups	80%
4	Gaining Commitment from Team Members	74%
5	Establishing Measurable Milestones	70%
6	Coping with Changes	60%
7	Working Out Project Plan Agreement with Team	57%
8	Gaining Commitment from Management	45%
9	Dealing with Conflict	42%
10	Managing Vendors and Subcontractors	38%
11	Other Challenges	35%

[1]This article was previously published in the *1985 Proceedings of the Project Management Institute,* 16th Annual Seminar/Symposium, Denver, Colorado.

data were collected mostly by questionnaires from attendees of project management workshops and seminars, as well as during in-plant consulting work conducted by the authors. Selectively, questionnaires were followed up by personal interviews. All data were checked for relevant sourcing to assure that the people who filled in the questionnaire had the minimum project leadership qualifications we established. These included: Two years of experience in managing multidisciplinary projects, leading a minimum of three other project professionals, and being formally accountable for final results.

Table 2

Potential Problems* (Subtle Reasons) Leading
to Schedule Slips and Budget Overruns

01 Difficulty of Defining Work in Sufficient Detail
02 Little Involvement of Project Personnel During Planning
03 Problems with Organizing and Building Project Team
04 No Firm Agreement to Project Plan by Functional Management
05 No Clear Charter for Key Project Personnel
06 Insufficiently Defined Project Team Organization
07 No Clear Role/Responsibility Definition for P-Personnel
08 Rush into Project Kick-off
09 Project Perceived as Not Important or Exciting
10 No Contingency Provisions
11 Inability to Measure True Project Performance
12 Poor Communications with Upper Management
13 Poor Communications with Customer or Sponsor
14 Poor Understanding of Organizational Interfaces
15 Difficulty in Working across Functional Lines
16 No Ties between Project Performance and Reward System
17 Poor Project Leadership
18 Weak Assistance and Help from Upper Management
19 Project Leader Not Involved with Team
20 Ignorant of Early Warning Signals and Feedback
21 Poor Ability to Manage Conflict
22 Credibility Problems with Task Leaders
23 Difficulties in Assessing Risks
24 Insensitivity to Organizational Culture/Value System
25 Insufficient Formal Procedural Project Guidelines
26 Apathy or Indifference by Project Team or Management
27 No Mutual Trust among Team Members
28 Too Much Unresolved/Dysfunctional Conflict
29 Power Struggles
30 Too Much Reliance on Established Cost Accounting System

*The tabulated potential problems represent summaries of data compiled during interviews with project personnel and management.

Sample Characteristics

The final qualifying sample included 304 project leaders from 183 technical projects. Each leader had an average of 5.2 years of project management experience. As shown by the sigma/standard deviation[2] the sample data are distributed widely:

Number of Project Leaders in Sample 304
Number of Projects in Sample 183
Number of Project Leaders
   per Project . . . . 1.66 ($\sigma = 1$)
Project Size (Average) . . . . $850K ($\sigma = 310K$)
Project Duration (Average) . . . 12 Months ($\sigma = 4$)
Multidisciplinary Nature
   (Average) . . . . 8 Team Members ($\sigma = 5$)
Project Management
   Experience/PM . . . . 5.2 Years ($\sigma = 2.5$)
Number of Previous Projects/PM . . . 6 ($\sigma = 4.5$)

Data were collected in three specific modes: (1) Open ended questions leading to a broad set of data, such as condensed in Table 2, and used for broad classifications and further, more detailed investigations; (2) Specific questions, requested to be answered on a tested five-point scale, such as shown in Figure 1. The scores enabled subsequent data ranking and correlation analysis; and (3) Interviews leading to a discussion of the previous findings and further qualitative investigations into the practices and experiences of project managers and their superiors.

All associations were measured by utilizing Kendall's Tau rank-order correlation. The agreement between project managers and their superiors on the reason for project control problems was tested by using the non-parametric Kruskal-Wallis one-way analysis of variance by ranks, setting the null-hypothesis for agreement at various confidence levels depending on the strength of the agreement or disagreement as specified in the write-up.

Discussion Of Results

The results of this study are being presented in four parts. First, the reasons for poor project control are analyzed as they relate to budget overruns and schedule slips. Second, the less tangible criteria for these control problems are discussed. This part shows that many of the reasons blamed for poor project perform-

[2]The distribution of the sample data is skewed. The sigma/standard deviation listed in parentheses corresponds to the positive side only.

Rank by		Reason or Problem	Rarely Sometimes Often Most Likely Always	Agreement Between GM & PM
General Managers	Project Managers		1 2 3 4 5	
1	10	Insufficient Front-End Planning	GM / PM	Disagree
2	3	Unrealistic Project Plan		Strongly Agree
3	8	Project Scope Underestimated		Disagree
4	1	Customer/Management Changes		Disagree
5	14	Insufficient Contingency Planning		Disagree
6	13	Inability to Track Progress	GM / PM	Disagree
7	5	Inablity to Detect Problems Early		Agree
8	9	Insufficient Number of Checkpoints		Agree
9	4	Staffing Problems		Disagree
10	2	Technical Complexities		Disagree
11	6	Priority Shifts		Disagree
12	10	No Commitment by Personnel to Plan		Agree
13	12	Uncooperative Support Groups		Agree
14	7	Sinking Team Spirit		Disagree
15	15	Unqualified Project Personnel		Agree

Directly Observed Reasons for Schedule Slips and Budget Overruns
Figure 1

ance, such as insufficient front-end planning and underestimating the complexities and scope, are really rooted in some less obvious organizational, managerial, and interpersonal problems. Third, the relationship between project performance and project management problems is discussed, and fourth, the criteria for effective project controls are summarized.

The Reasons for Poor Project Control

Figure 1 summarizes an investigation into 15 problem areas regarding their effects on poor project performance. Specifically, project managers and their superiors (such as senior functional managers and general managers) indicate on a five-point scale their perception of how frequently certain problems are responsible for schedule slips and budget overruns. The data indicate that project leaders perceive these problem areas in a somewhat different order than their superiors.

While *project leaders* most frequently blame the following reasons as being responsible for poor project performance:
1. Customer and Management Changes
2. Technical Complexities
3. Unrealistic Project Plans
4. Staffing Problems
5. Inability to Detect Problems Early,
senior management ranks these reasons somewhat differently:
1. Insufficient Front-End Planning
2. Unrealistic Project Plans
3. Underestimated Project Scope
4. Customer and Management Changes
5. Insufficient Contingency Planning
On balance, the data supports the findings of subsequent interviews that project leaders are more concerned with external influences such as changes, complexities, staffing, and priorities while senior

managers focus more on what should and can be done to avoid problems.

In fact, the differences between project leaders' and senior/superior management's perceptions were measured statistically by using a Kruskal-Wallis analysis of variance by ranks, based on the following test statistics:

Strong Agreement: If acceptable at > 99% confidence

Agreement: If acceptable at > 90% confidence

Weak Agreement: If acceptable at > 80% confidence

Disagreement: If rejected at 80% confidence

Project leaders disagree with their superiors on the ranking of importance for all but six reasons. What this means is that while both groups of management actually agree on the basic reasons behind schedule slips and budget overruns, they attach different weights. The practical implication of this finding is that senior management expects proper project planning, organizing, and tracking from project leaders. They further believe that the "external" criteria, such as customer changes and project complexities, impact project performance only if the project had not been defined properly and sound management practices were ignored. On the other side, management's view that some of the subtle problems, such as sinking team spirit, priority shifts, and staffing, are of lesser importance might point to a potential problem area. Management might be less sensitive to these struggles, get less involved, and provide less assistance in solving these problems.

Less Obvious and Less Visible
Reasons for Poor Performance

Managers at all levels have long lists of "real" reasons why the problems identified in Figure 1 occur. They point out, for instance, that while insufficient front-end planning eventually got the project into trouble, the real culprits are much less obvious and visible. These subtle reasons, summarized in Table 2, strike a common theme. They relate strongly to organizational, managerial, and human aspects. In fact, the most frequently mentioned reasons for poor project performance can be classified in five categories:

1. Problems with organizing project team
2. Weak project leadership
3. Communication problems
4. Conflict and confusion
5. Insufficient upper management involvement

Most of the problems in Table 2 relate to the manager's ability to foster a work environment conducive to multidisciplinary teamwork, rich on professionally stimulating and interesting activities, involvement, and mutual trust. The ability to foster such a high-performance project environment requires sophisticated skills in leadership, technical, interpersonal, and administrative areas. To be effective, project managers must consider all facets of the job. They must consider the task, the people, the tools, and the organization. The days of the manager who gets by with technical expertise or pure administrative skills alone, are gone. Today the project manager must relate socially as well as technically. He or she must understand the culture and value system of the organization. Research[3] and experience show that effective project management is directly related to the level of proficiency at which these skills are mastered. This is also reflected in the 30 potential problems of our study (See Table 2) and the rank order correlations summarized in Table 3. As indicated by the correlation figure of $\tau = +.45$, the stronger managers felt about the reasons in Figure 1, the stronger they also felt about the problems in Table 2 as reasons for poor project performance. This correlation is statistically significant at a confidence level of 99% and supports the conclusion that both sets of problem areas are related and require similar skills for effective management.

Management Practice and Project Performance

Managers appear very confident in citing actual and potential problems. These managers are sure in their own mind that these problems, summarized in Figure 1 and Table 2, are indeed related to poor project performance. However, no such conclusion could be drawn without additional data and the specific statistical test shown in Table 3. As indicated by the strongly negative correlations between project performance and (1) potential problems ($\tau = -.55$) and (2) actual problems ($\tau = -.40$), the presence of either problem will indeed result in lower performance. Specifically, the stronger and more frequently project managers experience these problems, the lower was the manager judged by supe-

---

[3]For a detailed discussion of skill requirements of project managers and their impact on project performance see H. J. Thamhain & D. L. Wilemon, "Skill Requirements of Project Managers," *Convention Record, IEEE Joint Engineering Management Conference,* October 1978, and H. J. Thamhain, "Developing Engineering Management Skills" in *Management of R & D and Engineering,* North Holland Publishing Company, 1986.

Potential Problems vs. Actual	Correlation of (1) Potential Problems (Table 2) and (2) Directly Observed Reasons for Budget and Schedule Slips (Figure 1)	$\tau = -.45$ **
Potential Problems vs. Performance	Correlation of (1) Potential Problems Leading for Budget and Schedule Slips (Table 2) and (2) Project Performance (Top Management Judgment)	$\tau = -.55$ **
Actual Problems vs. Performance	Correlation of (1) Directly Observed Reasons for Budget and Schedule Slips (Figure 1) and (2) Project Performance	$\tau = -.40$ **

All Tau values are   **99% Confidence Level (p = .01)
Kendall Tau
Rank-Order Correlation

Correlation of Project Management
Practices to Performance
Table 3

rior managers regarding overall on-time and on-budget performance.

Furthermore, it is interesting to note that the more subtle, potential problems correlate most strongly to poor performance ($\tau = -.55$). In fact, special insight has been gained by analyzing the association of each problem to project performance separately. Taken together, it shows that the following problems seem to be some of the most crucial *barriers* to high project performance:

• Team organization and staffing problems
• Work perceived not important, challenging, having growth potential
• Little team and management involvement during planning
• Conflict, confusion, power struggle
• Lacking commitment by team and management
• Poor project definition
• Difficulty in understanding and working across organizational interfaces
• Weak project leadership
• Measurability problems
• Changes, contingencies, and priority problems
• Poor communications, management involvement and support

To be effective, project leaders must not only recognize the potential barriers to performance, but also know where in the lifecycle of the project they most likely occur. The effective project leader takes preventive actions early in the project lifecycle and fosters a work environment that is conducive to active participation, interesting work, good communications, management involvement, and low conflict.

Criteria For Effective Project Control

The results presented so far focused on the reasons for poor project performance. That is, what went wrong and why were analyzed. This section concentrates on the lessons learned from the study and extensive interviews investigating the forces driving high project performance. Accordingly, this section summarizes the criteria which seem to be important for controlling projects according to plan. The write-up follows a recommendations format and flows with the project through its lifecycle wherever possible.

1. *Detailed Project Planning.* Develop a detailed project plan, involving all key personnel, defining the specific work to be performed, the timing, the resources, and the responsibilities.
2. *Break the overall program into phases and subsystems.* Use Work Breakdown Structure (WBS) as a planning tool.
3. *Results and Deliverables.* Define the program objectives and requirements in terms of specifications, schedule, resources and deliverable items for the total program and its subsystems.
4. *Measurable Milestones.* Define measurable milestones and checkpoints throughout the program. Measurability can be enhanced by defining specific results, deliverables, technical performance measures against schedule and budget.
5. *Commitment.* Obtain commitment from all key personnel regarding the program plan, its measures and results. This commitment can be enhanced and maintained by involving the team members early in the project planning, including the definition of results, measurable milestones, schedules and budgets. It is through this involvement that the team members gain a detailed understanding of the work to be performed, develop professional interests in the project and desires to succeed, and eventually make a firm commitment toward the specific task and the overall project objectives.
6. *Intra-Program Involvement.* Assure that the in-

terfacing project teams, such as engineering and manufacturing, work together, not only during the task transfer, but during the total life of the project. Such interphase involvement is necessary to assure effective implementation of the developments and to simply assure "doability" and responsiveness to the realities of the various functions supporting the project. It is enhanced by clearly defining the results/deliverables for each interphase point, agreed upon by both parties. In addition, a simple sign-off procedure, which defines who has to sign off on what items, is useful in establishing clear checkpoints for completion and to enhance involvement and cooperation of the interphasing team members.

7. *Project Tracking.* Define and implement a proper project tracking system which captures and processes project performance data conveniently summarized for reviews and management actions.

8. *Measurability.* Assure accurate measurements of project performance data, especially technical progress against schedule and budget.

9. *Regular Reviews.* Projects should be reviewed regularly, both on a work package (subsystem) level and total project level.

10. *Signing-On.* The process of "signing-on" project personnel during the initial phases of the project or each task seem to be very important to proper understanding of the project objectives, the specific tasks, and personal commitment. The sign-on process that is so well described in Tracy Kidders' book, *The Soul of a New Machine,* is greatly facilitated by sitting down with each team member and discussing the specific assignments, overall project objectives, as well as professional interests and support needs.

11. *Interesting Work.* The project leader should try to accommodate the professional interests and desires of supporting personnel when negotiating their tasks. Project effectiveness depends on the manager's ability to provide professionally stimulating and interesting work. This leads to increased project involvement, better communications, lower conflict, and stronger commitment. This is an environment where people work toward established objectives in a self-enforcing mode requiring a minimum of managerial controls. Although the scope of a project may be fixed, the project manager usually has a degree of flexibility in allocating task assignments among various contributors.

12. *Communication.* Good communication is essential for effective project work. It is the responsibility of the task leaders and ultimately the project manager to provide the appropriate communication tools, techniques, and systems. These tools are not only the status meetings, reviews, schedules, and reporting systems, but also the objective statements, specifications, list of deliverables, the sign-off procedure and critical path analysis. It is up to the project leaders to orchestrate the various tools and systems, and to use them effectively.

13. *Leadership.* Assure proper program direction and leadership throughout the project lifecycle. This includes project definition, team organization, task coordination, problem identification and a search for solutions.

14. *Minimize Threats.* Project managers must foster a work environment that is low on personal conflict, power struggles, surprises, and unrealistic demands. An atmosphere of mutual trust is necessary for project personnel to communicate problems and concerns candidly and at an early point in time.

15. *Design a Personnel Appraisal and Reward System.* This should be consistent with the responsibilities of the people.

16. *Assure Continuous Senior Management Involvement, Endorsement, and Support of the Project.* This will surround the project with a priority image, enhance its visibility, and refuel overall commitment to the project and its objectives.

17. *Personal Drive.* Project managers can influence the climate of the work environment by their own actions. Concern for project team members, ability to integrate personal goals and needs of project personnel with project goals, and ability to create personal enthusiasm for the project itself can foster a climate of high motivation, work involvement, open communication, and ultimately high project performance.

A Final Note

Managing engineering programs toward established performance, schedule, and cost targets requires more than just another plan. It requires the total commitment of the performing organization plus the involvement and help of the sponsor/customer community. Successful program managers stress the importance of carefully designing the project planning and control system as well as the structural and authority relationships. All are critical to the implementation of an effective project control system. Other organizational issues, such as management style, personnel appraisals and compensation, and intraproject communication, must be carefully considered to make the system self-forcing; that is, project personnel throughout the organization must feel that participation in the project is desirable regarding the fulfillment of their professional needs and wants. Furthermore, project personnel must be convinced that management involvement is helpful in their work. Personnel must be convinced that identifying the true project status and communicating potential problems early will provide them with more assistance to problem solving, more cross-functional support, and in the end will lead to project success and the desired recognition for their accomplishments.

In summary, effective control of engineering programs or projects involves the ability to:

- Work out a detailed project plan, involving all key personnel
- Reach agreement on the plan among the project team members and the customer/sponsor
- Obtain commitment from the project team members
- Obtain commitment from management
- Define measurable milestones
- Attract and hold quality people
- Establish a controlling authority for each work package
- Detect problems early

References

1. Adams, J. R., & Barndt, S. E. Behavioral Implications of the Project Life Cycle. Chapter 12 in *Project Management Handbook*. New York: Van Nostrand Reinhold, 1983.
2. Archibald, Russel C. Planning the Project. In *Managing High-Technology Programs and Projects*. New York: Wiley, 1976.
3. Casher, J. D. How to Control Project Risks and Ef-fectively Reduce the Chance of Failure. *Management Review,* June, 1984.
4. Delaney, W. A. Management by Phases. *Advanced Management Journal,* Winter, 1984.
5. King, W. R., & Cleland, D. I. Life Cycle Management. Chapter 11 in *Project Management Handbook*. New York: Van Nostrand Reinhold, 1983.
6. McDounough, E. F., & Kinnunen, R. M. Management Control of a New Product Development Project. *IEEE Transactions on Engineering Management,* February, 1984.
7. Pessemier, E. A. *Product Management*. New York: Wiley, 1982.
8. Spirer, H. F. Phasing out the Project. Chapter 13 in *Project Management Handbook*. New York: Van Nostrand Reinhold, 1983.
9. Stuckenbruck, L. C. Interface Management. Chapter 20 in *Matrix Management Systems Handbook*. New York: Van Nostrand Reinhold, 1984.
10. Thamhain, H. J. *Engineering Program Management*. New York: Wiley, 1984.
11. Thamhain, H. J., & Wilemon, D. L. Project Performance Measurement, The Keystone to Engineering Project Control. *Project Management Quarterly,* January, 1982.
12. Thamhain, H. J., & Wilemon, D. L. Conflict Management in Project Lifecycles. *Sloan Management Review,* Summer, 1975.
13. Tuminello, J. A Case Study of Information/Know-How Transfer. *IEEE Engineering Management Review,* June, 1984.
14. Urban, G. L., & Hauser, J. R. *Design and Marketing of New Products*. New York: Prentice Hall, 1980.
15. U.S. Air Force. *Systems Management - System Program Office Manual,* AFSCM 375-3, Washington, DC, 1964.

Dr. Hans J. Thamhain is an Associate Professor at the Management Department, Worcester Polytechnic Institute. Dr. David Wilemon is a Professor of Marketing Management at the School of Management, Syracuse University.

* * *

Reviews, Walkthroughs, and Inspections

GERALD M. WEINBERG AND DANIEL P. FREEDMAN

Reprinted from *IEEE Transactions on Software Engineering*, Volume SE-10, Number 1, January 1984, pages 68-72. Copyright © 1984 by Gerald M. Weinberg and Daniel P. Freedman.

Abstract—Formal technical reviews supply the quality measurement to the "cost effectiveness" equation in a project management system. There are several unique formal technical review procedures, each applicable to particular types of technical material and to the particular mix of the Review Committee. All formal technical reviews produce reports on the overall quality for project management, and specific technical information for the producers. These reports also serve as an historic account of the systems development process. Historic origins and future trends of formal and informal technical reviews are discussed.

Index Terms—Project management, software development management, technical reviews.

The Problem of Controlling Technical Information

ANY CONTROL system requires reliable information. A project management system normally obtains its information by two quite different routes, as indicated in Fig. 1. *Cost and schedule information* comes in channels relatively independent of the producing unit, and can thus be relied upon to detect cost overruns and schedule slippages. *Evaluation of technical output*, however, is often another matter.

If project management is not in a position to evaluate technical output directly, it must rely on the producing unit's own evaluation—a dangerous game if that unit is malfunctioning. If the unit is technically weak in a certain area, the unit's judgment will be weak in the same area. Just where the work is poorest, the evaluation sent to management will be least likely to show the weakness.

But even if the producing unit is not technically weak, the problem of unreliable information persists because of information overload. As a unit overloads, inadequate supervision may affect work quality—while at the same time affecting the quality of the evaluation. The unit *wants* to be done on schedule and *wants* the work to be correct. Under pressure, any human being will see what is wanted instead of what exists. Just when it is needed most, this control system utterly fails.

The Role of the Formal Technical Review

Formal technical reviews come in many variations, under many names, but all play the same role in project management, as indicated in Fig. 2. As in Fig. 1, the producing unit controls its own development work, perhaps even conducting informal reviews internally. At the level of the producing unit, in fact, the use of the formal technical review requires no

Manuscript received January 5, 1983.

G. M. Weinberg is with Weinberg and Weinberg, Rural Route Two, Lincoln, NE 68505.

D. P. Freedman is with Ethnotech, Inc., P. O. Box 6627, Lincoln, NE 68506.

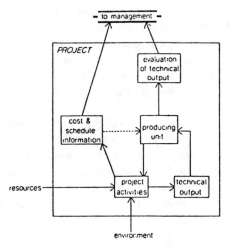

Fig. 1. Management's view of the output of a programming effort.

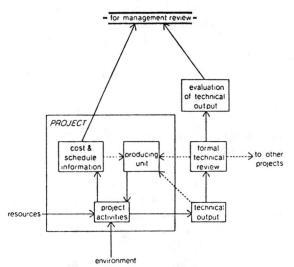

Fig. 2. The place of the formal technical review.

change, which simplifies its introduction as a project management tool.

As the diagram shows, the formal review is conducted by people who are *not part of that producing unit*. Hopefully, these are people who have no conscious or unconscious reason for favoring or disfavoring the project's work. Moreover, their report—the technical review summary report—goes to management, thus providing *reliable information* to be used in *management reviews* of the project.

Management Reviews Versus Technical Reviews

Fig. 2 also illustrates the difference between a *technical* review and a *management* review, sometimes called a "project review" or some similar name. The technical review committee is staffed by technical people and studies only technical issues. Its job is to put the evaluation of technical output on the same reliable basis as, say, cost and schedule information to management. Using both sorts of information, management can now make informed judgments of what is to be done in controlling the project.

It should also be noted that most "project control" systems do not concern themselves with the accurate and reliable evaluation of the quality of technical output. Instead, they concern themselves with measuring what can be measured *without* technical review, assuming, more or less, that one module of 300 lines of code is just like any other. If that assumption of quality is correct, then these systems can provide excellent management information for project control.

If that assumption is not correct, however, then only the "cost" side of the "cost effectiveness" ledger has any meaning. Under such conditions, even the best project control systems can provide only an illusion of control. The consequences are familiar enough—missed schedules, cost overruns, unmet specifications, inadequate performance, error-prone production, and huge and never ending maintenance.

Review Reports and Project Management

Whatever goes on *inside* it, the major project control function of *any* review is to provide *management* a reliable answer to the fundamental question:

Does this product do the job it is supposed to do?

Once any piece of work has been reviewed and accepted, it becomes part of the system. Subject to a very small risk factor, it is

1) complete,
2) correct,
3) dependable as a base for related work, and
4) measurable for purposes of tracking progress.

Without reviews, there are no *reliable* methods for measuring the progress of a project. *Sometimes* we get dependable reports from the producers themselves, but *sometimes* is not good enough. No matter how good their *intentions,* producers are simply not in a position to give consistently reliable reports on their own products.

For small, simple objects, with well-intentioned, competent producers, there is some chance of success without reliable progress measures. As projects grow larger and more complex, however, the chance of some self-report being overly optimistic becomes a certainty.

Whatever the system of formal reviews, the review reporting serves as a formal commitment by technically competent and unbiased people that a piece of work is complete, correct, and dependable. The review report states as accurately as possible the completeness and acceptability of a piece of software work, be it specifications, design, code, documentation, test plan, or whatever.

By themselves, these review reports do not guarantee that a project will not end up in crisis or failure. It is up to the management of the project to use the information in the review reports to make management decisions needed to keep the project on track. Well done review reports are not suf-ficient to make a project succeed, though poorly done reviews, or no reviews at all, are sure to get a project in trouble—no matter how skilled the management or how sophisticated the project management system.

Types of Technical Review Reports

The one report that is always generated by a *formal* review is the *technical review summary report*. This report carries the conclusions of the review to management, and thus is the fundamental link between the review process and the project management system.

Other reports *may* be generated. Issues raised that must be brought to the attention of the producers are placed on a *technical review issues list*.

If issues are raised about something other than the reviewed work itself, a *technical review related issues report* is created for each issue.

On occasion, an organization will institute some *research report*, such as a detailed breakdown of standards used and broken, or a report of hits and misses on a checklist.

Those cases where the review leader has to give a report of a failed review (not a failed product) lead to a *review process report*, the form and content of which will be unique to the situation and organization. For instance, on delicate matters the review process report may be verbal.

Other participants may also report on the process of the review itself. For instance, one or more participants might want to object to the behavior of the review leader.

The Review Summary Report

For effective project management, review summary reports must identify three items:

1) What was reviewed?
2) Who did the reviewing?
3) What was their conclusion?

Fig. 3 shows a widely used format containing these items. Although formats vary, the summary should generally be confined to a single page, lest its conclusion be lost in a forest of words.

The Technical Review Issues List

Whereas the summary report is primarily a report to management, the issues list is primarily a report to the producers. The issues list tells the producers *why* their work was not fully acceptable as is, hopefully in sufficient detail to enable them to remedy the situation.

The issues list is primarily a communication from one technical group to another. It is not intended for nontechnical readers and therefore need not be "translated" for their eyes. Moreover, it is a *transient* communication, in that once the issues are resolved, the list might as well disappear. (We exclude, for the moment, research use of the list). Therefore, the issues list need not be fancy, as long as it is clear.

Practices vary, but among our clients, management does not routinely get the issues list. The summary report already contains, in its assessment of the work, a weighted opinion of the seriousness of the issues, so management need not be burdened with extra paper and technical details.

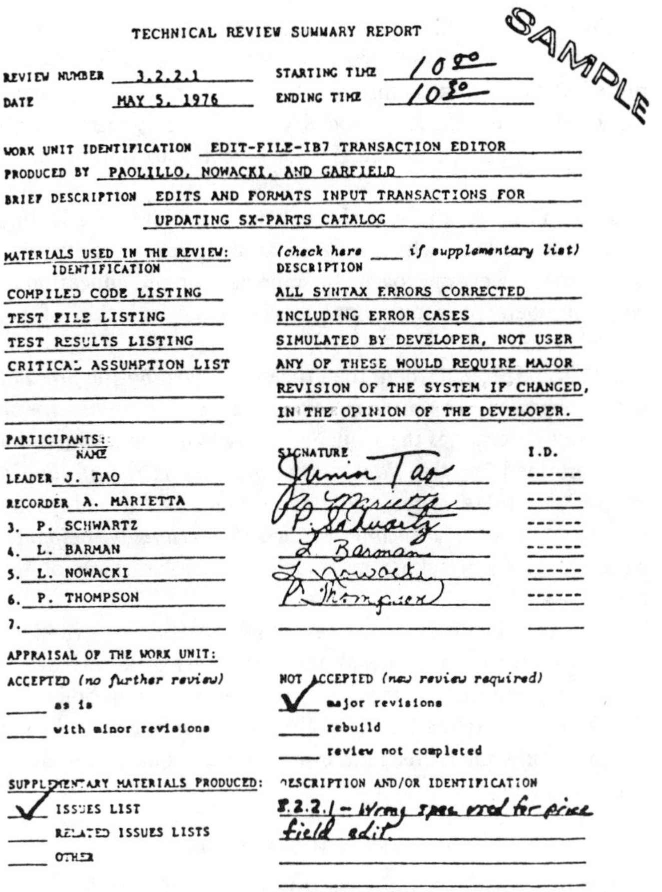

TECHNICAL REVIEW SUMMARY REPORT

SAMPLE

REVIEW NUMBER 3.2.2.1 STARTING TIME 10⁰⁰

DATE MAY 5, 1976 ENDING TIME 10³⁰

WORK UNIT IDENTIFICATION EDIT-FILE-IB7 TRANSACTION EDITOR

PRODUCED BY PAOLILLO, NOWACKI, AND GARFIELD

BRIEF DESCRIPTION EDITS AND FORMATS INPUT TRANSACTIONS FOR UPDATING SX-PARTS CATALOG

MATERIALS USED IN THE REVIEW: (check here ____ if supplementary list)

IDENTIFICATION	DESCRIPTION
COMPILED CODE LISTING	ALL SYNTAX ERRORS CORRECTED
TEST FILE LISTING	INCLUDING ERROR CASES
TEST RESULTS LISTING	SIMULATED BY DEVELOPER, NOT USER
CRITICAL ASSUMPTION LIST	ANY OF THESE WOULD REQUIRE MAJOR
	REVISION OF THE SYSTEM IF CHANGED,
	IN THE OPINION OF THE DEVELOPER.

PARTICIPANTS:

NAME	SIGNATURE	I.D.
LEADER J. TAO	Junior Tao	------
RECORDER A. MARIETTA	A. Marietta	------
3. P. SCHWARTZ	P. Schwartz	------
4. L. BARMAN	L. Barman	------
5. L. NOWACKI	L. Nowacki	------
6. P. THOMPSON	P. Thompson	------
7.		

APPRAISAL OF THE WORK UNIT:

ACCEPTED (no further review)

____ as is

____ with minor revisions

NOT ACCEPTED (new review required)

✓ major revisions

____ rebuild

____ review not completed

SUPPLEMENTARY MATERIALS PRODUCED: DESCRIPTION AND/OR IDENTIFICATION

✓ ISSUES LIST 3.2.2.1 – Wrong spec used for price field edit.

____ RELATED ISSUES LISTS

____ OTHER

Fig. 3. A technical review summary report.

The issues list need not be *concealed* from management, but when managers routinely receive lists of issues, they naturally try to use the information. For example, they may count issues as a means of evaluating producers or reviewers—a practice which tends to undermine the quality of future reviews.

Another common subversion of the review process is the attempt to make the issues list into a *solutions list*. The job of the review committee is to raise issues; the job of the producing unit is to resolve them. A review committee is generally no better at resolving issues than a producing unit is at raising them. Management may want to see issues lists from time to time to ensure that they are remaining issues lists, rather than solutions lists.

The Technical Review Related Issues Report

A related issue is something that comes up in the course of a review that does not happen to be the principal reason for the review. Examples of related issues might be:

1) a typographical error in a related document;

2) a hidden assumption in the specifications that makes part of one module obsolete;

3) a flaw in the original problem statement that makes the entire project plan invalid.

If an organization cannot handle issue 1) without alerting the management chain, it is probably in as bad a shape as an organization that handles issue 3) *without* alerting the management chain. The principal project management problem is with middle issues, such as 2). Such issues have always been troublesome to project control systems. When they are detected, the related issue report is a way of notifying *someone* who ought to be in a position to do something about them.

Because a related issue is, by definition, a deviation from smooth product development, there is really no way to develop a standard practice for handling all situations. A related issue report often descends like a bolt from the blue on some people who may not even know that a review is taking place. If it is not communicated in some standard, official form, people may not even recognize it. Therefore, if we want to keep related issue reports from passing directly into the wastebasket, we have got to give them *some* official status.

The mildest approach is to use a standard *transmittal sheet*, identifying the source of the material and attached to the actual communication, which may take any convenient form. Some organizations prefer a formal follow-up system that requires that each related issue report receive a reply within a few days. Another approach is to send the related issue report through the appropriate manager, leaving any action or follow-up decision on the managerial level.

Historical Analyses

Some of the information obtained from an historical analysis of review reports can be extremely specific. For instance, many organizations classify the types of problems turned up in each review and tabulate the frequency of each type. A similar tabulation is made of errors that slip through the review only to be caught at a later stage.

Comparison of these tabulations—in total, by review group, and by producer—provides clear guidance for future educational and reviewing practices. It is essential, however, that this information be used for improvement of project management, not for punishment of individuals, lest the whole scheme backfire and produce better methods of concealing errors and deficiencies.

To illustrate appropriate use of such historical analyses, let us say that most of the flaws detected during code reviews centered around the module interfaces. If this deficiency was project-wide, the training department could set up special training for everyone, guided by the specific types of interfacing errors recorded in the review reports.

Or perhaps the interfacing errors, upon analysis, reveal a weakness in project standards concerning interfaces. Whatever the problem, the historical records should first make it visible, them make it measurable, and finally help narrow it down to its true source.

Reviews and Phases

Any time after a project begins, an accurate, complete review report history can be compared with the schedule projected at the beginning of the development cycle. In which phases did the estimated time match the actual time? Where did the deviations occur? Were the deviations caused by problems in development? Were they mistakes in the original estimate?

Such historical information is obviously essential if project management is to improve from project to project. Yet such information will be meaningless if the "phases" of the project plan do not correspond to units of work marked at both beginning and end by reviews.

In order for any project control system to work, the system life cycle must be expressed in terms of measurable phases—some meaningful, reviewable product that represents the end of one phase and the beginning of the next. If there is nothing that can be reviewed, then nothing has been produced, and if nothing has been produced, how can it be controlled?

Varieties of Reviewed Materials

Much of the earliest public discussion of reviews focused on the varieties of *code reviews*, rather than reviews of other materials produced in the life cycle. In the early history of software development, we were primarily concerned with code accuracy, because the coding seemed to be the major stumbling block to reliable product development. As our coding improved, however, we began to see other problems that had been obscured by the tangle of coding errors.

At first we noticed that many of the difficulties were not coding errors but design errors, so more attention was devoted to *design reviews*. As these techniques begin to be effective at clearing up design problems, the whole cycle starts again, for we notice that design is no longer the major hurdle.

In many of these cases, we never clearly understood the problem the design was attempting to solve. We were solving a *situation*, not a problem. Currently, increased emphasis is being placed on the analysis process, which becomes the next area of application of technical reviews—*specification reviews*.

Other types of reviewed material include *documentation*, *test data* and *test plans*, *tools* and *packages*, *training materials*, *procedures* and *standards*, as well as any other "deliverable" used in a system.

Reviews of these materials are conducted not only during development, but also during operation and maintenance of the system.

Principal Varieties of Review Disciplines

It is possible to conduct a review without any particular discipline decided in advance, simply adjusting the course of the meeting to the demands of the product under review. Many reviews are conducted in just this way, but over time special disciplines tend to evolve which emphasize certain aspects of reviewing at the expense of others.

For instance, many of the best known review disciplines are attempts to "cover" a greater quantity of material in the review. The "inspection" approach tries to gain efficiency by focusing on a much narrower, much more sharply defined, set of questions. In some cases, an inspection consists of running through a checklist of faults, one after the other, over the entire product. Obviously, one danger of such an approach is from faults that do not appear on the checklist, so effective inspection systems generally evolve methods for augmenting checklists as experience grows.

Another way to try to cover more material is by having the

product "walked through" by someone who is very familiar with it—even specially prepared with a more or less formal presentation. Walking through the product, a lot of detail can be skipped—which is good if you are just trying to verify an overall approach or bad if your object is to find errors of detail.

In some cases, the walkthrough is very close to a lecture about the product—which suggests another reason for varying the formal review approach. In some cases, rapid education of large numbers of people may suggest some variation of the formal review.

In a walkthrough, then, the process is driven by the *product being reviewed*. In an inspection, *the list of points to be inspected* determines the sequence. In a plain review, the order is determined by the *flow of the meeting as it unfolds*. In contrast to these types, the various kinds of "round-robin" reviews emphasize a *cycling through the various participants*, with each person taking an equal and similar share of the entire task.

Round-robin reviews are especially useful in situations where the participants are at the same level of knowledge, a level that may not be too high. It ensures that nobody will shrink from participation through lack of confidence, while at the same time guaranteeing a more detailed look at the product, part by part.

Real Versus Ideal Reviews

Although many "pure" review systems have been described, people who observe actual reviews will never find one following all the "rules." By examining some of the real advantages and disadvantages of one of these "pure" systems, we can understand why every real review system involves aspects of all the major varieties. We will use the walkthrough as our example, but any system could be used to illustrate the same points.

With a walkthrough, because of the prior preparation of the presenter, a large amount of material can be moved through rather speedily. Moreover, since the reviews are far more passive than participating, larger numbers of people can become familiar with the walked through material. This larger audience can serve educational purposes, but it also can bring a great number of diverse viewpoints to bear on the presented material. If all in the audience are alert, and if they represent a broad cross section of skills and viewpoints, the walkthrough can give strong statistical assurance that no major oversight lies concealed in the material.

Another advantage of the walkthrough is that it does not make many demands on the participants for preparation in advance. Where there are large numbers of participants, or where the participants come from diverse organizations not under the same operational control, it may prove impossible to get everyone prepared for the review. In such cases, the walkthrough may be the only reasonable way to ensure that all those present have actually looked at the material.

The problems of the walkthrough spring rather directly from its unique advantages. Advance preparation is not required, so each participant may have a different depth of understanding. Those close to the work may be bored and not pay attention. Those who are seeing the work for the first time may not be able to keep up with the pace of presentation. In either case, the ability to raise penetrating issues is lost.

Why There is so Much Variety in Reviews

Although all reviews occupy the same role in project management as a control system, managers are justifiably confused by the great variety found in technical review practices. The practice of technical review differs from place to place for a variety of reasons, the principal ones being:

1) different external requirements, such as government contract provisions;

2) different internal organizations, such as the use or nonuse of teams;

3) continuity with past practices.

Continuity is probably the strongest reason. When it comes to social behavior, people tend to resist changing what they already do, even if it does not seem exceptionally productive in today's environment. In many project management systems, formal technical reviews have been introduced as a new form of some old practice, perhaps because it was easier to introduce reviews in this way.

How Reviews Evolved

The idea of reviews of software is as old as software itself. Every early software developer quickly came to understand that writing completely accurate programs was too great a problem for the unaided human mind—even the mind of a genius. Babbage showed his programs to Ada Lovelace, or to anyone else who would review them. John von Neumann regularly submitted his programs to his colleagues for review.

These reviews, in our terms, were *informal* reviews, because they did not involve formal procedures for connecting the review reports to a project management system. Informal review procedures were passed on from person to person in the general culture of computing for many years before they were acknowledged in print. The need for reviewing was so obvious to the best programmers that they rarely mentioned it in print, while the worst programmers believed they were so good that *their* work did not need reviewing.

Around the end of the 1950's, the creation of some large software projects began to make the need for some form of technical reviewing obvious to management all over the world. Most large projects had some sort of reviewing procedures, which evolved through the 1960's into more formalized ideas.

In the 1970's, publication espousing various review forms began to appear in the literature. For those interested in a history of publication, a bibliography appears in Freedman and Weinberg [1]. Publications, however, tend to conceal the grass-roots origin of reviews, giving the impression that they were "invented" by some person or company at a certain time and place.

Where Reviews Are Going

Today, the evolution of reviewing procedures continues, primarily on an experiential basis within projects. Reviews are a partial formalization of a natural social process, arising from the superhuman need for extreme precision in software. Therefore, the "science" of reviewing is a *social* science, and it is difficult to make general, quantifiable statements that apply to all reviews.

Some experimental work has been done on reviews, but these experiments generally suffer from the following problems:

1) Only one or two narrowly defined review procedures are examined.

2) Reviewers are novices in the procedures used.

3) The environment is significantly different from that of a real software development or maintenance environment.

Field reports overcome items 2) and 3), but introduce the problem of experimental control. Nevertheless, many of these reports indicate that effective project management is not possible without the technical review, in one form or another. These reports are sometimes puzzling to managers in other organizations, who have "tried reviews," but who have failed to overcome some of the human problems of changing entrenched social practices.

The best evidence for the effectiveness of reviews is that their use continues to spread. A body of practical knowledge has grown with this spread, particularly concerning the problems associated with starting a system of reviews. We anticipate that most future development of review technology will arise from such on-the-job experiments, rather than any theoretical or laboratory work.

References

[1] D. P. Freedman and G. M. Weinberg, *Handbook of Walkthroughs, Inspections, and Technical Reviews: Evaluating Programs, Projects, and Products*, 3rd ed. Boston, MA: Little, Brown and Company, 1982. (Because this reference contains an extensive bibliography, we are omitting further references here.)

Gerald M. Weinberg, photograph and biography not available at the time of publication.

Daniel P. Freedman, photograph and biography not available at the time of publication.

The Unit Development Folder (UDF): A Ten-Year Perspective

Frank S. Ingrassia
TRW Systems Engineering and Development Division
One Space Park
Redondo Beach, California 90278

Abstract

This paper is an annotated version of the original 1976 description of the content and application of the Unit Development Folder, a structured mechanism for organizing and collecting software development products (requirements, design, code, test plans/data) as they become available. Properly applied, the Unit Development Folder is an important part of an orderly development environment in which unit-level schedules and responsibilities are clearly delineated and their step-by-step accomplishment made visible to management. Unit Development Folders have been used on a number of projects at TRW and have been shown to reduce many of the problems associated with the development of software.

Ten years of application have not diminished the viability of this tool. This is probably due to the fact that it is a basic, simple, adaptable, and natural approach to software development. Experience has shown, however, that its effectiveness has been uneven. This is not surprising since the effectiveness of any tool is dependent on proper and diligent use. More fundamentally, tools will not resolve or compensate for intrinsic deficiencies in the software development environment. Everyone knows that the most critical aspect in developing software is to have a clear, consistent, well structured, and complete set of requirements at the beginning of the development process. Everyone knows this but many choose to compromise this principle. If you don't know where you are going, tools will not help you get to the right place.

One of the main side effects resulting from the invention of computers has been the creation of a new class of frustrated and harried managers responsible for software development. The frustration is a result of missed schedules, cost overruns, inadequate implementation and design, high operational error rates, and poor maintainability, which have historically characterized software development. In the early days of computer programming, these problems were often excused by the novelty of this unique endeavor and obscured by the language and experience gap that frequently existed between developers and managers. Today's maturity and the succession of computer-wise people to management positions does not appear to have reduced the frustration level in the industry. We are still making the same mistakes and getting into the same predicaments. The science of managing software development is still in its infancy and the lack of a good clear set of principles is apparent.

The problems associated with developing software are too numerous and too complex for anyone to pretend to have solved them, and this paper makes no such pretensions. The discussion that follows describes a simple but effective management tool which, when properly used, can reduce the chaos and alleviate many of the problems common in software development. The tool described in this paper is called the Unit Development Folder (UDF) and is being used at TRW in software development and management.

What is a UDF? Simply stated, it is a specific form of development notebook which has proven useful and effective in collecting and organizing software products as they are produced. In essence, however, it is much more; it is a means of imposing a management philosophy and a development methodology on an activity that is often chaotic. In physical appearance, a UDF is merely a three-ring binder containing a cover sheet and is organized into several predefined sections which are common to each UDF. The ultimate objectives that the content and format of the UDF must satisfy are to:

(1) Provide an orderly and consistent approach in the development of each of the units of a program or project

(2) Provide a uniform and visible collection point for all unit documentation and code

(3) Aid individual discipline in the establishment and attainment of scheduled unit-level milestones

(4) Provide low-level management visibility and control over the development process

Figure 1 illustrates the role of the UDF in the total software development process.

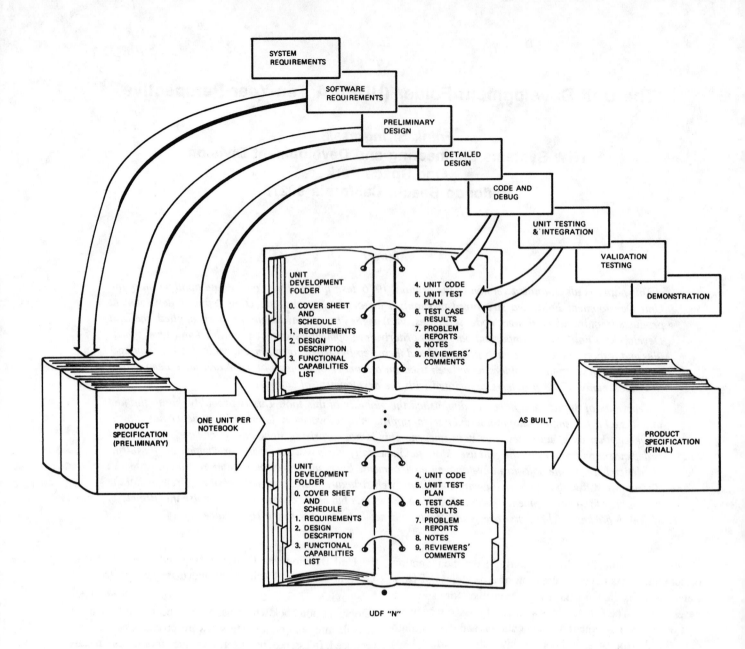

Figure 1. The UDF in the Development Process

If one follows a fairly standard design approach, the completion of the preliminary design activity marks the point at which UDFs are created and initiated for all units comprising the total product to be designed and coded. Therefore, the first question to be answered is, "What is a unit?" It was found that, for the purpose of implementing a practical and effective software development methodology to meet the management objectives stated earlier, a unique element of software architecture needed to be defined. This basic functional element is designated a "unit" of software and is defined independently of the language or type of application. Experience has indicated that it is unwise to attempt a simple-minded definition which will be useful and effective in all situations. What can be done is to bound the problem by means of some general considerations and delegate the specific implementation to management judgment for each particular application.

In retrospect, the preceding paragraph proved to be misleading. The intent was not to introduce and define a new software architectural entity, but a management entity which reflected the partitioning of the development effort. As a result, some people proceeded to define and establish "units" as architectural subdivisions, which often did not represent good functional delineations and were not logically addressable in the detailed description document. A more accurate concept of the UDF is that it encompasses a "unit of work."

At the lower end of the scale a "unit" can be defined to be a single routine or subroutine. At the upper end of the scale a "unit" may contain several routines comprising a subprogram or module. However it is defined, a unit of software should possess the following characteristics:

(1) It performs a specific defined function.

(2) It is amenable to development by one person within the assigned schedule.

(3) It is a level of software to which the satisfaction of requirements can be traced.

(4) It is amenable to thorough testing in a disciplined environment.

The keyword in the concept is manageability — in design, development, testing, and comprehension.

A natural question that may arise at this point is, "Why should a unit contain more than one routine?" The assumption for this proviso is that the design and development standards impose both size and functional modularity. Since functional modularity can be defined at various levels, the concept can become meaningless if it is not accompanied by a reasonable restriction of size. Consequently, the maximum-size constraint on routines may sometimes result in multiple-routine units.

There have been various attempts to establish simple, general rules for designating the units. In one situation, it was decided that there would be one UDF per routine. This resulted in a large number of UDFs, each with its own test plan/procedures, and a large number of requirements that were split and allocated to more than one unit. This strategy undoubtably had a negative effect on both cost and schedule since, 1) it increased the number of units and associated paperwork severalfold, 2) it did not take advantage of logical associations for requirements allocation and testing, and 3) it delayed the accomplishment of low-level integration.

In another situation, it was decided that each UDF would contain a Computer Program Component (CPC) as delineated in the preliminary design. Unfortunately, the CPCs were structured along strict, but high-level, functional aspects. That resulted in UDF size variation from one routine to two-hundred routines. This produced some extremely large UDFs that were practically unmanageable and had to be internally partitioned into smaller units. This strategy undoubtably also had a negative impact on cost and schedule due to the complexities and higher percentage of errors that occur as a function of size.

The lessons learned were:

(1) That the apportionment and allocation of software components into units can have a significant effect on cost and schedule results, and

(2) There is no general rule that can substitute for good judgment and planning.

Ideally, to assist both the documentation and the integration processes, it is advantageous if the units correspond directly to CPCs. However, this requires some thoughtful planning during architectural design, and may not always be feasible or practical.

The organization and content of a UDF can be adapted to reflect local conditions or individual project requirements. The important considerations in the structuring of a UDF are:

(1) The number of subdivisions is not so large as to be confusing or unmanageable.

(2) Each of the sections contributes to the management and visibility of the development process.

(3) The content and format of each section are adequately and unambiguously defined.

(4) The subdivisions are sufficiently flexible to be applicable to a variety of software types.

(5) The individual sections are chronologically ordered as nearly as possible.

The last item is very important since it is this aspect of the UDF that relates it to the development schedule and creates an auditable management instrument. An example of a typical cover sheet for a UDF is shown in Figure 2; the contents of each section will be briefly described in subsequent paragraphs.

The UDF is initiated when requirements are allocated to the unit level and at the onset of preliminary design. At this point it exists in the skeletal form of a binder with a cover sheet (indicating the unit name and responsible custodian) and a set of section separators. The first step in the process is for the responsible work area manager to integrate the development schedules and responsibilities for each of his UDFs into the overall schedule and milestones of the project. A due date is generated for the completion of each section and the responsibility for each section is assigned. The originators should participate in establishing their interim schedules within the constraints of the dictated end dates.

The first sentence of the preceding paragraph is badly written and somewhat misleading since it assumes that the software requirements are sufficiently detailed and well structured to allow the UDF definition process to proceed from consideration of the requirements alone. This is not always the case since requirements specifications vary considerably in their depth, structure, and level of detail. It may well be that the units cannot be adequately defined until near the end of the preliminary design phase. The exact time/date of UDF initiation is not as important as assuring that the allocation is reasonable and efficient.

The organization and subdivisions of the UDF are such that the UDF can accommodate a variety of development plans and approaches; it can be used in a situation where one person has total responsibility, or in the extreme where specialists are assigned to the particular sections. However, in the one-man approach it is still desirable that certain sections, indicated in the following discussion, be assigned to other individuals to gain the benefits of unbiased reviews and assessments.

The development of the UDF is geared to proceed logically and sequentially, and each section should be as complete as possible before proceeding to the next section. This is not always possible, and software development is usually an iterative rather than a sequential process. These situations only serve to reinforce the need for an ordered process that can be understood and tracked even under adverse conditions.

SECTION 0
COVER SHEET

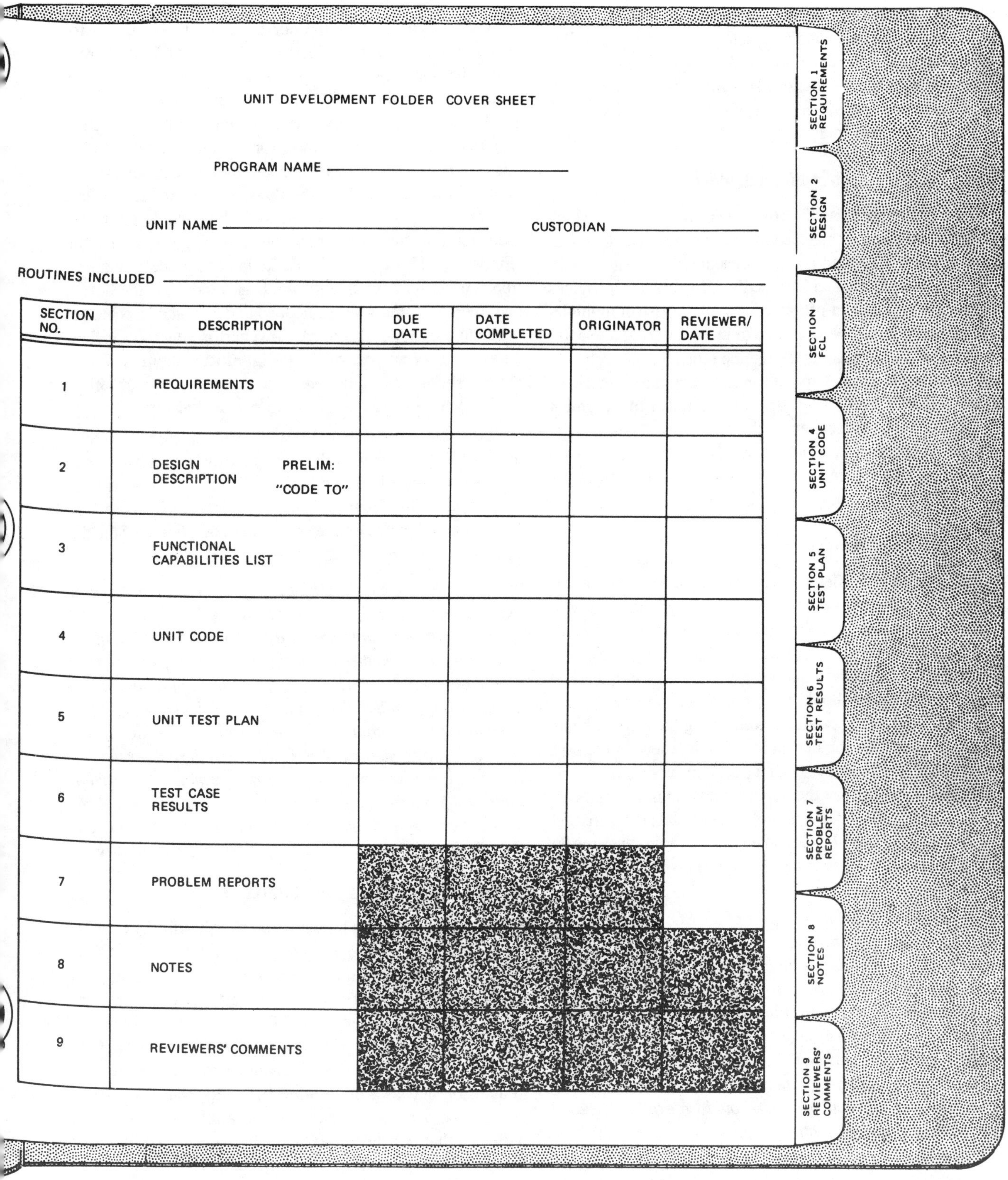

UNIT DEVELOPMENT FOLDER COVER SHEET

PROGRAM NAME _____

UNIT NAME _____   CUSTODIAN _____

ROUTINES INCLUDED _____

SECTION NO.	DESCRIPTION	DUE DATE	DATE COMPLETED	ORIGINATOR	REVIEWER/ DATE
1	REQUIREMENTS				
2	DESIGN DESCRIPTION PRELIM: "CODE TO"				
3	FUNCTIONAL CAPABILITIES LIST				
4	UNIT CODE				
5	UNIT TEST PLAN				
6	TEST CASE RESULTS				
7	PROBLEM REPORTS				
8	NOTES				
9	REVIEWERS' COMMENTS				

SECTION 1 REQUIREMENTS

SECTION 2 DESIGN

SECTION 3 FCL

SECTION 4 UNIT CODE

SECTION 5 TEST PLAN

SECTION 6 TEST RESULTS

SECTION 7 PROBLEM REPORTS

SECTION 8 NOTES

SECTION 9 REVIEWERS' COMMENTS

Figure 2. UDF Cover Sheet and Layout

Once a specific outline and UDF cover sheet have been established, it is imperative that the format and content of each section be clearly and completely defined as part of the project/company standards to avoid ambiguity and maintain consistency in the products. The following discussion expands and describes the contents of the UDF typified by the cover sheet shown in Figure 2.

Section 0: Cover Sheet and Schedule

This section contains the cover sheet for the unit, which identifies the routines included in the UDF and which delineates, for each of the sections, the scheduled due dates, actual completion dates, and assigned originators and provides space for reviewer sign-offs and dates. In the case of multiple-routine units, it may be advisable to include a one-page composite schedule illustrating the section schedules of each item for easy check-off and monitoring. Following each cover sheet, a UDF Change Log should be included to document all UDF changes subsequent to the time when the initial development is completed and the unit is put into a controlled test or maintenance environment. Figure 3 illustrates a typical UDF Change Log.

Section 1: Requirements

This section identifies the baseline requirements specification and enumerates the requirements which are allocated for implementation in the specific unit of software. A mapping to the system requirements specification (by paragraph number) should be made and, where practical, the statement of each requirement should be given. Any assumptions, ambiguities, deferrals or conflicts concerning the requirements and their impact on the design and development of the unit should be stated, and any design problem reports or deviations or waivers against the requirements should be indicated. In addition, if a requirement is only partially satisfied by this unit it will be so noted along with the unit(s) which share the responsibility for satisfaction of the requirement.

For units which comprise a part of a CPC, these will normally be a subset of the requirements that were allocated to the CPC during the preliminary design phase. In some instances, a particular unit of software may be totally or partially the result of a design solution for software implementation and, therefore, not directly traceable to the requirements. This may be the case, in particular, if the unit is composed of utility-type functions and routines. In this event, the lack of requirements should be explicitly stated and explained in this section.

The contents of this section may be a copy of the specific requirements paragraphs from the specification itself or an enumeration of the requirements paragraphs on a composed standard form.

Section 2: Design Description

This section contains the current design description for each of the routines included in the UDF. For multiple routine units, tabbed subsection separators are used for handy indexing. A preliminary design description may be included if available; however, the end item for this section is detailed design documentation for the unit, suitable to become (part of) a "code to" specification. The format and content of this section should conform to established documentation standards and should be suitable for direct inclusion into the appropriate detailed design specification (Figure 1). Throughout the development process this section represents the current, working version of the design and, therefore, must be maintained and annotated as changes occur to the initial design. A flowchart is generally included as an inherent part of the design documentation. Flowcharts should be generated in accordance with clear established standards for content, format, and symbol usage.

When the initial detailed design is completed and ready to be coded, a design walk-through may be held with one or more interested and knowledgeable co-workers. If such a walk-through is required, the completion of this section should be predicated on the successful completion of the design walk-through.

One of the common problems that occurs is in assuring that the design description contained in this section is maintained in current status and is an accurate reflection of the coded product. Whether the design is represented in the form of narrative plus flow charts or in the form of a design language listing, similar problems occur. It is not unusual for the coded product that is developed from the "code to" design to deviate somewhat from that initial design for various reasons. It is also not unusual for programmers to overlook the task of maintaining the design and code in sync. A design/code walk-through at the completion of the coding and test phase for each unit can help assure compatibility.

Section 3: Functional Capabilities List

This section contains a Functional Capabilities List (FCL) for the unit of software addressed by the UDF. An FCL is a list of the testable functions performed by the unit; i.e., it describes what a particular unit of software does, preferably in sequential order. The FCL is generated from the requirements and detailed design prior to development of the unit test plan. Its level of detail should correspond to the unit in question but, as a minimum, reflect the major segments of the code and the decisions which are being made. It is preferred that, whenever possible, functional capabilities be expressed in terms of the unit requirements (i.e., the functional capability is a requirement from Section 1 of the UDF). Requirements allocated to be tested at the unit level shall be included in the FCL. The FCL provides a vector from which

UDF CHANGE LOG

UNIT NAME _____ VERSION _____ CUSTODIAN_____

DATE	DPR/DR Number	Section(s) Affected and Page Numbers	Retest Method	Mod No.

NOTE: This revision change log is to be used for all changes made in the UDF after internal baseline (i.e., subsequent to mod number assignment). It is inserted immediately after the coversheet.

Figure 3. Example of a UDF Change Log

TEST CASE/REQUIREMENTS/FCL MATRIX

REQUIREMENTS DOCUMENT _____

DATE _____

Req'ts Paragraph Number	FCL NO.	1	2	3	4	5	6	7	8	9	0	OTHER ROUTINES

Above columns 1–0 labeled: TEST CASE NUMBER

INSTRUCTIONS: Mark an X in the appropriate box when a particular test case fully tests a particular requirement. Mark a "P" when a test partially tests a requirement. If a requirement is partially tested in another routine, mark a "P" in the "other routines" column. If more space is required, attach additional copies of this figure.

Figure 4. Example Test Case/Requirements/FCL Matrix

the Test Case Requirements/FCL matrix (Figure 4) is generated. The FCL should be reviewed and addressed as part of the test plan review process.

The rationale for Functional Capabilities Lists is as follows:

(1) They provide the basis for planned and controlled unit-level testing (i.e., a means for determining and organizing a set of test cases which will test all requirements/functional capabilities and all branches and transfers).

(2) They provide a consistent approach to testing which can be reviewed, audited, and understood by an outsider. When mapped to the test cases, they provide the rationale for each test case.

(3) They encourage another look at the design at a level where the "what if" questions can become apparent.

An FCL is particularly important for those portions of the design that are implementation-derived and not directly driven by requirements.

Section 4: Unit Code

This section contains the current source code listings for each of the routines included in the unit. Indexed subsection separators are used for multiple routine units. The completion date for this section is the scheduled date for the first error-free compilation or assembly when the code is ready for unit-level testing. Where code listings or other relevant computer output are too large or bulky to be contained in a normal three-ring binder, this material may be placed in a separate companion binder of appropriate size which is clearly identified with the associated UDF. In this event, the relevant sections of the UDF will contain a reference and identification of the binder with a history log of post-baselined updates. Figure 5 illustrates a typical reference form.

An independent review of the code may be optional; however, for time-critical or other technically critical units, a code walk-through or review is recommended.

Section 5: Unit Test Plan

This section contains a description of the overall testing approach for the unit along with a description of each test case to be employed in testing the unit. The description must identify any test tools or drivers used, a listing of all required test inputs to the unit and their values, and the expected output and acceptance criteria, including numerical outputs and other demonstrable results. Test cases shall address the functional capabilities of the unit, and a matrix shall be placed into this section which correlates requirements and functional capabilities to test cases. This matrix will be used to demonstrate that all requirements, partial requirements, and FCLs of the unit have been tested. An example of the test case matrix is shown in Figure 4. Check marks are placed in the appropriate squares to correlate test cases with the capabilities tested. Sufficient detail should be provided in the test

definition so that the test approach and objectives will be clear to an independent reviewer.

The primary criteria for the independent review will be to ascertain that the unit development test cases adequately test branch conditions, logic paths, input and output, error handling, and a reasonable range of values and will perform as stipulated by the requirements. This review should occur prior to the start of unit testing.

Section 6: Test Case Results

This section contains a compilation of all current successful test case results and analyses necessary to demonstrate that the unit has been tested as described in the test plan. Test output should be identified by test case number and listings clearly annotated to facilitate necessary reviews of these results by other qualified individuals. Revision status of test drivers, test tools, data bases and unit code should be shown to facilitate retesting. This material may also be placed in the separate companion binder to the UDF.

Section 7: Problem Reports

This section contains status logs and copies of all Design Problem Reports, Design Analysis Reports, and Discrepancy Reports (as required) which document all design and code problems and changes experienced by the unit subsequent to baselining. This ensures a clear and documented traceability for all problems and changes incurred. There should be separate subsections for each type of report with individual status logs that summarize the actions and dispositions made.

Section 8: Notes

This section contains any memos, notes, reports, etc., which expand on the contents of the unit or are related to problems and issues involved.

Section 9: Reviewers' Comments

This section contains a record of reviewers' comments (if any) on this UDF, which have resulted from the section-by-section review and sign-off, and from scheduled independent audits. These reviewers' comments are also usually provided to the project and line management supervisors responsible for development of the unit.

Summary

The UDF concept has evolved into a practical, effective and valuable tool not only for the management of software development but also for imposing a structured approach on the total software development process. The structure and content of the UDF are designed to create a set of milestones at the unit level, each of which can be easily observed and reviewed. The UDF approach has been employed on several software projects at TRW and continues to win converts from the ranks of the initiated. The concept has proved particu-

LISTINGS/TEST RESULTS

SEE SEPARATE NYLON PRONG BINDER IDENTIFIED AS
_____ FOR CODE LISTINGS
OR TEST RESULTS.

HISTORY LOG

CODE MOD NUMBER	DATE	REVIEWED BY
_____	_____	_____
_____	_____	_____
_____	_____	_____
_____	_____	_____
_____	_____	_____
_____	_____	_____
_____	_____	_____
_____	_____	_____
_____	_____	_____
_____	_____	_____
_____	_____	_____

Figure 5. Example Reference Log for Separately-Bound Material

larly effective when used in conjunction with good programming standards, documentation standards, a test discipline, and an independent quality assurance activity.

The principal merits of the UDF concept are:

(1) It imposes a development sequence on each unit and clearly establishes the responsibility for each step. Thus the reduction of the software development process into discrete activities is logically extended downward to the unit level.

(2) It establishes a clearly discernible timeline for the development of each unit and provides low-level management visibility into schedule problems. The status of the development effort becomes more visible and measurable.

(3) It creates an open and auditable software development environment and removes some of the mystery often associated with this activity. The UDFs are normally kept ''on the shelf'' and open to inspection at any time.

(4) It assures that the documentation is accomplished and maintained concurrent with development activities. The problem of emerging from the development tunnel with little or inadequate documentation is considerably reduced.

(5) It reduces the problems associated with programmer turnover. The discipline and organization inherent in the approach simplifies the substitution of personnel at any point in the process without a significant loss of effort.

(6) It supports the principles of modularity. The guidelines given for establishing the unit boundaries assure that at least a minimum level of modularity will result.

(7) It can accommodate a variety of development plans and approaches. All UDF sections may be assigned to one performer, or different sections can be assigned to different specialists. The various sections contained in the UDF may also be expanded, contracted or even resequenced to better suit specific situations.

As a final comment, it must be emphasized that no device or approach can be effective without a strong management commitment to see it through. Every level of management needs to be supportive and aware of its responsibilities. Once the method is established it also needs to be audited for proper implementation and problem resolution. An independent software quality assurance activity can be a valuable asset in helping to define, audit, and enforce management requirements.

Advances in Software Inspections

MICHAEL E. FAGAN, MEMBER, IEEE

Abstract—This paper presents new studies and experiences that enhance the use of the inspection process and improve its contribution to development of defect-free software on time and at lower costs. Examples of benefits are cited followed by descriptions of the process and some methods of obtaining the enhanced results.

Software inspection is a method of static testing to verify that software meets its requirements. It engages the developers and others in a formal process of investigation that usually detects more defects in the product—and at lower cost—than does machine testing. Users of the method report very significant improvements in quality that are accompanied by lower development costs and greatly reduced maintenance efforts. Excellent results have been obtained by small and large organizations in all aspects of new development as well as in maintenance. There is some evidence that developers who participate in the inspection of their own product actually create fewer defects in future work. Because inspections formalize the development process, productivity and quality enhancing tools can be adopted more easily and rapidly.

Index Terms—Defect detection, inspection, project management, quality assurance, software development, software engineering, software quality, testing, walkthru.

INTRODUCTION

THE software inspection process was created in 1972, in IBM Kingston, NY, for the dual purposes of improving software quality and increasing programmer productivity. Its accelerating rate of adoption throughout the software development and maintenance industry is an acknowledgment of its effectiveness in meeting its goals. Outlined in this paper are some enhancements to the inspection process, and the experiences of some of the many companies and organizations that have contributed to its evolution. The author is indebted to and thanks the many people who have given their help so liberally.

Because of the clear structure the inspection process has brought to the development process, it has enabled study of both itself and the conduct of development. The latter has enabled process control to be applied from the point at which the requirements are inspected—a much earlier point in the process than ever before—and throughout development. Inspections provide data on the performance of individual development operations, thus providing a unique opportunity to evaluate new tools and techniques. At the same time, studies of inspections have isolated and fostered improvement of its key characteristics such that very high defect detection efficiency inspections may now be conducted *routinely*. This simultaneous study of de-

Manuscript received September 30, 1985.

The author is with the IBM Thomas J. Watson Research Center, Yorktown Heights, NY 10598.

IEEE Log Number 8608192.

velopment and design and code inspections prompted the adaptation of the principles of the inspection process to inspections of requirements, user information, and documentation, and test plans and test cases. In each instance, the new uses of inspection were found to improve product quality and to be cost effective, i.e., it saved more than it cost. Thus, as the effectiveness of inspections are improving, they are being applied in many new and different ways to improve software quality and reduce costs.

BENEFITS: DEFECT REDUCTION, DEFECT PREVENTION, AND COST IMPROVEMENT

In March 1984, while addressing the IBM SHARE User Group on software service, L. H. Fenton, IBM Director of VM Programming Systems, made an important statement on quality improvement due to inspections [1]:

"Our goal is to provide defect free products and product information, and we believe the best way to do this is by refining and enhancing our existing software development process.

Since we introduced the inspection process in 1974, we have achieved significant improvements in quality. IBM has nearly doubled the number of lines of code shipped for System/370 software products since 1976, while the number of defects per thousand lines of code has been reduced by *two-thirds*. Feedback from early MVS/XA and VM/SP Release 3 users indicates these products met and, in many cases, exceeded our ever increasing quality expectations."

Observation of a small sample of programmers suggested that early experience gained from inspections caused programmers to reduce the number of defects that were injected in the design and code of programs created later during the same project [3]. Preliminary analysis of a much larger study of data from recent inspections is providing similar results.

It should be noted that the improvements reported by IBM were made while many of the enhancements to inspections that are mentioned here were being developed. As these improvements are incorporated into everyday practice, it is probable that inspections will help bring further reductions in defect injection and detection rates.

Additional reports showing that inspections improve quality *and* reduce costs follow. (In all these cases, the cost of inspections is included in project cost. Typically, all design and code inspection costs amount to 15 percent of project cost.)

Reprinted from *IEEE Transactions on Software Engineering*, Volume SE-12, Number 7, July 1986, pages 744-751. Copyright © 1986 by The Institute of Electrical and Electronics Engineers, Inc.

AETNA Life and Casualty. —0 Defects in use.
 4439 LOC [2]   —25 percent reduction in
           development resource.

IBM RESPOND, U.K.   —0 Defects in use.
 6271 LOC [3]   —9 percent reduction in
           cost compared to
           walkthrus.

Standard Bank of South Af- —0.15 Defects/KLOC in
rica. 143 000 LOC [4]   use.
           —95 percent reduction in
           corrective maintenance
           cost.

American Express,   —0.3 Defects in use.
System code). 13 000 LOC

In the AETNA and IBM examples, inspections found 82 and 93 percent, respectively, of all defects (that would cause malfunction) detected over the life cycle of the products. The other two cases each found over 50 percent of all defects by inspection. While the Standard Bank of South Africa and American Express were unable to use trained inspection moderators, and the former conducted only code inspections, both obtained outstanding results. The tremendous reduction in corrective maintenance at the Standard Bank of South Africa would also bring impressive savings in life cycle costs.

Naturally, reduction in maintenance allows redirection of programmers to work off the application backlog, which is reputed to contain at least two years of work at most locations. Impressive cost savings and quality improvements have been realized by inspecting test plans and then the test cases that implement those test plans. For a product of about 20 000 LOC, R. Larson [5] reported that test inspections resulted in:

• modification of approximately 30 percent of the functional matrices representing test coverage,

• detection of 176 major defects in the test plans and test cases (i.e., in 176 instances testing would have missed testing critical function or tested it incorrectly), and

• savings of more than 85 percent in programmer time by detecting the major defects by inspection as opposed to finding them during functional variation testing.

There are those who would use inspections whether or not they are cost justified for defect removal because of the nonquantifiable benefits the technique supplies toward improving the service provided to users and toward creating a more professional application development environment [6].

Experience has shown that inspections have the effect of slightly front-end loading the committment of people resources in development, adding to requirements and design, while greatly reducing the effort required during testing and for rework of design and code. The result is an overall *net* reduction in development resource, and usually in schedule too. Fig. 1 is a pictorial description of the familiar "snail" shaped curve of software development resource versus the time schedule including and without inspections.

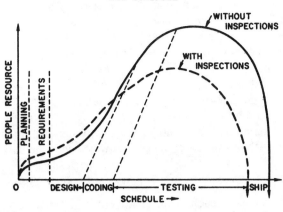

DEVELOPMENT PEOPLE RESOURCE AND SCHEDULE

Fig. 1.

THE SOFTWARE QUALITY PROBLEM

The software quality problem is the result of defects in code and documentation causing failure to satisfy user requirements. It also impedes the growth of the information processing industry. Validity of this statement is attested to by three of the many pieces of supporting evidence:

• The SHARE User Group Software Service Task Force Report, 1983 [1], that recommended an order of magnitude improvement in software quality over the next several years, with a like reduction in service. (Other manufacturers report similar recommendations from their users.)

• In 1979, 12 percent of programmer resource was consumed in post-shipment corrective maintenance alone and this figure was growing [8]. (Note that there is also a significant percentage of development and enhancement maintenance resource devoted to correcting defects. This is probably larger than the 12 percent expended in corrective maintenance, but there is no substantiating research.)

• The formal backlog of data processing tasks most quoted is three years [7].

At this point, a very important definition is in order:

A defect is an instance in which a requirement is not satisfied.

Here, it must be recognized that a requirement is any agreed upon commitment. It is not only the recognizable external product requirement, but can also include internal development requirements (e.g., the exit criteria of an operation) that must be met in order to satisfy the requirements of the end product. Examples of this would be the requirement that a test plan completely verifies that the product meets the agreed upon needs of the user, or that the code of a program must be complete before it is submitted to be tested.

While defects become manifest in the end product documentation or code, most of them are actually injected as the functional aspects of the product and its quality attributes are being created; during development of the requirements, the design and coding, or by insertion of changes. The author's research supports and supplements that of B. Boehm *et al.* [9] and indicates that there are eight attributes that must be considered when describing quality in a software product:

- intrinsic code quality,
- freedom from problems in operation,
- usability,
- installability,
- documentation for intended users,
- portability,
- maintainability and extendability, and "fitness for use"—that implicit conventional user needs are satisfied.

INSPECTIONS AND THE SOFTWARE QUALITY PROBLEM

Previously, each of these attributes of software quality were evaluated by testing and the end user. Now, some of them are being partly, and others entirely, verified against requirements by inspection. In fact, the product requirements themselves are often inspected to ascertain whether they meet user needs. In order to eliminate defects from the product it is necessary to address their prevention, or detection and resolution as soon as possible after their injection during development and maintenance. Prevention is the most desirable course to follow, and it is approached in many ways including the use of state machine representation of design, systematic programming, proof of correctness, process control, development standards, prototyping, and other methods. Defect detection, on the other hand, was once almost totally dependent upon testing during development and by the user. This has changed, and over the past decade walkthrus and inspections have assumed a large part of the defect detection burden; inspections finding from 60 to 90 percent defects. (See [2], [3], and other unpublished product experiences.) They are performed much nearer the point of injection of the defects than is testing, using less resource for rework and, thus, more than paying for themselves. In fact, inspections have been applied to most phases of development to verify that the key software attributes are present immediately after the point at which they should first be introduced into the product. They are also applied to test plans and test cases to improve the defect detection efficiency of testing. Thus, inspections have been instrumental in improving all aspects of software product quality, as well as the quality of logic design and code. In fact, inspections *supplement* defect prevention methods in improving quality.

Essential to the quality of inspection (or its defect detection efficiency) is proper definition of the development process. And, inspection quality is a direct contributor to product quality, as will be shown later.

DEFINITION OF THE DEVELOPMENT PROCESS

The software development process is a series of operations so arranged that its execution will deliver the desired end product. Typically, these operations are: Requirements Definition, System Design, High Level Design, Low Level Design, Coding, Unit Testing, Component or Function Testing, System Testing, and then user support and Maintenance. In practice, some of these operations are repeated as the product is recycled through them to insert functional changes and fixes.

The attributes of software quality are invested along with the functional characteristics of the product during the early operations, when the cost to remedy defects is 10–100 times less than it would be during testing or maintenance [2]. Consequently, it is advantageous to find and correct defects as near to their point of origin as possible. This is accomplished by inspecting the output product of each operation to verify that it satisfies the output requirements or *exit criteria* of the operation. In most cases, these exit criteria are not specified with sufficient precision to allow go/no verification. Specification of exit criteria in unambiguous terms that are objective and preferably quantitative is an essential characteristic of any well defined process. Exit criteria are the standard against which inspections measure completion of the product at the end of an operation, and verify the presence or absence of quality attributes. (A deviation from exit criteria is a defect.)

Shown below are the essence of 4 key criteria taken from the full set of 15 exit criteria items for the Coding operation:

- The source code must be at the "first clean compilation" level. That means it must be properly compiled and be free of syntax errors.
- The code must accurately implement the low level design (which was the verified output of the preceding process operation).
- All design changes to date are included in the code.
- All rework resulting from the code inspection has been included and verified.

The code inspection, I2, must verify that all 15 of these exit criteria have been satisfied before a module or other entity of the product is considered to have completed the Coding operation. Explicit exit criteria for several of the other inspection types in use will be contained in the author's book in software inspections. However, there is no reason why a particular project could not define its own sets of exit criteria. What is important is that exit criteria should be as objective as possible, so as to be repeatable; they should completely describe what is required to exit each operation; and, *they must be observed by all those involved.*

The objective of process control is to measure completion of the product during stages of its development, to compare the measurement against the project plan, and then to remedy any deviations from plan. In this context, the quality of both exit criteria and inspections are of vital importance. And, they must both be properly described in the manageable development process, for such a process must be controllable by definition.

Development is often considered a subset of the maintenance process. Therefore, the maintenance process must be treated in the same manner to make it equally manageable.

Software Inspection Overview

This paper will only give an overview description of the inspection process that is sufficient to enable discussion of updates and enhancements. The author's original paper on the software inspections process [2] gives a brief description of the inspection process and what goes on in an inspection, and is the base to which the enhancements are added. His forthcoming companion books on this subject and on building defect-free software will provide an implementation level description and will include all the points addressed in this paper and more.

To convey the principles of software inspections, it is only really necessary to understand how they apply to design and code. A good grasp on this application allows tailoring of the process to enable inspection of virtually any operation in development or maintenance, and also allows inspection for any desired quality attribute. With this in mind, the main points of inspections will be exposed through discussing how they apply in design and code inspections.

There are three essential requirements for the implementation of inspections:

- definition of the DEVELOPMENT PROCESS in terms of operations and their EXIT CRITERIA,
- proper DESCRIPTION of the INSPECTION PROCESS, and
- CORRECT EXECUTION of the INSPECTION PROCESS. (Yes, correct execution of the process is vital.)

The Inspection Process

The inspection process follows any development operation whose product must be verified. As shown below, it consists of six operations, each with a specific objective:

Operation	Objectives
PLANNING	Materials to be inspected must meet inspection entry criteria.
	Arrange the availability of the right participants.
	Arrange suitable meeting place and time.
OVERVIEW	Group education of participants in what is to be inspected.
	Assign inspection roles to participants.
PREPARATION	Participants learn the material and prepare to fulfill their assigned roles.
INSPECTION	*Find defects.* (Solution hunting and discussion of design alternatives is discouraged.)
REWORK	The author reworks all defects.
FOLLOW-UP	Verification by the inspection moderator or the entire inspection team to assure that all fixes are effective and that no secondary defects have been introduced.

Evaluation of hundreds of inspections involving thousands of programmers in which alternatives to the above steps have been tried has shown that all these operations are really necessary. Omitting or combining operations has led to degraded inspection efficiency that outweighs the apparent short-term benefits. OVERVIEW is the only operation that under certain conditions can be omitted with slight risk. Even FOLLOW-UP is justified as study has shown that approximately one of every six fixes are themselves incorrect, or create other defects.

From observing scores of inspections, it is evident that participation in inspection teams is extremely taxing and should be limited to periods of 2 hours. Continuing beyond 2 hours, the defect detection ability of the team seems to diminish, but is restored after a break of 2 hours or so during which other work may be done. Accordingly, no more than two 2 hour sessions of inspection per day are recommended.

To assist the inspectors in finding defects, for not all inspectors start off being good detectives, a checklist of defect types is created to help them identify defects appropriate to the exit criteria of each operation whose product is to be inspected. It also serves as a guide to classification of defects found by inspection prior to their entry to the inspection and test defect data base of the project. (A database containing these and other data is necessary for quality control of development.)

People and Inspections

Inspection participants are usually programmers who are drawn from the project involved. The roles they play for design and code inspections are those of the *Author* (Designer or Coder), *Reader* (who paraphrases the design or code as if they will implement it), *Tester* (who views the product from the testing standpoint), and *Moderator*. These roles are described more fully in [2], but that level of detail is not required here. Some inspections types, for instance those of system structure, may require more participants, but it is advantageous to keep the number of people to a minimum. Involving the end users in those inspections in which they can truly participate is also very helpful.

The Inspection Moderator is a *key player* and *requires special training* to be able to conduct inspections that are optimally effective. Ideally, to preserve objectivity, the moderator should not be involved in development of the product that is to be inspected, but should come from another similar project. The moderator functions as a "player-coach" and is responsible for conducting the inspection so as to bring a peak of synergy from the group. This is a quickly learned ability by those with some interpersonal skill. In fact, when participants in the moderator training classes are questioned about their case studies, they invariably say that they sensed the presence of the "*Phantom Inspector*," who materialized as a feeling that there had been an additional presence contributed by the way the inspection team worked together. The moderator's task is to invite the Phantom Inspector.

When they are properly approached by management, programmers respond well to inspections. In fact, after they become familiar with them, many programmers have been known to complain when they were not allowed enough time or appropriate help to conduct inspections correctly.

Three separate classes of education have been recognized as a necessity for proper long lasting implementation of inspections. First, *Management* requires a class of one day to familiarize them with inspections and their benefits to management, and *their role* in making them successful. Next, the *Moderators* need three days of education. And, finally, the other *Participants* should receive one half day of training on inspections, the benefits, and their roles. Some organizations have started inspections without proper education and have achieved some success, but less than others who prepared their participants fully. This has caused some amount of start-over, which was frustrating to everyone involved.

MANAGEMENT AND INSPECTIONS

A definite philosophy and set of attitudes regarding inspections and their results is essential. The management education class on inspections is one of the best ways found to gain the knowledge that must be built into day-to-day management behavior that is required to get the most from inspections on a continuing basis. For example, management must show encouragement for proper inspections. Requiring inspections and then asking for shortcuts will not do. And, people must be motivated to find defects by inspection. *Inspection results must never be used for personnel performance appraisal.* However, the results of testing should be used for performance appraisal. This promotes finding and reworking defects at the lowest cost, and allows testing for verification instead of debugging. In most situations programmers come to depend upon inspections; they prefer defect-free product. And, at those installations where management has taken and maintained a leadership role with inspections, they have been well accepted and very successful.

INSPECTION RESULTS AND THEIR USES

The defects found by inspection are immediately recorded and classified by the moderator before being entered into the project data base. Here is an example:

In module: *XXX*, Line: *YYY*, NAME-CHECK is performed one less time than required—LO/W/MAJ

The description of the defect is obvious. The classification on the right means that this is a defect in Logic, that the logic is Wrong (as opposed to Missing or Extra), and that it is a Major defect. A MAJOR defect is one that would cause a malfunction or unexpected result if left uncorrected. Inspections also find MINOR defects. They will not cause malfunction, but are more of the nature of poor workmanship, like misspellings that do not lead to erroneous product performance.

Major defects are of the same type as defects found by testing. (One unpublished study of defects found by system testing showed that more than 87 percent could have been detected by inspection.) Because Major defects are equivalent to test defects, inspection results can be used to identify *defect prone design and code*. This is enabled because empirical data indicates a directly proportional relationship between the inspection detected defect rate in a piece of code and the defect rate found in it by subsequent testing. Using inspection results in this way, it is possible to identify defect prone code and correct it, in effect, performing real-time quality control of the product as it is being developed, *before it is shipped or put into use*.

There are, of course, many Process and Quality Control uses for inspection data including:

- Feedback to improve the development process by identification and correction of the root causes of systematic defects before more code is developed;
- *Feed-forward* to prepare the process ahead to handle problems *or to evaluate corrective action in advance* (e.g., handling defect prone code);
- Continuing improvement and control of inspections.

An outstanding benefit of feedback, as reported in [3] was that designers and coders through involvement in inspections of their own work learned to find defects they had created more easily. This enabled them to *avoid* causing these defects in future work, thus providing much higher quality product.

VARIOUS APPLICATIONS OF INSPECTIONS

The inspection process was originally applied to hardware logic, and then to software logic design and code. It was in the latter case that it first gained notice. Since then it has been very successfully applied to software test plans and test cases, user documentation, high level design, system structure design, design changes, requirements development, and microcode. It has also been employed for special purposes such as cleaning up defect prone code, and improving the quality of code that has already been tested. And, finally, it has been resurrected to produce defect-free hardware. It appears that virtually anything that is created by a development process and that can be made visible and readable can be inspected. All that is necessary for an inspection is to define the exit criteria of the process operation that will make the product to be inspected, tailor the inspection defect checklists to the particular product and exit criteria, and then to execute the inspection process.

What's in a Name?

In contrast to inspections, walkthrus, which can range anywhere from cursory peer reviews to inspections, do not usually practice a process that is repeatable or collect data (as with inspections), and hence this process cannot be reasonably studied and improved. Consequently, their defect detection efficiencies are usually quite variable and, when studied, were found to be much lower than those of inspections [2], [3]. However, the name "walkthru" (or "walkthrough") has a place, for in some management and national cultures it is more desirable than the term "inspection" and, in fact, the walkthrus in *some* of these situations are identical to formal inspections. (In almost all instances, however, the author's experience has been that the term walkthru has been accurately applied to the less efficient method—which process is actually in use can be readily determined by examining whether a formally defined development process with exit criteria is in effect, and by applying the criteria in [2, Table 5] to the activity. In addition, initiating walkthrus as a migration path to inspections has led to a lot of frustration in many organizations because once they start with the informal, they seem to have much more difficulty moving to the formal process than do those that introduce inspections from the start. And, programmers involved in inspections are usually more pleased with the results. In fact, their major complaints are generally to do with things that detract from inspection quality.) What is important is that the same results should not be expected of walkthrus as is required of inspections, *unless a close scrutiny proves the process and conduct of the "walkthru" is identical to that required for inspections*. Therefore, although walkthrus do serve very useful though limited functions, they are not discussed further in this paper.

Recognizing many of the abovementioned points, the IBM Information Systems Management Institute course on this subject is named: "Inspections: Formal Application Walkthroughs." They teach about inspection.

Contributors to Software Inspection Quality

Quality of inspection is defined as its ability to detect all instances in which the product does not meet its requirements. Studies, evaluations, and the observations of many people who have been involved in inspections over the past decade provide insights into the contributors to inspection quality. Listing contributors is of little value in trying to manage them as many have relationships with each other. These relationships must be understood in order to isolate and deal with initiating root causes of problems rather than to waste effort dealing with symptoms. The ISHIKAWA or FISHBONE CAUSE/EFFECT DIAGRAM [11], shown in Fig. 2, shows the contributors and their cause/effect relationships.

As depicted in Fig. 2, the main contributors, shown as main branches on the diagram, are: *PRODUCT INSPECTABILITY, INSPECTION PROCESS, MANAGERS,* and *PROGRAMMERS*. Subcontributors, like *INSPECTION MATERIALS* and *CONFORMS WITH STANDARDS*, which contribute to the *PRODUCT INSPECTABILITY*, are shown as twigs on these branches. Contributors to the subcontributors are handled similarly. Several of the relationships have been proven by objective statistical analysis, others are supported by empirical data, and some are evident from project experience. For example, one set of relationships very thoroughly established in a controlled study by F. O. Buck, in "Indicators of Quality Inspections" [10], are:

- excessive SIZE OF MATERIALS to be inspected leads to a PREPARATION RATE that is too high.
- PREPARATION RATE that is too high contributes to an excessive RATE OF INSPECTION, and
- Excessive RATE OF INSPECTION *causes fewer defects to be found*.

This study indicated that the following rates should be used in planning the I2 code inspection:

OVERVIEW:	500 Noncommentary Source Statements per Hour.
PREPARATION:	125 Noncommentary Source Statements per Hour.
INSPECTION:	90 Noncommentary Source Statements per Hour.
Maximum Inspection Rate:	125 Noncommentary Source Statements per Hour.

The rate of inspection seems tied to the thoroughness of the inspection, and there is evidence that defect detection efficiency diminishes at rates above 125 NCSS/h. (Many projects require reinspection if this maximum rate is exceeded, and the reinspection usually finds more defects.) Separate from this study, project data show that inspections conducted by trained moderators are very much more likely to approximate the permissible inspection rates, and yield higher quality product than moderators who have not been trained. Meeting this rate is not a direct conscious purpose of the moderator, but rather is the result of proper conduct of the inspection. In any event, as the study shows, requiring too much material to be inspected will induce insufficient PREPARATION which, in turn, will cause the INSPECTION to be conducted too fast. Therefore, it is the responsibility of management and the moderator to start off with a plan that will lead to successful inspection.

The planning rate for high level design inspection of *systems design* is approximately twice the rate for code inspection, and low level (Logic) design inspection is nearly the same (rates are based upon the designer's estimate of the number of source lines of code that will be needed to implement the design). Both these rates *may* depend upon the complexity of the material to be inspected and the manner in which it is prepared (e.g., unstructured code is more difficult to read and requires the inspection rate to be lowered. Faster inspection rates while retaining high defect detection efficiency *may* be feasible with highly structured, easy to understand material, *but further study is needed*). Inspections of requirements, test plans, and user documentation are governed by the same rules as for code inspection, although inspection rates are not as clear for them and are probably more product and project dependent than is the case of code.

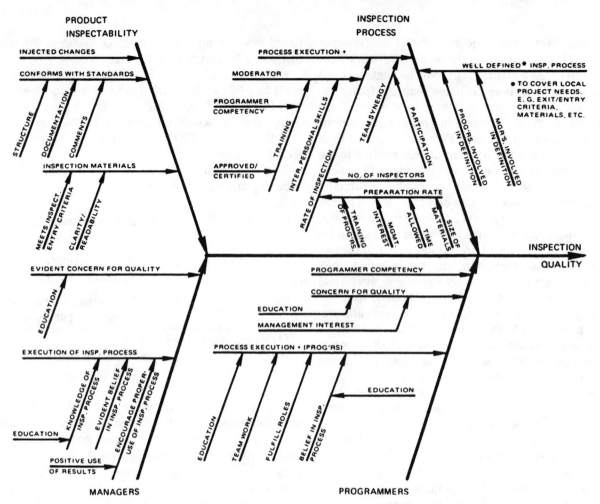

Fig. 2. Fishbone diagram of contributors to inspection quality.

With a good knowledge of and attention to the contributors to inspection quality, management can profoundly influence the quality, and the development and maintenance costs of the products for which they are responsible.

SUMMARY

Experience over the past decade has shown software inspections to be a potent defect detection method, finding 60–90 percent of all defects, as well as providing feedback that enables programmers to avoid injecting defects in future work. As well as providing checkpoints to facilitate process management, inspections enable measurement of the performance of many tools and techniques in individual process operations. Because inspection engages similar skills to those used in creating the product (and it has been applied to virtually every design technique and coding language), it appears that anything that can be created and described can also be inspected.

Study and observation have revealed the following key aspects that must be managed to take full advantage of the many benefits that inspections offer:

Capability	Action Needed to Enhance the Capability
• Defect Detection	— Management understanding and continuing support. This starts with education.

— Inspection moderator training (3 days).
— Programmer training.
— Continuing management of the contributors to inspection quality.
— Inspect all changes.
— Periodic review of effectiveness by management.
— Inspect test plans and test cases.
— Apply inspections to main defect generating operations in development *and* maintenance processes.

• Defect Prevention (or avoidance)
— Encourage programmers to understand how they created defects and what must be done to avoid them in future.
— Feedback inspection results promptly and removes root causes of systematic defects from the development or maintenance processes.
— Provide inspection results to

422

quality circles or quality improvement teams.

— Creation of requirements for expert system tools (for defect prevention) based upon analysis of inspection data.

• Process Management

— Use inspection completions as checkpoints in the development plan and measure accomplishment against them.

REFERENCES

[1] L. H. Fenton, "Response to the SHARE software service task force report," IBM Corp., Kingston, NY, Mar. 6, 1984.

[2] M. E. Fagan, "Design and code inspections to reduce errors in program development," *IBM Syst. J.*, vol. 15, no. 3, 1979.

[3] *IBM Technical Newsletter GN20-3814*, Base Publication GC20-2000-0, Aug. 15, 1978.

[4] T. D. Crossman, "Inspection teams, are they worth it?" in *Proc. 2nd Nat. Symp. EDP Quality Assurance*, Chicago, IL, Mar. 24–26, 1982.

[5] R. R. Larson, "Test plan and test case inspection specification," IBM Corp., Tech. Rep. TR21.585, Apr. 4, 1975.

[6] T. D. Crossman, "Some experiences in the use of inspection teams in application development," in *Proc. Applicat. Develop. Symp.*, Monterey, CA, 1979.

[7] G. D. Brown and D. H. Sefton, "The micro vs. the applications logjam," *Datamation*, Jan. 1984.

[8] J. H. Morrissey and L. S.-Y. Wu, "Software engineering: An economical perspective," in *Proc. IEEE Conf. Software Eng.*, Munich, West Germany, Sept. 14–19, 1979.

[9] B. Boehm *et al.*, *Characteristics of Software Quality*. New York: American Elsevier, 1978.

[10] F. O. Buck, "Indicators of quality inspections," IBM Corp., Tech. Rep. IBM TR21.802, Sept. 1981.

[11] K. Ishikawa, *Guide to Quality Control*. Tokyo, Japan: Asian Productivity Organization, 1982.

Michael E. Fagan (M'62) is a Senior Technical Staff Member at the IBM Corporation, Thomas J. Watson Research Center, Yorktown Heights, NY. While at IBM, he has had many interesting management and technical assignments in the fields of engineering, manufacturing, software development, and research. In 1972, he created the software inspection process, and has helped implement it within IBM and also promoted its use in the software industry. For this and other work, he has received IBM Outstanding Contribution and Corporate Achievement Awards. His area of interest is in studying and improving all the processes that comprise the software life cycle. For the past two years, he has been a Visiting Professor at, and is on the graduate council of, the University of Maryland.

ESTABLISHING SOFTWARE ENGINEERING STANDARDS IN AN INDUSTRIAL ORGANIZATION

by

Fletcher J. Buckley, RCA Missile and Surface Radar Division
Moorestown, NJ

ABSTRACT

This is a basic tutorial in establishing a viable set of software engineering standards in an industrial organization. The emphasis is on a practical implementation using proven techniques. The topic is approached in a step-by-step manner, and includes advice on format and content of the standards themselves as well as on the process of implementation.

INTRODUCTION

Purpose

This article provides a basic tutorial on how to establish a software engineering standards effort in an industrial organization. It is based on the experience of the author in such a program at RCA Missile and Surface Radar Division (MSRD), and the experiences of others who have trudged down the same roads. It should be carefully noted, however, that there is no intent to portray the one who wields the stylus as the one who slew the dragon. Furthermore, no one implementation was done in exactly this way, and so we experienced much pain that could have been avoided. In part, this tutorial incorporates lessons learned from the process.

Background

As software becomes more and more important to our industrial products, those in power come to an overwelming realization that there are better ways to produce software than to merely allow a stream-of-conscious flow. The work that leads to the realization of this moment of truth is beyond the scope of this paper. Suffice it to say that the happy moment has arrived, and you have been designated to do the job.

Assumption

This paper assumes that the reader is not at the forefront of the state-of-the-art of software development, but is content to plod at least two steps behind. Therefore, this paper does not address more esoteric methodologies such as rapid prototyping, etc. For those who use something other than a standard software life cycle, the basic approach will hold, but the details will differ.

IN THE BEGINNING

Announce Your Intentions

All of us hate to be surprised. This will include those who may be affected by the project. In addition, there will be those inside the organization who might harbor thoughts on the topic. So the first major rule is: LET EVERYBODY KNOW WHAT IS COMING. This can be done on paper, or by talking with those who, in turn, talk with others. One way is to announce a project organizational meeting and ask for the name of anyone who would like to be kept informed.

Having made the first announcement, make sure that the people in the existing power structures are informed. Touch base with all the software managers and other authorities who will have roles to play in developing the material. The last thing in the world that you want to have happen is to have someone come out of the woodwork at the end of the process and, with a few well-chosen words, reset the process to Step One. More importantly, there is a collective wisdom in the old timers that is hard to match; e.g., "This was tried before but failed due to ..." or, "It sounds like a good idea, but have you considered ... ."

Do Your Homework

Research the existing company policies, procedures, instructions, existing directives, etc. Gather material from other sources, such as the IEEE Software Engineering Standards Subcommittee (SESS), the Department of Defense (DoD), and other standards-producing organizations.

As a part of the Technical Committee on Software Engineering of the IEEE Computer Society, the SESS initiated a substantial effort in 1976 to establish an integrated set of standards. The current status of these efforts is shown in Tables 1 and 2. For a commercial organization, it is recommended that these standards be used as the basis for tailoring material that reflects your situation. The basic reason for this is that the standards represent a consensus of the concerned professionals in the field. For example, the use of formal military standards may invoke concerns that such an authoritative approach will prove to be a millstone around the neck of the organization, rather than a help.

TABLE 1 ANSI/IEEE APPROVED SOFTWARE ENGINEERING STANDARDS[1]	
NUMBER	TITLE
729-1983	IEEE STANDARD GLOSSARY OF SOFTWARE ENGINEERING TERMINOLOGY
730-1984	IEEE STANDARD FOR SOFTWARE QUALITY ASSURANCE PLANS
828-1983	IEEE STANDARD FOR SOFTWARE CONFIGURATION MANAGEMENT PLANS
829-1984	IEEE STANDARD FOR SOFTWARE TEST DOCUMENTATION
830-1984	IEEE GUIDE FOR SOFTWARE REQUIREMENTS SPECIFICATIONS
983-1986	IEEE GUIDE FOR SOFTWARE QUALITY ASSURANCE PLANNING
990-1987	IEEE RECOMMENDED PRACTICE FOR Ada AS A PROGRAM DESIGN LANGUAGE [2]
1002-1987	IEEE STANDARD TAXONOMY OF SOFTWARE ENGINEERING STANDARDS
1008-1987	IEEE STANDARD FOR SOFTWARE UNIT TESTING
1012-1987	IEEE STANDARD FOR SOFTWARE VERIFICATION AND VALIDATION PLANS

[1]Copies of approved ANSI/IEEE Standards may be obtained from the following:

- The IEEE Service Center
  (201) 981-0060
  201 Hoes Lane
  Piscataway, NJ 08854

- The IEEE Computer Society
  (800) 272-6657
  (714) 821-8380
  Worldway Postal Center
  Los Angeles, CA 90080

- The IEEE Computer Society
  Phone: 32.2660.11.43
  2 Avenue de la Tanche
  B-116
  Brussels, Belgium

[2]Ada is a registered trademark of the U.S. Government Department of Defense, Ada Joint Project Office.

The Department of Defense recently established a new series of comprehensive and exhaustive standards concerned with software development. They provide formats for 23 separate document types and an overwhelming mass of detail that applies to very large projects. If DoD standards are used for smaller projects, heavy use of a red pencil is recommended. However, recognizing that we are most productive when we are stealing from someone else, they serve as a good source for "cut-and-paste" customization. Table 3 shows the current status of these standards.

Additional sources to investigate are NASA, the European Space Agency (ESA), and other commercial organizations. However, when approaching commercial organizations, a certain amount of caution should be used. First, most commercial companies regard internal policies and standards as "Company Private" material. Company resources have been expended to produce them, and they see nothing to be gained by providing them to others. So do not be surprised if your professional contemporaries are not able to share their company standards with you. Second, the company policies that are most widely touted may be those that are completely out of touch with reality — they are the adult version of Show and Tell (while the boys and girls in the back room do different things).

CREATION

Establish a Framework

Install, typically, a framework of three documents, and install them inside the existing documentation set of your company - this is NOT the time to change structure. As shown in Figure 1, these consist of the following items:

(1) *Policy.* This establishes the legitimacy of the enterprise. It should state the overall concept of what is to be done, and the responsibilities of the various organizational elements for the implementation of that overall concept.

(2) *Implementing Instruction.* This is usually issued at the next organizational level. It states how the policy is to be executed.

(3) *Software Development Manual.* This documents the specific standards, including process requirements as well as the format and content requirements for products.

Policy. The major policy to be expressed is that EACH NEW SOFTWARE PROJECT SHALL HAVE A WRITTEN PLAN THAT IS APPROVED BY THE SOFTWARE MANAGER'S SUPERVISOR PRIOR TO THE START OF THE PROJECT. Associated with this policy should be:

(1) A Grandfather Clause — e.g., existing projects do not have to be retrofitted, but all projects starting on or after a specified date shall comply. This negates the fear that the rules are going to change for those projects already underway.

TABLE 2 APPROVED SOFTWARE ENGINEERING STANDARDS PROJECTS[3]

NUMBER	TITLE	PROJECTED DATE OF APPROVAL
P982	A STANDARD FOR SOFTWARE RELIABILITY MEASUREMENT	SEPT 1987
P1016	A GUIDE FOR SOFTWARE DESIGN DESCRIPTIONS	MAR 1987
P1028	A STANDARD FOR SOFTWARE REVIEWS AND AUDITS	JUNE 1987
P1042	A GUIDE FOR SOFTWARE CONFIGURATION MANAGEMENT PLANNING	MAR 1987
P1044	A STANDARD CLASSIFICATION FOR SOFTWARE ERRORS, FAULTS AND FAILURES	JUNE 1987
P1045	A STANDARD FOR SOFTWARE PRODUCTIVITY METRICS	JUNE 1987
P1058	A STANDARD FOR SOFTWARE PROJECT PLANS	JUNE 1987
P1059	A GUIDE FOR SOFTWARE VERIFICATION AND VALIDATION	SEPT 1987
P1061	A STANDARD FOR SOFTWARE QUALITY METRICS	SEPT 1987
P1062	A RECOMMENDED PRACTICE FOR SOFTWARE CERTIFICATION	SEPT 1987
P1063	A STANDARD FOR USER DOCUMENTATION	JUNE 1987
P1074	A STANDARD FOR THE SOFTWARE LIFE CYCLE PROCESSES	MAR 1988

[3]For information on on-going projects, contact:

John Horch
(205) 532-1100
Chairperson, Software Engineering Standards Subcommittee
Teledyne Brown, Cummings Research Park
Huntsville, AL 35807

TABLE 3 CURRENT DoD SOFTWARE ENGINEERING STANDARDS[4]	
STANDARD	COMMENTS
DOD-STD-2167, DEFENSE SYSTEM SOFTWARE DEVELOPMENT	BEING REVISED TO "A" VERSION
DOD-STD-2168, DEFENSE SYSTEM SOFTWARE QUALITY EVALUATION	IN DRAFT
MIL-STD-483A, CONFIGURATION MANAGEMENT PRACTICES	APPROVED, 4 JUNE 1985
MIL-STD-490A, SPECIFICATION PRACTICES	APPROVED, 4 JUNE 1985
MIL-STD-1521B, TECHNICAL REVIEWS AND AUDITS	APPROVED, 4 JUNE 1985

[4]Detailed information on the current status of these standards and associated handbooks may be obtained from:

SDS/SQS Information
ATTN: S. Kelly
IIT Research Institute
PO Box 180
Rome, New York 13440
(315) 336-2359

(2) An Escape Clause — e.g., requests for exceptions to this policy, together with the associated reasons, should be addressed to the Director of Engineering (a sufficiently high level to discourage frivolous requests).

(3) A Sunset Clause — e.g., this policy will expire in three years unless otherwise revised or reaffirmed within that period. This should be a standard clause on all policy directives; it automatically flushes the ash and trash that can otherwise clog up the pipes.

(4) An Implementing Instructions Clause — e.g., Implementing Instructions from subordinate units should be forwarded within 2 months of the effective date of this policy statement.

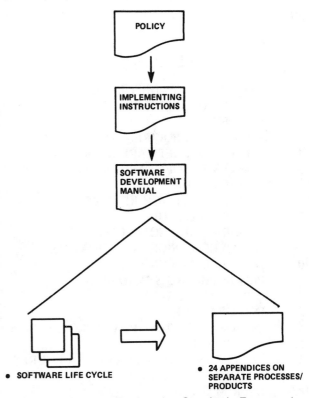

Figure 1. Software Engineering Standards Framework

Implementing Instruction. This has two major functions: (1) to reflect and expand the policy, and (2) to introduce the Software Development Manual (SDM). The thought here is that the standards in the SDM will evolve as the concepts are put into practice, and will be adjusted to fit the idiosyncrasies of the implementing organization. However, the Policy and the Implementing Instruction themselves should remain relatively stable.

The Software Development Manual. This can take many forms. One that has proven sucessful is that the basic section identifies the software life cycle and, with associated graphics, identifies the various processes and products that this life cycle includes. Additional detail on each of the processes and products is then provided in a specific appendix dealing only with that topic. The appendix should state who is responsible for a particular action, and provide guidance on coverage and implementation.

Table 4 identifies an example set of 24 appendices, each covering one specific item. Note that the topics are reasonably grouped, providing coverage of both processes and products. The items that apply to the complete process are grouped at the end.

The set of appendix topics does not have to be the absolute best set in existence, and the contents need not be extraordinarily polished prose. What is important is to identify a reasonable set of topics and write something about each. A consensus will come from the iterations and the detailed discussions.

Specific Content Guidance

Use the software life cycle and associated definitions in ANSI/IEEE Std 729-1983, IEEE Standards Glossary of Software Engineering Terminology. There are other life cycles and other definitions; however, in the long run, it does not really matter what life cycle and definitions are used, as long as there is agreement on what they are. A tremendous amount of time can be spent on definitions; the time could be better spent on more productive things. Use the IEEE definitions, and let the people who want to argue or define terms argue with the IEEE, while the rest of the group works on the other problems.

Use the material in the IEEE Standards and the current working drafts of the IEEE Standards Projects. Modify these to fit your situation, and then compare what you have written with the DoD Standards, NASA, ESA, and any others that are available to you. Fill in the holes, and then publish the first draft as a working paper.

COORDINATION

Provide the entire first draft in writing to all concerned, and request comments within 30 days. Then go around to the people on the coordination list and raise their consciousness that the document is out and that you consider their review to be essential. Then a week before the comments are due back, make the swing one more time.

Keep track of reviewers' comments, and the responses to them. The first draft will change as a result of the comments, and the cycle of coordination will probably reoccur as you seek consensus. To get good reviews and helpful comments, the reviewers will want to know what changes were made in the documents since the last time they saw them. To do this, provide a list of changes as an enclosure to the correspondence and place bars down the sides of the documents where changes were made. (To expect the reviewers to hunt through a large set of documents that they have previously reviewed, without indicating where the changes are, is extremely optimistic.) Before sending out the second draft, visit each person whose comments could not be incorporated and find out what their real problems are; seek alternate wording, etc.

IMPLEMENTATION

The happy day has arrived — the documents have been approved! Now the real work begins.

Help the First Implementors

Consider the position of the first project implementor. There are many immediate startup tasks, and now, as a result of your efforts, the project manager must also declare - in writing - how the project will be run for the next three years. Faced with this additional task, the project manager may:

(a)   despair, declare the new procedures are unworkable, and revert back to the previous manner of doing business. This, when and if it happens, is a "lose/lose" situation for everybody. Whoever wins, also loses.

(b)   ask for help to write the first Software Development Plan, and you may be assigned to do it. When you turn out a very good plan, it may be just rubber-stamped and filed. Then, once more, back to business as the firm used to conduct it.

To avoid this, you should provide enough help to overcome the familiarization problems associated with a new set of directives. But - at the same time - YOU MUST ENSURE THAT THE PROJECT MANAGER BECOMES SUFFICIENTLY INVOLVED IN THE PROCESS TO BECOME COMMITTED TO THE PLAN. One approach is to write the first draft yourself, and arrange for the project manager to complete it. At that point, THE PLAN BECOMES THE PROJECT MANAGER'S - AND NOT YOURS.

Ration Your Own Time

In the implementation process, there will be those that accept your standards and those that reject them. Spend your time with those who accept them. Don't waste your time on those that resist, because you will never convince them and they will absorb all your efforts.

Keep Previous SDPs

Start a file of old SDPs. This allows a series of iterations. Each new project can now build on the experiences of previous project plans, documentation, programming standards, etc. Concurrently, the organization starts to develop a lore of what worked and what didn't; gradually the company culture starts to change, to where developing a SDP becomes a matter of course. In effect, you are establishing a technical support group of peers who have walked a mile or two down the same road.

Revise the SDM

Revisit the entire structure - Policy, Implementing Instruction and SDM - once a year. The first two documents should be reasonably stable; the SDM may need tuning (year by year) to reflect changes in the business, lessons learned, etc. There is now actual experience on which to base these documents - a much better operating guide than academic theory. Perform these yearly reviews just as the initial establishment was performed: coordinate extensively, in writing, etc.

INITIATE IN-HOUSE TRAINING

Many a person is walking the streets of London tonight because the set of software engineering standards - documents on which vast quantities of resources were expended - did not pass the "dust test." (Try this test yourself. In any large corporation, reach over to any programmer's shelf and pull out the Standards Manual. Blow sharply on the top side. As the dust flies into the air and settles quietly all over the listings on the desk, you know that (1) the standards have either been memorized or (2) are not being used. The smart money bets on the latter case.) The best standards in the world are worthless unless used, and no one is going to use them unless time and effort is spent overcoming the "fluency barrier."

Not only must the software folks be trained, but everyone who must deal with either the software or the software folks also needs to be exposed to the topic. The amount will differ, ranging from a one-hour presentation to upper management to a formal in-plant course for those on the "firing line." When this is done, remember — it communicates management's committment to the working troops on the new way of doing business. So do it well the first time - and that means planning, rehearsals, etc.

SUMMARY

This article provided a tutorial on establishing software engineering standards in an industrial organization, including general guidance that applies to many varieties of organizations and environments, and specific guidance refering to one series of implementations. The major tasks involved are:

- Communicating the intentions within the organization.

- Establishing a framework of three documents: Policy, Implementing Instruction, and Software Development Manual.

- Coordinating iterations of review cycles.

- Implementing the standards.

- Training company personnel.

Elements of Software Configuration Management

EDWARD H. BERSOFF, SENIOR MEMBER, IEEE

Abstract—Software configuration management (SCM) is one of the disciplines of the 1980's which grew in response to the many failures of the software industry throughout the 1970's. Over the last ten years, computers have been applied to the solution of so many complex problems that our ability to manage these applications has all too frequently failed. This has resulted in the development of a series of "new" disciplines intended to help control the software process.

This paper will focus on the discipline of SCM by first placing it in its proper context with respect to the rest of the software development process, as well as to the goals of that process. It will examine the constituent components of SCM, dwelling at some length on one of those components, configuration control. It will conclude with a look at what the 1980's might have in store.

Index Terms—Configuration management, management, product assurance, software.

INTRODUCTION

SOFTWARE configuration management (SCM) is one of the disciplines of the 1980's which grew in response to the many failures of our industry throughout the 1970's. Over the last ten years, computers have been applied to the solution of so many complex problems that our ability to manage these applications in the "traditional" way has all too frequently failed. Of course, tradition in the software business began only 30 years ago or less, but even new habits are difficult to break. In the 1970's we learned the hard way that the tasks involved in managing a software project were not linearly dependent on the number of lines of code produced. The relationship was, in fact, highly exponential. As the decade closed, we looked back on our failures [1], [2] trying to understand what went wrong and how we could correct it. We began to dissect the software development process [3], [4] and to define techniques by which it could be effectively managed [5]–[8]. This self-examination by some of the most talented and experienced members of the software community led to the development of a series of "new" disciplines intended to help control the software process.

While this paper will focus on the particular discipline of SCM, we will first place it in its proper context with respect to the rest of the software development process, as well as to the goals of that process. We will examine the constituent components of SCM, dwelling at some length on one of those components, configuration control. Once we have woven our way through all the trees, we will once again stand back and take a brief look at the forest and see what the 1980's might have in store.

Manuscript received April 15, 1982; revised December 1, 1982 and October 18, 1983.

The author is with BTG, Inc., 1945 Gallows Rd., Vienna, VA 22180.

SCM IN CONTEXT

It has been said that if you do not know where you are going, any road will get you there. In order to properly understand the role that SCM plays in the software development process, we must first understand what the goal of that process is, i.e., where we are going. For now, and perhaps for some time to come, software developers are people, people who respond to the needs of another set of people creating computer programs designed to satisfy those needs. These computer programs are the tangible output of a thought process—the conversion of a thought process into a product. The goal of the software developer is, or should be, the construction of a product which closely matches the real needs of the set of people for whom the software is developed. We call this goal the achievement of "product integrity." More formally stated, product integrity (depicted in Fig. 1) is defined to be the intrinsic set of attributes that characterize a product [9]:

- that fulfills user functional needs;
- that can easily and completely be traced through its life cycle;
- that meets specified performance criteria;
- whose cost expectations are met;
- whose delivery expectations are met.

The above definition is pragmatically based. It demands that product integrity be a measure of the satisfaction of the real needs and expectations of the software user. It places the burden for achieving the software goal, product integrity, squarely on the shoulders of the developer, for it is he alone who is in control of the development process. While, as we shall see, the user can establish safeguards and checkpoints to gain visibility into the development process, the prime responsibility for software success is the developer's. So our goal is now clear; we want to build software which exhibits all the characteristics of product integrity. Let us make sure that we all understand, however, what this thing called software really is. We have learned in recent times that equating the terms "software" and "computer programs" improperly restricts our view of software. Software is much more. A definition which can be used to focus the discussion in this paper is that software is information that is:

- structured with logical and functional properties;
- created and maintained in various forms and representations during the life cycle;
- tailored for machine processing in its fully developed state.

So by our definition, software is not simply a set of computer programs, but includes the documentation required to define, develop, and maintain these programs. While this notion is not very new, it still frequently escapes the software

Reprinted from *IEEE Transactions on Software Engineering*, Volume SE-10, Number 1, January 1984, pages 79-87. Copyright © 1984 by The Institute of Electrical and Electronics Engineers, Inc.

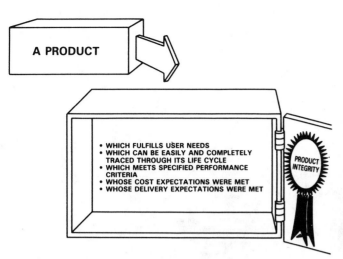

Fig. 1. Product integrity.

development manager who assumes that controlling a software product is the same as controlling computer code.

Now that we more fully appreciate what we are after, i.e., to build a software product with integrity, let us look at the one road which might get us there. We have, until now, used the term "developer" to characterize the organizational unit responsible for converting the software idea into a software product. But developers are, in reality, a complex set of interacting organizational entities. When undertaking a software project, most developers structure themselves into three basic discipline sets which include:

- project management,
- development, and
- product assurance.

Project management disciplines are both inwardly and outwardly directed. They support general management's need to see what is going on in a project and to ensure that the parent or host organization consistently develops products with integrity. At the same time, these disciplines look inside a project in support of the assignment, allocation, and control of all project resources. In that capacity, project management determines the relative allocation of resources to the set of development and product assurance disciplines. It is management's prerogative to specify the extent to which a given discipline will be applied to a given project. Historically, management has often been handicapped when it came to deciding how much of the product assurance disciplines were required. This was a result of both inexperience and organizational immaturity.

The development disciplines represent those traditionally applied to a software project. They include:

- analysis,
- design,
- engineering,
- production (coding),
- test (unit/subsystem),
- installation,
- documentation,
- training, and
- maintenance.

In the broadest sense, these are the disciplines required to take a system concept from its beginning through the development life cycle. It takes a well-structured, rigorous technical approach to system development, along with the right mix of development disciplines to attain product integrity, especially for software. The concept of an ordered, procedurally disciplined approach to system development is fundamental to product integrity. Such an approach provides successive development plateaus, each of which is an identifiable measure of progress which forms a part of the total foundation supporting the final product. Going sequentially from one baseline (plateau) to another with high probability of success, necessitates the use of the right development disciplines at precisely the right time.

The product assurance disciplines which are used by project management to gain visibility into the development process include:

- configuration management,
- quality assurance,
- validation and verification, and
- test and evaluation.

Proper employment of these product assurance disciplines by the project manager is basic to the success of a project since they provide the technical checks and balances over the product being developed. Fig. 2 represents the relationship among the management, development, and product assurance disciplines. Let us look at each of the product assurance disciplines briefly, in turn, before we explore the details of SCM.

Configuration management (CM) is the discipline of identifying the configuration of a system at discrete points in time for the purpose of systematically controlling changes to the configuration and maintaining the integrity and traceability of the configuration throughout the system life cycle. Software configuration management (SCM) is simply configuration management tailored to systems, or portions of systems, that are comprised predominantly of software. Thus, SCM does not differ substantially from the CM of hardware-oriented systems, which is generally well understood and effectively practiced. However, attempts to implement SCM have often failed because the particulars of SCM do not follow by direct analogy from the particulars of hardware CM and because SCM is a less mature discipline than that of hardware CM. We will return to this subject shortly.

Quality assurance (QA) as a discipline is commonly invoked throughout government and industry organizations with reasonable standardization when applied to systems comprised only of hardware. But there is enormous variation in thinking and practice when the QA discipline is invoked for a software development or for a system containing software components. QA has a long history, and much like CM, it has been largely developed and practiced on hardware projects. It is therefore mature, in that sense, as a discipline. Like CM, however, it is relatively immature when applied to software development. We define QA as consisting of the procedures, techniques, and tools applied by professionals to insure that a product meets or exceeds prespecified standards during a product's development cycle; and without specific prescribed standards, QA entails insuring that a product meets or

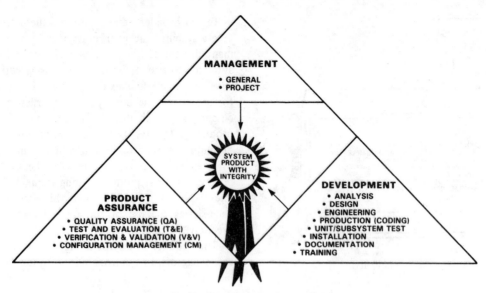

Fig. 2. The discipline triangle.

exceeds a minimum industrial and/or commercially acceptable level of excellence.

The QA discipline has not been uniformly treated, practiced or invoked relative to software development. First, very few organizations have software design and development standards that compare in any way with hardware standards for detail and completeness. Second, it takes a high level of software expertise to assess whether a software product meets prescribed standards. Third, few buyer organizations have provided for or have developed the capability to impose and then monitor software QA endeavors on seller organizations. Finally, few organizations have been concerned over precisely defining the difference between QA and other product assurance disciplines, CM often being subservient to QA or vice versa in a given development organization. Our definition of software given earlier suggests still another reason for the software QA discipline being in the same state as SCM so far as its universal application within the user, buyer, and seller communities. Software, as a form of information, cannot be standardized; only structures for defining/documenting software can be standardized. It follows that software development techniques can only be meaningfully standardized in relation to information structures, not information content.

The third of the four product assurance disciplines is validation and verification (V&V). Unlike CM and QA, V&V has come into being expressly for the purpose of coping with software and its development. Unlike QA, which prinicipally deals with the problem of a product's adherence to pre-established standards, V&V deals with the issue of how well software fulfills functional and performance requirements and the assurance that specified requirements are indeed stated and interpreted correctly. The verification part of V&V assures that a product meets its prescribed goals as defined through baseline documentation. That is, verification is a discipline imposed to ascertain that a product is what it was intended to be relative to its preceding baseline. The validation part of V&V, by contrast, is levied as a discipline to assure that a product not only meets the objectives specified through baseline documentation, but in addition, does the right job.

Stated another way, the validation discipline is invoked to insure that the end-user gets the right product. A buyer or seller may have misinterpreted user requirements or, perhaps, requirements have changed, or the user gets to know more about what he needs, or early specifications of requirements were wrong or incomplete or in a state of flux. The validation process serves to assure that such problems do not persist among the user, buyer, and seller. To enhance objectivity, it is often desirable to have an independent organization, from outside the developing organization, perform the V&V function.

The fourth of the product assurance disciplines is test and evaluation (T&E), perhaps the discipline most understood, and yet paradoxically, least practiced with uniformity. T&E is defined as the discipline imposed outside the development project organization to independently assess whether a product fulfills objectives. T&E does this through the execution of a set of test plans and procedures. Specifically in support of the end user, T&E entails evaluating product performance in a live or near-live environment. Frequently, particularly within the miliatry arena, T&E is a major undertaking involving one or more systems which are to operate together, but which have been individually developed and accepted as stand-alone items. Some organizations formally turn over T&E responsibility to a group outside the development project organization after the product reaches a certain stage of development, their philosophy being that developers cannot be objective to the point of fully testing/evaluating what they have produced.

The definitions given for CM, QA, V&V, and T&E suggest some overlap in required skills and functions to be performed in order to invoke these disciplines collectively for product assurance purposes. Depending on many factors, the actual overlap may be significant or little. In fact, there are those who would argue that V&V and T&E are but subset functions of QA. But the contesting argument is that V&V and T&E have come into being as separate disciplines because conventional QA methods and techniques have failed to do an adequate job with respect to providing product assurance, particularly for computer-centered systems with software components. Management must be concerned with minimizing the application of excessive and redundant resources to address the overlap of these disciplines. What is important is that all the functions defined above are performed, not what they are called or who carries them out.

THE ELEMENTS OF SCM

When the need for the discipline of configuration management finally achieved widespread recognition within the software engineering community, the question arose as to how closely the software CM discipline ought to parallel the extant hardware practice of configuration management. Early SCM authors and practitioners [10] wisely chose the path of commonality with the hardware world, at least at the highest level. Of course, hardware engineering is different from software engineering, but broad similarities do exist and terms applied to one segment of the engineering community can easily be applied to another, even if the specific meanings of those terms differ significantly in detail. For that reason, the elements of SCM were chosen to be the same as those for hardware CM. As for hardware, the four components of SCM are:

- identification,
- control,
- auditing, and
- status accounting.

Let us examine each one in turn.

Software Configuration Identification: Effective management of the development of a system requires careful definition of its baseline components; changes to these components also need to be defined since these changes, together with the baselines, specify the system evolution. A system baseline is like a snapshot of the aggregate of system components as they exist at a given point in time; updates to this baseline are like frames in a movie strip of the system life cycle. The role of software configuration identification in the SCM process is to provide labels for these snapshots and the movie strip.

A baseline can be characterized by two labels. One label identifies the baseline itself, while the second label identifies an update to a particular baseline. An update to a baseline represents a baseline plus a set of changes that have been incorporated into it. Each of the baselines established during a software system's life cycle controls subsequent system development. At the time it is first established a software baseline embodies the actual software in its most recent state. When changes are made to the most recently established baseline, then, from the viewpoint of the software configuration manager, this baseline and these changes embody the actual software in its most recent state (although, from the viewpoint of the software developer, the actual software may be in a more advanced state).

The most elementary entity in the software configuration identification labeling mechanism is the software configuration item (SCI). Viewed from an SCM perspective, a software baseline appears as a set of SCI's. The SCI's within a baseline are related to one another via a tree-like hierarchy. As the software system evolves through its life cycle, the number of

branches in this hierarchy generally increases; the first baseline may consist of no more than one SCI. The lowest level SCI's in the tree hierarchy may still be under development and not yet under SCM control. These entities are termed design objects or computer program components (see Fig. 3). Each baseline and each member in the associated family of updates will exist in one or more forms, such as a design document, source code on a disk, or executing object code.

In performing the identification function, the software configuration manager is, in effect, taking snapshots of the SCI's. Each baseline and its associated updates collectively represents the evolution of the software during each of its life cycle stages. These stages are staggered with respect to one another. Thus, the collection of life cycle stages looks like a collection of staggered and overlapping sequences of snapshots of SCI trees. Let us now imagine that this collection of snapshot sequences is threaded, in chronological order, onto a strip of movie film as in Fig. 4. Let us further imagine that the strip of movie film is run through a projector. Then we would see a history of the evolution of the software. Consequently, the identification of baselines and updates provides an explicit documentation trail linking all stages of the software life cycle. With the aid of this documentation trail, the software developer can assess the integrity of his product, and the software buyer can assess the integrity of the product he is paying for.

Software Configuration Control: The evolution of a software system is, in the language of SCM, the development of baselines and the incorporation of a series of changes into the baselines. In addition to these changes that explicitly affect existing baselines, there are changes that occur during early stages of the system life cycle that may affect baselines that do not yet exist. For example, some time before software coding begins (i.e., some time prior to the establishment of a design baseline), a contract may be modified to include a software warranty provision such as: system downtime due to software failures shall not exceed 30 minutes per day. This warranty provision will generally affect subsequent baselines but in a manner that cannot be explicitly determined *a priori*. One role of software configuration control is to provide the administrative mechanism for precipitating, preparing, evaluating, and approving or disapproving all change proposals throughout the system life cycle.

We have said that software, for configuration management purposes, is a collection of SCI's that are related to one another in a well-defined way. In early baselines and their associated updates, SCI's are specification documents (one or more volumes of text for each baseline or associated update); in later baselines and their associated updates, each SCI may manifest itself in any or all of the various software representations. Software configuration control focuses on managing changes to SCI's (existing or to be developed) in all of their representations. This process involves three basic ingredients.

1) Documentation (such as administrative forms and supporting technical and administrative material) for formally precipitating and defining a proposed change to a software system.

2) An organizational body for formally evaluating and

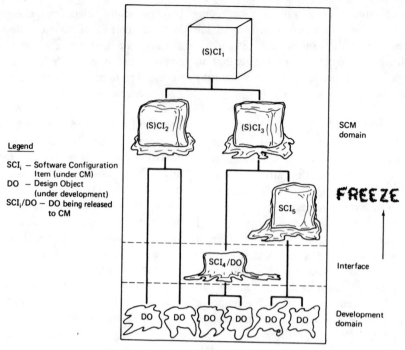

Fig. 3. The development/SCM interface.

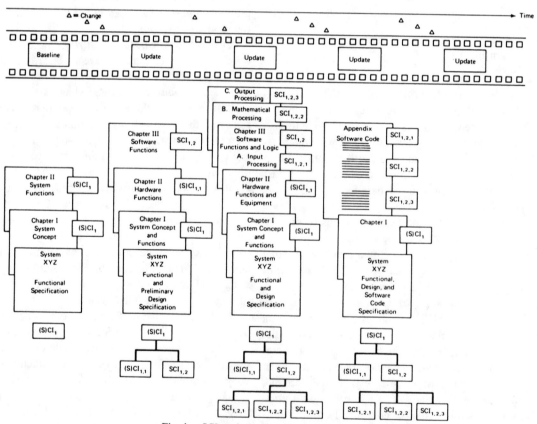

Fig. 4. SCI evolution in a single document.

approving or disapproving a proposed change to a software system (the Configuration Control Board).

3) Procedures for controlling changes to a software system.

The Engineering Change Proposal (ECP), a major control document, contains information such as a description of the proposed change, identification of the originating organization, rationale for the change, identification of affected baselines and SCI's (if appropriate), and specification of cost and schedule impacts. ECP's are reviewed and coordinated by the CCB, which is typically a body representing all organizational units which have a vested interest in proposed changes.

Fig. 5 depicts the software configuration control process.

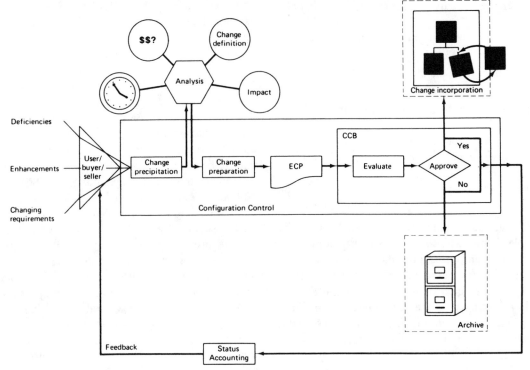

Fig. 5.   The control process.

As the figure suggests, change incorporation is not an SCM function, but monitoring the change implementation process resulting in change incorporation is. Fig. 5 also emphasizes that the analysis that may be required to prepare an ECP is also outside the SCM purview. Note also from the figure how ECP's not approved by the CCB are not simply discarded but are archived for possible future reference.

Many automated tools support the control process. The major ones aid in controlling software change once the coding stage has been reached, and are generically referred to as program support libraries (PSL's). The level of support provided by PSL's, however, varies greatly. As a minimum, a PSL should provide a centralized and readily available repository for authoritative versions of each component of a software system. It should contain the data necessary for the orderly development and control of each SCI. Automation of other functions, such as library access control, software and document version maintenance, change recording, and document reconstruction, greatly enhance both the control and maintenance processes. These capabilities are currently available in systems such as SOFTOOL's change and configuration control environment (CCC).

A PSL supports a developmental approach in which project personnel work on a common visible product rather than on independent components. In those PSL's which include access controls, project personnel can be separately assigned read/write access to each software document/component, from programs to lines of code. Thus, all project personnel are assured ready access to the critical interface information necessary for effective software development. At the same time, modifications to various software components, whether sanctioned baselines or modules under development, can be closely controlled.

Under the PSL concept, the programmer operates under a well-defined set of parameters and exercises a narrower span of detailed control. This minimizes the need for explicit communication between analysts and programmers and makes the inclusion of new project personnel less traumatic since interface requirements are well documented. It also minimizes the preparation effort for technical audits.

Responsibility for maintenance of the PSL data varies depending on the level of automation provided. For those systems which provide only a repository for data, a secretary/librarian is usually responsible for maintaining the notebooks which will contain the data developed and used by project personnel and for maintenance of the PSL archives. More advanced PSL systems provide real time, on-line access to data and programs and automatically create the records necessary to fully trace the history of the development. In either case the PSL provides standardization of project recordkeeping, ensures that system documentation corresponds to the current system configuration, and guarantees the existence of adequate documentation of previous versions.

A PSL should support three main activities: code development, software management, and configuration control. Support to the development process includes support to design, coding, testing, documentation, and program maintenance along with associated database schema and subschema. A PSL provides this support through:

• storage and maintenance of software documentation and code,
• support to program compilation/testing,
• support for the generation of program/system documentation.

Support to the management of the software development process involves the storage and output of programming data such as:

• collection and automatic reporting of management data related to program development,

435

- control over the integrity and security of the data in the PSL,
- separation of the clerical activity related to the programming process.

PSL's provide support to the configuration control process through:

- access and change authorization control for all data in the library,
- control of software code releases,
- automatic program and document reconstruction,
- automatic change tracking and reporting,
- assurance of the consistency between documentation, code, and listings.

A PSL has four major components: internal libraries in machine-readable form, external libraries in hardcopy form, computer procedures, and office procedures. The components of a PSL system are interlocked to establish an exact correspondence between the internal units of code and external versions (such as listings) of the developing systems. This continuous correspondence is the characteristic of a PSL that guarantees ongoing visibility and identification of the developing system.

Different PSL implementations exist for various system environments with the specifics of the implementation dependent upon the hardware, software, user, and operating environment. The fundamental correspondence between the internal and external libraries in each environment, however, is established by the PSL librarian and computer procedures. The office procedures are specified in a project CM Plan so that the format of the external libraries is standard across software projects, and internal and external libraries are easily maintainable.

Newer PSL systems minimize the need for both office and computer procedures through the implementation of extensive management functionality. This functionality provides significant flexibility in controlling the access to data and allocating change authority, while providing a variety of status reporting capabilities. The availability of management information, such as a list of all the software structures changed to solve a particular Software Trouble Report or the details on the latest changes to a particular software document, provides a means for the control function to effectively operate without burdening the development team with cumbersome procedures and administrative paperwork. Current efforts in PSL refinement/development are aimed at linking support of the development environment with that of the configuration control environment. The goal of such systems is to provide an integrated environment where control and management information is generated automatically as a part of a fully supported design and development process.

Software Configuration Auditing: Software configuration auditing provides the mechanism for determining the degree to which the current state of the software system mirrors the software system pictured in baseline and requirements documentation. It also provides the mechanism for formally establishing a baseline. A baseline in its formative stages (for example, a draft specification document that appears prior to the existence of the functional baseline) is referred to as a "to-be-established" baseline; the final state of the auditing process

conducted on a to-be-established baseline is a sanctioned baseline. The same may be said about baseline updates.

Software configuration auditing serves two purposes, configuration verification and configuration validation. Verification ensures that what is intended for each software configuration item as specified in one baseline or update is actually achieved in the succeeding baseline or update; validation ensures that the SCI configuration solves the right problem (i.e., that customer needs are satisfied). Software configuration auditing is applied to each baseline (and corresponding update) in its to-be-established state. An auditing process common to all baselines is the determination that an SCI structure exists and that its contents are based on all available information.

Software auditing is intended to increase software visibility and to establish traceability throughout the life cycle of the software product. Of course, this visibility and traceability are not achieved without cost. Software auditing costs time and money. But the judicious investment of time and money, particularly in the early stages of a project, pays dividends in the latter stages. These dividends include the avoidance of costly retrofits resulting from problems such as the sudden appearance of new requirements and the discovery of major design flaws. Conversely, failing to perform auditing, or constraining it to the later stages of the software life cycle, can jeopardize successful software development. Often in such cases, by the time discrepancies are discovered (if they are), the software cannot be easily or economically modified to rectify the discrepancies. The result is often a dissatisfied customer, large cost overruns, slipped schedules, or cancelled projects.

Software auditing makes visible to management the current status of the software in the life cycle product audited. It also reveals whether the project requirements are being satisfied and whether the intent of the preceding baseline has been fulfilled. With this visibility, project management can evaluate the integrity of the software product being developed, resolve issues that may have been raised by the audit, and correct defects in the development process. The visibility afforded by the software audit also provides a basis for the establishment of the audited life cycle product as a new baseline.

Software auditing provides traceability between a software life cycle product and the requirements for that product. Thus, as life cycle products are audited and baselines established, every requirement is traced successively from baseline to baseline. Disconnects are also made visible during the establishment of traceability. These disconnects include requirements not satisfied in the audited product and extraneous features observed in the product (i.e., features for which no stated requirement exists).

With the different point of view made possible by the visibility and traceability achieved in the software audit, management can make better decisions and exercise more incisive control over the software development process. The result of a software audit may be the establishment of a baseline, the redirection of project tasking, or an adjustment of applied project resources.

The responsibility for a successful software development project is shared by the buyer, seller, and user. Software auditing uniquely benefits each of these project participants. Appropriate auditing by each party provides checks and balances over the development effort. The scope and depth of the audits undertaken by the three parties may vary greatly. However, the purposes of these differing forms of software audit remain the same: to provide visibility and to establish traceability of the software life cycle products. An excellent overview of the software audit process, from which some of the above discussion has been extracted, appears in [11].

Software Configuration Status Accounting: A decision to make a change is generally followed by a time delay before the change is actually made, and changes to baselines generally occur over a protracted period of time before they are incorporated into baselines as updates. A mechanism is therefore needed for maintaining a record of how the system has evolved and where the system is at any time relative to what appears in published baseline documentation and written agreements. Software configuration status accounting provides this mechanism. Status accounting is the administrative tracking and reporting of all software items formally identified and controlled. It also involves the maintenance of records to support software configuration auditing. Thus, software configuration status accounting records the activity associated with the other three SCM functions and therefore provides the means by which the history of the software system life cycle can be traced.

Although administrative in nature, status accounting is a function that increases in complexity as the system life cycle progresses because of the multiple software representations that emerge with later baselines. This complexity generally results in large amounts of data to be recorded and reported. In particular, the scope of software configuration status accounting encompasses the recording and reporting of:

1) the time at which each representation of a baseline and update came into being;

2) the time at which each software configuration item came into being;

3) descriptive information about each SCI;

4) engineering change proposal status (approved, disapproved, awaiting action);

5) descriptive information about each ECP;

6) change status;

7) descriptive information about each change;

8) status of technical and administrative documentation associated with a baseline or update (such as a plan prescribing tests to be performed on a baseline for updating purposes);

9) deficiencies in a to-be-established baseline uncovered during a configuration audit.

Software configuration status accounting, because of its large data input and output requirements, is generally supported in part by automated processes such as the PSL described earlier. Data are collected and organized for input to a computer and reports giving the status of entities are compiled and generated by the computer.

THE MANAGEMENT DILEMMA

As we mentioned at the beginning of this paper, SCM and many of the other product assurance disciplines grew up in the 1970's in response to software failure. The new disciplines were designed to achieve visibility into the software engineering process and thereby exercise some measure of control over that process. Students of mathematical control theory are taught early in their studies a simple example of the control process. Consider being confronted with a cup of hot coffee, filled to the top, which you are expected to carry from the kitchen counter to the kitchen table. It is easily verified that if you watch the cup as you carry it, you are likely to spill more coffee than if you were to keep your head turned away from the cup. The problem with looking at the cup is one of overcompensation. As you observe slight deviations from the straight-and-level, you adjust, but often you adjust too much. To compensate for that overadjustment, you tend to overadjust again, with the result being hot coffee on your floor.

This little diversion from our main topic of SCM has an obvious moral. There is a fundamental propensity on the part of the practitioners of the product assurance disciplines to overadjust, to overcompensate for the failures of the development disciplines. There is one sure way to eliminate failure completely from the software development process, and that is to stop it completely. The software project manager must learn how to apply his resources intelligently. He must achieve visibility and control, but he must not so encumber the developer so as to bring progress to a virtual halt. The product assurers have a virtuous perspective. They strive for perfection and point out when and where perfection has not been achieved. We seem to have a binary attitude about software; it is either correct or it is not. That is perhaps true, but we cannot expect anyone to deliver perfect software in any reasonable time period or for a reasonable sum of money. What we need to develop is software that is good enough. Some of the controls that we have placed on the developer have the deleterious effect of increasing costs and expanding schedules rather than shrinking them.

The dilemma to management is real. We must have the visibility and control that the product assurance disciplines have the capacity to provide. But we must be careful not to overcompensate and overcontrol. This is the fine line which will distinguish the successful software managers of the 1980's from the rest of the software engineering community.

ACKNOWLEDGMENT

The author wishes to acknowledge the contribution of B. J. Gregor to the preparation and critique of the final manuscript.

REFERENCES

[1] "Contracting for computer software development—Serious problems require management attention to avoid wasting additional millions," General Accounting Office, Rep. FGMSD 80-4, Nov. 9, 1979.

[2] D. M. Weiss, "The MUDD report: A case study of Navy software development practices," Naval Res. Lab., Rep. 7909, May 21, 1975.

[3] B. W. Boehm, "Software engineering," *IEEE Trans. Comput.*, vol. C-25, pp. 1226–1241, Dec. 1976.

[4] *Proc. IEEE* (Special Issue on Software Engineering), vol. 68, Sept. 1980.

[5] E. Bersoff, V. Henderson, and S. Siegel, "Attaining software product integrity," *Tutorial: Software Configuration Management*, W. Bryan, C. Chadbourne, and S. Siegel, Eds., Los Alamitos, CA, IEEE Comput. Soc., Cat. EHO-169-3, 1981.

[6] B. W. Boehm et al., *Characteristics of Software Quality, TRW Series of Software Technology*, vol. 1. New York: North-Holland, 1978.

[7] T. A. Thayer, et al., *Software Reliability, TRW Series of Software Technology*, vol. 2. New York: North-Holland, 1978.

[8] D. J. Reifer, Ed., *Tutorial: Automated Tools for Software Eng.*, Los Alamitos, CA, IEEE Comput. Soc., Cat. EHO-169-3, 1979.

[9] E. Bersoff, V. Henderson, and S. Siegel, *Software Configuration Management*. Englewood Cliffs, NJ: Prentice-Hall, 1980.

[10] ——, "Software configuration management: A tutorial," *Computer*, vol. 12, pp. 6–14, Jan. 1979.

[11] W. Bryan, S. Siegel, and G. Whiteleather, "Auditing throughout the software life cycle: A primer," *Computer*, vol. 15, pp. 56–67, Mar. 1982.

[12] "Software configuration management," Naval Elec. Syst. Command, Software Management Guidebooks, vol. 2, undated.

Edward H. Bersoff (M'75–SM'78) received the A.B., M.S., and Ph.D. degrees in mathematics from New York University, New York.

He is President and Founder of BTG, Inc., a high technology, Washington, DC area based, systems analysis and engineering firm. In addition to his corporate responsibilities, he directs the company's research in software engineering, product assurance, and software management. BTG specializes in the application of modern systems engineering principles to the computer based system development process. At BTG, he has been actively involved in the FAA's Advanced Automation Program where he is focusing on software management and software configuration management issues on this extremely complex program. He also participates in the company's activities within the Naval Intelligence community, providing senior consulting services to a wide variety of system development efforts. He was previously President of CTEC, Inc. where he directed the concept formulation and development of the Navy Command and Control System (NCCS), Ocean Surveillance Information System (OSIS) Baseline now installed at all U.S. Navy Ocean Surveillance Centers. He also served as Experiment Director for the Joint ARPA, Navy, CINCPAC Military Message Experiment. This test was designed to examine the usefulness of secure, automated message processing systems in an operational military environment and to develop design criteria for future military message processing systems. Prior to joining CTEC, Inc., he was Manager of Engineering Operations and Manager of FAA Operations for Logicon, Inc.'s Process Systems Division. He joined Logicon from the NASA Electronics Research Center. He has taught mathematics at universities in Boston, New York, and Washington, DC. His technical contributions to the fields of software requirements and design range from early publications in computer architecture, reliability and programming languages, to more recent publications in software quality and configuration management. A textbook entitled *Software Configuration Management* (Prentice-Hall) represents the product of three years of research in the field by Dr. Bersoff and his colleagues.

Dr. Bersoff is a member of AFCEA, American Management Association, MENSA, and the Young Presidents' Organization.

Investigative Audit for Controlling Software Development

Gene F. Walters
Independent Software Consultant
Box 7785, Tahoe City, CA 95730

Abstract

Frequently, the program management staff of a software development project is unable to identify problem areas in the effort and initiate corrective action. The day-to-day activities can easily mask the more serious deficiencies. This paper provides detailed guidelines rather than a general methodology for an investigative audit to identify and remedy the problems. The author feels this approach will better enable others to more easily apply the technique.

Introduction

"Why an audit?"

All too often software development efforts miss the scheduled delivery date, overrun the budget, and result in a less than acceptable quality product. The origin of the approach to a structured audit described here was at the request of a contractor and his customer. The system the contractor was developing consisted of both hardware and software. The resultant software at the time the audit was performed was considerably greater than originally planned and had grown from 45,000 to 72,000 lines of code. The number of software personnel peaked at around 35. Both the contractor and the customer were dissatisfied with the progress. Schedule slips and cost overruns resulted. At the time the audit was performed, the fourth function out of twelve was going through integration test. Five overriding concerns at the beginning of the audit were:

1. Reduce the schedule risks as much as possible.

2. Reduce any risks which may lead to a poor quality product.

3. Minimize the impact of the audit upon the project personnel's daily activities.

4. Perform the audit as quickly as possible so that the recommendations could be enacted at the earliest time.

5. Recommend changes that would be viable so that the benefits to be gained outweigh any schedule impacts incurred for putting them in place.

From past experience and observations such audits have involved a task force of 5-10 persons, were done for larger projects, and had little predefined structure for the review process.

Before the audit was started a structured, disciplined methodology was established for the review.

Experience gained on this audit, has shown that this technique has considerable merit on software development projects ranging from a 10-50 person level over a 1-3 year period. Adjustments can be made to this methodology for smaller or larger efforts. These adjustments are described in the following section. The methodology addresses the five concerns listed above and does so with a minimum effort.

Audit Methodology

"Let's get an approach that will work."

The audit methodology is based upon getting all the pertinent information about the software development process as quickly as possible and providing the evaluation results with recommendations in the form of a written report and a presentation. The evaluation addresses the risks in completing the project and how to reduce these schedule risks to the maximum extent, but yet produce a high quality product. Included is the review of project controls, implementation methodologies, baselines, technical and management reviews, standards, configuration management, quality assurance, test controls, communication among personnel, and resources available to project personnel. The audit does not address the adequacy of the technical design by the management and control of the technical work. Cost is not considered directly: only the schedule impacts.

The overall flow of activities during the audit are shown in Figure 1. These activities are described in more detail in the following paragraphs. The structured interviews and the inspections are interleaved. The reasons are: 1) persons to be interviewed may not be available at the immediate convenience of the auditors, 2) many consecutive interviews can be taxing for the auditors, 3) interviews can identify items

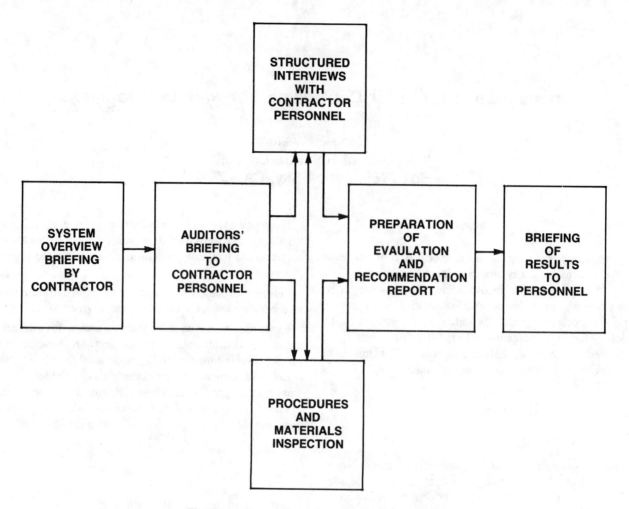

Figure 1: Flow Diagram of Audit Activities

or procedures to be inspected, and 4) inspections can identify the need for additional interviews.

The approximate times to be allocated for the activities shown in Figure 1 are:

1. System overview briefing by contractor   2-3 hours
2. Auditors' briefing to contractor personnel   1/2 hour
3. Structured interviews with contractor personnel & procedures and materials inspection   4 1/2 days
4. Preparation of evaluation and recommendations report   4 1/2 days
5. Presentation of results to contractor personnel   2 hours

For the size of a project in the range of 10-50 persons, there should be two auditors to ensure all the necessary information is captured quickly and accurately. Both of the auditors should be senior software system engineers or

managers who are knowledgeable on all phases and activities of software development.

If a project is quite small, one auditor would suffice since the resultant risks would not be large in the absolute sense. However, it would be preferable to still use two but perform the task over a shorter period of time.

For larger projects, the following approaches can be used:

1. Use additional auditors. One auditor will be the lead to coordinate the activities. Supporting auditors would have specialized areas of expertise. Additional effort is required for the coordination.
2. Use a team of two auditors to evaluate the overall software development process for identifying the specific areas of concern. Additional auditors, or the original team, would perform a detailed audit in the identified high risk areas.

The first alternative will likely accomplish the audit in less time but will require more person hours to complete.

Initial Activities

"Where are you now?"

At the outset of the audit it is important to find out briefly what the completed system is supposed to do and where the implementors think they are in the development effort. To accomplish this it is necessary to inform the project what the audit team is going to do and *not* do. Before the audit is started, the following activities should be completed:

1. Auditors and the software development organization agree on the overall activities that will take place. These are shown in Figure 1.

2. Prepare the forms to use for the structured interview before the audit. The items to include are discussed in the next section.

3. Request a briefing by the key project personnel, such as the project manager and the project systems engineer. The following information should be provided in the briefing:
   - Summary technical description of the system (e.g., functions, modules, size, languages, tools used)
   - Progress with respect to schedule
   - System baselines
   - Project organization and overall roles and responsibilities
   - Resources needed/used (e.g., development computers, word processors, other computers)

4. Request a meeting of all project personnel at which time the auditors will present the following information:
   - Introduction of the auditors
   - Objectives of the audit
   - Audit activities, e.g. (interviews and inspections)
   - How the results of the audit will be provided to the project

When the briefing is given to the project it must be made clear that the intent of the audit is to review the software development process, not to evaluate the project personnels' performance. There should be the opportunity for any project member to ask questions during and after the briefing.

Interviews

"How do you do? What do you do?"

Why interview the project personnel? Software development is labor intensive. Information can be gathered quickly by going directly to the source, the project personnel. Using interviews the auditors will be able to find out what work has been accomplished, is currently being done, and is planned. Specifically, how the work is performed should be addressed. An additional objective of the interview is to uncover past, current, and anticipated problems. Proposed solutions should be solicited.

Who should be interviewed? If the auditors have the patience and there is sufficient time, all the project personnel could be interviewed. Since this, in general, is not feasible, key individuals and others from the remaining software development team to make up at least 25 percent of the personnel should be interviewed. When the project briefing is given by the software development team, the first ones to be interviewed should be identified. It is essential to cover all the processes that are applicable for the current phase of the project (e.g., systems engineering, requirements analysis, design analysis, test management, configuration management, quality assurance, project control and document control). During the interviews additional personnel may be identified for individual discussions. The key project personnel should not be limited to managers and functional leaders. For example, individuals responsible for maintaining

Table 1: Typical Interview Topics

- **PERIOD OF TIME ON PROJECT**
- **PERCENT TIME ON PROJECT**
- **ACTIVITIES INVOLVED IN**
- **ROLES AND RESPONSIBLITIES**
- **RELATIONSHIPS WITH OTHERS**
- **DOCUMENTS USED IN WORK**
- **TECHNIQUES/AIDS USED IN WORK**
- **RESOURCES REQUIRED**
- **PROBLEMS ENCOUNTERED**
- **SOLUTIONS/PROPOSED SOLUTIONS**
- **WORK STILL TO BE DONE**
- **REQUIREMENTS ANALYSIS METHODOLOGY PLANNED/USED**
- **DESIGN METHODOLOGY PLANNED/USED**
- **DEVELOPMENT METHODOLOGY PLANNED/USED**
- **TESTING METHODOLOGY PLANNED/USED**
- **DESIGN & IMPLEMENTATION STANDARDS PLANNED/USED**
- **DOCUMENTATION STANDARDS PLANNED/USED**
- **INVOLVEMENT WITH CONFIGURATION MANAGEMENT**
- **INVOLVEMENT WITH QUALITY ASSURANCE**
- **INVOLVEMENT WITH FORMAL TESTING**
- **INVOLVEMENT WITH FORMAL TECHNICAL REVIEWS**
- **INVOLVEMENT WITH FORMAL MANAGEMENT REVIEWS**
- **INVOLVEMENT WITH PROJECT CONTROL**
- **INVOLVEMENT WITH TRAINING**
- **INVOLVEMENT WITH INSTALLATION**

configuration control records and project status information can provide considerable insight into how well the software development process is controlled.

A form with all the desired topics to cover should be used by the auditors during the interview. A list of typical topics is shown in Table 1. The information gathered from each individual for these topics include:

- Each individual's perception of his work and the methods used to accomplish it.

- How each individual relates to others on the project and the information flow.

- Resources required to accomplish the work yet to be done.

Cordiality is important to a successful interview. The likelihood of getting the necessary information during an interview is increased by friendly interaction between the auditors and the project personnel. The time for the auditors to be tough is after all the information is gathered and when the evaluation is being done.

The approach to conducting an interview uses many of the same techniques that are applied in a good job interview. The interviews should be held in a private office not belonging to the person being interviewed and with both auditors present. The setting should minimize interruptions. Since accurate and complete records are important, both auditors should take notes. All records from the interviews are to be handled in confidence and are not made available to the project staff.

In opening an interview the overall objectives of the discussion are to be explained to the individual. The fact that notes will be taken during the interview session should be mentioned. Any time conflicts which may limit the discussion should be established at the start of the interview.

In gathering information during the interviews, open-ended questions should be used. The interviewee should not be led to a yes or no answer or to an answer the auditor would like to hear. For example, do not ask: "Do you use top-down design techniques?" but rather "Would your describe the process you use in designing software?"

When the individual is responding to a topic, the auditor should probe by asking why, what, how, and when type questions. During these discussions, the auditors should refrain from making judgments. From the discussions the auditors should be able to identify the materials and procedures that are to be inspected. If the responsible individual is being interviewed, the auditors should establish when the inspection can be done.

In wrapping up the interview the auditors should thank the individual for his help and mention that a follow-up discussion may be required. Also, the individual should be given

Table 2. Project Control Information

- **OVERALL PROJECT SCHEDULE/STATUS INCLUDING DELIVERABLES**
- **PROJECT LEVEL MEMOS**
- **TECHNICAL AND MANAGEMENT REVIEW SCHEDULES/STATUS**
- **DETAILED TECHNICAL ACTIVIITY SCHEDULE/STATUS WITHIN A SPECIFIC PROJECT PHASE**
- **DETAILED DOCUMENTATION SCHEDULE/STATUS**
- **DISCREPANCY REPORTING AND CORRECTION STATUS**
- **ACTION ITEM LOGS**

the opportunity to come back if he has thought of additional information he has forgotten to bring up during the discussion.

The length of the sessions will vary from one to two hours. The total time with any individual should be less than four hours. The interviewee should not be hurried, but the auditors must keep the discussion focused to prevent lost time.

Inspections

"Let's see what you say you have."

The purpose of the inspections is twofold. First, the products that have been prepared or are used by the project are reviewed. Typical products that the auditors would look at are listed in Tables 2 and 3. The project control information is listed separately since it is so critical for both the project management and the customer. Second, the flow of information for key supporting activities is reviewed.

Table 3. Materials Inspected

- **STATEMENT OF WORK**
- **SOFTWARE IMPLEMENTATION PLAN**
- **SUPPORTING PLANS (E.G., CONFIGURATION MANAGEMENT AND QUALITY ASSURANCE)**
- **REQUIREMENTS SPECIFICATIONS**
- **DESIGN SPECIFICATIONS**
- **TEST PLANS AND PROCEDURES**
- **INSTALLATION AND TRAINING PLANS**
- **SOFTWARE DEVELOPMENT NOTEBOOKS/ FOLDERS**
- **STANDARDS DOCUMENTS**
- **FORMS (E.G., CONFIGURATION MANAGEMENT AND QUALITY ASSURANCE)**
- **MINUTES OF FORMAL MEETINGS**

Table 4. Activities Reviewed

- **MANAGEMENT REVIEWS**
- **TECHNICAL REVIEWS**
- **CONFIGURATION MANAGEMENT ACTIVITY FLOW**
- **QUALITY ASSURANCE ACTIVITY FLOW**
- **TEST ACTIVITY**
- **DATA FLOW FOR DOCUMENT PREPARATION**
- **PROBLEM REPORTING AND CORRECTION ACTIVITY FLOW**
- **CONFIGURATION CONTROL BOARD ACTIVITY**

Examples of such activities are listed in Table 4. Often these activities are slighted in a software development project while the concerted effort is on technically oriented tasks such as the design and coding activities.

Of the products to be reviewed, the first one should be the statement of work. Next, the various plans should be examined. The auditors should spot check the specifications, records, memos and folders for the type of information they contain, not the technical adequacy.

During the inspection of the project control information, the auditors should determine:

1. What schedule and status data exist.
2. Purpose of the schedules.
3. Present method of extracting and preparing schedule and status information.
4. Dynamics of the status data and the frequency of updates.
5. Degree of detail for schedule and status information.
6. Amount of effort spent in maintaining the schedule and status information.
7. Consistency and completeness of schedule and status information.

In reviewing the information flow for key supporting activities, the auditors should determine:

1. Compliance with plans.
2. Information flow from diagrams and descriptions, if they exist.
3. Formality of each activity.
4. Inconsistencies, conflicts, underlaps, and overlaps among activities.
5. Ease of completing, processing, and controlling forms.
6. How meetings are scheduled and conducted.
7. What information is maintained in logs, records, minutes, and action items lists.

During the process of inspecting the project control information and supporting activities, the auditors will be holding discussions with project personnel. The differences between these discussions and the interviews are that the subject matter will be sharply focused on one area and there may be more than one person from the project in the discussion.

Evaluation

"Hmmmm..., my diagnosis says you have..."

After the interviews and inspections have been completed, the auditors should, to the extent possible, isolate themselves from the project personnel to perform the evaluation and prepare the final report and presentation. A lot of notes will have been made up to this point of the audit. Organization of the material is essential. First the auditors should go over each form that was used for note taking during the interviews and list all the problems identified which are likely to impact the scheduled completion date or the product quality. Lack of quality will indirectly affect the schedule. Many of the problems must be derived from the information, or the lack of it. For example, the schedule and status information may be dispersed among several individuals and not integrated. In constructing the list, the auditors should maintain a cross reference index to the interview sheet. This will aid in the preparation of the report when specific examples are needed to support the discussion.

Once the list of problem areas has been established, the auditors should categorize and combine as necessary. The results can be given in two major sections, general and specific.

A parallel approach should be used in preparing the results of the inspections. It is expected that many of the results will be the same as for the interview.

Finally, the high risk areas must be identified. Examples of problem areas are: 1) project control, 2) configuration management, 3) quality assurance, 4) test planning/control/conducting, and 5) software implementation and test tools. For each identified problem area the risks should be listed which exist if no action is taken. Such risks could include: 1) delay in corrective actions, 2) incorrect decisions, 3) loss in software integrity, 4) lost motion because of rework, 5) reduced product quality, 6) difficult to maintain, and 7) schedule slippage. The problem areas should be ranked in order of criticality.

Final Report and Presentation

"To get well you can..."

Both a final report and a presentation should be provided by the auditors. The briefing provides the evaluation results

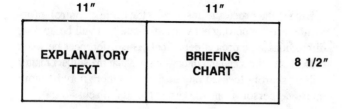

Figure 2: Report Layout

and recommendations quickly to a wide audience of key project personnel and management and permits interaction for clarifying the information. After the audit team has left, the final report provides an explanation of the presentation material which can later be referenced by the attendees at the briefing or by other project personnel.

The first step is to prepare the charts. Each chart is placed in the report with the accompanying explanatory text on the opposite page as is shown in Figure 2. The page layout shown is based upon the briefing charts being prepared with the longer dimension oriented horizontally.

Premature leaking out of the evaluation results should be avoided. Typing should be done by the auditors' staff or in an environment where confidentiality will be maintained.

A typical organization of the briefing and the report is shown in Table 5.

The last portion of the presentation and report consists of the recommendations, expected results, and implementation considerations.

The recommendations should be formulated by the problem areas which were identified in the risk assessment. The recommendations should be specific and, when appropriate, examples should be given to clarify them. For example, the configuration control activity may be ill-defined. A sample flow of a portion of this activity could be given which shows the necessary elements for a complete description: processes, responsible organizations, data flow, control flow, and decision points.

The expected results portion of the presentation and report

Table 5. Organization of Final Report and Presentation

- OBJECTIVES OF SOFTWARE REVIEW
- REVIEW CONSTRAINTS
- INTERVIEWS WITH PROJECT PERSONNEL
    - PERSONNEL MIX
    - TOPICS COVERED
    - GENERAL RESULTS
    - SPECIFIC RESULTS
- INSPECTIONS OF MATERIALS AND PROCEDURES
    - ITEMS INSPECTED
    - ACTIVITIES REVIEWED
    - PROJECT CONTROL INFORMATION REVIEWED
    - GENERAL RESULTS
    - SPECIFIC RESULTS
- RISK ASSESSMENT
- RECOMMENDATIONS
    - RISK AREA 1
    - RISK AREA 2
- EXPECTED RESULTS IF RECOMMENDATIONS ARE IMPLEMENTED
- IMPLEMENTATION CONSIDERATIONS FOR REVISED PROCEDURES

should address in summary form the benefits and reduced risks if the recommendations are implemented.

The final message that should be left is a brief plan on how the recommendations could be implemented with minimum impact on the day-to-day project activities. Without this plan the viability of the recommendations is questionable.

Conclusion and Recommendations for the Auditors

"Remember, it's the real world out there!"

In this final section, general considerations of how the auditors should conduct their work and a brief cost/benefit analysis of the investigative audit are given.

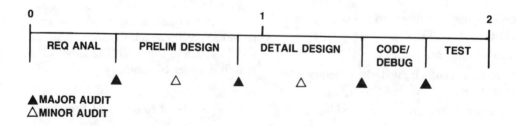

Figure 3: Project Schedule

Table 6: Audit vs Project Effort

AUDITS	
4 MAJOR AUDITS (160 HOURS EACH)	640 HOURS
2 MINOR AUDITS (96 HOURS EACH)	192 HOURS
TOTAL ....832 HOURS	

PROJECT	
2 YEARS X 20 PERSONS X 2000 HOURS/YEAR...................................80,000 HOURS	

RATIO OF AUDIT TO PROJECT EFFORT	
832/80,000 = 0.0104 ....1.04 PERCENT	

First, how should the auditors approach their task. A friendly, cooperative attitude is paramount. The auditors are there to help. The auditors should be as objective as possible. Remember that every project has its shortcomings. The project personnel have their noses to the grindstone and rarely have the time to back away from the daily activities and assess how well they are controlling the work. Also, the auditors should be careful not to be caught up in the myriad of details. It is easy to become overwhelmed.

The benefits have already been covered. Now, what is the cost of the investigative audit? The purpose of the audit is to assess how well a project is controlled and recommend redirection. To see what the typical cost is for auditing, an example project is given. Assume the project has an average of 20 persons for a period of two years with a schedule depicted in Figure 3.

Two types of audits are shown, major and minor. The major audit is of the type described in the previous sections and would require approximately 160 person-hours to complete using two auditors. This kind of audit would appropriately be used at the completion of one phase and before the start of the next. If incremental development is used, any time between the start of a new phase and the midpoint of the overlapping phases would be a good choice. When a phase is six months or longer it would be best to have a minor audit to spot check the development activity. The emphasis on this audit would be a review of the problem areas that were identified on the previous major audit. The estimated time for the minor audit is 96 person-hours.

Table 6. shows the effort required for the audits versus project effort.

The cost of audits will be slightly higher than one percent because the salary of the auditors will on the average be greater than that of the project personnel. Even so, the cost of the audits compared to the risks of proceeding without them would be reasonable and worth the investment.

445

Managing Software Development Projects for Maximum Productivity

NORMAN R. HOWES

Abstract—In the area of software development, data processing management often focuses more on coding techniques and system architecture than on how to manage the development. In recent years, "structured programming" and "structured analysis" have received more attention than the techniques software managers employ to manage. Moreover, these coding and architectural considerations are often advanced as the key to a smooth running, well managed project.

This paper documents a philosophy for software development and the tools used to support it. Those management techniques deal with quantifying such abstract terms as "productivity," "performance," and "progress," and with measuring these quantities and applying management controls to maximize them. The paper also documents the application of these techniques on a major software development effort.

Index Terms—Performance evaluation, productivity analysis, progress measurement, software development methodologies, work breakdown structure.

I. INTRODUCTION

IN 1977 we began developing a Project Management System to support worldwide operations. It was designed to assist with the day to day management of large engineering and construction jobs. As a management information system, it was necessary to interface with the company's financial and materials management systems. The result was that these systems had to be totally redesigned to support this new Project Management System.

The overall effort took about two million man-hours. The development of this system called BRICS (Brown & Root Integrated Control System) was managed using the system being developed but in a manual rather than automated mode. The key management concepts used to control this development effort; namely, performance evaluation, multibudgeting, and forecasting with the "variance" technique were documented in [1].

In order to give a complete self-contained treatment of these concepts, the scope of the paper was limited to these (somewhat technical) topics. This necessitated omitting the discussion of other BRICS capabilities such as productivity evaluation. Moreover the successful management of a large-scale software development project involves more than applying techniques such as these. An experienced software development manager has a fixed idea (philosophy) of how software development should be managed. If such a philosophy is a successful one it will automatically tend to maximize productivity and keep the work progressing as planned.

The purpose of this paper is to document such a philosophy,

to show the principle techniques necessary to support it, and to point out some common pitfalls that experience teaches one to avoid.

II. HOW ONE VIEWS SOFTWARE DEVELOPMENT

Scientists know that the way you "look at" a problem often influences whether you can solve it or not. Similarly, your viewpoint influences your ability to manage a software development project efficiently. The author has found it helpful to think of software development management as consisting of two separate but related parts: project planning and project execution. Both parts have five components. The planning components are:

subdivision of work
quantification
sequencing of work
budgeting
scheduling.

Subdivision of work is the decomposition of a job into manageable pieces which will be referred to as "work packages." This is sometimes called "packaging the work." Work packages should consist of one generic type of work, should be of short duration, should be logically related to how the work is to be performed, and it should be possible to assign responsibility for the completion of a given work package to one person.

Normally the subdivision of work is arrived at through a series of decompositions based on how the work will be performed. An example of this process is given in Fig. 1. Here, the job of developing the BRICS system was first decomposed into several major components such as developing a requirements specification, translating the requirements into a functional design, expanding the functional design into a technical design, implementing the design (coding), integration testing, acceptance testing, etc.

This is the first level of decomposition. Level 1 components are further subdivided as shown in Fig. 1 to product components at level 2. For example, the technical design component is subdivided into detailed design of processing modules, detailed design of data management modules, calculation of system timings, etc. These level 2 components are further decomposed into level 3 components and so on until the total effort has been subdivided into manageable components (work packages). When the work has been divided in this fashion, the resultant hierarchy is called a "work breakdown structure" (WBS).

Once the work has been subdivided, it can be quantified. Quantification is that component of planning which deter-

Manuscript received January 12, 1983.

The author is with Brown & Root, Inc., P. O. Box 3, Houston, TX 77001.

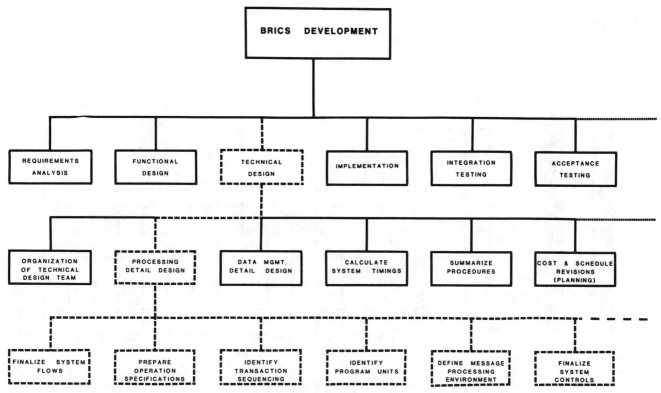

Fig. 1.   System development work breakdown structure (WBS).

mines the amount of work (man-hours), overhead, and computer resources required for each work package in the work breakdown structure. The estimated cost for each work package is based on this infomation.

Fig. 2 shows a copy of the "detailed estimate worksheet" used for quantifying and budgeting work packages for the BRICS software development effort. Note that BRICS work packages were referred to as "control packages" (a departure from standard WBS terminology peculiar to this project). The first step in quantification is to list the activities in each work package and their "unit of measure." The example shown in Fig. 2 is for the FINALIZE SYSTEM FLOWS work package shown in Fig. 1. The unit of measure for activities 2.2.20.1 and 2.2.20.2 is flowcharts. The unit of measure for activities 2.2.20.3 and 2.2.20.4 is reports.

The next step in quantification is to assign quantities to each activity (in the activity's unit of measure). How this was done for work package 2.2.20 (FINALIZE SYSTEM FLOWS) is shown in Fig. 2. The final step in the quantification process is to record the number of man-hours necessary to accomplish each activity in each work package. Depending on who you talk to, the man-hours may be considered as part of the quantification or part of the estimate. For the purposes of this paper it will be considered part of the quantification.

After the work packages have been quantified, the sequence in which the work packages are to be executed needs to be determined. This sequence of work provides the software development manager with an understanding of the order in which the work is to proceed. As the sequence of work is developed, the work breakdown structure needs to be reviewed to ensure that the subdivision of work is compatible with the sequence in which the work is to be completed. This may lead

to changes in the work breakdown structure such as changing or creating new work packages to better define the manner and order in which the work is to be accomplished.

After the work packages have been quantified and sequenced, they must be estimated. The estimate for each work package will specify the planned cost to complete the work in the work package. After the estimates are approved by manage-

DETAILED ESTIMATE WORKSHEET

PROJECT BRICS   PAGE 1 OF 1

PREPARED BY ____   CONTROL PACKAGE 2.2.20   DATE 9-19-79

ACTIVITY	DESCRIPTION	UNITS	QTY	MHRS	$	REF
2.2.20.1	Prepare Final Batch Flowcharts	Charts	60	720		101
2.2.20.2	Prepare Final On-Line Flowcharts	Charts	30	360		102
2.2.20.3	Prepare Batch Flow Narratives	Reports	60	360		
2.2.20.4	Prepare On-Line Flow Narratives	Reports	30	240		
	Total			1680		

Fig. 2.   Detailed estimate worksheet.

447

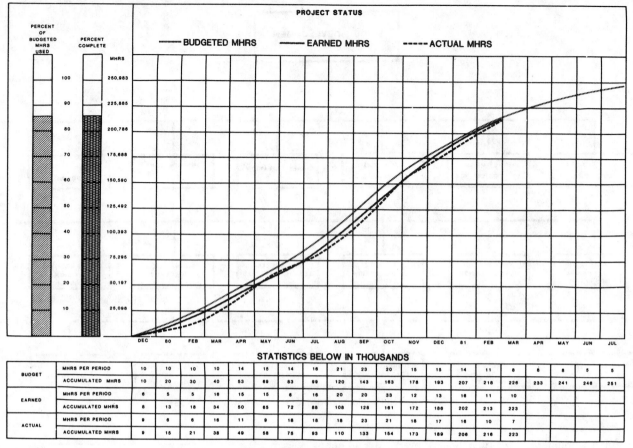

Fig. 3. Project status summary.

STATISTICS BELOW IN THOUSANDS

BUDGET	MHRS PER PERIOD	10	10	10	10	14	15	14	16	21	23	20	15	15	14	11	8	8	8	5	5
	ACCUMULATED MHRS	10	20	30	40	53	69	83	99	120	143	163	178	193	207	218	226	233	241	246	251
EARNED	MHRS PER PERIOD	8	5	5	16	15	15	8	16	20	20	33	12	13	16	11	10				
	ACCUMULATED MHRS	8	13	18	34	50	65	72	88	108	128	161	172	186	202	213	223				
ACTUAL	MHRS PER PERIOD	9	6	6	16	11	9	18	18	18	23	21	18	17	16	10	7				
	ACCUMULATED MHRS	9	15	21	38	49	58	76	93	110	133	154	173	189	206	216	223				

ment they will be called "budgets." The man-hours for a given work package are the "man-hour budget" for the package. The terms "work package budget" and "work package man-hour budget" imply a management allocation of resources in terms of cost and man-hours to complete the work package.

Finally, the work packages need to be scheduled to complete the planning process. The purpose of scheduling is not only to predict when a job can be completed given the sequence of work and the resources available but also to establish start and end dates for each work package. The software manager uses these scheduled dates for the work packages to control the work and communicate progress of the work.

III. THE PROJECT PLAN

The budget for your software development effort is the composite of all the budgets for all the work packages in your WBS and the schedule for your project is the composite of all work package schedules. Together the budget and the schedule are referred to as the "plan" or the "baseline."

Again, it is important how this plan is visualized. It is helpful to see an integrated picture of the budget and the schedule components of the plan. This is achieved by using the schedule to "time-phase" the budget. Time phasing shows graphically how the budget is to be expended over time. Fig. 3 shows the time phasing of the manhour budget for the TECHNICAL DESIGN and IMPLEMENTATION branches of the BRICS WBS hierarchy shown in Fig. 1.

The algorithm for time phasing the budget with the schedule is documented in [1]. It can be done manually, but if the number of work packages in your WBS exceeds 100 it becomes fairly difficult. One of the things BRICS does is to automatically produce time phasing graphs for work breakdown structures of any size whose budget and schedule have been entered into the system.

IV. PROJECT EXECUTION

Basically, the software manager's job is to control the development effort in accordance with the project plan discussed above. The five components of project control are:

accumulation of actual expenditures
progress measurement
performance evaluation
productivity measurement
change control and forecasting.

The activities of project control allow the software manager to monitor progress; anticipate and rectify problems; and to continue the "communication" established by the plan to meet requirements, cost objectives and the schedule.

Classical cost accounting methods are used to accumulate actual expenditures of manhours and costs. Each work package is considered as a ledger account and each expenditure incurred for each work package is posted to the appropriate account as it is incurred. Man-hour expenditures should be posted weekly to accommodate the productivity reporting discussed in a later section. Costs can be posted weekly or monthly. For plotting purposes it is advisable to maintain a historical record of the actual expenditure of man-hours for each work package at the end of each reporting period.

Collecting expenditures at the work package level allows for computing the actual expenditure for any element in the WBS at any level simply by summing. A plot of the actual expenditures against the baseline during the technical design and implementation of BRICS is also given in Fig. 3.

Progress measurement is that element of control that is involved with periodically (usually weekly) determining the status of each work package. Status is measured in percent complete. Usually the best method for measuring percent complete is to compare the actual number of units completed for each activity in a work package with the "budgeted quantity" (quantity shown on the detailed estimate worksheet) for that activity. The ratio obtained is the percent complete for the activity. Percent complete for the work package is computed using the formula

WP % comp

$$= \frac{\sum(\text{activity \% complete}) (\text{activity man-hour budget})}{\text{work package man-hour budget}}$$

where the summation is taken over all activities in the work package. It is the responsibility of the software manager to insure this data is collected periodically as it is the basis for the calculations used in performance evaluation.

V. PERFORMANCE EVALUATION

Performance evaluation is that element of control which compares actual progress and expenditures to the project plan, identifies deviations from the plan and determines solutions to correct for these deviations. Actual expenditures and the baseline are expressed in terms of manhours spread over time as shown in Fig. 3. But progress is measured in percent complete. In order to measure progress in the same units as the budget and expenditures so a comparison can be made one uses the concept of "earned value" (earned man-hours). Earned value (EV) for a work package is defined as

EV = (work package man-hour budger) (work package % complete).

Conceptually, earned value represents the (man-hour) value of work accomplished relative to the (manhour) budget. By computing earned value at the work package level it can be obtained for any element in the WBS hierarchy by summing the earned value for all work packages under the given hierarchy element.

A plot of earned value and actual manhour expenditure against the baseline for the BRICS technical design and implementation is given in Fig. 3. This plot is the software manager's principle performance evaluation tool. A detailed discussion of how to interpret such an earned value graph is given in [1]. Basically, if the earned value "curve" is tracking the baseline curve closely, work is progressing as planned and if it is tracking the actual expenditure curve closely, productivity is as planned.

VI. PRODUCTIVITY MEASUREMENT

If the earned value curve deviates significantly from either the baseline or the actual man-hour curve, or both there is

reason for concern. It is the responsibility of the software manager to take steps to rectify the problem but before this can be done the problem must first be isolated.

Suppose the earned value curve is tracking the baseline closely but deviates sharply from the actual expenditure curve with the "actuals" curve running "above" the earned value curve. This means the work content is being executed as planned (as scheduled) but the cost in man-hours is significantly more than planned. The obvious conclusion is low productivity. In order to know which work packages are experiencing low productivity, the software manager needs a weekly productivity report.

The calculation of productivity for a work package is as follows: first, the work package is assigned a unit of measure just like the activities in the work package. Each activity in the package may have a different unit of measure and it is not necessary that the work package unit of measure be the same as any of its activities. For instance, the unit of measure for work package 2.2.20 shown in Fig. 2 could be documents and its quantity could be 180.

The work package man-hour budget is obtained by summing the man-hours for each activity in the package. In this case it is 1680 man-hours. Dividing 1680 man-hours by 180 units gives 9.33 man-hours per unit or man-hours per document. This ratio will be referred to as the "budgeted cost per unit" or simply the "budgeted unit rate." Productivity is defined as output per man-hour. Consequently, the unit rate is the reciprocal of productivity since it is measured in terms of man-hours per unit (output).

The "actual unit rate" for an activity in the work package could be determined by dividing the actual manhour expenditure for the activity by the actual number of units completed on the activity. But to collect costs and compute unit rates for each activity would lead to far too much detail. This is the reason for "packaging" the work in the first place so it can be treated as manageable pieces instead of a mass of detail. What is desired is an actual unit rate for the work package. It is obtained using the formula

work package actual unit rate

$$= \frac{\text{work package actual man-hour expenditure}}{(\text{work pkg. \% complete}) (\text{work pkg. quantity})}$$

where the formula for work package % complete was given in Section IV. Similarly, budgeted unit rates and actual unit rates can be computed at summary levels of your work breakdown structure by assigning a quantity and unit of measure to each summary level WBS element and using the formulas

WBS element budgeted unit rate

$$= \frac{\text{WBS element man-hour budget}}{\text{WBS element quantity}}$$

WBS element actual unit rate

$$= \frac{\text{WBS element actual man-hour expenditure}}{(\text{WBS element \% comp.}) (\text{WBS element quantity})}$$

where the WBS element man-hour budget and the WBS

			QUANTITIES				MANHOURS				MANHOURS PER UNIT		
HIERARCHY	DESCRIPTION	: UOM	CONTROL BUDGET	ACTUAL	% CMP	FORECAST	: CONTROL BUDGET	ACTUAL	% BUD	FORECAST	: CONTROL BUDGET	ACTUAL	FORECAST
TECH DSGN 2.2	TECHNICAL DESIGN	: DOC	6214	138	2	6214	: 93210	1662	2	93210	: 15.00	12.04	15.00
PROC DSGN	PROCESS. DETAIL DSGN	: DOC	1688	138	6	1688	: 25151	1662	7	2515	: 14.90	12.04	14.90
2.2.20	FINALIZE SYST FLOWS	: DOC	180	138		178	: 1680	1662	99	1966	: 9.33	12.04	11.04
2.2.20.1	BATCH FLOWCHARTS	: CHT	60	58	100	58	: 720	752	100	752	: 12.00	12.97	12.97
2.2.20.2	ON-LINE FLOWCHARTS	: CHT	30	31	100	58	: 360	480	100	480	: 12.00	15.48	15.48
2.2.20.3	BATCH NARRATIVES	: REP	60	29	50	58	: 360	232	64	464	: 6.00	8.00	8.00
2.2.20.4	ON-LINE NARRATIVES	: REP	30	20	67	31	: 240	198	83	296	: 8.00	9.00	9.90
2.2.22	OPERATION SPECS.	: DOC	32	0	0	32	: 628	0	0	628	: 19.63		19.63
2.2.22.1	LIST JOB STREAMS	: LST	16	0	0	16	: 124	0	0	124	: 7.75		7.75
2.2.22.2	PRELIM OPER SPECS	: SPC	16	0	0	16	: 384	0	0	384	: 24.00		24.00
2.2.22.3	REVIEW WITH OPS MGMT	: RVW	5	0	0	5	: 120	0	0	120	: 24.00		24.00
2.2.24	IDENT TRANS SEQUENCE	: DOC	33	0	0	33	: 552	0	0	552	: 16.73		16.73
2.2.24.1	TRANS SEQ WORKSHEETS	: WKS	33	0	0	33	: 528	0	0	528	: 16.00		16.00
2.2.24.2	TEAM REVIEW OF WKSTS	: RVW	1	0	0	1	: 24	0	0	24	: 24.00		24.00
2.2.25	IDENTIFY PRGM UNITS	: DOC	734	0	0	734	: 11684	0	0	11684	: 15.92		15.92
2.2.25.1	PREPARE PRGM CHARTS	: CHT	398	0	0	398	: 6368	0	0	6368	: 16.00		16.00
2.2.25.2	PREPARE PSB WKSHEETS	: WKS	104	0	0	104	: 1132	0	0	1132	: 10.88		10.88
2.2.25.3	PREPARE DLI CALL PTN	: PTN	104	0	0	104	: 1132	0	0	1132	: 10.88		10.88
2.2.25.4	PREPARE ON-LINE HIER	: HIR	128	0	0	128	: 3052	0	0	3052	: 23.84		23.84

Fig. 4. Productivity report.

element actual man-hour expenditure are obtained by summing the work package man-hour budgets and actual man-hour expenditures for all the work packages under the given WBS element in the work breakdown structure hierarchy, and where the WBS % complete is given by

$$\text{WBS element \% complete} = \frac{\sum(\text{work pkg. \% comp.})(\text{work pkg. man-hour budget})}{\text{WBS element man-hour budget}}$$

where the summation is taken over all work packages under the given WBS element in the hierarchy.

An example of such a productivity report is given in Fig. 4. The software manager uses the performance report of Fig. 3 together with the productivity report to spot trends and isolate problem work packages. It is also necessary to consult the project schedule to spot problems. Even though productivity is satisfactory, work packages may not be starting or finishing as planned. Such a case would lead to the earned value curve tracking the actual curve closely but deviating significantly from the baseline curve on the performance report.

There are three reasons why software development work does not progress in accordance with the plan. They are:

1) changes in the scope of work,
2) quantity deviations, and
3) productivity deviations.

Changes in the scope of work are redefinitions of the original

requirement. Their basis can range from a change in the user procedures to a better design alternative. Quantity deviations arise from errors in the quantification process and productivity deviation arise from not accomplishing the work at the planned unit rate.

It is important for the software manager to distinguish among these three types of deviations. If work is not progressing as planned because of low productivity, pressure can be applied to increase productivity. Normally, the visibility given to productivity by this management approach tends to stimulate productivity. Applying pressure when productivity meets or exceeds planned unit rates may be counterproductive. Programmers and analysts need to be rewarded for exceeding planned productivity estimates even though the work is not progressing as planned for other reasons. Failure to do so may well introduce productivity problems where you did not have them before.

VII. CHANGE CONTROL AND FORECASTING

It is also important for the software manager to distinguish among the types of deviations in order to "keep the baseline current." This means providing for an up-to-date account of the scope of work and an audit trail of how the original budget evolved into the current baseline. If the baseline is not kept current, the percent complete and earned value computations will not be correct as will be seen in what follows.

A "variance" will denote the documentation of a deviation from the baseline. A "change order" is a variance that represents an agreed upon change in the scope of work. If the development is being done for a client, a change order will be a client approved variance and may result in a change to the contract. Then the original contract together with all change orders represents the current contractual environment under which the work is performed. The original budget for a work package together with all change orders affecting the package is the "client budget" (called control budget in [1]) for the package. The client budget for the project is the sum of the client budgets for all work packages.

Variances other than change orders will be designated as quantity or productivity variances depending on whether they arose as the result of a (current or projected) quantity or productivity deviation. Sometimes an observed deviation will have both a quantity and productivity component. It is important that the distinction be made and a separate variance be used to document each component. This is because quantity variances will be used to update the baseline whereas productivity variances will only update the forecast.

The client budget for a work package together with all quantity variances that affect the package is the "control budget" (called target budget in [1]) for the package. The control budget for the project is the sum of the control budgets for all work packages. It represents the real scope of work as currently understood and consequently is the true baseline to measure progress against. This is the budget the software manager uses to control the work and consequently this the budget used for calculating earned value.

The control budget for a work package together with all the productivity variances affecting the package is the "forecast" for the package. By constructing the forecast from the budget in this way the difference between the forecast and the budget is automatically quantified and estimated since each variance must be quantified and estimated. A comparison of the budgets and the forecast for a hypothetical development effort is given in Fig. 5.

One of the functional capabilities of BRICS is to provide the user with a means of storing his original quantifications and budgets in the computer and then as time progresses to enter expenditures as they are incurred, progress (percent complete) as it is measured and variances as they are recognized and quantified. BRICS then automatically produces plots of the earned value against the baseline and the "actuals," productivity reports, and an audit trail of how the budgets and the forecast evolved.

As a result the forecast should have more credibility than many of the "subjective guess" forecasts that occur on many software projects. Moreover, the contributions from scope changes, quantification errors, and productivity deviations can be determined. It is impractical to attempt tracking every single deviation from the plan. In practice one relies on the "Law of Compensating Error" to balance out small or insignificant variances and concentrates on tracking the significant ones.

Which variances to track is a matter of judgment, but normally enough of them should be tracked to ensure the forecast is accurate to a tolerance of approximately 5 percent. Also, it is more important to track quantity variances than productivity variances as they affect the baseline. All change orders should be tracked.

VIII. Selecting an Appropriate WBS

There are several software development methodologies on the market. Most of them are in essence a work breakdown structure for software development even though they may not be presented in that format. In any event, they are at least a subdivision of work in that they divide the software development process up into tasks that can be assigned to the analysts and programmers.

Which methodology to choose is probably less important than having a proven methodology and recognizing it for what it is. Many software development projects use these methodologies but few of them use them as the basis for deriving a project plan as described above. It is important that the tasks in the methodology either become the work packages in your subdivision of work or that they be packaged together to form work packages.

These work packages then need to be quantified, sequenced, budgeted, and scheduled as described above. The project plan (baseline) is then produced from this data. During execution of the plan, expenditures need to be accumulated, progress needs to be measured, and variances need to be posted against these work packages. Furthermore, a manual or automated system is needed to produce performance evaluation and productivity reports from these data.

The author has a software development WBS that will be discussed briefly in the next section. However, the BRICS development effort was managed using another methodology. The reader may be interested in the experience and it may shed some light on the problem of selecting an appropriate WBS for your job.

In 1978 Brown & Root purchased a software development methodology called SPECTRUM which is marketed by J. Toellner & Associates. SPECTRUM was used on a small to medium sized application prior to beginning the functional design of BRICS. From what the author could learn from some of those associated with the project, SPECTRUM worked as it was supposed to but the effort required to complete all the SPECTRUM forms was greater than the development effort itself. It may be that this methodology is targeted at larger development efforts and the "overhead" was too great for a smaller project.

So as not to lose their investment but in order to have a more streamlined methodology, Brown & Root undertook to rewrite SPECTRUM. At this time Brown & Root was employing a number of Arthur Andersen consultants and that firm had their own methodology. Both Arthur Andersen and Brown & Root personnel participated in the rewrite. The result was a mixture of SPECTRUM, Arthur Andersen's methodology and Brown & Root experience. This new methodology became the standard for use on the BRICS project. It was now small enough to fit in two rather large ring binders and became known as the "Black Book" methodology (a name derived from its black binders). Since that time Brown & Root has written a much small methodology called PROMPT for small to medium sized software projects. The WBS shown in Fig. 1 was extracted from the Black Book Methodology.

The author's experience with the Black Book methodology was that it was still too cumbersome. Many of the tasks were unnecessary and most of them required too elaborate forms that were never used again. The extensive documentation

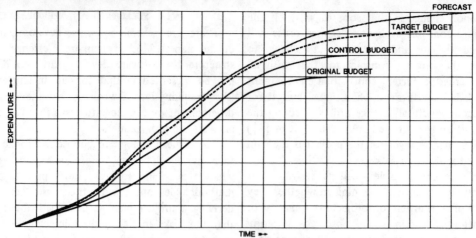

Fig. 5. Budget and forecast comparison.

tended to mask the reason for the individual tasks which often resulted in mechanical completion of forms in order to get a task over with rather than designing the system.

We partially circumvented the problem by distributing the author's methodology to development team members. When tasks were encountered that did not relate to the system being developed, they were "interpreted" in terms of the author's methodology and in several cases management granted permission to substitute other documents for the forms in the Black Book methodology. Proceeding in this manner we managed to finish the technical design phase exactly on schedule and 8 percent under the original estimate. Previously the functional design phase had exceeded the original estimate by 12 percent. In total the project succeeded in completing the design work at a tiny margin under the original estimate and on schedule. Even after acceptance testing the project was less than 6 weeks behind schedule after 4 years development.

IX. A Proposed Methodology

The author's methodology is a simple one. The document distributed to team members was only 20 pages. In the face of current thinking in the software engineering field it may seem old fashioned. It is based on the fundamentals of "top-down" architecture but pays little attention to structured programming or some of the activities referred to as structured analysis.

In summary the methodology works like this. First you determine what the system is to do. This is normally documented in something called a requirements specification. It can range from a list of report formats to be produced to satisy a business application to a formal analysis of how the system is to behave in a real-time environment as, for instance, in an air-defense system. How such a specification was developed for a military command and control system was documented in [2].

From here on the methodology centers around constructing something called a "system flowchart." A system flowchart is no ordinary flowchart like one used to describe a program. The system flowchart is constructed in a series of "levels." In fact, it is not a single chart but a family of charts.

The level 1 system flowchart is constrained to have no more than 6 "boxes" not counting the symbols for inputs, screens, files, and reports. The figure of 6 may seem arbitrary and is.

Another number could be used without altering the structure, but experience has shown 6 to be a good number. The boxes represent processing of some sort. At the first level the boxes usually represent subsystems. The level 1 system flowchart is a "first-cut" at visualizing how the system will be organized at the highest level.

At this point 6 catalogs are begun. These are the component catalog, the input catalog, the report catalog, the screen catalog, the file catalog, and the interface catalog. If a database management system is being used the file catalog may be named something more appropriate like a segment catalog. Each symbol on the level 1 flowchart is assigned an identifier. If the symbol represents a screen the identifier is logged in the screen catalog; if it represents a file it is logged in the file catalog, etc.

Even though the component catalog is limited to 6 components at level 1, the other catalogs are not. As many files, reports, etc. that can be defined at this level should be. The intent is that the level 1 system flowchart should be logically complete and as many files, screens, etc. as are needed to accomplish this is permissable. Also, at this time every member of each catalog must be documented as clearly as possible at this level of detail.

Finally, one normally begins drawing a system hierarchy showing how the components are decomposed at this point. The hierarchy is a shorthand notation for the system flowchart and is valuable for communicating system concepts where the detail of the system flowchart is not necessary.

Next, the level 1 system flowchart is expanded to level 2. Each level 1 component is decomposed into no more than 6 level 2 components. The flowchart is redrawn to reflect the new interfaces among the various level 2 components and new files to accommodate these interfaces, to handle temporary storage, etc. As the flowchart expands, each new interface, each new file and each new component needs to be labeled and cataloged. Just as with level 1, each item in each catalog needs to be documented as clearly and completely as is possible at this level of detail.

This decomposition process continues level by level until you reach components that are too small to decompose further. A general rule of thumb is if a component can be coded with no more that 200 lines of executable code (200 line of code in the procedure division for Cobol programs) that it is unnecessary to decompose it further. These low level compo-

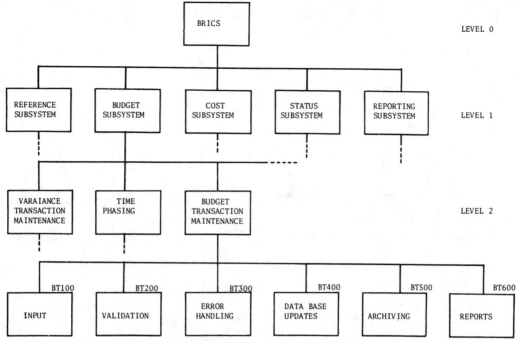

Fig. 6. System hierarchy for BRICS Project.

nents are called modules and eventually become the programs in your system. Figs. 6 and 7 show a simplified level 3 system hierarchy and flowchart, respectively.

When there is no longer anything left to decompose you are through with the design. Detail program specifications remain to be written for each module. Whether these modules adhere to the principles of structured programming or not is of less consequence than the structure induced on the system by this decomposition process. Care should be taken to document each program thoroughly by the liberal use of comment statements.

Modifications to this outline of a methodology will have to be made to accommodate special system requirements such as security, real-time operation, large database requirements, etc. This can be done by adding appropriate work packages to your work breakdown structure.

The Black Book methodology WBS shown in outline in Fig. 1 called for level 1 elements titled functional design, technical design, implementation, etc. Functional design corresponded roughly to developing the system flowchart down to level 2 in the author's methodology. At this point one of the hardest tasks is definition of the interfaces especially when interfacing with systems whose development or maintenance is outside your realm of responsibility.

Technical design corresponded roughly to developing the system flowchart down to level 4, but the parallel was imperfect. The Black Book methodology did not provide for the maintenance of the catalogs of the author's methodology and permitted substituting the system hierarchy diagrams for the system flowcharts. Moreover it possessed many forms to be filled out that were not relevant to the author's methodology.

The BRICS development was accomplished by adding those work packages from the authors methodology needed to develop the system flowchart to the Black Book methodology. The result was satisfactory. Other systems interfacing with BRICS and being developed concurrently used only the Black Book methodology and used only the system hierarchy dia-grams. These projects had difficulty with the methodology and eventually abandoned it.

X. Pitfalls to Avoid

The advice given in this section is likely to be at odds with the advice you may receive from other quarters. It is only the author's opinion and the only thing the author has to recommend it is that it has worked for the author.

First, do not embark on a large software development project without a proven methodology. It is more important to have a methodology and stick with it than not to use a methodology because of a perceived shortcoming with it. Do not be afraid to modify a methodology to meet your individual requirements. No methodology is universal. A methodology may work well in the hands of its author but not make sense to you. In this regard use common sense. Do not try to use something you do not understand.

Use the methodology to build a work breakdown structure. Base your estimates and schedule on this WBS. Use these to produce a project plan (baseline) and measure performance against it as was discussed in previous sections.

Avoid methodologies that avoid flowcharting. People with nontechnical backgrounds tend to have difficulty with flow-charting and consequently there has been a trend toward replacing them with various hierarchical diagramming schemes. Hierarchical diagrams appeal to our logical intuition whereas flowcharts appeal to our geometrical intuition. They give us a means of visualizing what the system is doing. It is important that the analysts designing the system have a highly developed visualization of the system under development just as an architect can visualize the structure he is designing.

Beware of advice from individuals who tell you that software development is intrinsically different from the development of "tangible" products and as such cannot be quantified and estimated accurately. This usually means they have little experience in the tasks to be estimated. Quantification and estimating may not be easy but they are "do-able."

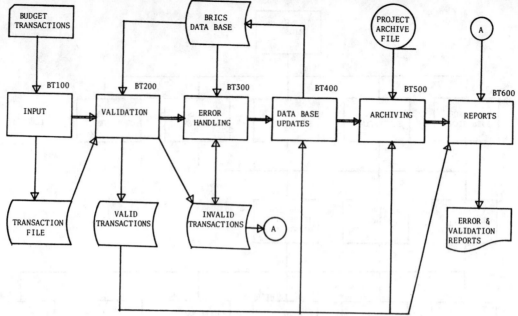

Fig. 7. Level 3 system flowchart for budget transaction maintenance subsystem.

It is true that during quantification and estimating some estimating assumptions may need to be documented as explained in [1, p. 247]. Furthermore, an estimating assumption may prove to be inaccurate at a later date causing a variance to be entered against the baseline. The quantity and criticality of these estimating assumptions will determine the amount of "contingency" built into the estimate, and there is no substitute for experience in correlating cost risk with your estimating assumptions. But the need for estimating assumptions is no reason to discard quantification and estimating as unrealistic.

Furthermore, the vast majority of software development is for products similar in nature to products that already exist, but reflecting the individual requirements of a certain organization. Thousands of multimillion dollar financial systems have been developed in the past and thousands more will be developed in the future. Beware of the one who tries to convince you that the system under consideration is uniquely different from anything in existence. The problem is in matching experience to the work at hand and often those responsible for making DP decisions do not have the background to discern whether the proposed software manager has the experience or not.

Management's need for a reasonably accurate assessment of the cost of development of a new product before deciding to undertake development is universally understood. But in the software development field, software managers frequently encourage general management to undertake risks they do not understand by failing to develop estimates based on detailed quantification.

Finally, avoid the temptation to begin coding before the detailed program specifications have been written for all the modules. Once programming gets underway, maintaining complete documentation will become more difficult. It is best to begin the programming effort with an accurate roadmap. Make implementation a summary level WBS element at a high level. This isolates coding work packages from design work packages.

Think of software as hardware. The modules should become as "chips" or IC's in your mind. Modularity is more important that structured programming. Enforce the limit on the number of lines of code in a module. Each module should be independent of other modules. The goal is to be able to change out modules without affecting other modules just as one changes out a character generator chip to produce a different type font on the screen. This is not a perfect analogy because some of the modules of a software system always correspond to the CPU chip of a computer. Nonetheless, this should be your viewpoint and goal.

You can gain a great deal of insight and advise from others about software development by reading the book containing [3].

REFERENCES

[1] N. R. Howes, "Project management systems," *Inform. & Management,* vol. 5, pp. 243–258, Dec. 1982.
[2] ——, "Development of effective command and control systems," *Signal Mag. (J. Armed Forces Commun. Electron. Ass.)* pp. 44–48, Feb. 1977.
[3] J. I. Schwartz, "Construction of software, problems and practicalities," in *1974 U.S.C. Seminar: Modern Techniques for the Design and Construction of Reliable Software.* Reading, MA: Addison-Wesley, 1975, pp. 15–54.

Norman R. Howes was born in Kansas City in 1939. He graduated from Eastern New Mexico University, Portales, in 1964 and received the Ph.D. degree in mathematics from Texas Christian University, Fort Worth, in 1968.

He is currently Project Manager for the BRICS project within Land Operations Group at Brown & Root, Inc., Houston, TX. He began his professional career at Texas Instruments in 1966 where he was Head of the Optronics Technical Staff and member of the Computer Advisory Board. He has authored several papers in the areas of mathematics, physics, and computer science and was a member of the Faculties of TCU and the University of Dallas between 1968 and 1971. Thereafter, he was Vice President of Alpha Systems, Inc. In 1973 he joined E-Systems, Inc. as Staff Scientist and later became Computer Consultant to Chief of Defense Denmark. He joined Brown and Root, Inc. in 1978.

"Self-Assessment Procedure X" by R.S. Gourd from *Communications of the ACM,* Volume 25, Number 12, December 1982, pages 883-887. Copyright © 1982, Association for Computing Machinery, Inc., reprinted by permission.

Self-Assessment Procedure X

A self-assessment procedure dealing with software project management

Roger S. Gourd, Gould Inc., S.E.L. Computer Systems Division

What is Self-Assessment Procedure X?

This is the tenth self-assessment procedure. The earlier ones appeared in *Communications* in May 1976, May 1977, September 1977, February 1978, August 1978, August 1979, August 1980, October 1981, and March 1982. The first seven are collected in a single volume available from ACM.*

This procedure deals with the management principles that apply to the development of computing software as exemplified in Brooks, Donaldson, Weinberg and other writers. Management topics touched on include personnel, planning, tasks, and monitoring.

Reader response to the earlier procedures showed that the basic educational aims of self-assessment can be achieved with small procedures that do not satisfy the requirements usually applied to testing or certification. Consequently, this procedure is short and is neither exhaustive nor balanced in its coverage. It merely provides a path to some self-assessment.

The next few paragraphs abbreviate the introduction and instructions given with the earlier procedures.

* Available from the ACM Order Department, P.O. Box 64145, Baltimore, MD 21264; for $7 to members and $15 to nonmembers.

What is Self-Assessment?

Self-assessment is based on the idea that a question and answer procedure can be devised that will help a person appraise and develop his or her knowledge about a particular topic.

It is important to note that although self-assessment, testing, and certification appear to have much in common, they actually are fundamentally different. Self-assessment is intended to be an educational experience for a participant. The availability of answers to the appraisal questions and reading lists for further study is an inherent characteristic of self-assessment. The appraisal questions are only the *beginning* of the procedure. Further, the appraisal questions are developed to help the participant think about the concepts and decide whether to pursue the references. This is in marked contrast to a certification test where the test items are designed to discriminate between test takers and to allow the tester to draw conclusions about the competence of participants.

The primary motivation of self-assessment is *not* for an individual to satisfy *others* about his or her knowledge; rather it is for a participant to appraise and develop his or her own knowledge. This means that there are several ways to use a self-assessment procedure. Some people will start with the questions. Others will read the answers and refer to the references first. These approaches and others devised by the participants are all acceptable if at the end of the procedure the participant can say, "Yes, this has been a worthwhile experience" or "I have learned something."

How to Use the Self-Assessment Procedure

We suggest the following way of using the procedure, but, as noted earlier, there are others. This is not a timed exercise; therefore plan to work with the procedure when you have an hour to spare, or you will be short-changing yourself on this educational experience. Go through the questions and mark the responses you think are most appropriate. Compare your responses with those suggested by the Committee, look up the references if the subject seems pertinent to you. In those cases in which you agree with the Committee, but you feel uncomfortable with the subject matter, *and* the subject is significant to you, look up the references.

Some ACM chapters may want to devote a session to discussing this self-assessment procedure or the concepts involved.

The Committee hopes some participants will send comments.

Approved and submitted by the ACM
COMMITTEE ON SELF-ASSESSMENT
a committee of the ACM EDUCATION BOARD

Chairman   Robert I. Winner
Computer Science Department
Vanderbilt University
Box 74, Station B
Nashville, TN 37235

Members   Neal S. Coulter
Florida Atlantic University

Howard Getz
General Motors Acceptance
Corporation

Charles Gold
IBM Corporation

Edward G. Pekarek
Appalachian State University

Eric A. Weiss

Self-Assessment Procedure X

This self-assessment procedure is not sanctioned as a test nor endorsed in any way by the Association for Computing Machinery. Any person using any of the questions in this procedure for the testing or certification of anyone other than himself or herself is violating the spirit of this self-assessment procedure and the copyright on this material.

Contents

Part I. Introduction

Software development project management cannot use a set of algorithms or procedures with hard and fast rules of application. At best it has subjective guidelines which help individuals and groups to contribute and cooperate toward understood goals and objectives. This procedure recognizes the subjective nature of software project management and combines the author's experience with the teachings of the suggested references. Some questions have more than one appropriate response.

Part II. Questions

1. When making decisions remember that
   (a) all relevant information must be gathered first
   (b) postponing a decision seldom has serious consequences
   (c) a nonoptimum decision is often better than no decision

2. General management is responsible for
   (a) planning and organizing
   (b) staffing and directing
   (c) controlling and communicating
   (d) decision making
   (e) all of the above

3. If managing consists of getting things done through people, then delegation is
   (a) setting policy for understanding authority
   (b) helping people do their job
   (c) giving people things to do and decisions to make
   (d) looking for results from subordinates

4. In a properly organized project
   (a) not every programmer need have all the talent required for the complete effort
   (b) all programmers will have the same talent levels
   (c) every programmer must understand the total project

3. Product requirements are best understood
   (a) when dictated by management
   (b) when jointly prepared by users and developers
   (c) when formulated by developers

6. Software project budgeting is difficult because
   (a) programmers are optimists
   (b) management wants to limit expenses
   (c) many decisions require unavailable information
   (d) it is hard to determine salaries

7. What effect can PERT or network scheduling have on a software project?
   (a) it helps identify critical tasks and project interdependencies
   (b) it holds programmers to schedules
   (c) it guarantees project completion on time
   (d) it allocates project budget appropriately per unit of work
   (e) it guarantees project completion within budget

8. A skills inventory of available programming talent will
   (a) help management understand project budgeting
   (b) allow programmers to define the necessary hardware environment
   (c) allow peers to evaluate each other
   (d) help management determine the talent available

9. What benefits are derived from project milestones?
   (a) they guarantee project completion on time
   (b) they guarantee project completion within budget
   (c) they help establish project objectives
   (d) they give programmers freedom to make technical trade-offs
   (e) they outline immediate goals

10. What should be considered prerequisites to project planning?
    (a) software requirements
    (b) programmer office environments
    (c) project goals and objectives
    (d) staffing availability
    (e) hardware malfunction reports

11. Project milestones are
    (a) statements of individual programmer activities
    (b) a set of significant measurable events
    (c) monthly progress reports

12. When interviewing prospective programmers a good technique for determining technical capacity is
    (a) to ask what the individual thought of his or her last boss
    (b) to probe the individual's relationships with previous employer
    (c) to ask about previous project tasks
    (d) to ask about preferences in work environments

13. Clearly written software functional specifications are necessary because
    (a) they form a basis for user reference documentation
    (b) they provide the software description against which satisfaction of requirements can be measured
    (c) they describe the external interfaces of a software product
    (d) all of the above

14. Progress measurement during software development is most readily done by
    (a) looking at cumulative expenses to date
    (b) looking at milestones accomplished to date
    (c) meeting with all the software developers
    (d) periodic management review

15. What is a reasonable time allocation mix for success in a software project?
    (a) 10% definition, 80% implementation, 10% testing and integration
    (b) 20% definition, 40% implementation, 40% testing and integration
    (c) 30% definition, 20% implementation, 50% testing and integration
    (d) none of the above

16. Maintaining a project history will
    (a) help programmers update their resumes
    (b) provide information useful for planning future projects
    (c) allow management to replace the project leader
    (d) provide peer pressure during the development phase
    (e) help analyze when hardware malfunctions occur

17. Beta test sites for software products are usually defined as
    (a) locations and environments with personnel able to measure programmer productivity
    (b) environments within which to satisfy early commitments to customer shipments of new software products
    (c) sites willing to help the software vendor evaluate product completeness and correctness
    (d) sites used to test product demand

18. Projects which are behind schedule can be recovered by
    (a) adding more resources
    (b) increasing the budget
    (c) changing the project's management
    (d) making trade-off decisions among functional, technical, cost, and schedule factors

19. Employee appraisal is intended to
    (a) correct an employee's shortcomings
    (b) recognize an employee's performance
    (c) evaluate an employee's performance
    (d) compare employees to a corporate norm

20. Project team code reviews are intended to
    (a) increase project team communication and identify potential implementation problems
    (b) measure debugged lines of code produced per unit time
    (c) inform management of the most commonly used algorithms
    (d) inform management of progress

21. Software product testing is
    (a) shared among developers, product evaluators, and Beta site users
    (b) a responsibility taken totally by development programmers
    (c) a technical writer's major task
    (d) shared among developers, product evaluators, and end users

22. What can be considered as project review mechanisms for software development efforts?
    (a) budget allocation
    (b) code review
    (c) milestone measurement
    (d) performance appraisal
    (e) design review

23. Structured programming is a set of techniques to increase the understanding of the software engineering discipline. Which of the following items relate to structured programming techniques?
    (a) program design languages
    (b) budget variance analysis
    (c) top-down development and integration
    (d) data collection
    (e) modular decomposition

24. Functional requirements within a specification are used to
    (a) set performance objectives for complied code
    (b) establish test and measurement criteria
    (c) identify inputs to a process, actions performed, and outputs generated

25. Software life cycle planning deals with
    (a) considerations for product maintenance and enhancement
    (b) design objectives for multiple hardware configurations
    (c) project analysis once staffing is in place
    (d) all of the above

26. Software engineers who are low performers or producers require attention from their supervisors. The supervisor's responsibilities include
    (a) praising the employee's progress
    (b) working with the employee to identify reasons for poor performance
    (c) pointing out the employee's failings to his or her peers
    (d) providing direction as to assignments and expectations

27. Project budget evaluation involves many factors. Which of the following relate to budget planning?
    (a) software engineer charge rates
    (b) timesharing or batch development
    (c) computing machinery capitalization rates
    (d) both (a) and (b) above

28. Software projects are often complex and involve varied tasks. For these reasons, individual contributors should
    (a) be able to select the pieces of work that interest them and complete the work in an order easiest for the individual
    (b) work with their supervisor to define discrete measurable task sets which will best achieve the schedule and objectives of the project
    (c) define the budget constraints which will minimize development costs, independent of how separate tasks are integrated into the project

29. Software project management's foremost challenge, given product requirements and understandable objectives, is to
    (a) provide an understandable, easy-to-use human interface to the software product
    (b) guarantee the highest performance possible within minimum address space constraints
    (c) select the functionality most meaningful to the development team's view of the product
    (d) define a realistic development and test schedule with an associated understanding of costs, and produce the product on time and within budget

30. Because of the abstract nature of software development, the larger a project is, the more difficult it is to understand the status of all individual components during development. A significant contributing factor to this problem is
    (a) management's overriding concern for timely status reports
    (b) software engineers' general frequent lack of training and understanding of how to define the tasks to be accomplished within an achievable schedule
    (c) end users' concern for having their product requirements fulfilled as soon as possible
    (d) programmer apathy toward the interests of management in avoiding budget overruns in large programs

Part III. Topic Groupings

Several management topics have been touched upon. The questions are grouped by topic below

TOPIC	QUESTIONS
Personnel	4, 8, 12, 19
Personnel/Management	26
Management	1, 2, 3
Management/Planning	28, 29
Planning	5, 6, 10, 15, 25, 27
Tasks	13, 16, 17, 20, 21, 23, 24
Tasks/Monitoring	7
Monitoring	9, 11, 14, 18, 22, 30

Part IV. Suggested Responses

1. c	7. a	13. d	19. c	25. a
2. e	8. d	14. b	20. a	26. b, d
3. c	9. e	15. c	21. a	27. a, c
4. a	10. a, c, d	16. b	22. b, c, e	28. b
5. b	11. b	17. c	23. a, c, e	29. d
6. c	12. c	18. d	24. b, c	30. b

Part V. Suggested References

Brooks, F.P. *The Mythical Man-Month.* Addison-Wesley, Reading, Mass., 1975.

Burrill, C.W., and Ellsworth, L.W. *Modern Project Management—Foundations for Quality and Productivity.* Burrill-Ellsworth Associates, Tenafly, N.J., 1980.

Donaldson, H. *A Guide to the Successful Management of Computer Projects.* Associated Business Press, London, England, 1978.

MacKenzie, R.A. *The Time Trap.* McGraw-Hill; New York, N.Y., 1975.

Rullo, T.A. (Ed.) *Advances in Computer Programming Management, Volume 1*; Heyden and Son, Philadelphia, Pa., 1980.

Weinberg, G.M. *The Psychology of Computer Programming.* Van Nostrand Reinhold Co., New York, N.Y., 1971.

OTHER REFERENCES

An independently developed home-study course on this subject sanctioned by the ACM is available from

ACM Professional Reference Programs
2 East Avenue
Suite 205
Larchmont, NY 10538

IBM Corporation has produced a detailed set of books on software project management. Many have found these books useful but their cost and limited availability prevented the Committee from basing this self-assessment procedure on them.

They are listed here for the reader's convenience and possible use.

Estimating Application Development Projects. IBM Corp, SR20-7333

Managing the Application Development Process. IBM Corp, SR20-7360

Managing the Application Development Process: Project Reviews. IBM Corp, SR20-7297

Managing the Requirements Definition Phase. IBM Corp, SR20-7400

Epilogue

Now that you have reviewed this self-assessment procedure, have checked your responses against those proposed by the Committee, and have reviewed the references for those questions about which you had any doubt or discomfort, you should ask yourself whether this has been a successful educational experience. The Committee suggests that you conclude that it has only if you have:

—discovered some concepts that you did not previously know about or understand,
   and
—increased your understanding of those concepts which were relevant to your work or valuable to you.

Glossary

Scope

This glossary defines the terms used in this tutorial in the field of software engineering and software engineering project management (SEPM). These definitions have their roots in a number of different management and technical domains: general (mainstream) management, project management, and system/hardware engineering, as well as new definitions and old terms with new meaning. The relationships between these domains and software engineering and software engineering project management can be seen in Figure 1.

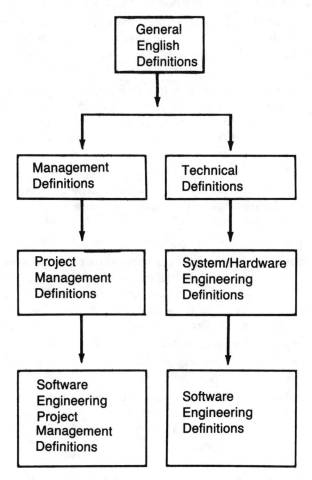

Figure 1: Hierarchical Domains of Software Engineering and Software Engineering Project Management Definitions

The definitions from any one particular domain in Figure 1, can generally be applied to any domain located lower on the hierarchy. For example, a *management* definition can apply to both *project management* and *software engineering project management,* and a project management definition can also apply to software engineering project management. But because of new technologies and meanings a software engineering project management definition will not necessarily apply to general management.

Since definitions for project management and software engineering project management, as well as definitions for hardware and software engineering and system and software system engineering are so similar the terms "hardware/software" and "system/software" are frequently used to mean applicability in both domains.

The concept of the *universality of management* (see definition) allows us to use many management terms in SEPM *without change.* These are usually identified along with their major function: planning, organizing, staffing, directing, or controlling.

The domain of the definition should be understood or identified in the first sentence of the definition. When the definition was taken from another source and the domain of definition was not obvious it was added.

Glossary Structure

Entries in the glossary are arranged alphabetically. An entry may consist of a single word, such as *project,* a phrase, such as *project management,* or an acronym such as SQA. Phrases are given in their natural order (*project management*) rather than reversed (*management, project*).

Blanks are taken into account in alphabetizing. They precede all other characters. Hyphens and slashes follow blanks. Alternative spellings are shown as separate glossary entries with cross-reference to the preferred spelling.

No distinction is made between acronyms and abbreviations. Where appropriate, a term that has a common acronym/abbreviation contains the acronym/abbreviation in parenthesis "( )" following the term. The abbreviate/ acronym might also be a separate entry. The definition will be with the term or abbreviation depending on which one has the most usage and the other will be cross referenced. For example, *PERT,* an acronym for *Program Evaluation and Review Technique,* has its definition after PERT. In contrast, *SQA* an acronym for *software quality assurance,* will have its definition after *software quality assurance (SQA).*

If a term has more than one definition, the definitions are listed with numerical prefixes. This ordering does not imply preference. Where necessary, examples and notes have been added to clarify the definitions.

The following cross-references are used to show a term's relationship to other terms in the glossary:

- *See* refers to a preferred term or to a term whose definition serves to define the term that has been looked up.
- *See also* refers to a related term.
- *Synonymous with* refers to a synonymous term.
- *Contrast with* refers to a term with an opposite or substantially different meaning.

In a few cases non-standard cross references are used to clarify a particular definition.

Source

In those cases in which a definition is taken from another source, the source is designated in brackets, "[ ]," following the definition. The use of a source reference does not imply an exact quote but an acknowledgement of the source of the definition. A list of all sources used in this glossary is given at the conclusion of the glossary.

In some cases the primary source of the definition is not the source listed, i.e., *they* got it from somebody else. In these cases the primary source is identified by parenthesis, "( )," as part of the definition. In most cases, the *Tutorial* author did not check the primary source. The primary sources are also listed at the conclusion of the glossary.

Acknowledgment

The author would like to acknowledge the hard work done by Jane Radatz, chair of the IEEE Computer Dictionary Standards Working Group, who gave us permission to use some of their terms even though the dictionary standard is not finished. I would like also to acknowledge that Mildred C. Thayer spent many hours researching terms and definitions for this glossary.

DEFINITIONS

a-a-a

acceptance — In project management, an official act by the customer to accept transfer of accountability, title, and delivery of a hardware/software configuration item or other items on a contract.

acceptance criteria — The criteria a hardware/software product must meet to successfully complete a test phase or meet delivery requirements. [IEEE SET Glossary, 1983]

acceptance testing — In a system engineering project, formal testing is conducted to determine whether or not a hardware/software system satisfies its acceptance criteria and enables the customer to determine whether or not to accept the system. *See also qualification testing, system testing.*

activity — A major unit of work to be completed in achieving the objectives of a hardware/software project. An activity has precise starting and ending times, incorporates a set of tasks to be completed, consumes resources, and produces tangible results. An activity may contain other activities and tasks in a hierarchical manner. The lowest level activities in the hierarchy is tasks. Dependencies often exist among activities, so that completion of one activity or task may provide necessary preconditions for initiation of subsequent activities and tasks.

activity network — In project management, a network graph using nodes with interconnecting edges to represent tasks and their planned sequence of completion, interdependence, and interrelationships that must be accomplished to reach the project goals.

activity report — A management report that provides the status of project activities over a period of time.

allocated baseline — The initial configuration identification established at the end of the allocation activity. This baseline is established by an approved hardware/software configuration item requirements specification.

allocated requirement — In system/software engineering, requirements that have been partitioned and allocated (assigned) to a particular hardware/software subsystem for implementation. The allocated requirements form the allocated baseline.

analysis — In system/software engineering the process of studying a system by partitioning the system into parts and by determining how the parts relate to each other in order to understand the whole

analysis phase — *See software requirements phase.*

analyst — A member of the software staff who is trained and experienced in analyzing existing systems for the purpose of determining and describing users' needs as a set of software requirements specifications. *See also programmer-analyst, programmer.*

annual performance review — A management appraisal of an employee given annually. *See also appraisal, management by objectives (MBO).*

application — The use to which a computer system is put; for example, a payroll application, a process control application, or a communications network application. [IEEE CAT Glossary, 1986]

application organization — A project structure built around a line of staff organization for the purpose of grouping similar software applications projects under one group (project) manager. The group manager is the project manager for all of the projects. The group manager makes the crucial project decisions and is the negotiating authority with the customer. The group manager routinely delegates certain authority to the subordinate supervisors for individual projects, retaining review and approval rights over their decisions. The group manager must meet his project goal within the resources of the organization. The manager usually has the responsibility to hire, discharge, train, and promote people within his project organization. [Fife, 1987] *See also project organizational structure.*

application program — *See application software.*

application software — Software specifically produced for the functional use of a particular application on a computer system; for example, software for a payroll system, gun fire control system, or general accounting ledger. *Sometimes called functional software. Contrast with system software.*

appraisal — A management process for evaluating and judging the performance of employees' work. *See also management by objectives (MBO).*

architecture design — 1. The process of defining a collection of hardware and software components and their interfaces to establish a framework for the development of a system/software system. 2. The result of the architectural design process. [IEEE SET Glossary, 1983] *Synonymous with system design.*

Argyris' motivation theory — A motivation technique based on the theory that the greater the disparity between company needs and individual needs the greater the dissatisfaction of the employee. *See also motivation theories by Herzberg, Lewin, Likert, Maslow, Mayo, McGregor, Patton, and Taylor. See also Theories X and Y and Theory Z.*

audit — 1. A project management review of a hardware/software project for the purpose of assessing compliance with software requirements, specifications, baselines, standards, procedures, instructions, codes, and contractual and licensing requirements. 2. An activity to determine through investigation the adequacy of, and adherence to, established procedures, instructions, specifications, codes, and standards or other applicable contractual and licensing requirements, and the effectiveness of implementation. (ANSI N45.2.10-1973) [IEEE SET Glossary, 1983] *See also code audit, independent audit.*

audit team — In project management an experienced group (team) of engineers and applications experts who are asked to audit a hardware/software engineering project to identify problems and initiate corrective action. *See also audit.*

auditing — *See configuration auditing.*

authority — In management (organizing), 1. The legal or delegated right to give directions to subordinates and to command resources. 2. The discretion given an employee or incumbent of an organizational position to use their judgment in decision making.

backup programmer — In software engineering the assistant leader of a chief programmer team; a senior-level programmer whose responsibilities include contributing significant portions of the software being developed by the team, aiding the chief programmer in reviewing the work of the other team members, substituting for the chief programmer when necessary, and having an overall technical understanding of the software being developed. [IEEE SET Glossary, 1983] *See also chief programmer team.*

balanced matrix — In a matrix organization, a balanced matrix means that both the functional and project organizations that contribute tangible and intangible resources to the project will have equivalent responsibilities, authority, and status. For example, the project manager and the functional manager will have equal pay and rank, equal availability to top management, equal status, equal privileges, and so on. *See matrix organization.*

bar chart — A management tool used to plan and control the time elements and schedule of a program. The bar chart lists the major activities of the project, its scheduled start and ending times, and its current status. The primary advantage of the bar-chart is that the plan (schedule) and progress of the project can be portrayed together graphically.

baseline — 1. A hardware/software work product that has been formally reviewed and agreed upon, which then serves as the basis for further development, and that can be changed only through formal change control procedures. Each baseline must specify items that form the baseline (for example, software requirements, design documentation, deliverable source code), the review and approval mechanisms, the acceptance criteria associated with the baseline, and the customer and project organization who participated in establishing the baseline. 2. A hardware/software configuration identification document or set of documents formally reviewed and agreed on at a specific time during the system's/software's life cycle, which completely describes the functional and/or physical characteristics of a hardware/software configuration item. Baselines, plus approved changes to those baselines, constitute the current hardware/software configuration identification of a product. See also configuration management, baseline document, milestone review.

Examples of system/software baselines are: [Lockheed, 1985]

Functional baseline—The initial configuration established at the end of the requirements definition phase.

Allocated baseline—The initial configuration established

at the end of either the system design review (large projects) or the preliminary design review (medium or small projects).

*Product baseline—*The initial configuration established at the end of system testing.

baseline document — System/software documents that establish one of the initial configuration identifications of a hardware/software configuration item. The system specifications, requirements specifications, and design specifications are examples of baseline identification documents. *See also configuration management, document, engineering document.*

baseline management model — A management and software life-cycle development strategy that integrates a series of life cycle phases, reviews, and baseline documents into a system for managing a software engineering project. Specifically it uses the waterfall life-cycle model to partition the project into manageable phases—requirements, design, implementation, and test—and establishes milestones, documents, and reviews at the end of each phase. *See also baseline, baseline document, life-cycle development model, milestone, milestone review, and waterfall model.*

baseline management review — *See milestone review, review.*

baseline management strategy — *See baseline management model.*

baseline review — *See milestone review, review.*

benefits — The monetary and non-monetary rewards, privileges, and bonuses used in management that can be used to compensate, motivate, or give incentive to employees.

biological survival needs — From Maslow's motivation theory, the basic needs to sustain human life, e.g., food, water, shelter, etc. *See also esteem and recognition needs, Maslow's motivation theory, Maslow's hierarchy of needs, security and safety needs, self-actualization needs, social needs.*

bonus — *See benefits.*

bottom-up — Pertaining to a software engineering approach that starts with the lowest level software components of a hierarchy and proceeds through progressively higher levels to the top level component; for example, bottom-up design, bottom-up programming, bottom-up testing. [IEEE SET Glossary, 1983] *Contrast with top-down.*

bottom-up design —The process of designing a system by identifying lower-level components, designing each component separately, then designing an integrating structure to integrate the lower-level components into larger and larger subsystems until the design is finished. *Contrast with top-down design.*

bottom-up testing — The process of checking out hierarchically organized programs, progressively, from bottom to top, using software drivers to simulation top-level components. *Contrast with top-down testing.*

budget — A statement of management plans and expected results expressed in numbered, quantitative, and monetary terms. Money is the only common denominator for expressing all resources required and used.

budget report — A management report that compares monetary expenditures to monetary estimates (budget). Differences between the budget estimates and actual project expenditures are explained.

budget review — A formal meeting at which the monetary expenditures for a system/software engineering project are presented to the user, customer, or other interested parties for comment and approval. The monetary expenditures are compared to the budget, and differences between the budget estimates and actual project expenditures are explained.

c-c-c

CDR — Acronym for critical design review.

change control — Within the context of hardware/software configuration management, the process by which a change is proposed, evaluated, approved or rejected, scheduled, and tracked [IEEE SET Glossary, 1983]. *See also configuration control, configuration management.*

change status report — In configuration management, details the status of all proposed changes to a hardware/software configuration item for which the contractor is responsible and for which existing documentation is listed in the configuration index. The purpose of the report is to provide the procuring activity (customer) and contractor (developer) with a summary of the current status of all proposed and approved engineering change proposals (ECPs). *See also configuration management.*

chief programmer — In software engineering, the leader of a chief programmer team; a senior-level programmer whose responsibilities include producing key portions of the software assigned to the team, coordinating the activities of the team, reviewing the work of the other team members, and having an overall technical understanding of the software being developed. [IEEE SET Glossary, 1983] *See also chief programmer team.*

chief programmer team —A software development team that consists of a chief programmer, a backup programmer, a secretary/librarian, and additional programmers and specialists as needed, and that employs support procedures designed to enhance group communication and to make optimum use of each member's skills. [IEEE SET Glossary, 1983] *See also egoless programming team, project team, project team structure.*

CI — Acronym for configuration item.

classic management model — The diagrammatic presentation of the five principal functions of management: planning, organizing, staffing, directing, and controlling (See Figure 2).

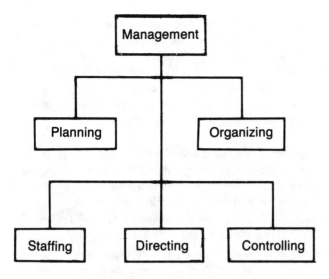

Figure 2: Classic Management Model

CM — Acronym for configuration management. *See also SCM (software configuration management).*

COCOMO — Acronym for Constructive Cost Model. *See also COCOMO software cost-estimation model.*

COCOMO software cost-estimation model —A software cost and schedule estimating method that was developed by Barry W. Boehm and documented in *Software Engineering Economics* [Boehm, 1981]. The model is an empirically derived, non-proprietary, cost-estimation model, based on a study by Boehm of 63 software development projects. The model accommodates three categories of software application, has a basic (simple), intermediate, and detailed version, and its primary input parameter is the estimated lines of uncommented, source code. The intermediate and detailed version of the model contain 15 cost multipliers that recognize differences in the project products and environment. Typically only the intermediate version is used. *See also the following software cost-estimation models: Doty, Putnam SLIM, RCA PRICE S, SDC, and TRW Wolverton. See also software cost-estimation model.*

code — 1. To represent data or a computer program in a symbolic form that can be accepted by a computer. (ISO) 2. To write a routine. (ANSI) 3. Loosely, one or more computer programs, or part of a computer program. [IEEE SET Glossary, 1983] *See also software.*

code audit — An (independent) review of source code by a person, team, or tool to verify compliance with software design documentation and programming standards. Correctness and efficiency may also be evaluated. [IEEE SET Glossary, 1983] *See also audit, inspection, walkthrough.*

code inspection — *See inspection.*

code walkthrough — *See walkthrough.*

coding phase — *See implementation phase.*

commercial computer environment — A collective term that is used to include computers, software, people, facilities, and so forth that are used to build, operate, and maintain software for business applications. *Contrast with embedded computer system.*

commitment — 1. A term used by managers to indicate the duty of an employee to follow through on an agreed-on plan or program. An obligation owed. To identify with a project, organization, manager, program, and so forth. 2. In contracts, a binding financial obligation.

communication — In management (directing), the process of transferring information from one person or group to another person or group with the understanding that the message being transmitted was understood by both groups or by both individuals.

component — A basic part of a hardware/software system.

computer — A functional programmable unit that consists of one or more associated processing units and peripheral equipment that is controlled by internally stored programs, and that can perform substantial computation, including numerous arithmetic operations or logic operations, without human intervention. [IEEE SET Glossary, 1983]

computer code — *See software.*

computer data — Data available for communication between or within computer equipment. Such data can be external (in computer-readable form) or resident within the computer equipment and can be in the form of analog or digital signals. [IEEE SET Glossary, 1983]

computer hardware — The physical portion of a computing system, including the electrical/electronic components, electromechanical components, and mechanical components. *Contrast with software. See also computer.*

computer program — *See software.*

computer program component (CPC) — A component of a computer program configuration item (CPCI). *See also software component.*

computer program configuration item (CPCI) — *See software configuration item (SCI). See also configuration management.*

computer science — The study of computers, their underlying principles and use. It comprises such topics as: compilers and operating systems; computer networks and interfaces; computer system architecture; hardware design and testing; information structures; programming languages; programming; software engineering; systems analysis and design; theories of information systems and computation; and applications from such disciplines as social, economics, political, engineering, business, and education sciences.

computer software — *See software.*

computer software component (CSC) — A component of a computer software configuration item (CSCI). *See also software component.*

computer software configuration item (CSCI) — *See software configuration item.*

computer system — A functional unit, consisting of one or more computers and associated software, that uses common storage for all or part of a program and also for all or part of the data necessary for the execution of the program; executes user-written or user-designated programs; performs user-designated data manipulation, including arithmetic operations and logic operations; and that can execute programs that modify themselves during their execution. A computer system may be a stand-alone unit or may consist of several interconnected units, or may be embedded in a larger non-data processing system. (ISO) [IEEE SET Glossary, 1983] *See also computer, software.*

configuration — 1. The arrangement of a system or network as defined by the nature, number, and chief characteristics of its functional units. More specifically, the term configuration may refer to a hardware configuration or a software configuration. 2. The requirements, design, and implementation that define a particular version of a system or system component. 3. The functional and/or physical characteristics of hardware/software as set forth in technical documentation and achieved in a product. (DoD-STD-480A) [IEEE SET Glossary, 1983] *See also configuration management.*

configuration accounting — In configuration management, the act of reporting and documenting changes made to a baseline configuration in order to establish a hardware/software configuration status. [Lockheed, 1985] *See also configuration management, configuration status accounting.*

configuration auditing — In configuration management, the process of verifying that all required hardware/software configuration items have been produced, that the current version agrees with specified requirements, that the technical documentation completely and accurately describes the configuration items, and that all change requests have been resolved. [IEEE SET Glossary, 1983] *See also configuration management.*

configuration control — In configuration management, 1. The process of evaluating, approving or disapproving, and coordinating changes to hardware/software configuration items after formal establishment of their configuration identification. 2. The systematic evaluation, coordination, approval or disapproval, and implementation of all approved changes in the configuration of a hardware/software configuration item after formal establishment of its configuration identification. (DoD-STD 480A) [IEEE SET Glossary, 1983] *Sometime erroneously used synonymously for configuration management. See also configuration management.*

configuration control board — In configuration management, the authority responsible for evaluating and approving or disapproving proposed engineering changes to the hardware/software configuration, and ensuring implementation of the approved changes. [IEEE SET Glossary, 1983] *See also configuration management.*

configuration identification — In configuration management, 1. The process of designating the hardware/software configuration items in a system and recording their characteristics. 2. The approved documentation that defines a hardware/software configuration item. 3. The current approved or conditionally approved technical documentation for a hardware/software configuration item as set forth in specifications, drawings, and associated lists, and documents referenced therein. (DoD-STD 480A) [IEEE SET Glossary, 1983] *See also configuration management.*

configuration item (CI) — An aggregation of hardware/software, or any of its discrete portions, which satisfies an end-use function and is designated by the customer for configuration management. CIs may vary widely in complexity, size, and type, from an aircraft, electronic or ship system to a test meter, circuit board, or teddy bear. During development and initial production, CIs are only those specification items that are referenced directly in a contract (or equivalent in-house agreement). During the operation and maintenance period, any repairable item designated for separate procurement is a configuration item. (DOD Directive 5010.19) *See also configuration management.*

configuration management (CM) — 1. The process of identifying and defining the hardware/software configuration items in a system, controlling the release and change of these items throughout the system life cycle, recording and reporting the status of configuration items and change requests, and verifying the completeness and correctness of configuration items. (DoD-STD 480A) [IEEE SET Glossary, 1983] *See also change control, change status report, configuration, configuration accounting, configuration auditing, configuration control, configuration control board, configuration identification, configuration item (CI), configuration management (CM), configuration management plan, and configuration status accounting, software component (SC), software configuration item (SCI).*

configuration management plan — In configuration management, a program for carrying out the project, design, or schedule for hardware/software configuration. *See also configuration management.*

configuration status accounting — In configuration management, the recording and reporting of the information that is needed to manage a hardware/software configuration effectively, including a listing of the approved configuration identification, the status of proposed changes to configuration, and the implementation status of approved changes. (DoD Directive 5010.19) [Lockheed, 1985] *See also configuration management.*

conflict — In management (directing), a clash between hostile or opposing elements or ideas. The state that exists when two individuals or groups have goals that clash or will affect each other differently.

conflict management — A modern management approach that does not see conflict as inherently bad, but inevitable between humans, and as a manageable and controllable force for the good of the organization or activity.

conflict resolution — A management activity for reducing conflict in an organization. The destructive effects of conflict should be avoided and the conflict resolved through the application of problem solving techniques.

Constructive Cost Model (COCOMO) — *See COCOMO software cost-estimation model.*

contract — In project management, a legally binding document agreed upon by the customer and the hardware/software developer or supplier. This includes the technical, organizational, cost, and schedule requirements of a product. [IEEE Requirements Guide, 1984]

contract data requirements list (CDRL) — Listing of all deliverable documentation required and made part of a contract. DoD usage. [Lockheed, 1985] *See also deliverable document, documentation, engineering document, interface control document (ICD), management document, software documentation, software maintenance documentation, system documentation, user documentation.*

contractor — An individual, partnership, company, corporation, or association having a contract with the procuring activity to deliver manufactured products, services, or data. Manufactured products can be hardware/software configuration items. [Lockheed, 1985]

control — *See configuration control, controlling.*

controlled-centralized team — From Mantei [1981], a software engineering project team similar to the chief programmer team. *See chief programmer team.*

controlled-decentralized team — From Mantei [1981], a software engineering project team similar to the egoless programming team. *See egoless programming team.*

controlling — All the management activities that ensure that actual work goes according to plan. It measures performance against goals and plans, reveals when and where deviation exists, and, by putting in motion actions to correct deviations, helps ensure the accomplishment of the plans.

conventional organization — An organizational structure that is either a line or staff organization. *Contrast with project organization. See also line organization, organizational structure, staff organization.*

coordinate — In management (directing), 1. To arrange for the organizational entities to work together toward a common goal with a minimum of friction. 2. A communication mechanism for informing interacting organizations of action that has been or will be taken that affects their organization. 3. Used as a term for obtaining agreement on actions (normally in advance of the action) with an interfacing organization that will be affected by that action.

cost-benefit analysis — In system/software engineering, the comparison of alternate courses of action, or alternate technical solutions, for the purpose of determining which alternative would realize the greatest cost benefit.

cost center — An organization or organizational entity that prepares its own budget and accounts for its own expenditures. The cost center may or may not be responsible for making a profit.

cost estimation — 1. The estimated cost to perform a stipulated task or acquire an item. 2. The product of a cost-estimation method or model. *See also software cost-estimation model.*

cost-tradeoff — In system engineering and management, that approach to problem solving that compares and evaluates alternative (technical) solutions especially where advantages and costs cannot be accurately measured in numbers, by considering costs of alternatives in comparison with benefits derived.

costing — The management activity of determining the cost of an activity or product. *See also cost estimation, software cost-estimation model.*

CPCI — Acronym for computer program configuration item.

CPM — Acronym for critical path method.

critical (detailed) design review (CDR) — A milestone review conducted for each hardware/software configuration item when the detail design is essentially complete. The purpose of this review will be to (1) determine that the detail design of the configuration item under review satisfies the functional and performance requirements of the configuration item requirement specifications, (2) establish the detail design compatibility among the configuration item and other items of equipment, facilities, software, and personnel, (3) assess configuration item risk area (on technical, cost, and schedule basis), and (4) review the detailed design description (specifications). [MIL-STD 1521A, 1982]. *See also milestone review, review.*

critical path — In the critical path method (CPM), a path through the activity net that takes a longer time than any other path. A path is the sum of all the activities on a particular route from the start of the overall activities until it is finished. *See also critical path method (CPM).*

critical path method (CPM) — A project management technique in which the activities that constitute a project are identified, dependencies among the activities are determined, an estimated time is assigned to each activity, and a sequence of activities taking the longest time (a critical path) is identified, and is used to determine the shortest possible completion time for the overall project. [IEEE CAT Glossary, 1986] *See also critical path, PERT.*

CSC — Acronym for computer software component.

CSCI — Acronym for computer software configuration item.

customer — 1. In system engineering, an individual or organization that specifies the requirements for and formally accepts delivery of a new or modified hardware/software product and its documentation. The customer may be internal or external to the parent organization of the project and does not necessarily imply a financial transaction between customer and developer. [IEEE SPMP STD, 1987] 2. The person, or persons, who pay for the project and usually (but not necessarily) decide the requirements; the customer may or may not be the user. [IEEE Requirements Guide, 1984]

d-d-d

data dictionary — 1. A collection of the names of all data items used in a software system, together with relevant properties of those items; for example, length of data item, representation, etc. 2. In software engineering, a central repository with descriptions of data flows, data elements, files, databases, and processes referred to in a data flow diagram set. [IEEE SET Glossary, 1983] *See also data flow diagram.*

data flow diagram (DFD) — A graphic representation of a software system, showing data sources, data sinks, storage, and processes performed on data as nodes, and logical flow of data as links between the nodes. It can also be used to represent hardware/software systems. [IEEE SET Glossary, 1983]

decision — A management (planning) activity for selecting a course of action from among alternatives.

decomposition — *See partitioning.*

definition phase — *See software requirements phase.*

delegate — 1. To be authorized to speak and act for another. 2. The management (directing) act of delegating authority.

delegation of authority — In management, the passing on, by one person to another, the responsibility for an activity or task and the right to command resources necessary to fulfill those responsibilities in the accomplishment of the activity or task.

deliverable document — In software engineering, a document that is deliverable to a customer, e.g., users' manual, operator's manual, programmer's maintenance manual. *See also documentation.*

delivery — 1. The point in the system/software development cycle at which a product is released to its intended user for operational use. 2. The point in the system/software development cycle at which a product is accepted by its intended user. [IEEE SET Glossary, 1983].

democratic-decentralized project team — From Mantei [1981], a software engineering project team similar to the (hierarchical) project team. *See hierarchical project team.*

design — *See software design.*

design constraint (requirement) — In software engineering, any requirement that impacts or constrains the design of a software system or software system component. For example, physical requirements, performance requirements, software development standards, software quality assurance standards. [IEEE SET Glossary, 1983] *See also software requirements specification.*

design phase — The period of time in the software development life cycle during which the designs for architecture, software components, interfaces, and data are created, documented, and verified to satisfy requirements. *See also detailed design phase, preliminary design phase. See also software development life-cycle phase.*

design process — *See software design.*

design review — 1. A review that will be conducted on a periodic basis to assess the degree of completion of technical efforts related to major milestones before proceeding with further technical effort associated with a particular element of the system. The schedule and plan for conduct of design reviews should be included in the developer's program plan and master schedule. [Lockheed, 1985] 2. A milestone review at which the preliminary or detailed design of a system is presented to the user, customer, or other interested parties for comment and approval. 3. The formal review of an existing or proposed design for the purpose of detection and correction of design deficiencies that could affect fitness-for-use and environmental aspects of the product, process or service, and/or for identification of potential improvements of performance, safety, and economic aspects. (ANSI/ASQC A3-1978) [IEEE SET Glossary, 1983] *See also milestone review, review.*

design verification — The evaluation of a design to determine correctness with respect to stated requirements, conformance to design standards, system efficiency, and other criteria. *See also verification and validation, verification.*

design-to-cost — An approach to managing a systems/software project in order to keep the project within cost and schedule. This is accomplished by ordering the individual requirements in order of importance, establishing rigorous cost goals for the design and implementation of each requirement, reserving a portion for contingencies (usually 15-20%), monitor the cost of developing individual requirements, and when cost overruns appear eminent either use part of the contingency fund or reduce the requirements starting with the least important requirement.

detailed design — 1. In software engineering, the process of refining and expanding the software preliminary design to contain more detailed descriptions of the processing logic, data structures, and data definitions, to the extent that the design is sufficiently complete to be implemented. 2. The result of the detailed design process. [IEEE SET Glossary, 1983] *Sometimes synonymous with detailed design specification. See detailed design description (specification).*

detailed design review — *See critical (detailed) design review.*

detailed design description (specification) — A document that describes the exact detailed configuration of a computer program. In DoD procurements, it is also called computer program product specification, a Type C5 specification, a Part II specification, or a program design specification. It is the primary product of the detailed design phase. [Lockheed, 1985] *See detailed design.*

detailed design phase — The software development life-cycle phase that uses the software system design and software architecture from the previous phase (preliminary design) to produce the detailed logic for each unit such that it is ready for coding. *See also software development life-cycle phase.*

detailed design specification — *See detailed design description (specification).*

developer — The person or persons who produce a product for a customer. The customer and the developer may be members of the same organization. Sometimes called a supplier. [IEEE Requirements Guide, 1984]

development method — *See software development methodology.*

development specification — Synonymous with *requirements specification.* DoD usage. [IEEE SET Glossary, 1983] *Synonymous with Part I specification (software), Type B5 specifications. See also software requirements specification.*

DFD — Acronyms for data flow diagram.

directing — All management activities that deal with the guidance and motivation of employees to follow the plan. Once employees are trained and oriented, the manager has a continuing responsibility for monitoring their assignments, guiding them towards improved performance, and motivating them to perform to the best of their abilities.

document —1. A data medium and the data recorded on it, that generally has permanence and that can be read by man or machine. (ISO) Often used to describe human-readable items only, for example, technical documents, design documents, and management documents. 2. To create a document. [IEEE SET Glossary, 1983] *See also deliverable document, documentation, engineering document, management document, milestone document.*

documentation — 1. A collection of documents on a given subject. (ISO) 2. The process of generating a document. 3. Any written or pictorial information describing, defining, specifying, reporting, or certifying activities, requirements, procedures, or results. (ANSI N45.2.10-1973) [IEEE SET Glossary, 1983] 4. Commonly used to mean users' document, software maintenance document, operator manual. *See also contract data requirements list (CDRL), deliverable document, document, software documentation, software maintenance documentation, system documentation, user documentation.*

DoD — Acronym for Department of Defense.

Doty software cost-estimation model — A macro software cost-estimation method that was developed in 1977 by Doty Associates for the Rome Air Development Center (U.S. Air Force). The model is an empirically derived, non-proprietary, cost-estimation model based on a study of 74 software development projects. The model accommodates five categories of software application, accommodates two phases of a life cycle, and its primary input parameter is the estimated lines of object or source code. The model is a set of nonlinear regression equations that estimate the costs. The model contains 14 cost multipliers that account for differences in project products and environment. *See also the following software cost-estimation models: COCOMO, Putnam SLIM, RCA PRICE S, SDC, and TRW Wolverton. See also software cost-estimation model.*

e-e-e

earned-value method — A project planning and control technique that compares project expenditures to a project's current earned value and budgeted cost. The earned-value system is initiated by allocating a budget to individual software deliverables, e.g., SCIs or software components. The ''earned value'' at any time on the project is the accumulated value of all the individual budgets from SCIs or software components that are completed. If the earned value is less than the actual expenditures to date, then the project is over budget. If the earned value is less than budget then the project is behind in schedule.

education — The process of developing the knowledge of basics, theory, and underlying concepts of a discipline usually provided by formal schooling at an institute of learning. This is in contrast to training in a skill or process.

For example, an individual would be educated in the principles of programming languages but trained in FORTRAN. Education is usually not needed immediately and is viewed as having a long-term payoff. *Contrast with training.*

effective technology — A software technology that will increase software productivity, reduce costs, and/or improve the quality of software produced. [Novaes-Card, *et al.* 1983] *See also software engineering technology.*

egoless programming — An approach to software development based upon the concept of team responsibility for program development. Its purpose is to prevent the programmer from identifying so closely with his or her output that objective evaluation is impaired. [IEEE SET Glossary, 1983]

egoless programming team — A software engineering project team that practices egoless programming. The egoless team structure was developed by Dr. Gerald Weinberg in 1971. An egoless team typically consists of approximately ten members. Discussions and decisions are made by consensus. Group leadership responsibility rotates; there is no permanent central authority. [Weinberg, 1971] *See also egoless programming, chief programmer team, project team, project team structure.*

embedded computer — A computer used in an embedded computer system. *See also embedded computer system.*

embedded computer system — A computer system that is integral to a larger system whose primary purpose is not computational. For example, a computer system in a weapon, aircraft, computer networking, intelligent point-of-sales systems, automatic teller machines, talking spelling checkers for children, and so on.

embedded software — Software for an embedded computer system. [IEEE SET Glossary, 1983] *See also embedded computer system.*

end user — *Synonymous with user.*

engineering — The science concerned with putting scientific knowledge to practical uses. *See also software engineering.*

engineering document — In software engineering, a document that is prepared as a result of a software engineering activity; e.g., software requirements specifications, test document, design description, etc. *See also documentation, management document.*

engineering management — The application of management principles and functions to managing an engineering activity. *See also project management, software engineering project management.*

engineering project management — *See project management.*

engineering standard — *See standard.*

esteem and recognition needs — From Maslow's motivation theory, the need to be held in esteem by themselves and by others. *See also biological survival needs, Maslow's motivation theory, Maslow's hierarchy of needs, security and safety needs, self-actualization needs, social needs.*

experience — In management (staffing), the state of having done something before. A person is said to be experienced in some skill or activity if they have been involved in that skill or activity as it occurred.

external interface requirement — A system/software requirement that specifies a hardware, software, or database element with which a system/software system or system/software component must interface, or that sets forth constraints on formats, timing, or other factors caused by such an interface

f-f-f

FCA — Acronym for functional configuration audit.

feedback — Signals or information that is taken from the output stage of a system and is fed back to the input stage of the same system to provide control. In project management, it is all the management reports that provide information as to whether or not the project is going according to plan and the degree and cause of the deviation.

forecasting — The managing (planning) process of attempting to predict future events. Forecasting has two views: view 1: to anticipate future events or make assumptions about the future; view 2: to predict future results or expectations from courses of action. To illustrate in project management; the first view requires the forecasting of future events such as availability of manpower, predicted inflation rate, or availability of new computer hardware and the impact these future events will have on the software engineering project. The second view requires the estimation of how the software engineering project will meet these future expectations and assumptions. Examples are expected expenditure of available resources and project funds against the project.

formal qualification review (FQR) — The test, inspection, or analytical process by which hardware/software products at the end item level are verified to have met specific procuring activities contractual performance requirements. This review does not apply to requirements verified at FCA. [MIL-STD 1521A, 1982]. *See also functional configuration audit (FCA).*

formal review — *See review. Contrast with informal review, walkthrough, inspection.*

FORTRAN — A programming language developed circa 1956, primarily for scientific computing applications.

FQR — Acronym for formal qualification review.

function — 1. In management, a major activity or group of activities that are continuous. For example, the principle functions of management are: planning, organizing, staffing, directing, and controlling. 2. In project management: an activity or set of activities that span the entire duration of a software project. Examples of project functions include configuration management, quality assurance, and project cost accounting. [IEEE SPMP STD, 1987] In programming: a specific, identifiable task performed by one or more software components. [Lockheed, 1985]

functional baseline — The initial hardware/software configuration identification established at the end of the conceptual phase. This baseline is established by an approved system specification.

functional configuration audit (FCA) — The formal examination of functional characteristics from test data for a hardware/software configuration item, prior to acceptance, to verify that the item has achieved the performance specified in its functional or allocated requirements. [MIL-STD 1521A, 1982] *See also formal qualification review (FQR).*

functional manager — The manager over a functional organization. *See also functional organization.*

functional organization — In management, a line or staff organization that is organized around one or more related sets of functions. The functional organization is used primarily to group together individuals with high technical skills such as programmers, engineers, and so forth. Functional organizations are normally continuous.

functional project organization — A project structure built around a functional organization or group of similar functional organizations. A project is accomplished either within the functional organization or, if multifunctioned, between two or more functional organizations. The project is accomplished by passing the project from functional organization to functional organization as the project passes through the life-cycle phases. *See also functional organization, project organizational structure, software development life cycle.*

functional requirement — A system/software requirement that specifies a function that a system/software system or system/software component must be capable of performing. [IEEE SET Glossary, 1983] *See also functional requirement specification.*

functional requirements specification — A specification that sets forth the functional requirements for a system/software system or system/software component. *See also functional requirement.*

functional software — *See application software.*

Gantt chart — A management technique for planning and controlling projects, activities, and tasks. Developed by Henry L. Gantt during World War I. *Synonymous with bar chart.*

group affinity — In management (staffing) the ability of an individual to get along with or fit into a group.

hardware/software component — A functionally or logically distinct part of a hardware/software configuration item. *See also configuration management.*

hardware/software configuration item — A hardware or software entity or a system entity comprised of both hardware and software which has been established as a configuration item. The hardware/software configuration item exists where functional allocations have been made which clearly define and describe the functions of the separate configuration items. *See also configuration management.*

hardware — *See computer hardware.*

headhunter — Originally an informal name for an executive recruiter who specialized in finding high-level executives and heads of corporations. Hence the name "headhunter." More recently individuals or companies that earn a fee recruiting highly paid, hard to find and hiring employees for other companies. Examples are electrical engineers, software engineers, programmers, and so forth.

Herzberg's motivation theory — A motivation technique based on the theory that a decrease in environment factors is dissatisfying; but an increase in environment factors is not satisfying. However a decrease in job content factors is not dissatisfying; but an increase in job content factors is satisfying. *See also motivation theories by Argyris, Lewin, Likert, Maslow, Mayo, McGregor, Patton, and Taylor. See also Theories X and Y and Theory Z.*

hierarchical team — *See project team.*

hierarchy — A structure whose components are ranked into levels of subordination according to a specific set of rules. For example, a hierarchy of software elements can be as follows: [Lockheed, 1985]

Pre-Ada Environment	Ada Environment
1. System	System
2. Segment	Segment
3. Element	Element
4. Program	Library
5. Subprogram	Sub-Library
6. Module	Library Unit/Module
7. Procedure/Routine	Secondary Unit/Subunit

hierarchy of needs — Psychologist Abraham Maslow's theory (1954) that basic human needs exist in an ascending order of importance and that once a lower-level need is satisfied, that need can no longer be used as a motivator. *See also Maslow's hierarchy of needs.*

i-i-i

IBM — Acronym for International Business Machines, Inc.

ICD — Acronym for interface control document.

identification — *See configuration identification.*

implementation phase — The software development life-cycle phase during which the detailed design is converted into a computer language that is executable by a computer. The implementation phase can also include unit testing. *Synonymous with coding phase. See also software development life-cycle phase.*

independent audit — An independent review of a software project by an outside agency or team that is separate from the organization responsible for the project for the purpose of assessing compliance with software requirements, specifications, baselines, standards, procedures, instructions, codes, and contractual and licensing requirements. *See also audit, review.*

independent verification and validation (IV&V) — 1. Verification and validation of a software product by an organization that is both technically and managerially separate from the organization responsible for developing the product. 2. Verification and validation of a software product by individuals or groups other than those who performed the original design, but who may be from the same organization. The degree of independence must be a function of the importance of the software. [IEEE SET Glossary, 1983] *See also validation, verification and validation, verification.*

informal organization — Generally in management (organizing), a loose knit or ad hoc organization existing parallel with or lying outside the formal organization structure which is typically connected together for non-organizational reasons. For example, the "members" of an informal organization may be retired military men and women, belong to the same lodge, graduated for the same university, and so forth. *See also line organization, staff organization.*

informal review — An informal review of existing or proposed software product and document typically by the originator's peers for the purpose of detection and correcting product and documentation errors. *Contrast with formal review. See also walkthrough, inspection.*

inspection — 1. A formal evaluation technique in which software requirements, design, or code are examined in detail by a person or group other than the originator to detect faults, violations of development standards, and other problems. *See also walkthrough, code audit.* 2. A phase of quality control that by means of examination, observation, or measurement determines the conformance of materials, supplies, components, parts, systems, processes, or structures to predetermined quality requirements. (ANSI N45.2.10-1973) [IEEE SET Glossary, 1983]

inspection system — In software engineering, a set of policies, procedures, and methods for performing inspections. *See also inspection.*

integration — 1. The act of merging a software element or elements with another; the act of merging a hardware component or components with another; the act of merging software CIs with hardware CIs in order to produce a total system which satisfies customer requirements. [Lockheed, 1985] 2. The process of combining software elements, hardware elements, or both into an overall system. [IEEE SET Glossary, 1983]

integration and test phase — The software development life-cycle phase that takes the computer code generated during the coding phase, integrates it into the environment, and tests it using real or simulated input. The output is then analyzed to determine whether the program performed as specified. *See also software development life-cycle phase.*

integration testing — An orderly progression of testing in which software elements, hardware elements, or both are combined and tested until the entire system has been integrated. [IEEE SET Glossary, 1983] *See also system testing.*

interface — 1. A shared boundary. An interface might be a hardware component to link two devices or it might be a portion of storage or registers accessed by two or more computer programs. (ANSI) 2. To interact or communicate with another system component or organizational entity.

interface control document (ICD) — That documentation used to define all interface requirements within and between hardware/software systems, or between hardware/software development contractors. The ICD constitutes a bilateral technical and administrative agreement between affected agencies and/or contractors. [Lockheed, 1985] *See also documentation.*

interface requirement — *See external interface requirements.*

interview — In management (staffing), to evaluate or question a job applicant.

investigative audit — *See audit.*

iteration — 1. In the software development life-cycle model, it is the act of repeating an earlier phase as faults are discovered or more efficient or effective designs are found. 2. In programming, the process of repeatedly executing a given sequence of programming language statements until a given condition is met or while a given condition is true.

[IEEE SET Glossary, 1983] *See also software development life-cycle phase, software life-cycle phase.*

IV&V — Acronym for independent verification and validation.

l-l-l

leadership — The management (directing) art of influencing others to willingly work toward the completion of group goals with enthusiasm and confidence. In project management, interpreting the plans and requirements to ensure that everybody on the project team is working toward a common goal.

Lewin's motivation theory — A motivation technique based on the theory that group forces can overcome the interest of an individual. *See also motivation theories by Argyris, Herzberg, Likert, Maslow, Mayo, McGregor, Patton, and Taylor. See also Theories X and Y and Theory Z.*

life cycle — All the the steps or phases an item passes through during its useful life. *See also software development life cycle, software life cycle.*

life-cycle development model — *See software development life-cycle model.*

life-cycle model — *See software life-cycle model.*

life-cycle review — *See milestone review.*

Likert's motivation theories — A motivation technique based on the theory that participative management is essential to personal motivation. *See also motivation theories by Argyris, Herzberg, Lewin, Maslow, Mayo, McGregor, Patton, and Taylor. See also Theories X and Y and Theory Z.*

line organization — In management, an organization within a larger organization or company with the responsibility and authority to do the work that represents the primary mission of the larger organizational unit. *Contrast with staff organization. See also conventional organization.*

lines of authority — In management (organizing), the connections between an individual, position, or activity and the individual, activity, or activity over which the authority is exercised. *See also authority.*

lines of code — 1. Source or object code on a program listing. 2. In software engineering, a line of source code as documented in a program listing. Used as input parameters for most software cost-estimation models. Usually does not include comments. 3. As used in COCOMO software cost-estimation model, all program instructions created by project personnel and processed into machine code by some combination of preprocessor, compilers, and assemblers. It excludes comment cards and unmodified utility software. It includes job control languages, format statements, and data declarations. Instructions are defined as lines or card

images—a line containing two or more source statements counts as one instruction; a five-line data declaration counts as five instructions. [Boehm, 1981] *See also COCOMO cost-estimation model, software cost-estimation model.*

LISP — 1. An abbreviation for LISt Processing. 2. An application-oriented language used for list processing. *See also application software.*

m-m-m

mainstream management — An informal term used to identify conventional or general management. *Contrast with project management, software engineering project management.*

maintenance phase — *See operation and maintenance phase.*

man-day by task report — A management report that identifies and lists tasks to be performed to accomplish a management goal, activity, or project, estimated man-days required or assigned for the task, organization, or individuals assigned to the tasks, and the number of days worked to date.

man-hour by activity report — A management report that identifies and reports on the number of staff hours that have been worked on a given activity, the organization or individuals assigned to the activity, compares the actual hours to the estimated hours, and whether or not the activity is going according to plan.

management — All the activities and tasks undertaken by one or more persons to plan and control the activities of others to achieve an objective or complete an activity that could not be achieved by the others acting independently.

management by objectives (MBO) — A management and motivation technique that requires an individual employee and his manager to establish and agree on a set of verifiable organizational and individual objectives that both the individual and his manager believe can be met over a given period of time. The employee's success or failure in meeting these goals frequently forms the basis of a performance appraisal. This approach is superior to an appraisal by personality traits and work characteristics, such as promptness, neatness, punctuality, golf scores, and so on. *See also appraisal, annual performance review.*

management document — A document that is prepared as a result of a project management activity; e.g., software project management plan.

management function — The set of activities that are continuous in relationship to the goals of the organization or activity. The principle functions of management are planning, organizing, staffing, directing, and controlling. *See also classic management model, function.*

management model — A representation or abstraction of some aspect of management for the purpose of explaining its behavior. *See also model, classic management model.*

management report — In management, to give an account or status of an activity or task at regular intervals. *See also activity report, budget report, man-day by task report, man-hour by activity report, milestone due or overdue report, project progress report, schedule report, significant change report, trend chart.*

management sciences — The study of the underlying principles of managing (planning, organizing, staffing, directing, and controlling) people, businesses, or institutions. The utilization of scientific methodology or principles in solving management problems.

manager — Anyone put in charge of a group of people, organization or activity. Someone who is recognized as having the ability to plan, organize, staff, direct, and control resources and personnel in accomplishing objectives. One who undertakes the tasks and functions of managing at any level of enterprise. *See also project manager, software engineering project manager.*

Maslow's hierarchy of needs — The classifications of human needs by Maslow placed in a hierarchical form. Once an individual's needs have been satisfied at a given level only the needs at a higher level can be motivators.

Maslow's hierarchy of needs are:

Biological survival needs—basic needs to sustain human life: food, water, shelter, etc.

Security and safety needs—freedom from physical danger.

Social needs—to belong; to be accepted by others.

Esteem and recognition needs—to be held in esteem by themselves and by others.

Self-actualization needs—to maximize one's potential and to accomplish something.

Maslow's motivation theory — A motivation technique based on the theory that human needs can be classified and that satisfied needs are not motivators. *See also biological survival needs, esteem and recognition needs, Maslow's hierarchy of needs, security and safety needs, self-actualization needs, social needs. See also motivation theories by Argyris, Herzberg, Lewin, Likert, Mayo, McGregor, Patton, and Taylor. See also Theories X and Y and Theory Z.*

matrix project organization — *See matrix organization.*

matrix organization — A project organizational structure built around a specific project in which personnel from two or more functional organizations are combined on a temporary basis under a project manager. The matrix organization is a compromise between the functional project organization and the project organization. Project managers are given responsibility and authority for com-

pletion of the project. The line or staff functions (usually called resource managers) provide skilled personnel (resources) when needed. The project manager usually does not have the authority to hire, discharge, train, or promote personnel within his project. *See also application organization, functional project organization, project organization, strong matrix organization, weak matrix organization.*

Mayo's motivation theory — A motivation technique based on the theory that interpersonal group values were superior to individual values. Personnel will respond to group pressure. *See also motivation theories by Argyris, Herzberg, Lewin, Likert, Maslow, McGregor, Patton, and Taylor. See also Theories X and Y and Theory Z.*

MBO — Acronym for management by objectives.

McGregor's motivation theory — A motivation technique based on the theory that managers must understand the nature of man in order to be able to motivate him. *See also motivation theories by Argyris, Herzberg, Lewin, Likert, Maslow, Mayo, Patton, and Taylor. See also Theories X and Y and Theory Z.*

methodology — *See software development methodology.*

metric — *See software quality metric.*

milestone — In project management, a scheduled event that is used to measure progress. Examples of major milestones include an issuance of a specification, completion of system integration, product delivery, and customer or managerial sign-off. Minor milestones might include baselining a software module or completing a chapter of the users' manual. A manager or an individual project member is identified and held accountable for achieving the milestone on time and within budget.

milestone chart — A management tool used to control milestone progress. The milestone chart lists the major activities of the project, their milestones (scheduled start and ending times plus others), and their current status. The primary advantage of the milestone chart is that the schedule and progress of the project can be portrayed together graphically. *See also bar chart.*

milestone document — A project document that describes and documents some part of a software development life cycle and the completion of the documents signals the completion of the milestone. For example, the completion of the software requirements specification (SRS) signals the completion of the software requirements analysis phase. *See also milestone.*

milestone due or overdue report — A management report that provides a status of the milestones that have been accomplished or missed and the reasons for missing the milestone.

milestone review — 1. A project management review that is conducted at the completion of each of the hardware/software development life-cycle phases (a milestone)—requirements phase, preliminary design, detailed design phase, implementation phase, test phase, and sometimes, installation and checkout phase. For example, a preliminary design review (PDR) is held at the completion of the preliminary design phase. 2. A formal review of the management and technical progress of a hardware/software development project. *See also system requirements review (SRR), system design review (SDR), software requirements review (SRR), preliminary design review (PDR), critical design review (CDR), test readiness review (TRR), physical configuration audit (PCA), functional configuration audit (FCA), formal qualification review (FQR). See also review.*

model — A representation of an artifact or activity intended to explain the behavior of some aspects of it. The model is less complex or complete than the activity or artifact modeled. A model is considered to be an abstraction of reality.

modern programming practices (MPP) — *Synonymous with software development methodology.*

motivate — *See motivation.*

motivation — In management, the act of influencing others with rewards or incentives to accomplish an activity or task.

motivation model — Management method that attempts to show how human energies and activity can be directed toward desired organizational goals. A description of a method for motivating individuals or groups and the expected outcome. *See also motivation theories by Argyris, Herzberg, Lewin, Likert, Maslow, Mayo, Patton, and Taylor. See also Theories X and Y and Theory Z.*

multi-disciplinary team — A project team that is comprised of individuals from more than one discipline, for example, a team comprised of electrical engineers, software designers, and physicists.

NASA — Acronym for National Aeronautics and Space Administration.

non-functional requirement — A software requirement that does not describe what the software will do but how the software will do it. For example, software performance requirements, software external interface requirements, software design constraints, and software quality attributes. *Contrast with functional requirements.*

non-phase dependent tool — A software tool that is applicable across all phases of the software development life-cycle. For example, a project management planning and control tools, a software verification tool, a budget reporting scheme. *Contrast with a phase dependent tool. See also software development life cycle.*

objectives — In management (planning), the goals toward which activities are directed. In project management, the technical requirements and management constraints of the project.

off-the-shelf computer — A general purpose computer system that can be purchased from a computer vendor that is applicable to many applications, for example, an IBM Personal Computer AT. *Contrast with a special purpose computer.*

on-the-job training (OJT) — In management (staffing), an informal method of training employees on the job through demonstration and hands-on experience rather than in a classroom using models and textbooks.

operation and maintenance phase — The software development life-cycle phase during which a software product is employed in its operational environment, monitored for satisfactory performance, and modified as necessary to correct problems or to respond to changing requirements. [IEEE SET Glossary, 1983] Note: this phase is not in the software development life-cycle phase. *See also software life-cycle phase.*

operation phase — *See operation and maintenance phase.*

operational constraint — In software engineering, performance and timing constraint placed on software developers caused by operational requirements.

organizational position — In management (organizing), a position in an organization designed for individuals to fill. The position should incorporate (1) clear description of the major duties or activities involved, (2) verifiable objectives, (3) the availability of information and resources necessary to accomplish a task, and (3) the authority granted to accomplish the assigned duties or activities.

organizational structure — In management (organizing), a defined relationship between certain functions, resources, and organizational positions. It is based on determining and itemizing the activities or tasks required to achieve the objects of the organization and the arrangement of these activities according to type, size, and other similar characteristics.

organizing — All management activities that result in the design of a formal structure of tasks and authority. Organizing involves the determination and enumeration of the activities required to achieve the objects of the organization, grouping of these activities, the assignment of such groups of activity to an organizational entity or group identifiers, the delegation of responsibilities and authority to carry them out, and provisions for coordination of authoritative relationships.

Part I specification — A software requirements specification. DoD usage. *Synonymous with Type B5 specification. See also software requirements specification.*

Part II specification — A (detailed) design specification. DoD usage. *Synonymous with Type C5 specification. See also detailed design specification.*

partitioning — The separation of the whole into its parts. [IEEE Requirements Guide, 1984] *Synonymous with decomposition.*

Patton's motivation theory — A motivation technique based on the theory that executives are motivated by the challenge in work, status, the urge to achieve leadership, the lash of competition, fear, and money. *See also motivation theories by Argyris, Herzberg, Lewin, Likert, Maslow, Mayo, McGregor, and Taylor. See also Theories X and Y and Theory Z.*

PCA — Acronym for physical configuration audit.

PDR — Acronym for preliminary design review.

performance — In software engineering 1. The ability of a computer system or subsystem to perform its functions. 2. A measure of the ability of a computer system or subsystem to perform its functions; for example, response time, throughput, number of transactions. [IEEE SET Glossary, 1983] *See also performance requirement.*

performance requirement — A system/software requirement that specifies a performance characteristic that a system/software system or system/software component must possess; for example, speed, accuracy, and frequency.

performance requirement specification — A specification that sets forth the performance requirements for a system/software or system/software component. [IEEE SET Glossary, 1983] *See also functional requirements specification, software requirements specification.*

performance standard — Standard that specifies the quality, quantity, cost, and time to complete a product or activity.

permanent promotion — *See promotion. Contrast with temporary promotion.*

personal power — In management (directing), power derived from the manager's personality and abilities to lead. *Contrast with positional power. See also power.*

personnel turnover — In management (staffing), the filling, terminating, and refilling the same organizational positions with qualified people.

PERT — 1. Acronym for Program Evaluation and Review Technique. 2. A variation of the critical path method in which minimum, maximum, and most likely times are used to estimate the mean and standard deviation of each activity item. These values are used to compute estimated path times and to find the critical path, and the critical path values are used to find the standard deviation of the completion time for the whole project. [IEEE CAT Glossary, 1986] *See also critical path method (CPM).*

phase — The stage of development in a product or activity. In project management, one of the stages of the life-cycle model. *See also software development life-cycle phase, software development phase.*

phase dependent tool — A software tool that is applicable across one (or several but less than all) phase of the software development life cycle, for example, a software cost-estimation tool, a structured analysis and design tool, a test case generator. *Contrast with a non-phase dependent tool.*

phase-down — In project management, the termination of the project.

physical configuration audit (PCA) — The formal examination of the configuration of a hardware/software configuration item against its technical documentation in order to establish the product or operational baseline. [MIL-STD 1521A, 1982]

planning — All management activities that lead to the selection from among alternatives of future courses of action for the enterprise. Planning involves selecting the objectives of the enterprise and the strategies, policies, programs and procedures for achieving them, either for the entire enterprise or for any organized part thereof.

PM — Abbreviation for project management, project manager.

policy — In management (planning), policies are concerned with predetermined management decisions. They are general statements or understandings that guide decision making and activities. Policies limit the freedom in making decisions but allow for some discretion.

position — *See organizational position.*

position description — In management (organizing), a description of the title, duties, responsibilities, and authority that go with each position identified in the organizational structure.

positional power — In management (directing), power derived from the manager's organizational position as manager. *Contrast with personal power. See also power.*

power — In management, the ability of one person to influence another. Control over resources. *See also positional power, personal power.*

practice — In engineering and management, to employ one's professional skill in performing an action or making a product.

preliminary design — 1. The process of analyzing design alternatives and defining the hardware/software system architecture. In software engineering, preliminary design typically includes definition and structuring of computer program components and data, definition of the interfaces, and preparation of timing and sizing estimates. 2. The result of the preliminary design process. [IEEE SET Glos-

sary, 1983] *Sometimes synonymous with preliminary design description. See also preliminary design description (specification).*

preliminary design description (specification) — A specification that sets forth the preliminary design of the software system. *Sometimes synonymous with preliminary design. See also preliminary design.*

preliminary design phase — The software development life-cycle phase that uses the software requirements defined in the previous phase to develop a software architecture and functional flow that will implement those requirements. *See also software development life-cycle phase.*

preliminary design review (PDR) — A milestone review conducted for each hardware/software configuration item prior to the detail design process to: (1) evaluate the progress and technical adequacy of the selected top-level design approach; (2) determine its compatibility with the functional and performance requirements of the configuration item requirements specification; and (3) establish the existence and compatibility of the physical and functional interfaces between the configuration item and other items of equipment or facilities [MIL-STD 1521A, 1982]. *See also milestone review, review.*

present value analysis — In software engineering, it is used in making life-cycle cost comparisons between alternative systems during the feasibility phase, in order to decide on the most cost-effective concept for development. [Boehm, 1981]

PRICE S cost model — *See RCA PRICE S software cost-estimation model.*

procedure — An act composed of steps to perform an activity, course of action, or a formalized technique. 1. In management, customary methods of handling future activities; guides to action rather than decision making. Procedures detail the exact manner in which an activity must be accomplished and allow very little if any discretion. 2. In software, a portion of a computer program which is named and which performs a specific task.

process — 1. A unique, finite course of events defined by its purpose or by its effect, achieved under given conditions. (ISO) 2. To perform operations on data in a computer process. (ISO) [IEEE SET Glossary, 1983]

process standard — A standard that defines the procedures or operations used in making or achieving a product. *See standard, product standard.*

process work breakdown structure (WBS) — A work breakdown structure (WBS) for a process, for example, a process WBS for a software project could include at the first level: requirement analysis, design, code, and software test. *See also product work breakdown structure, work breakdown structure (WBS).*

procuring agency — The agency of the customer that contracts for the hardware/software configuration items or systems. [Lockheed, 1985]

product — The results of a process.

product baseline — The hardware/software configuration identification established at the end of the full scale development phase. This baseline is established by an approved "as built" configuration item product specification. [Lockheed, 1985]

product specification — A (detailed) design specification. DoD usage. *Synonymous with Part II, Type C5 specification. See also detailed design specification.*

product standard — A standard that defines what constitutes completeness and acceptability of items which are produced as a result of a process. *See software engineering standard, process standard.*

product work breakdown structure (WBS) — A work breakdown structure (WBS) for a product, for example, a product WBS for a software project could include at the first level: application programs, utility programs, and operating systems. *See also process work breakdown structure, work breakdown structure (WBS).*

productivity — 1. In engineering, the act of producing. *Sometimes synonymous with productivity efficiency.* 2. A concept of managerial effectiveness that measures how well and efficiently managers accomplish their objectives.

productivity efficiency — Comparing goods produced or services accomplished to resources used (sometimes referred to as just productivity). In software engineering, a productivity efficiency measure is line of source code per resources used (usually people or cost). *See also productivity.*

profit margin — The amount of money and resources remaining after cost has been deducted from selling price.

program — 1. In management planning, an interrelated set of goals, policies, procedures, rules, tasks, assignments, resources to be employed, schedules, and other elements necessary to carry out a given course of action. 2. In software engineering, *synonymous with software. See also computer code, computer program.*

program librarian — In software engineering, an individual who administrates the program support library. The person responsible for establishing, controlling, and maintaining a software development library. An administrator/secretary/librarian who serves many teams and performs the following functions: maintains and controls all elements of the software configuration, i.e., documentation, source listings, data catalogs, and indexes "reusable" software models; and assists the team in research, evaluation, and document preparation. *See also program support library (PSL), secretary/librarian, software librarian.*

program library — An organized collection of computer programs. (ISO) [IEEE SET Glossary, 1983]

program manager — A senior manager over a group of projects. A senior manager over a large multi-discipline project. *Sometimes synonymous with project manager.*

program specification — 1. Any specification for a software system. *See detailed design description (specifica-*

tion), preliminary design description (specification), functional specification, performance specification, software requirements specification. 2. Synonymous with design specification. [IEEE SET Glossary, 1983]

program support librarian — *See program librarian.*

program support library (PSL) — In software engineering, provides a centralized and readily available repository for authorized versions of each component of a software system. The library should contain the data necessary for the orderly development and control of each software configuration item and engineering and deliverable documentation. *See also configuration management.*

program validation — *See validation.*

programmer — In SEPM (staffing), an individual who is experienced and qualified to write and document computer programs (software). An individual who is responsible for writing computer programs. *See also analysts, programmer-analysts.*

programmer-analysts — In SEPM (staffing), an individual who is both experienced and qualified as a programmer and as an analyst. *See also analysts, programmer.*

programming — The coding and unit testing of computer code.

programming team — *See project team structure.*

project — A temporary activity that is characterized by having a start date, specific objectives and constraints, established responsibilities, a budget and schedule, and a completion date. (If the objective of the project is to develop a software system, then it is sometimes called a software development or software engineering project.)

project activity — *See activity.*

project administrator — In SEPM (staffing), an individual who manages, directs, or governs some part of an activity or organization. Usually does not have supervisory responsibility over personnel. *See also project manager.*

project agreement — A document or set of documents accepted by the developer and the customer that specifies the scope, objectives, assumptions, management interfaces, risks, staffing plan, resource requirements, cost estimate, schedule, resource and budget allocations, project deliverables, and acceptance criteria for the project. Documents in a project agreement may include some or all of the following: a contract, a statement of work, system engineering specifications, user requirements specifications, functional specifications, the software project management plan, a business plan, or a project charter. [IEEE SPMP STD, 1987]

project deliverable — The item to be delivered to the customer, including quantities, delivery dates, and delivery locations, as specified in the project agreement. The project deliverables may include some or all of, but are not limited to, the following: customer requirements, functional specifications, design documentation, source code, object code, users' manuals, principles of operation, installation instructions, training aids, product development tools, and maintenance procedures. Project deliverables may be self contained or may be part of a larger system. *See also contract data requirements list (CDRL).*

Project Evaluation and Review Technique (PERT) — *See PERT.*

project file — *Synonymous with unit development folder (UDF).*

project leader — In project management, 1. a project supervisor who usually has less responsibility and authority than a project manager. 2. *Synonymous with project manager.*

project life cycle — *See software development life cycle, software life cycle.*

project management — A system of procedures, practices, technologies, and know-how that provides the planning, organizing, staffing, directing, and controlling necessary to successfully manage an engineering project. Know-how in this case means the skill, background, and wisdom to apply knowledge effectively in practice. *See also software engineering project management.*

project management plan — A management document describing the approach that will be taken for a project. The plan typically describes the work to be done, the resources required, the methods to be used, the configuration management and quality assurance procedures to be followed, the schedules to be met, the project organization, etc. [IEEE SET Glossary, 1983] *See also software project management plan.*

project manager — 1. A manager that has responsibility for planning, organizing, staffing, directing, and controlling a project. 2. In SEPM, a manager that has responsibility for planning, organizing, staffing, directing, and controlling a software engineering project. *See also project management, software engineering project management.*

project notebook — A central repository of written material such as memos, plans, technical reports, etc., pertaining to a project. *Loosely synonymous with project file, software development notebook, unit development folder (UDF).*

project organization — A project organizational structure built around a specific project. Project managers are given the responsibility, authority, and resources for completion of the project. (The project organization is sometimes called a *projectized* organization to get away from the term "project project organization.") The manager must meet his project goal within the resources of the organization. The manager usually has the responsibility to hire, discharge, train, and promote people within his project organization. *See also project organizational structure.*

project organizational structure — A special organization that has been established for the purpose of developing and building something that is too big to be done by only one or, at the most, a few people. In a software engineering project, the "something" is a software system. The project organizational structure can be superimposed on top of a line or staff organization. *See application organization, functional project organization, matrix organization, project organization.*

project plan — A management document that describes the approach that will be taken for a project. The plan typically describes the work to be done, the resources required, the methods to be used, the configuration management and quality assurance procedures to be followed, the schedules to be met, the project organization, etc. [IEEE SET Glossary, 1983] *See also software project management plan.*

project product — *See software engineering project product.*

project progress report — A narrative report indicating the status of the project and problems encountered.

project task — *See task.*

project team — 1. A designated group of people responsible for conducting a successful software development project from its planning through delivery. 2. The project team is a structured organization in which the project leader manages senior programmers and senior programmers manage junior programmers. The project team is sometimes called a hierarchical team because of its top-down flow of authority. It can be organized by component or phase. Many project teams practice egoless reviews (walkthroughs) and use a programmer support library. Senior programmers ensure quality of the product. *See also egoless programming team, chief programmer team, project team structure.*

project team structure — In project management, an organized group of 5-10 specialists (team members) with a defined relationship between certain functions, resources, and people. Several project team structures are usually part of a larger project organizational structure. *See also egoless programming team, chief programmer team, or project team.*

projectized organization — *See project organization.*

promotion — In managing (staffing), the transferring of an individual within a company or organization to a position with greater responsibilities which usually requires more advanced skills and knowledge than the previous position. The individual usually receives with the promotion greater compensation and greater recognition. *See permanent promotion, temporary promotion.*

prototype — *See software prototype.*

Putman software cost-estimation model — *See Putnam SLIM software cost-estimation model.*

Putnam SLIM software cost-estimation model — A proprietary, commercially available, macro software cost-estimation method and software package that is based on Putnam's analysis of the software life cycle in terms of the Rayleigh distribution of effort versus time. The model accommodates three categories of software application. Its primary input parameters are the estimated lines of uncommented source code, development technology environment, and estimated project development time. The SLIM was initially calibrated on 150 software development projects. It has since been calibrated on over 1400 software projects. *See also the following software cost-estimation models: COCOMO, Doty, RCA PRICE S, SDC, and TRW Wolverton. See also software cost-estimation model.*

q-q-q

QA — Acronym for quality assurance.

qualification testing — Formal testing, usually conducted by the developer for the customer, to demonstrate that the software meets its specified requirements. *See also acceptance testing, system testing.* [IEEE SET Glossary, 1983]

quality attributes requirement — A requirement that specifies the degree of an attribute that affects quality that the system/software must possess; e.g., reliability, maintainability. *See also software quality attributes (requirements).*

quality — 1. The totality of features and characteristics of a product or service that bears on its ability to satisfy given needs. (ANSI/ASQC A3-1978) 2. *See software quality.* [IEEE SET Glossary, 1983]

quality assurance — *See software quality assurance.*

quality assurance plan — *See software quality assurance plan.*

quality circle — A management and motivation technique in which employees meet periodically in small groups to develop suggestions for quality and productivity improvements. Often several people, usually non-managers, are involved in solving the problems. Sometimes called quality control circle.

quality metric — *See software quality metric.*

r-r-r

rapid prototyping — A software development strategy that incorporates the effective, rapid development of prototype software to enable customers to assess and recommend changes. To conduct rapid prototyping, four generic classes of methods and tools are available: fourth generation techniques, reusable software components, formal specification, and prototyping environments. Rapid prototyping helps reduce risk in high-risk projects. [Pressman, 1987] *See also spiral model.*

RCA — A large U.S. electronic and consumer goods corporation.

RCA PRICE S cost model — *See RCA PRICE S software cost-estimation model.*

RCA PRICE S software cost-estimation model — A proprietary, commercially available, macro, software cost-estimation method and software package. Price S was developed primarily for embedded system applications. Mathematical relationships between cost and parametric values based on historical experience allow the model to predict development costs. These parametric values are adjusted in a calibration mode to fit the model to a specific environment which represents the users' own situation. *See also the following software cost-estimation models: COCOMO, Doty, Putnam SLIM, SDC, and TRW Wolverton. See also software cost-estimation model.*

real time — 1. Pertaining to the processing of data by a computer in connection with another process outside the computer according to time requirements imposed by the outside process. This term is also used to describe systems operating in conversational mode, and processes that can be influenced by human intervention while they are in progress. (ISO) 2. Pertaining to the actual time during which a physical process transpires; for example, the performance of a computation during the actual time that the related physical process transpires, in order that results of the computation can be used in guiding the physical process. (ANSI) [IEEE SET Glossary, 1983]

recruit — In management (staffing), the process of searching out prospective employees for a particular job or organization.

reliability — *See software reliability.*

report — *See management report.*

reporting method — The approach or media for making management reports.

requirement — *See software requirement, system requirements.*

requirement analysis — 1. The process of studying user needs to arrive at a definition of system or software requirements. 2. The verification of system or software requirements. [IEEE SET Glossary, 1983] *See also software requirement analysis.*

requirements inspection — *See inspection.*

requirements phase — *See software requirements phase, system requirements phase.*

requirements review — *See software specification review (SSR), system requirements review (SRR).*

requirements specification — *See software requirements specification, system requirements specification.*

requirements verification — *See verification.*

resource manager — In project management (organizing), the manager of a functional organization who provides resources (people) for the project and matrix organizations. *See also functional organization, matrix organization.*

resources — In engineering and management, the people, money, equipment, facilities, transportation, and so forth that are needed or can be used to satisfactorily complete an activity or build a product. Resources can be expendable (money and materials) or nonexpendable (people and machines).

responsibility — In management (organizing), the accountability for actions taken, resources used, compliance with policy, and the attainment of results. It is "the obligation owed by subordinates to their supervisors for exercising authority delegated to them in a way to accomplish results expected." [Koontz and O'Donnell, 1976]

retirement phase — The period of time in the software life cycle during which support for a software product is terminated. [IEEE SET Glossary, 1983] NOTE: This phase does not appear in the software development life-cycle phase. *See also software development life-cycle phase, software life-cycle phase.*

retraining — In management (staffing), instructing workers to become proficient and qualified in a discipline other than that for which they are currently practicing or were originally schooled.

reusability — Effort to convert a software component for use in another application. [RADC, 1983]

review — 1. A formal meeting at which a product or document is presented to the user, customer, or other interested parties for comment and approval. It can be a review of the management and technical progress of the hardware/software development project. 2. The formal review of an existing or proposed design for the purpose of detection and remedy of design deficiencies that could affect fitness-for-use and environmental aspects of the product, process, or service, and/or for identification of potential improvements of performance, safety, or economic aspects. [IEEE SET Glossary, 1983] *See also audit, milestone review, budget review, code audit, critical (detailed) design review (CDR), independent audit, informal review, milestone review, preliminary design reviews (PDR), software specification review (SSR), system design review (SDR), system requirements review (SRR), physical configuration audit (PCA), functional configuration audit (FCA), formal qualification review (FQR). See also walkthrough, inspections.*

risk analysis — An approach to problem analysis which weighs risk in a situation by introducing risk probabilities to give a more accurate assessment of the risks involved. [Koontz, O'Donnell, and Weihrich, 1984]

rule — In management (planning), a requirement for specific and definite actions to be taken or not taken with respect to a situation. No discretion is allowed. *Contrast with procedure.*

SC — Acronym for software component.

schedule estimating method — *See software cost-estimation model. See also the following software cost-estimation models: COCOMO, Doty, Putnam SLIM, RCA PRICE S, and SDC.*

schedule report — A management report that provides the status of schedule and milestones completed.

scheduling — Determining and documenting the start and stop time for each activity and task in the project taking into account the precedence relation among tasks, the dependencies of tasks on external events and the required milestone dates. Schedules may be expressed in absolute calendar time or in increments relative to a key project milestone.

SCI — Acronym for software configuration items.

SCM — Acronym for software configuration management.

SDC — Acronym for Systems Development Corporation, an early systems and software engineering company.

SDC software cost-estimation model — A macro cost-estimation model developed in the mid-1960s by the Systems Development Corporation for the Electronics Systems Division (U.S. Air Force). The model is an empirically derived, non-proprietary, cost-estimation model based on a study of 104 attributes of 169 software development projects. Its primary input parameters are table driven, application describers. The model contains 13 cost multipliers that account for differences in project and environment. *See also the following software cost-estimation models: COCOMO, Doty, Putnam SLIM, RCA PRICE S, and TRW Wolverton. See also software cost-estimation model.*

SDF — Acronym for software development file.

SDR — Acronym for system design review.

secretary/librarian — The software librarian on a chief programmer team. [IEEE SET Glossary, 1983] *See also chief programmer team, program librarian.*

security — The establishment and application of safeguards to protect data, software, and computer hardware from accidental or malicious modification, destruction, or disclosure. [BCS, 1987]

security and safety needs — From Maslow's motivation theory, the need to be free from physical danger. *See also biological survival needs, esteem and recognition needs, Maslow's motivation theory, Maslow's hierarchy of needs, self-actualization needs, social needs.*

segment — In system engineering, a major part of a large hardware/software system. For example, a satellite system could have a satellite segment, a launch segment, and a guidance and control segment. 2. In software, a self-contained portion of a computer program that may be executed without the entire computer program necessarily being maintained in internal storage at any one time.

SEL — Acronym for Software Engineering Laboratory, NASA, Goddard Space Flight Center, Greenbelt, MD.

self determination — Deciding on and acting on your own decisions.

self-actualization needs — From Maslow's motivation theory, the need to maximize one's potential and to accomplish something. *See also biological survival needs, esteem and recognition needs, Maslow's motivation theory, Maslow's hierarchy of needs, security and safety needs, social needs.*

SEPM — Abbreviation for software engineering project management. [Thayer, Pyster, and Wood, 1981]

significant change report — A management report that identifies and calls attention to significant deviations from the plan.

SLIM cost model — *See Putnam SLIM software cost-estimation model.*

SLIM cost-estimation model — *See Putnam SLIM software cost-estimation model.*

social needs — From Maslow's motivation theory, the need to belong, to be accepted by others. *See also biological survival needs, esteem and recognition needs, Maslow's motivation theory, Maslow's hierarchy of needs, security and safety needs, self-actualization needs.*

software — A sequence of instructions suitable for processing by a computer. Processing may include the use of an assembler, a compiler, an interpreter, or a translator to prepare the program for execution as well as to execute it. [IEEE SET Glossary, 1983] *Synonymous with code, computer code, computer program. Contrast with hardware, computer hardware.*

software activity — *See activity.*

software component (SC) — A functionally or logically distinct part of a software configuration item distinguished for purposes of convenience in designing and specifying a complex software configuration item as an assembly of subordinate elements. Software components may be top-level or bottom-level. [DoD-STD-2167, 1985] *See also configuration management, software configuration item (SCI).*

software configuration auditing — *See configuration auditing.*

software configuration control — *See configuration control.*

software configuration identification — *See configuration identification.*

software configuration item (SCI) — A software entity which has been established as a configuration item. The software configuration item exists where functional allocations have been made which clearly delineate the separation between equipment functions and software functions and the software has been established as a configuration item. *See also configuration management.*

software configuration management (SCM) — *See configuration management.*

software configuration status accounting — *See configuration status accounting.*

software cost estimating method — *See software cost-estimation model.*

software cost model — *See software cost-estimation model.*

software cost-estimation model — Any one of several quantitative methods of estimating the expected cost (and some times schedule) of a software project. Quantitative techniques are generally based on empirically derived cost estimating relationships. Generally the major independent parameter (input) is lines of source code. *See also the following software cost-estimation models: COCOMO, Doty, Putnam SLIM, RCA PRICE S, SDC, and TRW Wolverton.*

software design — The process of defining the software architecture (structure), components, modules, interfaces, test approach, and data for a software system to satisfy specified requirements. [IEEE SET Glossary, 1983]

software design constraint (requirement) — *See design constraint.*

software detailed design specification — *See detailed design description (specification).*

software development — *See software engineering.*

software development activity — *See activity.*

software development cycle — *See software development life cycle.*

software development environment — *See software support environment.*

software development file (SDF) — A repository for a collection of material pertinent to the development or support of software. Contents typically include (either directly or by reference) design considerations and constraints, design documentation and data, schedule and status information, test requirements, test cases, test procedures, and test results. *Sometimes synonymous with unit development folder (UDF).*

software development library — A software library containing computer-readable and human-readable information relevant to a software development effort. [IEEE SET Glossary, 1983] *See also program support library.*

software development life cycle — A model of a software project that begins with the decision to develop a software product and ends when the product is delivered. It depicts the relationships among the major milestones, baselines, reviews, and project deliverables that span the life of the project. A project life cycle model must include project initiation and project termination activities. The software development life cycle typically includes a requirements phase, design phase, implementation (coding) phase, test phase, and sometimes installation and checkout phase. *See also software life cycle.*

software development life-cycle phase — One of the phases of the software development life-cycle. For example: software requirements phase, software design phase, implementation (coding) phase, software test phase, and sometimes, installation and checkout phase. *See also software development life cycle.*

software development methodology — (1) An integrated set of software engineering methods, policies, procedures, rules, standards, techniques, tools, languages, and other methodologies for analyzing, designing, implementing, and testing software; and (2) a set of rules for selecting for use the correct subsets of the methodology.

software development notebook — A collection of material pertinent to the development of a given software module or subsystem. Contents typically include the requirements, design, technical reports, code listings, test plans, test results, problem reports, schedules, notes, etc., for the module or subsystem. [IEEE SET Glossary, 1983] *See also project notebook, unit development folder (UDF).*

software development paradigm — Software engineering examples or models which can be used as a strategy for developing a software system. Examples are baseline management, top-down development, incremental development, rapid prototyping, and reusable software.

software development plan — *See software project management plan.*

software development process — The process by which user needs are translated into software requirements, software requirements are transformed into design, the design is implemented in code, and the code is tested, documented, and certified for operational use. [IEEE SET Glossary, 1983] *See also software development life cycle.*

software development project — *See software engineering project.*

software development project management — *See software engineering project manager.*

software development strategy — *See software development paradigm.*

software development tool — A software development tool is a computer program that assists a software engineer in analyzing, designing, coding, or testing a software system.

software documentation — Technical data or information, including computer listings and printouts, in human-readable form, that describe or specify the design or details, explain the capabilities, or provide operating instructions for using the software to obtain desired results from a software system. [IEEE SET Glossary, 1983] *See also contract data requirements list (CDRL), deliverable document, document, documentation, engineering docu-*

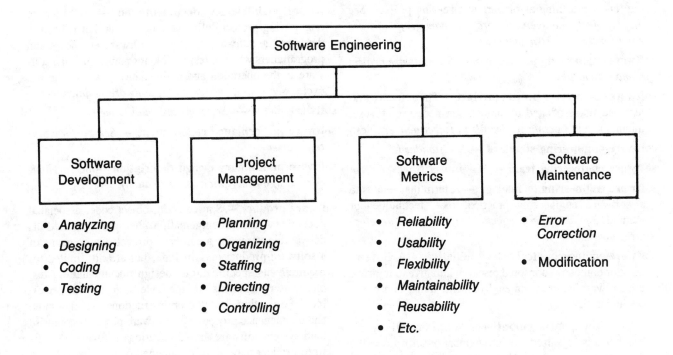

Figure 3: Software engineering model

ment, interface control document (ICD), software maintenance documentation, system documentation, user documentation, version description document (VDD).

software engineer — A person educated, trained and experienced in software engineering. *See also software engineering.*

software engineering — 1. The practical application of computer science, management, and other sciences to the analysis, design, construction, and maintenance of software and its associated documentation. 2. An engineering science that applies the concept of analysis, design, coding, testing, documentation, and management to the successful completion of large, custom-built computer programs. 3. The systematic application of methods, tools, and techniques to achieve a stated requirement or objective for an effective and efficient software system. *A hierarchical breakdown of software engineering can be seen in Figure 3.*

software engineering development — *See software development process.*

software engineering development model — *See software development life-cycle model.*

software engineering environment (SEE) — *See software support environment (SSE).*

software engineering methodology — *See software development methodology.*

software engineering model — A representation of software engineering functions and activities (see Figure 3).

software engineering project — The set of all activities, functions, and tasks, both technical and managerial, required to satisfy the terms and conditions of the project agreement. A software engineering project is a temporary activity that is characterized by having a start date, specific objectives and constraints, established responsibilities, a budget and schedule, and a completion date. A software engineering project consumes resources and has the goal of producing a product or set of products that satisfies the project requirements, as specified in the project agreement. A software engineering project may be self-contained or may be part of a larger project. In some cases, a software engineering project may span only a portion of the software product life cycle. In other cases, a software engineering project may span many years and consist of numerous subprojects, each in itself being a well-defined and self-contained software engineering project. [SPMS, 1986] *Synonymous with software project, software development project.*

software engineering project management — A system of procedures, practices, technologies, and know-how that provides the planning, organizing, staffing, directing, and controlling necessary to successfully manage a software engineering project. Know-how in this case means the skill, background, and wisdom to apply knowledge effectively in practice. *See also project management.*

software engineering project manager — A manager that has responsibility for planning, organizing, staffing, direct-

483

ing, and controlling a software engineering project. *See also project management, project manager, software engineering project management.*

software engineering project plan — *See software project management plan.*

software engineering project product — The software system and its associated documentation necessary to use, maintain, and operate it. *See also project deliverables.*

software engineering standard — *See standard.*

software engineering team — *See project team.*

software engineering technology — A term that relates to a software engineering practice, tool, technique, or method. *See also effective technology, software development methodology.*

software engineering technology initiative — A Government or company sponsored research initiative to improve the software engineering environment, tools, and methodologies.

software functional organization — A line or staff organization that is organized around a number of software skills. Personnel assigned could include software engineers, programmers, analysts, software managers, and sometimes machine operators, data entry, and other support personnel. The organization would provide a center of expertise in the software disciplines and a source of resources for project and matrix organizations. *See also functional organization, matrix organization, project organization.*

software functional requirement — *See functional requirement.*

software librarian — *Synonymous with program librarian.*

software life cycle — A model of the phases of a software system that starts when a software product is conceived and ends when the product is no longer available for use. It depicts the relationships among the major milestones, baselines, reviews, and project deliverables that span the life of the system. The software life cycle typically includes a requirements phase, design phase, implementation (coding) phase, installation and checkout phase, operation and maintenance phase, and sometimes, retirement phase. *See also software development life cycle.*

software life-cycle phase — One of the phases of the software life-cycle; for example, software requirements phase, software design phase, implementation (coding) phase, software test phase, installation and checkout phase, operation and maintenance phase, and sometimes, retirement phase. *See also software life-cycle, software development life-cycle phase.*

software life-cycle review — *See milestone review.*

software maintenance — Modification of a software product after delivery to correct faults, to improve performance or other attributes, or to adapt the product to a changed environment. [IEEE SET Glossary, 1983] *See also software maintenance documentation.*

software maintenance documentation — A software engineering project deliverable document that is used to describe the software system to software engineers and programmers who are responsible for maintaining the software in the operation and maintenance phase of the life cycle. *See also documentation, software maintenance.*

software metric — *See software quality metric.*

software performance requirement — *See performance requirement.*

software preliminary design description — *See preliminary design description (specification).*

software product — Source code, object code, associated documents, and documentation that are specified as deliverable items for a software project. Components of a software product may include, but are not limited to, requirements specifications, design documentation, test plans, users' manuals, source code, object code, principles of operation, installation instructions, training aids, and maintenance procedures. Software products comprise both system software and applications software. A software product may be self-contained or may be part of a larger system.

software product life cycle — 1. The set of all events and endeavors that occur within the birth-to-death cycle of a software product. 2. *Synonymous with software life cycle. See also software development life cycle.*

software productivity — *See productivity.*

software project — *See software engineering project.*

software project life cycle — *See software development life cycle.*

software project management — *See software engineering project management.*

software project management plan (SPMP) — The controlling document for managing a software project. A software project management plan defines the technical and managerial functions, activities, and tasks necessary to satisfy the requirements of a software project, as defined in the project agreement. [IEEE SPMP STD, 1987] *Synonymous with software development plan, software engineering project plan.*

software prototyping — *See rapid prototyping.*

software quality — 1. The totality of features and characteristics of a software product that bears on its ability to satisfy given needs; for example, conform to specifications. 2. The degree to which software possesses a desired combination of attributes. 3. The degree to which a customer or user perceives that software meets his or her composite expectations. 4. The composite characteristics of software that determine the degree to which the software in use will meet the expectations of the customer. [IEEE SET Glossary, 1983] 5. Attributes of software which affect its perceived value, e.g., correctness, reliability, maintainability, portability, etc.

software quality assurance — A planned and systematic pattern of all actions necessary to provide adequate confidence that the software and the delivered documentation conforms to established technical requirements. [IEEE SET Glossary, 1983]

software quality assurance plan — A project management plan for implementing a software quality assurance program within a company, organization, or project. The plan should include sections on: (1) purpose, (2) reference documents, (3) management, (4) documentation, (5) standards, practices, and conventions, (6) reviews and audits, (7) software configuration management, (8) problem reporting and corrective action, (9) tools, techniques, and methodologies, (10) code control, (11) media control, (12) supplier control, (13) record collection, maintenance, and retention. [IEEE STD 730-1984]

software quality attribute (requirement) — A requirement that specifies the degree of an attribute that affects quality that the software system must possess; e.g., correctness, reliability, maintainability, portability. *See also software quality metric, software requirements specification.*

software quality attribute — *See software quality attribute (requirement), software quality metrics.*

software quality metrics — In software engineering, a quantitative measure of the degree to which software possesses a given attribute that affects quality. An attribute of software which affects its perceived value; e.g., correctness, reliability, maintainability, portability, etc.

software reliability — Probability that the software will perform its logical operations in the specified environment without failure. [RADC, 1983] *See also reliability.*

software requirement — 1. A software capability needed by a user to solve a problem or achieve an objective. 2. A software capability that must be met or possessed by a system or system component to satisfy a contract, standard, specification, or other formally imposed document. 3. The set of all software requirements forms the basis for subsequent development of the software or software component. [IEEE SET Glossary, 1983] 4. Short description sometimes used in place of the term software requirements specification. *See also software requirements analysis, software requirements phase, software requirements specification.*

software requirements analysis — The process of studying user needs to arrive at a definition of software requirements. *See also software requirements specifications.*

software requirements phase — The software development life-cycle phase during which the requirements for a software product, such as the functional and performance capabilities, are defined and documented. [IEEE SET Glossary, 1983] *See also software life-cycle phase.*

software requirements review (SRR) — *Synonymous with software specification review (SSR).*

software requirements specification — A document that clearly and precisely describes, each of the essential requirements (functions, performance, design constraints, and quality attributes) of the software and the external interfaces. Each requirement being defined in such a way that its achievement is capable of being objectively verified by a prescribed method; for example, inspection, demonstration, analysis, or test. [IEEE Requirements Guide, 1983] *See also detailed design description (specification), preliminary design description (specification) software design constraint (requirement), software external interface requirement, software functional requirement, software performance requirement, software quality attribute (requirement), software requirements analysis, version description document (VDD).*

software reusability — A software development strategy that incorporates the reuse of existing software components. The reusable components are contained in a software library. *See reusability.*

software schedule model — *See software cost-estimation model.*

software specification review (SSR) — A milestone review conducted to finalize software configuration item requirements so that the software developer can initiate preliminary software design. The SSR shall be conducted when software configuration item requirements have been sufficiently defined to evaluate the developer's responsiveness to and interpretation of the system/segments level technical requirements. A successful SSR will be predicated upon the developer's determination that the software requirements specification and interface specifications form a satisfactory basis for proceeding into preliminary design phase. [MIL-STD 1521A, 1982] *See also milestone review, review.*

software support environment (SSE) — A system of computers, support software, facilities, procedures, and support personnel that makes available the necessary conditions, automatic processes, methodologies, and tools easily available to software developers. A minimum SSE would be a "software tool kit" that provides a set of diverse tools but with a common interface. A maximum SSE would be a complete "software factory." An SSE architecture allows (1) the distribution of computing power to all developers, (2) development machines that emulate the characteristics of the target machine, (3) improved human interface, (4) structured processing methodologies for good design and development, (5) improved product testing and analysis, (6) automatic trouble reporting and change control, (7) automatic project planning and scheduling, (8) continuous tracking of project activities, and automatic documentation preparation. *Synonymous with software development environment (SSE), software engineering environment (SEE).*

software system — A collection of software that relates in such a way as to allow the accomplishment of some system engineering requirement.

software system library — A controlled collection of system resident software that can be accessed for use or incorporated into other programs by reference; for example, a group of routines that a linkage editor can incorporate into a program as required. [IEEE SET Glossary, 1983] *See also software library.*

software technology transfer — The awareness, convincing, selling, motivating, collaboration, and special effort required to encourage industry, companies, organizations, and software engineering projects to make good use of new software development methodologies and technology products. *See also technology transfer, technology transfer gap.*

software tool — A software system or software package used by programmer or software engineers in the performance of their tasks. Software systems used to help develop, test, analyze, or maintain another software system or its documentation; for example, automated design tools, compilers, test tools, maintenance tools, word processors, and so forth. [IEEE SET Glossary, 1983]

SOW — Acronym for statement of work.

special-purpose computer — A computer system that is specified, designed, and built for a unique purpose. Contrast with an off-the-shelf (general purpose) computer. *See off-the-shelf computer.*

specification — 1. A document that prescribes, in a complete, precise, verifiable manner the requirements, design, behavior, or other characteristics of a hardware/software system or hardware/software system component. 2. The process of developing a specification. 3. A concise statement of a set of requirements to be satisfied by a product, a material, or process, indicating, whenever appropriate, the procedure by means of which it may be determined whether the requirements given are satisfied. (ANSI N45.2.10-1973) [IEEE SET Glossary, 1983] *See software requirements specification, system requirement specification. See also design specification, engineering document, formal specification, functional specification, interface specification, performance specification, software requirements specification.*

spiral model — A management strategy and life-cycle development model developed by Barry Boehm that incorporates a risk-driven approach to the software process. Contrast with prototyping-driven and specification-driven process. [Boehm, 1987] *Contrast with rapid prototyping, waterfall model.*

SPMP — Acronym for software project management plan.

SQA — Acronym for software quality assurance.

SRR — Acronym for software requirements review, system requirements review.

SRS — Acronym for system requirement specifications, software requirement specifications.

SSR — Acronym for software specification review.

staff — In management (staffing), a group of individuals assigned to one organization or activity.

staff organization — A group of functional experts who have the responsibility and authority to perform special activities which help the line organization do its work. A group of experts in their field that give advice or council. *Contrast with line organization. See also conventional organization.*

staffing — All the management activities that involve manning and keeping manned the positions which were established by the organizational structure. This includes selecting candidates for positions, training or otherwise developing both candidates and incumbents to accomplish their tasks effectively, appraising and compensating the incumbents, and terminating the incumbent when the organizational position is dissolved or the incumbent's performance is unsatisfactory.

staffing plan — In management (staffing) a plan that sees to the filling, and keeping filled, positions in the organization structure through defining staffing requirements, keeping an inventory of the available work force, and selecting and training the new hires. [Koontz, O'Donnell, and Weihrich, 1984]

stand-alone computer — A computer system or subsystem that is capable of operating without being connected to any other computer system or subsystem. *Contrast with embedded computer system.*

standard — 1. A standard is an approved, documented, and available set of criteria used to determine the adequacy of an action or object. 2. A document that sets forth the standards and procedures to be followed on a given project or by a given organization. 3. A software engineering standard is a set of (1) procedures that define the processes for and (2) descriptions that define the quantity and quality of a product from a software engineering project. *See also process standard, product standard.*

STARS (Software Technology for Adaptable, Reliable Systems) — A multimillion-dollar DoD software engineering research project.

state-of-the-art technique — In engineering, those technologies and methodologies that are the most effective and efficient available.

statement of work (SOW) — In system/software projects, a description of all the work required to complete a project. The SOW is normally part of a contract and is written by the customer or procuring agency. It may or may not include a procurement specification.

status accounting — *See configuration status accounting.*

strategic goal — In management (planning), a long-range goal of a company or organization. *See also strategy.*

strategic policy — In management (planning), an agreed on method of achieving the strategic goal. *See also strategy.*

strategy — In management (planning), the determination of the basic long-term objectives of an organization or enterprise, the adoption of courses of action, and allocation of resources necessary to achieve these goals.

strong matrix organization — In management (organizing), a matrix organizational structure with a full-time project manager and the majority of the staff assigned to the project organization. A strong matrix organization is not necessarily better than a weak matrix organization. *Contrast with weak matrix organization. See also matrix organization.*

structured analysis — In software engineering, a state-of-the-art software analysis technique that uses data flow diagrams, data dictionaries, and processes descriptions to analyze and represent a software requirement. *See also data flow diagram, data dictionary.*

supervise — In management (directing), the responsibility for overseeing the work and providing day-to-day control and direction to the personnel assigned to the manager or authorized for his control. It is the manager's responsibility to provide guidance and, when necessary, discipline to these people in order that they fulfill their assigned duties.

support personnel — In management (staffing), the staff personnel who provide assistance, advice, and auxiliary tasks in support of the personnel doing the primary duty of the organization.

support software — That software that is used to specify, develop, test, and manage the development of deliverable software and its associated documentation.

system — 1. A collection of hardware, software, people, facilities, and procedures organized to accomplish some common objectives. 2. In software engineering, a set of software programs that provide the cohesiveness and control of data that enables the system to solve problems.

system architecture — In system engineering, the structure and relationship among the components of a system. The system architecture may also include the system's interface with its operational environment. [IEEE SET Glossary, 1983]

system design — 1. The process of defining the hardware and software architectures, components, modules, interfaces, and data for a system to satisfy specified system requirements. 2. The result of the system design process. [IEEE SET Glossary, 1983] *Synonymous with architecture design. See also software design.*

system design phase — The period of time in the system life cycle (contrast to software life cycle) during which the designs for architecture, system components, interfaces, and data are created, documented, and verified to satisfy system requirements. *See also system requirement phase.*

system design review (SDR) — A system milestone review conducted when the definition effort has proceeded to the point where system requirements and the design approach are defined. Alternate design approaches and corresponding test requirements have been considered and the developer has defined and selected the required equipment, logistic support, personnel, procedural data, and facilities. This will normally be late in the definition phase. This review will be in sufficient detail to ensure a technical understanding between the system developer and the customer. The system segments are identified in the system design specification, and the hardware/software configuration items identified in the requirements specifications. [Lockheed, 1985] *See also milestone reviews, reviews.*

system development life cycle — A model of a hardware/software (system) project that begins with the decision to develop an engineering or hardware/software system and ends when the product is delivered. It depicts the relationships among the major milestones, baselines, reviews, and project deliverables that span the life of the project. A project life-cycle model must include project initiation and project termination activities. The system development life cycle typically includes a system requirements phase, system architectural design phase, design and development phase (normally done at the hardware/software segment/subsystem level), test phase, and sometimes installation and checkout phase. *See also software development life-cycle phase, system design phase, system requirement phase.*

system documentation — Technical data or information, including specifications, standards, engineering drawings, associated lists, manuals, computer listings and printouts that describe or specify the design or details, explain the capabilities, or provide operating instructions to obtain desired results from the system. *See also documentation.*

system engineering — The application of scientific, engineering, and management skills to transform an operational need into a description of a system configuration which best satisfies that operational need according to the system measures of effectiveness. [Lockheed, 1985]

system engineering project — The set of all activities, functions, and tasks, both technical and managerial, required to satisfy the terms and conditions of the project agreement. A system engineering project is a temporary activity that is characterized by having a start date, specific objectives and constraints, established responsibilities, a budget and schedule, and a completion date. A system engineering project consumes resources and has the goal of producing a product or set of products that satisfies the project requirements, as specified in the project agreement. In some cases, a system engineering project may span many years and consist of numerous subprojects, each being a well-defined and self-contained system engineering project. *See also software engineering project.*

system project managers — A manager that has responsibility for planning, organizing, staffing, directing, and controlling a system engineering project. *Synonymous with program manager. See also project manager, software engineering project manager.*

system requirement — 1. A system capability needed by a user to solve a problem or achieve an objective. 2. A system capability that must be met or possessed by a system or system component to satisfy a contract, standard, specification, or other formally imposed document. 3. The set of all system requirements forms the basis for subsequent development of the system or system component. [IEEE SET Glossary, 1983] *See also system requirement specifications, system requirements phase, software requirements.*

system requirements phase — The period of time in the system life cycle (contrast to software life cycle) during which the requirements for a system product, such as the functional and performance capabilities, are defined and documented. *See also system design phase.*

system requirements review (SRR) — A system milestone review that ascertains the adequacy of the system developer's efforts in defining system requirements. It will be conducted when a significant portion of the system functional and performance requirements has been established, normally in the definition phase (or equivalent effort). [Lockheed, 1985] *See also milestone review, review.*

system requirements specification (SRS) — A specification that sets forth the requirements for a system or system segment. Typically included are functional requirements, performance requirements, interface requirements, design requirements, and development standards. *Synonymous with system specifications.*

system software — Software designed for a specific computer system or family of computer systems to facilitate the operation and maintenance of the computer system and associated programs; for example, operating systems, compilers, utilities. [IEEE SET Glossary, 1983] *Contrast with application software. Sometimes synonymous with non-functional software.*

system specification — *Synonymous with system requirements specification.*

system testing — The process of testing an integrated hardware and software system to verify that the system meets its specified requirements. [IEEE SET Glossary, 1983] *See also acceptance testing, qualification testing.*

system validation — *See validation.*

system verification — *See verification.*

task — The smallest unit of management accountability for work assignment usually for one or a few individual project members. A task specification includes the specific objectives of the task, staffing requirements, the expected duration of the task, the resources to be used, and any special considerations. Similar tasks are usually grouped together to form functions and activities. [IEEE SPMP STD, 1987] *See also activity, function.*

task assignment — *See task.*

Taylor's motivation theory — A motivation technique based on the theory that workers will respond to an incentive wage. *See also motivation theories by Argyris, Herzberg, Lewin, Likert, Maslow, Mayo, McGregor, and Patton. See also Theories X and Y and Theory Z.*

team member — *See project team structure.*

team structure — *See project team structure.*

technique — An approach to performing a required function or job. *See also software development methodology.*

technology — A collective term that relates to a group of practices, tools, techniques, and methods. [Card, *et al.,* 1983] *See software engineering technology, effective technology.*

technology insertion — *Synonymous with technology transfer.*

technology transfer — The awareness, convincing, selling, motivating, collaboration, and special effort required to encourage industry, companies, organizations, and projects to make good use of new technology products. *Synonymous with technology insertion. See also software technology transfer, technology transfer gap.*

technology transfer gap — The time interval (measured in years) between the development of a new product, tool, or technique and its use by the consumers of that product, tool, or technique. *See software technology transfer, technology transfer*

temporary promotion — The promotion of an employee to a higher position in an organization for a fixed period of time. It is usually done when the incumbent is temporally absent. *Contrast to permanent promotion. See promotion.*

test — 1. A set of one or more test cases. 2. A set of one or more test procedures. 3. A set of one or more test cases and procedures. [IEEE Test Documentation, 1983] *See also test case specification, test design specification, test documents, test incident report, test item transmittal report, test log, test phase, test plan, test procedure specification, test readiness review (TRR), test report, test summary report, testing.*

test case specification — A document specifying inputs, predicted results, and a set of execution conditions for a test item. [IEEE Test Documents, 1983] *See also test, testing.*

test design specification — A document specifying the details of the test approach for a software feature or combination of software features and identifying the associated tests. [IEEE Test Documents, 1983] *See also test, testing.*

test document — *See test case specification, test design specification, test incident report, test log, test plan, test procedure specification, test report, test summary report.*

test incident report — A document that reports any event, which requires investigation, that occurs during the testing process. [IEEE Test Documents, 1983] *See also test, testing.*

test item transmittal report — A document identifying test items. It contains current status and location information. [IEEE Test Documents, 1983]

test log — A chronological record of relevant details about the execution of tests. [IEEE Test Documents, 1983] *See also test, testing.*

test phase — The period of time in the system/software development life cycle during which the components of a system/software product are evaluated and integrated, and the software product is evaluated to determine whether or not requirements have been satisfied. [IEEE SET Glossary, 1983] *See also software development life-cycle phase, test, testing.*

test plan — A document describing the scope, approach, resources, and schedule of intended testing activities. It identifies test items, the features to be tested, the testing tasks, who will do each task, and any risks requiring contingency planning. [IEEE Test Documents, 1983] *See also test, testing.*

test procedure specification — A document specifying a sequence of actions for the execution of a test. [IEEE Test Documents, 1983] *See also test, testing.*

test readiness review (TRR) — In software engineering, a milestone review to determine that the software test procedures are complete and to assure that the software developer is prepared for formal software performance testing. The results of informal testing will also be reviewed. [MIL-STD 1521A, 1982]. *See also milestone review, review, test, testing.*

test report — A document describing the conduct and results of the testing carried out for a system/software or system/software component. [IEEE SET Glossary, 1983] *See also test, testing.*

test specification — *See test case specification, test design specification, test procedure specification.*

test summary report — A document summarizing testing activities and results. It also contains an evaluation of the corresponding test items. [IEEE Test Documents, 1983] *See also test, testing.*

testing — The process of analyzing a system/software item to detect the differences between existing and required conditions and to evaluate the features of the system/software item. [IEEE SET Glossary, 1983]

Theories X and Y — A management motivation theory about the nature of people. Theory X suggests that people dislike work and will avoid it if they can. Theory Y suggests that the expenditure of physical and mental effort in work is as natural as play or rest. *See also McGregor's motivation theories.*

Theory Z — A combination of American and Japanese management style. [Ouchi, 1981] The basic principles of Theory Z are [Arthur, 1983]: (1) people need goals and objectives, otherwise they can easily impede their own progress and the progress of their company, (2) worker motivation is essential for good performance and must be both positively and negatively reinforced by management, (3) merely having goals and motivation will not prevent people from making mistakes, (4) the best interests of any given company are achieved when each individual's work is standardized to ensure that similar goals are attained by similar means, and (5) goals must change as working conditions and corporate needs change. In anticipation of such change Theory Z provides the mechanism for gradual change. *See also Theories X and Y.*

tool — *See software tool.*

top management — In management, an expression that equates to senior level management, for example, general manager, vice president for operations, director of computer services. Within a project management context, the project manager might refer to his and the customer's managers as "top management."

top-down — Pertaining to an approach that starts with the highest-level component of a hierarchy and proceeds through progressively lower levels; for example, top-down design, top-down programming, and top-down testing. [IEEE SET Glossary, 1983] *Contrast with bottom-up.*

top-down design — The process of designing a system by identifying its major components, decomposing them into their lower-level components, and iterating until the desired level of detail is achieved. *Contrast with bottom-up design.*

top-down testing — The process of checking out hierarchically organized programs, progressively, from top to bottom, using simulation of lower-level components (called stubs). [IEEE SET Glossary, 1983] *Contrast with bottom-up testing.*

training — The process of developing a skill, a knowledge on how to use, operate, or make something. This is in contrast to education in a concept of basic theory. For example, an individual would be trained in using FORTRAN but educated in the principles of programming languages. Training is typically used to satisfy a short-term requirement for skilled personnel on a particular activity or task. It has a short-term payoff. *Contrast with education.*

training plan — 1. In management (staffing), the career goal for each member of the staff and the training and education required to achieve those goals. 2. In project management, a description of the training needed by an organizations' personnel in order to complete a project. 3. In an engineering project, a deliverable configuration item. *See also education, training, training program.*

training program — In management (staffing), a collection of courses and training plans developed in response to the needs and demands of the company staff. Included are on-the-job training, formal company courses, courses through local universities and schools, self-study, and in-house formal or informal lectures. *See also education, training, training plan.*

trend chart — A management report that shows trends in such areas as budget, number of errors found in the system, man-hours of sick leave, and so on. Trend reports are used to predict the future.

TRW — An aerospace company located in Redondo Beach, California.

TRW Wolverton software cost-estimation model — A micro, software cost-estimation method that was developed in the early 1970s. The model uses a cost-per-instruction philosophy. The model was designed specifically to supply the detailed cost data required for proposals on government procurement. The model accommodates six software routines, seven life-cycle development phases, and a potential of eight software development activities in each phase. *See also the following software cost-estimation models: COCOMO, Doty, Putnam SLIM, RCA PRICE S, and SDC. See also software cost-estimation model.*

two-boss organization — *See matrix organization.*

Type A specification — A system specification. DoD usage. *Synonymous with system requirements specifications.*

Type B5 specification — A software requirements specification. DoD usage. *Synonymous with Part I specification (for software). See also software requirements specification.*

Type C5 specification — A software (detailed) design specification. DoD usage. *Synonymous with Part II specification (for software). See also detailed design specification.*

u-u-u

UDF — Acronym for Unit Development Folder.

uncertainty — In management (planning), a state of knowledge in which the decision maker is not knowledgeable about all the data and information necessary for accurate decisions or possible outcomes of an action.

unit development folder (UDF) — In SEPM, a central depository for recording the progress has been made toward "units" objectives. A unit can be a single project member or project team. A project management technique for monitoring software work accomplished. Initial development credited to Frank Ingrassia. *Sometimes synonymous with software development file.*

universality of management — From the management sciences [Koontz, O'Donnell, and Weihrich, 1984], [Fayol, 1949], a concept which means that: (1) management performs the same functions regardless of its position in the organization or the enterprise managed, and (2) management functions and fundamental activities are characteristic duties of managers; management practices, methods, detailed activities, and tasks are particular to the enterprise or job managed.

usability — 1. A software quality metric that defines the effort for training and software operation: familiarization, input preparation execution, and output interpretation. [RADC, 1983] 2. The extent to which a system facilitates ease of operation from a human viewpoint, covering both human engineering and ease of translation from current operation. [Lockheed, 1985]

user — 1. One who uses the services of a computer system. [IEEE CAT Glossary, 1986] 2. The person or persons who operate or interact directly with the computer system. The user and the customer are often not the same person. [IEEE Requirements Guide, 1984] *Synonymous with end user.*

user documentation — *See users' manual.*

user friendly — 1. Pertaining to a computer system, device, program, or document designed with ease of use as a primary design objective. [IEEE CAT Glossary, 1986] 2. A software system that has been designed for use by inexperienced people and includes one or more helpful features to assist the user. *Synonymous with user oriented.*

user interface — In software engineering, the software, input and output devices, screens, procedures, and dialogue between people and the software system. *See also interface.*

user oriented — *See user friendly.*

users' manual — In software engineering projects, a manual used to provide customer and/or contractor personnel with the necessary instructions concerning usage of software configuration items and instructions on how it is to be operated. The manual content and format is specifically designed to meet the needs of the intended user. [Lockheed, 1985]

v-v-v

V&V — Acronym for verification and validation.

validation — The process of evaluating software at the end of the software development process to ensure compliance with software requirements. [IEEE SET Glossary, 1983] *See also verification.*

verification — 1. The process of determining whether or not the products of a given phase of the software development cycle fulfill the requirements established during the previous phase. 2. The act of reviewing, inspecting, testing, checking, auditing, or otherwise establishing and documenting whether or not items, processes, services, or documents conform to specified requirements. 3. Formal proof of program correctness. (ANSI/ASQC A3-1978) [IEEE SET Glossary, 1983] *See also validation.*

verification and validation (V&V) — A software quality assurance procedure that includes both verification and validation. *See also independent verification and validation, validation, verification.*

version description document (VDD) — A specification that sets forth the exact version of a hardware/software configuration item and the interim changes thereto. It is used to identify the current version, and accordingly, accompanies each version of a hardware/software configuration item and each release of an interim version change to a configuration item. [Lockheed, 1985]

very-high-level language (VHLL) — In software development, a type of programming language in which the instructions to the computer closely reflect the natural language of the problem.

VHLL — Acronym for very-high-level language.

w-w-w

walkthrough (walkthru) — A software engineering review process in which a designer or programmer leads one or more other members of the development team through a segment of design or code that he or she has written, while the other members ask questions and make comments about technique, style, possible errors, violation of development standards, and other problems. [IEEE SET Glossary, 1983] *See also inspections.*

walkthru — Alternate spelling for walkthrough.

Warnier-Orr charts (diagram) — A software design tool and representation method developed by Warnier and modified by Orr that enable the analyst to represent the software system in a hierarchical manner.

waterfall model — A software development life-cycle strategy first developed by Winston W. Royce [1970], that partitions the project into manageable phases—requirements, design, implementation, and test—and establishes milestones, documents, and reviews at the end of each phase. In the model, the successful completion of one life-cycle phase in the waterfall chart corresponds to the achievement of the counterpart goal in the sequence of software engineering goals for the software process. The waterfall model recognizes the iteration between phases.

waterfall software development life-cycle model — *See waterfall model.*

WBS — Acronym for work breakdown structure.

weak matrix organization — In management (organizing), a matrix organizational structure with a part-time coordinator and where a majority of the staff are assigned to the functional organization on loan to the project organization. A weak matrix does not mean that is a bad organization or that a strong matrix is better. *Contrast with strong matrix organization. See also matrix organization.*

word processing — An office automation facility for computer aided authorship, editing, storage, revision, and printing of text.

work breakdown structure (WBS) — In project management, a method of representing in a hierarchical manner the parts of a product or process. A WBS can be used to represent a process (requirement analysis, design, code, software test, etc.) or a product (application programs, utility programs, operating systems, etc.). *See also process work breakdown structure, product work breakdown structure.*

work package — A specification of the work to be accomplished in completing a function, activity, or task. A work package specifies the objectives of the work, staffing requirements, the expected duration of the task, the resources to be used, the results to be produced and any special considerations for the work. [IEEE SPMP STD, 1987]

work product — Any document, documentation, or other tangible item that results from working on a project function, activity, or task. Examples of work products include the project plan, functional requirements, design documents, source code, test plans, meeting minutes, schedules, budgets, and problem reports. Some subset of the work products will form the set of project deliverables. [IEEE SPMP STD, 1987]

work-load chart — In management, a schedule of work to be done and the estimated amount of man-hours/days scheduled to accomplish the work.

References

(ANSI N45.2.10-1973) *Quality Assurance Terms and Definitions,* American National Standards Institute, NY, 1973.

(ANSI) — Definitions extracted from the *ANSI Technical Report, American National Dictionary for Information Processing,* X3/TR-1-77, American National Standards Institute, NY, September 1977.

(ANSI/ASQC A3-1978) *Quality Systems Terminology,* American National Standards Institute, NY, 1978.

(DoD-STD 480A) *Configuration Control Engineering Changes, Deviation and Waivers,* DoD Single Stock Point, Naval Publications and Forms Center, Philadelphia, PA.

(ISO) Definitions developed by Technical Committee 97 (Information Systems), Subcommittee 1, (Vocabulary) of The *International Organization for Standards (ISO).*

[ANSI/IEEE STD 730-1988] *IEEE Standard for Software Quality Assurance Plans,* IEEE, Inc., NY, 1984.

[Arthur, 1983] L.J. Arthur, *Programmer Productivity,* John Wiley & Sons, NY, 1983.

[BCS, 1987] *A Glossary of Computing Terms: An Introduction,* The British Computer Society, 5th Ed., Cambridge University Press, Cambridge, 1987.

[Boehm, 1981] B.W. Boehm, *Software Engineering Economics,* Prentice-Hall, Englewood Cliffs, NJ, 07632, 1981.

[Boehm, 1987] B.W. Boehm, "A Spiral Model of Software Development and Enhancement," *Tutorial: Software Engineering Project Management,* edited by R.H. Thayer, Computer Society of the IEEE, Washington D.C., 1987.

[Card, et al., 1983] D. N. Card, F. E. McGarry and G. Page, "Evaluating Software Engineering Techniques," *Proceedings from the Eighth Annual Software Engineering Workshop,* SEL-83-007, Nov. 1983.

[Fayol, 1949] H. Fayol, *General and Industrial Administration,* Sir Isaac Pitman & Sons, Ltd., London, 1949.

[Fife, 1987] D.W. Fife, "How to Know a Well-Organized Software Project When You Find One," *Tutorial: Software Engineering Project Management,* edited by R.H. Thayer, Computer Society of the IEEE, Washington D.C., 1987.

[IEEE CAT Glossary, 1986] Adapted from *IEEE Glossary of Computer Applications Terminology (Draft),* IEEE, Inc., NY, 1986.

[IEEE Requirements Guide, 1984] Adapted from *IEEE Guide for Software Requirements Specifications,* ANSI/IEEE Std 830-1984, IEEE, Inc., NY, 1984.

[IEEE SET Glossary, 1983] Adapted from *IEEE Standard Glossary of Software Engineering Terminology,* ANSI/IEEE Std 729-1983, IEEE, Inc., NY, 1983.

[IEEE SPMP STD, 1987] Adapted from *IEEE Standard for Software Project Management Plans (Draft),* P1058, IEEE, Inc., NY, 1987.

[IEEE Test Documentation, 1983] Adapted from *IEEE Standard Software Test Documentation,* ANSI/IEEE Std 829-1983, IEEE, Inc., NY, 1983.

[Koontz and O'Donnell, 1972] H. Koontz and C. O'Donnell, *Principles of Management: An Analysis of Managerial Functions,* 5th ed., McGraw-Hill Book Company, NY, 1972.

[Koontz, O'Donnell, and Weihrich, 1984] H. Koontz, C. O'Donnell and H. Weihrich, *Management,* 8th ed., McGraw-Hill Book Co., NY, 1984.

[Lockheed, 1985] Adapted from *Standards and Practices for Software Engineering,* Lockheed Missiles & Space Company, 1985.

[Mantei, 1981] M. Mantei, "The Effect of Programming Team Structures on Programming Tasks," *Communications of the ACM,* Vol. 24, No. 3, March 1981, pp. 106-113.

[MIL-STD 1521A, 1982] MIL-STD 1521A (USAF), *Technical Reviews and Audits for Systems, Equipment, and Computer programs (proposed revision),* Joint Policy Coordination Group on Computer Resource Management, April 15, 1982.

[Ouchi, 1981] W. Ouchi, *Theory Z: How American Business Can Meet the Japanese Challenge,* Addison-Wesley, Reading, MA, 1981.

[Pressman, 1987] R.S. Pressman, *Software Engineering: A Practitioner's Approach,* 2nd ed., McGraw-Hill Book Company, NY, 1987.

[RADC, 1983] *Software Quality Metrics for Distributed Systems,* RADC-TR-83-175, Vol. I (of three), prepared by Boeing Aerospace Company for Rome Air Development Center, Griffiss AFB, NY, July 1983.

[Royce, 1970] W.W. Royce, "Managing the Development of Large Software Systems," *Proceedings, IEEE WESCON,* August 1970, pp. 1-9. Reprinted in *Tutorial: Software Engineering Project Management,* edited by R.H. Thayer, Computer Society of the IEEE, Washington D.C., 1987.

[Thayer, Pyster, and Wood, 1981] R.H. Thayer, A.B. Pyster, and R C. Wood, "Major Issues in Software Engineering Project Management," *IEEE Transactions on Software Engineering,* Vol. SE-7, No. 4, July 1981, pp. 333-342.

[Weinberg, 1971] G. Weinberg, *The Psychology of Computer Programming,* Van Nostrand Reinhold, NY, 1971.

Bibliography

The following is an annotated list of books and publicly available reports on management and software engineering project management, as well as some general software engineering methodology books that every software manager should know about.

Abbott, J.R., *An Integrated Approach to Software Development*, John Wiley & Sons, Inc., NY, 1986, 359 pages.

This reference is useful in the development of requirements and software design documents. Its format is organized around a collection of annotated outlines for technical documents relevant to the development and maintenance of software. The annotations explain why the documents are organized as they are and why their contents are as shown.

Adams, J.R. and N.S. Kirchof, editors, *A Decade of Project Management*, Addison-Wesley Publishing Co., Reading, MA, 1981, 251 pages.

An excellent collection of project management papers from the Project Management Institute's quarterly magazine beginning in 1970 and running through 1980.

Addleman, D.R., M.J. Davis, and P.E. Presson, *Specification Technology Guidebook*, RADC-TR-85-135, prepared by Boeing Aerospace Company for Rome Air Development Center, Griffiss AFB, NY, August 1985, 214 pages.

This guidebook is for technical managers and provides for the selection of requirements and design specifications methodologies appropriate to various software development environments and types of software. The guidelines cover the requirements analysis, architectural design, and detailed design phases. A summary description of specification methodologies is provided. It also includes a method for selecting automated tools to support the selected methodologies. Three example problems are included.

Bailey, E.K., T.P. Frazier, and J.W. Bailey, *A Descriptive Evaluation of Automated Software Cost-Estimation Models*, Institute for Defense Analysis, IDA Paper P-1979, October 1986, 85 pages.

A technical report for project managers. This report provides an introduction to the usefulness of automated software cost-estimation tools and an evaluation of current, fully supported, commercially available, software cost and schedule estimation products. These tools can be used for the analysis of project planning, proposal evaluation, managing development and maintenance (i.e., tracking resources), and improving software productivity.

Beizer, B., *Software System Testing and Quality Assurance*, Van Nostrand Reinhold Co., NY, 1984, 380 pages.

An overview of testing and quality assurance methods for software development. It also covers all types of testing procedures, configuration management, and verification and validation.

Biggs, C.L., E.G. Birks, and W. Atkins, *Managing the Systems Development Process*, Prentice-Hall Inc., Englewood Cliffs, NJ, 1980, 408 pages.

This book is a very detailed description of methods used by one company to manage its software development project. The book contains a detailed step-by-step description from systems planning through systems implementation and maintenance of how to implement a computer-based system. The book also includes several blank forms that can be used for developing and managing a software system.

Blanchard, K. and S. Johnson, *The One Minute Manager*, Berkley Books, NY, 1984, 111 pages.

This very small, easy-to-read book provides, through short case studies, management approaches that will increase the manager's ability to lead people.

Block, R., *The Politics of Projects*, Yourdon Press, NY, 1986, 152 pages.

This book explores the political components of project failures and presents a process for taking control of the political situations. It provides examples, step-by-step guidelines, and a case study.

Boehm, B.W., *Software Engineering Economics*, Prentice-Hall, Inc., Englewood Cliffs, NJ, 1981, 775 pages.

This book tells you all you will ever want to know about software economics and software development cost estimating. This is the most referenced book in software engineering today. Every project manager should have a copy in his book shelf.

Bowen, T.P., G.B. Wigle, and J.T. Tsai, *Specification of Software Quality Attributes*, 108 pages Volume I: *Final Technical Report*, Volume II: *Software Quality Specifications Guidebook*, 142 pages, Volume III: *Software Quality Evaluation Guidebook*, 303 pages, RADC-TR-85-37, prepared by Boeing Aerospace Company for Rome Air Development Center, Griffiss AFB, NY, February 1985.

The most extensive and comprehensive information on software quality metrics available.

Brill, A.E., *Building Controls into Structured Systems*, Yourdon Press, NY, 1985, 168 pages.

The author shows the reader how to build and document internal controls as part of the formal systems development process. Like many of Yourdon Press's books, this book makes heavy use of structured analysis techniques.

Brill, A.E., *Techniques of EDP Project Management: A Book of Readings*, Yourdon Press, NY, 1986, 312 pages.

This book is a collection of papers addressing the special needs of project management. Each selected paper offers guidelines, methods, and advice to help managers successfully complete their projects. This book discusses everything from traditional subjects to areas such as burnout and family problems.

Brooks, Jr., F.P., *The Mythical Man-Month: Essays on Software Engineering*, Addison-Wesley Publishing Company, Reading, MA, 1975, 206 pages.

The software engineering project management best seller. Don't miss reading it.

Bruce, P. and S.M. Pederson, *The Software Development Project: Planning and Management*, John Wiley & Sons, Inc., NY, 1982, 234 pages.

This volume offers project managers a coherent framework on how to implement and control a software development project, from definition and analysis of requirements through the actual operation of a software system. All information is applicable to commercial and scientific projects in both public and private sectors. The techniques described provide a structured approach to planning, costing, and scheduling a software development effort, and to organizing and managing the project team. The book is augmented with a set of tear-out-charts suitable for quick reference or presentation material.

Cleland, D.I. and H. Kerzner, *A Project Management Dictionary of Terms*, Van Nostrand Reinhold Company, NY, 1985, 292 pages.

A very comprehensive dictionary of project management terms including: planning, organization, and control; matrix organization; cultural ambience and conflict; information systems; techniques, methodologies, and systems; and project cost/schedule management. A very useful book.

Cleland, D.I. and W.R. King, *Project Management Handbook*, Van Nostrand Reinhold Co., Inc., NY, 1983, 734 pages.

An excellent collection of papers by two of the leaders in the project management field. The purpose of the handbook is to provide project managers and those individuals concerned with project management a reference guide for the concepts and techniques in managing projects. This is not a superficial book. It goes into considerable depth on how to organize, plan, and control a "high tech" project.

Cooper, J.D. and M.J. Fisher, *Software Quality Management*, Petrocelli Books, Inc., NY, 1979, 294 pages.

This book provides a comprehensive treatment of the principles and practices embodied in the concept of software quality management. It defines measures of software quality, and discusses tools and practices to assure the development of quality software. Many references are listed for further study in this area.

DeMarco, T., *Controlling Software Projects: Management, Measurement, and Estimation*, Yourdon Press, NY, 1982, 296 pages.

This book shows managers how to organize a software engineering project and provides techniques for making early and accurate projections of time and cost to deliver a system. The author presents a set of function metrics which are quantifiable indications of system size and complexity derived directly from the requirements. The book makes good use of the DeMarco structured analysis method and, like so many of the Yourdon Press books, it is easy to read.

DeMarco, T., *Structured Analysis and System Specification*, Yourdon Press, NY, 1978, 366 pages.

This is the benchmark book and standard for structured software analysis and structured requirement specifications, to the extent that structured analysis is sometimes called the "DeMarco Technique." This book should be read by all those designers and managers who hope to use structured analysis on their software development system.

Deutsch, M.S., *Software Verification and Validation: Realistic Project Approach*, Prentice-Hall, Inc., Englewood Cliffs, NJ, 1982, 327 pages.

This book covers various topics in verification and validation. It also covers software testing activities, methods, and approaches. A short chapter is devoted to configuration management and quality assurance.

End, W., H. Gotthardt, and R. Winkemann, *Software Development*, John Wiley & Sons, Inc., NY, 1983, 345 pages.

Based on the experiences of several data-processing departments and training personnel, this manual is a comprehensive guide to the development of software for data processing systems. Each phase of development, from project proposal to implementation, is treated separately and in detail. Covers such aspects as monitoring projects, estimating the duration of a project, programming standards, estimating run times, minimizing test cases, and more.

Evans, M.W., *Productive Software Test Management*, John Wiley & Sons Inc., NY, 1984, 229 pages.

This book was based on experiences of the author as he both observed and worked in a variety of technical and managerial test situations. It is essentially a project management book centered around the testing phase. It includes test requirement identification, motivating the work force, and test development tooling and execution. Also included is a testing case history.

Evans, M.W., P. Piazza, and J.B. Dolkas, *Principles of Productive Software Management*, John Wiley & Sons, Inc., NY, 1983, 239 pages.

This book addresses the problems concerned with managing a software engineering project. The book presents an overall methodology for integrating software management and control techniques for the total software development process. The book shows how each phase of the project is monitored, controlled, and integrated with other phases to ensure a controlled, flow of work as it develops and proceeds.

Evans, M.W., and J. Marciniak, *Software Quality Assurance and Management*, John Wiley & Sons, Inc., NY, 1986, 400 pages.

This book examines the development process, with a view towards the methods that assure the highest quality possible in the finished product. The book treats every aspect and job function involved in the development process. Its integrated approach emphasizes the importance of having quality engineered into the software life cycle.

Fairley, R.E., *Software Engineering Concepts*, McGraw-Hill Book Company, NY, 1985, 376 pages.

This excellent text presents a thorough overview of software engineering. It includes two excellent chapters on project management with emphasis on project planning and life-cycle cost models. This general overview provides top-level information on software requirements, design, and verification and validation techniques. Also covered is a discussion on modern programming language features.

Fox, J.M., *Software and Its Development*, Prentice-Hall, Inc., Englewood Cliffs, NJ, 1982, 314 pages.

This is a very readable book by a former IBM employee and provides insight into software development problems. It discusses and makes a number of interesting points about managing software development.

Freedman, D.P., and G.M. Weinberg, *Handbook of Walkthroughs, Inspections, and Technical Reviews: Evaluating Programs, Projects, and Products*, 3rd ed., Little, Brown and Company, Boston, 1982, 450 pages.

The third edition of this handbook uses a question-and-answer format to explain how and why technical reviews are conducted. The authors discuss both formal and informal reviews. This is a very practical book and is based on their personal experiences in conducting formal technical reviews, walkthroughs, and inspections. The book covers how to conduct a review, reporting the results of the review, types of reviews, and types of materials reviewed.

Gane, C.P., and T. Sarson, *Structured Systems Analysis: Tools and Techniques*, Prentice-Hall, Inc., Englewood Cliffs, NJ, 1979, 253 pages.

This book describes the somewhat classic structured software requirements system entitled, "structured systems analysis." The book provides marvelous illustrations and examples of how to apply structured analysis methods and tools (manual) to analyzing a software system. It is a clearly written book and explains structured analysis at the management level.

Jensen, R.W., and C.C. Tonies, *Software Engineering*, Prentice-Hall, Inc., Englewood Cliffs, NJ, 1979, 591 pages.

This early book on software engineering provides an excellent review of software engineering as it pertains to systems. The chapters on project management fundamentals and software design are excellent.

Katzin, E., *How to Write a Really Good User's Manual*, Van Nostrand Reinhold Co., Inc., NY, 1985, 260 pages.

This reference is a book on writing a users' manual. It provides procedures and examples on how to document an interactive computer system. It also provides procedures for organizing and managing a documentation project as well as forms for recording and reporting project progress.

King, D., *Current Practices in Software Development: A Guide to Successful Systems*, Yourdon Press, NY, 1984, 232 pages.

A comprehensive guide to the latest software tools, practices, and techniques available to use with the system development life cycle. The author recommends a practical system development life cycle as framework in which to apply other techniques.

Koontz, H., C. O'Donnell, and H. Weihrich, *Management*, 8th ed., McGraw-Hill Book Company, NY, 1984, 702 pages.

This is the eighth and newest edition of the classic management book by Koontz and O'Donnell. It has been updated considerably with the addition of a third author, Heinz Weihrich, from the University of San Francisco. This book is a must for managers. If you only have time to read one book about management in your life, read this one. This book was formerly published under the title *Principles of Management: An Analysis of Managerial Functions*.

Lano, R.J., "The N^2 Chart," TRW, 1977, 227 pages (republished as *A Technique for Software and Systems Design*, North-Holland Publishing Co., NY, 1979, 119 pages).

This reference provides a comprehensive treatment of the types and uses of N^2 charts as shown here. Many illustrative examples are presented and discussed.

Martin, J. and C. McClure, *Diagramming Techniques for Analysts and Programmers*, Prentice-Hall, Inc., Englewood Cliffs, NJ, 1985, 412 pages.

This is a complete, easy to read, description of many of the modern software development methodologies and techniques. It makes an excellent reference for project managers who need to know more about the new methodologies of developing software systems.

McClure, C.L., *Managing Software Development and Maintenance*, Van Nostrand Reinhold Co., NY, 1981, 203 pages.

This book is separated into two parts. Part 1 is concerned with managing the software development and Part 2 with managing the software maintenance. The author talks about keeping maintenance in mind when managing a software development project. Also included is how to organize a software development team and how to control a software development project.

Mellor, S.J. and P.T. Ward, *Structured Development for Real-Time Systems: Volume 3: Implementation Modeling Techniques*, Yourdon Press, NY, 1986.

See entry after Ward, P.T. and S.J. Mellor.

Metzger, P.W., *Managing a Programming Project*, 2nd ed., Prentice-Hall, Inc., Englewood Cliffs, NJ, 1981, 201 pages.

This book was way ahead of its time when it was published in 1973. The current second edition is essentially the same as the earlier edition with the addition of a few pages on software development methodologies. This book starts with the software development life cycle as its basis and carries the reader from the beginning to the end of a software development project. It has an excellent case study on what can go wrong with a software development project. This case study, called "A War Story," is new to the second edition.

NASA, "Managers's Handbook for Software Development," technical report SEL-84-001, Goddard Space Flight Center, Software Engineering Laboratory, Greenbelt, MD, 61 pages.

This handbook presents a case study of methods and aids for the management of a software development project. The handbook information and data is based on the experiences of the Software Engineering Laboratory (SEL) in developing flight dynamics software. The management aspects of the following subjects are described: organizing the project; producing a development plan; estimating costs, scheduling, and staffing; preparing deliverable documents; using management tools; monitoring the project; conducting reviews; auditing; testing; and certifying. A free copy of the handbook can be obtained by writing to: Frank E. McGarry, Code 582, NASA/GSFC, Greenbelt, MD 20771

Page-Jones, M., *The Practical Guide to Structured Systems Design*, Yourdon Press, NY, 1980, 368 pages.

This is the benchmark and standard on structured design. It is extremely readable, full of interesting anecdotes and examples, and can be read and understood in a very short period of time.

Page-Jones, M., *Practical Project Management: Restoring Quality to DP Projects and Systems, 1985*, Dorset House Publishing, NY, 1985, 243 pages.

Page-Jones discusses the software quality crisis and provides specific and witty advice on ways to prevent project disaster. Like his earlier book, it makes very quick, very sensible, and very interesting reading.

Peters, L.J., *Software Design: Methods & Techniques*, Yourdon Press, NY, 1981, 248 pages.

This book is a well-written, easy to read, compendium of software analysis and design methodologies along with a description of various software engineering techniques and tools. Peters has done an excellent job of comparing the various techniques in a systematic manner by having each technique solve a simple but common problem.

Pressman, R.S., *Software Engineering: A Practitioner's Approach*, 2nd ed., McGraw-Hill Book Company NY, 1987, 587 pages.

This second edition is greatly expanded and improved over the first edition. This book on software engineering covers all aspects of software engineering. It contains new chapters on object-oriented and real-time design, additional emphasis on software quality assurance and configuration management, and virtually ignores coding as it should. The book devotes one chapter to project planning and software metrics.

Reifer, D.J., *Tutorial: Software Management*, 3rd ed., Computer Society of the IEEE Press, Washington, DC, 1985, 518 pages.

This is a companion book to the *Tutorial: Software Engineering Project Management* and contains many excellent papers on project management and software development.

Rosenau, Jr., M.D., *Successful Project Management*, Van Nostrand Reinhold Co., NY, 1981, 281 pages.

An excellent, readable book on the "big three" in planning a software project: determining the task, determining the schedule, and determining the cost. This book is unique; it takes a while to realize that it is a generic project management book which can be applied to the development of any artifact. While not devoted to software engineering projects, it does an excellent job of explaining how a software engineering project can be managed. The chapters are grouped according to the life cycle phases of definition, planning, implementation, control, and completion.

Sommerville, I., *Software Engineering*, 2nd. ed., International Computer Science Series, Addison-Wesley Publishing Company, Workingham, England, 1985, 327 pages.

This excellent second edition of a software engineering book has been thoroughly revised and updated since the first edition. (I recommend that you do not buy the first edition.) It is a very detailed software engineering book and covers all phases of the software development life cycle.

Steward, D.V., *Software Engineering with Systems Analysis and Design*, Brooks/Cole Publishing Company, Monterey, CA, 1987, 414 pages.

This is a very detailed book that covers all aspects of software engineering. The text presents the classical approaches to software engineering—data flow diagrams, structure charts, and Warnier-Orr Diagrams—and integates them with some of the newer techniques such as Trees. The book contains three chapters on managing the software development process: managing people and expectations, estimating the project, and scheduling and controlling the projects. Steward uses his Tree concept to estimate size and cost for a software development project.

Stuckenbruck, L.C., ed., *The Implementation of Project Management: The Professional's Handbook*, Addison-Wesley Publishing Company, Reading, MA, 1982, 254 pages.

This book is a collection of good articles on project management. Many of the articles are written by the editor L. C. Stuckenbruck and cover many aspects of managing a project. This book presents three histories for the implementation of project management concepts in three different organizations that were not using a project management organizational structure.

Tausworthe, R.C., *Standardized Development of Computer Software, Part I: Methods, Part II: Standards*, Jet Propulsion Laboratory, California Institute of Technology, Pasadena, CA, 1976 (republished as *Standardized Development of Computer Software*, Prentice-Hall, Inc., Englewood Cliffs, NJ, 1979, 375 pages.)

This early book on developing a computer software system involves not only the technology of developing a software system but covers the management as well. It presents an overall case study of the development of a software system by the Jet Propulsion Laboratory. It is based on the software standards and practice in use there at that particular time. The project that used this particular methodology was extremely successful with a schedule lapse of only 3%, a cost overrun of 6% and produced software which contained an average of approximately 3 errors per 1,000 lines of code. The two books can be obtained from the Government Printing Office at a nominal charge.

Ward P.T. and S.J. Mellor, *Structured Development for Real-Time Systems, Volume 1: Introduction & Tools* (166 pages), *Volume 2: Essential Modeling Techniques* (172 pages), *Volume 3: Implementation Modeling Techniques* (194 pages), Yourdon Press, NY, 1986. (Note: the principal author for Volume 3 is S.J. Mellor.)

These three small volumes update structured analysis and structured design. Written primarily for real-time applications they also update the structured techniques and terminology and as such should be read by both real-time and non-real-time professionals. Volume 1 is an introduction to the structured techniques. Volume 2 describes real-time structured analysis and Volume 3 describes real-time structured design.

Weinberg, G.M., *The Psychology of Computer Programming*, Van Nostrand Reinhold, NY, 1971.

Despite the apparent age of this book the information is still current. The psychology of programming is presented in an attempt to provide a better understanding of how people work together in a software development environment. Weinberg presents his concept of ''egoless programming'' and egoless technical reviews (walkthroughs) as a means of reducing programming errors.

Yourdon, E., *Classics in Software Engineering*, Yourdon Press, NY, 1986, 440 pages.

This a collection of 24 classic papers in software engineering. It represents the only place in which all these papers can be found under one cover. This book describes guidelines for project planning and control and details the involvement of the project team and the users at each life cycle.

Yourdon, E., *Managing the System Life Cycle: A Software Development Methodology Overview*, 2nd ed., Yourdon Press, NY, 1986, 292 pages.

This book provides a concise overview of the tools of structured analysis, structured design, and structured programming. It also presents a structured project life cycle that uses a structured technique for a typical MIS development project.

Yourdon, E., *Managing the Structured Techniques*, 3rd ed., Yourdon Press, NY, 1986, 296 pages.

This third edition of Ed Yourdon's book on managing structured techniques tells managers how to manage structured analysis, structured design, structured programming, chief programmer teams, and other techniques which together increase the effectiveness of a software engineering project. It extensively updates the technology advances since the second edition was published. Like all of Yourdon's books, it is extremely clear and readable.

Yourdon, E., *Structured Walkthroughs*, 3rd ed., Yourdon Press, NY, 1986, 196 pages.

This third edition of a very small book on structured walkthroughs provides a detailed description of how to apply this successful method of peer group review of such software engineering documents as functional specifications, design, and code. The book explains how to use walkthroughs to produce ''error free code'' to detect inefficiencies in design, and to improve communication between technicians. It can be read in one day.

Author Biography

Dr. Richard H. Thayer is a Professor in Computer Science at the California State University, Sacramento. On leave from the University, he is working on technology insertion for the Lockheed Software Technology Center, Austin, Texas. He is an international consultant and lecturer in software requirements, software engineering, project management, and software quality assurance.

Prior to this, he served over twenty years years in the U.S. Air Force as a senior officer in a variety of positions associated with engineering, programming, research, teaching, and management in computer science and data processing. His numerous positions include six years as a supervisor and technical leader of scientific programming groups, four years with the U.S. Air Force R&D program in computer science, and six years of managing large data processing organizations.

Dr. Thayer is a Senior Member of the Computer Society of the IEEE and the IEEE Software Engineering Standards Subcommittee. He is chairperson of the working group for *A Standard for Software Project Management Plans*. He is an associate fellow of the American Institute of Aeronautics and Astronautics where he served on the AIAA Technical Committee on Computer Systems, and is a member of the Association for Computing Machinery. He is also a registered professional engineer.

He has a BSEE and an MS degree from the University of Illinois at Urbana and a PhD from the University of California at Santa Barbara, in electrical engineering.

He is the author of over thirty technical papers and reports on software project management, software engineering, and software engineering standards and is an invited speaker at many national and international software engineering conferences and workshops.

Other titles from
IEEE Computer Society Press

Software Engineering: A European Perspective
edited by Richard H. Thayer and Andrew D. McGettrick

Concentrates on the areas in which Europe excels, such as formal methods, high-integrity systems, integrated software support environments, software quality management, and national and multinational government initiatives. The text contains a glossary of more than 1400 system/software engineering terms, an annotated bibliography with 25 entries describing the European approach, a glossary of information sources with 270 entries, and a list of publicly available software engineering standards used in Europe with more than 100 entries.

Sections: Background and Issues, Life Cycle Development Models/Processes, Requirements Analysis and Specifications, Software Design and Methodologies, High-Integrity Systems, Formal Methods, Software Project Management, Software Quality Management, Software Development Environments, Glossary of Terms, Software Engineering Standards.

696 pages. 1993. Hardcover. ISBN 0-8186-9117-4. Catalog # 2117-01 — $79.00 Members $64.00

Software Management, 4th Edition
edited by Donald J. Reifer

This newly updated text provides both the novice and experienced software manager with the materials necessary to comprehend and use the basic theories, concepts, techniques, and tools of software management. Includes both original material and reprints focusing on these four topics: general background information, the five basic functions of general management, advanced management topics, and support material for teachers.

Sections: Software Process, Project Management, Planning Fundamentals, Organizing for Success, Staffing Essentials, Direction Advice, Visibility and Control, Risk Management, Metrics and Measurement, Software Engineering Technology Transfer, Support Material.

664 pages. 1993. Hardcover. ISBN 0-8186-3342-5. Catalog # 3342-01 — $79.00 Members $64.00

Software Reengineering
edited by Robert S. Arnold

Explores software reengineering concepts and processes, tools and techniques, capabilities and limitations, risks and benefits, research possibilities, and case studies. Key sections of the text present, evaluate, and examine several examples of real-life reengineering projects, reengineering and CASE tools, data reengineering, processes for finding reusable parts, and metrics for measuring source codes.

Sections: Software Reengineering: Context and Definition, Business Process Reengineering, Strategies and Economics, Reengineering Experience and Evaluation, Technology for Reengineering, Data Reengineering and Migration, Source Code Analysis, Software Restructuring and Translation, Annotating and Documenting Existing Programs, Reengineering for Reuse, Reverse Engineering and Design Recovery, Object Recovery, Knowledge-Based Program Analysis.

688 pages. 1993. Hardcover. ISBN 0-8186-3272-0. Catalog # 3272-01 — $79.00 Members $64.00

Computer-Aided Software Engineering (CASE), 2nd Edition
edited by Elliot Chikofsky

Describes new information on CASE technology, background, and evolution. The papers in this text illustrate the present state of CASE, how its concepts have fared over time, and how it looks as a technology for the future.

Sections: CASE Environments and Tools: Overview, Evolution of Software Development Environment Concepts, Role of Data Browsing Technology in CASE, Role of Assistants and Expert System Technology in CASE, Role of Prototyping in CASE, Tailoring Environments (Extension, Meta-Specification, and Generation), Issues of Evaluating Tools and Managing CASE, Bibliography.

184 pages. 1993. Softcover. ISBN 0-8186-3590-8. Catalog # 3590-05 — $35.00 Members $25.00

 IEEE COMPUTER SOCIETY PRESS

▼ **To order call toll-free: 1-800-CS-BOOKS** ▼

▼ **Fax: (714) 821-4641** ▼ **E-Mail: cs.books @ computer.org** ▼

10662 Los Vaqueros Circle **Los Alamitos, CA 90720-1264** **Phone: (714) 821-8380**

IEEE Computer Society

IEEE Computer Society Press Publications

Monographs: A monograph is an authored book consisting of 100-percent original material.

Tutorials: A tutorial is a collection of original materials prepared by the editors and reprints of the best articles published in a subject area. Tutorials must contain at least five percent of original material (although we recommend 15 to 20 percent of original material).

Reprint collections: A reprint collection contains reprints (divided into sections) with a preface, table of contents, and section introductions discussing the reprints and why they were selected. Collections contain less than five percent of original material.

Technology series: Each technology series is a brief reprint collection — approximately 126-136 pages and containing 12 to 13 papers, each paper focusing on a subset of a specific discipline, such as networks, architecture, software, or robotics.

Submission of proposals: For guidelines on preparing CS Press books, write the Managing Editor, IEEE Computer Society Press, PO Box 3014, 10662 Los Vaqueros Circle, Los Alamitos, CA 90720-1264, or telephone (714) 821-8380.

Purpose

The IEEE Computer Society advances the theory and practice of computer science and engineering, promotes the exchange of technical information among 100,000 members worldwide, and provides a wide range of services to members and nonmembers.

Membership

All members receive the acclaimed monthly magazine *Computer*, discounts, and opportunities to serve (all activities are led by volunteer members). Membership is open to all IEEE members, affiliate society members, and others seriously interested in the computer field.

Publications and Activities

Computer **magazine:** An authoritative, easy-to-read magazine containing tutorials and in-depth articles on topics across the computer field, plus news, conference reports, book reviews, calendars, calls for papers, interviews, and new products.

Periodicals: The society publishes six magazines and five research transactions. For more details, refer to our membership application or request information as noted above.

Conference proceedings, tutorial texts, and standards documents: The IEEE Computer Society Press publishes more than 100 titles every year.

Standards working groups: Over 100 of these groups produce IEEE standards used throughout the industrial world.

Technical committees: Over 30 TCs publish newsletters, provide interaction with peers in specialty areas, and directly influence standards, conferences, and education.

Conferences/Education: The society holds about 100 conferences each year and sponsors many educational activities, including computing science accreditation.

Chapters: Regular and student chapters worldwide provide the opportunity to interact with colleagues, hear technical experts, and serve the local professional community.